THE MOST
TRUSTED NAME
IN TRAVEL

FROMMER'S

NEW ZEALAND

By Diana Balham,
Kate Fraser &
Renée Lang

FROMMER'S STAR RATINGS SYSTEM

Every hotel, restaurant, and attraction listed in this guide has been ranked for quality and value. Here's what the stars mean:

★   Recommended
★★   Highly Recommended
★★★   A must! Don't miss!

AN IMPORTANT NOTE

The world is a dynamic place. Hotels change ownership, restaurants hike their prices, museums alter their opening hours, and busses and trains change their routings. And all of this can occur in the several months after our authors have visited, inspected, and written about, these hotels, restaurants, museums and transportation services. Though we have made valiant efforts to keep all our information fresh and up-to-date, some few changes can inevitably occur in the periods before a revised edition of this guidebook is published. So please bear with us if a tiny number of the details in this book have changed. Please also note that we have no responsibility or liability for any inaccuracy or errors or omissions, or for inconvenience, loss, damage, or expenses suffered by anyone as a result of assertions in this guide.

Golden Bay (see p. 282).

CONTENTS

A LOOK AT NEW ZEALAND

For a small country with a sparse population, New Zealand is a scenic powerhouse, with landscapes of such beauty and diversity they rival that of any of the five continents. Consider this: In a couple of days of travel, you can see sun-drenched beaches, rolling vineyards, fjords and glaciers, and sleek cityscapes. This Pacific island nation is split into two large landmasses: North Island and South Island. North Island is home to New Zealand's most cosmoplitan city, Auckland, not to mention mountains and sparkling bays, Maori homelands and Hobbits—plus the country's buzzing capital, Wellington. The South Island holds its own in the scenery department, with fjords and falls, icy sounds, and charming small towns. Here are just a few reasons to visit New Zealand.

Named for the first European explorer to see New Zealand, Abel Tasman National Park is the smallest of the country's national parks (at 87 square miles) but still offers plenty of natural beauty. See p. 280.

An aerial shot of the ZEALANDIA wildlife sanctuary (p. 246), an innovative wildlife sanctuary surrounded by a first-in-the-world "pest exclusion fence" to restore the area to its original biological profile. It's home to a number of rare species.

In a country this lightly populated, sheep are more likely to cause traffic jams than cars.

A traditional Maori "Greeting Show" near Rotorua Town.

Waiotapu—or "Sacred Waters," see p. 146—is a hub of geothermal activity.

The Auckland cityscape.

A lemur at the world-class Auckland Zoo, p. 69.

A "museum of gardening," the Hamilton Gardens (see p. 111) features 21 themed gardens that are meant to illuminate cultures and gardening techniques from around the globe. Some one million people visit yearly.

Hand-raised because of illness as a chick, and "imprinted" on humans ever since, Sirocco, a critically endangered kakapo parrot, is a friendly star at ZEALANDIA wildlife sanctuary (p. 246). Here, he is greeting a fan.

The set for the *Lord of the Rings* film trilogy, called Hobbiton (see p. 114), is among the country's most popular tourist attractions.

Thousands of glow worms illuminate the famed Waitomo Cave, p. 114.

Interactive exhibits enthrall visitors at New Zealand's National Museum, "Te Papa," p. 244.

The Rotorua Museum, p. 142, is set in a handsome former spa resort, built in 1908.

Inside the Rotorua Museum are important works of Maori art, like this mask from the Te Arawa people.

Girls on a school field trip enjoy the bucolic beauty just outside of Wellington.

SOUTH ISLAND

The picturesque settlement of Akaroa (p. 321) is nestled in a volcanic valley.

Bungee jumping is hugely popular across New Zealand. Here a brave soul tries it from a St. Helen's bridge in Canterbury.

Kayakers on Milford Sound, p. 352.

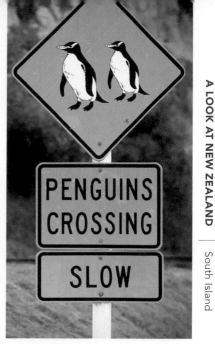

Penguin crossing sign in Oamaru, p. 367.

Oamaru's colony of blue penguins, p. 367.

Lupins blooming in the town of Oamaru.

Hikers cross the swing bridge over the turquoise river running through Hokitika Gorge, p. 299.

Skiing in July means great powder and awe-inspiring views in the Remarkables Mountain Range.

The triple-tiered Purakaunui Falls, in the Catlins, p. 381.

Sipping a cold one at the Minus 5° Ice Bar in Queenstown, p. 340.

The dank tunnels of the 1880s-era Banning Mine are a major touristic attraction, known today as the Denniston Mine Experience, p. 291.

The century-old TSS *Earnslaw* (p. 332) steamboat chugs along scenic Lake Wakatipu, near Queenstown.

Queenstown (p. 325) may be one of the most scenic cities on Earth. It's set on an inlet Lake Wakatipu and surrounded by soaring mountain ranges (including the Remarkables).

Christchurch's Transitional Cathedral (p. 315), crafted of such materials as cardboard tubes and shipping containers, was built after the city's cathedral was damaged in a 2011 earthquake.

Whale-watching charters are a major lure for visitors to Kaikoura, p. 322. Here, a humpback cavorts near a sightseeing boat.

Christchurch Art Gallery (p. 314) is known for its cutting-edge, contemporary exhibits. Here, young visitors examine a sculpture by Ron Mueck.

Snow-dusted Mount Cook rises some 12,000 feet into the sky.

Hikers carefully wend their way along Franz Josef Glacier.

The Marlborough wine region is thought by many to produce the finest sauvignon blanc on the planet. Winery and vineyard tours are available year-round; see p. 272.

THE BEST OF NEW ZEALAND

"Last, loneliest, loveliest, exquisite, apart," wrote Victorian author Anthony Trollope when describing New Zealand after a visit in 1891. His observation has been echoed by many who have visited the country in the years since. About the size of Japan, but with a population of only 4.5 million, New Zealand is endlessly described as "punching well above its weight"—a saying that applies not just to the country's successes on the sporting field. Yes, we do collect a swag of cups and medals, but there is much, much more to the country and its people than winning at games.

Let's talk diversity. New Zealand is like a cleverly wrapped gift that continually reveals surprises. There are heart-stopping thrills for adventure seekers. Ecotourists have national parks, penguin colonies, marine parks (whales, sea lions, dolphins), and forest walkways to explore. The landscape can change from gently charming to towering majesty within an hour's driving time. It switches pace so smoothly you can go from wondering if anyone's home to plunging into resort razzle-dazzle, areas buzzing with taxis, buses, museums, galleries, wine bars, and smart shops.

New Zealand eats well and drinks well. We have achieved international recognition and awards for our wines and our craft beers. Our coffee roasteries and baristas produce outstanding coffees. We grow, catch, and rear fabulous food for a lineup of classy chefs and not-so-classy (but fun) food trucks.

We go a bit overboard about our history, and hardly a hamlet or town exists that doesn't have its own small but polished museum (see the **Nelson Provincial Museum,** p. 276), let alone the big-city treasure houses of collections, such as **Toitu Otago Settlers Museum** (p. 375).

We are an artistic lot too. Please don't miss **Christchurch Art Gallery,** or the **Eastern Southland gallery** in Gore with its John Money collection.

For a small country, the main cities in both North and South islands keep their distance from each other, and this, combined with challenging geography (mountains, rivers, sea crossings), mean many miles must be traveled to reach the best attractions. Fortunately the travel links are easy. National airline Air New Zealand is backed up by smaller regional airlines, the InterCity coach system connects business centers with practically every visitor attraction, and in-between are busy shuttle buses and helicopters whizzing smaller groups to popular destinations. It is ridiculously easy to have lunch in a waterfront bistro in Auckland, drive to Rotorua for an evening *hangi* experience, and in the morning catch a flight south to Christchurch, Dunedin, Queenstown, or Invercargill for the best of the south. It's all so easy, and so brilliantly different.

But the biggest asset of all is ourselves. The New Zealanders. We like it when visitors admire our country, but we are absolutely certain that the images and memories taken away are not only the sandhills of Hokianga, the hubbub of Rotorua, and the wineries and restaurants of Queenstown but also the good folk you meet along the way. From the coach driver in Northland to the publican on Stewart Island, the New Zealand welcome is genuine.

THE most authentic NEW ZEALAND EXPERIENCES

- o **Aerial Sightseeing:** When you are enveloped in snow-covered peaks and glacial ice, the very landscape can almost overwhelm. Tackling the heights in a plane or helicopter puts it all in a different perspective. See Greymouth and Franz Josef/Fox Glaciers in chapter 10; Queenstown and Milford Sound in chapter 11.
- o **See a City Rise Again:** There are few places in the world where you can see in one city block the devastation of an earthquake and the beauty of a city rebuilt. A renewed Christchurch is taking shape, and the results are impressive. See chapter 9.
- o **Stargazing:** Stars, galaxies, and planets look close enough to touch when a knowledgeable guide is to hand to identify and point them out in the clear night skies of the Mackenzie Country. See Tekapo and Aoraki/Mount Cook in the Mackenzie Country in chapter 15.
- o **Take a Jetboat:** "Jetting away" takes on new meaning when you are zooming up a wilderness river. The jetboat was invented here, and boaties have had plenty of practice skimming white-water rapids in deep canyons, sliding by rocky cliffs, and delivering a thrill a second. See chapter 11.
- o **Visit a Maori Marae:** Experience the *hongi* (the formal nose-to-nose Maori greeting), see deeply moving song-and-dance performances, and eat from a traditional underground *hangi* (oven). Do this in Rotorua as part of an organized tour experience, or seek permission to visit one of the dozens of East Cape marae (village commons).
- o **Watching the Birds:** Make a date with a baby **kiwi** in Franz Josef (p. 303), or shine your spotlight on a foraging kiwi on Stewart Island (p. 391). The **kotuku** (white heron) nesting season is short (Nov–Feb), but the chicks and parents are at home for visitors (p. 301). December to February is the time

to visit the only **royal albatross** colony in New Zealand (p. 377). Penguins are found in many coastal crannies, but sighting them is not that simple. Luckily, a colony of **blue-eyed penguins** puts on a nightly show in Oamaru as they rush up from the sea to nesting places (p. 367). And last but not least, wave off thousands of **godwits and gannets** at Farewell Spit (p. 283).

o **Whale-Watch in Kaikoura:** When a mighty sperm whale flaps its tail at you, you won't forget it soon. These big sea monsters come to this particular stretch of water for a marine habitat rich in their kind of plankton. Don't be surprised to see dolphins aplenty, too. See chapter 13.

NEW ZEALAND'S best ARCHITECTURAL LANDMARKS

North Island

o **Auckland War Memorial Museum ★★★** (Auckland): Auckland's monumental war museum lies on the rim of an ancient volcano enveloped in parks and gardens. (The museum's colonnades are said to be a near-replica of the Greek Parthenon.) A newer dome entrance in the Atrium shows off contemporary New Zealand architecture. See p. 64.

o **The Sky Tower ★★★** (Auckland): The tallest manmade structure in the Southern Hemisphere soars above the cityscape at 328m (1,076 ft.), affording unforgettable views from two observation decks. Three glass-fronted elevators can whiz up the building in a speedy 40 seconds. See p. 66.

o **St. Mary's Church ★★★** (Tikitiki, East Cape): This ornate Maori church was built in 1924 to honor the soldiers of Ngati Porou who lost their lives in World War I. The interior is a masterpiece of intricate Maori design, the carvings by local Ngati Porou. See p. 190.

South Island

o **The Christchurch Transitional Cardboard Cathedral** (234 Hereford St., Christchurch): When the original Christ Church Cathedral was badly damaged in the Christchurch earthquake in February 2011, the Anglican diocese came up with a temporary solution: the Transitional Cathedral. Designed by Japanese architect Shigeru Ibu, it is constructed largely of cardboard and light timbers, most visible in the exterior walls of huge cardboard "tubes." The interior of the cathedral is bathed in the natural light streaming between the tubes. See p. 315.

o **Stranges Building** (219 High St., Christchurch): A striking building on a tight triangular corner in the rebuilt Christchurch CBD, it contains offfices, shops, bars, and cafes. Multicolored glazing belies the strength of the building; it has been built to 180% of the seismic code.

o **The Arts Centre** (30 Worcester Blvd., Christchurch): Designed by architects Benjamin Mountford and Hurst Seager and built in 1876 as an education facility, this pleasing collection of neo-Gothic buildings is clustered around a lovely quadrangle. In 1973 it became the Christchurch Arts Centre, housing artist studios, theaters, a dance school, galleries, shops, cafes, and restaurants. Badly damaged in the 2011 earthquake, it has undergone a NZ$20-million restoration, and today much of the facility has reopened. See p. 313.

o **Ilex Event Centre** (Christchurch Botanic Gardens, Christchurch): A zigzag structure of tall glass walls wraps around a souvenir shop, cafe, and plant nursery in the Botanic Gardens. Designed by Patterson Associates Ltd., Christchurch, it is cleverly sited just above the Avon River, making it part of river walk. See p. 314.

o **Oamaru's Victorian Harbour Precinct** (Harbour/Tyne sts., Oamaru): Left behind when the harbor closed to coastal shipping, this Victorian-era cluster of streets, ornate limestone buildings, and warehouses has been reinvented, reinvigorated, and restored as a commercial hub of shops, cafes, bars, hotels, and galleries. See p. 366.

o **Oamaru Opera House** (Thames St., Oamaru): Designed by architect J. M. Forrester, the Opera House opened in 1907. Its grandeur faded, but the building remained largely in its original condition until it was fully restored in 2010. The facade is less ornate than might be expected, but nothing has been held back in the auditorium: Think ornate plastering, gilding galore, and an Edwardian proscenium arch. And it works. Everything from opera to indie bands have taken the stage in the decade since restoration. See p. 367.

o **Dunedin Railway Station** (Anzac Ave., Dunedin): Opened in 1906, this impressive decorative building was described by its architect as "Flemish Renaissance." We're a long way from Belgium, but you have to love such a flamboyant face for a port cargo railway station. See p. 374.

THE best PLACES TO STAY IN NEW ZEALAND

North Island

o **Sofitel Auckland Viaduct Harbour ★★★** (Auckland): Five-star luxury in the heart of Auckland, with gorgeous harbor views and boutique extras like candle rituals at night. See p. 48.

o **Eagles Nest ★★★** (Bay of Islands): This eco-friendly retreat is fit for a rock star, with luxurious appointments and boutique touches. The views overlooking the Bay of Islands are soul-stirring, and you've a good chance of spotting a kiwi lurking in the native bush. See p. 100.

o **The French Country House ★★★** (Pahoia, Tauranga): Tasteful elegance in a manor-style home set on 16 hectares (40 acres) of rolling countryside with horses, cattle, and enormous chickens. Settle in to one of the plump sofas and warm yourself by the blazing fire. See p. 125.

○ **Treetops Lodge & Estate** ★★★ (Horohoro): For privacy and posh, this luxury lodge is hard to beat. Its vast grounds include an 800-year-old forest, trout streams, and lakes. Go horseback riding, fish for trout, or dine on Michelin-starred meals. See p. 154.

○ **Huka Lodge** ★★★ (Taupa): The grounds (7 hectares/17 acres of immaculate riverside privacy), the gorgeous rooms, the wonderful food and—take my word for it—the best service will stay in your memory long after you have moved on. They'll arrange anything you may want to do, but you and the family may find it hard to venture off-lodge. It has numerous places to dine: from the formal Trophy Room, where you'll be watched by lots of dead animal heads, to a nice spot down by the river. A stay in the four-suite **Owner's Cottage** or the two-suite **Alan Pye Cottage** will practically melt your credit card, but you won't regret it. Both have infinity swimming pools and Jacuzzis and many luxurious touches. Enjoy. See p. 167.

○ **Chateau Tongariro Hotel** ★★★ (Whakapapa Village): This grande dame and New Zealand icon enjoys a choice perch at the base of Mount Ruapehu. It's solidly gracious, with lobby and lounges full of plump armchairs and sparkling chandeliers. See p. 180.

○ **Ahu Ahu Beach Villas** ★★★ (Oakura): This lovely beach accommodation of four units and three family villas was crafted from all manner of recycled and repurposed bits and pieces—100-year-old French clay tiles, power poles, driftwood. They're as amazing as their location, overlooking the Tasman Sea. See p. 218.

○ **Wharekauhau Country Estate** ★★★ (Featherstone): The current Duke and Duchess of Cambridge (William and Kate) stayed at this 2,000-hectare (5,000-acre) working sheep station, with views out over Palliser Bay. This award-winning estate offers royals and non-royals alike loads of luxury and comfort. See p. 264.

South Island

○ **Wakefield Quay House** ★★★ (Nelson): Perched high above Nelson's Wakefield Quay, the Wakefield Quay House, a heritage villa from 1905, incorporates a luxurious guest area comprising ensuite guest rooms, the Crow's Nest, the Captain's Room, and a grand breakfast room. The large veranda is the perfect setting for evening drinks as the sun sets over the bay. See p. 278.

○ **The Theatre Royal Hotel** ★★ (Kumara): Enjoying a resurgence of style, the Theatre Royal Hotel was rescued from dishevelment and restored to its Victorian glory days, with deliciously cozy ensuite rooms, a busy bar, and a good restaurant. There's nary a hint of ghostly miners, flash floozies, or music-hall actors, but you can't have everything. See p. 296.

○ **The Limetree Lodge** ★★★ (Wanaka): In a previous life hosts Pauline and John were farming in an isolated part of the South Island—meaning they were always ready and well prepared to welcome callers. They have brought a great hospitality ethos to their Wanaka property, where comfort abounds. Options of B&B or bed, breakfast, and dinner. See p. 346.

o **Observation Rock Lodge** ★★★ (Halfmoon Bay): Wake to panoramic views of the blue waters of Paterson Inlet—plus gourmet breakfasts, hot tub soaks, and kayakiing expeditions at this boutique lodge. See p. 392.

THE best RESTAURANTS IN NEW ZEALAND

North Island

o **The French Café** ★★★ (Auckland): The accolades and awards keep coming, but you should experience this fine-dining destination yourself, where exquisitely prepared food meets impeccable service and a smartly designed modern-farmhouse ambience. See p. 57.

o **'a Deco** ★★★ (Whangarei): With a name that's shorthand for the handsome Art Deco building it occupies, this Whangarei award-winner showcases regional foods with a modern twist. See p. 108.

o **Chim Choo Ree** ★★★ (Hamilton): This hip city restaurant is located by the river in a tree-shrouded spot in the lovely old Waikato Brewery building. The kitchen produces interesting mashups (cured venison with puffed buckwheat and chèvre), accompanied by an eclectic wine list and good craft beers. See p. 117.

o **Plateau Bar & Eatery** ★★★ (Taupo): Serving local cuisine with an emphasis on carnivore fare, Plateau has won awards and the hearts of happy locals, who can be seen here on Friday nights kicking back and enjoying the good food and drink in the festive, casual atmosphere. See p. 170.

o **Elephant Hill** ★★★ (Te Awanga): This strikingly modern winery restaurant takes advantage of its setting with floor-to-ceiling glass windows and a large deck overlooking rows of grapevines, the blue Pacific and the flat-topped Kidnapper Cliffs. The food rambles the countryside, from smoked venison to grilled whitefish to glazed duck with softshell crab. See p. 209.

o **Logan Brown** ★★★ (Wellington): This 20-year-old city icon still excels in the business of feeding and pampering diners. It's smack-dab in the inner city, and the afternoon high tea on Friday and Saturday is a nice way to soak in the ambience without paying dinner prices. See p. 238.

South Island

o **Arbour** ★★★ (Blenheim): We love it for its culinary finesse, use of seasonal ingredients, and wine-matching flair. See p. 274.

o **Fat Pipi Pizzas** ★★★ (Hokitika): Makes the best pizza. (Even one with whitebait.) End of story. See p. 301.

o **Harlequin Public House** ★★★ (Christchurch): The city is not short of good restaurants, and picking the best is like naming one of your children as your favorite. Harlequin Public House takes top prize thanks to the determination of owner/chef Jonny Schwass to push local/fresh/innovative. The menu features cheap cuts as well as extravagances, and the service is swift, professional, and friendly. See p. 320.

o **Caffeine Laboratory** ★★★ (Christchurch): Sure it's small, but its coffee is fantastic and the food is big on flavors and innovation, such as fish tacos with cucumber cress and radish salad and a saffron-infused mayonnaise. See p. 319.

o **Madam Woo** ★★★ (Queenstown): Both fancy and friendly, Madam Woo gets the tick of approval for its take on Malaysian/New Zealand/European dishes. See p. 338.

o **Amisfield Winery Estate** ★★★ (Arrowtown): Famous firstly for its Trust the Chef menu, it continues to take the top prize for innovation. A great eating experience accompanied by—it goes without saying—terrific wines. See p. 330.

o **Gentil Bistro** ★★★ (Wanaka): Masters at the helm make a huge difference to a destination restaurant, even in a popular lakeside resort. The owner is French, the executive chef is English, and both are culinary masters. The menu is outstanding, the wine list is amazing, and plenty of attention is paid to the beer list. See p. 346.

o **Plato Dunedin** ★★★ (Dunedin): The decor has definitely changed, but the attention is really all on the food. Simple classics with many a tweak keep the flavors interesting. See p. 379.

THE best CYCLE TRAILS IN NEW ZEALAND

o **Alps to Ocean** (310km, 6 days): A sweeping landscape is viewed from behind the handlebars along this trail, which runs from the Tasman Valley in Mount Cook National Park to Oamaru's Victorian Harbor Precinct. The mountains nudging Aoraki/Mount Cook are gigantic and jagged. The lakes are huge and about 50 shades of blue, and the trail rides on and on past rivers and plains and villages, cliffs of clay and hydro dams. Ancient drawings in limestone caves, vineyards, mobs of sheep, and finally the curious sight of perfectly preserved Victorian buildings. Accommodation includes former schoolhouses, country cottages, restored railway sheds, and farm lodges.

o **Otago Rail Trail** (150km, 1–5 days): This is the bike ride that has inspired thousands to hop on a bike and follow an old train track bed through the glorious Central Otago countryside. It's like being in a landscape painting, albeit one that puffs out the cleanest, sweetest air you might ever breathe. Rail bridges and a tunnel or two add a touch of drama, and at the end of each day you're rewarded with a restaurant or pub and a charming place to lay down your head (and bicycle).

o **Little River Trail** (50km, 1 day): Perhaps the easiest South Island trail, this gets the popular vote from those who enjoy a quiet bike ride along a pretty route. The landscape flicks from the busy hub of Hornby to glimpses of old settlements, the flanks of ancient volcanoes, wildlife habitats, and the pretty township of Little River where the local gallery/craft store is a must-see.

THE best MUSEUMS IN NEW ZEALAND

North Island

o **Auckland War Memorial Museum** ★★★ (Auckland): This top-flight museum experience holds the largest collection of Maori and Polynesian artifacts in the world, plus an interactive volcanoes gallery and a lovely sculpture walk. See p. 64.

o **New Zealand Maritime Museum** ★★★ (Auckland): Located right on the harbor, this museum contains working displays and exhibitions documenting 1,000 years of New Zealand maritime history. Watch traditional boat craftsmen, peruse the exhibit on America's Cup history, and take a breezy harbor ride on a heritage sailing ship. See p. 68.

o **Waikato Museum** ★★★ (Hamilton): Waikato history, culture, and place in the world are center stage here, with impressive Maori art and weaving and carving from the area's Tainui people, plus a very good World War I exhibition. See p. 112.

o **Rotorua Museum** ★★★ (Rotorua): This spa town's historical treasure house is set in the old Bath House building, a delightful Edwardian assemblage of fairy-tale gables and turrets. It tells the story of the Te Arawa (the first people to live in this area) and subsequent settlers, not to mention the history of the world-famous Bath House itself, built in 1908 as the "Great South Seas Spa." See p. 142.

o **Tawhiti Museum** ★★★ (Hawera): This delightful collection may just be the best private museum in the country. Former art teacher Nigel Ogle created life-size exhibits and scale models that encapsulate the history of Taranaki. Take a ride around the museum environs on the **Tawhiti Bush Railway,** a little logging train. See p. 214.

o **Museum of New Zealand–Te Papa Tongarewa** ★★★ (Wellington): New Zealand's so-called "national" museum has been the capital's top attraction since it opened in 1998. Te Papa, as it's known, brings the fun into the museum experience with interactive technology and world-class exhibitions that eloquently tell the story of New Zealand—its art, culture, history, and environment. It's a beautiful piece of architecture as well, a beacon of modernity facing the waterfront. See p. 244.

South Island

o **Aviation Heritage Aircraft** ★★★ (Omaka, near Blenheim): This is a must-visit for everyone with an interest in aviation, WW1, or history in general. Who knew those early flyboys had so many aircraft at their disposal, or that so many clever chaps could actually manufacture these planes, let alone fly them? Fascinating, funny, and inspirational. See p. 271.

o **WOW: The World of Wearable Art** ★★★ (Nelson): WOW took Nelson by storm when it was first staged. It took a year or two to gain a wider audience, but just look at the show now! It's a world-beater that sadly is now staged in Wellington, but Nelson has the back story. The fantastical, fabulous entries come from all over the world, and we should all be thankful that a museum has opened to display them. See p. 276.

o **Toitu Otago Settlers Museum** ★★★ (Dunedin): This museum not only focuses on how our great-granny lived and worked, but it pays attention to 20th-century details as well. Vintage washing machine anyone? Or a Buick? Plan on a couple of hours, maybe more, as every corner of this very urbane museum has interesting objects and exhibitions. See p. 375.

o **Transport World** ★★★ (Invercargill): So who knew old trucks could hold so much interest for so many people? The collection holds exhibits garnered not only from local Invercargill sheds, but pretty flash treasures trawled in the U.S. as well, including Henry Ford's first cars right up to the Model T. Gas (petrol) pumps of yesteryear, old paddy waggons, and who knows what all. It's so well-exhibited that no overload is detected. See p. 385.

THE best BEACHES IN NEW ZEALAND

North Island

o **Waiheke Island's Onetangi Bay:** Stand on the bay's wide stretch of golden sand, and you can see for miles. On a clear day, throw yourself down into the sand and gaze at the steep pinnacles of Great Barrier Island and Little Barrier, off in the hazy distance. There might even be a few glimpses of the Coromandel in between deliciously warm swims.

o **Karikari Peninsula's Beaches:** This is the Far North at its subtropical best, where endless sweeps of sparkling white sand are lapped by crystal-clear, azure-blue waters. And from Tokerau Beach to Rangiputa to Matai Bay, you may have miles of it to yourself for beachcombing, sunbathing, and swimming (with care).

South Island

o **Tahunanui** (Nelson): The sea is shallow and warm here, with gentle waves and a good-for-families beach with attached activities: bumpa cars, paddleboarding, and a skating rink. See p. 278.

o **Marahau to Totarunui** (Abel Tasman National Park): The sand here is golden unlike that the east coast, where it is universally beige. The beaches are tucked between rocky (often limestone) outcrops and bush that reaches almost to the tide mark. It's hard to beat for sheer romanticism, which might be a reason for the popularity of kayaking here, blessed by the whoosh of paddles rather than the whine of powerboats. See p. 281.

o **Wharariki** (Golden Bay): This is a walking beach, not a beach for swimming. Wild seas pound it, giant sandhills are shaped by the strong winds off the Tasman Seas, and all is drama. It is a wilderness place with dramatic caves and quiet rock pools. See p. 283.

NEW ZEALAND IN CONTEXT

*K*ia ora, welcome to New Zealand! Get used to this greeting because you will hear it—and likely use it—plenty during your New Zealand experience. It means "hello" as a greeting or "go well" as a farewell. This chapter is designed to help you understand a little more about New Zealand's fascinating culture, language, history, and people.

LOOKING BACK: NEW ZEALAND HISTORY

EARLY MAORI SETTLEMENT   There's more than one theory on how New Zealand's first inhabitants settled here. The Maori legend tells of Kupe, who in A.D. 950 sailed from Hawaiiki, the traditional homeland of the Polynesians. The legend doesn't tell us exactly where Hawaiiki was located in the South Pacific, but present-day authorities believe it belonged to the Society Islands group that includes Tahiti.

It wasn't until the mid–14th century that Maori arrived in great numbers. They found abundant supplies of seafood and berries, which they supplemented with tropical plants like taro, yams, and kumara (sweet potato) they'd brought from Hawaiiki. Dogs and rats also made the voyage, and they were added to the protein source. The cultivation of these imported vegetables and animals gradually led to an agricultural society with permanent villages based on a central *marae* (village common or courtyard) and *whare runanga* (meetinghouse). This is where the distinctive Maori art forms of woodcarving and tattooing evolved.

ABEL TASMAN & DUTCH DISCOVERY   The first recorded sighting of New Zealand by Europeans occurred in December 1642. Abel Tasman, who was scouting territory for the Dutch East India Company, spied the west coast of the South Island and entered Golden Bay. As his two ships anchored, several Maori war canoes launched and paddlers shouted hostile challenges. The next day, Maori attacked, killing four sailors. Tasman fired at the retreating canoes and departed.

CAPTAIN COOK When Captain James Cook left England in 1768 on the *Endeavour*, he carried orders from King George III to sail south in search of the "continent" reported by Abel Tasman. If he found it uninhabited, he was to plant the English flag and claim it for the king; if not, he was to take possession of "convenient situations," but only with the consent of the indigenous people.

On October 7, 1769, Nicholas Young, son of the ship's surgeon, spotted New Zealand from his perch in the mast. Naming the headland (in the Gisborne area) Young Nick's Head, Cook sailed into a bay and anchored. With the help of a young Tahitian chief, Tupea, who had sailed with the crew as a guide and interpreter, Cook tried to make contact with the Maori, but to no avail. They remained hostile. Disappointed, Cook claimed the country for King George and England.

THE BRITISH ARRIVE The immigration of Europeans, mostly from Great Britain, had a devastating impact on Maori culture. Most destructive was the introduction of liquor, muskets, and diseases. Missionaries arriving in New Zealand at this time translated the oral language of Maori and put it in writing, established schools, and upgraded tribal agricultural methods through the use of ploughs and windmills.

THE TREATY OF WAITANGI From 1829 the "New Zealand Company," an English organization, began sending emissaries to buy land from the Maori and establish settlements. Between 1839 and 1843, it sent 57 ships carrying 19,000 settlers, as the nucleus of a permanent British population.

In 1839, Captain William Hobson was sent by the British government to sort out the concerns over land purchased and land taken. He arranged an assembly of Maori chiefs at Waitangi in the Bay of Islands and on February 6, 1840, the Treaty of Waitangi was signed. The treaty guaranteed Maori "all the rights and privileges of British subjects" in exchange for their acknowledgment of British sovereignty, while granting the Crown exclusive rights to buy land from the Maori. Instead of easing tensions, though, the Treaty of Waitangi ushered in one of the bloodiest periods in New Zealand's history. The British were eager to exercise their right to purchase Maori land, and while some chiefs were eager to sell, others were not. As pressures forced them to sell, the Maori revolted, and when Chief Hone Heke hacked down the British flagpole at Kororareka (Russell) in 1844, it signaled the beginning of some 20 years of fierce battles. The British would emerge victorious, but the seizure of that Maori land continues to be a subject of debate today.

FROM WAITANGI TO THE PRESENT By the time the 1860s arrived, gold had been discovered in the South Island. The gold rushes opened up huge tracts of Westland and Otago. Cobb & Co, the stagecoach company, extended their operations to link the major centers with Christchurch and Dunedin. Advances in rail transport followed, and with waves of new immigrants keen to seek a (golden) fortune, New Zealand entered a period of lively economic activity.

In 1892, the introduction of the first refrigerated shipment of lamb to England heralded a new era in New Zealand meat exports.

History was made again in 1893 when New Zealand became the first country in the world to allow women to vote.

In 1914, 100, 000 New Zealanders joined the Australia–New Zealand Army Corps (ANZAC) and joined Britain to fight in World War I. Some 2,000 young New Zealand men—and some women in the Nursing Corp—died in this conflict and are still remembered in Europe for their sacrifice. "THEY CAME FROM THE UTTERMOST ENDS OF THE EARTH" is the inscription on many memorials on the old battlefields. ANZAC Day is a national holiday in New Zealand.

The Depression of the 1930s brought unemployment, work camps, and riots. In 1939, New Zealand soldiers returned to battle with the advent of World War II. In 1947 the Statute of Westminster gave New Zealand full independence from Britain, and by the 1950s the country was enjoying what is referred to as a golden era. (although older people remember it as gray rather than golden for its many rules and restrictions). Prices for farmed wool and meat ensured a booming rural economy, and unemployment was so low the then Prime Minister claimed to know all 11 of the jobless by name. Air travel was affordable, and young and old left the country for months at a time on what has become known as the OE (overseas experience).

By the 1980s, New Zealand was no longer seen as "Britain's Farm," and meat, wool, and butter strove to find new markets. Today, those primary products are sold to a global market, but it is now wine, a wide range of dairy products, fishing, and tourism that are the major movers in the nation's economy.

NEW ZEALAND TODAY

New Zealand is a young nation, growing and changing rapidly, but like the rest of the world we too are affected by global changes; we too have issues with urban drift, city infrastructure and housing. We have cleared old-growth forests, extracted coal and gold, and too often shown little respect for our unique-ness. We think differently now.

Multiculturalism is changing the way we live. In 1987 when the concern was biculturism, a tribunal was set up to address Maori issues dating from the settlement years (1839–43). A balance of that land was returned to Maori ownership, and many tribes have established lucrative business and corporate entities in the seafood, forestry, farming, and tourism industries. Since that time we have welcomed immigrants from the wider Pacific, predominately Samoa and Tonga and more recently Korea, Thailand, India, and China. Each immigrant enriches and adds to our nation—be it in education, music, hospitality, or agriculture.

Our cultural heart beats strongly, adding vibrancy to daily life. New Zealand artists, writers, musicians, actors, and filmmakers have developed an enthusiastic international audience.

ART, BOOKS & FILMS

ART New Zealand's artistic roots are embedded in a mix of European tradition and Maori influences. The early European tradition favored an emblematic and literary pairing of image and subject matter leaned toward the land. The Maori tradition of figurative imagery (traditionally expressed in carving) asserted a strong genealogical identity.

Among the most collectible of our 20th-century artists whose work shows an identity with the land are **Colin McCahon** (1919–87), **Toss Woollaston** (1910–98), **Rita Angus** (1908–70), **Doris Lusk** (1916–90), **Trevor Moffitt** (1936–2006), and **Ralph Hotere** (1931–2013). Among a plethora of current sought-after artists, **Shane Cotton, Michael Parekowhai, Philip Trusttum, Barry Cleavin, Neil Dawson, Bing Dawe, Séraphine Pick, Richard Killeen,** and **Gretchen Albrecht** stand out. As ever, art lovers and collectors should seek out dealers and art galleries for advice and direction.

BOOKS Appreciating a land and its people is never easy in a few days or weeks, but there are many New Zealand writers whose work reveals much of their country. A suggested reading list includes *The Collected Stories of Katherine Mansfield* (Wordsworth, 2006); *Owls Do Cry,* by Janet Frame (George Braziller, 1982); *Potiki* by Patricia Grace (University of Hawaii Press, 1995); *Essential NZ Short Stories,* by Owen Marshall (Random House New Zealand, 2002); *Once Were Warriors,* by Alan Duff (University of Hawaii Press, 1990); **NZ Wars Trilogy,** by Maurice Shadbolt (David Ling Publishing Limited, 2005); and *The Luminaries,* by Eleanor Catton (Little, Brown and Company, 2013).

FILM Director and New Zealand native **Sir Peter Jackson** grabbed headlines when he secured Hollywood funding for *The Lord of the Rings,* which was filmed in 2000 with the biggest film budget ever. His *Heavenly Creatures* (1994) was the winner of the Silver Lion at the Venice Film Festival; and of course the *Lord of the Rings* trilogy went on to win a cluster of Oscars. Jackson has since added to his success with *King Kong* and *The Hobbit* trilogy. The Weta Studios in Wellington are closely associated with Jackson's productions and its studio is now a major tourism venture, spurred on by Jackson's success, we now have a thriving film industry.

Two of Maori author Alan Duff's novels have also been made into successful films: *Once Were Warriors* and *What Becomes of the Broken Hearted* shocked audiences with their true-to-life violent portrayal of Maori gang society. Niki Caro's *Whale Rider* in 2002 won international acclaim.

EATING & DRINKING
Dining Customs

o Tipping is not customary in New Zealand, although an extra 5% to 10% gratuity showing thanks for good service and good food is appreciated.

o A restaurant or cafe stating that it "serves wine, beer, spirits, cocktails" is fully licensed to serve alcohol and likely to have a bar. A restaurant or cafe advertising itself as BYO is licensed to sell and serve alcohol but also allows diners to Bring Your Own. *Note:* BYO usually means wine only. If in doubt ask when making a booking. A corkage fee is generally charged (NZ$4–$15).

o New Zealand restaurants and cafes are legally allowed to charge extra on public holidays (a surcharge) to cover the extra cost of the increase in hourly wages on such days. Not every restaurant adds the surcharge. The information will be included on menus.

o All eateries are now smoke-free. This is the law, with smoking banned across the board in all public buildings.

o Fast-food joints, takeout meals, and snack shops including McDonald's, BurgerFuel, KFC, Pizza Hut, Starbucks, sushi bars, and muffin stops are widely available. Homegrown favorite snacks include **fish 'n' chips**— deep-fried battered fish filets and potato chips/fries firmly wrapped in paper (deep-fried sausages, onion rings, oysters, pineapple rings, and hot dogs are usually available in the same outlet). Small **meat pies** (hand pies) are another popular snack and are widely available, with many small convenience stores and even service stations keeping them warm in a ubiquitous pie-warmer. A sweet tomato-based sauce is the popular accompaniment, and fillings are usually mince (ground beef) and/or cheese (NZ$5).

o A **Maori** *hangi,* where food is cooked underground, is a must-do experience. Traditionally, it involves lighting a fire and putting large stones in the embers to heat. Simultaneously, a large pit is dug. The heated rocks are then transferred into the pit, covered with wet sacking and/or wet newspapers. Prepared lamb, chicken, pork, fish, shellfish, and vegetables (most commonly sweet potato, pumpkin, and cabbage) are wrapped in leaves, placed in flax baskets (now made of wire or mesh), and lowered into the cooking pit, covered with more newspaper and earth, and left to steam. The moist, tender, melt-in-your-mouth food is lifted out a few hours later.

o Restaurants that offer à **la carte menus** serve (a) **entrées** or starters; (b) **mains,** or main event; and (c) **desserts** or sweet courses, or to finish. Entrees include breads and spreads, tasty morsels such as oysters and clams, and soups. Mains feature meat, fish, pasta or vegetarian dishes, any of which may or may not include vegetables. Desserts may include crème brulee, pannacotta, fruit crumble, hot soufflé, or a cheese suggestion. Other menu inclusions: **sides** (vegetables, fries) and **salads** (green, slaw, rice, etc.). Many restaurants offer gluten-free, dairy-free, and nut-free dishes.

WHEN TO GO

New Zealand is in the Southern Hemisphere; therefore, all seasons are the opposite of those in North America, Europe, and other Northern Hemisphere locations.

There really isn't a bad time to travel to New Zealand., though most New Zealanders take their main annual holidays between Christmas and mid-January, which puts pressure on accommodations in major summer destinations. During the Easter break and school holidays in April, June to July, and September to October (see "Holidays," below, for dates), it also pays to reserve well in advance.

Weather

New Zealand's climate, especially by Northern Hemisphere standards, is pretty mellow for much of the year. You'll find a far greater seasonal difference in the South Island than in the subtropical North, and don't believe anyone who says it never gets cold here or that there are no extremes. In Central Otago, winter temperatures are often 14°F (–10°C) and sometimes as low as –4°F (–20°C), with summers up to 100°F to 104°F (38°C–40°C). By comparison, the northern part of the North Island is subtropical. That means *lots* of winter/spring rain, and often daily light showers.

The west coast of the South Island can get up to 100 inches or more of rain a year on its side of the Southern Alps, while just over the mountains to the east, rainfall is a moderate 20 to 30 inches annually. Rain is also heavier on the west coast of the North Island, averaging 40 to 70 inches annually. Milford Sound, though, beats the lot; it's the wettest place in the country, with a phenomenal 365 inches of rain a year.

THE SEASONS

SPRING (SEPT, OCT, NOV)   The countryside is flush with new green grass, baby lambs, and blooming trees. Christchurch in the spring means blossoms, bluebells, and daffodils in abundance; Dunedin is a splurge of rhododendron color. The weather can still be very changeable right up to mid-October, so come prepared with light rain gear. In the South Island, it's not unusual to get a late snowfall.

SUMMER (DEC, JAN, FEB)   From Christmas to mid-January, New Zealand goes on holiday and visitor hotspots are filling up. Planning and booking ahead is the way to go. Foodies take note: This is stone fruit season, with cherries, apricots, peaches, and nectarines at their ripest best. In Otago the wildflowers and mountain herbs are blooming and vineyards are heavy with fruit. The fruitful season has arrived.

AUTUMN (MAR, APR, MAY)   The best months to visit are February, March, and April. The temperatures are pleasant, and in April you'll be wearing summer clothes in the upper North Island. The most spectacular autumn colors are found in Queenstown, Central Otago, and Christchurch. Late April sees the grape harvest coming in.

WINTER (JUNE, JULY, AUG)   Ski season! Ski areas in Queenstown, mid-Canterbury, and the Central Plateau in the North Island should be open for business. Resort towns around ski areas will be bustling.

Average Seasonal Temperature & Rainfall

Temperatures reflected are daily average (°C/°F). Rainfall reflects the daily average in millimeters/inches (mm/in.) and is accurate within 1 millimeter.

	SUMMER	FALL	WINTER	SPRING
BAY OF ISLANDS				
MAX. TEMP	25/77	21/70	16/61	19/66
MIN. TEMP	14/57	11/52	7/45	9/48
RAINFALL	7/0.28	1/0.44	16/0.64	11/0.44
WESTPORT				
MAX. TEMP	22/72	17/63	13/55	15/59
MIN. TEMP	12/54	10/50	5/41	8/46
RAINFALL	12/0.48	14/0.56	15/0.6	16/0.64
AUCKLAND				
MAX. TEMP	24/75	20/68	15/59	18/65
MIN. TEMP	12/54	13/55	9/48	11/52
RAINFALL	8/0.32	11/0.44	15/0.6	12/0.48
CHRISTCHURCH				
MAX. TEMP	22/72	18/65	12/54	17/63
MIN. TEMP	12/54	8/46	3/37	7/45
RAINFALL	7/0.28	7/0.28	7/0.28	7/0.28
ROTORUA				
MAX. TEMP	24/75	18/65	13/55	17/63
MIN. TEMP	12/54	9/48	4/39	7/45
RAINFALL	9/0.36	9/0.36	13/0.52	11/0.44
MOUNT COOK				
MAX. TEMP	20/68	14/57	8/46	14/57
MIN. TEMP	9/48	4/39	-1/30	4/39
RAINFALL	12/0.48	13/0.52	13/0.52	14/0.56
WELLINGTON				
MAX. TEMP	20/68	17/63	12/54	15/59
MIN. TEMP	13/55	11/52	6/43	9/48
RAINFALL	7/0.28	10/0.4	13/0.52	11/0.44
QUEENSTOWN				
MAX. TEMP	22/72	16/61	10/50	16/61
MIN. TEMP	10/50	6/43	1/34	5/41
RAINFALL	8/0.32	8/0.32	7/0.28	9/0.36
NELSON				
MAX. TEMP	22/72	18/65	13/55	17/63
MIN. TEMP	13/55	8/46	3/37	7/45
RAINFALL	6/0.24	8/0.32	10/0.4	10/0.4
INVERCARGILL				
MAX. TEMP	18/65	15/59	11/52	15/59
MIN. TEMP	9/48	6/43	1/34	5/41
RAINFALL	13/0.52	14/0.56	12/0.48	13/0.52

Public holidays: New Year's Day (Jan 1), New Year's Holiday (Jan 2), Waitangi Day (Feb 6), Easter Good Friday, Easter and Easter Monday (varies), ANZAC Day (Apr 25), Queen's Birthday (first Mon in June), Labour Day (last Mon in Oct), Christmas Day (Dec 25), and Boxing Day (Dec 26).

Regional holidays: Wellington (Jan 22), Auckland (Jan 29), Northland (Jan 29), Nelson Region (Feb 1), Otago (Mar 23), Southland (Mar 23), Taranaki (Mar 31), Hawke's Bay (Nov 1), Marlborough (Nov 1), Westland (Dec 1), and Canterbury (observed on the Fri of the second week in Nov).

School holidays: Four school terms are observed. Dates may vary, but as a guide Term 1 is January 27 to April 3. Term 2 is April 20 to July 3. Term 3 is July 20 to September 26. Term 4 (summer term) is October 12 to December 17 Dates can vary between schools, but the longest holiday period is December to January, when NZ families also take a summer holiday.

For a calendar of **special events and local festivals,** see the individual destination chapters.

SPEAKING ENZED

The common language might be English, but here in NZ conversation is peppered with quintessentially Kiwi words, phrases, and colloquialisms. Here are some everyday New Zealand words and phrases and what they mean.

Bach   North Island term for vacation house (plural: baches)

Bath   Bathtub

Bathroom   Where one bathes; bath

Biscuits/bikkies   Cookies

Bludge   Borrow

Bonnet   Hood of car

Boot   Trunk of car

Bro   Slang for "brother"; a friendly term used widely

Bush   Forest but usually only smaller trees

Chemist shop   Drugstore

Chilly bin   Cooler (U.S.), esky (Aus.)

Cocky   A farmer

Cot   Crib (place where a baby or toddler sleeps)

Crib   Term for holiday house in Otago or Southland

Cuppa   Cup of tea

Dairy   Convenience store

Do   As in "a bit of a do"; a party

Duvet   Comforter, quilt or doona (Aus.)

En suite   Bathroom attached to a bedroom and used only those using the bedroom

Fanny   Female genitalia; you'll shock Kiwis if you call the thing you wear around your waist a "fanny pack"

Footpath   Sidewalk

Gallops   Thoroughbred horse racing

Get stuck in   Get started

Gidday   Hello

Grizzle   Complain

Grog   alcoholic drinks as in "where's the grog?"

Hire   Rent

Hooker   Front-row rugby player

Hotties   Hot-water bottles used to heat beds when there is no electricity or electric blankets

Jandals   Flip-flops
Judder bars   Speed bumps
Jug   Electric kettle or a pitcher
Knickers   Underwear, undies
Knock up   Wake up
Loo   Toilet
Lounge   Living or sitting room
Mate   Friend
Mossie   Mosquito
Nappy   Diaper
Queue   Line, to wait in line
Return ticket   Round-trip ticket
Serviette   Napkin
Shout   Treat someone (usually refers to a meal or a drink), buy a round
Single bed   Twin bed
Singlet   Sleeveless undershirt or fashion top
Sister   Nurse
Smoko   Morning or afternoon break
Strides   Trousers as worn by a man
Ta   Thank you
To call   To visit or to contact by telephone
Togs   Swimsuit
To ring   To phone
Track trail for hiking
Tramping   Hiking
Trots   Harness racing. Or a stomach complaint involving diarrhea
Varsity   University, college

Food Terms

Afghans   Popular Kiwi cookies made with cornflakes and cocoa
ANZAC biscuits   Cookies popular during WW2 but not actually posted overseas as often believed. They were made with golden syrup rather than sugar to get around sugar rationing.
Bangers   Sausages
Beetroot   Beets
Blue vein   Bleu cheese
Chips   French-fried potatoes
Chook   Chicken
Dinner   The main meal of the day; can be the meal eaten in the middle of the day
Entrée   Appetizer or first course. The second course in NZ is the "main"
Hogget   A lamb that is more than 1 year old
Jelly   Gelatin dessert
Marmite   A popular yeast-based breakfast spread
Meat pie   A two-crust pie filled with stewed, cubed, or ground meat and gravy. Can be any size but in fast-food outlets, it will be a hand pie.

maori

The Maori language is a Polynesian dialect. It was first given a written form in the early 19th century by missionaries and British linguists. Today, there are Maori radio stations and television channels, and Maori terms and words are in common use.

Many place names can be explained by their prefixes and suffixes. For example:

Ao   Cloud
Ika   Fish
Nui   Big, or plenty of
Roto   Lake
Rua   Cave, or hollow, or two (Rotorua's two lakes)
Tahi   One, single
Te   The
Wai   Water
Whanga   Bay, inlet, or stretch of water

Then there are frequently used words. For example:

Haka   Dance (war, funeral, and so on)

Hangi   Oven made by filling a hole with heated stones, and the feast roasted in it
Hongi   The traditional greeting that involves a pressing together of noses in traditional greeting
Karakia   Prayer or spell
Kia ora   Hello, Go well
Kumara   Sweet potato
Marae   Courtyard, village common
Pa   Stockade or fortified place
Pakeha   Caucasian person; primarily used to refer to those of European descent
Poi   A ball—traditionally made with flax—with string attached, twirled in action song
Tangi   Funeral with mourning and lamentation
Taonga   Treasure
Tapu   Taboo; a religious or superstitious restriction
Tiki   Human image, sometimes carved of greenstone
Whare   House

Pavlova   Popular dessert named after ballerina Anna Pavlova, consists of layeerred meringue, cream and topped with fruit or chocolate.

Pikelets   Small pancakes served with a cup of tea, Often topped with jam and cream.

Pipis   Shellfish similar to cockles

Pudding   Dessert

Saveloy or sav   A cooked smoked sausage

Scone   A biscuit served with morning or afternoon tea

Silverbeet   Swiss chard

Snarlers   Sausages

Takeaway   Takeout

Tamarillo   Tree tomato

Tomato sauce   Ketchup

Water biscuit   Cracker

Weet-Bix   A breakfast cereal similar to shredded wheat packed flat to a brick shape

Whitebait   Very tiny fish, with an elusive delicate taste. May be served floured and fried or mixed in a batter as a pattie.

White tea   Tea with milk added

SUGGESTED NEW ZEALAND ITINERARIES

3

We hear it all the time: "This is such a small country; we never realized there would be so much to see!" We're talking white-sand beaches and sweeping vineyards, sprawling glaciers and jagged peaks. On the cultural side, you have moving Maori performances, heritage architecture, and smart and quirky museums. Country comes to city in restaurants big and small, where farm-to-table menus draw from a bounty of produce, seafood, and wines. Make the most of your New Zealand trip—and your time—with the following suggested itineraries.

THE REGIONS IN BRIEF

The North Island

AUCKLAND ★★★   Far too often overlooked as little more than a landing port, Auckland has first-rate attractions, quality accommodations, and diverse leisure opportunities. It is without doubt the most cosmopolitan of the cities, and its balmy climate has a special appeal. Waitemata Harbour and Hauraki Gulf offer some of the world's finest sailing, boating, and fishing. Cultural offerings abound in museums, galleries, and performing arts centers, and the shopping is the most diverse in the country. The city has more than 1,000 restaurants and a wild nightlife scene, and if you're into a beach lifestyle, you'll find numerous choices within easy reach. In addition to its big-city attractions, Auckland has a Polynesian backbone that makes it truly unique. If you're touring only the North Island, Auckland is a perfect base.

NORTHLAND ★ & COROMANDEL   Both are within easy reach of Auckland and can be tackled as a day trip if you're short on time. Although each warrants at least a couple of days' exploration, if you have to choose between the two, I'd definitely swing up to the far north. Northland is served by a far better infrastructure in terms of transportation, hotels, and restaurants, and its beach attractions (on the east coast) are too numerous to itemize. That

North Island at a Glance

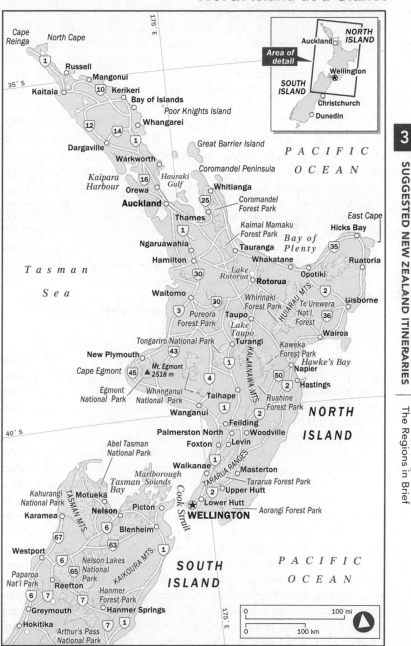

175° E

Cape Reinga

North Cape

1

Russell

Mangonui

35° S

Kaitaia

10

Kerikeri

Bay of Islands

Poor Knights Island

12

14

Whangarei

1

Dargaville

Great Barrier Island

Warkworth

Kaipara Harbour

16

Hauraki Gulf

Coromandel Peninsula

Orewa

Whitianga

Auckland

25

Coromandel Forest Park

Thames

1

Kaimai Mamaku Forest Park

East Cape

Hicks Bay

Ngaruawahia

Tauranga

Bay of Plenty

35

Hamilton

Whakatane

Ruatoria

30

Lake Rotorua

Rotorua

Opotiki

2

Tasman Sea

Waitomo

30

Whirinaki Forest Park

Te Urewera Nat'l Forest

Gisborne

3

Pureora Forest Park

Taupo

Lake Taupo

36

Wairoa

Tongariro National Park

43

Turangi

Kaweka Forest Park

New Plymouth

1

Hawke's Bay

Cape Egmont

45

Mt. Egmont 2518 m

4

50

Napier

2

Hastings

Egmont National Park

Whanganui National Park

Taihape

Ruahine Forest Park

NORTH

Wanganui

1

2

ISLAND

Feilding

40° S

Palmerston North

Woodville

Abel Tasman National Park

Foxton

Levin

Waikanae

1

Marlborough

Masterton

Tasman Sounds

Tararua Forest Park

Kahurangi National Park

Motueka

Bay

2

Upper Hutt

Karamea

Nelson

Picton

Lower Hutt

Aorangi Forest Park

6

WELLINGTON

Blenheim

67

63

1

Westport

6

Nelson Lakes National Park

SOUTH

PACIFIC

65

ISLAND

OCEAN

Paparoa Nat'l Park

Reefton

Hanmer Forest Park

6

7

7

Greymouth

Hanmer Springs

Hokitika

7

1

Arthur's Pass National Park

PACIFIC OCEAN

Area of detail

NORTH ISLAND

Auckland

Wellington

SOUTH ISLAND

Christchurch

Dunedin

0   100 mi

0   100 km

HUIARAU MTS.

KAIMANAWA MTS.

TARARUA RANGES

TASMAN MTS.

KAIKOURA MTS.

Cook Strait

175° E

21

said, you'll find far more tourists here, too, at least in the Bay of Islands area. Head farther north, though, and a whole world of unpopulated beaches awaits. Fishing, diving, boating, and camping are all big draws. The area's rich Maori culture is also an excellent introduction to New Zealand's history.

The Coromandel Peninsula, to the south of Auckland, is a slightly more rugged version of Northland. It has a craggier coastline, a more remote landscape, and sections with very poor roads. Accommodations are middling to say the least (with a few exceptions). Still, there's color and character here, and it's long been a favorite with New Zealand campers and beach bunnies— especially the eastern side of the peninsula, where you'll find top surf beaches.

WAIKATO & BAY OF PLENTY ★   The **Waitomo Caves** have traditionally been Waikato's biggest attraction, and although their natural splendor is undeniable, Waikato itself is a strange hive of tourist buses, darting in and out of otherwise undisturbed farmland. The region's largest city, **Hamilton,** has long been in Auckland's shadow, but this university town has come of age, offering plenty of treasures, including the gorgeous **Hamilton Gardens** and the award-winning **Waikato Museum.**

The sun-drenched paradise known as the Bay of Plenty has become a hot spot, from the ports and harbors of fast-growing **Tauranga** to the beautiful stretch of beach at **Mount Maunganui.** Again, the emphasis is on a beach lifestyle—boating, fishing, surfing, sunbathing, and golf are the main attractions—and some stunning accommodations are available. If you've been to Australia's Gold Coast, you'll sense a hint of that style here.

ROTORUA ★★★, TAUPO ★ & TONGARIRO NATIONAL PARK ★★
Rotorua is on almost every visitor's hit list, and some would say that makes the area objectionably touristy. We disagree. Rotorua has spent millions refining its attractions and accommodations, of which there are many, and it offers a unique geographic and Maori cultural slice of New Zealand life. In terms of adventure tourism, it is biting at the heels of Queenstown.

Taupo and Tongariro National Park, in combination with Rotorua, make the whole central region an unbeatable value in terms of volcanic landscape and adventure variety. Come here for volcanic and Maori attractions, the world's best trout fishing, mountaineering, skiing (water and snow), mountain biking, and tramping.

GISBORNE & HAWKE'S BAY ★★★   This is one of the most underrated areas of the country. The East Cape and Gisborne offer a rare insight into Maori culture, free of tourist hype. The area has amazing beaches and world-class surfing conditions, and, in combination with Hawke's Bay, is probably the country's most important wine-producing region. Gisborne's laid-back rural approach doesn't always find favor with visitors. Hawke's Bay, on the other hand, has the best range of boutique B&Bs and cottages in the country. **Napier**'s Art Deco charms are legendary and definitely worthy of inspection.

TARANAKI & WANGANUI   Let's put it this way—if you want the best of small-town, provincial New Zealand, this is it. **New Plymouth** is surprisingly vibrant in its own right, and you can't help but feel that, stuck out here on its own western limb, it couldn't care less about the rest of the country. Mount Taranaki and the sea are big attractions for trampers and surfers, and the region's gardens are stunning.

WELLINGTON ★★★   The capital has come alive in almost every aspect—today's it's the country's coolest and most sophisticated city. Take a ride on the **Wellington Cable Car** for glorious harbor and city views, and explore the **Museum of New Zealand–Te Papa Tongarewa**—it's a remarkable collection that will help you understand what you have seen, or are about to see, on your New Zealand adventure. Wellington is also home to several national performing-arts companies, so you'll find a rich arts culture.

The South Island

NELSON ★★★   Characterized by three national parks and good swimming beaches with golden sand, this is a top region to visit for those interested in arts, crafts, wines, and gourmet restaurants. Outdoor pursuits run the gamut, from wet and wild (white water rafting) to calm and sunny (kayaking in **Abel Tasman National Park**).

MARLBOROUGH ★★   Blenheim is a sea of vineyards, with winemakers, wineries, and cellar doors eager to present the best of the best. One day is scarcely enough to do the tastings justice. The **Marlborough Sounds** is a destination in itself, with its bush-rimmed bays and inlets offering superb sailing and boating opportunities. Water taxis provide easy affordable access, and accommodation ranges from water's-edge lodges to campsites.

CHRISTCHURCH & CANTERBURY ★★   After Auckland, Christchurch is the second major destination for overseas tourists and the choice of many as the starting point for South Island explorations. Two massive earthquakes (Sept 2010 and Feb 2011) caused much damage, but the city's rebuild is seeing a new Christchurch rise. Canterbury's physical attractions are many, and its outdoor lifestyle features cycling, hiking, climbing, and surfing.

WEST COAST ★★ **& THE GLACIERS** ★★   This warm, friendly region has many contrasting landscapes, from the palm trees of **Karamea** in the north to the river towns of **Westport, Greymouth,** and **Hokitika** to the raw beauty of Westland with its massive mountains and glaciers.

QUEENSTOWN & ENVIRONS ★★   For sheer impact, this southwestern portion of New Zealand stands on its own, offering scenic majesty, marvelous walks, and loads of fun. Queenstown is a must-see. It's an international tourist resort, with a well-earned reputation as a work-hard, play-hard destination. **Milford Sound** ★★ is simply stunning, drawing big numbers of sightseers daily—yet somehow retaining its air of remoteness. **Wanaka** ★★★, with its wide-open lake and distant mountains, is a lakeside town that believes

South Island at a Glance

Area of detail

Auckland

NORTH ISLAND

SOUTH ISLAND

Wellington

Christchurch

Dunedin

New Plymouth

Cape Egmont 45

Egmont National Park

Mt. Egmont 2518 m

43

Wanganui

NORTH ISLAND

40° S

Abel Tasman Nat'l Park

Marlborough Sounds

Tasman Bay

Cook Strait

Kahurangi National Park

Motueka

Nelson 6

Picton

WELLINGTON

Karamea

TASMAN MTS.

Blenheim

67

6

63

Westport

6

Nelson Lakes National Park

KAIKOURA MTS.

1

Paparoa Nat'l Park

65

Reefton

Hanmer Forest Park

Greymouth

6

7

7

Hanmer Springs

Hokitika

7

1

Tasman Sea

SOUTH ISLAND

Arthur's Pass National Park

Kaiapoi

6

73

73

Christchurch

Franz Josef Glacier

Fox Glacier

Westland National Park

Mt. Cook Nat'l Park

Methven

1

75

Akaroa

Mt. Cook 3754 m

Lake Tekapo

Lake Tekapo

Ashburton

Haast

6

Lake Pukaki

8

Twizel

8

Timaru

Canterbury Bight

Mount Aspiring National Park

Lake Wanaka

8

83

45° S

Milford Sound

Wanaka

Oamaru

Doubtful Sound

Queenstown

6

Cromwell

Lake Wakatipu

85

Alexandra

1

Palmerston

Fiordland National Park

Te Anau

Lake Te Anau

6

GARVIE MTS.

8

87

Roxburgh

Dunedin

94

Lake Manapouri

8

Milton

PACIFIC OCEAN

96

Gore

94

1

99

Invercargill

Foveaux Strait

Oban

170° E

0   100 mi

0   100 km

Stewart Island

24

in the good life. It lies on the doorstep to big-adventure country reaching to Haast Pass and beyond.

THE MACKENZIE COUNTRY/AORAKI/MOUNT COOK & WAITAKI DISTRICT ★★★   This is the region of superlatives. Highest mountain, longest glacier, big rivers! Experiences include mountaineering, bush walks, glacier hikes, seeing native birdlife, and trekking mighty forests. It has a string of picture-perfect lakes, and, in **Oamaru,** a town that's preserved its Victorian-era buildings and added steampunk to the culture.

DUNEDIN ★★★, SOUTHLAND & STEWART ISLAND ★★   Dunedin is gorgeous and gothic, with grand buildings and a smart take on ecotourism. And Southland? This quiet achiever has so many outstanding natural features that authorities have seen fit to designate an entire coastal circuit as the "Southern Scenic Route." Stewart Island is a surprise: Large, barely populated, with awesome skies and landscapes, it is one of the world's very special places.

NEW ZEALAND IN 2 WEEKS

Two weeks in New Zealand gives you more opportunities to drive between destinations and take in the color of the provinces. Still, don't underestimate the time your journey will take. New Zealand has good roads, but 20km (12 miles) in some parts of the country could be narrow, steep, and winding—which means it might take you twice as long to negotiate them as it would back home. In general, roads are well maintained and all major roads are paved. Drive with care on narrow, unpaved roads if you venture into more remote areas. This itinerary gives you a taste of both main islands, sticking to main centers with the greatest concentration of activities.

Day 1: Arrive in Auckland ★★★

Arrive in Auckland and head to **Viaduct Basin** (p. 67), aka "The Viaduct," the city's buzzing harborside village complex with restaurants, cafes, hotels, shops, and people-watching aplenty. What you do next depends on your post-arrival energy level: You may just want to stretch your legs with a stroll or sample Kiwi food and wine in one of the Viaduct's cutting-edge eateries. If you land early enough and feel like getting out on the water, you can experience grand-prix sailing on an authentic America's Cup yacht, *NZL 41*—and even get in a little crewing action if you're so inclined. Sailings are 11am and 2pm daily.

Day 2: Auckland's Major Sights

Prepare to sightsee until you drop. Get on the double-decker **Auckland Explorer Bus** (p. 41)—the cheapest and easiest way to see as much as possible in 1 day. You'll set eyes on **Mission Bay**'s pretty beach promenade, get a taste of Maori culture at **Auckland War Memorial Museum**

(p. 64), and zoom up to a **Sky Tower observation deck** via a 40-second glass lift. The bus drives through the leafy **Botanic Gardens** (p. 71) and through Parnell village. At night, dine in one of the restaurants in the **SKYCITY complex** (p. 56)—you won't go wrong sampling fusion cuisine in the sky-high **Sugar Club** (p. 56) or rustic Italian at **Gusto at the Grand** (p. 56).

Day 3: Waiheke Island ★★★

Rise early and catch a ferry to **Waiheke Island** (p. 83). Rent a car and drive around the island, visiting wineries, olive groves, artists' studios, and unspoiled beaches. Some of the best surprises are in the little bays away from Oneroa township. Following visits to **Whittaker's Musical Museum** (p. 85) and **Connells Bay Sculpture Park** (p. 85), have lunch at the picturesque **Stonyridge winery** (p. 86) or **Cable Bay Vineyards** (p. 88). Later in the day, sit on the beach at **Onetangi Bay** and watch the sunset. Stay in style at the **Te Whau Lodge** (p. 88) or the **Boatshed** (p. 87).

Day 4: Rotorua ★★★

Arrive back in Auckland by midday and fly to Rotorua. Rent a car. If you want a day of complete rest and solitude in unabashed luxury, head for **Treetops Lodge** (p. 154). If you want to see the sights, go straight to **Rotorua Museum** (p. 142) for an excellent overview of geothermal and volcanic history. Spend the rest of the afternoon at **Te Puia** (p. 144) to see bubbling mud and Maori cultural performances. Watch the sun set over the lake and relax in a hot rock pool at **Polynesian Spa** (p. 143).

Day 5: The Thermal Attractions ★★★

Drive 30 minutes south to see the geothermal wonders of **Waimangu** and **Waiotapu** (p. 146), with trails, steaming fumeroles, gluggy mud pools, and boat cruises on **Lake Rotomahana.** If you're back in town by early afternoon you could take a guided tour of **Whakarewarewa Living Maori Village** (p. 149), a working, modern Maori village on the lakefront, followed by a walk among the **Whakarewarewa Forest** redwoods (p. 152). Finish the night with a tour and cultural performance at **Mitai Maori Village** (p. 148).

Day 6: Drive to Wellington

Rise early for a day of driving, but *be careful,* as roads in the Rotorua region are busy with huge logging trucks. A 5-hour journey will take you around **Lake Taupo** (p. 163), where there are plenty of lake-edge stops for photographs, through the stark beauty of **Tongariro National Park** (p. 172), and through heartland farming provinces. You could stop off for a night in the **Wairarapa** (p. 256)—or at least stop to eat in one of **Greytown's cute cafes** (p. 264)—or drive the last taxing, winding, uphill leg over the Rimutaka Hills to Wellington. Alternatively, go the coastal route along the Kapiti Coast.

New Zealand in 2 Weeks

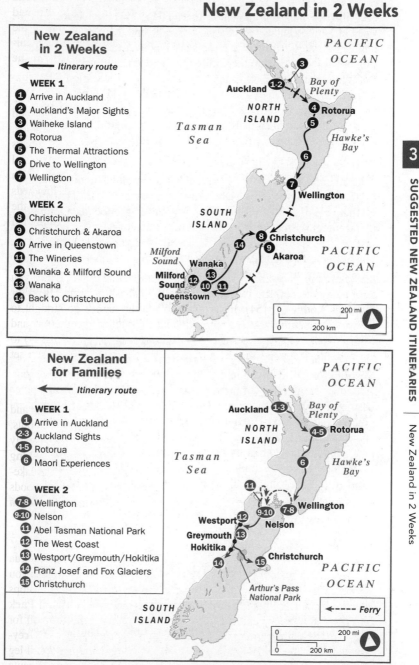

New Zealand in 2 Weeks

← *Itinerary route*

WEEK 1
1. Arrive in Auckland
2. Auckland's Major Sights
3. Waiheke Island
4. Rotorua
5. The Thermal Attractions
6. Drive to Wellington
7. Wellington

WEEK 2
8. Christchurch
9. Christchurch & Akaroa
10. Arrive in Queenstown
11. The Wineries
12. Wanaka & Milford Sound
13. Wanaka
14. Back to Christchurch

New Zealand for Families

← *Itinerary route*

WEEK 1
1. Arrive in Auckland
2-3. Auckland Sights
4-5. Rotorua
6. Maori Experiences

WEEK 2
7-8. Wellington
9-10. Nelson
11. Abel Tasman National Park
12. The West Coast
13. Westport/Greymouth/Hokitika
14. Franz Josef and Fox Glaciers
15. Christchurch

Day 7: Wellington ★★★

The first-rate museum known as **Te Papa** (p. 244) eloquently tells the story of New Zealand and is a must-visit. Spend 2 to 3 hours here and don't miss the gift shop for top-quality crafts. And you can't visit the capital without a ride up the **Cable Car** (p. 245), a wander through the **Botanic Garden** (p. 246) at the top, and a sit-in at a session of **Parliament** (p. 247). Art lovers should see **City Gallery Wellington** (p. 248), and if you like the funky side of life, wander up **Cuba Street** (p. 242). Late afternoon, amble around the waterfront to **Oriental Parade** (p. 243). Have dinner at **Logan Brown** (p. 238) or **Shed 5** (p. 241).

Day 8: Christchurch ★★★

Take an early flight to Christchurch. Hit the ground running and head to the central city area. Don't miss the remarkable **Transitional Cathedral** (p. 315)—designed by a Japanese architect as a temporary replacement for the city's iconic Anglican cathedral, severely damaged in the 2011 earthquake. The **Christchurch Art Gallery** (p. 314) is bound to impress—not only for its huge waves of glass on the western facade but its many outstanding New Zealand and international works. Stroll down the boulevard and visit the **Canterbury Museum** (p. 313), the **Arts Centre** (p. 313), and the **Botanic Gardens** (p. 314). Dine on inventive bistro food at the **Harlequin Public House** (p. 320).

Day 9: Christchurch & Akaroa ★★★

Head to the i-SITE office in Rolleston Avenue beside Canterbury Museum for the Akaroa Shuttle's 8:45am departure to the pretty harborside town of Akaroa. On arrival, stop to pick up a coffee and French pastries to go from **L'Escargot Rouge Deli** (p. 322), then at 11am board your 2-hour **Akaroa Harbour Nature Cruise** (p. 322), with views of ancient volcanic sights and Hector's dolphins. Have lunch along the pleasant waterfront at **Bully Hayes Restaurant & Bar** (p. 322). Afterward, pick up the brochure for the self-guided **Akaroa & Bays Art Trail** ★ (p. 322), which leads to the homes and studios of 18 local artists and craftspeople. The shuttle departs Akaroa at 3:45pm for a 5:15pm arrival in Christchurch. Refresh yourself at your hotel and then choose one of the many restaurants/bars around Victoria, Montreal, and Worcester streets for your evening meal.

Day 10: Arrive in Queenstown ★★★

Queenstown is a 6-hour road trip drive from Christchurch, so for those short on time, skip the coach or rental car and fly. Morning flights depart around 7am and flight time is only 1 hour 10 minutes—giving you a whole full day to make the most of the many and varied attractions in this scenic resort. For that first coffee (or breakfast), **Vudu** (p. 340) is close to many attractions including Queenstown i-Site. At 9am be the early rider up the **Skyline Queenstown** (p. 328) to get a bird's-eye view of Lake Wakatipu and the ragged, jagged peaks of The Remarkables. From here you can also ride the **Skyline Luge.** Then, head down to **Kiwi Birdlife Park** (p. 329) for a close-up look at local wildlife. In the afternoon take a cruise on Lake Wakatipu on the vintage steamship TSS *Earnslaw* to Walter Peak (p. 328). Back in Queenstown, refresh in your hotel room for dinner in one of Queenstown's many outstanding eateries, maybe **Botswana Butchery** (p. 338) or the **Bunker** (p. 338).

Day 11: The Wineries

Take a guided winery tour or rent a car and drive yourself around the best of Central Otago's wineries. The top four closest to Queenstown are **Gibbston Valley Wines** (p. 334), **Peregrine** (p. 334), **Amisfield** (p. 330), and **Chard Farm** (p. 333). Don't miss Gibbston's wine cave and cheesery, and have a fabulous lunch at Amisfield. Head back into Queenstown and enjoy one of the world's best burgers at **Fergburger** (p. 339) and a little gaming action at one of the city's two **casinos** (p. 341).

Day 12: Wanaka & Milford Sound

Rise early; it's a big day. Catch an early Wanaka Connexions (bus) to Wanaka for your **scenic flight to Milford Sound,** which includes Lake Wanaka, Mount Aspiring, Fiordland, and a boat cruise on Milford Sound. Back on Wanaka terra firma, take a late afternoon stroll in this pleasant lakeside town. Dinner tonight? Sample wonderful French bistro food at **Gentil Bistro** (p. 346) or enjoy lake views with your regional food at the **Trout Café Restaurant & Bar** (p. 347). Depending on your budget, enjoy sweet dreams at the luxury **Limetree Lodge** (p. 346) or the **YHA Wanaka Purple Cow** (p. 346).

Day 13: Wanaka

Visit **Stuart Landsborough's Puzzling World** (p. 347) and the **Warbirds & Wheels Museum** (p. 342). In the afternoon take a wine tour with **Funny French Cars** (p. 345), a complete change of scene as you rattle down country roads to view two or three local wineries. Take the Wanaka Alpine ConneXions bus back to Queenstown and enjoy dinner at **Madam Woo** (p. 338) or **Eichardt's Bar** (p. 338).

Day 14: Christchurch

Enjoy a lazy morning in Queenstown before flying to Christchurch to connect with your international flight. If you have time between the two flights, go to the **International Antarctic Centre** (p. 314) near the airport.

NEW ZEALAND FOR FAMILIES

Kids will love New Zealand. There are enough weird, wonderful, curious, funny, and interesting things on these islands to amuse the most inquiring child's mind. This itinerary runs a little over 2 weeks and hits the kid-friendly highlights of both North Island and South Island.

Day 1: Arrive in Auckland ★★★

Start slowly with an easy day, checking out combo deals and family passes at the visitor center at **Viaduct Basin** (p. 67), where the kids can watch the boats and visit the **New Zealand Maritime Museum** (p. 68). Be sure to take a ride on the historic scow *Ted Ashby*. Give kids a bird's-eye view of the city from the **Sky Tower** (p. 66), taking them up in the exterior glass lift and letting them walk over the glass floor. Dine in the revolving restaurant at the top.

Day 2: Auckland Sights

Impress the kids right from the start with **Kelly Tarlton's Sea Life Aquarium** (p. 66)—where they stay dry in Underwater World beneath an acrylic dome while sharks and stingrays swim overhead. Spend the afternoon at **Auckland War Memorial Museum** (p. 64) and make sure you let the kids loose in the superb **Weird & Wonderful Discovery Centre,** where they can open drawers and touch exhibits.

Day 3: More of Auckland

Get off to an early start at **Auckland Zoo** (p. 69), which has heaps of great stuff for kids. Check out the daily animal encounters and view sea lions through underwater viewing windows. Drive to **Butterfly Creek** (p. 69), flirt with winged beauties, ride on the Red Admiral Express, and see animals at Buttermilk Farm.

Day 4: Drive to Rotorua

Hire a car and start the 3-hour drive to Rotorua early. Stop at **Hamilton** (p. 109) along the way and feed the ducks at **Hamilton Lake.** In the afternoon, visit **Rotorua Museum** (p. 142) and "experience" a volcanic eruption in the theater there. Follow this with a trip to **Rainbow Springs Nature Park** (p. 145) to see kiwi, tuatara, and other native species—as well as take a ride on the Big Splash.

Day 5: Rotorua ★★★

The kids will be screwing their noses up at the smell of sulfur in the air, so get out there and show them what it's all about. Drive down to **Waimangu** and **Waiotapu** (p. 146). Allow half a day for both, or, if you have to choose, 2 hours for Waiotapu. Back in town, feed the kids from one of the takeaway stands at the lakefront and then let them loose at **Skyline**

Skyrides (p. 144), where they can plummet downhill on a luge, or better still, have an adventure in the **Zorb** (p. 144). The **Agrodome** (p. 144) is a hive of kids' activities—I'd plan to spend the afternoon here. Finish with a relaxing dip at **Polynesian Spa** (p. 143).

Day 6: Maori Experiences

Spend the morning investigating the wonders of **Te Puia** (p. 144), which includes the Whakarewarewa Thermal Reserve and the New Zealand Maori Arts & Crafts Institute. Stay and watch Pohutu Geyser blow its top. In the afternoon, take a guided tour of **Ohinemutu Maori Village** (p. 149) on the lakefront. Set the evening aside for a hangi meal and a Maori experience at **Tamaki Maori Village** (p. 159).

Day 7: Drive to Wellington

The drive south normally takes about 5 hours, but allow a day. Stop at **Lake Taupo** (p. 163) and visit **Huka Falls** (p. 162), just off the main highway north of Taupo. Have a picnic at one of the little beaches around the lake and then head into **Tongariro National Park** (p. 172) for beautiful mountain landscapes. Maybe there'll be time to squeeze in a snack stop at **Greytown** (p. 264) before you wind your way across the Rimutaka Ranges and down into Wellington by late afternoon.

Day 8: Wellington ★★★

Spend your morning hours exploring the **Museum of New Zealand–Te Papa Tongarewa** (p. 244). Let the kids run free along the waterfront after that—there'll be boats and people aplenty for them to watch. Head up the **Cable Car** (p. 245), then take the short walk to the **Botanic Garden** (p. 246) and the Space Place planetarium in the **Carter Observatory** (p. 246) for a bit of stargazing. Don't miss **Zealandia,** the world's first urban wildlife sanctuary, where you can stroll and spot rare native species (p. 246). Wander down **Cuba Mall** (p. 253) for an early dinner and let the kids get splashed by the iconic **Bucket Fountain** (p. 253).

Day 9: Wellington to Nelson

Leave Wellington on the 9am ferry and have an early lunch or late breakfast on board (the ferry has movies and play areas for children). Arrive in Picton and collect your rental car near the ferry wharf for your trip to Nelson. Ten minutes shy of Nelson, **Happy Valley Adventures** has 4WD bike adventures and the irresistible Skywire, a sort of flying fox meets ski chairlift (p. 278). In Nelson head to the **Nelson Provincial Museum**—this small museum has a children's section that includes a Taniwha Cave (p. 276). Give the kids a "bambino" ice cream from **Penguino Gelato Café** (p. 276) in Montgomery Square. The **Boat Shed** (p. 279) is an iconic Nelson restaurant; try the All Day Menu if the dinner menu looks too grownup.

Day 10: Nelson ★★★

The **World of Wearable Art** (p. 276) is an eye-stopper with flights of fanciful fashion. In the same building, the posh and polished **Classic Cars Museum** (p. 276) is an amazing experience for kids of all ages. For lunch pick up the makings of a picnic and head to **Tahuna Beach** (p. 278)—one of the most popular beaches in the area. If the kids tire of water play, they can have a blast on the rides at **Nelson Fun Park** (p. 276) or thrill to close encounters with wallabies, meerkats, and monkeys at the **Natureland Zoo** (p. 276)—both at Tahuna Beach.

Day 11: Abel Tasman National Park ★★★

Drive to **Kaiteriteri** and its lovely golden-sand beaches. **Abel Tasman National Park** (p. 281) is famous for its kayaking experiences, and **Marahau** is your launching place for this must-do water experience. While you're there, sample the big, untidy, delicious burgers sold at the celebrated **Fat Tui** burger truck (p. 282); picnic benches are nearby. Hop on a water taxi to check out other bays and coves. Return to Nelson.

Day 12: The West Coast ★★★

SH6 takes you through the Buller Gorge to Westport. In the morning, take a horse trek and swim with **Buller Adventure Tours** (p. 288)—it's great fun. In Westport visit the **Coal Town Museum** (p. 286) and get the picture for tomorrow's **Denniston Experience** (p. 288). In the late afternoon, take a short walk around the Tauranga Bay; you'll likely see seals sunning themselves in the last of the sun's rays on this wild and beautiful coast. Dine close to the beach at **The Bay House** (p. 289) in Tauranga Bay.

Day 13: Westport/Greymouth/Hokitika ★★

Take the SH67 out of Westport and drive 20 minutes to the turnoff for Denniston for a journey into a retired coalmine at the **Denniston Experience** (p. 288). *Note:* This unique tour is not suitable for small children or those who have difficulty on uneven surfaces. The tour takes 2 hours. Head back to SH6 for the scenic **Great Coast Road** from Westport to Greymouth. Stop at **Punakaiki** and take the signposted track to the **Pancake Rocks** ★★★ (p. 292). Then travel on to Greymouth. Continue on SH6 to Hokitika with a side trip to **Shantytown Heritage Park** ★★ (p. 294), a replica gold-mining town with a steam train and some 30 heritage buildings. **On Yer Bike** ★★ (p. 295) is another fun activity, going off-road in a rainforest on quad bikes, go-karts, and an 8WD Argo. Take the 20-minute drive to Hokitika with time to watch the sunset from the beach. Add in a pizza from **Fat Pipi's** ★★★ (p. 301; close to the beach), and the kids will declare this a perfect day.

Day 14: Franz Josef & Fox Glaciers ★★★

The glaciers are waiting! If you are traveling in mid-February, stop in **Whataroa** and check to see if the **White Heron Sanctuary Tour** ★★ (p. 301) is on that day. If it is, do it. As soon as you arrive in Franz Josef, confirm your **heli-hike glacier adventure** (p. 302). Weather can change abruptly, so take the first available flight. Tour the interactive glacier exhibits and indoor hatching home for the Rowo kiwi at the **West Coast Wildlife Centre** (p. 303). The **Glacier Hot Pools** (p. 303) in Franz Josef are open until 10pm.

Day 15: Christchurch

This is a long day's drive to Christchurch, so take plenty of stops. Backtrack along SH6 to Kumara Junction for SH 73 via Otira and **Arthur's Pass** to Christchurch. If you decide to break up the journey, an overnight stop at the **Theatre Royal Hotel** ★★★ (p. 296) in Kumara is recommended.

7-DAY SOUTH ISLAND MOTORHOME TOUR

The point of traveling by motorhome is the ability to set your own route and timetable—not to mention enjoying budget-wise self-catering facilities and a holiday free of lodging concerns. This itinerary is based on motorhome pickup in Christchurch and drop-off in Queenstown. Check that your proposed motor home provider has a depot in Queenstown, if it incurs a drop-off fee and how much, and if there is a free transfer to/from the drop-off point to the airport at Frankton and/or the town center in Queenstown. Motorhome driving tips and freedom camping laws are detailed in Chapter 17.

Day 1: Christchurch to Aoraki/Mount Cook

Collect your motorhome from the company's Christchurch depot. Stop in **Lake Tekapo** (p. 355) for a walk around the lakefront to the hot pools/ ice rink and cafe. Travel alongside **Lake Pukaki** into the mountains of **Aoraki/Mount Cook National Park** (p. 357). In the township find your spot among the camping/power sites. Take an evening walk to the **Sir Edmund Hillary Alpine Centre** (p. 363) for the truly amazing planetarium and night sky exploration.

Day 2: Aoraki/Mount Cook

Wow! Waking up in the alpine majesty of Aoraki/Mount Cook National Park is special—the dawn chorus can be deafening. First adventure of the day is a exploration of the township (pick up a map from the **Department of Conservation (DOC) National Park Visitor Centre,** which also has excellent displays detailing the natural and human history of the national park) and your choice of the park's many tourism activities: from glacier cruises to bush walks to aerial flightseeing. Return to SH8 and shop for groceries if necessary in **Twizel.** At Omarama take SH83. Stop to see local mammal fossils at the **Vanished World Centre** (p. 363) in Duntroon, and then rejoin SH1 at Pukeuri for the short drive to Oamaru. Drive through town on Thames Street to Itchen Street and tour the **Victorian Oamaru Historic Precinct ★★★** (p. 367) and visit the **Oamaru Blue Penguin Colony ★** (p. 367).

Day 3: Oamaru to Dunedin

Leave Oamaru early for Dunedin, following SH1. Dunedin's one-way street system will deliver you neatly to Anzac Avenue and a carpark for your motorhome by the **Dunedin Railway Station,** a short walk to the city's major attractions: **Toitu Otago Settlers Museum ★★★**; the **Dunedin Public Art Gallery ★★; the Dunedin Chinese Garden ★★;** and **Cadbury World.** The **Dunedin Holiday Park** in **St. Kilda** has powered campsites and is well sited to visit neighboring **St. Clair Hot Salt Water Pool** (open daily 6am–7pm). If you have time, take a cruise of Dunedin Harbour on a **Monarch Wildlife Tour ★★★** to Tairoa Head and the albatross rookery. See chapter 15.

Day 4: Dunedin to Stewart Island via the Catlins, Invercargill & Bluff

Follow SH1 to the Owaka turnoff (SH82) and take the Southern Scenic Route via the Catlins to Invercargill, and SH1 to Bluff and the ferry terminal for Stewart Island. The **Catlins** (p. 381) has so many magnificent natural features (**Purakaunui Falls, Tautuka Beach, Lake Wilkie, Cathedral Caves, Curio Bay**) that it's a surprise to discover it also has a quirky side, including Blair Somerville's whimsical creations at the **Lost Gypsy Gallery** (p. 382) at Papatowai. The last ferry from Bluff to Stewart Island departs at 5pm (Dec–Apr; check website for winter hours). It is a passenger ferry only, but there is suitable parking for your motorhome in the adjacent carpark. Accommodation options on Stewart Island range from budget to luxury. The island village of **Oban** is the last to lose the light of day so you'll have plenty of time after your 6:30pm arrival to explore the hillside and beachside streets, either by foot or rented scooter. When it is dark, go kiwi spotting in Glory Bay with **Bravo Adventure cruises** (p. 391).

Day 5: Stewart Island to Te Anau via Riverton, Tuatapere & Manapouri

Rise early and hire a water taxi to take you to **Ulva Island** to experience the amazing birdlife. Catch your prearranged ferry ride back to Bluff and your parked motorhome. Backtrack on SH1 to the turnoff for the continuation of your journey on the Southern Scenic Route, this time via Riverton, Tuatapere, and Manapouri to Te Anau. **Riverton** is a fishing and holiday destination nestled into the rocky coastline with sweeping views of the ocean and a gem of a museum: **Te Hikoi Southern Journey ★★**. Tuatapere is the starting point of the Hump Ridge Track, which has the largest wooden viaduct in the world (as of 2015 anyway) and takes 3

Other Suggested New Zealand Itineraries

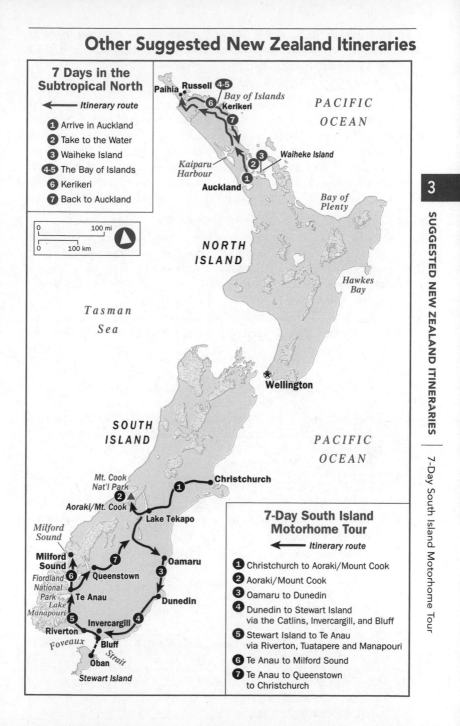

7 Days in the Subtropical North

← *Itinerary route*

1 Arrive in Auckland
2 Take to the Water
3 Waiheke Island
4-5 The Bay of Islands
6 Kerikeri
7 Back to Auckland

0 ___ 100 mi
0 ___ 100 km

Paihia
Russell 4-5
Bay of Islands
Kerikeri
6
7
Kaiparu Harbour
Waiheke Island
3
2
1
Auckland
Bay of Plenty

PACIFIC OCEAN

NORTH ISLAND

Hawkes Bay

Tasman Sea

★ **Wellington**

SOUTH ISLAND

PACIFIC OCEAN

Mt. Cook Nat'l Park
Christchurch
1
2
Aoraki/Mt. Cook
Lake Tekapo
Milford Sound
Milford Sound
7
Oamaru
Fiordland National Park
6 **Queenstown**
3
Lake Manapouri
Te Anau
Dunedin
5
Riverton
4
Invercargill
Foveaux
Bluff
Strait
Oban
Stewart Island

7-Day South Island Motorhome Tour

← *Itinerary route*

1 Christchurch to Aoraki/Mount Cook
2 Aoraki/Mount Cook
3 Oamaru to Dunedin
4 Dunedin to Stewart Island via the Catlins, Invercargill, and Bluff
5 Stewart Island to Te Anau via Riverton, Tuatapere and Manapouri
6 Te Anau to Milford Sound
7 Te Anau to Queenstown to Christchurch

days. Manapouri is the gateway to the **Sounds of Fiordland** (tours to Doubtful Sound start here), and in about 15 minutes you will be in Te Anau.

Day 6: Te Anau to Milford Sound

No driving today. Catch a coach (bus) for a day trip to **Milford Sound** (p. 335). It is not that distant, but the road is tricky, the scenery can distract, and it is better viewed than driven, especially in a motorhome. Choose a day tour (such as **Fiordland Tours**) that includes coach travel, optional lunch, photo opportunities, short walks, and a boat cruise on Milford Sound (seeing seals, dolphins, and waterfalls). Back in Te Anau take the evening **Te Anau Glowworm Caves tour.**

Day 7: Te Anau to Queenstown to Christchurch

On your last day in the ruggedly beautiful south, take time on your drive back to Queenstown via Mossburn, Athol, and Kingston—where the road from here to near Queenstown follows the shore of Lake Wakatipu—to stop in the rural settlements for coffee, snacks, or souvenirs. And photographs! Drop off your motorhome at the depot.

7 DAYS IN THE SUBTROPICAL NORTH

It always astounds us that so many overseas visitors arrive in Auckland and immediately drive or fly south—or that they avoid the North Island altogether in favor of the south. Sure, the South Island landscapes are more dramatic, but the top of the North, especially in summer, is a quintessential Kiwi experience: white-sand beaches, warm oceans, endless days of swimming and sunbathing, barbecues at the beach, campfires, parties, boats, surf, and sun. Here are 7 days that include islands close to Auckland to give you a feel for the more laid-back side of New Zealand life. Waiheke Island is the most populated and the most popular and heaven for wine drinkers.

Day 1: Arrive in Auckland ★★★

Rest for a while before heading off to **Viaduct Harbour** (p. 67), which will give you an instant appreciation of New Zealanders' obsessions with boats. Sit in one of the stylish cafes and restaurants, and watch the boats come and go. Visit the **New Zealand National Maritime Museum** (p. 68) for an insight into what the ocean really means to northerners. In the afternoon, take the **Auckland Explorer Bus** (p. 41) to the **Auckland War Memorial Museum** (p. 64), where you can admire the views and the grassy green swathe of the **Botanic Gardens** (p. 71). Drive around to **Mission Bay's seaside promenade** (p. 55) and have a picnic dinner as you watch people swim at sunset.

Day 2: Take to the Water

Have a rare sailing experience on America's Cup yacht *NZL 41* (p. 67). It's all sea spray, sunshine, and flapping sails out there, plus you'll have great views of the city skyline. Enjoy lunch wharf-side and then go up the **Sky Tower** (p. 66) for the best views in New Zealand.

Day 3: Waiheke Island ★★★

Rise early and take the ferry to **Waiheke Island** (p. 83). Save time and go straight into a guided tour of the island, or rent a car and drive around the beaches, wineries, and pretty, unpopulated bays. There's something intangible at work here and you'll quickly be seduced into the relaxed pace of island life. Have lunch at **Stonyridge Vineyard** (p. 86) and dinner at **Mudbrick Vineyard** (p. 88) or **Cable Bay Vineyards** (p. 88), or eat fish and chips on **Onetangi Bay** (p. 85) after a late-afternoon swim.

Days 4–5: The Bay of Islands ★★★

Back on the mainland, drive north to **Paihia** (p. 93). Base yourself here if you want to try all the attractions, or go to **Russell** (p. 94) if you're after a peaceful retreat. Visit **Waitangi Treaty Grounds** (p. 93) for a dose of Maori culture and some lovely boardwalks through native bush and mangrove swamps. Wander through the cool, green leafy grounds to find **Waikokopu Café** and the massive Maori *waka* (canoe) on display by the beach. Sit on the beach and enjoy the sun.

Day 6: Kerikeri

This is our northern fruit capital. Enjoy citrus, persimmons, kiwifruit, and macadamia nuts. Stop at **Kerikeri Bakehouse Café** (p. 104) for picture-perfect picnic food. Take your bounty down to the **Kerikeri River Walk** and eat by the river before exploring the local sights. Spend the afternoon at **Marsden Estate Winery** (p. 104) or drive to a local beach and swim until the sun goes down.

Day 7: Drive to Auckland

Drive back to Auckland and do some more sightseeing. See **Kelly Tarlton's Sea Life Aquarium** ★ (p. 66) or visit the **Auckland Zoo** ★★ (p. 69).

AUCKLAND

This is it: our biggish, brashest, and really quite cosmopolitan center, the City of Sails, where you can almost always see the Sky Tower, even when you're wandering in the Waitakere ranges or sipping a pinot gris on Waiheke Island. And you can quite possibly see the sea: Auckland sprawls its way around two glorious harbors—the Waitemata and the Manukau—and its residents keenly identify with all things watery. Aucklanders tend to be laid-back, but this is a city that is going places. Hey, it's not New York, but we love it here.

4

ESSENTIALS

Getting There & Arrival

BY PLANE **Auckland Airport** (www.aucklandairport.co.nz; ℂ **0800/247-767** in NZ or 09/275-0789) is 21km (14 miles) south of the city beside the Manukau Harbour. It's about 30 minutes from the CBD when traffic is flowing normally. The **Jean Batten International Terminal** has a huge shopping area with around 100 retail outlets, including convenience stores and pharmacies. Two competing **duty-free agencies,** LS Travel Retail Pacific and Aer Rianta, have good deals on fashion, fragrances, and the usual stuff. They are open for all incoming and outgoing flights. There's an arrival pickup service, which means you can leave your duty-free goods at the airport and pick them up when you fly out.

If you have time to kill in the airport, you can store your bags at the **Collection Point** (NZ$3 per bag; nothing left overnight; daily 6am–11pm). They also sell toiletries and rent out towels and hair dryers for use in the free showers for transiting and non-transiting passengers.

For currency exchange, 10 **Travelex** (www.travelex.co.nz; ℂ **0800/666-391** in NZ) booths are located in the international and domestic terminals and open daily for all arriving and departing flights. A number of **ATMs** can be found in both the international and domestic terminals and accept Visa, MasterCard, American Express, Diner's Club and all Plus cards. Rental-car agencies are on the ground floor. Luggage trolleys are free of charge and are available throughout both terminals. There are wireless hotspots throughout both terminals and the first 30 minutes is free.

For information about the region and free booking services, the **Auckland Airport i-SITE Visitor Centre** (www.aucklandnz.com; ✆ **09/365-9925**) is in the arrivals hall on the ground floor (near door 11). It's open daily from 6am to 10pm.

The **Domestic Terminal** is a 10-minute walk from the International Terminal (follow the signs), or take the free inter-terminal bus, which departs every 15 minutes between 5am and 10:30pm. It has similar facilities to the international terminal. See the airport website for more details.

The **Airbus Express** (www.airbus.co.nz; ✆ **0800/103-080** in NZ or 09/366-6400) is the cheapest transport between the airport and the city. The blue buses travel from the airport to the city and back every 10 to 30 minutes (depending on the day and time), stopping at designated bus stops if requested. It's a 24-hour service to and from the international terminal (bus stop and ticket kiosk outside door 8), and runs from 6am until the last scheduled flight from the domestic terminal (bus stop and ticket kiosk outside door 4). The fare is NZ$16 one-way (NZ$28 round-trip) for adults, and NZ$6 one-way (NZ$12 round-trip) for children 5 to 15 years old or NZ$38 and NZ$72 for a family. Allow 1 hour travel time. You can board with two large bags and one carry-on bag. Check the website for route details.

Catch a **taxi** from outside the arrivals area (door 8) at the international terminal and outside the luggage collection area (door 4) at the domestic terminal; the fare between the airport and city center is typically NZ$75 to NZ$90 one-way, although **Discount Taxis** (www.discounttaxis.co.nz; ✆ **09/529-1000**) and **Cheap Cabs** (www.cheaptaxi.co.nz; ✆ **09/621-0505**) post fares online from as little as NZ$33. Otherwise, try **Auckland Co-op Taxis** (www.cooptaxi.co.nz; ✆ **09/300-3000**) or **Corporate Cabs** (www.corporatecabs.co.nz; ✆ **09/377-0773**).

A number of shuttle companies will transport you from the airport to your hotel and vice versa for NZ$30 to NZ$60, depending on the length of the journey. **Super Shuttle** (www.supershuttle.co.nz; ✆ **0800/748-885** in NZ, or 09/522-5100) and **Auckland Airport Shuttle** (www.aucklandairportshuttle.co.nz; ✆ **0800/855-557** in NZ, or 09/303-1973) are both reliable.

BY TRAIN & COACH (BUS) The **Britomart Transport Centre**, operated by Auckland Transport (www.at.govt.nz; ✆ **09/366-4467**), is the city's major transportation hub, located at the bottom of Queen Street in the CBD by the ferry terminals. It's where intercity and commuter rail, buses, taxis, and ferry services connect. Britomart is open Monday to Thursday 5am to 11pm, Friday 5:20am to 1am, Saturday 6:30am to 12:30am, and Sunday 6:30am to 11pm. There you'll find food outlets, news agents, coin-operated lockers, toilets, ticketing agents, and a transport information booth.

For information on **KiwiRail**'s Northern Explorer train, which travels 6 days a week between Auckland and Wellington, contact KiwiRail (www.kiwirailscenic.co.nz; ✆ **0800/872-467** in NZ, or 04/495-0775). **InterCity** (www.intercity.co.nz; ✆ **09/623-1503**) buses arrive and depart from the SKYCITY bus terminal, 102 Hobson St.

Maori Auckland

The Maori name for Auckland is **Tamaki Makaurau,** which roughly translates as "the place of 1000 lovers." It's not because Aucklanders have loose morals: In pre-European times, the area was coveted by many tribes for its fertile, volcanic soils and its handy locations between two resource-rich coasts. Over the centuries, it was claimed by at least 18 tribes. The Hauraki Gulf was first settled by Maori about 1,000 years ago, with the earliest settlement, on Motutapu Island (next to Rangitoto), dating back to the 12th century. There are 48 cones in the Auckland volcanic field—all within about 20km (12 miles) of the city center—and most display the horizontal terracing that signifies a Maori *pa* site (a fortification built on a hill).

BY CAR **State Highway 1 (SH1)** goes through Auckland and out the other side: You'll be arriving in the city from the south if you come from the airport. Traffic congestion is a real problem in Auckland, especially during morning and evening rush hours, so avoid driving if you can. Parking is also quite expensive.

Visitor Information

The official website for **Auckland Tourism** is **www.aucklandnz.com**. There are six official i-SITE visitor centers in the Auckland region. Two are in Auckland city: The **Auckland i-SITE Visitor Information Centre–Princes Wharf,** 137 Quay St. (✆ **09/365-9914**), is open Monday to Friday 8:30am to 6pm and weekends 9am to 5pm in the summer and daily from 9am to 5pm in the winter. The **Auckland SKYCITY i-SITE Visitor Information Centre** (✆ **09/365-9918**) is in the SKYCITY Atrium, on the corner of Victoria and Federal streets. It's open daily from 9am to 6pm in the summer (to 5pm in the winter).

The **Devonport i-SITE Visitor Centre,** Devonport Wharf (✆ **09/365-9906**), is open daily from 10am to 5pm.

Other useful information can be found at **www.doc.govt.nz**. The Department of Conservation's website has information about national parks, marine reserves, walks, and DOC campgrounds.

Special Events

The annual **Auckland Anniversary Day Regatta** ★★★ (www.regatta.org.nz; ✆ **0800/734-2882** in NZ), held on the last Monday in January, is a brilliant spectacle on the water. The annual **Auckland Arts Festival** ★★★ (www.aucklandfestival.co.nz; ✆ **09/309-0101**) finishes off the summer with an eclectic mix of the best local and international arts and cultural events, in particular ones that celebrate its Pacific flavor. In October, **New Zealand Fashion Week** ★★★ (www.nzfashionweek.com) brings together the best in Kiwi fashion when more than 80 New Zealand designers unveil their latest collections to fashionistas, buyers, and media. Foodies gather at Western

Springs each November for a **Taste of Auckland** (www.tasteofauckland. co.nz), the biggest culinary celebration in the country.

Go to www.aucklandnz.com for more events.

City Layout

Greater Auckland is really four cities—cosmopolitan Auckland, multicultural Manukau, beachy North Shore, and wild-west Waitakere. You can pick up a city map from the visitor center, but the **Automobile Association** (✆ **0800/500-543**) has a better one.

MAIN ARTERIES & STREETS   Auckland's main drag is **Queen Street,** which ends at **Customs Street,** 1 block from waterfront **Quay Street.** At the other end of Queen St is **Karangahape Road** (known as "K'Rd."). Within this small area are most of the inner city's major hotels, restaurants, shops, nightspots, and bus, rail, and air terminals. **Parnell** and **Ponsonby** are the inner-city suburbs with the best eating establishments.

Neighborhoods in Brief

Inner City   As well as the "big box" hotels and numerous restaurants, Auckland's inner city is home to many top attractions, including the vibrant and ever-evolving Viaduct Harbour, Britomart, and Wynyard Quarter precincts. Head down to Quay Street to get out on the water or hang out in High Street and Vulcan Lane, get a coffee, and watch the world go by. Or maybe shock your mother by getting a tattoo on K'Road!

Ponsonby/Herne Bay   Bohemian (Ponsonby) meets rich (Herne Bay): These two stylish suburbs are full of trendy cafes and restaurants, TV stars and wannabes. But the lovely old wooden buildings also house some gorgeous specialty shops and delightful B&Bs.

Mount Eden/Epsom   Leafy suburbs where rich folk live in enormous wooden mansions, next door to students in rather more run-down villas! The villages are pretty and filled with good eateries and shops, not to mention B&Bs if you want somewhere quiet to base yourself. One Tree Hill and Cornwall Park are close by.

Parnell/Newmarket   Two more well-heeled suburbs. Parnell Village is so visitable but you'll damage your credit cards if you linger too long; it's got great restaurants and cafes and is handy to the museum and the lovely Auckland Domain. Newmarket is great for clothes and shoe shopping.

Mission Bay/St. Heliers   Did you bring your rollerblades? This is where you can show off your prowess on a sunny day when all you have to worry about is which restaurant-with-a-million-dollar-view to eat at later.

Devonport/Takapuna   Devonport is another "old money" suburb. Takapuna is a bit more nouveau riche. Both are across the water. "Devo" has some terrific B&Bs and pretty shops. Don't tackle the Harbour Bridge at rush hour; take a ferry instead. That's what the locals do.

Getting Around

BY BUS   Your best bet might be to get the **Auckland Explorer Bus** (www. explorerbus.co.nz; ✆ **0800/439-756** in NZ). This sightseeing double-decker bus leaves daily from the Ferry Building every 30 minutes from 9am to 4pm in the summer and 10am to 3pm in the winter with free pickup from major city hotels. It visits 14 top attractions, including Kelly Tarlton's Sea Life

A Safe Bet

Auckland is pretty safe by international standards, but use your common sense. It's best to avoid the Auckland Domain and Albert Park after dark, and Aotea Square can get a bit boisterous when the pubs close.

Aquarium, Mount Eden, and the Auckland Zoo, and you can get off and on as you please. It's from NZ$45 per day for adults, NZ$20 for children, and NZ$100 for a family pass. Two-day passes are also available.

Auckland Transport (https://at.govt.nz; ℗ **0800/10-30-80** in NZ) runs most of the other buses, trains, and ferries around the city. Pick up timetables at the visitor center or at Britomart Transport Centre.

The **CityLink Bus** (red) does a circuit from the Wynyard Quarter, along Queen Street, along K'Road and back again every 7 to 8 minutes from 6:25am to 11:25pm Monday to Saturday and every 10 minutes from 7am to 11:20pm Sunday. It's NZ$1 for adults and NZ50c for children. The **InnerLink Bus** (green) makes a slightly bigger circle, from Britomart to Parnell, Newmarket, along K'Road and Ponsonby Road and back to Britomart via SKYCITY. It runs every 10 or 15 minutes from 6:30am to 11pm Monday to Friday, 6:30am to 11pm Saturday and 7am to 11pm Sunday. The fare is NZ$2.50 maximum for adults and NZ$1.50 for children. The **OuterLink Bus** (amber) leaves from Wellesley Street to inner-city suburbs Parnell, Newmarket, Epsom, Balmoral, Mt. Eden, St. Lukes, Mt. Albert, Pt. Chevalier, Westmere, and Herne Bay. It's every 15 minutes from 6:30am to 11pm Monday to Friday and 7am to 11pm on Sunday: NZ$4.50 and NZ$2.50 maximum. For bus travel farther out, inquire at the visitor center.

AT HOP is the money-saving Auckland Transport smartcard ticketing system that you can use on buses, trains, and ferries. You can either buy a card for NZ$5 (at stations, visitor centers, and many convenience stores) and load as much money as you want onto it or get a **Discovery Day Pass** for NZ$16 to NZ$22 (plus NZ$5 for the card), depending on the zones. (If you get a NZ$32 pass, it includes a one-way airport transfer as well.) For more information, go to https://at.govt.nz.

BY TAXI   Typical rates for taxis start at about NZ$5 and go up NZ$2 per kilometer (0.62 mile). You can flag one down, phone for one, or go to the main taxi stand on the corner of Customs Street West and Queen Street. **Auckland Co-Op Taxis** (www.cooptaxi.co.nz; ℗ **09/300-3000**) and **Corporate Cabs** (www.corporatecabs.co.nz; ℗ **09/377-0773**) are both reliable.

BY TRAIN   **Auckland Transport** (https://at.govt.nz) also runs the suburban train system from Britomart in Auckland on four lines: the Eastern (to Manukau), the Western (to Waitakere), the Southern to Pukekohe, and the Onehunga (to Onehunga). Fares are from NZ$2.50 for adults and NZ$1.70 for children for one stage but you'll probably save money by buying a Discovery Day Pass (see "By Bus," above).

BY FERRY You can catch a ferry to the seaside village of **Devonport** from Pier 1 beside Queen's Wharf, Quay St (www.fullers.co.nz; ℰ **09/367-9111**). It's NZ$12 round-trip for adults, NZ$6.50 for children ages 5 to 15, and NZ$35 for a family, and ferries leave about every half hour. Some ferries sailing to and from Rangitoto and Waiheke islands also stop at Devonport. (For more on Waiheke ferries, see "A Side Trip to Waiheke Island," p. 83.)

BY CAR Driving in the CBD can be a nightmare, but if you must, there's metered parking and parking lots all over the city, all open 24 hours. For details, go to https://at.govt.nz.

[FastFACTS] AUCKLAND

Area Code Auckland's area code (STD) is **09.**

Currency Exchange Most banks, both in the city and in the suburbs, will be able to help you with this. They are generally open Monday to Friday from 9am to 4:30pm. You'll find several **Travelex NZ** branches at Auckland International Airport and the Domestic Airport, which are open daily during normal business hours (www.travelex.co.nz; ℰ **0800/666-391**).

Dentists There are usually emergency dentists in the **White Cross accident and urgent medical centers,** which are all over Auckland. Go to www.whitecross.co.nz to find the nearest one. These have different opening hours, usually closing between 8pm and 10pm or staying open 24 hours a day.

Doctors For genuine emergencies, dial ℰ **111.** Otherwise, the **CityMed Medical Centre,** 8 Albert St. (www.citymed.co.nz; ℰ **09/377-5525**), is centrally located, or try one of

the **White Cross clinics** (www.whitecross.co.nz).

Embassies & Consulates Embassies are in Wellington (see "Fast Facts: Wellington," in chapter 17). For additional information, contact the **Ministry of Foreign Affairs & Trade** in Wellington (www.mfat.govt.nz; ℰ **04/439-8000**).

Auckland has consulates of the **United States,** Level 3, 23 Customs St. E. (ℰ **09/303-2724**); **Canada,** Level 9, 48 Emily Place (ℰ **09/309-3690**), **Ireland,** Level 3, 205 Queen St. (ℰ **09/977-2252**); and the **United Kingdom,** IAG House, 151 Queen St. (ℰ **09/303-2973**).

Emergencies Dial ℰ **111** to call the police, fire, or ambulance services. For non-urgent police matters, call the **Central Police Station** (ℰ **09/302-6400**).

Hospitals Auckland **City Hospital,** 2 Park Rd., Grafton (ℰ **09/367-0000**), is the main trauma and accident hospital in the city. Also see "Doctors," above.

Lost Property Call the Central Police Station

(ℰ **09/302-6400**) or any local police station.

Luggage Storage & Lockers "You can leave a few pieces of luggage at the Princes Wharf i-SITE during business hours. The latest pickup is 5pm; it's NZ$5 per bag for up to 4 hours and NZ$10 for a day. There are also coin-operated luggage lockers at the **Britomart Transport Centre** (ℰ **0800/467-536** in NZ), which you can access 24 hours a day.

Newspapers & Magazines The *New Zealand Herald* is the daily Auckland paper. The *Sunday Star-Times* and *Herald on Sunday* are Sunday-morning publications.

Post Office The Auckland City Post Shop is at 23 Customs St. (ℰ **0800/501-501** in NZ). it's open Monday to Friday from 9am to 5:30pm and Saturday from 9am to 2pm. For *poste restante* (held mail) pickup, go to the Post Shop in the Bledisloe Building at 24 Wellesley St. (ℰ **0800/501-501** in NZ). For other branches, go to www.nzpost.co.nz.

WHERE TO STAY

Over recent years Auckland really has grown into the city it has always wanted to be, complete with a terrific range of accommodations. Like any growing city, at certain times of year (especially over the summer months) there can be high demand for beds at every level, so it pays to book ahead.

For longer stays, the city has a number of fully serviced apartments, including **CityLife Auckland** ★, 171 Queen St. (www.heritagehotels.co.nz; **⦿ 0800/368-888** in NZ, or **09/379-9222**), with 164 hotel rooms and a variety of one- to three-bedroom suites and hotel rooms that range from NZ$179 to NZ$189. It's located directly above central Queen Street and is a handy walk to all the main attractions. The self-rated **VR hotel chain** (www.vrhotels. co.nz; **⦿ 09/565-1177**) also offers good-value longer-stay accommodation with several properties in central locations, including **Ascotia off Queen,** 3–5 Scotia Place.

Centrally located B&Bs are harder to find, but they are plentiful a little further out in the suburbs.

In the Inner City
EXPENSIVE

Heritage Auckland ★★ The Heritage has size, location, and friendly service on its side—and a Qualmark Enviro-Gold rating. Just a short walk from main shopping and entertainment areas, the hotel comprises two distinct parts—the Hotel wing in a restored, landmark Art Deco building; and the purpose-built contemporary Tower wing—completed in 1998 and 1999, respectively. All rooms are generous suite-style units with good-size bathrooms. A slight premium applies on the self-contained Tower suites, many of which boast great harbor views. Speaking of views, the rooftop with its generously proportioned swimming pool was recently refurbished and is now a great spot to enjoy some R&R. There's even a tennis court if you're feeling suitably energetic. Heritage Auckland was the first hotel in New Zealand to receive an accreditation by the NZ Vegetarian Society for its special menu options for vegan and vegetarian diners (see "Where to Eat"), and its lobby cafe recently introduced a local raw breakfast-bar concept.

Hotel Wing, 35 Hobson St.; Tower Wing, 22 Nelson St. www.heritagehotels.co.nz. **⦿ 0800/368-888** in NZ, or 09/379-8553. 274 units. NZ$399 superior room; NZ$449–NZ$649 suite. Long-stay, off-peak, and special rates. Valet parking NZ$35. **Amenities:** 2 restaurants; 2 bars; babysitting; concierge; 2 gyms; 2 Jacuzzis; rooftop heated outdoor pool; heated indoor lap pool; room service; sauna; all-weather outdoor lit tennis court; Wi-Fi (free).

Hotel DeBrett ★★★ Step out the door and you'll be on hip High Street, then return to the chic oasis that is the Hotel DeBrett: a boutique labor of love that started life as the Commercial Hotel in 1841. The interiors are a hymn to Midcentury Modern: 25 stylish and surprising rooms and suites in the same quirky palette of funky colors. I've rarely enjoyed just being in a hotel room and doing nothing more strenuous than soaking in its fun, fab flavor. Owners John Courtney and Michelle Deery have poured their hearts and souls into this multi-award-winning establishment, and it shows. Request the Loft Suite with its mad, stripy-carpeted spiral staircase. The restaurant is terrific, the bar atmospheric, there's a drawing room filled with art, books, movies, and music, and I was so totally in love with my acid-green velvet bathrobe that I simply had to buy it after staying here.

2 High St. www.hoteldebrett.com. ⓒ **09/925-9000.** 25 units. Rooms and suites from NZ$275–NZ$675. Rates include continental breakfast, pre-dinner drink, and free local calls. Valet parking. **Amenities:** Restaurant; bar; babysitting; concierge; nearby gym; massage; Wi-Fi (free).

Hilton Auckland ★★★   There's no other Hilton in the world quite like this boutique-style property, opened in 2001 and located right in the heart of Viaduct Harbor. Recently extensively refurbished, it's almost completely surrounded by water, perched on the end of Princes Wharf like the giant ship that inspired it and like those that dock alongside it. Rooms are modern, sophisticated, stylish—not overly large in some cases, but always exquisitely furnished, with fabulous bathrooms and amazing sea views. For even better views, opt for 1 of the 12 deluxe corner rooms that feature two whole walls of glass. The suites are shaped like the bow of a ship and boast vast decks. Ask about the presidential suite for ultimate luxury. And you could do far worse if you choose to eat in-house at **Fish**—head chef Shane Yardley's exciting menu is well worth staying in for.

Princes Wharf, 137–147 Quay St. www.hilton.com. ⓒ **0800/448-002** in NZ, or 09/978-2000. 165 units. Guest and deluxe rooms NZ$710–NZ$880 and NZ$1,310–NZ$2,210. Suites POA. Off-season and special rates available. Valet parking NZ$40. **Amenities:** Restaurant; bar; babysitting; concierge; gym with trainer; heated outdoor pool suspended from 4th-floor bridge; room service; Wi-Fi (free).

The Langham Auckland ★★★   In keeping with the brand worldwide, Auckland's Langham is plush and rather formally elegant but with excellent, friendly service. All the rooms here are opulent, but the four floors of Club Rooms offer that little bit extra: king-size beds and lovely marble bathrooms, plus Club Lounge access and business facilities. The hotel has Green Globe Certification and was awarded Qualmark Enviro-Gold status in 2008. As for the restaurant, or should I say restaurants, lunch or dinner at Eight involves choosing from eight—count 'em—international cuisines. Overall, the Langham is more traditional than the Hilton and much larger.

83 Symonds St. www.langhamhotels.com. ⓒ **0800/616-261** in NZ, or 09/379-5132. 411 units. NZ$275–NZ$425 classic & executive; NZ$570–NZ$2,445 suite. Leisure packages and long-stay rates. Valet parking NZ$45. **Amenities:** 3 restaurants; 2 bars; limousine airport transfers; babysitting; concierge; concierge-level rooms; health club with gym and trainer; Jacuzzi; heated rooftop lap pool; room service; 2 saunas; Chuan day spa; Wi-Fi (free).

SKYCITY Grand Hotel ★★★   The Grand is SKYCITY's five-star pride and joy and it sits proudly on Federal Street, right next to the 328m (1,076-ft.)

Central Auckland

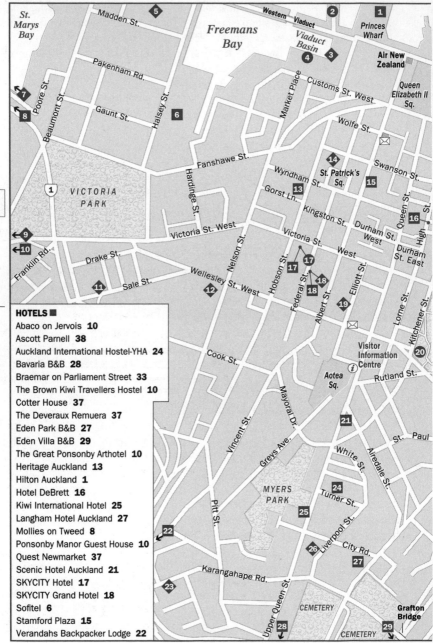

St. Marys Bay
Madden St.
Pakenham Rd.
Poore St.
Beaumont St.
Gaunt St.
Halsey St.
Franklin Rd.
Drake St.
Sale St.

VICTORIA PARK

Freemans Bay
Western Viaduct
Viaduct Basin
Princes Wharf
Air New Zealand
Queen Elizabeth II Sq.
Customs St. West
Market Place
Wolfe St.
Swanson St.
Fanshawe St.
Hardinge St.
Victoria St. West
Wellesley St. West
Wyndham St.
Gorst Ln.
St. Patrick's Sq.
Kingston St.
Victoria St. West
Nelson St.
Hobson St.
Federal St.
Albert St.
Elliott St.
Durham St. West
Durham St. East
Queen St.
High St.
Lorne St.
Kitchener St.
Cook St.
Vincent St.
Greys Ave.
Mayoral Dr.
Pitt St.
MYERS PARK
Aotea Sq.
Visitor Information Centre
Rutland St.
St. Paul
White St.
Airedale St.
Turner St.
Liverpool St.
City Rd.
Karangahape Rd.
Upper Queen St.
CEMETERY
CEMETERY
Grafton Bridge

HOTELS ■

Abaco on Jervois **10**
Ascott Parnell **38**
Auckland International Hostel-YHA **24**
Bavaria B&B **28**
Braemar on Parliament Street **33**
The Brown Kiwi Travellers Hostel **10**
Cotter House **37**
The Deveraux Remuera **37**
Eden Park B&B **27**
Eden Villa B&B **29**
The Great Ponsonby Arthotel **10**
Heritage Auckland **13**
Hilton Auckland **1**
Hotel DeBrett **16**
Kiwi International Hotel **25**
Langham Hotel Auckland **27**
Mollies on Tweed **8**
Ponsonby Manor Guest House **10**
Quest Newmarket **37**
Scenic Hotel Auckland **21**
SKYCITY Hotel **17**
SKYCITY Grand Hotel **18**
Sofitel **6**
Stamford Plaza **15**
Verandahs Backpacker Lodge **22**

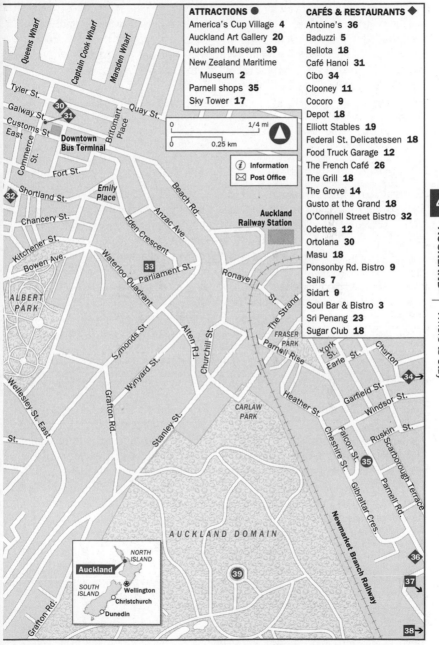

ATTRACTIONS ●
America's Cup Village **4**
Auckland Art Gallery **20**
Auckland Museum **39**
New Zealand Maritime
   Museum **2**
Parnell shops **35**
Sky Tower **17**

CAFÉS & RESTAURANTS ◆
Antoine's **36**
Baduzzi **5**
Bellota **18**
Café Hanoi **31**
Cibo **34**
Clooney **11**
Cocoro **9**
Depot **18**
Elliott Stables **19**
Federal St. Delicatessen **18**
Food Truck Garage **12**
The French Café **26**
The Grill **18**
The Grove **14**
Gusto at the Grand **18**
O'Connell Street Bistro **32**
Odettes **12**
Ortolana **30**
Masu **18**
Ponsonby Rd. Bistro **9**
Sails **7**
Sidart **9**
Soul Bar & Bistro **3**
Sri Penang **23**
Sugar Club **18**

ⓘ Information
✉ Post Office

Sky Tower. Even the standard rooms are gorgeous, and if you, er, splash out for one of the Grand Presidential Suites, splashing is probably what you'll want to do a lot of in your enormous shower with numerous jets. The Grand has original New Zealand artwork on the walls, an award-winning and very beautiful Balinese-themed day spa downstairs, three outrageously good restaurants in the hotel itself (**The Grill** by Sean Connolly, **MASU** by Nic Watt, and **Gusto at the Grand;** see "Where to Eat," below), as well as SKY-CITY'S other eateries on Federal Street.

90 Federal St. www.skycitygrand.co.nz. ℂ **0800/759-2489** in NZ, or 09/363-6000. 320 rooms. Rooms from NZ$259; suites from NZ$489; Grand Presidential Suites from NZ$1,929. Long-stay, off-peak, and special rates. Valet parking NZ$35. **Amenities:** 3 restaurants; 3 bars; Mercedes airport transfers from NZ$140 one-way; babysitting; concierge; gym; Jacuzzi; heated indoor lap pool; room service; sauna; East Day Spa; Wi-Fi (free).

Sofitel Auckland Viaduct Harbour ★★★   They're very big on rituals in the Sofitel chain, and this lovely five-star hotel right on the Viaduct Harbour is no exception: It has candle rituals at night, greenstone hot-stone rituals in the day spa, and a rather startling *sabrage* ritual in the eponymous bar where a French-trained master of the art will slice open a champagne bottle with a sabre, à la Napoleon. Sacre bleu! Plus you get gorgeous harbor and marina views wherever you go (but if you don't want to go anywhere, lie back and savor them from your room's Juliet balcony).

21 Viaduct Harbour Ave. www.sofitel.com. ℂ **09/909-9000.** 171 rooms. Superior rooms from NZ$320; Luxury Atrium View rooms from NZ$395; Luxury Marina View rooms from NZ$470; Junior Suites from NZ$520. Long-stay, off-peak and special rates. Valet parking. **Amenities:** 2 restaurants; 1 bar; babysitting; concierge; gym; Jacuzzi; heated indoor lap pool; room service; sauna; Wi-Fi in lobby; day spa and beauty salon; Wi-Fi (free).

Stamford Plaza ★★★   Another five-star centrally located hotel that's been recently refurbished from top to bottom. Although not old in a historical sense, this hotel was built at a time when space was not an issue, thus most of the rooms measure a cat-swinging 36m2 while the 11 executive suites are a generous 66m2. Still not big enough for you? Then go for one of the two Raffles Suites at 97m2. And if money is no object, there's either the Stamford Suite with its black marble bathroom measuring an impressive 133 sq. m or the Governors Suite, which not only squeaks in at being the biggest (134 sq. m) but also has floor sensors that will light your way to the bathroom in the night.

22–26 Albert St. www.stamford.com.au/spak. ℂ **09/309-8888.** 286 rooms. Superior rooms from NZ$389; Executive rooms from NZ$429; suites from NZ$589. Valet parking. **Amenities:** 3 restaurants; 1 bar; concierge; fully equipped gym; heated indoor lap pool, spa pool and sauna; 24-hour room service; interconnecting rooms; Wi-Fi (free).

MODERATE

Braemar on Parliament Street ★★   History and character are at the heart of this three-story Edwardian gentleman's townhouse (ca. 1901); you feel it as soon as you walk in. The four rooms in this delightful B&B—two

with en-suite bathrooms, two with shared bathroom—are packed with charm, right up to the impressive 11-ft. stud in each room. The Batten Suite (once home to legendary pilot Jean Batten's father) is the best and biggest. Your hosts, John Sweetman and his wife, have an astonishing collection of historic Auckland photographs, and their welcoming manner make this place a home away from home. It's the only upmarket B&B in the central business district, and it's just a short walk from trendy High Street, downtown activities, restaurants, and transport systems. Braemar earned its Qualmark Enviro-Gold rating for its ecofriendly approach to hosting, energy conservation, and recycling.

7 Parliament St. www.aucklandbedandbreakfast.com. ℗ **0800/155-463** in NZ, or 09/377-5463. 4 units. From NZ$250 double. Rates include breakfast. Free parking. Long-stay rates. **Amenities:** Babysitting; free bikes; nearby golf course, pool, and tennis courts; Wi-Fi (free).

SKYCITY Hotel ★★　Part of the SkyCity complex, this four-star hotel has been awarded Trip Advisor's Certificate of Excellence for 4 years in a row now, which is not really surprising as management has absolutely got it together in terms of quality accommodation and amazing service. Of the 340+ rooms available, you can choose one with a premium city view or a deluxe harbor view—and despite the bustling activity just a few floors below, you're guaranteed that your room will be a quiet cocoon of restfulness. The lobby, which is the ground floor of the complex, recently underwent a NZ$24 million refurbishment and is, of course, just a matter of steps away from some of the city's finest dining experiences (see "Where to Eat").

72 Victoria St. W. www.skycityauckland.co.nz. ℗ **09/363-6000.** Rooms and suites from NZ$249–NZ$429. Carpark and valet parking. **Amenities:** 8 restaurants and bars; baby-sitting, business center; full concierge service; 24-hour room service; Wi-Fi (free).

INEXPENSIVE

For a sensibly priced stay in a landmark building right in the heart of the city, **Scenic Hotel Auckland** ★, 380 Queen St. (www.scenichotelgroup.co.nz; ℗ **0800/696-963** or 09/374-1741), offers 100 very comfortable rooms priced from NZ$230 to NZ$529. Ask for one of the eight rooms on the northwest face, which boast incredible views straight down Queen Street. It's a modest but perfectly situated option with a good cafe and bar at street level.

　　Budget travelers will find a clean, affordable spot right in the heart of the city at the 120-room **Kiwi International Hotel** ★, 411 Queen St. (www.kiwihotel.co.nz; ℗ **0800/100-411** in NZ, or 09/379-6487). It offers ensuite (from NZ$95–NZ$125), economy (NZ$79–NZ$85), or family rooms (NZ$139–NZ$145), plus a family apartment (NZ$179–NZ$195) that sleeps five. It's within walking distance to all major attractions, shops, and restaurants, and it has its own bar and restaurant and Internet access.

In Ponsonby
EXPENSIVE

Mollies on Tweed ★★★　A member of the Small Luxury Hotels of the World, this five-star property has accumulated plenty of international accolades, and its award-winning gourmet restaurant, **The Dining Room,** complete with dining terrace, is definitely a must-do experience. The grand old 1870s home has been extensively renovated and expanded to provide 13 stylish suites and apartments. Mollies combines the comforts of home with the privacy of apartment living. If you take the upstairs level, you'll have a balcony; downstairs rooms open onto the garden. Nothing has been spared to create gorgeous interiors filled with antiques and smart furniture. The location is handy to Ponsonby Road restaurants, bars, and boutique shopping.

6 Tweed St., St. Mary's Bay. www.mollies.co.nz. ℭ **09/376-3489.** 10 suites. Junior suite NZ$695; premier villa suite NZ$845; Mollies suite $1075. Off-season, long-stay and weekend rates. Rates include breakfast. Free off-street parking. **Amenities:** Restaurant; bar; airport transfer (NZ$140 one-way); babysitting; concierge; day spa; 24-hr room service, valet parking; Wi-Fi (free).

MODERATE

If you want an excellent motel close to the Ponsonby action, **Abaco on Jervois** ★★, 59 Jervois Rd. (www.abaco.co.nz; ℭ **0800/220-066** in NZ, or 09/360-6850), offers a range of immaculate, modern rooms priced from NZ$145 to NZ$235. Executive and premium suites on the middle and top levels are the best and biggest. Premium suites have a Jacuzzi, shower, separate lounge, desk, and kitchen. The complex is directly across the road from popular restaurants, bars, and cafes.

The Great Ponsonby Arthotel ★★ This restored villa, owned by hosts Sally James and Gerard Hill, enjoys a quiet location within walking distance of the best of Ponsonby. Comfortable rooms reflect a colorful Pacific mood. Three suites have both bathtubs and showers. The lovely Dunedin Room has its own deck, while the upstairs penthouse has a sitting room and balcony. Don't overlook the Palm Garden studios if you want extra space and privacy; some of these come with kitchenette, minibar, and DVD player. It's a great place for relaxing, with a sunlit lounge bulging with books, lots of New Zealand art and magazines, verandas for unwinding, and breakfasts to linger over. The property has a Qualmark Enviro-Gold rating and participates in recycling and energy conservation programs.

30 Ponsonby Terrace. www.greatpons.co.nz. ℭ **0800/766-792** in NZ, or 09/376-5989. 11 units. Villa rooms NZ$245; courtyard studios NZ$265; palm garden suite NZ$325; penthouse NZ$400. Rates include full breakfast. Ask about off-peark rates. Free off-street parking. Dog-friendly rooms available. **Amenities:** Fixed-price taxi airport transfers; babysitting; free use of bikes; Wi-Fi (free).

Ponsonby Manor Guest House ★★ Beginning life back in the 1870s as a boarding school for girls, this charming establishment then began to take in private boarders, a practice that continued until 2011 when it underwent a massive renovation—fortunately retaining some of the beautiful architectural features as well as amazing views over the city—and changed its name. These days it offers a range of rooms, each with an ensuite, and is a perfect choice if you're looking to stay for a week or longer. Although Ponsonby Manor is in the very heart of Ponsonby with its myriad dining options, self-catering facilities are available along with a burgeoning vegetable and herb garden, which the guests are encouraged to plunder at will.

229 Ponsonby Rd. www.ponsonbymanor.co.nz. © **09/360-7977.** 14 rooms, including a family room that sleeps 5. NZ$770–NZ$875 double room weekly rates. **Amenities:** Self-catering facilities; bathroom with disabled access; garden and deck; Wi-Fi (free).

INEXPENSIVE

The Brown Kiwi Travellers Hostel ★   Another Victorian gem, this 100+-year-old house is on a quiet street just a block from the main Ponsonby action. The best deals here are the two rooms in the lovely little garden house, a purpose-built corrugated-iron dwelling tucked among banana palms and ponds. It serves as a double or triple facility and is less sardinelike than the in-house rooms. Overall, this place offers a good atmosphere and a terrific garden courtyard in which to while away summer days and nights. It also has a well-equipped kitchen and a TV room.

7 Prosford St. www.brownkiwi.co.nz. © **09/378-0191.** 32 beds, all with shared bathroom (4 bathrooms in total). NZ$30–NZ$33 dorm per person weekly rates; NZ$70–NZ$78 twin/double. Rates include free local calls. Discount for BBH Club Card members. **Amenities:** Kitchen; TV room; Wi-Fi (60 min. free daily; $10/week).

Verandahs Backpacker Lodge ★★   Another cheap and cheerful option, Verandahs comprises two substantial Victorian dwellings, smack-bang next door to each other and just off Ponsonby Road. Renovated to a good standard, both buildings back on to Western Park, which can serve as a short-cut into the city and are on all the important bus routes. It has two good-sized lounges and a huge kitchen full of every pot or utensil you'll ever need. With access to Wi-Fi at reasonable rates, this lodge is very popular with young international travelers, although the size and variety of rooms available make it suitable for all age groups and budgets.

4–6 Hopetoun St. www.verandahs.co.nz. © **09/360-4180.** 17 rooms, including singles, doubles, dorms and a family room. NZ$31–NZ$105. Discount for BBH Club Card members. **Amenities:** Kitchen; lounge; travel desk; Wi-Fi (free).

In Mount Eden/Epsom

MODERATE

Bavaria Bed & Breakfast Hotel ★★   While it's not ultra-modern, this big old villa comprising 11 units feels very comfortable and is close to the city (10 min. by bus). The three upstairs rooms are the sunniest, and all have doors leading out onto the balcony. All units have ensuite bathrooms, which were updated relatively recently. It's also close to Mount Eden village, which has a growing number of restaurants and hip cafes.

83 Valley Rd., Mount Eden. www.bavariabandbhotel.co.nz. © **09/638-9641.** 11 units. NZ$185 double; NZ$70 each extra adult; NZ$50 children 2–12; free for children under 2. Rates include full breakfast. Off-season and long-stay rates. Free off-street parking. **Amenities:** Nearby golf course; nearby tennis courts; Wi-Fi (free).

Eden Park B&B ★★ Elegance is the word that comes to mind when you step inside the door of this immaculately restored early-20th-century villa on the city fringe. Although it appears to be on one level from the front, the ground slopes away at the rear, allowing plenty of room for the gently swaying trees that filter the light in the breakfast room. Each of the four rooms in this beautifully appointed property is named after a color, thus the Cream Room, the Blue Room, the Yellow Room (each with an ensuite bathroom), and the Green Room, which has its own private bathroom. The guest lounge features a 55-inch TV, but if you come during rugby season, you're very handy to Eden Park so you can watch the real thing if you're so inclined. Hosts Marlene and Anthony are justly proud of their charming establishment, which is handy to local public transport including buses and trains.

20 Bellwood Ave., Mount Eden. http://bedandbreakfastnz.com. bookings@bedandbreakfastnz.com. © **09/630-5721.** 4 rooms, from NZ$250 each. Rates include breakfast. Free off-street parking. **Amenities:** Nearby tennis courts; Wi-Fi (free).

Eden Villa B&B ★★ Your friendly hosts, Christine and Anthony, enjoy sharing their gracious early-20th-century villa, literally a stone's throw from Mt. Eden village, with guests. TLC is the house specialty; they like to describe their B&B with its three tastefully furnished and generously proportioned rooms as a "home away from home." Guests are encouraged to relax on the deck or in the north-facing sunny garden, but if the lure of TV is too strong, there's a dedicated guest lounge where the small screen rules. Two of the rooms have their own ensuite while the third has a private bathroom. Christine and Anthony are happy to share their local knowledge and recommend cafes and restaurants in their neighborhood and beyond.

16 Poronui St., Mount Eden. www.edenvilla.co.nz. © **09/630-1165.** 3 rooms. NZ$250. Rates include breakfast. Free off-street parking. **Amenities:** Nearby tennis courts; Wi-Fi (free).

In Parnell/Newmarket/Remuera
EXPENSIVE

Cotter House ★★★ You know you've arrived somewhere special on first sight of this historic lodge set in parklike manicured grounds in Remuera, one of Auckland's leafy, genteel suburbs. Although Cotter House offers only two rooms and one suite, nothing has been spared to make each one the last word in luxury—from the underfloor heating and lavish drapes to the tasteful artworks on walls that soar to a high ceiling stud. As you move from your room to one of the two elegant guest lounges, you'll be captivated by the attention to detail lavished on the hallway and on the staircase. You'll also quickly become aware that there is much more to a stay here than simply bunking down for a night or two, such as a customized meal in the dining room, where the resident chef will create a themed dinner for you, or a spa treatment. Alternatively, you could just bask in the glorious grounds. How tempting to just stay on and let the rest of the world drift by…. By the way, Cotter House has a 98% Qualmark rating.

2 St. Vincent Ave., Remuera. www.cotterhouse.com. © **09/529-5156.** From NZ$605. **Amenities:** Laundry services, chef on call, dedicated laptops; spa services; Wi-Fi (free).

MODERATE

Ascot Parnell ★★ Experienced hosts Bart and Therese Blommaert have been welcoming guests since the 1990s and are more than happy to meet travelers at the airport, which can make early or late arrivals a lot less daunting. Their modern apartment complex, complete with an elevator, is in a lovely location down a long, private driveway and just a short walk up the street to Parnell Village. Rooms are exceptionally comfortable and spacious, with views of the harbor or the subtropical gardens. The lovely 12m (40-ft.) pool is enveloped in garden greenery.

32 St. Stephens Ave., Parnell. www.ascotparnell.com. ⓒ **09/309-9012.** 3 units. NZ$225–NZ$385 double. Extra person (by request only) $50. Long-stay & off-peak rates. Rates include full breakfast and off-street parking. Children over 10 only. **Amenities:** Airport transfers (POA); guest kitchen; laundry facilities; shop; swimming pool; nearby tennis courts; Wi-Fi (free).

The Deveraux Remuera ★ Another delightful old mansion that was once home to one of Auckland's more affluent families, the Deveraux has been offering accommodation at modest prices on and off since the late 1930s. Although situated on a very busy road, the hotel is set well back down a driveway with another unrelated building in front to act as a buffer. In addition to four nicely appointed master suites, there are also several executive and standard suites, each with its own bathroom.

267 Remuera Rd., Remuera. www.devereux.co.nz. ⓒ **09/524-5044.** NZ$115 standard room; NZ$135–NZ$155 suite. Long-stay & off-peak rates. **Amenities:** Free off-street parking; Wi-Fi (free).

Quest Newmarket ★ If you like to cook up a storm while you're traveling, then these modern serviced apartments are ideal in more than one way: Not only do they come equipped with excellent kitchens, but there's a quality supermarket within walking distance. If that idea doesn't appeal, you'll be pleased to know you're close to any number of adjacent cafes and restaurants, plus some of Auckland's best boutique shopping. Quest Newmarket has been recently refurbished, and all the studios and apartments now have a light and airy ambience. It's just a short walk up the street to Parnell Village.

31–39 Davis Crescent, Newmarket. www.questapartments.co.nz. ⓒ **09/520-3000.** 49 units: studio, 1-, 2-, and 3-bedroom apartments. NZ$195–NZ$430. Long-stay rates. **Amenities:** Gym; undercover parking; Wi-Fi (free).

In Takapuna & Devonport
EXPENSIVE

Peace and Plenty Inn ★★ Romantics will love this gorgeous old Devonport home, which Judy Machin has transformed into the ultimate sumptuous, floral-themed haven. Every room has an ensuite bathroom—two with tub and shower, the rest shower only. The downstairs Albert room is the smallest unit but has the best bathroom; the Windsor is the biggest. Three upstairs rooms are sunny, with views and balconies. The whole place oozes character and ambience. The garden suite overlooks the lush subtropical garden, and the property has a Qualmark Enviro Gold Award.

6 Flagstaff Terrace, Devonport. www.peaceandplenty.co.nz. ℂ **09/445-2925.** 7 units. From NZ$195–$465. Extra person (and children 5–13) $50. Long-stay and off-peak rates. Rates include full gourmet breakfast. **Amenities:** Airport transfers (POA); babysitting; bike available; library; Wi-Fi (free).

MODERATE

Admirals Landing Bed & Breakfast ★★ This waterfront home owned by well-traveled Howard and Joy Mace is typical of all that's good about staying in Devonport. It's just a short walk to a good range of restaurants and cafes, village shops, a golf course, and some of Auckland's best beaches. The two rooms (Waterfront and Paua) are light and bright with everything you'll need for a comfortable stay; the Waterfront Room, which boasts 11 windows, offers excellent views in almost every direction. If you're keen to know more about this attractive seaside suburb, book yourself on one of Joy's guided heritage walks up Mt. Victoria and around the village.

11 Queens Parade, Devonport. www.admiralslanding.co.nz. ℂ **09/445-4394.** 2 units. NZ$230–NZ$300 double. Rates include breakfast and fresh fruit. Off-peak rates available. Children accepted by special arrangement. **Amenities:** Nearby golf course; Wi-Fi (free).

Emerald Inn Motel ★★ For those who want to be practically on the beach, the self-catering options available here are many and varied. Although parts of the exterior look a little dated, the rooms are fresh and clean and have all the amenities you'd expect from good quality holiday accommodation. Best of all, it's only a few steps to one of Takapuna's most popular cafes (daytime only), where you can watch all the comings and goings to your heart's content. If sand is not your thing, you can lounge by the pool. Longer-term (and minimum-stay) holiday accommodation in the complex is in the form of duplex units (basic but comfortable), Emerald Villas (fabulous location), and Emerald Cottage (luxury accommodation).

16 The Promenade, Takapuna. www.emerald-inn.co.nz. ℂ **09/488-3500.** NZ$182–NZ$250 studio; NZ$255–NZ$330 suite; NZ$550 villa; NZ$690 cottage. **Amenities:** BBQ; guest laundry; parking; swimming pool; Wi-Fi (free).

The Esplanade Hotel ★ As one of Auckland's oldest suburbs, Devonport has its fair share of beautiful old buildings, and the Esplanade Hotel, built in the Edwardian era, is one of them. Its location is pretty special, too—across the road from the ferry terminal and just a few steps from any number of shops, galleries, and cafes. On the ground floor you'll find the **Esplanade Restaurant and Bar,** serving breakfast, lunch, and dinner; then wander up the grand staircase to your choice of 15 character-filled rooms, which, while not terribly flash and in some cases even a wee bit tired, are certainly comfortable enough.

1 Victoria Rd., Devonport. www.esplanadehotel.co.nz. ℂ **09/445-1291.** 15 units. NZ$225–NZ$375 double. Off-peak rates. **Amenities:** Restaurant; 2 bars; business venues; room service; Wi-Fi (free).

The Spencer on Byron ★★   Fancy being just 500m (546 yards) from arguably the North Shore's best beach with the Takapuna shopping precinct even closer? Then this four-star high-rise hotel with 150 rooms, many of which have stunning views of Rangitoto Island, could fit the bill in more ways than one. If you're into hitting a ball around, you might like to choose from the handful of studio rooms and suites that open onto the courtyard running alongside the hotel's tennis court. There's also an outdoor heated pool, a family-sized spa pool, and a well-equipped gym.

9–17 Byron Ave., Takapuna. www.spencerhotel.co.nz. Ⓒ **09/916-6111.** 150 units. NZ$200–NZ$562. **Amenities:** Restaurant; bar; library; parking; Wi-Fi (free).

Out West

Beach lovers should consider **Bethells Beach Cottages** ★★, 267 Bethells Rd., Bethells Beach, Waitakere (www.bethellsbeach.com; Ⓒ **09/810-9581;** 2-night minimum stay), where two boutique cottages and a self-contained apartment are set in lush, private gardens—the ultimate Kiwi getaway—for NZ$190 to NZ$355, plus NZ$40 for each extra adult guest and NZ$20 for each child (low-season rates available). Owners John Paice and Trude Bethell have won a number of eco and environmental awards, and their accommodation has been designed to reflect this in every way possible.

Spend your nights in a rainforest restreat at **Waitakere Estate** ★★, 573 Scenic Dr., Waiatarua (www.waitakereestate.co.nz; Ⓒ **09/814-9622**), which offers four-star hotel rooms, villas, and apartment accommodation—a total of 21 rooms. A fine-dining restaurant is part of the complex, and if money's no object, take advantage of their helipad and arrive via helicopter. Rates run from NZ$165 for loft rooms, from $180 for deluxe rooms, from $200 for a garden spa apartment, and approximately $800 for the Gate Villa.

Near the Airport

There are now lots of accommodation choices out near the airport. The **Novotel Auckland Airport** ★, Ray Emery Drive (www.novotel.com; Ⓒ **09/365-0000**), is not so much close to the international terminal as almost attached to it. It has 263 rooms and suites from NZ$289 and good online specials. For truly budget deals, the **ibis Budget** ★, 2 Leonard Isitt Dr. (www.accorhotels.com; Ⓒ **09/255-5152**), has 125 simple, comfy rooms from NZ$99 plus free parking.

WHERE TO EAT

It's been many years since eating out in Auckland meant overcooked meat-and-three-vege in a hotel restaurant, although, ironically, this is where some of the very best establishments can be found these days. Nowadays Auckland offers world-class cuisine at good prices, specializing in fresh-produce-rich "New Zealand modern" cooking, Pacific Rim fusion and ethnic fare in all quarters of the city but especially in the Viaduct Harbor/Wynyard Quarter/Britomart precincts of the CBD, on Ponsonby Rd., Parnell and further around

skycity & FABULOUS FEDERAL ST.

More accurately called **Federal St at SKYCITY,** this formerly nondescript inner-city side street is now a premium dining destination, with the beautiful, five-star SKYCITY Grand Hotel—and several of its flagship restaurants—at its center. Kiwi cooking wunderkind Peter Gordon is the brains behind two of them, the tapas bar **Bellota ★★** and the sky-high and very successful **Sugar Club ★★**. The ambience in the former will have you thinking you've been transported to the back streets of Barcelona—right down to the guitarist and the mostly Spanish-speaking waitstaff. Bellota is a great place to sip on an authentic Spanish sherry and whet your appetite on some tapas or maybe a few pintxos while you decide where to go for dinner. If the Sugar Club is your choice, I do hope you've booked well in advance (but any wait will be worth it—on a clear evening the view is nothing short of stunning). For more casual dining, pop across the road to Al Brown's **Depot ★** or—right next door—his **Federal Delicatessen ★**. But wait, there's more. **Masu by Nic Watt ★★** (an acclaimed chef), which features the traditional Japanese robata style of cooking over an open charcoal grill, won Best New Restaurant in *Cuisine* NZ's Good Food Awards 2014. Not only is the food fabulous, but watching the incredible range of activity in the open kitchen is positively addictive. Hungry for a good cut of meat? Right next door you'll find **The Grill by Sean Connolly ★★**, where both grain- and pasture-fed Angus and Wagyu take pride of place on the menu alongside a range of sustainable seafood. Sean Connolly is also in charge of **Gusto at the Grand ★★**, which features his personal take on rustic Italian food—be sure to leave any dainty appetites behind.

the waterfront at Mission Bay and over the bridge at Devonport and Takapuna. European, Asian, casual bistro or silver-service posh: There are thousands of great and surprising restaurants to choose from—not to mention fantastic cafes, delis and bakeries anywhere you can squeeze in a couple of chairs and tables.

In the Inner City

Given the choice available, it's almost impossible to come up with a short list of not-to-be-missed eating establishments in this category, but I'll give it my best shot. Designed in the spirit of a "European back-street bistro," **O'Connell Street Bistro ★★**, 3 O'Connell St. (www.oconnellstbistro.com; ℂ **09/377-1884**), has more than stood the test of time—but you absolutely have to book in advance, since it can only seat 28 people. Note that a fire closed the restaurant in January 2016, but at press time it was scheduled to reopen 3 or 4 months down the road. Another restaurant that never disappoints is **Soul Bar & Bistro ★★**, Hobson and Customs Street West (ℂ **09/356-7249;** www.soulbar.co.nz), where the international food is not only excellent but the prime Viaduct Harbor location with fabulous people-watching potential has made it an Auckland institution. On any given day you're likely to spot the odd famous (well, famous in New Zealand) face along with international travelers, the business crowd, and high-flyers in general.

The French Café ★★★, 210 Symonds St., Newton (www.thefrenchcafe. co.nz; ✆ 09/377-1911), just keeps on picking up awards of the international as well as local variety—visit its website (a work of art in itself) and count 'em for yourself (I can't keep up; the list gets longer each year). But for the purposes of this guide, suffice to say that dining here is a totally unforgettable experience combining exquisite food (a recent summer menu featured king-fish ceviche with coconut and avocado; seared duck breast with peaches, shallots, wild fennel and lavendar; and organic lamb with a goat-cheese mash) with impeccable service and a wonderful ambience. The attention to detail at every level really has to be experienced to be believed.

EXPENSIVE

Baduzzi ★ INTERNATIONAL   Okay, so the name translates to "meat-balls," but you're going to get a whole lot more than your mom's go-to dinner when you rock up here. I actually thought I'd died and gone to heaven when I first tasted the crayfish meatballs here. For starters, Baduzzi is in a very cool location, right near the water and close to a bunch of other cool eating places, and while many of the dishes have an Italian bent, it also serves some excel-lent steak and seafood. And in the unlikely event that you need further con-vincing, it's run by two of the most experienced and well-respected chefs in town. Trust me—it's good.

10-26 Jellicoe St., Wynyard Quarter. www.baduzzi.co.nz. ✆ **09/309-9339.** Reservations required. Main courses NZ$32–NZ$48. Daily 11:30am–late.

Cocoro ★★ JAPANESE   The really serious foodies in Auckland rate this as the city's best Japanese restaurant, and having experienced chef Makoto Tokuyama's magic touch, I'm inclined to agree. The freshest of seafood is front and center (and the chef's specialty), but a sprinkling of meaty dishes includes grilled Wagyu filet and charcoal-finished duck leg confit. Although a

---

The Hip Group Cafes

Any one of the sophisticated cafes run by the entity known as the Hip Group is definitely the place to be. Finding one should not be a problem; at last count there were 10 of them, most centrally located. So what makes these cafes so special? Personally, I think it's the win-ning combination of attractive yet totally professional waitstaff, really good food (much of it grown in a purpose-developed market garden on the out-skirts of Auckland), and buzzy atmosphere. Not all are open for dinner; check first with a quick visit to the web-site (www.hipgroup.co.nz). Here's the list of central ones: **Ortolana** (✆ 09/ 368-9487) and **Milse** (✆ 09/215-8996) at Britomart in the city; **Rosie** at 82 Gladstone Rd., Parnell (✆ 09/369-1182); **Richmond Road Café** in Grey Lynn (✆ 09/360-5559); **Takapuna Beach Café** in Takapuna (✆ 09/484-0002); and **St. Heliers Bistro & Café** in (surprise!) St. Heliers.

la carte dining is an option, I highly recommend one of the three degustation menus, which can be paired with either sake or wine.

56a Brown St., Ponsonby. http://cocoro.co.nz. ℭ **09/360-0927.** Reservations essential. Degustation menu from NZ$90. Tues–Sat noon–2pm and 5:30–10pm.

Clooney ★★ INTERNATIONAL   Once an industrial warehouse and now one of Auckland's top dining experiences presided over by an award-winning chef, Clooney is a highly desirable night out. From its elegant main dining area, favored by Auckland's elite, to its private dining rooms and basement lounge, it's all about style and delicious tastes. Indulge in a seven-course tasting menu or eat a la carte—whichever option you choose, you can expect top flavors. Think hapuka with paua crème and pork flavors, or lamb with yogurt, eggplant, sunflower, and olives.

33 Sale St. www.clooney.co.nz. ℭ **09/358-1702.** Reservations required. Two courses NZ$80; three courses $95. Daily 11am–late.

The Grove ★★ MODERN NEW ZEALAND   Another illustrious award-winning restaurant that can be counted on to deliver the goods in the form of dishes that appear modern but are heavily influenced by classic French cooking techniques. Your dining experience at The Grove is on a prix-fixe (fixed-price) basis with either five or nine courses with optional wine matching. Because renowned chef Ben Bayly uses organic and sustainable meats along with seasonal fruits and vegetables, the menu is never static, but there's almost always at least one delicious game dish available. To complete a memorable night, there's even valet parking available.

St. Patrick's Square, Wyndham St. www.thegroverestaurant.co.nz. ℭ **09/368-4129.** Reservations required. Prix fixe from NZ$90 (wine extra). Mon–Fri noon–late; Sat 6pm–late.

Sails ★ SEAFOOD   Bart Littlejohn's family established this Auckland icon set smack in the middle of Auckland's biggest marina many years ago. For a long time it was the go-to place for special occasions, but a recent revamp has seen it take on a more relaxed ambience. It's the perfect spot to enjoy a magnificent array of seafood while looking out over the marina and deciding on which yacht you'd like to sail away. By the way, it's pretty hard to go past the oysters—and then there's the always beautifully cooked catch of the day.

103–113 Westhaven Dr., Westhaven Marina. www.sailsrestaurant.co.nz. ℭ **09/378-9890.** Reservations required. Main courses from NZ$40. Mon–Fri noon–3:30pm and daily 6:30–9pm daily.

MODERATE

Café Hanoi ★ MODERN VIETNAMESE   This place found favor with locals and visitors alike from the day it opened back in mid-2010. Serving zesty food with a twist, Café Hanoi uses heaps of fresh herbs, delicious seafood, and, among other things, free-range chicken and pork. Be prepared to share—not only is the menu designed for this, but it's just too hard to choose otherwise. If you're after more of a snack than a meal, consider its sister

CHEAP eats: FOOD HALLS ★

A long-time favorite with impoverished locals, Asian students, and travelers, Auckland's food halls offer undeniably good-value eating. Not all food stalls are created equal, however, so it's worth noting the really good ones, which include two great Thai choices: **Marigold Thai** in the **Food Alley food court,** 9–11 Albert St. (www.facebook.com/Food-Alley-189107124443118/;

(© **09/373-4917**), and **Som Tum** in the **Mercury Plaza food court,** 23–31 Mercury Rd. ((© **09/309-9387**). At **Ponsonby Village International Foodcourt,** 106 Ponsonby Rd. (www.ponsonbyfoodcourt. co.nz), the seriously hip, not to mention well-dressed, clientele is almost as interesting as the assorted food stalls. Food halls are generally open from around 10am to 10pm.

operation just a few steps away, **Xuxu Dumpling Bar** ★, where you can indulge your dumpling cravings to your heart's contenet. Excelsior Bldg, Galway St. & Commerce St., Britomart. www.cafehanoi.co.nz. (© **09/302-3478.** Reservations required. Dinner from NZ$45. Mon–Sat midday–late, Sun 5pm–late.

Odettes ★★ NEW ZEALAND/FUSION For a seriously good casual eating experience from breakfast through to dinner, this place hits the spot. The emphasis is on sharing plates, but not just *any* sharing plates—expect some very interesting flavor and texture combos, especially with the accompaniments. The food changes seasonally, but a recent menu of small bites included such delectables as avocado hummus, pork belly dumplings, duck parfait, confit octopus, and yellowfin tartare. Be warned that if you go at night and actually want to *see* what's on your plate, it's best to choose a table against the wall where the lighting is sufficient. Shed 5, City Works Depot, 90 Wellesley St. West. www.odettes.co.nz. (© **09/309-0304.** No reservations required. Dinner from NZ$35. Mon 7am–4pm, Tues–Fri 7am–9pm, Sat 8am–9pm, and Sun 8am–3pm.

Ponsonby Central ★ INTERNATIONAL Located in the heart of Ponsonby, this hugely popular complex offers great ambience and a fabulous range of eateries serving designer burgers, modern Chinese, crêpes, authentic pizzas, Japanese, Argentinian BBQ, and even South American street food. Most are open well into the night, so it's always hopping—there really is something for everyone and every budget. And did I mention the most excellent cafe/bakeries on the Richmond Road side for a coffee and snack on the run? 136 Ponsonby Rd. www.ponsonbycentral.co.nz. (© **09/376-8300.** Daily 7am–11pm.

INEXPENSIVE

Most of the cheap eats in and around the city tend to be Asian eateries. Several notable exceptions are in Ponsonby: **Bird on a Wire,** 136 Ponsonby Rd. (http://birdonawire.co.nz), serves finger-lickin'-good free-range rotisserie chicken, burgers, and fresh salads. The bird at **Boy and Bird,** 222 Ponsonby Rd. (www.boyandbird.co.nz), is citrus-brined, house-rubbed, rotisseried, and

If you're lucky enough to be visiting Auckland over the summer months and you fancy doing the "When in Rome" thing, head to one of the following establishments and invest in a fragrant package of piping-hot golden chips (French fries to you) and fish coated in a delicious crisp batter all wrapped in newspaper: **FishSmith** (200 Jervois Rd., Herne Bay); **Greenwoods Fresh Catch** (1 Pah Rd., Epsom); **Jimmy the Fish** (136 Ponsonby Rd., Ponsonby); or **Mt. Eden Village Fish Shop** (438 Mt Eden Rd., Mt. Eden). And where should you go to eat it? I highly recommend a beach or maybe a park. Anywhere outdoors on a fine evening is good.

chopped. **Burger Burger,** 136 Ponsonby Rd. (http://burgerburger.co.nz), serves gourmet burgers. **Il Buco,** 113 Ponsonby Rd. (www.ilbuco.co.nz), sells damn good pizza by the slice—perfect when you're in a hurry.

In the heart of town, don't pass by **Bonz Cajun Kitchen** and **Ela Cuisine** at the **Elliott Stables** (www.elliottstables.co.nz) marketplace on Elliott Street. The former is known for its classic Cajun dishes and the latter for wonderfully fragrant Indian delicacies. The market also has a variety of cheap and cheerful Spanish, Italian, and German options. Slightly farther afield in Grafton is **Café Karadeniz** (www.cafekaradeniz.co.nz) with tasty Turkish offerings.

As for the best Asian eateries, my top five are **Angie's Kitchen,** Mount Street (© **09/368-1618**), a popular hangout for anyone with a taste for Nyonya flavors; **Barilla Dumpling,** Dominion Road (© **09/638-8032**), where the Chinese treats are positively addictive; **Bian Sushi,** not far from the CBD in Symonds Street (© **09/309-5609**), for excellent sushi; **Dak Hanmari,** Upper Queen Street (© **09/369-5656**), for sizzlingly good Korean; and **Indochine Kitchen,** on Fort Street in the central city (© **09/309-5609**), for deliciously smoky Hanoi-style street food.

Sri Pinang ★ MALAYSIAN   Located on Auckland's most colorful street, this popular restaurant never disappoints—but it can get awfully busy at lunchtime and evenings, so phone ahead or get there early. Angie's Roti Curry at NZ$9 is, in my book, the best value around, but I can sometimes be tempted by the Nasi Lemak.

356 Karangahape Rd. © **09/358-3886.** NZ$10–NZ$15. Mon 5–10pm, Tues–Fri 11am–10pm, Sat–Sun 5:30–10pm.

Food Truck Garage ★ HEALTHY FAST FOOD   The subject of a TV series, this star truck now has a permanent home in a "garage" at the City Works Depot in Wellesley Street West where it dispenses healthy burgers and tacos featuring zucchini and beetroot. The sides—Buffalo Cauliflower, Loaded Spuds, Truck Slaw, etc—are almost too yummy to be healthy, but believe me, they really are good for you.

1/90 Wellesley St. W. © **09/973-2305.** NZ$15–NZ$20. Mon–Thurs 11am–8:30pm, Fri & Sat 11am–9pm, Sun 11am–4:30pm.

In Ponsonby

EXPENSIVE

Ponsonby Road Bistro ★ INTERNATIONAL Although the menu is presented in quite a casual fashion, this utterly reliable yet award-winning restaurant excels in attentive yet professional service. My eye filet steak was cooked to perfection, and the delicious simplicity of the rotating side dishes (steamed broccoli with miso butter; beetroot, carrot, and apple slaw; chunky chips with aioli) do a wonderful job in supporting the main act.

165 Ponsonby Rd. www.ponsonbyroadbistro.co.nz. ℭ **09/360-1611.** Reservations required. Mains from NZ$35. Mon–Sat noon–3pm; Mon–Sat from 5:30pm; reduced menu served Mon–Fri 3–5:30pm.

Sidart ★★ INTERNATIONAL/FUSION In the event that your tastebuds are feeling a little jaded, get refreshed and rejuvenated by some really inspirational food at this innovative restaurant. No a la carte dining here—it's all about the tasting menu which, on Tuesdays, comes in the form of a Test Kitchen comprising eight courses designed by award-winning owner/chef Sid Sahwawat. One recent menu featured quail with kale, cashews, and apple, while pork came with eggplant, radish, and lime.

Three Lamps Plaza, 283 Ponsonby Rd. www.sidart.co.nz. ℭ **09/360-2122.** Reservations required. Degustation menu from NZ$80. Tues–Sat dinner from 6pm, Fri lunch (5-course tasting menu) from midday.

MODERATE

This inner-city suburb is now so full of eateries—from casual to fine dining and with more popping up all the time that it is not an easy task to identify any in particular. But among those that have stood the test of time is *la grande signora* of the strip, **Prego** (it's been here since the 1980s, a long time in Auckland restaurant history), at 226 Ponsonby Rd. (www.prego.co.nz; ℭ **09/376-3095**). It's open daily for lunch and dinner from noon until late and is as good as it ever was. Expect to pay upwards of $35 for a main course, but you can nibble more cheaply. Then there's **SPQR** at 150 Ponsonby Rd. (www. spqr.co.nz; ℭ **09/360-1710**), where since the '90s the main sport has been people-watching—this is where much of the film and media crowd, the gay community, and your average run-of-the-mill Joe Bloggs all hang out, from lunchtime through to the wee hours, looking supercool. Well known for their

---

Food Trucks

Following the trend in Australia and elsewhere, food trucks are now making their culinary presence felt throughout the inner city. The good news is that they regularly congregate in one place, giving those with a peripatetic bias the chance to pick and choose. Particularly recommended is The Lucky Taco, presided over by the super-friendly and colorful Otis and Sarah Frizzell. Check **www.thestreetfoodcollective.co.nz** to track them down.

platters, SPQR also serves up a good range of pizzas, along with the usual bistro meat and fish suspects.

A newer contender on the Ponsonby strip, **Blue Breeze Inn,** 146 Ponsonby Rd., Ponsonby Central complex (http://thebluebreezeinn.co.nz; ✆ **09/360-0303**), will have your taste buds thinking they are in China (main dishes around $28), and the rest of your senses reveling in the Pacific Island atmosphere, complete with complimentary cocktails. It's open daily lunch and dinner.

In Mount Eden
MODERATE

Looking for bistro-style food and atmosphere? Then head for **Molten ★** at 422 Mt. Eden Rd. (www.molten.co.nz; ✆ **09/638-7236**), in the heart of Mt. Eden village where you can nibble in the wine bar or partake of heartier fare next door, depending on your appetite. The brined chicken (NZ$29) is a wonderfully tender treat, while the slow-cooked lamb shoulder (NZ$30) literally melts in your mouth. And if there are four or more of you I recommend choosing from the Feasting Menu, served family style with large platters in the middle of the table (from NZ$55). The previous edition of this guide paid homage to **Bowmans** at 597 Mount Eden Rd., which sadly is no more. However, the good news is that **Bolaven** (www.bolaven.co.nz; ✆ **09/631-7520**), named after the plateau in Laos where the French first planted coffee (who knew?), has now taken up residence at this address and is open for breakfast and lunch Tuesday through Sunday and dinner Wednesday through Saturday. Expect some seriously good and well-priced Asian food with a Laotian bent.

The Healthy Stuff

Over recent years the rise of organic cafes has been an interesting phenomenon, and the inner-city suburbs are now spoiled for choice. One of the first—if not the first—to appear on the scene was **Little Bird Unbakery,** which now has three outlets: the flagship premises on 385 New North Rd., Kingsland (✆ **09/550-7377**); 1A Summer St., Ponsonby; and in the city on 14 Customs St. E. (www.littlebirdorganics.co.nz). Little Bird not only offers fabulous smoothies and raw treats—I personally recommend its Spring Bird Bowl, packed with seasonal goodies—but each of its establishments are a pleasure to visit, thanks to the creative spaces they are housed in. Just up the road a little in the heart of Grey Lynn is **Kokako** (www.kokako.

co.nz; ✆ **09/379-2868**), in the suburb's old post office (with some original fixtures) at 537 Great North Rd. Choose from organic cabinet food or an innovative seasonal menu (chili scrambled eggs with avocado and cornbread; a potato, carrot, parsnip, egg, and relish hash with hollandaise). The good folk here are committed to sustainability and have awards to prove it—and by the way, the coffee is superb. A little farther out, on 1087 New North Rd., Mt. Albert, **Cosset** (www.cosset.co.nz; ✆ **09/846-0655**) is a vegetarian establishment that prides itself on its delicious vegan and gluten-free baked goods. It's a great place to enjoy a healthy breakfast—"happy hour" is between 8am and 9am.

ice cream, YOU SCREAM . . .

Giapo Grazioli's amazing ice cream creations, which have thrilled as well as satisfied so many customers since first opening **Giapo** ★★ at 279 Queen St. in the city in 2008, are definitely worth screaming about. Every single ingredient (and I mean *everything*) is made on the premises, so it's little wonder that this haute ice cream establishment just keeps on cleaning up all the relevant awards. They're artworks in their own right. Go. Just as soon as you can.

INEXPENSIVE

Just over the road from Molten, **Rad** (www.returnofrad.co.nz; ℰ **09/631-5218**) is a hip fusion joint that's open for breakfast and lunch. Personally, I can't go past Grandma's pork banh mi—trust me, it's exceptional value.

In Parnell/Newmarket
EXPENSIVE

Going strong now for more than 40 years, **Antoine's** ★★ at 333 Parnell Rd. (www.antoinesrestaurant.co.nz; ℰ **09/379-8756**), continues to attract a well-heeled clientele with rich French cuisine and impeccable service. It's open for dinner Monday to Saturday and lunch Wednesday to Friday; however you really need to book. By the way, if you're one of the minority that enjoys a dish of tripe, acclaimed chef Tony Astle is your man.

Another spot that's been on the scene for many years is **Cibo** ★, 91 St. Georges Bay Rd. (www.cibo.co.nz; ℰ **09/303-9660**), a favorite among the expense-account crowd. Actually, the quality and range of dishes food adds up to much more than the bill at the end. And a menu that at first glance looks fairly traditional has some interesting twists.

MODERATE

In Newmarket, wander down Nuffield Street and choose **Tasca** (ℰ **09/522-4443**), for Spanish food; **Caffe Massimo** (ℰ **09/522-6700**), for excellent counter food; **Nuffield St. Café** (ℰ **09/520-2240**), for European-style food; **Wagamama** (ℰ **09/524-4975**), for a bowl of Japanese goodness; or **Basque Kitchen Bar,** 61–73 Davis Crescent (ℰ **09/523-1057**), for more Spanish.

On the North Shore

The Engine Room ★ at 115 Queen St., Northcote Point (www.engineroom. net.nz; ℰ **09/480-9502**), is still among the best the North Shore has to offer. Its fabulous cookbook makes a very worthy souvenir of a meal there. Up the road, **Eight.Two** ★ at 82 Hinemoa St., Birkenhead (www.eightpointtwo. co.nz; ℰ **09/419-9082**), serves innovative New Zealand cuisine. In Takapuna, things have really heated up with **Madam Woo** at 486 Lake Rd. (www. madamwoo.co.nz; ℰ **09/489-4601**), giving Asian fusion a run for its money. Not far away at 21 Hurstmere Rd. and not far from the golden sands of Takapuna Beach is the slightly more established **The Commons** (www.

WEST meets EAST

If you're searching for a good range of ethnic cuisines without having to travel all over the city, look no further than **Dominion Road** (a major arterial road that runs north-south across most of the central isthmus and is so well known to locals that it even had a song written about it years ago). It was recently estimated that over 80 different ethnic groups are represented up and down this colorful route across the city. Some are relatively smart, while others are not much more than hole-in-the-wall dumpling and noodle houses where the number of people crammed in at any time is testament to the good, cheap food. Wherever possible, make a reservation, especially on weekends, but a number of the most cheap and cheerful don't take bookings, so you'll have to take your chances. As for tipping, it's now expected (although not compulsory) in the more upmarket establishments. Bon appétit!

thecommons.co.nz; © **09/929-2791**), where the extensive menu should satisfy most appetites.

If venturing down the peninsula to Devonport, be aware that there are no really standout eateries but plenty of perfectly pleasant options.

EXPLORING AUCKLAND

Pick up the bimonthly "The Auckland Gallery Guide" for everything you need to know about the city's best galleries and their current exhibitions. It's free from information centers and art galleries and has user-friendly maps.

The Top Attractions

Auckland War Memorial Museum ★★★ Auckland's imposing museum building, crafted from Portland stone and designed to reflect the heroic valor of the New Zealand soldier and the "classical" tragedy of battles such as Gallipoli, stands in the Auckland Domain on the rim of an ancient volcano surrounded by parks and gardens. (The museum's colonnades are said to be almost a replica of the Parthenon's in Greece.) Of the two entrances, the original harbor entrance has stunning views; the newer rear dome entrance in the Atrium shows off contemporary New Zealand architecture.

Get a shaky start at **Volcanoes,** a gallery that introduces you to Auckland's turbulent natural history. It's the only city in the world built on a volcano field, and the interactive movie room, simulating the birth of a new volcano, will have you thinking we're slightly crazy for living here at all. And in case you think this sounds a bit dry and "museumy," it's perfectly illustrated by the cool but pretty thought-provoking "volcano house," in which you go into a typical Kiwi lounge, sit down and watch a TV news broadcast as Mount Rangitoto erupts all over the city.

This first-rate museum experience gives a marvelous introduction to New Zealand history and culture. The largest collection of Maori and Polynesian artifacts in the world alone is worth a visit and a must-see. Key attractions in the extensive **Maori Treasures Gallery** include the impressive 25m (80-ft.) war canoe chiseled from one enormous totara trunk and covered with intricate carvings. That same artistry is reflected in the 26m (85-ft.) meetinghouse, with its carved and painted walls and rafters. Also on display are magnificent greenstone weapons, tools, and feather cloaks. Three times a day—at 11am, noon, and 1:30pm (plus an extra 2:30pm performance Jan–Apr)—concerts by the local Ngati Whatua *iwi* (tribe) bring the culture to life.

The museum is easy to negotiate. Just remember that the first floor is about the people, the second is about the land, and the third is our war memorial. The moody **Pacific Pathways** houses a world-renowned collection of Pacific artifacts; "New Zealand at War: Scars on the Heart" tells an emotional story of New Zealand in conflict, from the Land Wars of the 1840s to its present-day peacekeeping operations.

The first-floor Natural History Galleries showcase everything from dinosaur skeletons to live seaside rock pools. It's a fascinating area well supported by the superb **Weird & Wonderful Discovery Centre.**

To get the most of your visit, allow 2 to 3 hours minimum. An on-site cafe is open during museum hours, although the service can be patchy and the coffee isn't always the best. There are two very good shops worth a visit. Booking ahead is essential, or check the website for holiday activity timetables. Be sure to take a stroll around the magnificent **sculpture walk** featuring eight works by New Zealand artists. The museum supplies a map.

Auckland Domain. www.aucklandmuseum.com. © **09/309-0443.** Admission to permanent collection NZ$25 per adult and NZ$10 per child. Charges for special exhibitions may apply. Museum entrance plus Museum Highlights Tour: Adults NZ$40, children NZ$20. Museum entrance plus Maori Cultural Performance: Adults NZ$45, children $20. Museum entrance plus Maori Cultural Performance and Museum Highlights Tour: Adults NZ$55, children NZ$25. Daily 10am–5pm. Wheelchair access throughout. Explorer Bus stops every 60 min. (30 min. Oct–Mar).

Auckland Food Tours

With its wealth of incredibly fresh foods and delicious produce—think seafood, top-quality beef and lamb, world-renowned wine—it's no secret that New Zealand is becoming a very attractive foodie destination. A food tour is a great way to meet some artisan producers and sample their wares. You won't go wrong with **The Big Foody** (http://thebigfoody.com; © **0800/366-386**), which offers a variety of tempting options, including the Queen Street Food Tour and the Takapuna Beach Food & Culture Tour (both NZ$125 per person). **Finding Flavour** (www.finding-flavour.co.nz; © **09/3727-344** or mobile **021/550-510**) is another great option for gourmands to get behind the scenes and meet the food makers. And if you fancy giving your taste buds a spicy hit, spend a couple of hours on Eat Auckland's **Sandringham Food and Spice Tour** (www.eatauckland.co.nz).

Sky Tower ★★★ In the first 18 months after it opened in August 1997, Sky Tower drew over a million visitors, making it New Zealand's most popular paid attraction. At 328m (1,076 ft.), it is the tallest manmade structure in the Southern Hemisphere, affording unforgettable views over the sprawling mass of Auckland. It has two observation decks, including a glass lift and glass floor panels. Access to the observation decks is by three glass-fronted elevators, which can whiz up the building in a speedy 40 seconds. I'm petrified of heights but even I got a thrill out of going to the top. I just closed my eyes in the glass lift!

The Sky Tower has two restaurants and one cafe: Peter Gordon's restaurant **The Sugar Club** is on level 53; **Orbit** (a revolving restaurant) is on level 52, and the **Sky Café** is on level 51. The Main Observation level features the latest technology. The Sky Deck is the highest public viewing area, with 360-degree views through seamless glass.

SKYCITY, Victoria and Federal sts. www.skytower.co.nz. ℭ **0800/759-2489** in NZ, or **09/363-6000.** Admission NZ$28 adults, NZ$11 children 6–14, NZ$61 family. Daily 8:30am–late. Underground parking is available.

Kelly Tarlton's Sea Life Aquarium ★ Board the amazing toothy Shark Bus from your hotel and head around the bays to the last big dream of Kiwi diver Kelly Tarlton, who died in 1985. He envisaged an **Underwater World** where the whole family could make like divers without getting wet: moving along a conveyor belt beneath an acrylic dome while sharks, stingrays, eels, and numerous other species swam overhead. And that's what you can do here, as well as watching rays clamber up their keepers during feeding time in **Stingray Bay,** meeting king and gentoo penguins in a **Penguin Discovery Experience,** freaking yourself out in a **Shark Dive,** or taking a **Behind the Scenes Tour,** plus seahorses, jellyfish, and more. The new **Antarctic Ice Adventure** allows visitors to see penguins with just the aquarium glass between them, but I kinda liked creaking around the penguin enclosure in the old "Snow Cat" train, which has gone now. Still, it's a great place and puts Auckland's old sewage storage tanks to ingenious use. Give yourself 2 hours and ring ahead to find out daily feeding times.

23 Tamaki Dr., Orakei. www.kellytarltons.co.nz. ℭ **0800/805-050** in NZ, or 09/531-5065. Admission NZ$39 adults, NZ$22 children 3–14, free for children 2 and under. Special rates for families and seniors; book online to save up to 20%. Shark Dive Extreme from NZ$200; Shark Cage Adventure from NZ$124; Penguin Discovery from NZ$199; Behind the Scenes tour adults from NZ$40, children 3+ from NZ$20. Daily 9:30am–5pm (last entry 4pm). Take free Shark Bus from 172 Quay St., Mission Bay city bus (bus stop D13 at Tyler St), Explorer Bus.

Auckland Art Gallery Toi o Tamaki ★★ New Zealand's most important art space, this is the best place to see people stroking their little beards and opining intelligently about what they see in front of them. And what they see is a really pretty impressive collection of more than 15,000 artworks set on four floors: historic, modern, and contemporary New Zealand art, international paintings, sculpture, and prints from the 11th century to today, all

AUCKLAND | Exploring Auckland

Iconic Rangitoto

Rising up from the Hauraki Gulf, the symmetrical cone of Rangitoto Island is one of Auckland's most visible icons. Of the 48 dormant volcanoes scattered across the Auckland region, it is the largest and the youngest. The island is accessible by ferry during the day and visitors can walk up a scoria path that leads from the wharf to the crater rim.

Fullers, Ferry Terminal, 99 Quay St. (www.fullers.co.nz; *C* **09/367-9111**), has a **Volcanic Explorer Tour** that visits Rangitoto Island (NZ$59 adults, NZ$30 children 5–15). It's a 25-minute cruise from downtown Auckland. You can also get to Rangitoto via **kayak** on a night paddle with **Fergs Kayaks** (www.fergskayaks.co.nz); see "Kayaking," below.

enclosed in a complex that melds an early French Renaissance–style building from 1887 with a rather expensive extension completed in 2011. It won the World Architecture Festival's World Building of the Year award in 2013, so enjoy the extraordinary space as well as the artwork. This is the place to gaze at everything from the world's greatest Old Masters to groundbreaking Maori and Pacific work you simply won't see anywhere else. Exhibitions change regularly. There are free tours every day at 11:30am and 1:30pm—highly recommended!

Cnr Wellesley and Kitchener sts. www.aucklandartgallery.com. *C* **09/379-1349** for 24-hr. information. Free admission; fees for some special exhibitions. Daily 10am–5pm.

The Viaduct Harbor

Auckland's Viaduct Basin, more commonly called "The Viaduct," is a glistening creation that includes apartment blocks, hotels, restaurants, cafes, bars, shops, markets, and every facility an earnest yachtie could want. The village complex was created in 2000 to support America's Cup–related syndicates, corporations, superyachts, and the public together in one venue.

Between October 1999 and March 2000, and again from October 2002 to March 2003, the village was the place to soak up the excitement of the America's Cup challenge. Millions of visitors crammed in over the two periods, along with some 2,000 competitors and team personnel, plus 200 international media representatives during each challenge. In addition to the America's Cup action, the village played host to up to 80 **superyachts** on each occasion, the largest gatherings in the Southern Hemisphere, turning Auckland into a Pacific Monte Carlo. Superyachts are luxury motor and sailing vessels in excess of 30m (98 ft.) long, ranging in value from NZ$4 million to over NZ$40 million. Viaduct Harbor can accommodate 88 superyachts of up to 50m (165 ft.)!

Visitors can experience grand-prix sailing on an authentic America's Cup yacht, *NZL 41,* built for the 1995 San Diego Challenge, or *NZL 68.* You can be as involved as you want in the crewing action, no sailing experience required. The price per person is NZ$170 for 2 hours of sailing and $120 for children 10 to 15 years. Sailings are 11am and 2pm daily. A challenge race between the two boats is held every Saturday from November to March at 2pm. The price per person is NZ$230 for a 3-hour race and $170 for children 10 to 15 years. For details on the daily sailings from Viaduct Harbor, contact **Explore NZ** (www.exploregroup.net; ⓒ **0800/397-567** in NZ, or **09/359-5987**). Children 9 and under are not permitted to sail.

The Viaduct Basin development has changed the face of Auckland forever, providing a fistful of fabulous restaurants, clubs, and bars that have endured—despite the fact that Team New Zealand relinquished the America's Cup in the 2002–03 challenge. It is a marvelous place to explore, and given that some of Auckland's best eateries are here, you'd be silly to miss it.

Viaduct Harbor has also been a stopover point in the epic Volvo Ocean Race (formerly the Whitbread Round-the-World Race).

Other Museums, Monkeys & More

Museum of Transport & Technology (MOTAT) ★ Victorian brass-helmeted firemen pedaling around on ancient bikes with hoses attached, bewhiskered gentlemen working at a forge, ladies in period costume doing pioneer things—these are all sights you might see at MOTAT, along with a plethora of planes, trains, and automobiles, including an enormous old steam engine you can play on, scientific phenomena you can fiddle with in the kids' exploration area, early-settler shops, and glimpses into New Zealand's past. Take a tram ride to the Sir Keith Park Memorial Aviation display, located in a separate building down the road, or jump off at the zoo. It's the biggest museum of its type in the country, covering 16 hectares (40 acres) in beautiful Western Springs park, 5km (3 miles) from the city center, and has permanent exhibitions, such as 90 Degrees South (Ed Hillary's 1956–58 Antarctic expedition) as well as changing displays. Skip the overpriced cafe and have a picnic at Western Springs.

805 Great North Rd., Western Springs. www.motat.org.nz. ⓒ **0800/668-2869** in NZ, or 09/815-5800. Admission NZ$16 adults, NZ$8 children 5–16, NZ$40 families. Daily 10am–5pm. Explorer Bus.

New Zealand Maritime Museum ★★★ The National Maritime Museum is perfectly placed beside the harbor. Inside are intricate working displays and fascinating exhibitions documenting 1,000 years of New Zealand maritime history. Watch traditional craftsmen restoring historical vessels, wood-turning, and working on sails. Of course there's an exhibit on America's Cup history. Plus, you get the chance to hit the high seas yourself: Ride the historic scow *Ted Ashby*, which takes to the water for a 60-minute ride every day except Monday (sailings 11:30am and 1:30pm weekdays; noon and 2pm weekends). Inside the museum I particularly like the 1950s beach shop and bach (holiday house) display, which sums up much of the quintessential Kiwi seaside holiday experience. The 14 galleries and interactive displays in this acclaimed museum will keep you busy for quite a while.

Hobson Wharf, Viaduct Basin. www.maritimemuseum.co.nz. ⓒ **09/373-0800**. Admission NZ$20 adults, NZ$10 children 5–14, free children 4 and under; NZ$40 families.

AUCKLAND | Exploring Auckland

Museum Combo (museum entry plus *Ted Ashby* harbor cruise) NZ$50 adults, NZ$25 children 5–14, NZ$50 Auckland families, $95 non-Auckland families. Summer daily 9am–5pm; winter daily 9am–5pm. Park in Downtown Car park & purchase a discounted parking pass at the Museum ticket desk for 4 hours' parking.

Auckland Zoo ★★ I have friends who live near the zoo whose kids have grown up with lions roaring grumpy lullabies to them at dusk. It's a beautiful property owned by Auckland City and next to fabulous Western Springs park, and even people who don't like zoos should enjoy this one. Conservation and natural environments drive everything here: It's one of Australasia's leading zoos, and the animals inhabiting it have better lives than a lot of humans I know! It's made up of a number of precincts, such as Pridelands (including cheetahs, hippos, giraffes, lions, zebras), the Primate Trail (orangutans and lemurs), and Te Wao Nui (indigenous species, such as little blue penguins, New Zealand fur seals, kiwi, and weta). There are daily animal encounters and Junior Keeper and behind-the-scenes experiences. On Safari Nights you sleep in the old elephant house. (Don't worry, they've cleaned it out.)

Motions Rd., Western Springs. www.aucklandzoo.co.nz. ✆ **09/360-3805.** Admission NZ$28 adults, NZ$23 students and seniors, NZ$12 children 4–15, family passes NZ$47–NZ$72. Daily 9:30am–5:30pm (5pm in winter); last admission 4:15pm. Blue Circle Explorer Bus or Pt. Chevalier 045, which departs from Downtown Centre, inner city. Free parking.

Butterfly Creek ★★ This is a great thing to do if you've time to kill before taking a flight—it's just a few minutes' drive from Auckland International Airport. You'd have to be fairly weird not to like butterflies (there are more than 20 glorious species here, mainly from Asia and Central America, which you can encounter in the Butterfly House), but if you do fall into this category and prefer crocodiles, there are two of them here, too. There are also giant weta (like grasshoppers on steroids), tarantulas, cute fluffy things at Buttermilk Farm, a tropical aquarium, the interactive Dinosaur Kingdom, a pretty freaky range of reptiles, and some cotton-top tamarin monkeys. Yep, it's more like a zoo.

10 Tom Pearce Dr., Manukau. www.butterflycreek.co.nz. ✆ **0800/132 101** in NZ, or 09/275-8800. NZ$13–NZ$27 adult and NZ$10–NZ$16 child, depending on areas visited. Family passes NZ$39–NZ$73. Daily 9am–5:30pm in summer; daily 9:30am–5pm in winter.

Historic Houses

Alberton ★★, 100 Mount Albert Rd. (www.alberton.co.nz; ✆ **09/846-7367**), is perhaps the finest of all of Auckland's historic homes that are open to the public. The once-simple farmhouse built in 1863 grew into the fairy-tale mansion that stands today. Owned by Heritage New Zealand (previously the New Zealand Historic Places Trust), it provides an intimate glimpse into Victorian life. It's open Wednesday through Sunday, 10:30am to 4pm; admission is NZ$11 adults and NZ$3.50 children.

Ewelme Cottage, 14 Ayr St., Parnell (www.historic.org.nz; (C) **09/379-0202**), was built for the Rev. Vicesimus Lush from 1863 to 1864 and named for Ewelme Village in England. The roomy *kauri* cottage is authentically preserved, right down to its 19th-century wallpaper. It contains an important collection of more than 800 books. Admission is NZ$8.50 adults, free for accompanied children. It's open Sunday only 10:30am to 4:30pm.

Highwic, 40 Gillies Ave., Epsom (www.highwic.co.nz; (C) **09/524-5729**), is one of New Zealand's finest Gothic Revival houses. Built in 1862, it gained additions modeled from an American pattern book in 1873. Its distinctive architecture and gardens offer insight into the lives of the wealthy Victorian family who retained possession of it until 1978. Admission is NZ$10 adults, free for accompanied children. It's open Wednesday through Sunday 10:30am to 4:30pm.

Kid Magnets

In addition to Rainbow's End (below), the **Auckland Zoo, Kelly Tarlton's,** the **Sky Tower, Butterfly Creek,** the **Museum of Transport & Technology,** and the **Auckland Museum's Weird & Wonderful Discovery Centre** are designed for kids and fun-loving adults.

Rainbow's End ★   Here's one attraction you really need to have a couple of rug rats in tow to get the most out of. Get ready for the Stratosfear, the Fear Fall, the Power Surge, and the double-loop Corkscrew Coaster. If this sounds like your idea of a good time, New Zealand's biggest theme park is the place for you. It's not Disneyland, but these rides combined with more gentle activities like the Enchanted Forest Log Flume, Gold Rush, and the big swingin' Pirate Ship should keep everyone happy. For the wee ones, there's magical fun to be had in the Kidz Kingdom.

Cnr of Manukau Stations and Great South roads, Manukau City. http://rainbowsend. co.nz. (C) **0800/438-672** in NZ, or 09/262-2030. All-day Super Pass (includes unlimited rides) NZ$55 adults (14 & up), NZ$44 children 2–13, NZ$27 Kidz Kingdom (children 2–5), NZ$7–15 spectator pass, also family passes and combos. Daily 10am–5pm. Take the Manukau motorway exit 15 min. south of Auckland and drive to the end of the Rainbow. Free parking.

Parks & Gardens

The Auckland area has 22 regional parks, covering 37,038 hectares (91,484 acres) and more than 500km (310 miles) of walking tracks. The **Auckland Domain ★**, the city's oldest park, is an imposing crown of green just minutes from the city center. Within it, the **Wintergarden,** the steamy **Tropical House,** and **Fernz Fernery** are botanical showcases for indigenous and exotic plant specimens. Admission is free. The Wintergarden is open daily from 10am to 4pm. There are also extensive formal gardens, sweeping lawns, statuary, duck ponds, sports grounds, and dozens of picnic spots. Summer Sundays bring free jazz and rock concerts in the band rotunda, chamber music in the Wintergarden, and megaconcerts on the sports fields. Call (C) **09/379-2020** for details. There are several well-signposted entrances to the Auckland Domain. Two of the busiest are on Stanley Street and Parnell Road. There are also entrances on Grafton Road and Park Road.

The **Parnell Rose Garden** and **Dove-Myer Robinson Park** (named after a popular former city mayor) are off Gladstone and Judges Bay roads in Parnell. One of the city's first churches, little St. Stephen's Chapel, is also here.

The **Auckland Botanic Gardens,** 102 Hill Rd., Manurewa (www.aucklandbotanicgardens.co.nz; ☏ **09/267-1457**), cover 64 hectares (158 acres). It's home to more than 10,000 plants. The gardens are open daily from 8am to 8pm in summer and 8am to 6pm in winter. The Visitor Centre is open Monday through Friday 8am to 4:30pm (till 4pm in winter) and Saturday and Sunday 9am to 5pm (till 4pm in winter); the cafe is open daily from 8:30am to 4:30pm. Free guided walks are available every Wednesday at 1pm. Other guided tours are available by arrangement. Call ☏ **09/266-3698**, e-mail botanicgardens@arc.govt.nz, or ask at the visitor center. To get here from the city, travel south and take the Manurewa motorway exit, turn left onto Hill Road, and drive to the entrance.

Also worth a look are **Eden Gardens,** 24 Omana Ave., Mt. Eden (www.edengarden.co.nz; ☏ **09/638-8395**). Once a quarry, it is now a showplace for an amazing collection of rhododendron, vireya, hibiscus, bromeliads, palms, and many other subtropical species. The gardens are open daily 9am to 4:30pm (till 4pm in winter); the on-site cafe is open 9am to 4pm. Admission is NZ$8 adults, NZ$6 seniors and students, and free for children.

Exploring Devonport

The village of Devonport is all about atmosphere, charm, historic buildings, the arts, and cafes. It has a summer holiday feel, even in the middle of winter, and especially on weekends. Stop at the **Devonport i-SITE Visitor Center,** Devonport Wharf (www.aucklandnz.com or www.devonportnz.com; ☏ **09/446-0677**), where you can find out about things to see and do. It's open daily from 8:30am to 5pm.

TAKING THE FERRY Catching the **Fullers Ferry** ★★ (www.fullers.co.nz; ☏ **09/367-9111**) to Devonport is one of the nicest day's outings you can have in Auckland. Make your way to Pier 1, Ferry Terminal at 99 Quay St.,

---

Rustic Roaming

Epsom's **Cornwall Park** (Auckland's largest) is like the countryside in the middle of the city: There are sheep, stone walls, and lovely walks. In the middle of it is **One Tree Hill,** which should be called None Tree Hill, following a protesting Maori's handiwork with an axe in 2000

(negotiations over a replacement tree are nearing an end). The **Cornwall Park Visitor Center** (www.cornwallpark.co.nz; ☏ **09/630-8485**) has maps and information on walks. Access is via Greenlane Road, Manukau Road, or Campbell Road.

WINE OUT west

Greater Auckland is home to more than 110 vineyards. The main regions are Waiheke Island, Matakana, and Kumeu. Henderson Valley is the country's oldest grape-growing area, dating to the arrival of Croatian and other Northern Hemisphere immigrants in the early 1900s. Today, the western suburbs and areas north to Kumeu are a major grape-growing region. Cabernet sauvignon is the most commonly planted grape; merlot and pinot noir are also important. Chardonnay and sauvignon blanc are the main white varieties. Most West Auckland wineries also draw fruit from other regions, mostly Gisborne, Marlborough, and Hawke's Bay. The Kumeu area, about 30 minutes from Central City, is the most accessible for a day's outing. Waiheke Island is about 30 to 40 minutes away by ferry; it's by far the prettiest region and worth the time.

If you're short on time and must forego a winery tour, call at **Glengarry Wines ★★**, with 15 retail wine outlets around Auckland, see www.glengarry.co.nz for locations (🕿 **0800/733-505** in NZ, or 09/308-8346). These stores hold an extensive range of varietals from most New Zealand regions and offer tax-free wine sales, wine tastings, worldwide home delivery, and wine-tour information. They're open Monday through Saturday 9am to 8pm and Sunday 11am to 7pm.

For information on Waiheke Island wineries, see "A Side Trip to Waiheke Island" later in this chapter.

You'll find a good cluster of wineries along Lincoln and Henderson Valley roads and nestled in the surrounding hills. The small townships of Kumeu, Huapai, and Waimauku also have good selections. For information on wine tours, see "Organized Tours & Cruises," below. For further details on the area, pick up the free vineyard brochures from a visitor center. Following are the notables.

○ **Babich Wines,** 10 Babich Rd., Henderson (www.babichwines.co.nz; 🕿 **09/833-7859**): One of the most picturesque wineries, Babich has a pleasant picnic area near its shop and vintages going back to 1990. It's only 20 minutes from Central City and open for tastings Monday through Friday from 9am to 5pm and Saturday from 10am to 5pm (closed Sun).

○ **Soljans Estate,** 366 St. Hwy. 16, Kumeu (www.soljans.co.nz; 🕿 **09/412-5858**): Soljans produces internationally competitive wines. It has cellar sales and tastings, a cafe, and a winery complex. Daily winery tours (11:30am–2:30pm) followed by a tasting cost NZ$12 per person. Tastings without the tour are free except for groups of 6 people or more ($6 per person). The winery is open daily 9am to 5:30pm; the cafe is open Monday through Friday 11am to 3pm and on weekends 9am to 3pm.

○ **Coopers Creek,** 601 SH16, Huapai (www.cooperscreek.co.nz; 🕿 **09/412-8560**): Coopers Creek has wine tasting and Sunday summer jazz performances. It's open Monday through Friday 9:30am to 5:30pm and weekends from 10:30am to 5:30pm.

○ **West Brook Winery,** 215 Ararimu Valley Rd., Waimauku (🕿 **09/4119924**): With lovely parklike grounds, petanque, and giant chess in the garden, this is a pleasant place for a picnic; snacks are available for purchase. It's open Monday to Friday 9am to 5pm, Saturday 10am to 5pm, and Sunday 11am to 5pm. Tastings are free except for groups of 8 or more people ($6 per person).

and take to the water. You'll get great views of the city as you head out aboard the catamaran *Kea.* The ferry operates daily every half-hour from 7:15am to 8pm and every hour from 8 to 11pm, and the trip takes 12 minutes. The round-trip fare is NZ$12 adults, NZ$6.50 children ages 5–15. If you plan to base yourself in Devonport, buy a 10-trip or weekly ferry pass.

DEVONPORT VILLAGE TOURS   The two historic backbones of the village are Victoria and Church streets, now the main business area. Many of the buildings here date to the first European settlement. Pick up a self-guided walking-tour brochure called **"The Old Devonport Walk"** from the visitor center, and meander the seaside village. If you decide to stay for dinner in Devonport, you'll find numerous cafes along the main street.

Another fun way to see Devonport is by Segway. **Magic Broomstick Segway Tours** (www.magicbroomstickstours.co.nz; ℂ **09/445-4035** or **027/3393155**) does two Segway tours a day in summer (Nov–Apr) and two daily in winter. A family tour (45 min.) is NZ$60 per person, the Taste of Segway tour (1 hr.) is NZ$80, the Mount Victoria tour (1.5 hr.) is $120, and the Northhead Tour (2.5 hr.) is $150.

BEACHES
There are three excellent white-sand beaches in close range—**Devonport,** a good swimming spot with a playground; **Cheltenham,** a safe tidal beach; and **Narrow Neck Beach,** with safe swimming and a playground. Not far from the village center is **Mount Victoria,** from the top of which are great harbor views. Visit **North Head,** which was once a significant defense spot for both Maori and the Europeans. The volcanic hill was developed during World War II and is honeycombed with underground tunnels, chambers, and gun emplacements. **Devonport Explorer Tours** (www.devonporttours.co.nz; ℂ **09/357-6366**) take in both Mount Victoria and Northhead beaches on a 1-hour minibus tour (allow 2 hr. if you include the ferry trip from Auckland). The cost is NZ$40 per adult (including ferry ride); booking ahead is essential. Tours run daily every hour from 10am to 3pm all year round.

ART GALLERIES
At the colorful **Art by the Sea,** King Edward Parade and Church St. (www.artbythesea.co.nz; ℂ **09/445-6665**), you'll find top-quality work by New Zealand artists. It's right next door to cafes and across the road from the sea; hours are Monday through Saturday 10am to 5pm and Sunday 11am to 4pm. **Peter Raos Glass Gallery ★★**, Shop 5, 2 Queens Parade (www.peter-raos.com; ℂ **09/445-4278**), is also worth checking out for handmade art glass and jewelry by local resident and master glass artist Peter Raos. It's open Tuesday through Saturday from 11am to 5pm.

MUSEUMS & MORE
Two museums worth visiting are the **Devonport Museum,** 31A Vauxhall Rd. (www.devonportmuseum.org.nz; ℂ **09/445-2661**), open Saturday and Sunday from 2 to 4pm with free admission, and the **Devonport Naval Museum,** 64

King Edward Parade, Torpedo Bay, Devonport (www.navymuseum.mil.nz; ✆ 09/445-5186), open daily from 10am to 5pm, with free admission. The former tells the story of Devonport through historical artifacts and natural-history displays. The latter is housed in a 19th-century submarine mining station and showcases the story of the New Zealand Navy.

For something completely different, check out **Devonport Chocolates** ★, 17 Wynyard St. (www.devonportchocolates.co.nz; ✆ 09/445-6001), where you can see chocolate being made. The shop is open Monday through Sunday 9:30am to 5pm.

Organized Tours & Cruises

You can book several half- and full-day tours of Auckland and its environs at the visitor center. Half-day tours cover city highlights, while all-day tours usually include something of the east or west suburbs, the zoo, or the vineyards.

BUSH & BEACH

Bush & Beach ★★ (www.bushandbeach.co.nz; ✆ 09/837-4130) will take you out to the wild west coast to experience the elemental side of Auckland. Half- or full-day tours may include visits to a gannet colony, a winery, or a virgin rainforest (NZ$150–NZ$235 per person). Bush & Beach also has an all-day tour to the Hobbiton movie set in Matamata ($285 adults, half-price children under 11); wear comfortable walking shoes. The **Best of Both Worlds Tour** provides a good overview of Auckland's diversity, taking in the city in the morning and the bush and beaches of West Auckland in the afternoon.

WINE TRAILS

Auckland Wine Trail Tours ★★ (http://winetrailtours.co.nz; ✆ 09/630-1540) specializes in introducing small groups of people to leading growers. The five tour options covere the best wine areas in the area and scenic highlights along the way. Half- and full-day tours are available. The full-day **Waterfalls & Wines Tour,** for instance, includes city views, rainforest and waterfalls, black-sand beaches, visits to four wineries, and a winery lunch (NZ$265 per person). **Fine Wine Tours** ★★ (www.finewinetours.co.nz; ✆ 0800/023-111 in NZ, or 021/626-529) also has a great selection of half- and full-day food and wine tours (NZ$179–NZ$299). Especially good is the **Great Auckland Food & Wine Lovers Tour** (Mon–Sat; NZ$299 per person, including cafe lunch), which introduces you to cheesemaking, ice cream, a busy fish market, delis, a chocolate boutique, a distillery, and a winery, all in Auckland.

ON THE WATER

Auckland won't deprive you of an opportunity to get out on the waves. **Fullers** (www.fullers.co.nz; ✆ 09/367-9111) is one company that makes it easy. If you're on a tight itinerary, one of Fullers' best-value deals is the **Harbor Cruise,** a 1½-hour sightseeing excursion that shows off Viaduct Harbor,

Island Escape

If you feel like spoiling yourself, join **Hauraki Blue Cruises** ★★★, Viaduct Harbour Marina (www.haurakibluecruises.co.nz; ✆ **0800/334-339** in NZ) for a lunch cruise around the harbor (from NZ$99 for adults and NZ$50 for children), departing daily at 11am. Or how about an overnight trip around some of the Hauraki Gulf islands (from NZ$299 for adults and NZ$225 for children), departing at 3pm. Their vessel *Ipipiri* is the largest cruise ship permanently based in New Zealand, so expeditions are year-round.

Devonport Naval Base, and the Harbor Bridge, with coffee and commentary. Fares are NZ$38 adults, NZ$19 children ages 5 to 15. The cruise includes a round-trip ticket to Devonport so that passengers can visit the seaside village at their leisure, or on any scheduled Fullers sailing. Tours depart from Pier 2, Ferry Terminal, 99 Quay St., at 10:30am and 1:30pm. Fullers' **Volcanic Explorer Tour** option visits Rangitoto Island for NZ$59 adults, NZ$30 children ages 5 to 15. Among Waiheke Island Explorer options, a **Taste of Waiheke Tour** ★ visits three award-winning wineries and a top olive oil producer. It costs NZ$129 and includes a light lunch at Stonyridge.

New Zealand's only research-based marine mammal experience, **Auckland Whale & Dolphin Safari** (www.awads.co.nz; ✆ **09/357-6032** or freephone 050/8365744) works closely with the Department of Conservation and local universities, combining close-up viewing of whales, dolphins, and seabirds with scientific research. The eco-safari departs from the Auckland Viaduct at 12:30 daily and lasts for 4½ hours (NZ$160 adults, $105 children 15 and under).

Auckland Seaplanes (www.aucklandseaplanes.com ✆ **09/8872-456**) has a variety of tours flying over Auckland's harbors and islands in a Havilland Beaver Float Plane, which seats up to eight passengers. It operates 7 days a week during daylight hours.

Yachting is big in New Zealand. **Exploregroup NZ** ★★★ (www.exploregroupnz.co.nz; ✆ **0800/397-567** in NZ, or 09/359-5987) offers some exciting ways to experience Auckland from the water. As well as the rides on America Cup boats *NZL41* and *NZL68,* the company operates a fleet of purpose-built sailboats, which offer lunch, dinner, coffee, and half-day cruises in Auckland and the Bay of Island. Cruises with the **Maritime Museum** (p. 68) on the heritage scow *Ted Ashby* offer a very different type of experience.

OUTDOOR ACTIVITIES & SPECTATOR SPORTS

Outdoor Pursuits

GOLF You'll find more than 40 golf courses in the Auckland region. For details call the **Auckland Golf Association** (www.auckgolf.co.nz;

4

AUCKLAND | Outdoor Activities & Spectator Sports

© **09/522-0491** or 027/437-3822), Monday through Thursday between 9am and 5pm, and ask for the course nearest you and current greens fees.

HORSEBACK RIDING   The Auckland region is home to about 20 riding operations. Visitor centers can give you advice about the outfitter nearest you. The most popular rides are at **Muriwai Beach** (www.murawaibeachhorsetreks.co.nz), **Pakiri Beach** (www.horseride-nz.co.nz), and **Warkworth** (www.horseridingwarkworth.co.nz).

JETBOATING   **Auckland Adventure Jet** (www.aucklandadventurejet. co.nz; © **0800/255-538** in NZ) will whisk you out onto Waitemata Harbour for a thrilling 35-minute high-speed ride for NZ$98. Jetboats depart hourly from Pier 3A at the ferry Terminal at 99 Quay Street, at the bottom of Queen Street.

KAYAKING   Ian Ferguson was one of New Zealand's top athletes; he competed in five Olympic games, won four gold medals and one silver, and in 1996 was named New Zealand Olympian of the century. He is also the man behind **Fergs Kayaks** ★★, located at **Ian Ferguson Marine Sports Centre,** 12 Tamaki Dr., Okahu Bay (www.fergskayaks.co.nz; © **09/529-2230**). It has several kayaking options; the most fun, perhaps, is the **Rangitoto Night Trip,** which involves a 75-minute paddle out to the island and a 45-minute walk to the top of Rangitoto for a spectacular night view of Auckland. The trip leaves at 6pm, returns by 11pm, and costs around NZ$150.

Other fantastic watery trips are run by **Auckland Kayak Tours** (www. aucklandseakayaks.co.nz; © **0800/999-089** or 09/2134-545) and take kayaking trips up river to the Riverhead Tavern, Rangitoto Island, and Motukorea/ Browns Island. Tours start at the St. Heliers Central Boat Ramp, Tamaki Drive, and the company includes free city pickup (NZ$95–NZ$185); meals are included for day trips and morning or afternoon tea for half-day trips.

MOUNTAIN BIKING & TOURING   Downhill mountain biking is what you get with **Auckland Adventures** (www.aucklandadventures.co.nz; © **09/379-4545**). It offers a number of mountain bike tours for groups of five people or more, taking in the best of West Auckland. Costs range from NZ$85 to NZ$135 per person, and a full-day tour is NZ$185 per person. Biking time varies from 1 to 3 hours, depending on your level of fitness. For mountain and touring bike rentals, self-guided cycle tours, and guided cycle holidays, try **Natural High** (www.naturalhigh.co.nz; © **09/257-4673**), conveniently located minutes from the Auckland Airport (10 Uenuku Way). A mountain bike park is just around the corner. It's open Monday to Friday 9am to 5pm and Saturday 10am to 4pm. Bikes rent from NZ$50 a day.

SAILING   You'll find numerous brochures about sailing charters at the Auckland visitor center. See also "Organized Tours & Cruises," above. If you'd like to learn the basics of sailing, contact **Sailing Away School of Sailing** ★★ (www.sailingaway.co.nz; © **09/521-2387**), and sailing master Suzanne Bourke will take you out on the *French Connection.*

SURFING New Zealand Surf 'n' Snow Tours (www.newzealandsurf-tours.com; ℂ **0800/787-386** in NZ, or 09/828-0426) offers 1- and 2-day surf tours for NZ$50 to NZ$199 and a 5-day surf tour at NZ$899 in the Auckland and Northland regions. If you've never taken to the board or want to improve your skills, **Piha Surf School** (www.pihasurfschool.com; ℂ **09/8128-1230**) at Piha Beach offers lessons by internationally qualified instructors (1½ hr.; $120 for one-on-one instruction and $80 group lesson).

SWIMMING Accessible from Tamaki Drive (where there's frequent bus service from Britomart), the beaches at Judges Bay, Okahu Bay, Mission Bay, Kohimarama, and St. Heliers Bay are popular inner-harbor swimming spots.

SHOPPING

Auckland's shops are generally open from Monday to Friday 9am to 5:30pm, and many stay open later on Thursday and Friday. Saturday hours are normally 10am to 4pm, although many shops stay open all day, and a number are open on Sunday. *Tip:* Some shops will post your purchases home, thereby avoiding the 15% Goods and Services Tax you pay on most items in this country.

Inner City

Britomart (www.britomart.org) is a whole lot more than the headquarters of Auckland's public transport system at the bottom of Queen St.—it's a precinct in the heart of the CBD where some of the hippest designers and coolest eateries can be found. Top Kiwi designers **Karen Walker, Trelise Cooper, World, Zambesi, Juliette Hogan,** and **Kate Sylvester** all have stores here.

Head for the **High St.–Vulcan Lane–O'Connell St. areas ★★★** (www. heartofthecity.co.nz)—the place to go for the best in New Zealand fashion houses, accessories, art—not to mention coffee and interesting food. Also here is the excellent bookstore **Unity** (www.unitybooks.co.nz; ℂ **09/307-0731**). The lovely and innovative **Pauanesia ★★**, 35 High St. (www.

Antiques Hunting

The most popular concentrations of antiques stores are around the Epsom area and in Parnell, Remuera, and the inner city. Parnell's happy hunting grounds include **Murdoch McLennan,** 367 Parnell Rd. (ℂ **09/309-4757**), which has a beautiful range of English antiques; and a few doors down, **Baran de Bordeaux,** 367 Parnell Rd. (ℂ **09/307-1201**), filled with exquisite imported French antiques and decorative items from the 17th through 19th centuries.

In Epsom, check out **John Stephens Antiques,** 15 Shore Rd., Epsom (ℂ **09/529-1660**); and **Country Antiques,** 489 Manukau Rd. (ℂ **09/630-5252**). In Remuera, look for **Abbey Antiques,** 87 Great South Rd. (ℂ **09/520-2045**), and several others on the same stretch of Great South Road. And if you like old china—especially English brands—you'll adore fossicking at **Babushka,** 156 Garnet Rd., Westmere (ℂ **09/378-9226**).

GOING TO market

For an excellent Pacific experience, visit the **Otara Market ★★★**, Newbury St., Otara (© **09/274-0830**), on Saturday from 6am to noon. It's the largest Polynesian market in the world, with larger-than-life personalities, exotic foods and smells, wonderful *tapa* cloth, flax mats and baskets, and bone carvings.

The extensive **Avondale Market,** Avondale Racecourse, Ash Street (www.avondalesundaymarkets.co.nz; © **09/818-4931**), is held on Sunday from 5am to noon and has a strong Polynesian and Asian influence. It features a mass of fruit, vegetables, new and used clothes, and bric-a-brac. There are no fast-food or drink stalls at this market. An excellent **City Farmers' Market** is held every Saturday morning from 8am to noon in the large courtyards behind the Britomart Transport Centre on Gore Street. **La Cigale,** 69 St. Georges Bay Rd., Parnell, is a French-style market held every Saturday 8am to 1:30pm and Sunday 9am to 1:30pm.

The **Silo Park Markets** (www.silopark. co.nz) operate every fine Friday evening during summer. Silo Park is in the Wynyard Quarter—a revitalized area of Auckland's waterfront west of Viaduct Harbor. Just look out for the giant silos! Grab dinner, gifts, and arts and crafts from an eclectic array of stalls and toast the end of the week at the **Silo Park Bar,** with local DJs there to entertain. Silo Day markets are on Saturday and Sunday noon to 6pm.

Enjoy a great day in the country at the acclaimed **Matakana Village Farmer's Market** (www.visitmatakana.co.nz), which showcases artisan foodstuffs, gourmet delicacies, and produce. It's within an hour's striking distance from Auckland by car.

---

pauanesia.co.nz; © **09/366-7282**), sells the very best in contemporary New Zealand and Pacific homeware. The **Vault,** 13 High St. (www.thevaultnz.com; © **09/377-7665**), is the perfect place for reasonably priced New Zealand and international design items—everything from jewelry to stationery to small gifts. **Chancery Square** (www.chancerysq.co.nz) is also packed with international brand stores, exclusive fashion names, cafes, and restaurants.

All manner of middle-of-the-road stores line **Queen Street** from top to bottom, but I think you find much better shops down the little side streets running off it. Among the excellent specialty shops, **Fingers ★★**, 2 Kitchener St. (www.fingers.co.nz; © **09/373-3974**), is Auckland's most established New Zealand jewelry collective. Also at 2 Kitchener Street is the excellent **FHE dealer gallery** (www.fhegalleries.com; © **09/302-4108**), exhibiting and selling ever-changing works from some of New Zealand's best artists and craftspeople. **Kura Gallery,** 188 Quay St. (www.kuragallery.co.nz; © **09/302-1151**), has a great range of original New Zealand art and crafts.

Ponsonby/Herne Bay/K'Road

The inner-city suburb of Ponsonby is best known for its fabulous bars and eateries, but you could spend all day just browsing in its gorgeous design and fashion stores and boutiques. Some of New Zealand's best designers have branches here, including **World, Andrea Moore, Cybèle,** and **Ruby. Carlson Ponsonby,** 120

Ponsonby Rd. (http://tanyacarlson.com), stocks a number of fab Kiwi designers, and **Clothesline,** 132 Ponsonby Rd. (www.clothesline.co.nz), will sell you a homegrown designer T-shirt you won't see back home. You'll find local art and design treasures at **Texan Art Schools,** several locations (http://texanartschools. co.nz), **Bijoux Gallery,** 8 Ponsonby Rd. (www.bijoux.co.nz), and **Chan Andreassend,** 5 Rose Rd. (www.chanandreassend.co.nz).

Karangahape Road is worth browsing for its diversity and cultural mix, but don't expect high-quality goods here; it's better known for art galleries, featuring both the quirky and the bizarre. Check out **www.iloveponsonby. co.nz** and **www.kroad.com** for more on both Ponsonby and K'Road.

Parnell/Newmarket

Shopping Parnell is a special experience, albeit an expensive one, with everything from Timberland to Cartier. You'll find all sorts of exclusive gifts in a rabbit's warren of little historic buildings, restored to picturesque splendor, that stretch along a mile of **Parnell Road** (www.parnell.net.nz). Visit Newmarket's latest hot spots, **Nuffield and Teed streets ★★★,** for the high-end stores of iconic international and Kiwi fashion brands like **Karen Walker, Trelise Cooper, Kate Sylvester,** and **Zambesi.** There are a number of excellent cafes and restaurants here too—the ideal place to pause between parcels. Altogether, **Newmarket** (www.newmarket.co.nz) has over 40 designer fashion stores and New Zealand's largest concentration of shoe stores—20 of them! In this area check out the **Poi Room,** 17 Osborne St., Newmarket (✆ **09/520-0399;** www.thepoiroom.co.nz), for high-quality New Zealand art, design, jewelry, prints, glass, and textiles.

AUCKLAND AFTER DARK

Auckland has something for everyone—the adventurous, the sophisticated, the young, and the young at heart. From 24-hour casinos and live theater to cinema, clubs, pubs, bars, and dance spots, you can party all the way to breakfast time.

For information about what's on here and around New Zealand, contact **Ticketek** (www.ticketek.co.nz; ✆ **09/307-5000**) or **Ticketmaster** (www.ticketmaster.co.nz; ✆ **09/970-9700**). You can make credit-card bookings for events and get your tickets couriered to you.

The Performing Arts

Auckland Live, 50 Mayoral Dr. (www.aucklandlive.co.nz; ✆ **09/309-2677**), is the cultural core of Auckland. Located in the central area bordered by Mayoral Drive and Albert, Wellesley, and Queen streets, it includes the modern Aotea Centre, the impressive Auckland Town Hall, and the refurbished Civic theater. The **Aotea Centre** (✆ **09/307-5060**), opened in 1990 by Dame Kiri Te Kanawa, features theater, ballet, dance, opera, major stage productions, art exhibitions, and lots of local drama. The **Auckland Town Hall**'s Great Hall seats over 1,600 and is modeled after the Gewandhaus Concert Hall in

Leipzig, Germany, which was bombed during World War II. It is regarded as one of the finest acoustically tuned concert halls in the world, and it schedules regular performances by the Auckland Philharmonia and the New Zealand Symphony Orchestra.

The **SKYCITY Theatre** is the newest addition to the city's performance venues. The 700-seat theater features state-of-the-art technology and major local and international performers in dance, theater, rock, pop, jazz, and cabaret. For details on events, call ℂ **0800/759-2489** or visit www.skycity.co.nz.

The **Maidment Theatre** at Auckland University (www.maidment.auckland.ac.nz; ℂ **09/308-2383**) is well known for New Zealand drama and theater sports; the **Bruce Mason Centre,** in Takapuna (www.bmcentre.co.nz; ℂ **0800/005-959** in NZ, or 09/488-2940), offers a little of everything.

The Live Music Scene

Pick up the free *Auckland What's On* guide from the visitor center for the latest on the music scene. You'll find jazz and rhythm-and-blues gigs at bars, restaurants, and hotels around the city, such as at **Orleans Cajun and Creole Restaurant,** 48 Customs St East. (www.orleans.co.nz; ℂ **09/3095-854**). For punk or rock, head to the funky **Whammy Bar,** St. Kevin's Arcade 183 Karangahape Rd. (www.undertheradar.co.nz).

For a thumping good night, try **Studio The Venue,** at 340 Karangahape Rd. (www.studiovenue.co.nz; ℂ **09/3580-994**), not far from the CBD, which has a great lineup of local and international artists of rap, hip hop, hard rock, pop rock and more. The large **Vector Arena,** 42–80 Mahuhu Crescent, Parnell (www.vectorarena.co.nz; bookings through Ticketmaster at www.ticketmaster.co.nz or ℂ **0800/111-999**), is where you can catch a star-studded concert or top international artist. The venue holds 12,000 people. Catch a bus from the CBD or walk (about 20 min.).

If Irish music is your thing, you'll find it at **Danny Doolan's** ★, Viaduct Basin (ℂ **09/358-2554**), offering food and live entertainment 7 nights a week. **The Dogs Bollix** ★★★, at the intersection of Karangahape and Newton roads, Newton (ℂ **09/376-4600**), is one of the city's premium music venues. It's a pub environment with a large garden bar, showcasing the best homegrown and international rock, Celtic, folk, and blues talent. **Kings Arms** ★★★, 59 France St., Newton (www.kingsarms.co.nz; ℂ **09/373-3420**), is another top live music venue featuring international and local favorites. The **Powerstation** ★★★, 33 Mount Eden Rd., Eden Terrace (www.powerstation.net.nz; no phone), has been the iconic starting point for many well-known New Zealand groups including internationally recognized Shihad. It features local talent as well as high-profile international names.

The Club & Bar Scene

No matter how many nightspots are listed here, somebody's favorite will always be overlooked. If you want a night with the work-hard, play-hard business crowd, head for **Parnell;** older, richer, devil-may-care types flock to

The Britomart Bars

Development is ongoing at Britomart (www.britomart.org), where classy, cool new bars seem to spring up by the minute. Some faves: **Mac's Brewbar** (www.macs.co.nz) at the Northern Steamship Company, 122 Quay St. (*C* **09/374-3952;** www.northernsteamship.co.nz), housed in a historic building; **The Britomart Country Club,** 31 Galway St. (www.britomartcountryclub.co.nz; *C* **09/303-2541**), with a large garden and a night-and-day buzz as punters enjoy a beer, a meal ,or the tunes of top DJs; former parking garage **Tyler Street Garage,** 48 Tyler St. (www.tylerstreetgarage.co.nz; *C* **09/300-5279**), now an über-cool industrial-style bar; **Orleans Music Liquor Kitchen,** Roukai Lane, 44 Customs St. E (www.orleans.co.nz; *C* **09/309-5854**), is a sophisticated tapas and wine bar; **Racket,** 6–10 Roukai Lane (www.racket-bar.co.nz; *C* **09/309-5854**); and the glamorous **Xuxu Dumpling Bar,** Galway and Commerce streets (www.xuxu.co.nz; *C* **09/309-5529**), the perfect spot to have Asian-inspired cocktails while you wait for a table at **Café Hanoi** just across the road. If you fancy a wee dram, try Auckland's sophisticated whisky bar, **Jefferson Whisky Bar,** Imperial Building, 7 Fort Lane (www.thejefferson.co.nz; *C* **021/044-0494**), featuring 500 varieties of the golden nectar along with mouthwatering meat dishes.

Viaduct Harbor and its many night-time haunts. A younger, funkier set hangs out in **High St./Vulcan Lane** or at **Britomart** in the inner city; most of the all-night clubs, drag clubs, and gay bars are along **Karangahape Road;** and **Ponsonby** is a favored upmarket place for drinks, dinner, and a general wind-up before hitting the club scene.

INNER CITY **Sweat Shop Brew Kitchen,** 7 Sale St., Freemans Bay (www.sweatshopbrew co.nz; *C* **09/307-8148**), has a restaurant, live music stages, a microbrewery, private bars, and a huge outdoor deck. And don't miss chef Peter Gordon's **Bellota,** 91 Federal St., opposite SKYCITY Grand Hotel, a dark, supercool, sensuously modern take on a Spanish tapas bar. **La Zeppa,** 33 Drake St., Freemans Bay (www.lazeppa.co.nz; *C* **09/379-8167**), is another popular tapas and wine bar in the Victoria market area. It's popular with the corporate crowd.

PONSONBY **SPQR,** 150 Ponsonby Rd. (www.spqrnz.co.nz; *C* **09/360-1710**), is the staple of Ponsonby Road. It has a great bar scene late Friday and Saturday nights; you'll see all sorts, both gay and straight, indulging in cocktails with fanciful names such as Horny Monkey and the Slapper. **Lime,** 167 Ponsonby Rd. (www.worldsbestbars.com; *C* **09/360-7167**), is the smallest bar of all, and everyone, just everyone, is determined to be first or second here—after that, there's always a queue to get in.

At **Little Easy,** 198 Ponsonby Rd. (www.littleeasy.co.nz; *C* **09/360-0098**), grab a burger and drink downstairs; upstairs at night an old VW van turns into a DJ booth; and **Whiskey,** 210 Ponsonby Rd. (www.whiskeybars.com; *C* **09/361-2666**), has a chic interior and a great late-night scene on Friday and

PLACE YOUR bets: A NIGHT AT THE CASINO

The largest casino in New Zealand, **SKY-CITY Auckland Casino,** Victoria and Federal streets (www.skycityauckland.co.nz; ✆ **0800/759-2489** in NZ, or 09/363-6000), gets some 12,000 visitors per day. This vast expanse of gaming tables (blackjack, roulette, craps, Caribbean stud poker, baccarat, tai sai, pai gow, and money wheel), 80-seat keno lounge, and more than 1,200 slot machines should have you keen to try your luck. Note the strict dress code (jeans, shorts, active sportswear, and sports shoes not permitted; jackets required for men). The casino is not the only aspect of this multifaceted complex. It holds several excellent restaurants, the Sky Tower, the SKYCITY Theatre complex, and one of the best contemporary New Zealand art collections in the country (see "Exploring Auckland," above). The casino is open 24/7.

Saturday. The very popular **Malt,** 442 Richmond Rd., Grey Lynn (www.maltbar.co.nz; ✆ **09/360-9537**), feels like a local corner pub, but with more warmth and style. **Chapel Bar and Bistro** is right in the heart of Ponsonby at 147 Ponsonby Rd. (www.chapel.co.nz; ✆ **09/360-4528**). The atmosphere is stylish and relaxed, a bit like a neighborhood local. At the popular **Bedford and Soda,** 4 Brown St., Ponsonby (www.bedfordsodaliquor.co.nz; ✆ **09/3787-5362**), you can imbibe hand-made sodas, innovative alcoholic and non-alcoholic cocktails, and tasty meatballs. Join the throng at **Ponsonby Social Club,** 152 Ponsonby Rd. (www.ponsonbysocialclub.co.nz; ✆ **09/361-2320**), and tap your toes to the '90s hip hop and R&B tunes or get up and dance. It's noisy, relaxed and fun.

PARNELL The sophisticated and friendly **46&York,** 46 Parnell Rd., on the corner of York Street, has a great selection of wines, spirits, and craft beers in an old heritage building (www.46onyork.co.nz; ✆ **09/3779-675**).

The Gay Scene

There is always something new going on, but a number of reliable favorites form the backbone of the gay nightlife scene. Karangahape Road is the home of most venues: **Eagle Bar,** 259 Karangahape Rd. (✆ **09/309-4979**), is a down-to-earth mixed-crowd kind of bar (open 7 days until late), while **Family Bar,** 270 Karangahape Rd. (✆ **09/309-0213**), is Auckland's popular drag/DJ bar/club (also open 7 days until late). The latter has been proudly gay-owned and -operated for many years now and always keeps up with fashion. Two others in this colorful area are **Caluzzi Bar and Cabaret,** 461 Karangahape Rd. (www.caluzzi.co.nz; ✆ **09/357-0778**), which offers drag cabaret shows with dinner and random club get-togethers on Wednesday evenings.

If you are just after a coffee in a friendly gay environment, check out **Alleluya Bar & Café** in St. Kevins Arcade just off 183 Karangahape Rd. (✆ **09/377-8424**), or **Garnet Station** (www.garnetstation.com; ✆ **09/360-3397**) at 85 Garnet Rd., Westmere. **Shanghai Lil's,** 212 Ponsonby Rd. (www.

shanghailil.co.nz; ⓒ **09/309-0213**), has long been an Auckland institution and often features live piano music. In February each year nearby Ponsonby Road hosts the **Pride Parade** during Auckland's Pride Festival. If you are keen to meet someone, try **Centurian Sauna for Men,** 18 Beresford Sq. (www.centuriansauna.co.nz; ⓒ **09/377-5571**), Auckland Central. Alternatively, there is **Lateshift Gay Mens Club** (www.lateshift.co.nz; ⓒ **09/373-2657**) on the lower level at 25 Dundonald St., Newton. Need to do some adult shopping? Visit **Grinder K'rd** (www.thegrinder.co.nz; ⓒ **09/307-9191**), located at 348 Karangahape Rd. And last but not least, for LGBT (and mainstream) books go to the **Women's Bookshop,** 105 Ponsonby Rd. (ⓒ **09/376-4399**), or **Unity Books,** 19 High St. in the city (ⓒ **09/307-0731**).

A SIDE TRIP TO WAIHEKE ISLAND ★★★

This divine little paradise is just 35 minutes from downtown Auckland by ferry. Of its permanent population of about 8,000, nearly 1,500 commute to the city each day to work; in summer, the island's population swells to over 40,000 as visitors come to languish in the enchanting mix of white-sand beaches, lush native bush, green farmland, top wineries and vineyards, and swish little cafes and restaurants. I strongly recommend a stay of at least 1 or 2 nights.

Essentials

GETTING THERE By Ferry Fullers Ferries (www.fullers.co.nz; ⓒ **09/367-9111**) offers hourly service (20 sailings daily) from downtown Auckland to Waiheke Island. Ferries depart from Pier 2, Quay St., in Central City. Most sailings are met by buses, shuttles, and taxis at Matiatia, near the main township of Oneroa. The Fullers trip takes 35 minutes and costs NZ$35 round-trip for adults and NZ$18 children 5 to 15.

The passenger and vehicular ferry of the **SeaLink Travel Group** (www.sealink.co.nz; ⓒ **0800/732-546** in NZ, or 09/300-5900) leaves from Half Moon Bay, Pakuranga, and arrives at the Kennedy Point Wharf farther east across the Surfdale Causeway. Ferries run every hour daily between 6am and 6pm. The fare is NZ$136 round-trip for a car and driver. Passengers without cars pay NZ$32 adults and NZ$20 children 5 to 15. Reservations are essential.

Pine Harbour Ferry, Jack Lachlan Drive, Pine Harbour, Auckland (www.pineharbour.co.nz; ⓒ **09/536-4725**), operates regular service to Waiheke between 8:30am and 5:40pm, with extended hours between December 27 and January 31. The round-trip fare is NZ$28 adults, NZ$20 children, and NZ$64 for a family. It's a shorter, cheaper ferry trip, but you'll have to drive farther on the Auckland side if you're staying in the city.

By Tour Fullers' **Waiheke Explorer Tour** ★★ (www.fullers.co.nz; © 09/367-9111) gives you the option of being met on the island by a bus and taken on one of four tours, which last from 1½ hours to all day. It's an excellent choice if you're short on time, and it includes unlimited bus travel on the island for the rest of the day. It departs daily at 10am and noon and costs NZ$49 adults and NZ$25 children 5 to 15.

By Air Contact **Auckland Seaplanes** (www.aucklandseaplanes.com; © 09/390-1121) for the cost of being whisked to the location of your choice on the island in no time.

GETTING AROUND **By Car** If you don't want to take a car to the island, hire a rental when you arrive. **Waiheke Auto Rentals,** Matiatia Wharf (www.waihekerentals.co.nz; © 09/372-8998), has good hourly rates and offers pickup and key drop-off service. Four-wheel-drive vehicles, scooters, motorbikes, and mountain bikes are also available. For bicycle rental, contact **Waiheke Bike Hire,** Matiatia Wharf car park (www.waihekebikehire.co.nz; © 09/372-7937), open daily from 9am (except Dec 25). Rates begin at NZ$35 per day and subsequent days are NZ$15 each (cash only).

By Bus For information on Waiheke Island bus services, visit **Maxx** (www.maxx.co.nz; © 09/366-6400). Buses serve most bays and beaches at the west end of the island. Pick up a schedule from bus drivers. Inquire about the **All-Day Bus Pass,** which costs NZ$8.50 adults, NZ$5 children ages 5 to 15, and NZ$22 family.

By Tour An excellent way to get a feel for Waiheke is to go with **Ananda Tours** ★★ (www.ananda.co.nz; © 09/372-7530 or 027/233-4565). It offers art studio, gourmet food and wine, and ecowalking tours with knowledgeable guides; prices begin at NZ$105 per person.

VISITOR INFORMATION The best place to get information, maps, and travel tips is at **Waiheke i-SITE,** 118 Ocean View Rd., Oneroa (www.waiheke.aucklandnz.com; © 09/372-1234), open daily from 9am to 5pm. The staff has extensive knowledge of available accommodations on the island. There is also an information kiosk at Matiatia Wharf.

For more on Waiheke Island, check out **www.waihekeonline.com** and **www.gotowaiheke.co.nz**.

ORIENTATION Waiheke Island is approximately 19km (12 miles) long and has 90km (56 miles) of coastline, 40km (25 miles) of which is white-sand beaches. **Oneroa,** the largest shopping village on Waiheke, is a 15- to 20-minute uphill walk from Matiatia Wharf, where the passenger ferries dock. It's a 10-minute drive from the Kennedy Point Wharf, where the vehicular ferry docks. This western end of the island has the most settlement around **Sandy** and **Enclosure bays** and **Palm Beach. Ostend** and **Surfdale** also have shops and cafes, including a substantial supermarket in Ostend. Oneroa has an excellent grocery store as well, but the best supermarket is inSurfdale.

SPECIAL EVENTS The **Waiheke Island Wine Festival** (www.auck-landnz.com; $\circled{c}$ **09/372-7676**), in February, is a great chance to taste the island's terrific, award-winning wines. Tickets go on sale in October. **Headland Sculpture on the Gulf** (www.sculptureonthegulf.co.nz; $\circled{c}$ **09/372-9907**) is a must-see in late January and early February. This unforgettable outdoor exhibition of large-scale contemporary sculpture along Waiheke Island's coastal walkway is held every year.

Exploring the Island

In Oneroa, visit the **Waiheke Community Art Gallery,** 2 Korora Rd. (www.waihekeartgallery.org.nz; $\circled{c}$ **09/372-9907**), where you'll find a wide range of works from the many resident artists and craftspeople on the island. It's open daily from 10am to 4pm. You can pick up a copy of the Waiheke Art Guide there (or at the i-SITE visitor center). It lists about 20 local artists, many of whom open their studios to visitors. The guide also marks the location of six large public sculptures acquired from previous Headland Sculpture on the Gulf exhibitions. Nearby is the fascinating **Whittaker's Music Museum** ★, 2 Korora Rd. (www.musical-museum.org; $\circled{c}$ **09/372-9627;** about NZ$12), where Lloyd and Joan Whittaker will hold you spellbound with a 90-minute live performance on a range of antique musical instruments, including organs, concertinas, pianolas, and mouth organs (Sat at 1:30pm). A screening of a recorded show is shown Sunday through Friday at 1:30pm. The museum is open daily 1 to 4pm.

The **Waiheke Island Historic Village & Museum,** 165 Onetangi Rd. (www.waihekemuseum.org.nz; $\circled{c}$ **09/372-7143** or 09/373-6861), is overlooked by a fortified Maori settlement site first inhabited some 700 years ago. Inside old cottages are collections of furniture, books, documents, and photographs. It's open Wednesday and weekends year-round from noon to 4pm; entry is by donation. Catch the Onetangi Bus no. 1 to get there.

Be up early to experience a bit of local culture at the **Ostend Market** ★, Ostend Hall, on the corner of Ostend Road and Belgium Street (www.ostend-market.co.nz; $\circled{c}$ **09/372-4475**). A colorful assemblage of local pottery, island-made goods, fruit and vegetables, herbal remedies, massage, plants, herbs, and more, it's held every Saturday from 8:30am to 12:30pm. On Sunday between 10am and 2pm, visit the **Waiheke Island Farmer's Market** at 7 Belgium St., Ostend.

Another "must" activity is a drive to the glorious **Onetangi Bay** ★★—in my mind, one of the best beaches in New Zealand. Here you can swim and surf in crystal-clear water with views as far as the eye can see. If you want to feel the true spirit of freedom, take it all off at the western end of **Palm Beach,** a small bay used for nude swimming.

For a peek into a fabulous private garden, check out Lance and Kay Peterson's **Dead Dog Bay** (formerly Te Whau Garden), 31 Vintage Lane (www.deaddogbayco.nz; $\circled{c}$ **09/372-6748**), which features a stunning combination of art and native bush. Even better is **Connells Bay Sculpture Park** ★★★, 142

Cowes Bay Rd. (http://connellsbay.co.nz; ✆ **09/372-8957**), where you'll find a superb display of work by top New Zealand sculptors set into the magnificent native bush landscape. Admission is NZ$30 adults and NZ$15 children 14 and under. This outstanding guided experience is by appointment only from late October through April. If you're a real art fan, you might consider a stay at the property's seaside cottage accommodations for one or two couples (see p. 87).

For additional, delightful walks pick up the excellent **"Waiheke Island Walkways"** ★ brochure from the i-SITE visitor center. It maps out and details eight great island walks.

Another fabulous way to see the island is to **Drive the Loop** ★★, a 1-day self-drive tour that starts and finishes at Waiheke Auto Rentals on Matiatia Wharf (see "Getting Around," above). The company provides the rental vehicle and loop tour package, which includes maps with all the most interesting people and places highlighted. It takes 4 to 8 hours (65km/40 miles) to complete the loop, depending on how often you stop, and costs NZ$120 to NZ$175, depending on the vehicle category. For information, call ✆ **09/372-8998.**

Visiting Vineyards

To the surprise of many, more than 40 vineyards operate on Waiheke Island, where the Mediterranean-style climate is perfect for growing grapes (and olives). Some of the country's best reds come from the island. Pick up the free **"Waiheke Winegrowers' Map,"** or check out the **Waiheke Winegrowers' Association website** (www.waihekewine.co.nz). Plan your visits around mealtimes, because several growers have excellent restaurants.

One of the leaders among the Waiheke vineyards is undoubtedly **Stonyridge** ★★★, 80 Onetangi Rd. (www.stonyridge.com; ✆ **09/372-8822**). In 1987, Stonyridge produced the first Larose vintage, immediately judged one of the world's top reds by the *London World Guide to Cabernet*. Stonyridge has the dreamiest vineyard, with an incredibly picturesque view from its restaurant, which just happens to be one of the nicest places on the island to dine (lunch only). Tours of the cellar, vineyard, and olive grove (with two wine tastings) begin at 11:30am on Saturday and Sunday; admission is NZ$12 per person.

Mudbrick Vineyard & Restaurant ★★, 126 Church Bay Rd., Oneroa (www.mudbrick.co.nz; ✆ **09/372-9050**), is another magical setting for a meal. **Goldwater Estate,** 18 Causeway Rd., Ostend (www.goldwaterwine.com; ✆ **09/372-7493**), is a small, premium winegrower producing top cabernet/merlots. It's open daily noon to 4pm from December through February with reduced hours for the rest of the year. It offers tasting sessions and tours by arrangement. **Cable Bay Vineyards** ★★★, 12 Nick Johnstone Dr., Oneroa (http://cablebay.nz; ✆ **09/372-5889**), is a beautiful, architecturally arresting complex that includes the winery, tasting room, restaurant, bar, and an art gallery. Cable Bay boasts dramatic views over Motukaha Island. It's open for lunch daily from 11am, and offers dinner Thursday through Saturday from 6pm.

The Good Oil

Waiheke is fast becoming known for its premium extra-virgin olive oils, with some 20,000 olive trees growing on the island. Harvest season is April through May or June, and there is no better place to sample than **Rangihoua Estate ★**, 1 Gordons Rd., Rocky Bay (www.rangihoua.co.nz; ℰ **09/372-6214**). The Frantoio Room is open Monday to Saturday in January and February; otherwise, tours and tastings are held Saturdays from 11am until 4pm, or by appointment. You'll find more award-winning olive oils at **Azzuro Olives**, 152 Te Whau Dr. (www.azzurogroves.com; ℰ **09/372-2700**). Azzuro's farm shop offers olive tastings and sales, and includes fine alpaca clothing made from the alpaca herd on the property.

Kennedy Point Wines & Olive Oil ★, 44 Donald Bruce Rd., Kennedy Point (www.kennedypointvineyard.com; ℰ 09/372-5600), has a winery and tasting room in a lovely setting. **Te Whau Vineyard & Cafe ★★★**, 218 Te Whau Dr. (www.tewhau.com; ℰ 09/372-7191), has a smart cafe that serves lunch daily in summer and dinner Thursday through Saturday, with reduced winter hours. Tours are NZ$12 per person. With more than 500 cellared wines, Te Whau houses the most diverse collection of New Zealand wine in the world. **Passage Rock Wines,** 438 Orapiu Rd. (www.passagerockwines. co.nz; ℰ 09/372-7257), is in a tranquil bay setting. Its award-winning wines have grabbed international attention—as have the wood-fired pizzas in its cafe bistro.

For a **wine tour** of several vineyards, contact **Waiheke Island Wine Tours** (www.waihekeislandwinetours.co.nz; ℰ 09/372-2140). Wayne Eagleton will pick you up from the 10am ferry at 10:35am, and your tour will be finished in time for the 4pm ferry. A shared tour is NZ$99 person (over 18). A private exclusive tour can be tailored to your tastes and costs NZ$230 per person. **Fullers** and **Ananda Tours** also offer vineyard tours; see "Getting There," above, for more information.

Where to Stay

The island has plenty of good backpacker and hostel options, priced from NZ$22 to NZ$85 per night; or go to **www.visitwaiheke.co.nz** (ℰ 021/709-302) for a range of excellent self-contained holiday houses to rent.

You'll find plenty to be pleased about at the **Estate Church Bay ★★**, 56 Church Bay Rd. (www.theestatechurchbay.com; ℰ 09/372-2637). Four beautiful rooms overlook vineyards and country views and go for NZ$525 to NZ$725. Or enjoy a self-contained stay at the lovely two-bedroom **Connells Bay Cottage ★★**, Cowes Bay Road, Connells Bay (www.connellsbay.co.nz; ℰ 09/372-8957; NZ$400 a night), which sleeps one or two couples.

The Boatshed Hotel ★★ There's a real feel of New Zealand about this gorgeous spot above the beach, overlooking little Oneroa. To call it "relaxed luxury" is a little vague; suffice to say you'll love the clean-cut elegance of the marine-themed suites—so much so you may never want to leave. The Boat-shed offers terrific sea views from private balconies and every comfort, right down to heated bathroom floors. For something special, splurge on the three-story Lighthouse Suite, which has a private top-floor lounge and a first-floor bedroom with commanding views and a balcony. Ground-floor rooms are more spacious.

Tawa and Huia sts., Oneroa. www.boatshed.co.nz. ⓒ **09/372-3242.** 7 units. NZ$630–NZ$955. Rates include breakfast and airport and ferry transport. Off-season rates. Children 11 and under not accepted. **Amenities:** Dining room; bar; bikes; concierge; nearby golf course; room service; watersports equipment rentals; Wi-Fi (free).

Te Whau Lodge ★★★   In Te Whau Lodge, Gene O'Neill and Liz Eglinton have an unbeatable combination: awesome views, dynamite culinary skills, and a relaxed, friendly vibe. Built to blend with the landscape, the lodge utilizes timber finishes and that intrinsic New Zealand building material, corrugated iron. Every spacious room has its own theme, its own bathroom, and its own fabulous balcony. Gene and Liz will take care of all your activity bookings. And just when you think it can't get any better, Gene will present you with one of his delectable two-course table d'hôte dinners, using vegetables fresh from the lodge garden. The lodge has its own sewage disposal and gray-water treatment plant, too. Te Whau doesn't have some of the extras of the Boatshed, but in my view it's a more intimate, friendly experience.

36 Vintage Lane, Te Whau Point, Waiheke. www.tewhaulodge.co.nz. ⓒ **09/372-2288.** 4 units. NZ$585. Reduced rate for 2 or more nights. Off-peak rates. Rates include breakfast, predinner canapés, and airport and ferry transport. Dinner NZ$70–NZ$100. Children 11 and under not accepted. **Amenities:** Bar; concierge; nearby golf course; outdoor Jacuzzi; spa treatments; room service; Wi-Fi (free; in lounge and main reception areas only).

Where to Eat

One of the best Waiheke restaurants is **Te Whau Vineyard Café** ★★★, 218 Te Whau Dr. (www.tewhau.co.nz; ⓒ **09/372-7191**). *Wine Spectator* rated it one of the country's top restaurants for wine lovers, and it has an amazing collection of over 500 New Zealand wines. It offers lunch daily 11am to 5pm and dinner Thursday to Saturday 6:30 to 11pm (Fri–Sun in winter). Mains average NZ$38.

At **Mudbrick Vineyard & Restaurant** ★★, Church Bay Road, Oneroa (www.mudbrick.co.nz; ⓒ **09/372-9050**), diners gaze out over rolling farmland to the waters of Hauraki Gulf while enjoying French rural cuisine; main courses are NZ$28 to NZ$38. Stonyridge Vineyard's **Veranda Café** ★★, 80 Onetangi Rd. (www.stonyridge.com; ⓒ **09/372-8822**), serves excellent Pacific Rim cuisine in a glorious romantic setting. It serves lunch only (daily in summer; Sat and Sun in winter). Main courses are NZ$25 to NZ$35; reservations are required. Also great for lunch (and dinner Fri–Sat nights from 6pm) is **Cable Bay Vineyard** ★★, 12 Nick Johnstone Dr., Oneroa (http://cablebay. nz; ⓒ **09/372-5889**).

In Oneroa village, **Vino Vino** ★, behind Green Hills Wines & Spirits, Oneroa (www.vinovino.co.nz; ⓒ **09/372-9888**), is a local favorite for big Mediterranean platters and a la carte dining on a huge deck with stunning views. **Nourish Café** ★, 3 Belgium St., Ostend (www.nourish.co.nz; ⓒ **09/372-3557**), has a fresh seasonal menu with main courses around NZ$26, plus great baked goods. It's open daily 8am to 4pm, with late nights on Friday and Saturday. If you're after a tasty pizza or a light pasta dish, **Stefano's,** located in Surfdale Village (ⓒ **09/372-5309**), has takeaways and a delivery service (and gluten-free pizzas on request).

En Route to Northland: The Hibiscus Coast

Located 48km (30 miles) north of Auckland, the Hibiscus Coast comprises the communities of Silverdale, Whangaparaoa, Orewa, Waiwera, and Puhoi. It's a 45-minute drive from Auckland, and **InterCity** coaches (www.intercity.co.nz; ⓒ **64/9/583-5780**) offer service that makes a day's outing a reasonable option.

The **Hibiscus Coast Information Centre,** 214A Hibiscus Coast Hwy. (next to KFC), Orewa (ⓒ **09/426-0076;** hbcvic@rodney.govt.nz), is open Monday through Friday from 9am to 5pm and Saturday and Sunday from 10am to 4pm.

On the drive north, stop at **Waiwera Thermal Resort** ★★, State Hwy. 1 (www.waiwera.co.nz; ⓒ **0800/924-937** in NZ, or 09/427-8800), open daily 9am to 9pm. Nineteen indoor and outdoor pools are kept at 82°F to 113°F (28°C–45°C), with both private and communal pools. A spa offers excellent treatment packages. Admission to the pools is NZ$26 adults, NZ$15 children 5 to 14, NZ$22 students, and NZ$10 seniors and spectators.

En Route to the Coromandel Peninsula: The Pacific Coast Highway

From Auckland the Pacific Coast Highway (not exactly a highway in the American sense of the word) leads down the west coast of the Firth of Thames and west again to Thames and the Coromandel Peninsula. It moves along the **Seabird Coast** ★ where **Kaiaua Fisheries Licensed Seafood Restaurant,** 939 E. Coast Rd., Kaiaua (ⓒ **09/232-2776**), serves some of the best fish and chips in the country; it's open daily 9am to 9pm. Once you've filled your bellies, check out the **Miranda Shorebird Centre** ★, East Coast Road (www.miranda-shorebird.org.nz; ⓒ **09/232-2781**), The 8,500 hectares (21,000 acres) of tidal flats are the summer feeding grounds for millions of migratory birds.

You can also relax in one of the largest hot mineral pools in the Southern Hemisphere or unwind in a private Jacuzzi at **Miranda Hot Springs Thermal Pools** (www.mirandahotsprings.co.nz; ⓒ **07/867-3055**). It's open 9am to 9pm. Admission is NZ$14 adults (ages 14 and over) and NZ$7 for children.

NORTHLAND

How was Auckland? Ready for a change of scene? (I know what you're thinking: New Zealanders are rubbish at naming things: Northland, Southland, Westland, Eastland, North Island, South Island . . .). Northland is where our founding document, the Treaty of Waitangi, was signed, in 1840. It's where the Waitangi National Reserve and Treaty Grounds make a delightful place to sit and consider the past. This long, skinny bit north of Auckland even has a prettier name: Maori call Northland *Te Tai Tokerau*, which means "the northern tide."

Explore **Waitangi** in the extraordinary **Bay of Islands** to your heart's content, but know that Northland has much more to show you. Take in the heart-stoppingly beautiful beaches and harbors up the east coast, pause to honor Maori spirits as they depart for the underworld at **Cape Reinga** on the country's northernmost tip, and go over the wild primeval kauri forests on the windswept west coast as you head south again. (You *could* just go back down SH1, but where's the fun in that if you have your own car?) And there's hardly anyone here: Northland's five main areas—**Whangarei and the east coast, the Bay of Islands, the Far North, Hokianga,** and the **Kauri Coast**—are home to fewer than 160,000 permanent residents. You'll practically have it all to yourself.

THE BAY OF ISLANDS & THE FAR NORTH

Bay of Islands: 237km (147 miles) N of Auckland; Cape Reinga: 431km (267 miles) N of Auckland

Subtropical Northland is basically one big swimming pool, so if it's summer, you'll want to spend much of your time up to your neck in its warm blue waters, fishing, exploring, diving, or lying on a gorgeous beach just about anywhere in the region.

Essentials

GETTING THERE & GETTING AROUND   **By Plane**   There are three Northland airports: **Whangarei, Kerikeri and Kaitaia. Air New Zealand** (www.airnewzealand.co.nz; © **0800/737-000** in NZ) flies from Auckland to Whangarei and Kerikeri daily, with a shuttle bus to Paihia. **Great Barrier Airlines** (www.

Northland

greatbarrierairlines.co.nz; ℭ **0800/900-600** in NZ, or 09/275-9120) flies daily from Auckland to Whangarei and Kaitaia and also provides a charter service. **Salt Air** (www.saltair.co.nz; ℭ **0800/472-582** in NZ, or 09/402-8338) offers scenic flights and charters between Auckland, Whangarei, and Kerikeri.

By Coach (Bus)   InterCity (www.intercity.co.nz; ℭ **09/583-5780**) provides daily service to Paihia, Kerikeri, and Kaitaia.

By Car   You'll have tons of options for renting a car in Northland, so ask at a visitor center for a list of operators. Also request the free "Twin Coast Discovery Highway" map from any visitor center: It's more scenic than just sticking to the main drag. You might want to visit the Whangarei area on your way north (about 1½ hr.) or head straight to the Bay of Islands (about 3 hr.). The drive from Auckland to Kaitaia via the east coast takes about 5 hours.

By Ferry   A passenger ferry connects Paihia and Russell, running half-hourly from 7am till 7:30pm and till 10:30pm in summer. Fares are NZ$12 per round-trip for adults, NZ$6 per round-trip for children 5 to 14. If you're driving to Russell, take the car ferry at Opua. It goes back and forth every 10 minutes, daily from 6:40am to 10pm, and costs NZ$11 one-way for a car and driver and NZ$1 per extra adult and 50¢ per child. Camper vans are up to NZ$28, depending on the size, and motorcycles are NZ$5.50 one-way. The car ferry lands at Okiato, about a 10-minute drive from Russell township.

By Water Taxi   Bay of Islands Island Water Taxi (ℭ **09/402-5454**) offers 24-hour service and charters; fares depend on the time of day and the number of passengers.

By Tour   Several companies in Auckland offer 1- to 5-day tours to the Bay of Islands and beyond. **GreatSights** (www.greatsights.co.nz; ℭ **0800/744-487** in NZ) is one of the best.

ORIENTATION   Paihia and Waitangi pretty much join up and are the beating heart of tourism in the region, with all tours and cruises for the Bay of Islands starting here. It's just 1.5km (1 mile) to Waitangi, the "birthplace of the nation" and where the historic Treaty House can be found.

The historic village of **Russell** is across the water and its main street, The Strand, runs along the waterfront. Most of the local charter boats live here.

Kerikeri is a 20-minute drive north of Paihia off State Highway 10.

Farther north, there's glorious **Doubtless Bay.** The delightful fishing village of **Mangonui** (82km/51 miles from Paihia) and **Coopers Beach, Cable Bay, Taipa,** and **Tokerau Beach** are close by. From here, the big bay extends in a sandy arc along the eastern side of the **Karikari Peninsula.**

Kaitaia is the biggest town in the Far North, 116km (72 miles) south of Cape Reinga, which is at the tippy-top of the country. To the southwest is **Ahipara** at the bottom of **Ninety Mile Beach,** which runs in an unbroken sandy sweep to the Cape.

Opononi is a peaceful settlement at the mouth of the west coast's Hokianga Harbour, 89km (55 miles) south of Kaitaia.

THE TOILETS THAT SAVED A town

Kawakawa, 16km/10 miles south of Paihia, was mildly famous for being the only town in New Zealand to have a railway line running through the middle of it. (Gabriel, the vintage steam train, trundles through town on Fridays, weekends, and public holidays.) Then a gallant public convenience came to the rescue back in 1999, and everything changed. Kawakawa now boasts what is the only building in the Southern Hemisphere designed by the late Austrian artist Frederick Hundertwasser until the decision was made to build the fabulous new **Hundertwasser Art Centre** (p. 105). Possibly the most glorious comfort stop in the world, this is a kaleidoscopic riot of mosaic tiles, wonky walls, bottle windows, and glowing ceramic pillars—and there's a tree growing out of the middle of it. Pee (free) in paradise!

VISITOR INFORMATION   The **Bay of Islands i-SITE Visitor Information Centre** is at the Wharf, Marsden Road, Paihia (© **09/402-7345**), and is open 8am to 5pm in winter, 8am to 7pm in summer. They'll help with Kerikeri information as well. The main Northland website is **www.northlandnz.com.** Also go to **www.paihia.co.nz, www.russell.co.nz,** or **www.kerikeri.co.nz.**

The **Far North i-SITE Visitor Centre** is at the Te Ahu Civic and Community Centre, on the corner of Matthews Avenue and South Road, Kaitaia (www.teahu.org.nz; © **09/408-9450**). It's open daily from 8:30am to 5pm. For information on Ahipara, Ninety Mile Beach, and Far North activities, see www.ahipara.co.nz or www.topofnz.co.nz.

SPECIAL EVENTS   A 3-day **Bay of Islands Sailing Week** is feted at the end of January. February 6 is **Waitangi Day,** a national holiday and commemoration of the Treaty signing. Watch hopeful fliers jump off the wharf at the **Russell Birdman Festival** in (comparatively) chilly July. In early August, look for the **Bay of Islands Jazz & Blues Festival** at various venues around Paihia and Russell. The **Bay of Islands Show & Festival of Food and Wine** is in November.

Exploring the Towns
IN PAIHIA/WAITANGI
Waitangi Treaty Grounds ★★★   This magnificent 506-hectare (1,250-acre) reserve tells the story of modern New Zealand: The flagstaff that stands tall in these grounds marks the spot where the Confederation of Maori Chiefs signed the first treaty with the British Government on February 6, 1840. It granted Maori the rights of British subjects in exchange for recognition of its sovereignty. The rather dainty Treaty House, home to British Resident James Busby from 1833 to 1840, looks out on the sweeping lawn where negotiations between Maori and Pakeha (non-Maori) were thrashed out prior to the signing. You can go inside and see how James, his wife, Agnes, and their six children lived in the 19th century and see a copy of the treaty in Maori and the room where it was drawn up.

Paddle a *Waka* on a Heritage Journey

Take cultural immersion to the next level and paddle a traditional *waka* (canoe) with Hone Mihaka of award-winning **Taiamai Tours Heritage Journeys ★★★** (www.taiamaitours.co.nz; © **09/405-9990**) and members of the Ngapuhi tribe. They also offer *marae* (temple) visits, *hangi* (food cooked in an earth oven), *karakia* (traditional prayers), hot springs trips and, if you're there around Waitangi Day, a splendid **6-night *marae* and war canoe experience** paddling during the national celebrations. The standard *waka* tour is from NZ$135 per person.

You'll be welcomed into one of New Zealand's most fabulous *whare runanga* (meeting houses) as an honored visitor, and whether you're a fan of cultural shows or not, you'd have to be pretty blasé not to be impressed by the *kapa haka* (Maori performance) group. These are among the best in the country, and give it heaps, as we say here! The meeting house, built in 1840 during the centenary of the Treaty signing, contains beautifully carved panels from the signatory tribes. A short walk will take you to Hobson's Beach and the 35m-long (115-ft.) Maori *waka* (war canoe), Ngatokimatawhaorua, which needs a minimum of 76 paddlers! It was constructed out of three huge kauri trees also during the centenary.

Take a tour to get the most out of Waitangi, but if you go on February 6, be prepared to be an ant on the bottom rung of history: It gets *busy* as Maori warriors, *kapa haka* groups, and folks in period costume mingle with dignitaries, politicians, and the occasional protestor as well as loads of Kiwis on a public holiday.

Waitangi Treaty Grounds, Tau Henare Dr., Waitangi. © **0800/9248-2644** in NZ, or 09/402-7437. www.waitangi.org.nz. Admission (valid for 2 consecutive days) NZ$25 adults, free for children 18 and under accompanied by an adult. Tours NZ$10 adults, free for children 18 and under accompanied by an adult. Maori cultural performances NZ$10 adult, free for children 18 and under accompanied by an adult. Hangi and concert NZ$105 adults, NZ$50 children. Jan–Feb daily 9am–7pm, Mar–Dec daily 9am–5pm.

IN RUSSELL

Many New Zealand towns look as if they have been designed by roving packs of depressed accountants. Russell is so not like this. It's a delightful little place chock-full of historic wooden houses, where you can stroll along the waterfront soaking it all in. Hike up Flagstaff Hill for jaw-dropping views of the Bay of Islands and you'll see the eponymous flagstaff that was hacked down by the Maori chief Hone Heke four times between 1844 and 1845.

Make a point of visiting the excellent **Russell Museum,** 2 York St. (www.russellmuseum.org.nz; © **09/403-7701**), open daily 10am to 4pm (till 5pm in Jan). Admission is NZ$10 for adults and NZ$3 for children. There are all sorts of bits and bobs from Maori and European early days, including a one-fifth replica of Captain Cook's *Endeavour,* moa bones you can touch, barbaric artifacts from the whaling years, and some souvenirs from American author Zane Grey's swordfishing years, when he dubbed the Bay of Islands "the angler's Eldorado." New Zealand's oldest wooden church, the Anglican Christ Church, established in 1836, is behind the museum. You can still make out the holes made by musket balls during the sacking of Russell by the Maori chief Hone Heke in 1845. It's open every day from 9am to 5pm.

At the south end of The Strand, prepare to be fascinated by an artisan time capsule masquerading as a house of God. **Pompallier Mission** ★ (www. pompallier.co.nz; ℂ **09/403-9015**) was built in 1841 by the eponymous French bishop who hoped to convert Maori to the Roman Catholic faith. He and the Marist brothers spent 7 years (1842–49) printing and binding bibles in Maori, and this beautiful French Lyonnaise mission house (New Zealand's oldest surviving Catholic building) houses the printing works and tannery. The very interesting tour tells the story of these exhausting processes—how hard those early settlers worked, especially the religious ones! Admission includes the tour and is NZ$10 for adults and free for accompanied children. It's open from 10am to 4pm (May–Oct) and 10am to 5pm (Nov–Apr).

IN KERIKERI

Kerikeri is a bustling and prosperous town surrounded by orchards and vineyards: Kerikeri oranges are famed throughout the land! It's also big on gourmet food products and arts and crafts, and it has some important historical sites, too. The **Kerikeri Mission Station** ★, 246 Kerikeri Rd. (www.historic. org.nz; ℂ **09/407-9236**), is where two of New Zealand's oldest buildings can be found. **Kemp House** was completed in 1822 and is home to the godly folk of the Anglican Church Missionary Society. The **Stone Store** next door is New Zealand's oldest stone building (1835), and ground-floor entry is free. It's been set up as a kind of period gift shop, selling anything from candle snuffers to toy soldiers. The stuff is all new but looks old. For NZ$10 per person (accompanied children free), you can visit the Stone Store's upper floor and take a tour of Kemp House. The two buildings are open daily, 10am to 5pm November to April and until 4pm the rest of the year.

To see how Maori lived in this area, visit **Kororipo Pa,** an easy 20-minute walk to the Maori fort site, which was home to the very scary chief Hongi Hika. To be honest, you can't see much at a pa site because Maori constructed all their pre-European buildings out of wood and none have survived, but the

Hell Hole No More

Russell was New Zealand's biggest town before 1840 and was dubbed "the hell hole of the Pacific" thanks to the uncouth behavior of its whalers, traders, and sailors. In those exciting days Russell was called "Kororareka," which translates as "sweet penguin" after a local Maori chief who was hurt in battle asked for some penguin broth while he was convalescing. "How sweet is the penguin!" he is reputed to have said.

ingenious warfare trenches are interesting. You'll have more to see at nearby **Rewa's Village** (✆ **09/407-6454**), a reconstruction of a *kainga* (fortified pre-European Maori fishing settlement). It's open daily from 9:30am to 5:30pm November to April (9am–5pm in Jan–Feb), and 10am to 4pm May to October; admission is NZ$5 for adults and free for accompanied children.

If you like your greenery, check out **Wharepuke,** 190 Kerikeri Rd. (www.wharepuke.co.nz; ✆ **09/407-8933**), a subtropical "garden of national significance" lovingly tended by plant freak Robin Booth. Wander around by yourself for nothing or let Booth take you on an eco-garden tour (advance bookings required). Be sure to have a look at the art gallery and really quite revolutionary non-toxic printmaking studio, run by Booth's son-in-law Mark Graver, while you're here. Oh, and there's an award-winning cafe and restaurant and some splendid ecofriendly cottages to stay in (see p. 101). It's open daily 9am to 5pm.

Lots of Kerikeri folk are arty, and the "Kerikeri Art & Craft Trail" brochure (free at information centers) will direct you to 17 artists close by. If you're around on a Sunday, make a beeline for the **Bay of Islands Farmer's Market ★★** for the best in Northland produce (Hobson Ave, Kerikeri; Sun 8:30am–noon). You can take your goodies down to lovely **Rainbow Falls** in Rainbow Falls Rd. (by car) or meander along the **Kerikeri River Walk.**

Love wine? This area has a couple of good wineries: **Cottle Hill Winery,** 28 Cottle Hill Drive (www.cottlehill.co.nz; ✆ **09/407-5203**) is open daily in summer (closed Mon–Tues the rest of the year) from 10am to 5:30pm. **Marsden Estate Winery,** 56 Wiroa Rd. (www.marsdenestate.co.nz; ✆ **09/407-9398**), is open daily 10am to 5pm (till 4pm in winter), and closed Good Friday and December 25 and 26.

IN THE FAR NORTH & HOKIANGA

Doubtless Bay boasts the rather special **Matthews Vintage Collection,** State Highway 10, 5km (3 miles) north of Taipa (www.matthewsvintage.com; ✆ **09/406-0203**). It's run by Win and Lyn (Matthews), who have an amazing array of vintage cars and machinery dating back to the early 20th century—the vehicles that helped shaped this country. It's open Monday to Friday 10am to 4pm; admission is NZ$10 adults, NZ$5 children ages 5 to 15 years. The **Te Ahu Heritage Museum,** Te Ahu Centre, corner of Matthews Avenue and South Road, Kaitaia (www.teahuheritage.co.nz; ✆ **09/408-9454**), tells the overlapping story of early Maori settlement and the new immigrants, many from Dalmatia. These hardy Europeans played a large part in the kauri gum industry and there's much to see here.

Yes, these folks want to sell you stuff, but the **Ancient Kauri Kingdom,** SH1, Awanui, 7km (4 miles) north of Kaitaia (www.ancientkauri.co.nz; ✆ **09/406-7172**), is interesting nonetheless. Mighty kauri logs 30,000 to 50,000 years old have been pulled from local swamps and transformed from gray lumps of wood into satiny-smooth golden works of art. It's open daily, and admission is free—because you'll surely want you to take something home with you.

NORTHLAND'S magical TREES

In **Waipoua Forest ★★★** and the smaller **Trounson Kauri Park,** experience the awesome—in the proper sense of the word—power of these forest giants, some more than 1,000 years old: in Waipoua, *Tane Mahuta* **(God of the Forest) ★★**, the largest known kauri in New Zealand, and **Te Matua Ngahere (Father of the Forest),** the second biggest by volume. Go to the **Hokianga i-SITE Visitor Information Centre,** SH12, Opononi (www.northlandnz.com; ℭ **09/405-8869**), for more. The Maori guides with **Footprints Waipoua ★★★**, 29 SH12, Opononi (www.footprintswaipoua.co.nz; ℭ **0800/687-836** in NZ, or 09/405-8207), can take you to see *Tane Mahuta,* but it's only a few minutes' walk from the road so a guide isn't essential, although the 4-hour Twilight Encounter (NZ$95 adults and NZ$35 children 5–12) is very good.

To see what happened to the trees after humans got hold of them, you could visit the **Kauri Museum** in Matakohe (www.kauri-museum.com; ℭ **09/431-7417**), open daily), but at NZ$25 per adult, I think it's a rip-off. Love the way they say the guided tours are complimentary! Try the **Ancient Kauri Kingdom** (above) instead.

Organized Tours & Cruises

Head to Paihia for the following. You needn't prebook unless you're visiting during the peak period between December 23 and January 15. You'll have lots to choose from, but here are some standouts.

Get your dolphin fix on a cruise with **Fullers GreatSights Dolphin Cruise,** Maritime Building, Waterfront, Paihia (www.dolphincruises.co.nz; ℭ **0800/653-339** in NZ, or 09/402-7421). On the ever-popular **Cream Trip ★**, you can swim with dolphins and visit the Hole in the Rock (a natural rock arch that boats can pass through), stopping at Urupukapuka Island for lunch (not provided). It's NZ$125 for adults, NZ$63 for children, and NZ$15 extra per person to swim with the dolphins, offered daily from 9:30am to 4:30pm, picking up from Russell. The **Dolphin Eco Experience ★★** gets you up close and personal with these lovely creatures, and there's a boom net so less-confident swimmers can go in too. It's NZ$115 for adults and NZ$58 for children, daily 8am to noon, also picking up from Russell.

TOURS TO CAPE REINGA

Cape Reinga ★★★ is the northernmost tip of New Zealand, where the Tasman Sea and the Pacific Ocean meet. It's super-scenic and spiritually significant to Maori. The cape, with its lighthouse standing sentinel, is perched at the top of the Aupouri Peninsula, with **Ninety Mile Beach** running all the way down its west coast.

Kiwis love to drive on Ninety Mile Beach, but your car-rental firm won't like it as people frequently get stuck in the sand. So leave this to the experts or take a coach tour, which will bring you back down the cape via the beach and let you go sand boarding on the **Te Paki Sand Dunes.**

LET'S go SAILING

What could be lovelier than exploring the Bay of Islands by yacht? A trip on the tall ship **R Tucker Thompson ★★**, Maritime Building, Paihia (www.tucker.co.nz; © **0800/882-537** in NZ, or 09/402-8430), is the ultimate in romantic sailing. The 19th-century replica schooner operates from November to April, and a day out costs NZ$145 for adults and NZ$73 for children over 5. Morning tea, lunch, and an island swim are included. **Gungha's**

Super Cruise ★ (www.bayofislandssailing.co.nz; © **0800/478-900** in NZ) is a good-value day trip around the Bay of Islands on the 20m (65-ft.) maxi yacht *Gungha II* and includes an island stopover, snorkeling, and lunch for NZ$95. For three eco-friendly days on the water, join the crew of the 22m (72-ft) ketch *Manawanui* with **Ecocruz**, The Wharf, Paihia (www.ecocruz.co.nz; © **0800/432-627** in NZ), from NZ$650 per person.

Note: The round-trip from the Bay of Islands to Cape Reinga by car takes about 7 hours; it's more pleasant to take a day tour from Kaitaia or Doubtless Bay.

FROM PAIHIA   **Fullers GreatSights Bay of Islands** (www.greatsights. co.nz; © **0800/653-339** in NZ, or 09/402-7421) does an 11-hour Cape Reinga tour. It's NZ$145 for adults and NZ$73 for children ages 5 to 15.

FROM KAITAIA   **Sand Safaris Cape Reinga Tours,** 36 Wireless Rd., Kaitaia (www.sandsafaris.co.nz; © **0800/869-090** in NZ, or 09/408-1778), charges NZ$50 for adults and NZ$30 for children under 15; or you could try **Harrisons Cape Runner Tours,** 123 North Rd., Kaitaia (www.harrisonscapereingatours.co.nz; © **0800/227-373** in NZ, or 09/408-1033); tours are NZ$50 for adults, NZ$25 for children.

FROM MANGONUI Dune Rider (www.capereingatours.co.nz; © **0800/386-369** in NZ, or 09/408-2411) does an 11-hour Cape Reinga tour. It's NZ$55 for adults and NZ$30 for children under 15 and also picks up from Kaitaia.

Outdoor Pursuits

FAST BOATING   **Mack Attack,** Maritime Building, Paihia (www.mackattack.co.nz; © **0800/622-528** in NZ, or 09/402-8180), can take you out to the Hole in the Rock very quickly for NZ$99 adults, NZ$49 children 14 and under.

FISHING   The Paihia visitor center has a list of light-line fishing charters, most of which supply rods and bait and range for about NZ$100 per person for a 4-hour snapper excursion. For game fishing, try **Earl Grey Fishing Charters,** Paihia and Russell Wharf (www.earlgreyfishing.co.nz; © **09/407-7165**), which will customize a trip to your requirements.

GOLF   Tee off in paradise at the **Waitangi Golf Club** (www.waitangigolf. co.nz; © **09/402-8105**). Greens fees are NZ$49 for 18 holes. Clubs, shoes, and cart rentals are available.

KAYAKING Paddle to idyllic waterfalls and islands with **Coastal Kayakers,** Te Karuwha Parade, Waitangi (www.coastalkayakers.co.nz; ✆ **0800/334-661** in NZ, or 09/402-7421). You'll pay from NZ$85 per person for a half-day trip to NZ$685 for a 3-day tour.

WALKING Of course you'll be checking out the walks around the **Waitangi National Trust Estate ★★★,** won't you? Ask the good people at the Paihia visitor center about other trails, and be sure to pick up the booklet "Walking in the Bay of Islands Maritime and Historic Park" (NZ$5). Check the **Department of Conservation (DOC) website** (www.doc.govt.nz) for hikes farther afield.

Where to Stay

During December and January, the population in the Bay of Islands balloons from about 2,000 to more than 30,000—so book in advance during these times.

Paihia might be cheaper, but it's a Las Vegas showgirl to Russell's Met Opera star. It has some nice places, but the town lacks the charm of Russell and is the first choice for party-hard hedonists and backpackers. On the other hand, it's a more convenient place to stay if you're taking tours, and it has more places to eat (and you don't need to gulp down your dessert for fear of missing the last ferry back to Russell).

IN PAIHIA/OPUA

The **Bounty Motel,** 42 Selwyn Rd., Paihia ★ (www.bountyinn.co.nz; ✆ **09/402-7088**), is a good budget option in a town heaving with motels. It's close to the beach and 2 minutes from the shops. Summer rates are from NZ$120 double per night; winter from NZ$99. The **Copthorne Hotel & Resort ★★,** Tau Henare Dr. (www.millenniumhotels.co.nz; ✆ **09/402-7411**), is a rather sprawling "big box" hotel, but it enjoys a dress-circle location right next to the Waitangi Treaty Grounds. The Copthorne has 180 rooms, including four suites, and a totally fabulous free-form rock swimming pool (although you could just swim in the sea!). Rates are from NZ$127 for a standard double to NZ$279 for a suite with breakfast.

The Sanctuary @ the Bay of Islands ★★ If you want to be (almost) alone or holed up with just your significant other, this modern and attractive retreat is the place to do it: It'll just be you, a handful of other lucky folk, and the native birds, although it's only 5 minutes from Paihia. State of the art and totally luxurious (with views to die for): You'll be so relaxed it'll be hard to lift that glass to your lips!

SH11, Port Opua. www.sanctuarybayofislands.co.nz. ✆ **09/402-6075.** 4 units. NZ$450–NZ$593 per couple; NZ$50 extra person; no children under 12. Rates include cooked breakfast and open bar. Dinner by arrangement (NZ$95 per person). Call for off-peak rates. **Amenities:** Chef for in-house dining; heated outdoor pool; spa treatments; Wi-Fi (free).

Paihia Beach Resort & Spa Hotel ★★ Apartment and studio living at its opulent best is what you get here after a fairly recent revamp. These suites have everything you need, making them ideal for those desiring a stay longer than a couple of days (with long-stay deals sweetening the pot). Enjoy your own little (or extensive) makeover at the super-pampering spa (one of the best in Northland) and then dine at the very fine restaurant, **Provenir** (p. 103). The resort is close to Waitangi and has splendid views of Te Ti Bay.

116 Marsden Rd., Paihia. www.paihiabeach.co.nz. ℭ **0800/870-111** in NZ or 09/402-0111. 21 units. NZ$555–NZ$834 double; NZ$62 extra person. Long-stay rates and packages available. Rates include breakfast. **Amenities:** Restaurant; bar; babysitting; four Jacuzzis; heated outdoor pool; room service; health spa and sauna rooms; watersports equipment; Wi-Fi.

IN RUSSELL

If you want to be in Russell and save your dollars while admiring the views, try the **Top 10 Holiday Park,** 1 James St. (www.russelltop10.co.nz; ℭ **0800/148-671** in NZ, or 09/403-7826). Cabins and motels are from NZ$65 to NZ$198, and powered sites are NZ$52.

The Duke of Marlborough ★★ New Zealand's first licensed hotel announces that it has been "refreshing rascals and reprobates since 1827," but it serves a more discerning crowd these days. Little wonder, as the lovely old historic building has been beautifully done up in a modern style that nods at the past and the beachfront location is a winner. You're right in the heart of the action here. Get a sea-facing room and you can sit on your balcony and a drink and watch old salts rowing their dinghies home as the sun sets over the water. The establishment has a nice sense of humor, too. Loved the Duke of Marlborough crest painted on my wall to look like a bedhead!

The Strand, Russell. www.theduke.co.nz. ℭ **09/403-7869.** 25 rooms and self-contained bungalow with kitchenette. NZ$125–NZ$360 double, NZ$195–NZ$360 bungalow. Rates include continental breakfast. **Amenities:** Restaurant; Wi-Fi (free).

Eagles Nest ★★★ You know you're in good hands when a hostelry boldly advertises itself as "somewhere between seven stars and heaven." Is this an idle boast? Well, the numerous international awards suggest it's not: This place won the World Travel Awards' World's Leading Boutique Villa Resort in 2013 and is consistently picked as the best resort in New Zealand and Australasia. The owners are committed to making this an eco-friendly retreat as well as a super-luxurious one—are you feeling the love? There is that small matter of needing a very springy wallet to stay here, of course, but if you book the ultimate in luxury, the four-bedroom villa Rahimoana, they'll throw in a Porsche Cayenne, chef, butler, and concierge for your personal use. The villas Sacred Space, First Light Temple, Eagle Spirit, and The Eyrie are slightly less sumptuous, but it's totally relative: No matter where you stay, you'll be enveloped in the kind of rarefied cocoon that means you're a rock star already or you're planning to become one soon.

60 Tapeka Rd., Russell. www.eaglesnest.co.nz. ℭ **09/403-8333.** 19 rooms in 6 self-contained units. NZ$2,295–NZ$3,995 per villa; NZ$12,995 for Rahimoana. Rates include

breakfast. Long-stay, off-peak and special deals. **Amenities:** Exclusive dining room; free use of bikes; concierge; 2 helipads; helicopter access to 5 local golf courses; Jacuzzi; resident personal trainer and massage therapists; heated outdoor pool (5 villas only); room service; Wi-Fi.

IN KERIKERI

Kauri Cliffs ★★★ This super-luxury retreat 25 minutes from Kerikeri snaps up the golfing set, but non-players will find plenty to keep them blissed out here, too. The gorgeous property sprawls over 2,630 hectares (6,500 acres) of undulating coastal farmland with an award-winning par-72 David Harman–designed golf course (voted 49th best in the world by *Golf* magazine) providing eye-popping views while you sink your balls. It's bigger than Eagles Nest (see above), but you'll still feel cosseted in your fabulous suite. Oh, and a world-class day spa is set in a native forest. Convinced?

Tepene Tablelands Rd., Matauri Bay. www.kauricliffs.com. ✆ **09/407-0010.** 22 suites, one 2-bedroom cottage. Suites from NZ$775 per person Cottage fromNZ$8,950 per night. Rates include full breakfast, pre-dinner drinks, à la carte dinner, use of all facilities except golf and spa treatments. Off-season rates and special deals. Closed June. **Amenities:** Restaurant; bar; babysitting; mountain bikes; concierge; world-class golf course; large gym; Jacuzzi; outdoor heated pool, indoor heated lap pool; limited room service; sauna; full-service spa; 2 tennis courts; Wi-Fi.

Stone Store Lodge ★ A very nice man called Richard runs this select little place tucked into the native bush close to Kerikeri Inlet. He has three lovely modern suites, each with its own bathroom, of course, but you can have a soak in the outdoor bath among the trees if that's what floats your rubber ducky. Richard will throw together a tasty pizza on his wood fired oven if that appeals. This place has a Kiwi Green rating denoting sustainable tourism.

201 Kerikeri Rd., Kerikeri. www.stonestorelodge.co.nz. ✆ **09/407-6693.** 3 units. NZ$175–NZ$230 double; NZ$50 each extra person. Longer stay and off-peak rates available. Rates include breakfast. No children 11 and under. **Amenities:** Outdoor tub set in bush (NZ$35); massage services; Wi-Fi.

Wharepuke ★ This little place is really, er, branching out: You can now eat at the award-winning cafe (p. 104), check out the art gallery and non-toxic printmaking studio (p. 96), do a garden tour and stay in one of five self-contained eco-cottages nestled in the subtropical grounds. The Booth family has owned this land since 1938, and patriarch Robin has been lovingly planting subtropicals since 1993. Apart from his dad's misfire with the wrong sort of kiwifruit, it's been a howling success botanically. The cottages are smart and stylish while also being eco-friendly in terms of waste and building materials—and you'll sleep well, take my word for it.

190 Kerikeri Rd., Kerikeri. www.wharepuke.co.nz. ✆ **09/407-89333.** 5 units. NZ$130-NZ$180 double; NZ$15 per extra person. **Amenities:** Restaurant; airport shuttle; library; tour desk; Wif-Fi.

IN THE FAR NORTH & HOKIANGA

Beach Lodge, 121 SH10, Coopers Beach (www.beachlodge.co.nz; ✆ **09/406-0068**), has stunning views and is just a few steps from the smooth, sandy beach of your dreams. It has five self-contained apartments, but kiddies are discouraged, so don't bring them! It's NZ$175 to NZ$400 per night per double.

In **Kaitaia,** the **Loredo Motel** (✆ **09/408-3200**) is a good bet (from NZ$115 for a double), but if it's absolute beachfront you want, go a bit farther north to Houhora Heads and the family-oriented **Wagener Holiday Park** (www.northlandholiday.co.nz; (✆) **09/409-8511**). Cabins are from NZ$25 per person; a powered site is from NZ$18 per adult. If you make it as far as the stunning **Hokianga Harbour,** you might see a new blushing bride posing coyly on the grounds of the waterfront **Copthorne Hotel and Resort Hokianga** (www.copthornehokianga.co.nz; (✆) **09/405-8737**), with 33 rooms (from NZ$93 double) and a pleasant restaurant. Just south of Waipoua Forest is the lovely **Waipoua Lodge** ★★ (www.waipoualodge.co.nz; (✆) **09/439-0422**), if you want to spring for a bit of luxury. Four apartments are set apart from the 120-year-old kauri villa and dining room (B&B: NZ$485–NZ$585 suite, NZ$50 children 6–11, free children 5 and under; NZ$80 extra per person).

Kokohuia Lodge ★★   Steve and Suzanne run this one-suite-only luxury eco B&B in Omapere overlooking the sublime Hokianga Harbour. (Omapere pretty much joins on to the other "O" settlement of Opononi at the mouth of the harbour.) They're fairly passionate about the environment and are "off the grid," producing their own solar electricity and hot water and feeding guests wherever possible from the organic garden. (They've earned an Enviro Gold award, which is a big deal in the Kiwi tourism industry.) The house and the location are simply beautiful: Hokianga's famous dunes shimmer gold on the far side of the harbour at sunrise and sunset. It's truly heavenly, and these lovely people are very happy in their work!

101 Kokohuia Rd, Omapere. www.kokohuialodge.co.nz. (✆) **021/779-927.** 1 suite. NZ$295 double. Rates include breakfast. Dinner available on request (NZ$50 per person for 2 courses). **Amenities:** Barbecue grills; pizza oven.

The Old Oak ★★   Atmosphere, history, and a steady eye for crisp, fresh decor bring this fabulous Mangonui landmark alive. It's a simply gorgeous old inn dating from 1861 that had its heyday in the 19th century, fell on hard times as a grotty backpacker lodge, and has now been restored to its former glory for visitors to enjoy. And enjoy it they will: It's in one of the prettiest villages in the country, and each room retains a little piece of history: One features a cross over the bed made from the fussy Victorian curlicues added to the front veranda. If you appreciate a sense of place, you'll fall for this very special boutique hotel. Play a game of pétanque in the garden, which features organic herbs and veggies and a formal rose bed, before heading for a bite to eat. If you don't want to go far, a very good Indian restaurant (Indian Spice; (✆) **09/406-0896**) is attached to the hotel but operates as a separate business.

66 Waterfront Rd., Mangonui. www.theoldoak.co.nz. (✆) **09/406-1250.** 7 rooms and suites. NZ$135–NZ$295 double. **Amenities:** BBQ; pétanque court; restaurant next door; Wi-Fi.

Where to Eat

Don't assume the best food is in the main centers: You'll find culinary gems all over Northland these days. This is a short list; ask for more recommendations at visitor centers—staff are happy to tell you where they like to eat.

IN PAIHIA/WAITANGI

Whare Waka Café (✆ 09/402-7437) is a daytime venue on the Treaty Grounds with a rather unusual view: overlooking a lake and the war canoe (in Maori, "whare" means house and "waka" means canoe). It serves yummy cabinet (cold prepared foods) and à la carte food and a *hangi* (meat and veggies cooked in the ground) on Wednesdays and Saturdays in the summer. The unimaginatively named **Waterfront Restaurant & Bar,** 48 Marsden Rd., Paihia (✆ 09/402-6701), fortunately scores more points for its food, doing a fine line in fresh local produce, including great seafood like rock oysters. **Alongside** and **35° South,** 69 Marsden Rd., Paihia (✆ 09/402-6220), are, well, alongside each other: The first is a funky bar and restaurant by Marsden Wharf that boasts one of the biggest selections of rums in Northland, and the latter is an all-day eatery on the wharf with its own aquarium, so you can ogle some fishy creatures while waiting to eat some other ones, if that doesn't put you off. **Provenir,** 116 Marsden Rd. (✆ **0800/870-111** in NZ, or 09/402-0111), is the restaurant at the Paihia Beach Resort & Spa Hotel, and, although an emphasis on fresh local ingredients isn't the most original philosophy for a New Zealand restaurant these days, it's usually a good bet for stuff you're paying a goodly amount to eat. The best seats in the house are actually out on the terrace, where you can see and be seen. The food—from local farmers, fishermen, producers, and winemakers—is fresh and delicious: The "Revive at 5" option—NZ$6 tapas choices and a good selection of wines for NZ$8 a glass between 5pm and 7pm—is a great way to kick off your evening.

IN RUSSELL

The Gables, The Strand (✆ 09/403-7670), is an old favorite that's been around since 1847 (the building, not the restaurant). It capitalizes on its prime location on the waterfront, but the interesting menu should distract you; try rabbit, black pudding, and rare omak beef fillet (whatever that is!). For something less formal, **Hone's Pizza, Salad & Beer Garden Restaurant,** 10 York St. (✆ 09/403-7670), used to have a large purple octopus as the main element of its decor, but it must have slid back into the sea. Pizzas, burgers, salads, and good old fish and chips here.

The Duke of Marlborough ★ MODERN NEW ZEALAND   The Duke has gone from serving pretty good pub-style food with pretty so-so service to making Kiwi gourmet food mag Cuisine's top 150 restaurants list in 2011. For visitors, know that the food is fab and so close to the waterfront action that you could spit pomegranate pips at the tourists as they pass, if you were particularly badly brought up. It leans towards seafood—or in my case, "C food": chowder, calamari, and chocolate mousse—but caters masterfully for other tastes too, and terrific desserts plus an ambience that can't be manufactured. The multinational staff are now delightful, so there!

The Strand, Russell. www.theduke.co.nz. © **09/403-7869.** Reservations required for dinner in summer. Main courses NZ$25–NZ$36. Daily till late.

IN KERIKERI

If you love vineyard restaurants, try **Marsden Estate Winery** ★ (www.marsdenestate.co.nz; © **09/407-9398**), which serves antipasti, calamari, scallops— yum!—with their own wine (naturally) in a grape-bedecked courtyard. **Ake Ake Vineyard** ★★ (www.akeakevineyard.co.nz; © **09/407-8230**) has the location, the homegrown wine, and whole lot of beautiful local produce for lunch and dinner. If you're heading off to view Kerikeri's beauty spots in picnic mode, try the **Kerikeri Bakehouse Café,** 334 Kerikeri Rd. (© **09/407-7266**), a bustling little joint cheerfully decorated with Polynesian tapa cloth and full of homemade goodies. That caramel and pecan tart did slip down easily.

Food at Wharepuke ★ MODERN THAI-EUROPEAN   Chef Colin Ashton has amassed plenty of accolades, including inclusion in *The Great New Zealand Cookbook,* winning Northland cafe of the year several times, being named a *Cuisine* Local Fave in 2013, and working as tour chef for Shania Twain and the Red Hot Chilli Peppers! So if you want to eat like famous people, this is a top-drawer place nestled in the subtropical loveliness of **Wharepuke subtropical gardens** (p. 96) near the Stone Store; it's open for breakfast, lunch, and dinner. The building might be plain (it's an old U.S. Army barracks; long story), but the food is fancy and the coffee organic.

190 Kerikeri Rd., Kerikeri. www.foodatwharepuke.co.nz. © **09/407-8936.** Main courses NZ$28–NZ$39. Reservations required for dinner in summer. Daily till late.

IN THE FAR NORTH & HOKIANGA

Newsflash! **The World Famous Mangonui Fish Shop,** Waterfront Drive (© **09/406-0478**), has a rival. Sure, the fish practically leap out of the water onto your plate here, and yes, they are delicious, but all the tour buses stop here and so does every other tourist coming to this quaint little town in Doubtless Bay. Locals tell me they get their "shark and taters," as we say around here, from **Fresh & Tasty Takeaways,** Waterfront Drive (© **09/406-0082**), which is attached to the beautiful old Mangonui Hotel, just down the road from the more famous one. It's cheaper, quicker, and every bit as good, and you can go and say gidday to the cockatoo in the public bar while you're waiting for your takeout.

WHANGAREI

169km (105 miles) NE of Auckland; 62km (38 miles) S of Paihia; 58km (36 miles) E of Dargaville

Whangarei (population 50,000) used to be a town you passed through on your way to "sexier" destinations farther north, but it has bucked its ideas up no end in recent years and is now a great place to linger on a Northland odyssey. The Town Basin is now humming with activity as locals and visitors gather to enjoy the town's cafes and restaurants, historic places, and galleries while ogling fancy yachts in the marina. It's also the gateway to the wonderful but largely unsung Whangarei Heads and the Tutukaka Coast: The Poor Knights Islands Marine Reserve has some of the best diving in the world, and big-game fishing (not in the marine reserve, of course) is another drawcard.

Essentials

GETTING THERE & GETTING AROUND **By Plane** Whangarei is a 40-minute flight from Auckland with **Air New Zealand** (www.airnewzealand.co.nz; ✆ **0800/737-000** in NZ), which offers several flights a day. **Great Barrier Airlines** (www.greatbarrierairlines.co.nz; ✆ **0800/900-600** in NZ) operates a charter service from Auckland on Fridays and Sundays in summer. The **Whangarei Bus Service airport shuttle** (✆ **09/438-6005**) will take you into Whangarei.

By Coach (Bus) InterCity (www.intercity.co.nz; ✆ **09/623-1503**) passes through Whangarei several times a day.

By Car Whangarei is a 2-hour drive from Auckland. If you need a rental car, the major companies have offices at the airport.

VISITOR INFORMATION The **Whangarei i-SITE Visitor Centre,** 92 Otaika Rd., Whangarei (www.whangareinz.com; ✆ **09/438-107**), is open daily from 8:30am to 5pm weekdays and 9:30am to 4:30pm on weekends and public holidays, with extended hours over summer. A second center, **Te Manawa The HUB,** is located in the Town Basin (✆ **09/430-1188**).

For general regional information, go to **www.northlandnz.com**.

Exploring the Town

The **Town Basin** ★★ by the harbor is a splendid place for a wander. There you will find the rather eccentric **Claphams National Clock Museum** (www.claphamsclocks.com; ✆ **09/438-3993**), the collection of Archibald Clapham, who came to New Zealand in 1903 and amassed 400 clocks and music boxes. It's open daily 9am to 5pm; admission is NZ$10 for adults and NZ$4 for kids.

The Town Basin is also home to the **Whangarei Art Museum** (www.whangareiartmuseum.co.nz; ✆ **09/430-4240**), which features some pretty important local and national exhibitions and is also the venue for live music performances from time to time. It's open daily from 10am to 4pm; entry is by donation. But the biggest news for Whangarei's art scene is the decision to build the **Hundertwasser Arts Centre and Wairau Maori Art Gallery,** which will be the last authentic (and somewhat mad) building in the world to be designed by the celebrated Austrian architect Friedensreich Hundertwasser, who spent many years in New Zealand and died in 2000 (see Kawakawa, p. 93). A magnificent folly in the heart of the city, it is scheduled for completion by 2019.

DIVE, DIVE, dive!

Established in 1981, the pristine underwater sanctuary known as the **Poor Knights Islands Marine Reserve** ★★★ lies 1 hour offshore by powerboat, and **Tutukaka** (a 30-min. drive from Whangarei) is where you go to access it. Here, the clear waters near the edge of the Continental Shelf are met by subtropical currents—which means the marine life here differs from what you find in other parts of New Zealand. It's a paradise for divers, with sheer cliffs, rock stacks, and sea caves to explore.

The marine reserve is one of the world's 10 most popular sites for scuba diving and is strictly controlled by the Department of Conservation. The major operator (and New Zealand's largest dive company) is **Dive! Tutukaka,** the Poor Knights Dive Centre, Marina Rd., Tutukaka (www.diving.co.nz; ✆ **0800/288-882** in NZ, or 09/434-3867), which offers a range of diving and snorkeling trips. Some of their fully qualified dive masters are award-winning underwater photographers, so if you have a camera that likes to get wet, this is the place to get it out.

Wrecks dive (NZ$249 per person) will take you to two ex–New Zealand Navy ships *Tui* and *Waikato,* which were sunk to provide artificial reefs for divers to enjoy. Dives are from NZ$269 with hired gear; snorkeling is NZ$169.

If you don't dive but still want to experience the Poor Knights, Dive! Tutukaka also operates **A Perfect Day** (www.aperfectday.co.nz), a cruise company that aims to provide just that in a day trip featuring sightseeing, kayaking, cave explorations, snorkeling, swimming, and lunch. There's even a "fish-cam" so you can see what's happening underwater. It costs NZ$169 adults, NZ$85 children under 15.

Kiwi North ★ (www.kiwinorth.co.nz; ✆ **09/438-9630**) is a short name with a long agenda: It encompasses the Whangarei Museum, Kiwi House, and Heritage Park and is situated on a 25-hectare (62-acre) historic farm just 3 minutes from town. The museum has fascinating natural-history, historic Maori, and early-settler collections. The kiwi house has a nocturnal house with a number of these iconic species, as well as tuatara (our last living relative of the dinosaurs) and native geckos. The heritage park tells our early European story with a series of historic buildings. Kiwi North is open daily from 10am to 4pm and costs NZ$15 adults, NZ$10 seniors and adult students, and NZ$5 children 5 and older (children 4 and under free) for all attractions; a family pass (two adults and three children) is NZ$35.

Next door, the **Whangarei Native Bird Recovery Centre** (www.nbr.org.nz; ✆ **09/438-1457**) is open Monday and Friday 1pm to 4:30pm and Tuesday to Thursday 10am to 4:30pm. It holds all sorts of endearing native birds in various stages of recovery: penguins, kiwi, white herons, moreporks (native owls), and even albatrosses. Sparky the one-legged kiwi lives here permanently! Donations are welcome.

Whangarei Quarry Gardens ★, Russell Road (www.whangareigardens.org.nz; ✆ **09/437-7210**), tells a nice story of resurrection: This old quarry site has been converted into a lush subtropical paradise by volunteers. It has tracks leading into the Coronation Scenic Reserve and is open daily from 9am to 5pm; entry is by voluntary donation.

Ducks and a cheeky eel are on hand to help you eat your lunch at the lovely **Whangarei Falls,** 5km (about 3 miles) from the town center on the Tutukaka road. The falls are very photogenic, and surrounded as they are by lush native bush, it's hard to believe they're so close to Whangarei.

Where to Stay

If motels are your thing, there are plenty here; just ask the friendly folk at the visitor center for recommendations. But for something a little more interesting (and still not too pricey), try **Parkhill Fine Accommodation,** 7D Dent St. (www.parkhillwhangarei.co.nz; ✆ **09/438-8977**), right next to the Town Basin and the CBD. It's a B&B with two lovely rooms (one with a spa bath) and everything you'd expect in a more expensive place. Rates are NZ$150 and NZ$155 and breakfast is included.

If you're on your way up to Tutukaka, the **Pacific Rendezvous Motel Resort,** 73 Motel Rd., Tutukaka (www.pacificrendezvous.co.nz; ✆ **0800/999-800** in NZ), has 30 one-, two-, and three-bedroom apartments and is on a spectacular headland with direct access to two beaches, with loads of activities for families. Apartments are from NZ$170 for one bedroom to NZ$210 for three bedrooms.

Lupton Lodge ★★ The outskirts of Whangarei are characterized by mature trees and dry stone walls encircling contented cows, much like the setting for this lovely B&B. It's a bit like being in Thomas Hardy's Wessex, except the lodge is a beautiful, sparkling-white villa built in 1896 instead of a crumbling farmhouse. There's also a converted two-story barn and a nice cat called Peanut. If you wish to start your day with a bagel with creamed mushrooms, bleu cheese, and spinach served by very congenial hosts, this is your place.

555 Ngunguru Rd. www.luptonlodge.co.nz. ✆ **09/437-2989.** 5 rooms and suites and one detached two-bedroom apartment. Rooms from NZ$145 double; apartment from NZ$275. Rates include breakfast. Dinner available on request. **Amenities:** Dining room; outdoor pool; pool/snooker table; Wi-Fi.

The Guesthouse ★★★ It's a thundering great cliché to say the photos don't do this place justice—either the extraordinary accommodation or the picture-perfect panorama that this Whangarei Heads five-star luxury guesthouse offers. But there it is. You will feel very privileged when you wake up in an unspoilt paradise that isn't just around the corner from a tourist trap of any description. Every extra little something has been provided in the lovely three-bedroom house, built in 2001 but in a modern colonial style: They even lay on wild kiwi on the 42-hectare (100-acre), intensely conservation-minded property. The only low point? Intense disappointment that, even after all my skulking around at midnight, I never got to see one of these treasured birds.

Taihararu, Whangarei Heads. www.taihararulodge.com. ✆ **021/938-879.** 3 bedroom house with kitchen. Rates NZ$320–NZ$530. Breakfast basket can be provided. **Amenities:** Gym; helipad; watersports equipment; Wi-Fi.

Where to Eat

Topsail, 206 Beach Rd., Onerahi (www.topsail.co.nz; ℂ **09/436-2955**), is one of the pricier places in these parts. It does modern Kiwi cuisine with great views of the Whangarei Harbour, serving dinner Wednesday to Saturday from 6pm. The style-y **Red Pizzeria,** 3 Kensington Ave. (www.redpizzeria.co.nz; ℂ **09/459-5380**), is home to the Metre Long Pizza, and you've got to admit that the 3-foot, 2-inch pizza doesn't sound nearly as tempting! It's open daily for dinner from 5pm and does lunch on Sunday. For lunch in the Town Basin, try **Mokaba,** 206 Beach Rd, Onerahi (www.mokabacafe.co.nz; ℂ **09/438-7557**). It's open daily from 8am to 5pm and will cater to the gluten-wary in your party. If you make it out to Tutukaka, you've got to try the very popular **Schnappa Rock ★**, Marina Rd., Tutukaka (www.schnapparock.co.nz; ℂ **09/434-3774**), a humming beach spot that serves great seafood and is open daily from 8am till late. You might even get some live music.

'a Deco ★★★ MODERN NEW ZEALAND New Zealand foodies' magazine *Cuisine* really rates this award-winning fine-dining establishment, which does rather stand out like a dog's dangly bits in relatively unsophisticated Whangarei. Chef Brenton Low is a clever guy who knows just how much fancy stuff he can get away with here, but he's onto a winner with beautifully cooked and presented local produce offset by the gorgeous Art Deco building that gives the restaurant its name.

70 Kamo Rd. www.facebook.com/aDeco.restaurant. ℂ **09/459-4957.** Main courses NZ$38–NZ$42. Reservations required for dinner in summer. Tues–Sat dinner and Fri lunch.

WAIKATO, THE BAY OF PLENTY & THE COROMANDEL

Ask a Kiwi to describe the following, and he or she might say: The Bay of Plenty? Sun. The Coromandel? Beaches. Waikato? Cows. So if you're tempted to detour around the Waikato and its mighty river (New Zealand's longest), please reconsider. This energetic and ever-changing region has much to explore scenically: outstanding caves, award-winning gardens, Hobbiton! And, yes, a few (million) cows.

Early Maori quickly realized the agricultural potential of the fertile **Waikato,** one of three regions sandwiched between Auckland and the tourist mecca of Rotorua (see chapter 8). In the aptly named **Bay of Plenty,** many New Zealanders have a favorite seaside spot, whether Mount Maunganui, Whakatane, or Ohope. The Bay of Plenty is awash with fabulous beaches, but inland BOP (as it's often abbreviated) has its charms, too: **Te Puke,** for example, is synonymous with those luscious little hairy kiwifruit. *Note:* We don't call them "kiwis"; that's what we call ourselves, with a big "k."

The **Coromandel Peninsula** is a much-loved outdoor playground for North Islanders, with a fascinating gold-mining history and contrasting coasts—the jagged but sheltered west coast, which borders the Firth of Thames, and the beautiful sandy bays of the east coast.

HAMILTON & THE WAIKATO

127km (79 miles) S of Auckland; 107km (66 miles) NE of Rotorua; 107km (66 miles) E of Tauranga

Hamilton is New Zealand's largest inland city, with a population of around 145,000, and it's a quick drive from Auckland on some of our fanciest roads! It's always been a bit of a Cinderella hiding behind the skirts of its northern big sister, but this university town has found its footing in recent years and offers plenty of treasures, if you know where to look. The Waikato region boasts the renowned Waitomo Caves, but we suggest stopping awhile in the pretty town of Cambridge, soaking in the hot springs at Te Aroha or catching a wave out on the west coast in Raglan.

Essentials

GETTING THERE & GETTING AROUND **By Plane** **Air New Zealand** (© **0800/737-000** in NZ) has daily flights to Hamilton from the main centers. The airport is about 15 minutes' drive south of the city. **Roadcat Transport** (www.roadcat.co.nz; © **0800/153-159** in NZ or **07/823-2559**) and **Super Shuttle** (www.supershuttle.co.nz; © **0800/748-885**) will transport you there from the airport.

By Coach (Bus) **InterCity** (www.intercity.co.nz; © **09/583-5780**) links Hamilton to other major centers. The **Hamilton Transport Centre,** 373 Anglesea St. (© **07/859-0509**), is the central hub for all local and regional buses, shuttles, taxis, and car rentals. The staffed counter is open Monday to Friday 8am to 4:30pm.

By Train The **Northern Explorer** ★★★ passes through Hamilton on the Auckland to Wellington route every day except Wednesday. Call © **0800/872-467** or 04/495-0775 or visit **www.kiwirailscenic.co.nz**. This is a journey not to be missed.

By Car Nice and central, Hamilton is on SH1, about 1½ hours from Auckland, Rotorua, Tauranga, and Taupo. If you haven't already rented a car from one of the major firms, try **Waikato Car Rentals,** Brooklyn Rd., Hamilton (www.waikatocarrentals.co.nz; © **0800/154-444** in NZ, or 07/855-0094).

By Taxi **Hamilton Taxis** (www.hamiltontaxis.co.nz; © **0800/477-477** in NZ, or 07/847-7477) is a 24-hour service.

ORIENTATION SH1 and the Waikato River run through Hamilton; follow the bypass to avoid the city. The main street is Victoria, and the CBD is small enough to navigate on foot.

VISITOR INFORMATION The main website is **www.hamiltonwaikato. com**. The **Hamilton i-SITE Visitor Centre,** on the corner of Caro and Alexandra streets (www.visithamilton.co.nz; © **0800/242-645** in NZ, or 07/958-5960), is open Monday to Friday 9am to 5pm; weekends 9:30am to 3:30pm. The **Cambridge i-SITE,** corner of Queen and Victoria streets (www.cambridgeinfo.co.nz; © **07/823-3456**), is open Monday to Friday 9am to 5pm and weekends 10am to 4pm. The **Waitomo Caves Discovery Centre and i-SITE** is at 21 Waitomo Caves Rd. (www.waitomocaves.com; © **0800/474-839** in NZ, or 07/878-7640); see the website for open hours. The very Hobbity **Matamata i-SITE,** 45 Broadway (www.matamatanz.co.nz; © **07/888-7260**), is open Monday to Friday 9am to 5pm and weekends 9am to 4:15pm.

SPECIAL EVENTS   The most Kiwi of these would have to be the **New Zealand National Agricultural Fieldays** (www.fieldays.co.nz; ℂ **07/843-4499**), the biggest agricultural trade show in the Southern Hemisphere. From black singlets to the latest gadgets for the farm, this mid-June event is also entertaining for those not rurally inclined. For culture vultures, the **Hamilton Gardens Arts Festival** (www.hgaf.co.nz; ℂ **07/859-1317**) is held annually in mid-February.

Exploring the Area
IN HAMILTON
Heaven for the green-thumbed, **Hamilton Gardens** ★★, Cobham Drive (www.hamiltongardens.co.nz; ℂ **07/838-6782**), was named the International Garden Tourism Network's Garden of the Year in 2014. It has a staggering 18 specialty gardens—from Tudor to traditional Maori to Italian Renaissance and even a Children's Discovery Trail—set in 54 hectares (133 acres) of land beside the Waikato River; admission is free. The themed gardens are open

WAIKATO, THE BAY OF PLENTY & THE COROMANDEL | Hamilton & the Waikato

Play Me, I'm Yours!

How's this for a nice idea? The Hamilton City Council thought it would be cool to have a few pianos dotted around the city streets so that anyone could wander past and tickle the ivories if the spirit moved them. So if you see one of Hamilton's brightly painted **Street Pianos,** don't be shy. Give us a tune.

daily from 7:30am to 7:30pm in summer and 5:30pm in winter, the information center and shop are open from 9am to 5pm; and the cafe is open from 9am to 6pm in summer and 9:30am to 5pm in winter.

The award-winning **Waikato Museum** ★★★, 1 Grantham St. (www.waikatomuseum.co.nz; © **07/838-6606**), is a great hulking modern building next to the river that suffers slightly from being strangely set out, so that you strike a lot of art gallery before you reach the actual museum—but both bits are definitely worth pursuing. As is usually the case with regional museums, Waikato history, culture, and place in the world are center stage in its 13 galleries: The collections hold more than 38,000 objects and include impressive Maori art and weaving and carving from the area's Tainui people. Te Winika, a 200-year-old carved *waka taua* (war canoe), is a favorite exhibit. Like many other New Zealand museums of a similar vintage, it has a very good World War I exhibition that is continuing until Armistice Day, November 11, 2018: *For Us They Fell* tells the human stories of Waikato people who served in the Great War. **Exscite** and **Planet Warriors** ★★★ (© **07/838-6553**) are fun, colorful hands-on science galleries designed for children to learn about the world. Next door but still part of the museum, in the lovely old post office building, is **ArtsPost** (www.waikatomuseum.co.nz; © **07/838-6923**), comprising three galleries specializing in work by emerging artists and a shop that stocks beautiful New Zealand art and design pieces. Entry to the museum is free, but a donation is requested. Admission to Exscite and Planet Warriors is NZ$5 for adults, NZ$8 for children 4 to 14 and NZ$18 for a small family. All are open daily from 10am to 4:30pm.

If you thought tea just grew in places like Ceylon, you'd be wrong. It grows here in Waikato, on the only tea plantation in New Zealand. **Zealong Tea Estate,** 495 Gordonton Rd. (© **07/853-3018;** www.zealong.com), is a 5-minute drive north of Hamilton. You can sit on the Zealong Pavilion balcony and look out on rows of tea growing happily in the Waikato countryside. Zealong offers two "Discover Tea Experience" tours a day (9:30am and 2:30pm). It's NZ$20 per person for the tour and a tea-flavored macaron to take away or NZ$49 including tiffin: a selection of sweet and savory goodies served on multilayered cake stands. If you liked the tea, you can buy some to take home. It's open Tuesday to Sunday 10am to 5pm.

IN CAMBRIDGE

Cambridge is a very pretty town with sprawling oak trees and lovely old churches (some of which have been repurposed to attract arts-and-crafts shoppers), and if you settle in at a handy cafe, you'll soon realize as the SUVs roll past that this is a serious horse town. It's the center of the Australasian bloodstock industry and, like neighboring Matamata, is surrounded by beautiful, flat pastures full of sleek, expensive racehorses. If you'd like to see some of this region's equine perfection in action, try to time your visit to coincide with a night when there's **harness racing at the Cambridge Raceway,** Taylor Street (www.harnessracingwaikato.co.nz; ℂ **07/827-5506**), and you might see some greyhounds running as well. There are about 70 race dates a year. In keeping with the moneyed vibe, Cambridge also has a large concentration of **antiques shops.** Antiques fairs are held in September and April; the visitor center has a brochure on the best dealers in these parts.

IN OTOROHANGA

Have you spotted a kiwi (the bird, not the fruit) yet? If not, the **Otorohanga Kiwi House & Native Bird Park ★★★**, 20 Alex Telfer Dr. (www.kiwihouse.org.nz; ℂ **07/873-7391**), is the place to go. This small town has been associated with our national bird ever since the sanctuary opened in 1971, when three locals—a pharmacist, a bricklayer, and a doctor—heard that some wild kiwi had been left homeless after a fire in Northland. They rescued the kiwi before they even had anywhere to put them—the first kiwi eggs were incubated in a Thermos flask! All these years later, some 200 kiwi have been successfully raised from eggs, and many have been reintroduced to the wild. Kiwi (three species) are the stars here, of course, but you can also see our rare ancient reptile the tuatara and other native species like the blue duck, weka, kaka, kakariki, and several species of gecko. Everything is bigger and better following a major rebuilding program in 2015, but a visit here still feels very personalized and special. It's open daily from 9am to 5pm: Admission is NZ$24 for adults, NZ$8 for children 5 to 15 and NZ$59 for a family pass.

IN RAGLAN

This seaside village with a primo left-hand surfing break is worth a visit if you've got your own transport. It's full of buff boardriders and laid-back artists, and you can hang out in a funky cafe (try **Raglan Roast**). It's a 45-minute drive from Hamilton on SH23.

Biking Through the Bush

The **Timber Trail** (www.thetimbertrail. com; ℂ **07/878-4997**) is a great bike ride that's part of the New Zealand Cycle Trail Network. It starts in the village of Pureora, in the south of the Waikato region, and winds through beautiful Pureora Forest, ending up, 2 days and 85km (53 miles) later, in Ongarue, in the Ruapehu Region (see chapter 8). The grade 2/3 trail follows old bush tramways and bulldozer and haul roads from logging days and includes 35 bridges, including eight large suspension bridges. A real highlight is the historic Ongarue Spiral, a triumph of bush engineering complete with a lower-level bridge, a very deep cutting, a curved tunnel, a complete circle of track, and an overbridge. Bike rental is around NZ$30 for half a day and NZ$40 per day. Visit the website for more on bikes and accommodations.

THERE BE hobbits!

If you get the whole Middle-earth thing, you're going to want to beat a path to **Hobbiton Movie Set & Farm Tours,** 501 Buckland Rd., Matamata (www.hobbitontours.com; ℭ **0508/446-224** in NZ, or 07/888-1505), like an army of Orcs after an enchantment of Elves—or something like that. "Lord of the Rings" mania calmed down a few years after Peter Jackson released the last film in 2003, and then it all started up again with the shooting of the three new "Hobbit" films, when the set was pressed into service again. The standard tour of the Shire includes a visit to the Hobbit holes, the Green Dragon Inn, and the Mill, and you might just spy some hairy-footed folk along the way. The tour costs NZ$75 to NZ$125 adults, NZ$38 children 10–14, and NZ$10 children 5–9 (free children 4 and under). If you can, we recommend the evening dinner tour. There's a look around the 4.8-hectare (12-acre) site, followed by a drink in front of the open fire at the Green Dragon Inn, then a banquet in the dining room.

But the best bit comes last, as visitors make their way back through the Shire holding lanterns. The evening tours are held on Wednesday and Sunday nights (and Tues in summer) and cost NZ$190 adults, NZ$150 children 10–14, and NZ$100 children 5–9 (free for children 4 and under). There's a shuttle bus from the Matamata i-SITE (see above), which is a Hobbity work of art in its own right.

Hobbiton doesn't have a monopoly on Tolkien film locations, however. On the small and low-key tours offered by **Hairy Feet Waitomo,** 1411 Mangaotaki Rd., Piopio, near Waitomo (www.hairyfeetwaitomo.co.nz; ℭ **07/877-8003**), you can visit a private farm with spectacular limestone cliffs and see locations where key scenes from "The Hobbit: An Unexpected Journey" were filmed. These include the spot where Gandalf gives Bilbo the sword known as "Sting." Tours run daily at 10am and 1pm and cost NZ$50 adults and NZ$25 children up to 14.

IN WAITOMO: CAVES, CAVES & MORE CAVES

A little dot on the map, Waitomo is famous for just one thing: its vast network of ancient limestone caves. September 2014 marked 125 years that local people have been guiding visitors through the system.

To get here, you can take the **Waitomo Shuttle** (ℭ **0800/808-279** in NZ, or 07/873-8279) from Hamilton; the shuttle also meets InterCity coach services and Northern Explorer trains in nearby Otorohanga. The **Waitomo Caves Discovery Centre and i-SITE Visitor Information Centre** (see above) has a neat little museum about the area, and you can book tours here.

Waitomo has three main "tourist caves": the **Waitomo Glowworm Caves, Aranui Cave,** and **Ruakuri Cave.**

With a flash visitor center, a restaurant, and a theater, the **Waitomo Glowworm Caves ★★★**, 39 Waitomo Caves Rd. (www.waitomo.com; ℭ **0800/456-922** in NZ, or 07/878-8228), has certainly certainly seen some changes in the last 30 million years! It's touristy, no doubt, but it's also undeniably impressive: A guided tour takes you through 250m (820 ft.) of spectacular underground scenery that includes **The Cathedral,** a cavern with such good acoustics that Dame Kiri Te Kanawa and the Vienna Boys' Choir have sung here. The tour includes a boat trip through the magical and twinkly **Glow-worm Grotto** (perfect for the 10-year-old girl in your party). Tours depart every half hour from 9am to 5pm and are NZ$49 for adults, NZ$22 for children 4–14, and NZ$118 for a family pass.

Another 15 minutes down the road, **Aranui Cave ★★** doesn't have glowworms, but some of the most spectacular natural formations can be found here. This tour is the same price as for the Glowworm Caves or you can get a combo for NZ$70, NZ$31 and NZ$153.

Ruakuri Cave was first discovered by Maori almost 500 years ago. You can do New Zealand's longest guided underground walking tour here, which includes a walk down the amazing spiral entranceway. Two-hour tours depart daily from the **Legendary Black Water Rafting Company,** 585 Waitomo Caves Rd., from 9am to 3:30pm and are NZ$69 for adults, NZ$27 for children 4–14, or NZ$169 for a family pass.

On the **Spellbound Glowworm and Cave Tour ★★★**, Waitomo Caves Road (beside Huhu Café; www.glowworm.co.nz; ✆ **0800/773-552** in NZ or 07/878-7622), you'll see an unbelievable display by glowworms that impressed renowned British naturalist Sir David Attenborough enough that he featured them in two BBC documentaries. This is a terrific tour, less touristy and more personalized (with smaller groups) than the ones above. It includes a 20-minute drive into the hinterland, two cave visits, and two short scenic walks and is safe, easy, and suitable for children. It runs daily from 10am to 3pm and costs NZ$75 for adults and NZ$26 for kids 14 and under accompanied by a parent.

Where to Stay
IN HAMILTON
You won't be overwhelmed by the sheer number of chic city lodgings in Hamilton, but if you want to stay in town, the **Novotel Tainui Hamilton,** 7 Alma St. (www.novotel.co.nz/Hamilton; ✆ **0800/450-050** in NZ or 07/838-1366), is one of the more reliable ones and has all the restaurant/bar/gym/spa stuff on offer. Rates are from NZ$189. **Titoki Boutique Accommodation ★★**, 1846C River Rd. N., Hamilton (www.titokiboutiqueaccommodation.co.nz; ✆ **07/854-4044**), offers two suites in a separate guest wing from gracious hosts Jude and John, complete with lounge and dining room. This home is

---

Springing to Life

If you venture east in the Waikato, you'll come across a sleepy little town with some rather delightful hot springs: **Te Aroha Mineral Spas,** Te Aroha Domain (www.tearohamineralspas.co.nz; ✆ **07/884-8717**), is situated in a restored Edwardian bathhouse and offers private mineral hot tubs (from NZ$18 per adult and NZ$11 per child) and massage and beauty treatments (from NZ$40). There's also a free foot pool in the domain if you're happy just to dip a toe in the warm water.

modern and comfortable, great for those chilly Waikato winter nights. Rooms are NZ$275 to NZ$295 and include breakfast, chocolates, and a bottle of New Zealand wine—and you won't get woken up by squawking children because under-15s are not allowed.

This little oasis gets full marks, both for ambience and Peter and Anne's hospitality: The **City Centre Bed and Breakfast** ★, 3 Anglesea St. (www.citycentrebnb.co.nz; ✆ **07/838-1671**), is close to everything, but once again, no children (under 7) are allowed. Rates are from NZ$90 to NZ$165 or NZ$119 per night for the studio cottage. Twenty minutes out of town in Ngahinapouri you'll find **Uliveto B&B Country Stay & Olive Grove** ★, 164 Finlayson Rd. (www.uliveto.co.nz; ✆ **07/825-2116**), a lovely rural Waikato property run by Daphne and Peter. Each of the two very nice rooms is NZ$170 nightly, and you can stroll in the garden and among the olives.

IN CAMBRIDGE

Enjoy sweeping rural vistas and home comforts at **Maungatautari View,** 1006 SH1, Karapiro (www.maungatautariview.co.nz; ✆ **07/823-4165**), a B&B and farmstay near Lake Karapiro and 10km (6 miles) from Cambridge. It has a swimming pool and a Jacuzzi, and you can get to know the pet sheep and cattle. Suitable for families, it's got four rooms, from NZ$150 per night with breakfast, and can accommodate up to 10 people.

Huntington Stables Retreat ★★ This rural retreat just 5 minutes' drive from Cambridge has two self-contained luxury suites (the Stables) with trundle beds (can accommodate four), a compact studio (the Loft), and a guest room in the main house (the Stall). Each is beautifully furnished and spacious, and the property has a pool, Jacuzzi, and sauna for guest use. If you book either of the Stables, you'll get a complimentary bottle of wine and an anti-pasto platter plus a well-stocked pantry and fridge. You're encouraged to put your teenagers in the Stall for a bit of peace and quiet!

106 Maungakawa Rd., RD4, Cambridge. www.huntington.co.nz. ✆ **07/823-4136.** 4 units. NZ$135–NZ$470. Rates include breakfast except for the Stall. Long-stay and weekend packages. **Amenities:** Babysitting (charged); badminton; bikes for rent; Jacuzzi; pétanque, outdoor pool; sauna; Wi-Fi except for the Stall.

IN WAITOMO/OTOROHANGA

Very handy to the caves is **Abseil Breakfast Inn,** Waitomo Caves Village (www.abseilinn.co.nz; ✆ **07/878-7815**), which has four themed rooms that are far more romantic than they sound: Bush, Cave, Farm, and Swamp! They do a great first meal of the day; breakfast, after all, is their middle name (NZ$145–NZ$180 double).

Kamahi Cottage ★★★ This utterly charming and very romantic one-bedroom cottage describes itself as New Zealand's only five-star farmstay, and it's definitely the nicest B&B around, with modcons you didn't know you couldn't live without and old-fashioned touches that set it apart from similar places—love the basket of cozy bed socks and the hammock chairs on the little porch, perfect for enjoying the lovely rural views. It's also environmentally friendly (it has Qualmark Enviro Gold status), and owners Liz and Evan have covenanted more than 283 hectares (700 acres) of their family farm so that the native bush can never be cut down. It has gardens to linger in, and and Liz will cook you a superb dinner if you request it.

229 Barber Rd., RD5, Otorohanga. www.kamahi.co.nz. ⓒ **07/873-0849.** 1 cottage. NZ$375—NZ$495 for 2–4 people. Rates include breakfast. Dinner on request. Long-stay and weekend packages available. **Amenities:** Complimentary port and schnapps; Wi-Fi in the main house.

IN MATAMATA

After a hard day's Hobbit hunting, you'll welcome the modern comforts of Joy and Ian's **de Preaux Lodge ★**, 441 Taihoa S. Rd. (www.depreauxlodge. com; ⓒ **0274/629-936**). It's a luxury B&B in the lush Matamata countryside that also caters to families (NZ$135 per person with breakfast and NZ$175 including dinner and a farm tour).

Where to Eat
IN HAMILTON

Get the free *Dine Out* guide from the visitor center for ideas on where to eat. The south end of Victoria Street is where most of the good restaurants, cafes, and bars can be found.

Hamilton has some really good eating establishments these days, serving innovative and very appealing food. The very popular **Palate,** 20 Alma St. ★ (www.palaterestaurant.co.nz; ⓒ **07/834-2921**), is an award-winning fine-dining restaurant that serves fresh local produce with loads of style. It's in a great location right by the river and next door to the Novotel (Tues–Fri 11:30am–2pm and Mon–Sat 5:30pm till late; closed Sun). In the same building, **Indian Star,** 20 Alma St. (www.indianstar.co.nz; ⓒ **07/834-3122**), is considered a best-kept secret by locals. (There's a sister restaurant in Rotorua if you want to repeat the experience.) This one is open daily for lunch from 11am to 2:30pm, then dinner from 5pm till late. If you're looking for a good breakfast, brunch, and lunch choice, try the award-winning **River Kitchen ★**, 237 Victoria St. (www.theriv-erkitchen.co.nz; ⓒ **07/839-2906**), which does interesting items like pickled pork pies and has what some reckon is the best coffee in Hamilton (Mon–Fri 7am–4pm, Sat 8am–4pm, and Sun 8am–3pm). **Scotts Epicurean,** 181 Victoria St. (www.scottsepicurean.co.nz; ⓒ **07/839-6680**), is also very good in this department, with fairly simple food done really well. It's run by two Scotts: brother and sister Jason and Mandy (Mon–Fri 7am–3pm and weekends 8am–4pm). Right by the river, **Gothenburg,** 21 Grantham St. (www.gothenburg. co.nz; ⓒ **07/834-3562**), does terrific tapas and desserts with good selections of wine and beer, including the best sampling of Belgian beer in the country, if that's your thing (Mon–Fri 8am till late, Sat 11:30am till late; closed Sun).

Chim Choo Ree ★★★ MODERN NEW ZEALAND Cameron Farmi-lo's hip and innovative city restaurant won *Cuisine* magazine's Best Regional Restaurant award in 2014, and it's easy to see why. It's in a great spot by the river surrounded by mature trees, and even though the lovely old Waikato

Brewery building suffers from Industrial Small Window Syndrome, the sun was streaming in the day I visited. It's an appealing place, where water for the table is served in old Waikato Draught beer bottles and botanical drawings from a book have been torn out and stuck on the wall. The atmosphere is playful and fun, even on a quiet day. The mains put interesting things together, like cured venison, pickled heirloom beetroot, puffed buckwheat, and chèvre, but the desserts also sing of an original talent: How about rice pudding mousse with sour raspberry ambrosia, lime marscarpone, and sherbert? It may sound like a plate of stodge, but it's the lightest, tastiest thing I've had in a long time. You'll get a New Zealand–centric wine list and a good range of craft beers to choose from. Provincial perfection!

14 Bridge St. www.chimchooree.co.nz. *①* **07/839-4329.** Main courses NZ$34–NZ$37. Open Mon–Fri 11:30am–2pm and Mon–Sat 5pm–late; closed Sun.

Victoria Street Bistro ★★★ MODERN NEW ZEALAND Hamilton seems to be cornering the market in top restaurants at the moment. This busy spot won *Cuisine* magazine's Best Regional Restaurant award the year before Chim Choo Ree (above) and has garnered lots of other awards as well for its smart fine dining and successful combination of Andrew Clarke rattling the pans and Julia Clarke keeping everything running smoothly. Try the contrasting flavors of the lamb loin, which delicately melds lamb belly, onion, aubergine, pinenuts, kumara (sweet potato), dates, and preserved lemon. Expensive for around here but worth every penny.

153 Victoria St. www.victoriastreetbistro.co.nz. *①* **07/839-4444.** Main courses NZ$34–NZ$42. Tues–Sun 11:30am till late.

IN CAMBRIDGE

The pretty town of Cambridge has a number of decent eateries these days and is a nice place to linger. Try breakfast or lunch at **Alpino Cucina e Vino,** 43 Victoria St. (www.alpino.co.nz; *①* **07/827-5595**), which serves mainly genuine Italian food and has a lovely atmosphere. It's open Wednesday to Sunday 8am to 11pm. **Rouge,** 11 Empire St. (www.rougeempire.co.nz; *①* **07/823-9178**), is another great breakfast and lunch venue that uses free-range, organic, and fair-trade products wherever possible. The coffee brings back many repeat customers. It's open daily 7:30am to 4pm. For lunch or dinner, you could try **Onyx,** 70 Alpha St. (www.onyxcambridge.co.nz; *①* **07/827-7740**), a licensed cafe and restaurant that does great wood-fired pizzas, among other treats, and serves beer from Hamilton's Good George Brewing; it's open daily from 9am. And for something a little farther out, the **Boatshed Café,** 21 Amber Lane, Cambridge (www.theboatshedkarapiro.co.nz; *①* **0800/743-321** in NZ), overlooks picturesque Lake Karapiro and is a delightful spot for lunch. On Thursday, it offers a NZ$10 lunch special on selected items. It's open Thursday to Sunday 10am to 3pm.

IN WAITOMO

Order up, get a strong person to help you carry it out, then take a selfie of you and your ginormous ice cream from **Big Azz Ice Creams** ★, 543 SH3,

Waitomo (℗ **07/873-8282**). You're not going to believe this: Ask for one scoop and you'll get three; ask for two and you'll get five. (My child nearly ate himself to death when he asked for three.) It has at least 14 yummy Tip-Top (a local brand) flavors, like Goody Goody Gum Drops and Raspberry Lemonade Fizz, plus real fruit "soft serve" ice creams. The shop is part of an orchard/fruit and produce/grocery store/gift stop—it has something for everyone but especially those massive ice creams!

If you want some real food, try the **Huhu Café**, 10 Waitomo Caves Rd., Waitomo (www.huhucafe.co.nz; ℗ **07/878-6674**), a slick and popular little operation that's open all day to warm you up after your underground adventure (with a log burner in winter). It's open daily from 11am till late and serves a menu that goes around the world but comes back to ice cream sundaes—although you probably won't need these if you've been to Big Azz Ice Creams (see above). They don't *actually* serve huhus, the large, crazy beetles that beat on your windows at night, although Maori do eat the gooey grubs!

TAURANGA & THE BAY OF PLENTY

208km (129 miles) SE of Auckland; 86km (53 miles) NW of Rotorua

They don't call it the Bay of Plenty for nothing: This region, from **Waihi Beach** in the north to **Ohope** in the south, is a paradise of sun-drenched orchards, peaceful towns and 125km (78 miles) of wonderful white-sand beaches. **Tauranga,** the fifth largest city in New Zealand and the fastest growing, numbers around 128,000 lucky souls. It has the country's largest and most efficient port, and the harbor boasts two marinas full of pleasure craft for locals and visitors to explore its bounty. Nearby **Mount Maunganui** is home to a glorious stretch of ocean beach that keeps on getting voted New Zealand's best by Trip Advisor, beloved by surfers, swimmers, dog owners and beach strollers alike. The Bay is also home to **White Island,** which has been smoking away continuously since long before Captain Cook first sighted it in 1769: A trip out to the island is an experience that will stay with you forever. It was on this expedition that Cook christened the region and the very appealing name stuck.

Essentials

GETTING THERE   By Plane   Air New Zealand (www.airnewzealand. co.nz; ℗ **0800/767-767** in NZ) offers daily direct flights from Tauranga to Auckland, Wellington, and Christchurch. The airport is in Mt Maunganui, which is 5km (about 3 miles) from Tauranga city. **Luxury Airport Shuttles** (www.luxuryairportshuttles.co.nz; ℗ **0800/454-678** in NZ, or 07/547-4444) will transport you to and from the airport from NZ$10 per person.

By Coach (Bus)   InterCity (www.intercity.co.nz; ℗ **09/583-5780**) has daily services between Tauranga and Auckland, Napier, Rotorua, Taupo, Thames, and Wellington.

By Car   It takes about 2½ hours to drive from Auckland to Tauranga, about 1½ hours from the Coromandel and Hamilton and 1 hour from Rotorua.

ORIENTATION   **Cameron Road** is the main thoroughfare that runs right through Tauranga. The main bridge offers a shortcut to **Mt. Maunganui,** which is a continuous stretch of white-sand beach running 60km (37 miles) east all the way to Whakatane.

GETTING AROUND   There are a lot of big trucks on the road heading to and from the very busy port, so be aware of this if you are driving. For getting around the city and "the Mount", there's a council-subsidized public transport system, Bay Bus. Phone the call centre (www.baybus.co.nz; ℂ **0800/422-928** in NZ) for information. It's open Monday to Friday from 7am to 6pm.

VISITOR INFORMATION   The **Tauranga i-SITE Visitor Information Centre,** Civic Centre, 95 Willow St. (ℂ **07/578-8103**), is open 8:30am to 5:30pm daily. Pick up a free copy of the *Bay of Plenty Visitor Guide* while you're here. The **Whakatane Visitor Centre,** Quay Street (www.whakatane. com; ℂ **0800/942-528** in NZ, or 07/306-2030), is open Monday to Friday from 8:30am to 5:30pm and weekends from 10am to 4pm.

SPECIAL EVENTS   Many events in the Bay center around summer, sea and sand, like the **Port of Tauranga Half Ironman** (www.tgahalf.co.nz; ℂ **09/523-4212**), which is a triathlon event that takes place in Mt. Maunganui each January. For something that's a bit more cultural, the very well-established **National Jazz Festival** (www.jazz.org.nz; ℂ **09/577-7460**) takes place in Tauranga for 4 days each Easter, and the annual 10-day **Tauranga Arts Festival** (www.taurangafestival.co.nz; ℂ **09/577-7018**) is held at the end of October or the beginning of November.

Exploring the Area
IN & NEAR TAURANGA

The **Tauranga Art Gallery** ★★, 108 Willow St. (www.artgallery.org.nz; ℂ **07/578-7933**), is right across the road from the visitor center. It presents historical and contemporary art but with more of an emphasis on the latter, which is appropriate given the modernity of the building. As with most regional galleries, it exhibits a mix of touring exhibitions from other institutions and artist projects that speak about this locality. The gallery is open daily from 10am to 4:30pm; admission is free.

From mostly new to old, the lovely **Elms Mission Station,** 15 Mission St. (www.theelms.org.nz; ℂ **07/577-9772**), is the oldest European heritage site in the Bay of Plenty. Built in 1847, it also happens to be one of the finest examples of colonial architecture of its time, with the clean, simple lines of our earliest settler buildings. The mission station was established in 1838 by Archdeacon Alfred Brown, who built his freestanding library the following year, before the main homestead, so important were his books to him. You can visit daily from 10am to 4pm. It's free to walk in the gardens and NZ$5 per person for a house and library tour. If you'd like to know more about Tauranga's history, pick up the "Historic Tauranga" brochure from the information

Fly Back in Time

For a unique sightseeing experience, call **Classic Fliers,** 9 Jean Batten Dr., Mt. Maunganui (www.classicflyersnz.com; ℭ **07/572-4000**). Take flight over Tauranga in a classic open-cockpit biplane—choose from a Boeing Stearman or a Grumman Ag-Cat. A 25-minute flight is NZ$355; the deluxe version, including a DVD, certificate, and photo, is NZ$377. Afterward, have a beer and a bite at the **Avgas Café and Bar** and check out the very interesting aviation museum.

center. Also appealing to garden lovers is **McLaren Falls Park ★**, McLaren Falls Road, Tauranga (ℭ **07/577-7000**), just a 10-minute drive from central Tauranga. It's 190 hectares (470 acres) of parkland next to a very pretty lake where you can go on a number of walking trails, have a picnic, or even fish for trout if you have a New Zealand license. If you stay till it gets dark and take the Waterfall Track, you'll pass a rather lovely glowworm dell. The park also has one of the best botanical tree collections in the North Island. It's open daily from 7am to 7:30pm in summer and until 5:30pm in winter. For still more garden attractions in the region, ask for the "Garden Trail" brochure at the visitor center.

A 20-minute drive from Tauranga is the little town of Te Puke, which all but sustains the kiwifruit industry in New Zealand. Not surprisingly, it has a visitor attraction that can tell you about this multimillion-dollar export in all sorts of fun ways—and you'll know you're there when you see the giant plastic slice of fruit. **Kiwi360,** SH2, Te Puke (www.kiwi360.com; ℭ **07/573-6340**), is 5km (3 miles) south of the town. The 40-minute Kiwi Kart tour involves traveling around the property in a little plastic carriage shaped like (what else?) a kiwifruit. These run on the hour and cost NZ$20 for adults and NZ$6 for children 5 to 15. You can also get free tastings of fresh kiwifruit and feijoas, and buy jams, relishes, honey, and wine and liqueurs made from these fruit. There's a cafe (don't miss the kiwifruit ice cream!) and a large gift shop with many items completely unrelated to kiwifruit. It's open daily 9am to 5pm in summer (10am–3pm in winter).

IN WAIHI BEACH

A magnificent 9km (5.5-mile) swath of white sand at the northern end of the Bay of Plenty, **Waihi Beach** is popular with Kiwi holidaymakers, who come here in droves during the summer to swim, fish, and surf—Waihi Beach has one of the safest surf breaks in the country. The good people at **Waihi Beach Surf School,** Brighton Recreational Reserve (www.beachsurfschool.co.nz; ℭ **027/245-8593**), will rent you a board for NZ$30 to NZ$40 for half a day or NZ$50 for a full day. Paddleboards are NZ$30 per hour or NZ$40 for half a day. Or you might prefer to walk this beautiful coastline: From the north end of the beach, there's an easy 45-minute walk to pohutukawa-fringed **Orokawa Bay,** or you could continue on to **Homunga Bay** (2½ hr.). Note that you'll need to return the same way or arrange a pickup at Ngatitangata Road.

IN MT. MAUNGANUI

In summer, Mt. Maunganui is a happening hotspot full of young surfy types wandering around in their swimwear, but the Tauranga area is also a favorite place for retirees, so the rest of the year a good proportion of its population tends to be a lot older. Looming over the long expanse of beach is "the Mount," an extinct volcano known to Maori as **Mauao** ★★. Walking around or to the top of Mauao will give you stunning 360-degree views of the bay, the harbor, and long, skinny Matakana Island to the north. It's 3.5km (2 miles) around and 252m (827 ft.) to the summit on well-formed, grassy tracks through native bush. You'll pass other walkers, joggers, and possibly some paraglider pilots lugging their wings to the takeoff. (Look up and you'll see them soaring overhead like colored birds.) Pick up the free "Walker's Guide to Mauao" brochure from the visitor center if you need more information.

The **Mount Maunganui Hot Salt Water Pools,** 9 Adams Ave. (© **07/577-8551**), situated at the base of Mauao, are a nice place to warm up and chill out. These are saltwater pools, not mineral springs, with temps up to 39°C (102°F); the active and children's pools are 32°C (90°F). There is a large public pool, two outdoor Jacuzzis, three private Jacuzzis and a toddlers' pool with a slide. You can get a massage onsite as well. General admission is NZ$11 for adults and NZ$8.10 for children 5 to 15. Private pools are NZ$16 for adults or NZ$21 and NZ$17 for admission to both. They're open Monday to Saturday from 6am to 10pm and Sunday from 8am to 10pm.

The Mount is also the place to take a scenic spin on the water with **Kewpie Cruises,** Pilot Bay Wharf, Mt. Maunganui (www.kewpiecruises.co.nz; © **0800/539-743**). The good ship *Kewpie* is a beautifully restored 14m (46-ft.) solid kauri ferryboat that used to ply the waves farther north on the Bay of Islands Cream Trip run. Nowadays, it does several pleasure cruises around the Bay of Plenty, including a 1-hour inner harbor cruise, stopping off at Matakana Island, where you can hop off and catch the boat when it comes around again. It's remarkably good value (NZ$20 adults, NZ$15 children 12–17, and free for under-12s) and runs every day on the hour from 10am to 4pm daily in summer and winter weekends from 11am to 3pm.

IN & AROUND WHAKATANE

Quieter than Tauranga but just as perfectly sited, **Whakatane** is the sunniest place in the North Island, with great beaches. It's provincial New Zealand at its best—relaxed, friendly, and offering so many ways to make your holiday perfect. Check out the **Whakatane Library and Exhibition Centre—Te Koputu a te Whanga,** 46 Kakahoroa Dr. (www.whakatanemuseum.org.nz; © **07/306-0509**), which houses the **Whakatane District Museum,** telling the stories of the district, and three gallery spaces that offer local and touring exhibitions. It's open Monday to Friday 9am to 5pm and weekends 10am to 2pm. You might also want to check out **Mataatua Wharenui,** 105 Muriwai Dr. (www.mataatua.com; © **07/308-4271**), "The House That Came Home." This authentic *marae* experience tells the story of a Maori meeting house that was built in 1875 and traveled to Sydney and Melbourne in Australia, then to the Victoria and Albert Museum

WHITE magic

White Island ★★★ is the fascinating if not conventionally beautiful jewel in the Bay of Plenty's crown. The only active marine volcano in New Zealand, it is a place that awakens all your senses at once—and you might want to add fear to the list, although the capable and very experienced operators on these trips will look after you. Maori know it as Whakaari: It sits 48km (29 miles) out to sea and is privately owned but has been a scenic reserve since 1953. You'll need to take a guided tour if you want to get closer than peering at its steam plume from the distant shore.

It's possibly one of the most accessible marine volcanoes in the world, and so it draws vulcanologists and other scientists like clever moths to a sulfurous flame. You can experience the bleak lunar landscape where geothermal steam vents spout and bubbling mud pools gurgle and examine the remains of a doomed sulfur-mining enterprise that was destroyed by a lahar (volcanic mudslide) in 1914, killing 10 miners. The volcano was very active from 1981 to 1983, which decimated the island's pohutukawa forest; another eruption in 2000 covered its surface in scoria and mud. Know that White Island is constantly monitored by the latest seismographic equipment, and operators shut up shop at even the slightest rise in activity.

You can visit by sea or air: the award-winning eco-operator **White Island Tours ★★★**, 15 The Strand East, Whakatane (www.whiteisland.co.nz; ℂ 0800/733-529 in NZ, or 07/308-9588), takes visitors out on a launch for a 6-hour tour that includes lunch and safety gear (gas mask and hard hat). You spend up to 2 hours of that on a guided walking tour of the volcano's inner crater (don't wear your dancing shoes!), and on the boat journey back you may also experience closeup encounters with marine mammals (dolphins, whales). The tours leave every day at 9:15am, weather permitting, and cost NZ$199 adults and NZ$130 children. (This tour isn't recommended for kids under 8.) For an aerial view, try **Frontier Helicopters ★★★**, 216 Aerodrome Rd., Whakatane Airport (www.frontierhelicopters. co.nz; ℂ 0800/804-354 in NZ, or 07/308-4188). I've done this and I can attest that flying over a volcano belching steam and sulfur is a surreal experience. The 20-minute flight is followed by a 1-hour guided tour of the crater, leaving daily from 8am. It's rather pricey at NZ$650 per person but absolutely unforgettable. You can also do this trip from Rotorua, but it's more expensive still.

in London and back to New Zealand via Dunedin, finally being rebuilt in Whakatane in 2011. The 1.5-hour tour looks at the importance of this sacred place to Ngati Awa Maori of the Bay of Plenty. It's open Thursday to Sunday from 9:30am to 4pm and costs NZ$49 for adults and NZ$15 for children.

Nearby **Ohope** is home to one of New Zealand's best-loved beaches, which sweeps for 11km (6¾ miles) along the Pacific Coast. If you take a short walk over the hill at its north end, you'll come to an absolute gem in the wilderness: Otarawairere Beach, where ancient pohutukawa trees fringe the bay and bloom brilliant crimson in the weeks before Christmas. **Ohiwa Harbour** is another lovely place to explore on foot or by water. It's safe for swimming and kayaking and is also a haven for birdlife: Godwits migrate from Alaska every year to nest on its shores.

Outdoor Pursuits

BLOKARTING   Blokart Recreation Park, 176 Parton Rd., Papamoa (www.blokartrecreationpark.co.nz; ✆ **0800/4256-5278** in NZ, or 07/572-4256), is the place to sail around a track on your Blokart, a Kiwi invention similar to a land yacht. It's great fun as long as there's wind. If not, you can always try another home-grown idea: drift karting, which is a motorized trike you kneel on and deliberately try to skid around corners. Kids love it! Blokarts are NZ$30 for 30 minutes and NZ$50 for 1 hour; drift karts are NZ$25 for one 1-minute practice round and three 3-minute drift sessions. You can do a combo for NZ$50.

DOLPHIN SWIMMING   Dolphin Seafari ★★, 101 Te Awanui Dr., Mt. Maunganui (www.nzdolphin.com; ✆ **07/577-0105**), boasts a 95% chance of seeing wild populations of dolphins and gives you an 85% chance to swim with them. You may also see whales, which are common in the Bay of Plenty. The 5-hour tour departs daily at 8am in summer, and the price includes all gear and light refreshments: It's NZ$140 for adults and NZ$95 for children 6 to 12. This company is fully licensed by New Zealand's Department of Conservation.

FISHING   Blue Ocean Charters, Tauranga Bridge Marina, Tauranga (www.blueocean.co.nz; ✆ **0800/224-278** in NZ, or 07/544-3072), offers full-day, twilight, and overnight trips in the abundant waters around White Island. Full-day reef fishing trips are NZ$100 for adults and NZ$50 for children under 13; overnight is NZ$165 per person. Overnight hapuka fishing trips are NZ$185 per person. For more operators, ask at the visitor center.

KAYAKING   Waimarino, 36 Taniwha Place, Bethlehem, Tauranga (www.waimarino.com; ✆ **07/576-4233**), offers a range of guided and unguided kayaking adventures, from sea kayaking to New Zealand's only glowworm kayak tour, on Lake McLaren. Prices range from NZ$99 per person for a guided tour of Lake McLaren to NZ$190 for a gourmet dinner tour. If you're in the Whakatane area, **KG Kayaks** ★★, 93 Kutarere Wharf Rd., near Ohope (www.kgkayaks.co.nz; ✆ **07/315-4005**), offers freedom hires (rentals with safety briefings, life jackets, and route maps) and guided tours around the Ohope Beach area, Ohiwa Harbour, and out to Whale Island, 9km (5½ miles) off the Whakatane coast. Freedom hires are from NZ$28 per hour and guided tours are from NZ$85 for adults and NZ$50 for children under 16.

SURFING   Guy and Rebecca from Hibiscus Surf School, Main Beach, Mt. Maunganui (http://surfschool.co.nz; ✆ **07/575-3792**), will teach you how to surf. They'll also give you the lowdown on local surf and ocean conditions. Beginner lessons, held daily at 1:30pm, are from NZ$85 for 2 hours. If you're already a surfhound and just want to rent a board, head to the **Mount Surf Shop,** 96 Maunganui Rd. (www.mountsurfshop.co.nz; ✆ **07/575-9133**); it's NZ$30 for a half-day rental.

DIVING   Diveworks, 96 The Strand, Whakatane (www.diveworks-charters.com; ✆ **0800/354-7737** in NZ, or 07/308-2001), will take you out to explore the rich, clear waters around White Island and Whale Island for hourly, half-day, and full-day trips. A 4-hour guided dive tour around Whale Island and an island walk is NZ$120 for adults and NZ$75 for children.

Where to Stay

By New Zealand standards, the Bay of Plenty beaches are heaving with tourists over the summer, so if you're planning to visit between December and February, it's a good idea to call in advance to make your booking.

IN & NEAR TAURANGA

For a chic, inner-city stay, try the boutique **Hotel on Devonport** ★★, 72 Devonport Rd. (www.hotelondevonport.net.nz; ⓒ **0800/322-856** in NZ, or 07/578-2668). You get a lovely big room, free Wi-Fi, a free newspaper every morning, and they hand you a drink when you walk in! Rooms are from NZ$170 to NZ$270. **Tauranga Lodge,** 10 Adrine Lane, Ohauiti, Tauranga (www.taurangalodge.co.nz; ⓒ **07/544-4465**), is a more intimate, country experience: a B&B where your every wish is catered to by hosts John and Karla. There are home-baked goodies in the tins and pre-dinner drinks and canapés in the evening, if you so desire. Have a glass of wine in the Jacuzzi, which looks out onto Tauranga, the Mount, and the Pacific Ocean. The three suites range from NZ$250 to NZ$290 per night.

Trinity Wharf Tauranga ★★ Do you fancy the idea of tying up your craft at the private floating dock and walking straight into the lovely, light-filled **Halo** restaurant? Don't have a boat? You could arrive by helicopter. Plenty of people have done this (especially brides-to-be), but more make their appearance the motorized way, of course—this bright, white 4.5-star boutique hotel sits over the water on Tauranga Harbour. However you arrive, this is a stunning location, especially on a fine day. Guest rooms, suites, and apartments are chic, somewhat enormous, and inviting. Gaze at the reflections on the infinity pool and the harbor water from a deck built for relaxing with a long, cold drink.

51 Dive Cres. www.trinitywharf.co.nz. ⓒ **07/577-8700.** 122 rooms. Standard rooms from NZ$$176–NZ$230; premium waterview spa rooms from NZ$256–NZ$326; garden view apartments from NZ$426–NZ$526; penthouse apartment from NZ$686–NZ$730. Long-stay and off-peak rates. **Amenities:** Restaurant; bar; baby grand piano in lobby; babysitting; gym; outdoor infinity pool; room service; Wi-Fi (free).

The French Country House ★★★ There is absolutely nothing even remotely New Zealandy about this extraordinary boutique accommodation in the countryside 20 minutes from Tauranga, but that shouldn't stop you from booking several nights in unashamed Euro-style luxury right away! This gorgeous home set in 16 hectares (40 acres) of rolling countryside and parklike grounds (with horses, cattle, a donkey, and enormous chickens) looks as if it has been teleported direct from some French Hansel and Gretel fairy tale, complete with chandeliers, antique fittings and furniture, and wrought-iron spiral staircase. It's so over the top it meets itself coming back down again, but you'll love it, right down to the heart-shaped spoons that come with Kay's divine carrot cake, which she serves with tea in bone china cups. If this doesn't put the romance back into your life, you're might want to check your pulse.

163 Esdaile Rd., Pahoia, Tauranga. www.thefrenchcountryhouse.co.nz. © **07/548-2339.** 3 suites. NZ$795 double. Rates include breakfast, afternoon tea on arrival, pre-dinner drinks and canapés. Dinner on request (from NZ$90 per person). Long-stay and off-peak rates. Riding lessons or horse trekking on-site. **Amenities:** Dining room; Wi-Fi (free).

IN & NEAR MT. MAUNGANUI

For something cost-effective and self-contained, try **Quest Mount Maunganui,** 424 Maunganui Rd., Mt. Maunganui (www.questmountmaunganui. co.nz; © **0800/944-400** in NZ, or 07/575/5615). Choose from one-, two-, and three-bedroom apartments. It also has a gym, a Jacuzzi, and a swimming pool. Rates are from NZ$170 to NZ$499.

Oceanside Resort & Twin Towers ★★   The Mount's very own "twin towers" are a landmark around here and continue to offer superior two-bedroom apartment accommodation with unbeatable views. The three-level resort part of the complex sits behind the towers and has cheaper but still very nice studios and one- and two-bedroom suites. All rooms have private patios or balconies. There's no restaurant on-site, but you're just moments from the Mount's numerous eateries and right across from Le Marie in the Pacific Apartments (but given that they're in direct competition, Oceanside might not be too keen to send you in this direction!).

1 Maunganui Rd., Mt. Maunganui. www.oceanside.co.nz and www.twintowers.co.nz. © **0800/466-868** in NZ, or 07/575-5371. 60 rooms. Resort executive studios from NZ$159–NZ$220; resort 1 bedroom suites from NZ$199–NZ$290; resort 2 bedroom suites from NZ$235–NZ$310; twin tower 2 bedroom apartments from NZ$310–NZ$485; twin tower 3 bedroom penthouse from NZ$515–NZ$620. Long-stay and off-peak rates. **Amenities:** Babysitting; gym; sauna; Jacuzzi; heated outdoor pool; laundry (tower suites); free underground car parking; free Wi-Fi for 1 hour, then NZ$10 per day for 250Mb.

Pacific Apartments ★★   With nine floors of smart, luxurious accommodation ranging from studios to a four-bedroom apartment, this lovely property gets full marks for convenience. Every room has a full laundry and kitchen, and you're seconds away from Mt. Maunganui beach, "The Mount," and the hot saltwater pools. Plus there's a terrific French restaurant on-site (see "Where to Eat"). Sit on your deck and enjoy great harbor views—you can watch the cruise and container ships go by—or ocean views from the other side. (Ask for a room on the third floor or higher.)

8 Maunganui Rd., Mt. Maunganui. www.thepacificapartments.co.nz. © **0800/862-864** in NZ, or 07/929-7474. 33 rooms. Studios from NZ$175–NZ$220; 1 bedroom apartments from NZ$195–NZ$240; 2 bedrooms from NZ$300–NZ$500; 3 bedrooms from NZ$400–NZ$700; 4 bedrooms from NZ$600–NZ$850. Long-stay and off-peak rates. **Amenities:** Restaurant; bar; babysitting; gym; large Jacuzzi; heated outdoor pool; room service; Wi-Fi (free).

Papamoa Beach Resort ★★★ There'll be no complaints about the views if you stay here: This holiday park in the ocean suburb of Papamoa couldn't be closer to the long, white-sand beach that stretches for miles in either direction. The upmarket villas and units are light, bright, modern, and spacious. Ask for a beachfront room; you'll love sitting on your deck and watching the sun set over the water.

535 Papamoa Beach Rd., Papamoa. www.papamoabeach.co.nz. ✆ **0800/232-243** in NZ, or 07/572-0816. 38 units. Powered sites from NZ$42–54 for two people. Cabins from NZ$88–NZ$100; holiday units from NZ$130–NZ$189; 2 bedroom garden villas from NZ$185–NZ$242; beachfront villas from NZ$200–NZ$273; 3 bedroom baches from NZ$350–NZ$500. Long-stay and off-peak rates. **Amenities:** Family barbecue area; bikes for hires; children's playground with jumping pillow; holiday kids' club; Jacuzzi; mini-tennis court; pétanque; free Wi-Fi in villas.

IN WAIHI BEACH

Waihi Beach Top 10 Holiday Resort ★ Kiwi families have been making this holiday park on beautiful Waihi Beach their regular destination for years, but the accommodation has been refurbished and looks brand-new. It offers four different motel options, several self-contained units, and cabins that sleep four, five, or six people (and tent sites) on the lovely native-bush and garden part of the park or across the road right on the beach. In addition to attractive covered areas for eating, barbecuing, or cooking a pizza on the wood-fired pizza oven, this place has something other places don't—eels! They're not for eating, though; you feed them in the stream that runs through this lovely property.

15 Beach Rd. Waihi Beach. www.top10.co.nz/parks/waihi-beach. ✆ **0800/924-428** in NZ, or 07/863-5504. 23 units. Powered sites from NZ$50–NZ$66 for two people; park motels from NZ$145–NZ$275; self-contained units from NZ$100–NZ$270; cabins from NZ$100–NZ$200. Long-stay and off-peak rates. **Amenities:** Gym; children's playground with jumping pillow; library; Jacuzzi; heated outdoor pool; sauna; surfboards, body boards, mountain bikes and trikes for hire; 30 min. free Wi-Fi per device, then NZ$5 for 2 hours/500Mb–NZ$25 for 7 days/1Tb.

IN WHAKATANE/OHOPE

A rather prominent 4.5-star motel, **White Island Rendezvous,** 15 The Strand East, Whakatane (www.whiteislandrendezvous.co.nz; ✆ **0800/242-299** in NZ, or 07/308-9588), is tucked in between the Whakatane River and a pohutukawa-topped cliff. The only accommodation of its type in town with its own cafe, this is very handy if you're planning to take a trip with White Island Tours (see "White Magic," above), which operates out of the same building. The motel has numerous options, from twin studios and two-bedroom apartments to two lovely old villas next door. You'll pay from NZ$119 to NZ$179 for the motel accommodation and NZ$190 for a villa. The **Ohope Beach Top 10 Holiday Park,** 367 Harbour Rd., Ohope Beach (www.ohopebeach.co.nz; ✆ **0800/264-673** in NZ, or 07/312-4460), has cabin, motel, and apartment accommodation right on a fabulous beach. Rates are from NZ$88 for a standard cabin to NZ$320 for a two-bedroom apartment. Powered camp sites are from NZ$42 to NZ$51 for two people. **Ohope Beach Resort,** 307 Harbour

Rd., Ohope (www.ohopebeachresort.net; © **0800/464-673** in NZ, or 07/312-4120), is, as its name would suggest, more resorty, offering two-bedroom and three-bedroom penthouse accommodations that are a home away from home—if home is a flash (that would be fancy, in New Zealandese) apartment. There's a gym and a tennis court and a pool, although why wouldn't you take advantage of the beautiful beach on your doorstep? It's nice but lacks the Kiwi camping holiday appeal of the Top 10. Apartments are NZ$200 to NZ$350 for a two-bedroom and NZ$295 to NZ$450 for a penthouse.

Where to Eat

IN TAURANGA

There are some good places on The Strand, around Wharf Street, and on Devonport Road, but they don't have a monopoly on Tauranga's dining scene. For more ideas, ask for the free *Dine Out* guide from the visitor center. The Old Yacht Club building is home to popular **Harbourside ★**, 150 The Strand (www.harboursidetauranga.co.nz; © **07/571-0520**), which is packed with locals in all weather. You can get wonderful seafood here (to go with the harbor views), but the menu takes in everything from miso-roasted quail to a wagyu sirloin fillet (NZ$66). It's open daily from 11:30am until late. For great contemporary Asian cuisine, try **Macau ★**, 59 The Strand (www.dinemacau.co.nz; © **07/578-8717**), where the presentation is as beautiful as the food. They get pretty creative with their cocktails too: Anyone for a Popcorn Paloma, featuring popcorn-infused tequila, vanilla syrup, lime juice, and pink grapefruit soda? It's open Monday to Friday from 11am till late and on Saturday 10am till late. **Halo,** 51 Dive Crescent (www.trinitywharf.co.nz; © **07/577-8700**), is the restaurant in the wonderfully situated Trinity Wharf Tauranga hotel, offering fresh, modern alfresco dining on the balcony or indoors in the evening or when the sun doesn't shine—rare for this part of the world! It's open daily from 7am till late.

Bethlehem, a suburb of Tauranga and just a few minutes' drive from the city center, has a couple of choice options. There aren't many wineries in the Bay of Plenty, but **Mills Reef Winery ★★**, 143 Moffat Rd., Bethlehem, Tauranga (www.millsreef.co.nz; © **07/808-3203**), is one of them and it does great brunches and lunches (from 9:30am on) and dinner by appointment, serving Pacific Rim cuisine matched with Mills Reef wines. The winery is set in 8 hectares (20 acres) of lovely grounds, and it's ideal for larger groups or intimate meals. You can also visit for a wine tasting daily from 10am to 5pm.

Somerset Cottage ★★ MODERN NEW ZEALAND   They take their food pretty seriously at Somerset Cottage, which is a fine-dining restaurant, a cooking school (four series a year), and an online food store all wrapped into one yummy package. The restaurant part of the enterprise has been pleasing locals and visitors since 1986 and the cooking school was established the following year. Chef Rick Lowe says he's not allowed to take certain favorite dishes off the menu, including Momufuku-style steamed pork buns with pork belly, twice-baked cheese soufflé with oven-roasted paprika pears, and oven-roasted duck with vanilla and coconut-scented kumara mash and orange sauce—and we suggest you see why.

30 Bethlehem Rd., Bethlehem, Tauranga. www.somersetcottage.co.nz. ✆ **07/576-6889.** Main courses NZ$38–NZ$40. Lunch Wed–Fri noon–2:30pm and dinner Mon–Sat from 5pm; closed Sun.

Phil's Place ★ MODERN NEW ZEALAND   From this delightful setting you can watch expensive yachts and launches bobbing around on their moorings as you enjoy tapas, lunch, or dinner. The very hospitable Penny and Jo welcome diners like long-lost friends. In the evening, the restaurant becomes an intimately lit, warm, and invitingly cozy space that serves innovative choices and hearty, delicious classics like seafood chowder that's absolutely stuffed with whole mussels, fish, prawns, and scallops. Don't be fooled by the size of the meals: This is very good food indeed. It just isn't the sort of place where you get a tiny serving with an enormous price.

101 Tauranga Bridge Marina. www.philsplacenz.com. ✆ **07/574-4147.** Main courses NZ$23–NZ$37. Daily from 11:30am till late.

IN MOUNT MAUNGANUI

Astrolabe Brew Bar ★★, 82 Maunganui Rd. (www.astrolabe.co.nz; ✆ **07/574-8155**), has restyled itself from a cafe that serves drinks to a cool gastrobar to come for a tasty bite accompanied by Mac's beer (a Kiwi brand) and other beverages. It offers themed nights, lots of à la carte choices, and set menus (NZ$45, NZ$34, and NZ$27) and is open daily from noon till late. For a slightly more sedate dinner right by the Mount, try the aptly named **Mount Bistro,** 6 Adams Ave. (www.mountbistro.co.nz; ✆ **07/575-3872**), a fine-dining place with a great location and innovative food. Opening hours are Tuesday to Sunday from 5:30pm to 10pm. If you're in the mood for a little French cuisine, head to **Le Marie,** 8 Maunganui Rd. (www.le-marie.com; ✆ **07/575-9033**), the restaurant in the ground floor of **Pacific Apartments** (see "Where to Stay," above). This very good restaurant is slightly less Gallic earlier in the day, but you can still get a splendid *champignons à la crème* with cabanossi sausage at 9am. Things get more serious as the day wears on, and really, you'd have to be a complete philistine to pass up the chance to eat lavender crème brulée. It's open Tuesday to Sunday from 7am till late. You can get a great thin-crust pizza that will fill you up and then some at **Pizza Library,** 314 Rata St. (www.thepizzalibrary.co.nz; ✆ **07/574-2928**). The surroundings (like a library!) and atmosphere are equally nice, and so is the service; it's open Monday to Wednesday 5pm to 8:30pm and Thursday to Sunday midday to 8:30pm. **Café Eighty Eight,** 88 Maunganui Rd. (✆ **07/574-0384**), is a busy little place crammed with gorgeous counter food and happy locals. It's open daily from 7am till 4:30am.

IN WHAKATANE/OHOPE

These beach towns are not overflowing with great eateries, but you'll enjoy **Soulsa** ★, 126 The Strand, Whakatane (✆ **07/307-8689**), which prides itself on taking very good care of its customers, right down to chef Jono

Marr coming out of the kitchen to chat. This is widely thought to be the best restaurant in Whakatane, serving sophisticated food in a relaxed setting. It's open Tuesday to Saturday from 5:30 to 9pm. Fancy strolling along the beach with a baguette and some fine French cheese for a seaside picnic? Try **L'Epicerie Café Deli Bakery ★**, 73 The Strand, Whakatane (www.lepicerie. co.nz; ℭ **07/308-5981**), a delightful establishment that brings all things French and delicious to the Bay of Plenty and is run with love and passion by Guilhem and Chloé. Take it to go or stay for a great coffee and a pastry from the divine selection. It's open Tuesday to Friday from 7:30am to 2:30pm, Saturday 8am to 2:30pm, and Sunday 8am to 2pm. In Ohope, **Chez Louis,** 63 Pohutukawa Ave., Ohope Beach (ℭ **07/312-5342**), does authentic European-style wood-fired pizzas, including a country French version (sour cream, mushrooms, onion, bacon, garlic, cheese, and herbs), breads, pastries, and damned fine coffee. Louie and Anais are the real deal and love what they do. They're open Wednesday from 8am to 8pm and Thursday to Sunday from 4:30pm to 8pm.

THE COROMANDEL

119km (74 miles) E of Auckland

The towns of the Coromandel Peninsula heaved with glinty-eyed gold prospectors at the height of the gold rush in the 19th century. These hard-living characters in particular thronged to Thames, at the base of the peninsula, and drank away their cares at the 100-plus pubs that filled the town by 1868. Of these, just four remain today, and it's a quieter place altogether, but there's still plenty of colorful history to be discovered here.

From Thames you can access the peninsula's water wonderland, which offers limitless opportunities for swimming, diving, fishing, and boating. The two coasts are divided by the native-bush-covered Coromandel Range, but wherever you are, you'll come across interesting people: The area has always been a magnet for folk who like to do things differently. You could whiz around in a day, but this is truly a place to settle into and savor, preferably with a cold drink in one hand and a toe in the balmy waters.

Essentials

GETTING THERE & GETTING AROUND By Plane Sunair (www. sunair.co.nz; ℭ **0800/786-247** in NZ) runs a twice-daily service to Whitianga from Auckland and Tauranga and will also arrange scenic and charter flights.

By Ferry 360 Discovery Cruises (www.360discovery.co.nz; ℭ **0800/360-3472** in NZ) runs between Auckland and Coromandel town. The 4-hour round-trip is NZ$70 for adults (same-day return), NZ$40 children 5 to 15, which includes a free transfer into town. They can also arrange tours from Coromandel.

By Coach (Bus) InterCity (www.intercity.co.nz; ℭ **09/583-5780**) runs regular services between Auckland, Thames, Whitianga, and Coromandel.

By Car Thames is about a 1½-hour drive from Auckland. If you're driving to the top of the peninsula, be warned that the road just north of Colville is unsealed. It's a gorgeous trip, but the road is steep and narrow with precipitous drops straight down to the sea—so you'll need to keep your wits about you. The 309 Road, between Coromandel and Whitianga, and the Tapu-Coroglen Road are also mostly gravel. SH25 is easier and offers better views.

By Taxi Contact **Whiti City Cabs** in Whitianga (© **07/866-4777**).

VISITOR INFORMATION The Coromandel's main tourism website is **www.thecoromandel.com**. The **Thames i-SITE Visitor Centre,** 206 Pollen St. (www.thamesinfo.co.nz; © **07/868-7284**), is open Monday to Friday from 8:30am to 5pm and Saturday, Sunday, and public holidays 9am to 4pm. The **Coromandel Information Centre,** Samuel James Reserve (© **07/866-8598;** www.coromandeltown.co.nz), is open Sunday to Thursday 10am to 4pm and Friday and Saturday 10am to 5pm in summer; and Monday to Friday 10am to 4pm and Saturday and Sunday 11am to 3pm in winter. The **Whitianga i-SITE Visitor Centre,** 66 Albert St. (www.thecoromandel.com/whitianga/; © **07/866-5555**), is open daily from 9am to 5pm.

SPECIAL EVENTS Two unique celebrations that happen in this region are the March **Whangamata Beach Hop** (www.beachhop.co.nz), a 5-day celebration of '50s hot rods, classic cars, and a whole lotta rock 'n' roll; and the annual **Whitianga Scallop Festival** in September, featuring scenery, sounds, and of course those delicious shellfish (www.scallopfestival.co.nz).

Exploring the Peninsula

If you visit in December or January, you'll be in one of the best places to see the glorious "New Zealand Christmas tree," the pohutukawa, in bloom. The trees cling to the coast or spread out across the sands, then drop their stamens in scarlet mounds that might make you think you've stumbled across a murder. Nothing could be further from the truth; for Kiwis, they signify summer and good times.

At **Goldmine Experience** on SH25 in Thames (www.goldmine-experience.co.nz; © **07/868-8514**), you can take a 40-minute guided tour through a 19th-century gold stamper battery. It's open daily from 10am to 4pm in summer (reduced hours in winter), and admission is NZ$15 adults, NZ$5 children ages 5 to 12.

Although the **Thames Historical Museum,** corner of Pollen and Cochrane streets, Grahamstown (© **07/868-8509**), has surprisingly little about mining, it's a fascinating window into the world of pioneer New Zealand. It's open daily 1 to 4pm. Admission is NZ$5 adults and NZ$2 children. Pick up the "Historic Grahamstown" brochure from the information center to guide you around some of this attractive town's many historic buildings.

North of Thames just past Tapu take the Tapu-Coroglen road to the lovely **Rapaura Watergardens** ★ (www.rapaurawatergardens.co.nz; © **07/868-4821**), a New Zealand Garden of Distinction. It's 26 hectares (64 acres) of

Ride 'em Cowboy!

Bike rides are so hot right now! The **Hauraki Rail Trail ★★★**, 407 Mackay St., Thames (www.haurakirailtrail.co.nz; ℂ **07/868-5140**), is part of the New Zealand Cycle Trail network and claims to be the easiest bike trail in the country. It's 2 days and 77km (47 miles) of lovely and varied riding from the Thames coast into the Waikato through the historic gold-mining town of Waihi and on through the stunning Karangahake Gorge, ending in Waikino. You can rent comfort bikes (NZ$45 per day), mountain bikes (NZ$55 per day), and child buggies (NZ$40 per day) from stations along the way and also arrange lodging; see the website for details.

gardens of peaceful beauty, with lots of waterlilies! The garden is open daily from 9am to 5pm; admission is NZ$15 for adults, NZ$6 for children ages 5 to 15. It has a cafe onsite as well. You'll have to climb 187 steps, but they'll take you to the most famous tree in these parts—the **Square Kauri.** This beauty, the 15th-largest on the peninsula, is about 1,200 years old and has a trunk that's completely square. The track is about 2.5km (1½ miles) past Rapaura Gardens. For regular-shaped kauri, you can see one of the peninsula's best and most easily accessible trees if you do the 5-minute **Waiau Falls** walk, 11km (7 miles) east of Coromandel town on the 309 Road, then continue for a few minutes down the track.

The **Driving Creek Railway and Potteries ★★★**, 380 Driving Creek Rd. (www.drivingcreekrailway.co.nz; ℂ **07/866-8703**), is the heartwarming labor of love of potter Barry Brickell, a hippie with a heart of gold who arrived here in the 1970s and decided to leave his mark on the world by replanting an entire kauri forest *and* building New Zealand's only narrow-gauge mountain railway (over 27 years). He's done both, and it's hard to say which you'll love more. Personally, I think he should be knighted immediately for services to the planet. There are six delightful 1-hour train trips per day in summer from 10:15am: Adults are NZ$30 adults, NZ$13 children ages 4 to 16, and NZ$73 for families. There's also a working pottery and kiln onsite. Kiwi magic.

For really gorgeous local art and crafts, go to **Weta Design ★★**, 46 Kapanga Rd., Coromandel Town (www.wetadesign.co.nz; ℂ **07/866-8823**), open daily from 10am to 5pm, or the slightly edgier **The Source Artist Collective ★★** across the road (ℂ **07/866-7345**).

Over on the east coast, if you can drag yourself away from Whitianga's beaches, check out the excellent **Mercury Bay Museum ★**, opposite the wharf (www.mercurybaymuseum.co.nz; ℂ **07/866-0730**), open daily from 10am to 4pm. It's a fascinating potted history of the area from the arrival of the Polynesian navigator Kupe onwards (NZ$7.50 adults, NZ50¢ children, and families NZ$15). Then get busy at **Arts @ Bay Carving ★★**, 5 Coghill St., Whitianga (www.baycarving.com; ℂ **021/105-2151**), and carve your own bone, shell, wood, stone, or kauri gum work of art (from NZ$45 per person, per piece). Its opening times are flexible, depending on bookings.

Pack your walking shoes and take the **Whitianga Ferry** (www.whitianga-ferry.co.nz; ℭ **07/866-5140**) passenger boat across to Ferry Landing, which has the oldest hand-hewn stone wharf in Australasia, built in 1837. The ferry operates daily from 7:30am to 10:30pm and 11pm on Saturdays (return trip NZ$6 adults, NZ$4 children). It's just a few minutes to Front Beach for a swim or walk on to the **Shakespeare Cliff Lookout,** which has an impressive memorial to Captain Cook's visit to these parts and is a 3km (1-mile) loop track. Around the corner is lovely **Flaxmill Bay.** Stop for a bite at **Eggsentric Café & Restaurant** (p. 138).

After all this activity, you'd probably appreciate a long, hot soak. The **Lost Spring,** 121A Cook Dr., Whitianga (www.thelostspring.co.nz; ℭ **07/866-0456**), has gone from being one man's obsessive search for hot water to quite a big deal in the thermal springs/day spa business. It's open daily from 10:30am to 6pm daily (till 8pm on Sat) and costs NZ$36 for an hour or NZ$60 for a day pass; must be 14 or over.

Organized Tours

Aotearoa Lodge & Tours, 70 Racecourse Rd., Whitianga (www.tournz.co.nz; ℭ **0508/868-769** in NZ, or 07/866-2807), offers 2-, 3-, and 4-day tours of the peninsula around the upper North Island. The 3-day A Touch of Coromandel tour (from Auckland) costs from NZ$1,029 per person.

Doug and Jan from **Kiwi Dundee Adventures** ★★★, McBeth Road, Hikuai (www.kiwidundee.co.nz; ℭ **07/865-8809**), are two of the top guides in the country and will show you the peninsula or the whole of New Zealand if you wish, hiking or touring, in 1 to 16 days. Day tours are from NZ$262 per person.

Cathedral Cove Scenic Cruises ★ (www.cathedralcovecruises.co.nz; ℭ **0800/888-688** in NZ or 027/5555-152) will take you to one of the most beautiful beaches in the region, exploring sea caves and islands. The 2½-hour

---

Wacky Water

Where science meets eccentricity: **The Waterworks** ★★★, 471 The 309 Rd., Coromandel (www.thewaterworks.co.nz; ℭ **07/866-7191**), bills itself as a theme park, but its low-tech, tongue-in-cheek approach to getting kids (and big people) to have fun with the physics and mechanics of water makes this a standout. It has dozens of interactive gadgets and sculptures to keep everyone happy firing water cannons, riding bikes to power fountains, and firing up giant barrel-and-kitchen-knife music boxes for hours. Get even wetter in the lovely swimming hole with the eels! (They don't bite, but might nuzzle your leg if you're lucky.) It's open daily 10am to 6pm in summer and till 4pm in winter (admission NZ$24 adults and NZ$18 children 4–15).

Bathing Beauty

This is weird and wonderful: At Hot Water Beach ★★★, you can dig a hole in the sand and wallow around in natural thermally heated salt water—up to 147°F (64°C)—for 2 hours on either side of low tide. Ask at the visitor center to find out the best time to go.

Magical Scenery Cruise is NZ$75 adults and NZ$45 children 5 to 15. **Sea Cave Adventures** ★★ (www.whitianga-adventures.co.nz; © **0800/806-060** in NZ) does much the same thing for NZ$65 adults and NZ$40 children 5 to 11. Try the **Glass Bottom Boat** ★★ (www.glassbottomboatwhitianga.co.nz; © **07/867-1962**) to get a better look at the marine life of the area. The 2-hour tour to Cathedral Cove (snorkeling included) is NZ$95 adults, NZ$50 children ages 3 to 15. All depart from Whitianga Wharf daily.

Outdoor Pursuits

BEACHES Where to start? Tell your friendly visitor-center staff what you want to do (swim, dive, surf), and they'll recommend the perfect beaches for you.

FISHING A good number of charter operators work from Whitianga, Whangamata, and Waihi: Ask for recommendations at the visitor centers. Tairua Beach is great for surf-casting, while Coromandel's northern islands are good for snapper. Try **Epic Adventures** (www.epicadventures.co.nz; © **0800/374-269**) for half- and full-day excursions (prices on application), and you could end up on their website holding an enormous, scaly creature and wearing a big grin.

WALKING You'll find lots of good walks in the region, or you could step it up a notch and go tramping (hiking) in the **Coromandel Forest Park.** Go to the DOC visitor center near Thames, Kauaeranga Valley Road (www.kauaerangavc.govt.nz; © **07/867-9080**), for details. There's another DOC office in Coromandel town at the i-SITE Visitor Centre (see above) as well. Don't miss the unforgettable walk to beautiful Cathedral Cove, which is part of the Hahei Marine Reserve and has an extraordinary sea cave. You can walk from Hahei.

GOLF The **Lakes Resort Pauanui,** 100 Augusta Dr., Pauanui (www.lakes-resort.com; © **07/864-9999**), is a championship 18-hole course and heaven if you like this kind of thing, with accommodations, a restaurant, the whole works. Greens fees are a substantial NZ$110. The **Dunes Golf Resort,** Mata-rangi (www.thedunesmatarangi.com; © **07/866-5394**), is another top course with food and lodgings; fees are NZ$80 for 18 holes and NZ$50 for 9 holes. Greens fees for the 18-hole **Mercury Bay Golf & Country Club,** Golf Road, Whitianga (© **07/866-5479;** www.mercurybaygolf.co.nz), are just NZ$40. The **Thames Golf Club,** SH26, Thames (www.sportsground.co.nz/thames-golfclub; © **07/868-9062**), is an 18-hole course with greens fees of NZ$40.

SCUBA DIVING **Cathedral Cove Dive & Snorkel,** 48 Hahei Beach Rd., Hahei (www.hahei.co.nz/diving; © **09/866-3955**), does diving and snorkeling trips from NZ$85 and PADI courses from NZ$599. **Dive Zone Whitianga,**

SEE THE sea FROM A KAYAK

A lovely way to view the sheltered bays of the east coast is by kayak. **Cathedral Cove Kayaks** ★★★ (www.seakayaktours.co.nz; ℂ **0800/529-258** in NZ, or 07/866-3877) does half-day tours from Hahei, costing from NZ$105 adult and NZ$65 children 4 to 15. A full-day trip is NZ$170 (NZ$120 for kids).

7 Blacksmith Lane (www.divezone.co.nz/whitianga; ℂ **09/867-1580**), does a similar diving trip (from NZ$175 per person); PADI courses are priced on application.

Where to Stay

Book ahead if you're visiting between December and February. Accommodation tends to be a little more rustic on the east coast.

Campervan sites in **Department of Conservation** campsites are available on a first-come, first-served basis; camping fees are from NZ$10 per adult and NZ$5 per child. Go to www.doc.govt.nz for details.

IN OR NEAR THAMES

Tararu, just north of Thames, has one of the most attractive motels you'll find anywhere. **Coastal Motor Lodge** ★★, 608 Tararu Rd. (www.stayatcoastal.co.nz; ℂ) **07/868-6843**), has delightful A-frame chalets, motel units, and cottages framed by bush and beautifully kept gardens. Get an upstairs unit and you'll think you're sleeping in a cathedral. Rates range from NZ$135 to NZ$170 double. **Cotswold Cottage** ★★, 46 Maramarahi Rd., Totara (www.cotswoldcottage.co.nz; ℂ **07/868-6306**), is a lovely 100-year-old kauri villa (not something you'd find a lot of in the Cotswolds). This very charming B&B has scenic views, and they'll do dinner if you give them a bit of notice. Rooms are from NZ$155 double.

IN OR NEAR COROMANDEL

The best budget choice here is the very roomy and central **Coromandel Top 10 Holiday Park & Backpackers,** 636 Rings Rd., Coromandel (www.coromandelholidaypark.co.nz; ℂ **07/866-8830**), set on 1.5 hectares (3½ acres) of grounds. Rates are from NZ$36 to NZ$350 for two. The three luxury two-bedroom cottages that comprise **Driving Creek Villas** ★★, 21A Colville Rd., Coromandel Town (www.drivingcreekvillas.com; ℂ **07/866-7755**), are as stylish and mod as the delightful Driving Creek Railway nearby is quaint and bohemian: Both are great finds in their own way. The cottages are NZ$325 for two and NZ$40 per extra person. Or sleep surrounded by native bush overlooking Coromandel Harbour in one of the 25 units at **Anchor Lodge** (www.anchorlodgecoromandel.co.nz; ℂ **07/866-7992**); rooms range from NZ$95 to NZ$300.

IN OR NEAR WHITIANGA

If you like apartment living, try **Asure Marina Park Apartments** ★★, 84 Albert St. (www.marinapark.co.nz ℂ **0800/743-784** in NZ or 07/866-0599).

The 60 good-size one-, two-, and three-bedroom apartments overlook the marina, so you can watch fisherpersons and pleasure seekers take to the water as you soak in one of two Jacuzzis. Rates are from NZ$175 for one bedroom to NZ$385 for three bedrooms. At the other end of the scale, the luxury eco-friendly B&B **Within the Bays,** 49 Tarapatiki Dr. (© **07/866-2848,** www. withinthebays.co.nz), has just two guest rooms, both with extraordinary views of Shakespeare Cliffs (from NZ$250 double).

Villa Toscana ★★ Personally, I am of two minds when it comes to replicating Tuscan villas. There's a lot to be said for going to Tuscany for the real thing, but if you pine for cypresses, this is a pretty good substitute. Giorgio and Margherita Allemano certainly are the real deal: Their five-star fully self-contained two-bedroom suite uses lots of Italian fixtures and fittings, but the view is Kiwi all the way. You get your own fancy kitchen and a spacious lounge for kicking back after a hard day on the tourist trail. Giorgio is very proud of his wine cellar, and he's also a marine biologist and keen angler, so if these are also your passions, head straight for this peaceful hideaway.

65 Tarapatiki Dr., Whitianga. www.villatoscana.co.nz. © **07/866-2293.** 1 2-bedroom suite. From NZ$580 double; NZ$100 each extra person. Rates include breakfast and a 750ml bottle of Italian wine. Ask about off-season rates. Located 4km (2½ miles) north of Whitianga. **Amenities:** Washing machine; Jacuzzi; Wi-Fi (free).

IN PAUANUI/TAIRUA

Colleith Lodge ★, 8 Rewa Rewa Valley Rd., Tairua (www.colleithlodge.co.nz; © **07/864-7970**), is a modern luxury B&B with three rooms, a lap pool, and a Jacuzzi. Margaret and Colin speak French and Spanish, which could be *très bon* and *bueno* if your English isn't so great. Rooms are NZ$495; no children under 15. **Harbourview Lodge ★**, 179 Main Rd., Tairua (www.harbourviewlodge. co.nz; © **07/864-7040**), is similar but a bit cheaper, at NZ$275 for two. They'll also lend you spades to dig yourself a warm bath at Hot Water Beach!

Grand Mercure Puka Park Resort ★★★ This lovely upmarket accommodation has always been the posh place to stay in Pauanui (unless you're on very good terms with some of the super-rich boaties who have holiday homes in the nearby Waterways subdivision). It's been done up in recent years and is better than ever. The kindly staff will lug your bags to your luxury "treehouse" in the bush. Standard chalets have a shower-only bathroom; superiors are larger and have a bath and shower. Executive chalets have separate lounge/dining areas, and the Royal Puka Apartment is a freestanding two-story, three-bedroom chalet.

Mount Ave., Pauanui Beach. © **07/864-8088.** www.pukapark.co.nz. 50 units. From NZ$315 for a standard chalet to NZ$1,145 for the apartment. Long-stay and off-peak rates. **Amenities:** Restaurant; bar; babysitting; bikes; concierge; gym; pétanque; Jacuzzi; heated outdoor pool; room service; sauna; day spa beauty treatments; tennis court; watersports equipment rentals; Wi-Fi (in reception only; free).

IN WHANGAMATA/OPOUTERE

If you scan the website for **Brenton Lodge ★★**, 2 Brenton Place, Whangamata (www.brentonlodge.co.nz; © **07/865-8400**), and your eyes stop at

"Chocolate and Us," you'll be thrilled to know the people who run this luxury accommodation *also make liqueur chocolates and truffles.* What's not to love? They'll ply you with yummy treats and even show you how to make them. The rooms and the location are quite heavenly, too, with pretty gardens and private suites. Breakfast is supplied (chocolate for breakfast?) and dinner too if you request it. The suites are NZ$425 double and NZ$100 for extra adults or children. Or you could deny your chocolate fix and venture a little farther north to Opoutere, which has a fine, unspoiled beach, and a small campground: **Opoutere Coastal Camping,** 460 Ohui Rd. (www.opoutere-beach.co.nz; © **07/865-9152**), with comfy cabins (from NZ$75 for two) and chalets (from NZ$100 for two).

Where to Eat

IN THAMES

Thames has traditionally been a town you pass through on your way somewhere else, but its numerous historic buildings are being put to better use these days. The attractive exposed brick and pretty courtyard of the spacious **Café Melbourne ★★,** 715 Pollen St. (www.cafemelbourne.co.nz; © **07/868-3159**), is a great setting. Kim is from Melbourne; husband and chef, Russell, is from Thames. They've started a nice little operation offering treats like pork and apple salad with coriander, very refreshing on a hot day. The cafe is open Monday to Thursday 8am to 5pm, Friday 8am to 9pm, and weekends 9am to 4pm. Behind this cafe is a little strip of (mostly) **specialty food shops** that includes a deli, a juice bar, and an organic butcher—a perfect lineup for picnic dinners on the beach. Open daily from 8am to 4pm, **Sola Café ★★,** 720B Pollen St. (www.solacafe.co.nz; © **07/868-8781**), is a friendly and welcoming vegetarian place with great coffee and a green vibe; it's a member of the environmentally aware Conscious Consumer organization. It's also a funky art space, where changing exhibitions showcase local artists' work.

IN COROMANDEL

Driving Creek Café ★★, 180 Driving Creek Rd. (www.drivingcreekcafe. com; © **07/866-7066**), is the ideal place for lunch after a visit to the railway next door, while you're still feeling the love from Barry Brickell's efforts for the planet (p. 132). These friendly hippies serve great vegetarian food with names like Peace Platter and World Peace Platter (Update Your Peace)—falafel, hummus, dolmades, olives, and other antipasto delights—plus soups, tofu burgers, and more. There's a secondhand bookstore, too. It's open from 9:30am to 4pm and closed Wednesday and Thursday.

    Pepper Tree Restaurant and Bar ★, 31 Kapanga Rd. (www.pepper-treerestaurant.co.nz; © **07/866-8211**), is a different kettle of organically smoked fish altogether: It's an upmarket place on the main street of Coromandel town in a nice old homestead with wraparound verandas—great if you want the passing parade to see you chowing down on your market-fresh seafood dish. It's open daily from 10am to 9pm. Seafood is quite the thing around here: Get your fresh-smoked fish, mussels, scallops, salmon, or roe from the

Coromandel Smoking Co. ★★★, SH25, Tiki Road (www.corosmoke.co.nz; ℘ 07/866-8793), open daily 9am until 5pm with reduced winter hours. But wait, there's more: The **Coromandel Oyster Company** ★, SH25, Tiki Road, Coromandel (℘ **07/866-8028**), is nirvana if you crave these slimy characters. It also sells mussels, *paua* (abalone), crayfish, and other seafood at wholesale prices.

IN WHITIANGA & CLOSE BY
The days of having to choose between one crummy and derivative "greasy spoon" diner and another are pretty much over in the provinces, and nowhere is this more true than in Whitianga, which now has its fair share of interesting eateries. In nearby Whenuakite, try the **Hot Water Brewing Co.,** SH25 (www. hotwaterbrewingco.com; ℘ **07/866-3830;** daily from 11am), which proudly advertises real food and real beer and that they like it real fresh, and, although I'm not crazy about their grammar (what has happened to the adverb?), the grub is great. It offers lunch, dinner, and beer tastings in a lovely, bushy setting; try a refreshing Golden Steamer Ale. **Salt Restaurant & Bar** ★★, 2 Blacksmith Lane (www.salt-whitianga.co.nz; ℘ **07/866-5818**), is the place for fine dining in town and has a beachfront view of the marina. But children are happily welcomed, and the youngsters' menu includes vanilla ice cream and chocolate sauce no matter what you order. Sweet! It's open daily from 11:30am until late. Slightly less upmarket but equally appealing is the **Eggsentric Café & Restaurant** ★★, 1049 Purangi Rd., Flaxmill Bay (www.eggsentriccafe. co.nz; ℘ **07/866-0307**). If you take the little ferry from Whitianga, they'll pick you up at night. Chances are there will be live music; eclectic artwork and great ambience are a given. It's open every day except Monday from 9am till late.

IN PAUANUI/TAIRUA
If you're feeling flush or celebratory, the sumptuous **Miha** at the **Grand Mercure Puka Park Resort** ★★★ (p. 136) is everything you could hope for. The scallops and pork belly were so delicious as a starter I could have ordered it for the main course and dessert. Kids are made to feel very welcome here. Miha is memorable but not cheap: Mains are NZ$30 to NZ$40 (open daily till late). Alternatively, drive to Tairua and eat at **Manaia Kitchen & Bar,** 228 Main Rd. (℘ **07/864-9050**). It's a lively spot that's big on organic produce (open Thurs–Mon 10am till late; closed Tues–Wed). *Note:* An hourly daytime passenger ferry that runs from Pauanui to Tairua stops at 6pm in the summer and earlier in winter, but Mahaia is equally fine as a lunch excursion.

IN WHANGAMATA
Argo, 328A Ocean Rd. (www.argorestaurant.co.nz; ℘ **07/865-7157**), is your designated formal restaurant and wine bar in these parts. It's in the heart of Whangamata, so the views aren't great, but the local produce, craft beer, and boutique wines on offer make up for that. It's open for dinner daily in summer and until 5:30pm in winter. Otherwise, have a look at **Sixfortysix,** 646 Port Rd. (www.sixfortysix.co.nz; ℘ **07/865-6117**), on the main drag and doing roughly the same thing with great coffee and the best local ingredients. It's open daily from 8am but lunch only on Thursdays and Sundays.

ROTORUA, TAUPO & THE RUAPEHU REGION

The thermal cauldron of Rotorua draws visitors from every corner of the globe to marvel at its gushing geysers and rumbling mud pools. Technically it's in the Bay of Plenty, but really should be bracketed with the Central Plateau–Taupo and the major North Island volcanoes in the Ruapehu region: These are the must-sees in this part of the world.

Rotorua was settled by Te Arawa Maori in the 1300s, who must have appreciated having hot baths to cook and bathe in, and the rest of the world eventually caught up. Rotorua's roots as a tourist draw go back to the 19th century, when Maori guides took visitors to see the extraordinary Pink and White Terraces. These were obliterated by the devastating eruption of Mount Tarawera in 1886, but Maori hospitality is still alive and well here.

Volcanic activity also led to the formation of Lake Taupo—the largest in New Zealand. Around 26,500 years ago, a massive eruption left a crater 30km (20 miles) wide and 180m (600 ft.) deep. Today that great big hole is one of our favorite playgrounds for fishing, swimming, boating, and simply chilling out.

Southwest of Taupo is the otherworldly volcanic region known as Ruapehu, which includes the three volcanoes Mount Tongariro, Mount Ruapehu, and Mount Ngauruhoe. Home to two Great Walks, two national cycle trails, three ski areas, a dual UNESCO World Heritage Site, and the longest navigable river in New Zealand, the region is a magnet for adventure junkies. Mount Ruapehu attracts thousands of skiers and snowboarders to its slopes each winter. The mystical Whanganui River also has its source in this region, deep in the national park that takes its name.

ROTORUA ★★★

221km (137 miles) SE of Auckland; 86km (53 miles) S of Tauranga

By New Zealand standards, Rotorua is Tourist Central—we don't call it "Rotovegas" for nothing! But at heart it's still a Kiwi town that smells like rotten eggs (thanks to the sulfur produced by thermal activity), where you can have just about any kind of adventure and be blown away by the power of nature.

About a third of Rotorua's 69,000 residents are Maori—the highest percentage of any city in New Zealand—so this is the place to immerse yourself in their culture.

Essentials

GETTING THERE **By Plane** **Air New Zealand** (www.airnewzealand. co.nz; ℂ **0800/767-767** in NZ) has daily services to and from the major centers. **Super Shuttle** (ℂ **07/349-3444**) will transport you to and from the airport, which is 15 minutes out of town, from about NZ$21 per person.

By Coach (Bus) **InterCity** (www.intercity.co.nz; ℂ **07/348-0388**) also has daily services to and from the major centers, which depart from and arrive at the visitor center.

By Car Rotorua is just an hour's drive from Taupo, Hamilton, and Tauranga, a 2½-hour drive from Auckland, and 5½ hours from Wellington. The roads are good, but watch out for logging trucks, which frequent the highways in this area.

ORIENTATION Rotorua lies on Lake Rotorua's southwestern shore. **Fenton Street** is the main road. It runs south from the lake for 3.5km (2 miles) to **Whakarewarewa Village,** and this is the area's most accessible thermal area. **Tutanekai Street** is the major shopping street, with **City Focus** right in the center, under an eye-catching sail-like structure.

GETTING AROUND Bay Bus (www.baybus.co.nz; ℂ 0800/422-928 in NZ) has a CityRide bus service around Rotorua with 10 different routes to choose from.

You can hail a **taxi** from the visitor center or call **Rotorua Taxis** (www. rotoruataxis.co.nz; ℂ **07/348-1111**). Rotorua has lots of **car rental agencies;** you can get details at the visitor center. The staff will also have information on shuttle services to the main geothermal areas. Shuttles generally cost NZ$25 to NZ$45 per person, and prices sometimes include admission.

VISITOR INFORMATION Go to www.rotoruanz.com, the website for **Destination Rotorua,** the city's official tourism marketing arm. Rotorua i-SITE & Visitor Centre, 1167 Fenton St. (ℂ 07/348-5179), is open daily from 7:30am to 6pm and 7pm in winter. Grab a free copy of the "Rotorua Visitor Guide," a local publication that lists activities, attractions, eateries, and events in the area. And don't forget to soak your feet in the free thermal footbath at the entrance. Redwoods i-SITE & Visitor Centre, Long Mile Rd., Whakarewarewa Forest (www.redwoods.co.nz; ℂ 07/350-0110), caters to recreational

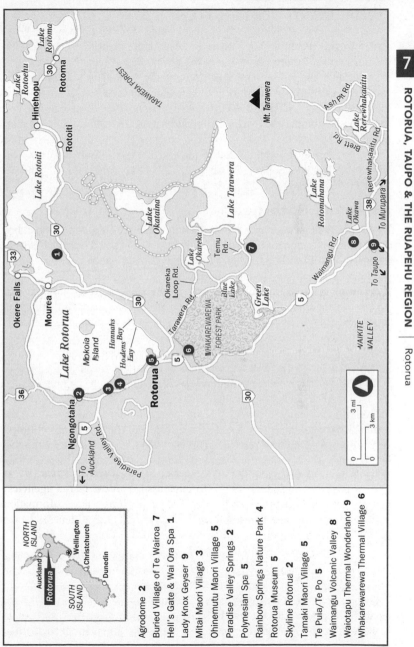

Agrodome **2**
Buried Village of Te Wairoa **7**
Hell's Gate & Wai Ora Spa **1**
Lady Knox Geyser **9**
Mitai Maori Village **3**
Ohinemutu Maori Village **5**
Paradise Valley Springs **2**
Polynesian Spa **5**
Rainbow Springs Nature Park **4**
Rotorua Museum **5**
Skyline Rotorua **2**
Tamaki Maori Village **5**
Te Puia/Te Po **5**
Waimangu Volcanic Valley **8**
Waiotapu Thermal Wonderland **9**
Whakarewarewa Thermal Village **6**

pursuits in the 5,600-hectare (13,838-acre) exotic-pine plantation forest, a popular spot for walking, mountain biking, and horseback riding.

SPECIAL EVENTS The biennial **Opera in the Pa (℃ 07/348-9047)** is a lovely event featuring New Zealand's best young Maori, European, and Polynesian singers performing at a range of Maori cultural locations. It's usually held in January. Rotorua is also very big on sporting events of all kinds, and it can be quite fun to watch other people pushing themselves to the max; you can even join in, if you're up for it! The **Rotorua Marathon** (www.rotorua-marathon.co.nz; ℃ 07/348-3301), which sees thousands of people heading around Lake Rotorua each year, also includes a half marathon, a quarter marathon, and a 5.5km (3½-mile) fun run. It happens in late April or early May. And if you're a winter-visiting music fan, check out the **Rotorua Blues Festival** (www.bopblues.com/bluesfest; ℃ 027/273-8881), which is held annually around the end of May.

Exploring Rotorua

Most visitors to New Zealand come to Rotorua to see its thermal attractions and immerse themselves in Maori culture, but **Mount Tarawera ★★★**, located 24km (15 miles) southeast of the city, should not be overlooked as a destination. The mountain made its presence known back in 1886, when it dramatically blew its stack, destroying Maori villages, killing around 150 people and engulfing the beautiful Pink and White Terraces. But it's peaceful today, and a 4WD drive tour or a scenic flight over the mountain's sizeable crater is a wonderful experience—which I can attest to, having taken a chopper flight to the extraordinary bleak and blasted landscape of the mountain's summit, where you feel like an insignificant creature perched on the head of a sleeping monster. You can get out and walk around, which is a pretty amazing feeling. (See "Outdoor Pursuits," below.)

Even if your time is limited, try to do the scenic flight, and also add these destinations to your must-see list: **Te Puia, Rotorua Museum,** and **Waiotapu** or **Waimangu** geothermal reserves. This way, you'll get to experience the best of Rotorua's Maori culture and natural thermal uniqueness and learn something about its history and place in the world in the process. You can easily do these in 2 days.

Don't Go Jump in the Lake

There are 16 major lakes in the region and you can swim or boat in many of them—but not Lake Rotokakahi, the Green Lake. It's *tapu* (sacred) and thus off-limits even for a little dip. You may get seriously growled at by local Maori if you try.

THE MAJOR SIGHTS & ATTRACTIONS
In the City Area
Rotorua Museum ★★★ The wonderfully elaborate Edwardian building that is home to Rotorua's historical treasure house is a big part of the story here. As well as telling the stories of Te Arawa (the first people to live in this area) and subsequent settlers, the museum

Ask at the visitor center or check the official tourism website (www.rotoruanz. com) for specials and combo deals on Rotorua's attractions. New packages and hot deals are added throughout the year but typically include Tamaki Tours, the Polynesian Spa, Agrodome, Skyline, and other top activities. The **Rotorua Super Pass** (www.rotoruasuperpasses. co.nz; © **07/349-0388**) offers a variety of deals; the standard superpass, for example, will get you into Paradise Valley Springs, Skyline, the Polynesian Spa, and Te Puia from NZ$240.

reveals in sometimes bizarre detail the history of Rotorua's world-famous Bath House, built in 1908 as the "Great South Seas Spa." It chronicles the weird and wonderful lengths predominantly wealthy overseas visitors went to to benefit from the mineral-rich waters of the area. These included taking "electric baths," where electric currents were fed directly into the water. It's a wonder anyone survived. Some of the private treatment rooms, with their fittings hideously stained by the corrosive chemicals in the water, have been left in situ. By the time the bathhouse closed in 1966, it was a maintenance nightmare, described by a visitor as "a place out of hell. The building smelled: salty, dampness, sulfur, a decayed monster." Not so today: A state-of-the-art technology and a sophisticated air-cleaning system keeps all exhibits safe and corrosion-free. Of the two very good 20-minute films, one brings to life the 1886 eruption of Mount Tarawera (love the shaking seats!), and the other is the story of the B Company Maori Battalion that fought in World War II. You can explore the museum from its spooky basement to the rooftop viewing platform.

Queen's Dr., Government Gardens. www.rotoruamuseum.co.nz. © **07/350-1814.** Admission NZ$20 adults, NZ$8 children 5–15. Open daily 9am–6pm in summer and 9am–5pm in winter. Free tours daily on the hour from 10am. Rotorua Stories Cinema every 20 min. from 9am; Maori Battalion Cinema every 30 min. from 9:30am. Cafe and gift shop.

Polynesian Spa ★★★ Hot therapeutic bathing doesn't come much more highly recommended than this: *Condé Nast Traveller* has voted the Polynesian Spa among its top 10 natural spas in the world six times in the past decade. It's divine to wallow in beautifully landscaped pools of hot or warm water right on Rotorua's lakeside. Two types of mineral waters flow into this complex. The Priest springs have high acidity levels and are great for aching muscles, and the Rachael springs are alkaline and wonderful for the skin, thanks to the antiseptic quality of sodium silica in the water. There are 26 pools in total (14 have lake views) in four different bathing areas: the family spa, the adult pools and priest spa, private pools and the lake spa. The last is the most expensive: It has four Japanese rotenburo pools set among rocks and waterfalls beside the lake. You'll pay extra for exquisite treatments at the Deluxe Lake Spa, which has a private bar, relaxation lounge, and free shampoo and conditioner. In the family spa, your little ones can play in the warm freshwater pool or toddlers' pool with mini waterslide while you sit back and

KID magnets

Rotorua has a bunch of attractions and activities with special appeal for younger family members. Take a **gondola** up to **Skyline Rotorua** ★, Fairy Springs Rd., Ngongotaha (www.skyline.co.nz; ✆ **07/347-0027**), and marvel at the amazing views as you hurtle down the intermediate or advanced track on your luge (the little sleddy thing on wheels). You can also do the **Skyswing** here— three people go up, then away like a crazy pendulum at speeds of up to 140kmph (90mph)—or ride a **zipline** or do the **mountain bike trail.** There's also a cafe, a restaurant, a gift shop, a wine tasting room, and a jellybean shop! Actually, you could just live here. Admission is from NZ$28 adults and NZ$14 children 5 to 14 for the gondola to NZ$125 for a family luge pass; adventure passes are NZ$139 and NZ$125. It's open daily 9am to 8pm.

Meet some real Kiwi characters— human and animal—at the **Agrodome** ★, 141 Western Rd., Ngongotaha (www. agrodome.co.nz; ✆ **07/357-1050**). You'll see farm shows (with 19 breeds of sheep!), farm tours, sheep shearing, and sheepdogs in action and find out what

"Get in behind!" means. Clue: It's not rude. You can also book activities like helicopter flights and jetskiing from here. Farm shows are NZ$33 adults, NZ$16 children 5 to 15 and NZ$85 for a family pass. Farm tours on this 142-hectare (350-acre) property are NZ$45 and NZ$22 (NZ$115 for the family). Combos are NZ$62, NZ$31, and NZ$149, and it's open daily from 9am to 5pm.

At **Paradise Valley Springs** ★, 467 Paradise Valley Rd., Ngongotaha (www. paradisevalleysprings.co.nz; ✆ **07/348-9667**), you can see New Zealand birds (such as kea, the world's only mountain parrot), trout, eels, and assorted exotic wildlife, including—somewhat unexpectedly—lions! It's NZ$30 adults and NZ$15 kids 5 to 15; a family pass is NZ$83. It's open daily 8am until dark (last entry 5pm).

Parents might want to sit this one out: **Zorbing,** 149 Western Rd., Ngongotaha (www.zorb.com/world/rotorua; ✆ **07/357-5100**), is a Kiwi invention that involves rolling down a 250m (820-ft.) slope—wet or dry—in a big plastic bubble. It costs from NZ$39 to NZ$78, depending on the ride, and is open daily 9am to 5pm.

supervise in one of two hot mineral pools. Adults can use the large hot mineral pool and the three priest spa pools. The private pools are walled off from the rest of the rabble, if you don't like to bathe in public! Onsite, a spa shop sells skin and body products and a cafe serves healthy snacks and beverages.

Government Gardens, lakefront end of Hinemoa St. www.polynesianspa.co.nz. ✆ **0508/765-977** in NZ, or 07/348-1328. Admission adult pools and priest Spa NZ$27; lake spa NZ$45 adults, NZ$16 children 5–14; family spa NZ$15 adults, NZ$7 children, NZ$39 family; private pools NZ$18–27 adults, NZ$7 children. Spa therapies from NZ$89–NZ$170. Daily 8am–11pm.

Te Puia ★★★ Just 5 minutes from the CBD, this is one of Rotorua's top attractions—it's like a one-stop shop for Maori culture, nature, and conservation. The 60-hectare (148-acre) Te Puia complex is situated in the Whakarewarewa geothermal valley and is home to the **New Zealand Maori Arts and Crafts Institute,** a live kiwi enclosure, the famous and very obliging **Pohutu**

Geyser, and more than 500 steaming, bubbling, seething geothermal features. Established in 1963, the institute has two interactive galleries, and you can watch stone, bone, and wood carvers and flax weavers at work. Over in the geothermal area, the Pohutu Geyser erupts up to 20 times a day, to a height of up to 30m (98 ft.). You can also see rare kiwi in the nocturnal kiwi house, which has been housing the national bird since 1976. If you come back at 6pm for the Te Po Maori cultural performance, you'll get the chance to try food from a *hangi* (earth oven). Spending the day and evening here can add up, cost-wise, but the Te Po Maori performers are among the best in the country.

Hemo Rd., Te Whakarewarewa Valley, Rotorua. www.tepuia.com. ℭ **0800/837-842** in NZ, or 07/348-9047. Day pass NZ$50 adults, NZ$25 children 5–15, NZ$135 family; with cultural performance NZ$63 adult, NZ$32 children, NZ$170 family. Te Po performance NZ$115 adults, NZ$76 children, NZ$410 family. Daily 8am–6pm (winter until 5pm). Guided tours hourly 9am–4pm. Daytime cultural performances are at 10:15am, 12:15pm, and 3:15pm.

Rainbow Springs Nature Park ★★★

Although this is a very kid-friendly place, *every* visitor to New Zealand—young or old—should see a kiwi. And unless you go to a dedicated kiwi sanctuary, it's extremely unlikely you'll see one in the wild. These aren't wild, but they're the next best thing, and you can also see tuatara—our wonderful prehistoric reptiles—plus other native species like kea and geckos and some exotics. The park is built around one of New Zealand's biggest and most successful kiwi conservation operations. The excellent Kiwi Encounter tour takes you behind the scenes at the kiwi nursery, from which some 1,350 Rainbow Springs kiwi chicks have been released into the wild since 1995. Also try the Big Splash, a theme-park style ride that whizzes you through the ecological evolution of New Zealand. Your pass allows you to return the same night and see the nocturnal kiwi as they go about their business.

192 Fairy Springs Rd. www.rainbowsprings.co.nz and www.kiwiencounter.co.nz. ℭ **0800/724-626** in NZ, or 07/350-0440. Admission NZ$40 adults, NZ$20 children 3–15; family passes NZ$99. Admission & Kiwi Encounter NZ$46 adults, NZ$30 children; family passes from NZ$129. Combos with Agrodome also available. Daily 8:30am–10pm (9:30pm in winter).

Volcanic Hills Winery ★

Rotorua might have been lacking a winery in recent times, but it isn't now! Exclusive vintages are made at the base of the Skyline Rotorua site (see above), where you can have a look at the process. Then you can take a gondola up the hill to sample the, er, fruits of their labor in the tasting and wine sales room. The extraordinary panorama is a little different from the gentle, rustic scenes you get in most wineries. (The grapes are grown elsewhere in New Zealand; it's the winemaking process that goes on here.) If you go when Annie is on duty, she'll probably give you a hug and definitely communicate her incredible passion for the product. The funniest thing? One of the two winemakers is called Sean Beer!

176 Fairy Springs Rd. www.volcanichills.co.nz. ℭ **021/750-200.** 3 wine tastings NZ$7.50; 5 wine tastings NZ$13. Wine available by the glass; food platters NZ$6.50–NZ$25. Daily 11am–7pm (11am–6pm in winter).

WHAT'S COOKING? geothermal gems

If you're new to geothermal activity, the whiff of sulfur and the sight of steam wafting from holes in the ground all around can be a little unsettling. But humans have been living alongside this peculiarity in the Earth's crust for a long time now. There are lots of places you can see this energy force at work. **Waimangu Volcanic Valley ★★★**, 587 Waimangu Rd. (www.waimangu.com; ℂ **07/366-6137**), a 20-minute drive south of Rotorua, calls itself "the world's youngest geothermal system." It appeared after the dust (and steam) had settled following the eruption of Mount Tarawera on June 10, 1886, making it the only hydrothermal system in the world completely formed in historic times as a result of a volcanic eruption. There are a number of walks to do here. The main, 1.5-hour walk through the valley takes you past the best sites in the first 45 minutes, including **Frying Pan Lake,** the world's largest hot-water spring, and the extraordinarily blue lake within the **Inferno Crater ★★**, the level of which rises and falls on a regular 38-day cycle. You can also do a boat cruise on **Lake Rotomahana** to visit a separate geothermal system, but you'll see better features on foot. The cruise departs five or six times a day and is NZ$43 adults and NZ$12 children 6 to 16. Walking the valley costs NZ$36 adults and NZ$12 children ages 6 to 16. Only do the 2-hour **Mt. Haszard Hiking Trail** if you're feeling fairly energetic—it

takes up you and over a mountain. Waimangu is open daily from 8:30am; the last admission is 3:40pm (4:40pm in Jan).

Another 10 minutes down the road, **Waiotapu Thermal Wonderland ★★★** (www.waiotapu.co.nz; ℂ **07/366-6333**) could well be New Zealand's most colorful geothermal area. Allow up to 2 hours to wander around the park, although the most impressive bits are mostly in the shorter 40-minute walk. You'll see the **Artist's Palette,** a huge silica terrace of hot and cold pools and steaming fumeroles where minerals turn the ground everything from burnt orange and red to bright yellow, white, and purple; the ochre-fringed **Champagne Pool,** which lies inside this area; bubbling mud pools and the extraordinary chartreuse-green **Devil's Bath,** which is full of sulfur but looks like the makings of a really nasty cocktail. The famously reliable **Lady Knox Geyser** is a short drive down the road but is part of the ticket price and performs daily at 10:15am—a very civilized hour! Waiotapu is open daily from 8:30am to 6pm in summer and till 5pm in winter. Admission is NZ$33 adults, NZ$11 children 5 to 15, and NZ$80 families. If you want to see quite a large mud pool for nothing, look out for the signpost just before the park. Also free is **Kuirau Park,** a good little geothermal area off Pukuatua and Ranolf streets in the city. It's full of gluggy mud pools, steamy seams, and boiling lakes. As with all these sites, keep to the designated

Just Outside Rotorua
Buried Village of Te Wairoa ★ The Pink and White Terraces were once known as the Eighth Wonder of the Natural World, so it's not surprising that visiting Europeans were staying in the village of Te Wairoa when Mount Tarawera erupted in 1886, obliterating everything for miles around. Here, the story of this natural disaster is brought to life. The excellent museum has some interesting objects excavated from the village. You can also explore the

paths. A few stupid people have climbed the barrier fences at night and taken a fatal header into the scalding pools. The watchword, obviously, is be careful at all times.

Located 15km (9 miles) northeast of Rotorua on SH30, **Hell's Gate Geothermal Park & Mud Spa ★★★** (www. hellsgate.co.nz; ℂ **07/345-3151**) calls itself "the beast of all geothermal parks" and also claims to be Rotorua's most active geothermal field. We have playwright George Bernard Shaw to thank for the name: He was told by his religious friends that this was where his atheist soul would go, and the 20-hectare (50-acre) Maori-owned reserve is indeed a rumbling, steaming moonscape of hot-water lakes, sulfur formations, gloopy mud volcano, and the largest hot waterfall in the Southern Hemisphere. There's also a pretty and rather unexpected native bush walk in the middle of it. After your walk, it's heaven to sit in an outdoor mud pool and slather the silky stuff all over yourself, then shower and have a soak in an ordinary hot mineral pool. A spa area has massage and mud therapies. It's open daily from 8:30am to 10pm. Admission is NZ$35 adults, NZ$18 children under 16, and NZ$85 families (or NZ$90, NZ$45, and NZ$215 if you include the mud bath and sulfur spa).

If you need more mud pampering, Hell's Gate's sister property, **Wai Ora Spa,** 77 Robinson Ave., Holdens Bay (www.waioraresort.co.nz; ℂ **07/343-5100**), in the **Wai Ora Lakeside Spa Resort,** blends Maori healing traditions and wellness practices with natural spa products (also available at Hell's Gate). You can also get standard, non-mud beauty treatments in this relaxing space, which won the "Best Luxury Destination Spa" in New Zealand in the 2014 World Luxury Awards.

You can also get mud treatments at the **Spa at QE ★**, 1073 Whakaue St. (www.spaatqe.co.nz; ℂ **07/343-1665**), in the city's old Queen Elizabeth Hospital, which is open on weekdays from 9am to 9pm and weekends from 9am to 5pm. They do massage, mineral, and mud. It's NZ$70 for a single bath and NZ$99 for a double.

Orakei Korako Cave and Thermal Park ★★★ (www.orakeikorako.co.nz; ℂ **07/378-3131**) is a rather lovely and unspoiled geothermal area on SH5, closer to Taupo than Rotorua. It involves a very short ferry ride across the Waikato River and an energetic walk around the reserve and features one of only two geothermal caves in the world. (You'll have to go to Italy to see the other one.) Poignantly, a plaque honors two young Maori men and former guides who died in Libya during World War II. Entry is NZ$36 adults, NZ$15 children 6 to 16, and NZ$92 for a family. It's open from 8am; the last boat trip leaves at 4:30pm in summer and 4pm in winter.

archaeological site and see the remains of Maori *whare* (houses), the Rotomahana Hotel, a flour mill, and other buildings—it's a bit like Pompeii, sans the Romans! Thirty-minute guided tours are part of the admission price. A nice uphill walk winds through native bush to a waterfall.

1180 Tarawera Rd. www.buriedvillage.co.nz. ℂ **07/362-8287.** Admission NZ$33 adults, NZ$10 children 13–18, NZ$5 children 5–12, family NZ$65. Daily 9am–5pm (winter until 4:30pm).

MAORI CULTURAL EXPERIENCES

It's probably fair to say that Rotorua is the capital of Maori culture in New Zealand, so this is a good place to experience it. A number of cultural performances are on offer, which include a *kapa haka* (traditional song and dance) show and a *hangi* (earth oven banquet). The *hangi* is the traditional Maori method of cooking, in which a large pit is dug in the ground and filled with a wood fire topped by stones. These are heated through, and then flax baskets of food are placed on top and covered with damp cloths. Earth is piled on top to create a natural oven. It generally takes about 3 hours of cooking time, and then dinner is served—and everything tastes of wood smoke! The flavor may be a bit of an acquired taste, but you should definitely partake while you're here. Meat and vegetables make up most of the food on offer.

Three major players specialize in these multifaceted cultural performances: **Tamaki Maori Village, Mitai Maori Village,** and **Te Po** (which is part of **Te Puia**). All start their evening extravaganzas around 6:30pm and include lodging pickup and drop-off.

The fact that **Tamaki Maori Village ★**, 1220 Hinemaru St. (www.tamakimaorivillage.co.nz; © **0508/826-254** in NZ, or 07/349-2999), is probably New Zealand's most awarded cultural attraction may have gone to its head a little—the operation is now so large and commercial there's little chance you'll actually imagine you're living in a Maori village in pre-European times. The 3-hour evening tour is very popular nonetheless and offers visitors the opportunity to see ancestors of an ancient tribe going about their daily life for your entertainment: carving, weaving, receiving *ta moko* (spiritual tattoos), singing, dancing, and cooking in the old ways. The cultural performance takes place in the village's meetinghouse and is followed by a *hangi*. You can also do an **overnight *marae* stay** in the village, which includes all food and accommodation in a traditional carved sleeping house. The village experience is NZ$110 adults, NZ$60 children 10 to 15, NZ$20 children 5 to 9, and NZ$280 a family. The *marae* stay is NZ$230 adults, NZ$165 children 10 to 15, and NZ$155 children 5 to 9. It's open daily.

Mitai Maori Village ★★★, 196 Fairy Springs Rd., Rotorua (www.mitai. co.nz; © **07/343-9132**), has a village experience, concert performance, and *hangi* every night (NZ$116 adults, NZ$58 children 10–15, NZ$23 children 5–9, NZ$315 family). Your warriors for the evening arrive rather impressively, paddling down the stream in a *waka* (war canoe). Many visitors feel this is a more genuine performance than what you get at Tamaki—and you get the chance to see glowworms in their natural habitat. As with all these operations, there's a **reconstructed village** where you can see the daily activities and traditional rituals of the local tribes, and you can learn how Maori use indigenous plants for medicinal purposes on **guided bush walks.**

Te Po ★★★ at Te Puia puts on a very good evening show along the same lines. It costs NZ$104 adults, NZ$52 children 5 to 15, and NZ$279 family. You can also see its cultural performance if you visit during the day.

Whakarewarewa Living Maori Village ★★★, 17 Tryon St., Rotorua (www.whakarewarewa.com; © **07/349-3463**), is the original Maori cultural tourism veteran and worth a look. The Tuhourangi/Ngati Wahiao people have been hosting visitors (and their kids have been diving off the bridge to retrieve coins) since the early 1800s. It's a working, modern Maori village in the middle of a geothermal area where the locals still use the hot water for cooking and washing, as they have been doing for hundreds of years. A guided village tour with a cultural performance (11:15am and 2pm daily) is NZ$35 adults, NZ$15 children 5 to 15, and NZ$85 family. Add a *hangi* meal and it's NZ$66 adults and NZ$38 children, which is pretty good value. You can also see the Pohutu Geyser from here for much less than you'll pay at Te Puia. Whakarewarewa is open daily from 8:30am to 5pm.

In addition to these specialists, all the major hotels put on their own cultural performances and *hangi*. These tend to be quite a bit cheaper, and you don't have to travel far. The **Novotel**'s four-course steamed *hangi* and cultural performance is one of the best and good value at NZ$69 per adult.

You are also welcome to visit **Ohinemutu Maori Village** ★ on the lakefront. Go to the end of Fenton Street and keep heading west until you see the historic Tama-te-Kapua meetinghouse, cemetery, and the lovely little **St. Faith's Anglican Church.** Admission to the church is by gold coin donation, and you must ask permission before entering: There's usually someone there who will show you around but you're not allowed to take photographs inside. The church is beautifully decorated with *whakairo* (carvings) and woven *tukutuku* wall panels. A modern but rather wonderful feature is the window that depicts Jesus wearing a Maori cloak—if you sit in the right place with the lake behind him, he appears to be walking on water. The village has lots of thermal activity: The local ladies even cook their Christmas hams over grates in a couple of places. Please be courteous and thoughtful—the village isn't a tourist attraction; it's where people live.

Organized Tours

The visitor center has quite a hefty pile of brochures for half- and full-day tours. Most take in the main geothermal attractions and are similarly priced. For a good-value introduction to some of the city's best features, try **Kia Ora Guided City Walks** (www.nzmaoritourism.com; © **021/782-777**). The guides are locals who know their city inside out and provide a knowledgeable commentary as you walk around landmarks such as the lovely Government Gardens, Ohinemutu Maori village, and St. Faith's Church. Two-hour tours are NZ$30 per adult and leave from the visitor center at 10am and 2pm daily.

Here's something really special that will stay with you forever but requires a good chunk of your time: **Walking Legends Guided Walks** (www.walkinglegends.co.nz; © **0800/925-569** in NZ, or 021/545-068) does two fully guided 4-day treks from Rotorua, on the beautiful **Lake Waikaremoana Track** ★★★, a **Great Walk of New Zealand.** The lake is in the Te Urewera forest, 150km (93 miles) southeast of Rotorua, which, until 2014, was a national park but is now managed by Maori from the Tuhoe tribe. On the 46km (28-mile) **Lake Waikaremoana Walk,** you stay in simple huts. Boat transport carries most of your gear, but you do need to be moderately fit. All gear, food, and transport to and from Rotorua are included (NZ$1,450 for adults and NZ$1,000 for children 15 and under). The 30 to 40km (18- to 24-mile) **Waikaremoana Discovery** is flexible in its itinerary. The main difference is that the accommodation is a lot flasher (you stay in lodges). It's NZ$1550 for adults and NZ$1000 for children.

Outdoor Pursuits

Rotorua almost rivals Queenstown as an adventure-activity destination these days. Here are just some of the things you can do—with the emphasis on exhilarating rather than hair-raising.

FISHING   Overseas visitors to Rotorua are frequently surprised at how close you are to some of the best wild trout fishing in New Zealand. Rotorua, Tarawera, Okataina, and Rotoiti offer the best chance of catching a fish you can post on Facebook! The season is from October to the end of June. Eleven fishable lakes hold both wild and stocked trout. The greatest trout population is in Lake Rotorua, where wild rainbow trout average 1.5 to 2kg (3–4½ lb.) and brown trout 3kg (6½ lb.), and it's open all year round. Your fishing guide can sort out your fishing license. **Trout Fishing with Bryan Colman** ★★ (www.troutfishingrotorua.com; ℂ **07/348-7766**) is run by an acknowledged expert—the longest-serving in Rotorua—who offers light-tackle trolling and fly- and spin-fishing for NZ$120 per person per hour, minimum 2 hours, which can be shared by four people. **Cruise and Fish Rotorua** (www.cruise-andfish.co.nz; ℂ **021/951-959**) will take you out by 4WD or helicopter (and then in a boat, obviously) for fly- and spin-fishing around the central North Island from NZ$50 to NZ$875.

FLIGHTSEEING   **Volcanic Air,** Memorial Drive (www.volcanicair.co.nz; ℂ **0800/800-848** in NZ, or 07/348-9984), does a selection of helicopter and floatplane tours, from NZ$95 to NZ$915 per person. Many of its flights include a tour over (and stop off at) **Mount Tarawera** ★★★ in either craft. **Helicorp,** Rotorua Airport (www.helicorp.co.nz; ℂ **0800/694-354** in NZ, or 07/345-8021), does much the same thing but without the floatplane. Their prices range from NZ$85 to NZ$642 per person.

4WD SAFARIS   **Kaitiaki Adventures,** 1135 Te Ngae Rd., Rotorua (www. nzmaoritourism.com; ℂ **0800/338-736** in NZ, or 07/357-2236), will take you up Mt. Tarawera in a 4WD where you can walk around the crater and learn about this bleakly beautiful landscape and the history of the volcano. It's NZ$149 per person (no under-7s).

GOLF   The Arikikapakapa course at the **Rotorua Golf Club,** 399 Fenton St. (www.rotoruagolfclub.kiwi.nz; ℂ **07/348-4051**), is a links-style 18-hole course that's unique because you can tee off next to a boiling mud pool! Greens fees are NZ$70 and club hire is NZ$30. The company with the genteel name of **Government Gardens Golf** has been bought out by a crowd called **Ballbusters (Our Balls Are Bigger!)**, Government Gardens (www.ballbusters. co.nz; ✆ **07/348-9126**). You can still play a round on the Motutara Golf Course (9 holes) for the ridiculously cheap price of NZ$16, or NZ$40 including your clubs and everything else you'll need. It also has a driving range, mini-golf, paintball, baseball batting and footgolf. Their balls really are bigger.

HORSEBACK RIDING   Claiming to be the biggest horse-trekking facility in this country, the **Farmhouse Rotorua,** 55 Sunnex Rd. (www.thefarm-house.co.nz; ✆ **07/332-3771**), has more than 80 horses suitable for all ages and abilities. You can ride on this working farm over rolling hills and through native bush; all gear is provided. There's also budget accommodation, which you can book with or without a horse ride. Treks range from 30 minutes (NZ$30) to 2 hours (NZ$80). It's open daily, and rides are generally from 10am to 2:30pm.

JETBOATING   Experience the thrill of jet-sprinting on the **Agrojet,** one of a number of pulse-quickening activities at **Agroventures Adventure Park,** 1335 Paradise Valley Rd. (www.agroventures.co.nz; ✆ **0800/949-888** in NZ, or 07/357-4747). They call it a Ferrari on water—you'll reach speeds of 100kmph (62 mph) in just 4.5 seconds, for NZ$49. For a more lasting jetboat experience, try **New Zealand Riverjet** ★★, Tutukau Rd., 34km (21 miles) north of Taupo (www.riverjet.co.nz; ✆ **0800/748-375** in NZ, or 07/333-7111). It offers a range of trips, including the 3-hour Thermal Safari through the very scenic Tutukau Gorge, with free entry to the **Orakei Korako** geothermal park and some thrilling fast stuff on the way back. It's NZ$169 adults, NZ$89 children under 15, and NZ$455 family. (See also "Outdoor Pursuits," in Taupo.)

MOUNTAIN BIKING   Rotorua is the mountain-biking capital of New Zealand and holds all sorts of mad extreme events like Crankworx. For something energetic but a bit less insane, check out the mountain bike tracks in **Whakare-warewa Forest**—about 130km (81 miles) in all. **The Redwoods** is a section of the commercially harvested exotic pine forest that's been set aside for activities that include mountain biking; it has its own visitor center (see "Visitor Information," above). **Mountain Bike Rotorua,** 1 Waipa State Mill Rd., Whakarewarewa Forest (www.mtbrotorua.co.nz; ✆ **0800/682-768** in NZ, or 07/348-4295), will rent you a bike from 2 hours to several days. Depending on the kind of bike, 2 hours costs NZ$35 or NZ$60 for adults and NZ$20 for children, right through to 3 or 4 days (NZ$50 or NZ$100, respectively, per day for adults). Mountain Bike also does guided adventures that may include rafting, kayaking, and hot pools. The operation runs daily 9am to 5pm and has a cafe on-site. Or try **Planet Bike Mountain Biking Planet Bike** ★★, 8 Waipa Bypass Rd., Whakarewarewa Forest (www.planetbike.co.nz; ✆ **07/346-1717**), which does freedom bike rentals from NZ$35 for 2 hours to NZ$55 for a full day. Its guided tours cost from NZ$75 for 2 hours to NZ$115 for half a day.

Go to **www.riderotorua.com** for everything you need to know about Rotorua's world-class trails, maps, and activities.

A Cruise Fit for a Queen

See Lake Rotorua via a breakfast, lunch, dinner, or coffee cruise. The paddleboat *Lakeland Queen*, Memorial Drive, Ohinemutu (www.lakelandqueen.com; ✆ 07/348-0265), was purpose-built in 1986 and overhauled in 2006 thanks to popular demand, ending up 10m (33 ft.) longer and equipped to carry 300 guests. The breakfast cruise (NZ$40 adults, NZ$20 children 5–12) departs daily at 8am; the 1-hour lunch cruise (from NZ$50 adults and NZ$25 children) departs daily at 1pm. The 2-hour twilight dinner cruises, departing Saturdays in the summer months at 7pm, is NZ$65 adults, NZ$33 children. The 1-hour coffee cruise (NZ$25 adults and NZ$10 children) departs daily at 8am and 1pm.

WALKING   You can take any number of delightful free walks in Rotorua, particularly around the region's picturesque lakes. Pick up the *Rotorua Walkways* brochure from the visitor center, which features eight walks ranging from 10 minutes to 2 hours and 45 minutes. The whole walkway is 26km in total and is broken into eight shorter sections. One of these is the 25-minute **Motutara Walkway ★★**, which meanders around the lakefront to Sulphur Bay, passing mud pools and sulfur vents along the way. Some 12km (7 miles) southeast of Rotorua is the lovely **Lake Okareka Walkway,** a 2.5km (about 1½-mile) stroll around the lake and back again. It takes about 1.5 hours and you'll see plenty of bird life. Farther afield, **Whakarewarewa Forest** is not just for mountain bikers. It has a number of well-marked walking tracks for all ages and levels of fitness. Keep in mind that this is exotic pine forest, not native bush, so it's certainly not a must-see, in my opinion. Trail walks range from 30 minutes to 3.5 hours. The 2km (1¼-mile) **Redwood Memorial Grove Track** is the most popular and features giant 67m (219-ft.) California coastal redwoods that were planted in 1901; it takes 30 minutes if you leave from the visitor center.

If you have more time, **Whirinaki Rainforest Experiences ★★★**, Whirinaki Forest Park, Te Urewera (www.whirinaki.com; ✆ 0800/869-255 in NZ), offers 1- to 3-day fully guided walks into this part of the beautiful **Te Urewera Forest,** led by local Maori. You'll pay from NZ$155 to NZ$325.

Where to Stay

With more than 13,000 visitor beds in Rotorua you should be able to find something to suit your needs and budget. There are numerous hotels and motels: Fenton St. is "motel mile" and many boast private Jacuzzis in each room. However, not all of them are thermally heated mineral pools: Some are just ordinary old hot water.

EXPENSIVE

The **Novotel Rotorua Lakeside ★**, at the lake end of Tutanekai Street (www. novotelrotorua.co.nz; ✆ 07/346-3888), is one of the best "big box" hotels (that's pretty much what it looks like) in the city and is very handy to the action. You'll get lovely views of the lake if you book one of the superior rooms. There are 199 rooms—the lake-view superior ones are the nicest—ranging from standard to the Royal Suite, which is huge! This hotel is very kid-friendly, with the Cartoon Channel, free stay and breakfast, and presents for your young ones on arrival. Rooms range from NZ$179 to NZ$650. You might also like the **Millennium Hotel Rotorua ★**, corner of Eruera and Hinemaru streets (www.millenniumhotels.co.nz/millenniumrotorua/; ✆ **07/347-1234**), which is next door to the Polynesian Spa. You'll get great views of the lake, but only if you're higher than the first floor, so it might pay to ask. It has 227 guest rooms, two restaurants, and a bar, and rates range from NZ$120 to NZ$350.

Black Swan Lakeside Boutique Hotel ★★★ This upmarket little five-star gem is packed with style and personality and sits right down on the lake in beautifully tended formal gardens and a conservatory with lots of lovely spots for relaxation. The decor is classic black and white with shots of cobalt blue—love the black dressmakers' dummies with their classy bling! Arthur and Denise are gracious hosts, with Denise heading a team of four spa and beauty therapists in a well-stocked spa with just two rooms (so you won't be deafened by a hen party in full swing). A fulltime chef bakes tasty treats for your room and also whips up delicious dinners on request.

171 Kawaha Point Rd., Rotorua. www.blackswanhotel.co.nz. ✆ **07/346-3602.** 8 rooms. Pool-view rooms NZ$$399–NZ795, lakeview rooms NZ$599–NZ$995. Special deals & packages. Rates include breakfast. Dinner on request. **Amenities:** Croquet & pétanque lawns; Jacuzzi; pool; room service; day spa; Wi-Fi (free).

Koura Lodge ★★ Let hosts David and Gina Wells look after you in secluded luxury in their five-star boutique B&B haven beside the lake. The rooms and apartments make the most of the stunning views and have verandas so you can sit outside for breakfast and maximize your relaxation possibilities. They're all lovely but the upper level two-bedroom apartment is a proper home away from home with a log burner for chilly winter nights and a billiard table to keep you entertained.

209 Kawaha Point Rd. www.kouralodge.co.nz. ✆ **07/348-5868.** 10 rooms. NZ$465–NZ$990. Rates include breakfast. Long-stay rates. **Amenities:** Jacuzzi; free use of kayaks and tennis court; sauna; free Wi-Fi.

Peppers on the Point ★★ This is a lovely property, an imposing 1930s mansion perched on a finger of land jutting out into Lake Rotorua and looking towards Mokoia Island. It has been converted into a nine-suite lodge and there's also a modern four-bedroom villa—and a tiny chapel, should you need one! Although there are other boutique properties on Kawaha Point, this one is set on 2 hectares (5 acres) and remains very private and peaceful. All the suites are large, luxurious, and tastefully decorated; plus, children are welcome. Everything is geared toward your relaxation and enjoyment: I had one of the best therapeutic massages of my life here.

214 Kawaha Point Rd., Rotorua. www.peppers.co.nz/on-the-point/. ✆ **07/348-4868.** 10 units: 9 suites (including a 2-bedroom lake villa cottage suite) and a 4-bedroom villa.

Lake and lodge suites from NZ$985, premier suite from NZ$1185; villa and cottage price on application. Long-stay, off-peak, and special deals. Rates include breakfast, pre-dinner drinks and canapés and dinner. **Amenities:** In-house chef, bar and wine cellar; babysitting; concierge; room service; therapeutic massage room, day spa, gym; Jacuzzis in lake cottages and villa; sauna; outdoor tennis court; Wi-Fi (free).

Solitaire Lodge ★★★   I had a magical stay at this gob-smackingly perfect location. It's perched in splendid isolation on a finger of land edging into beautiful Lake Tarawera just 20 minutes from Rotorua. It's difficult to describe just how special this place is. The buildings are locked into a rather quaint '70s time warp, but the interiors certainly aren't—but you won't be spending too much time inside anyway, unless you're gazing out of the picture windows at the view of the lake and Mount Tarawera. Have I mentioned the view? The good people here will take you trout fishing, up in a helicopter, to the waterfall track, or to the hot spring on the lake and then send you off to bed after a splendid five-course dinner. Privacy, perfection: Please can I go back?

16 Ronald Rd., Lake Tarawera. www.solitairelodge.co.nz. ℂ **07/362-8208.** 10 suites. NZ$1,550–NZ$2,500 per night. Rates include breakfast, light lunch, pre-dinner cocktails, dinner, and selected lodge activities. **Amenities:** Restaurant, bar; use of kayaks, motorized dinghies, fishing equipment; room service; Wi-Fi (free).

The Springs ★★   Classy B&B accommodation in the central city with super-professional hosts Murray and Colleen Ward. This single-level property was purpose-built to house guests, and each of the four lovely rooms has a private terrace leading into the rose garden. You'll love Colleen's buttermilk pancakes with locally grown blueberries, which she whips up at breakfast time.

16 Devon St. www.thesprings.co.nz. ℂ **07/348-9922.** 4 rooms. NZ$325–NZ$420. Rates include breakfast. Long-stay rates. Closed July–Aug. **Amenities:** Guest lounge with library; Wi-Fi (free).

Treetops Lodge & Estate ★★★   Treetops has the feel of a large and very luxurious hunting lodge, which is what it is, but much more besides. The region's poshest accommodation, Treetops is also about preserving things—the native creatures that live on the 1,000-hectare (2,470-acre) property, which includes an 800-year-old forest surrounded by an additional 24,300 hectares (60,000 acres) of Department of Conservation (DOC) land, seven trout streams, and four lakes. You don't need to crunch the numbers to realize that this is a pretty private place to stay, although it's just a 30-minute drive from Rotorua. Seeing it from the back of a horse with an experienced guide is a sublime experience, and it will make settling back in your large and stylishly appointed suite even more of a delight. The place is so spacious you drive a golf cart down to the main lodge for dinner, cooked by Michelin-star chefs, a very fine experience indeed.

351 Kearoa Rd., RD1, Horohoro. www.treetops.co.nz. ℂ **0800/000-313** in NZ, or 07/333-2066. 14 units: 8 villas, 4 lodge rooms, a family retreat, and a cottage. Pheasant

Cottage from NZ$534; lodge rooms from NZ$1,162; lodge apartments from NZ$1,818; villas from NZ$1,968; Owner's Retreat for up to 8 guests from NZ$4620. Rates include breakfast, pre-dinner cocktails, four-course dinner, and selected lodge activities. Long-stay rates and special deals. **Amenities:** Restaurant, bar/lounge; babysitting; bike rentals; concierge; room service; watersports equipment rentals, games room, library, day spa, sauna, gym; Wi-Fi (free).

MODERATE

The smallish, 44-room **VR Rotorua Lake Resort,** 366 SH33, Mourea, Rotorua (www.vrrotorua.co.nz; ℭ **0800/655-555** in NZ, or 07/362-4599), sits on the shores of lovely Lake Rotoiti and is built to make the most of the stunning views. This is a place to relax and enjoy your surroundings, perhaps play a game of giant outdoor chess on the lawn before heading out to **Hell's Gate** or **Whakarewarewa Forest,** both of which are close by. It's only a 15-minute drive from the city and good value, with rooms from just NZ$125. **Regal Palms 5 Star City Resort,** 350 Fenton St. (www.regalpalms.co.nz; ℭ **0800/743-000** in NZ, or 07/350-3232), is a bit of a find in the central city. This multi-award-winning property has a Jacuzzi in every apartment-style room and plenty of entertainment for the family (mini-golf, tennis, gym, a heated outdoor pool) if you're all a bit sick of staring into boiling mud pools. You'll pay between NZ$185 and NZ$375 for a room.

Wai Ora Lakeside Spa Resort ★★ This lovely resort sitting right beside Lake Rotorua is 10 minutes' drive out of the city and your reward is peace and quiet, absolute lakefront, pleasant rooms, a very nice restaurant and an award-winning spa (see "What's Cooking?" and "What to Eat"). It's a small, modern 4.5-star property, perfect for a spa pampering session: You can get a treatment and order a platter of food while you loll around in your bathrobe! Try to get back into your clothes in time to watch the sun set over the lake, however.

77 Robinson Ave., Rotorua. www.waioraresort.co.nz. ℭ **07/343-5100.** 30 units. NZ$189–NZ$495. Long-stay, off peak and special deals. **Amenities:** Restaurant; bar; 2 outdoor pools; 3 Jacuzzis, sauna; gym; day spa; valet parking; complimentary shuttle transfers; room service; free Wi-Fi.

Regent of Rotorua ★★ This is a stylish five-star boutique hotel that everyone seems to love. If you think it's reminiscent of the lovely **Black Swan** (above), that's because the owners used to own the out-of-town property as well. The Regent has been transformed from a run-of-the-mill 1960s motel complex into a glamorous inner-city spot with gorgeous suites (from "Cutie" to two-bedroom executive) that have all the modcons and yet are surprisingly good value. And it's nice to know that the warmth of your heating and water come from environmentally friendly geothermal energy.

1191 Pukaki St. www.regentrotorua.co.nz. ℭ **0508/734-368** in NZ, or 07/348-4079. 35 rooms. NZ$200–NZ$495. Ask about special deals. **Amenities:** Regent Room Restaurant; bar; concierge; mini-gym; laundry; heated outdoor pool & thermal indoor pool; day spa; Wi-Fi (free).

Maori Hospitality at Its Best

Manaakitanga, or the concept of hospitality, is very important to Maori, and here's a place where you can experience it firsthand. **Maruata Rotorua** ★★, 2 Kuirau St. (www.maruata.co.nz; ✆ 021/801-559), run by the Nathan family, who are Te Arawa Maori, is a modern and stylish self-contained four-star holiday house right next to the inner-city geothermal wonderland that is Kuirau Park. You can learn more about Maori culture here through art, music, videos, books, wine, and food. It has contemporary Maori art on the walls (some for sale), free Wi-Fi throughout, and a thermal pool for your exclusive use. Rares run from NZ$295 per night but drop for longer stays.

INEXPENSIVE

Quest Rotorua Central ★, 1192 Hinemoa St. (www.questrotoruacentral. co.nz; ✆ 07/929-9808), is a centrally located complex with 36 self-contained apartments from studio to executive. Rooms are from NZ$155 to NZ$199, but special packages are often available. Wi-Fi throughout the complex is free, which is another plus. The **Sport of Kings Motel,** 6 Peace St., Fenton Park (www.sportofkings.motel.co.nz; ✆ 0800/508-246 in NZ, or 07/348-2135), is a very reasonably priced 4.5-star motel that's owned and operated by local Kiwis who know Rotorua inside and out. The motel has 16 ground-floor rooms, from studios to two-bedroom apartments, many with their own private Jacuzzi. The reception area is a mini-gallery featuring the owners' original native-bird artwork: You can take a little piece of them home with you! Rooms are from NZ$139 to NZ$225.

Silver Fern Rotorua ★ You'll get very friendly service and clean, spacious rooms at this five-star motel on the main drag. Accommodation ranges from studios to two-bedroom suites. Every room comes with a spa bath or spa pool, which is good news if you need a massage to round out the pampering—the day spa is way cheaper than many others in town.

326 Fenton St. www.silverfernrotorua.co.nz. ✆0800/118-808 in NZ, or 07/346-3849. 25 units. NZ$135–NZ$280. Ask about special deals and packages. Breakfast on request. **Amenities:** Babysitting; bikes; laundry; room service; day spa; Wi-Fi (free).

Where to Eat

It's hasn't been that long since lunch in Rotorua meant a sausage roll and a terrible coffee in a polystyrene cup, but as tourism has flourished, so too have good places to eat. Hardly any of the big attractions are without a cafe now, and although some are better than others, you'll have plenty of good options to choose from all over the region—and that goes for dinner choices, too. Most decent places serve vegetarian, vegan, and gluten-free options.

EXPENSIVE

Mokoia Restaurant ★★ CONTEMPORARY/PACIFIC RIM Stunning lake views and what many consider to be the best food in Rotorua are what you get at this resort restaurant that's open to the public. Expect interesting combinations that show off indigenous ingredients like *kawakawa* (a peppery leaf), *manuka* (tea tree), *piko piko* (fern shoots), and Maori potatoes. The delicate yet crunchy quail tempura infused with horopito and Mata beer on Pacific slaw with mango salsa and lotus crisps is a winner. The avocado ice cream is surprising!

77 Robinson Ave., Holdens Bay, Rotorua. www.mokoiarestaurant.co.nz. © **07/345-4117.** Dinner reservations recommended. Main courses NZ$36–NZ$44. Daily from 7am; dinner 6–10:30pm.

Stratosfare ★★ CONTEMPORARY NEW ZEALAND You can't really come to Rotorua and not take a gondola ride up to the everexpanding Skyline complex. Whether or not you luge or mountain bike your way down is up to you, but eating here is quite cost-effective, as your lunch or dinner includes the price of the gondola ride. The big, swanky dining room with stunning views has been reworked from a standard restaurant to a cross between a very good buffet and an à la carte place. Lots of delicious, freshly prepared items are grouped into food or ethnic families (seafood, Mediterranean, antipasti, and so on), and in the cooked-to-order meat section, the chefs will grill standard and premium cuts or seafood, like wagyu beef and crayfish (these cost a little extra). Desserts? But of course: Crêpes are a specialty, but the crème brulée—always a good test of a restaurant—was one of the best I've ever had.

Fairy Springs Rd., Rotorua. www.skyline.co.nz. © **07/347-0027.** Dinner reservations recommended. Lunch/gondola NZ$54 for adults, NZ$29 for children 11–14, and NZ$19 for children 5–10. Dinner/gondola NZ$77 for adults, NZ$39 for children 11–14, and NZ$29 for children 5–10. Daily 11:30am till late.

Regent Room Restaurant & Wine Bar ★★ CONTEMPORARY PACIFIC FUSION In keeping with everything else about this boutique hotel, the restaurant, which is open to the public, is stylish and sumptuous. That goes for the food as well. It serves all things fresh and seasonal, but the meat courses are particularly good—this place has won New Zealand Beef and Lamb excellence awards twice in recent years and was crowned Rotorua Hotel Restaurant of the Year in 2013. And isn't it a good sign when you've already chosen your dessert before your main course arrives?

1191 Pukaki St. www.regentrotorua.co.nz. © **07/348-4079.** Dinner reservations recommended. Main courses NZ$34–NZ$38. Daily 6:30am till late.

MODERATE

Urbano, 289 Fenton St. (www.urbanobistro.co.nz; © **07/349-3770**), is a modern bistro that does contemporary, unfussy breakfast, brunch, lunch, and dinner located in the "motel mile" area of Rotorua, if you happen to be staying out that way. It's open Monday to Saturday from 9am till 11pm and Sunday from 9am to 3pm. Smiling staff and a lean towards Moroccan cuisine keep bringing customers back to **Abracadabra Café,** 1263 Amohia St. (www.abracadabracafe.com; © **07/348-3883**), an all-day eatery in a funky 1940s house with a groovy garden bar that really lends itself to tapas and a glass of wine. It's open Tuesday to Saturday from 10:30am to 11pm and Sunday from 10:30am to 6pm. **Relish Café,** 1149 Tutanekai St. (www.relishcafe.co.nz; ℗ **07/343-9195**), is in the next block down from Eat Streat (see above) and is the place to go if you fancy a wood-fired pizza. It would probably draw the line at making you a pizza for breakfast, but there are plenty of other delicious options for breakfast, lunch, and dinner, including very yummy seafood chowder. It's open Tuesday to Sunday from 7:30am to 3pm and then 5:30pm till late. The rather underwhelming sounding **Picnic Café,** 1174 Whakaue St. (℗ **07/343-9239**), delivers up reliably good breakfasts, brunches, and lunches with excellent, friendly service, really good coffee, and ample portions. It's open daily from 7:30am to 4pm.

Sabroso ★★★ LATIN AMERICAN   Sarah and John from Sabroso serve up all good things from the Latin American continent, and people just can't get enough. One happy customer even says she runs the Rotorua Marathon each year just so she can eat here! It's got great, friendly service, wonderful, authentic food, and loads of atmosphere, with vegan options, if this is your thing. And yes, you can get sangria, margaritas, and mojitos. Make sure you book in advance; it's small and very popular.

1184 Haupapa St. www.sabroso.co.nz ℗ **07/349-0591.** Dinner reservations recommended. Main courses NZ$18–NZ$46. Wed–Sun 5–9pm.

Leonardo's Pure Italian ★★ ITALIAN   Genuine Italian food cooked by a genuine Italian: Leonardo Baldi. It's got such a good reputation (the number-one restaurant in Rotorua on Trip Advisor for 2014), that this is where the rich and famous come when they're in town (Robert Redford!). It's also where locals in the know head for. These guys go much further than pizza and pasta: After someone found a bullet in the wild pork stew, the management decided to turn a negative into a positive and offered a $50 Leonardo's voucher to the next customer who found one! That's attitude.

1099 Tutanekai St. ℗ **07/347-7084.** Dinner reservations recommended. Main courses NZ$23–NZ$35. Daily 5–10pm.

Capers Epicurean ★★ CAFE/DELI   This award-winning place is a bit of an Aladdin's Cave. It's a busy spot that takes its food and coffee very seriously. It's also a purveyor of delicious local and imported goodies like sauces, chocolates, teas, balsamic vinegars, and dressings, many of which make good presents to take home. It transforms from a nice breakfast and lunch venue (eat in or takeaway) to a great spot for dinner, serving dishes like peri-peri-marinated lamb rump, spiced puy lentils, and pan-seared venison.

1181 Eruera St. www.capers.co.nz. ℗ **07/348-8818.** Dinner reservations recommended. Main courses NZ$30–NZ$34. Daily 7am–9pm.

Fat Dog Café & Bar ★★ CAFE/LIGHT MEALS   This cafe has been here so long that the original fat dog must have gone to the great kennel in the sky years ago. It's a crazy, colorful, chaotic gathering place for every man and his (fat) dog, and nobody stands on ceremony. It's fun, casual, and still good value,

STREAT food

Eat Street is a bustling, pedestrian-only dining precinct at the lake end of Tutanekai Street in the city center furnished with a covered central walkway with retractable roofing, making it ideal for eating out of doors. It's home to a wide variety of bars and restaurants—from fine dining and contemporary food to the coolest places to be caught enjoying yourself with a glass in hands. Three of the best are **Atticus Finch** (www.atticusfinch.co.nz; *C* **07/406-0400**), which describes itself as "Rotorua's only Mediterranean rim al fresco shared dining experience." You can get main courses too, and they're big on cocktails made with fresh herbs and fruit, with a good selection of wines and craft beers. It's open Monday to Thursday from 5pm till late and Friday to Sunday 11:30am till late. **Ponsonby Rd.** (www.ponsonbyrd.co.nz; *C* **021/151-2036**) is a gorgeous, red-painted, over-the-top cocktail lounge with chandeliers and bling as

far as the eye can see. (The joke may be lost on international visitors: The other Ponsonby Rd. is a very trendy bar and restaurant strip in inner-city Auckland.) The owners have come up with their own locally inspired cocktails, like the Mokoia Sunset and the Hinemoa and Tutanekai, plus you can get a range of wines, beers, and spirits and light meals and, if you're lucky, live music. Opening hours are Monday to Thursday from 4pm till late and Friday to Sunday from noon till late. **CBK** (www.cbkrotorua.co.nz; *C* **07/347-2700**), which stands for Craft Bar & Kitchen, is open all day every day (9am till late) and is Rotorua's only stone grill restaurant—think generous cuts of meat sizzled before your very eyes. But this is not all it serves; in fact, the menu is enormous, with kids and vegetarians (although not vegetarian kids!) well catered for and a great range of craft beers and cider on offer.

although not as ridiculously cheap as it used to be. Some of the food is a bit mad (fried ice cream, anyone?), but you won't leave hungry or wearing a frown. 1161 Arawa St. www.fatdogcafe.co.nz. *C* **07/347-7586.** Main courses NZ$28–NZ$32. Daily 7am–9pm.

Shopping

If you want to see what top artists, jewelers, and craftspeople in this region have to offer, pick up the "Rotorua Arts Trail" brochure from the visitor center. The best places to find traditional Maori arts and crafts are **Te Puia** (www.tepuia.com; *C* **07/348-9047**), which has wonderful stone, bone, and wood carvings for sale, and **Tamaki Maori Village** (www.tamakimaorivillage.co.nz; *C* **07/349-2999**), which has displays of indigenous work at the replica village (but you have to go on a paid tour to access the shops).

Simply New Zealand, corner of Pukuatua and Fenton streets (www.simplynewzealand.com; *C* **07/348-8273**), has New Zealand–made Merino wool knitwear, toiletries, and a whole lot of souvenirs. Be warned: Some of the cheaper lines (like soft toy kiwis and budget jewelry, including suspiciously cheap greenstone) are made in China. This goes for any cheapish souvenir store, not just this one, which has branches around New Zealand. If in doubt, read the label.

Rainbow Springs and Agrodome (see "The Major Sights & Attractions") have good shops that stock wool products. At **Mountain Jade,** 1288 Fenton St. (www.mountainjade.co.nz; ℂ **07/349-3968**), you can watch master carvers working with greenstone (or *pounamu,* as Maori call it). They're fairly open about the fact that some of their stone has been imported, and the piece you've got your eye on might in fact have been carved in China from Chinese jade, not New Zealand greenstone. Just ask. They're open daily from 9am to 6pm.

En Route to Taupo

It's only 84km (52 miles) to Taupo via SH5 on very good roads. You'll pass one of the three main geothermal reserves—**Orakei Korako Cave and Thermal Park**—although it's closer to Taupo than Rotorua (see "Geothermal Gems," above). Eight kilometers (5 miles) before you reach Taupo, you'll see the **Wairakei Geothermal Power Station,** which performs the neat trick of turning underground energy into electric power. Steamy stuff!

TAUPO ★

287km (178 miles) SE of Auckland; 84km (52 miles) S of Rotorua; 155km (96 miles) NW of Napier

In the past couple of decades, Taupo has gone from being a little town by a large lake to a tourism hub for the region with more accommodation providers, food outlets, and activities operators than you can shake a stick at. Because of this rapid growth, the town is something of an architectural hodgepodge, but it has some nice public sculptures and green spaces to relax in and, the focal point—Lake Taupo—is undeniably lovely. The lake has long been a haven for Kiwi families thanks to its great boating, swimming, and fishing opportunities. In the summer months, the city's small population of 23,000 more than doubles, so expect it to be a little crowded during these times—and book in advance.

Essentials

GETTING THERE & GETTING AROUND By Plane Air New Zealand Link (www.airnewzealand.co.nz; ℂ **0800/737-000**) flies to Taupo from Auckland five times a day, with connections to other destinations. **Great Lake Taxis** provides a shuttle service (ℂ **07/377-8990**).

By Coach (Bus) InterCity (www.intercity.co.nz; ℂ **09/583-5780**) buses from all over the North Island arrive and depart daily from the Taupo i-SITE (see below).

By Taxi For service in and around Taupo, call **Great Lake Taxis** (ℂ **07/377-8990**) or **Blue Bubble Taxis** (ℂ **07/378-5100**).

By Car SH1 and SH5 pass through Taupo. Roads in the area are very good, but this part of the world gets pretty cold in winter, so beware of ice. Also watch out for logging trucks. It's 1 hour to Rotorua, 2 hours to Napier, Waitomo, Hamilton, and Tauranga, 3.5 hours to Auckland, and about 5.5 hours to Wellington.

Taupo & the Ruapehu Region

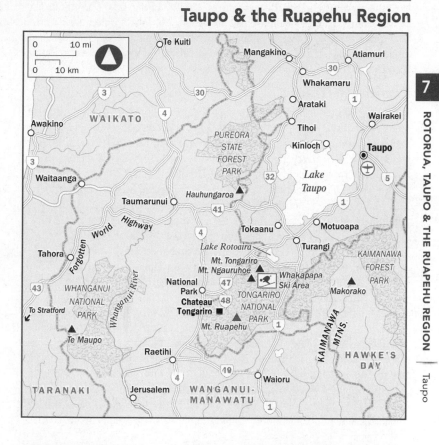

ORIENTATION Taupo township sits at the northeastern tip of the lake, where the Waikato River, New Zealand's longest, flows out of the lake's Tapuaeharuru Bay. **Tongariro Street** is the main drag. Perpendicular to that are **Heu Heu** and **Horomatangi streets,** two of several that form the main shopping area. Tongariro Street runs into **Lake Terrace,** the continuation of SH1 that runs around the lake and where most of the motels are situated.

VISITOR INFORMATION Go to **www.GreatLakeTaupo.com**, the website for **Destination Great Lake Taupo,** the district's Regional Tourism Organization. The **Taupo i-SITE Visitor Information Centre** (✆ **0800/525-382** in NZ, or 07/376-0027) is at 30 Tongariro St. It's open daily from 8:30am to 5pm. The **Turangi i-SITE** (✆ **0800/288-726** in NZ, or 07/386-8999) is at Ngawaka Place and is also open daily from 8:30am to 5pm.

SPECIAL EVENTS If you like to watch other people just about wrecking themselves with exertion, the **Ironman New Zealand,** in March and April, will be just your thing (www.ironmannewzealand.com; ✆ **09/303-0193**). Then there's the **Lake Taupo Cycle Challenge,** held on the last Saturday in

November (www.cyclechallenge.com; ⓒ **07/378-1546**). Come to think of it, there seem to be a lot of masochists in Taupo. Ah, this is better: The **Taupo Summer Concert** (www.greenstoneentertainment.co.nz; ⓒ **07/378-9542**) has top international acts in January each year. Check out www.GreatLakeTaupo. com/Events for a full rundown on what's on.

7 | Exploring Taupo

The **Wairakei Tourist Park,** north of Taupo, is home to many "manufactured" attractions (see "Kid Magnets," below), but one of the best sights manages without our help: **Huka Falls ★★★** is at the top of the hill before you reach Taupo. Here, 22,000 liters (nearly 9,000 gallons) of water squeeze through a narrow chasm before crashing 20 meters (65 ft.) into a super-turbo washing machine of churning mayhem. ("Huka" is the Maori word for foam.) It's not a huge drop, but the power of the falls is incredible. A path will take you alongside the falls, and there's a footbridge so you can get a safe bird's eye view. You can also walk here from town (see "Outdoor Pursuits," below). This area is prone to theft, so lock your car and don't leave valuables inside.

The **Taupo Museum ★**, 4 Story Place (www.taupodc.govt.nz; ⓒ **07/376-0414**), is a fine little regional museum that blends the story of settlement here with the things that make this place what it is—namely, volcanic activity and the lake, which are intertwined, given that one was formed by the other. Add in fishing, logging, and Kiwis on holiday and you've got yourself a museum. The 1960s caravan with its collection of period bathing suits, crockery, and other accouterments is nice, as is the Busy Corner Store. Another thing that sets this apart is the permanent exhibition of the **Ora Garden of Wellbeing,** the New Zealand garden based on Maori spiritual beliefs that won a gold medal at the Chelsea Flower Show in the U.K. in 2004. Admission is NZ$5 for adults and free for children 17 and under. It's open daily from 10am to 4:30pm.

GETTING INTO HOT WATER

Taupo is a great place to steep your body in the natural mineral waters that pop out of the ground. **Taupo DeBretts Hot Springs ★★**, Napier/Taupo Road, SH5 (www.taupodebretts.co.nz; ⓒ **07/378-8559**), in the native-bush-filled Onekeneke Thermal Valley, has been helping Kiwis (and others) to relax for more than 120 years. The water here is thought to have almost magical properties: providing therapeutic relief for muscular, bone, and skin ailments. It has two thermal outdoor pools, 12 private pools, a children's warm-water playground, and a giant dragon hydroslide, as well as a barbecue and picnic area and a day spa. Admission is NZ$22 for adults, NZ$11 for children ages 3 to 12, and NZ$60 for a family pass (NZ$7 for the hydroslide). The complex is open daily from 8:30am to 9:30pm. Like DeBrett's, the **AC Baths,** 26 AC Baths Ave. (ⓒ **07/376-0350**), is a Kiwi institution, and it's great for kids because the water is geothermally heated but not mineral in content, so you can jump in and put your head under. It's a lot flasher these days than it was when I was a kid: It has a large outdoor pool, two lap pools, toddler pools, two hydroslides, a Tarzan swing, four private

KID magnets

7

The **Volcanic Activity Centre**, Wairakei Tourist Park (www.volcanoes.co.nz; 𝄢 **07/374-8375**), does a great job of explaining what's happening in this volcanic region—one of the largest in the world. There are 3D maps and touch-screen computers, a geyser that spouts, a tornado machine, an earthquake simulator, and more. (Maybe don't take your more imaginative kids just before bedtime.) Admission is NZ$12 adults, NZ$7 children 5 to 15, and NZ$31 for a family pass. Okay, so you can get bees and prawns (shrimp) anywhere, but these two attractions (also in the Wairakei Tourist Park) are fun if you want to stop thinking about volcanoes and hot water. At the **Huka Honey Hive** (www.hukahoneyhive. com; 𝄢 **07/374-8553**), you can watch busy bees in glass-fronted hives, and then hit the shop for one of the lovely

jars of honey or ice cream made from the stuff. The shop also has a wide range of honey-based chocolates, fruit wines, and even woolly bees, as well as manuka honey skin and healthcare products. It's open daily from 9am to 5pm in summer and 10am to 5pm in winter; entry is free. At the **Huka Prawn Park** (www.huka-prawnpark.co.nz; 𝄢 **07/374-8474**), the prawns live the good life (for a time) in a Jacuzzi—actually water geothermally heated by the Wairakei plant nearby. You can go on a tour, hand-feed them, fish them up, and then eat them at the **Riverside Restaurant and Bar!** If you're not totally sick of prawns by then, you might wish to play **Killer Prawn Golf.** An all-day pass is NZ$28 for adults and NZ$16 for children 5 to 15 or NZ$69 for a family pass. It's open daily from 9am to 4pm in summer and 9:30am to 3:30pm in winter.

mineral pools, a sauna, and a cafe. But it's still cheap as! (as we say around here): NZ$7 for adults, NZ$3 for children up to 15, and NZ$18 for a family pass. It's open daily from 6am to 9pm.

The little ones are not welcome in the pools at Wairakei Terraces & Thermal Health Spa ★★, next to the Wairakei steamfield (www.wairakeiterraces. co.nz; 𝄢 07/378-0913), which is so aimed at the overseas market it's not funny: You can get the whole cultural experience here if you come in the evening or get your pores steamed if you opt for a spa treatment. It looks pretty, though: They've replicated the original silica terraces that disappeared with the development of the geothermal power plant in the 1950s, but it's an eye-watering NZ$25 just to get into the pools (no kids under 14). Spa treatments range from NZ$80 to NZ$145, and the hangi, concert, and Maori village tour are NZ$105 for adults and NZ$53 for children 5 to 12. (They're just not allowed in the pools.)

If you don't have time for a soak in Taupo, stop at the **Tokaanu Thermal Pools,** at the south end of Lake Taupo (see "En Route to Taupo," p. 160).

EXPLORING LAKE TAUPO

Taupo is New Zealand's biggest lake by a large margin: It's about the size of Greater London. If you want to have a closer look, a number of operators are keen to help. How about chugging around on a replica steamboat? **Ernest**

Hot Dip Tip

For a free geothermal thrill, take the **Huka Falls Track** (see "Walking," below), and you'll find a hot stream that runs into the Waikato River at the Spa Park end of the track. Just after the start of the track, you cross a bridge over the stream; access to the pool is below that. **Note:** As with all natural mineral pools, you mustn't put your head under (in rare cases, dangerous amoeba in unchlorinated thermal pools can be picked up through the nose).

Kemp Cruises (www.ernestkemp. co.nz; ℂ **07/378-9222**) operates 2-hour cruises two or three times a day (depending on the time of year) daily for NZ$40 per adult (or two for NZ$70) and NZ$10 children ages 5 to 15. This is a pleasant way to see the lake, and Ian, the skipper, is a good sport with an entertaining commentary. On board are free tea, coffee, and biscuits. Like most operators, this one visits the **Maori rock carvings** ★★, which are accessible only by boat. Carved in the late 1970s, they're not old but look impressive, looming up out of the water. See if you can spot the numerous small carvings, including one that is reputedly a naked depiction of one of the two artists' girlfriends!

Chris Jolly Outdoors (www.chrisjolly.co.nz; ℂ **07/378-0623;** NZ$44 adults and NZ$16 children) has four nice big launches that ferry passengers around in comfort three times a day—and the homemade muffins are very nice!

If you want to feel the wind in your hair, hop aboard a beautiful old yacht with **Sail Fearless** (www.sailfearless.co.nz; ℂ **022/189-1847;** NZ$35 adults and NZ$10 children). You can even swim if you wish.

All boat trips leave from **Taupo Marina.** Book at the visitor center or harbor office.

Outdoor Pursuits

CYCLING   Bike tours and rentals can be arranged through **Rapid Sensations,** 413 Huka Falls Rd. (www.rapids.co.nz; ℂ **0800/353-435** in NZ, or 07/374-8117). Guided tours include the **Craters of the Moon** thermal area and the **Huka Falls** track, a 2.5-hour ride that costs NZ$75 per person. Freedom bike hire is from NZ$40 for 2 hours for an adult and from NZ$25 for a child. **Pack & Pedal,** 5 Tamamutu St. (www.skiandbiketaupo.wix.com/pack-and-pedal; ℂ **07/377-4346**), do rentals only—NZ$40 for up to 4 hours and NZ$60 for a full day—and they'll help out with kids' bikes, too.

For more information, go to **www.biketaupo.org.nz**.

FISHING   If trapping a trout floats your boat, Lake Taupo—and especially Turangi (known as the trout fishing capital of New Zealand)—is the place to be. The first little baby trout were released into this lake more than 100 years ago. In the 1920s, U.S. author Zane Grey discovered the Tongariro River (the most important spawning river in the region) and raved about it in his book *Tales of the Angler's Eldorado.* These days you need a Taupo-issued fishing license, which is good for a day or a full season. The minimum legal size is 40cm (16 in.), and the daily limit is three fish. The best river fishing is during the winter spawning runs (June–Sept), but lake fishing is good all year. There are dozens of fishing guides and charter operators in these parts, with widely varying prices, depending on whether they offer you tea and bikkies or a basic service, so inquire at the visitor center for recommendations.

FLIGHTSEEING   Take off and land in the water with a scenic ride in **Taupo's Floatplane** ★★ (www.tauposfloatplane.co.nz; ☏ **07/378-7500**). Flights leave from the lakefront near Taupo Boat Harbor and range from 10 minutes whizzing over Taupo (NZ$105 adults; NZ$52 children) to a 2-hour White Island excursion (NZ$790 adults; NZ$395 children). If you want to go up in a chopper, try **Heli Adventure Flights** (www.helicoptertours.co.nz; ☏ **0508/435-474** in NZ; NZ$99–NZ$740 per person) or **Inflite Charters** (www.inflitecharters.com; ☏ **0800/435-488** in NZ; NZ$99 for 9 min. to NZ$790 for 90 min).

GOLF   **Wairakei Golf and Sanctuary,** SH1 (www.wairakeigolfcourse.co.nz; ☏ **07/374-8152**), is a championship course that has expanded in recent years. It's pretty expensive: Greens fees are NZ$185 for nonaffiliated members, and you'll need to book in advance. This establishment now also includes a predator-free wildlife sanctuary, a pro shop, bar, and cafe. **The Kinloch Club,** 261 Kinloch Rd. (www.thekinlochclub.com; ☏ **07/378-6933**), is one of New Zealand's top courses, and greens fees are a staggering NZ$235. You may prefer the **Taupo Golf Club,** 32 Centennial Dr. (www.taupogolf.co.nz; ☏ **07/378-6933**), one of the very few New Zealand clubs to have two 18-hole courses—choose between the Centennial or the Tauhara courses. Greens fees are NZ$69 and NZ$49 for nonaffiliated members.

JETBOATING   Jetboats operate in three areas on the Waikato River. **Hukafalls Jet** ★★★, Wairakei Tourist Park (www.hukafallsjet.co.nz; ☏ **0800/485-253** in NZ, or 07/374-8572), streaks around the base of the Huka Falls, doing fancy 360-degree spins. It's the only company working the falls. A 30-minute ride is NZ$115 for adults and NZ$69 for children under 15. **Rapids Jet,** Rapids Road, Aratiatia (www.rapidsjet.com; ☏ **0800/727-437** in NZ, or 07/374-8066), runs upstream in the Nga Awa Purua rapids; 35 minutes is NZ$105 for adults and NZ$60 for children 5 to 15. A third operator, **New Zealand Riverjet,** takes visitors through the magnificent Tutukau Gorge and Orakei Korako geothermal park. (See also "Outdoor Pursuits" in Rotorua.)

Hobbit Watch

The **Aratiatia Rapids** (down Aratiatia Rd. near Taupo) are the result of damming the Waikato River for hydroelectric power generation. The gates are opened several times a day, and a huge volume of water cascades down. Apart from being impressive, these rapids are also film stars—in "The Hobbit: The Desolation of Smaug," the dwarfs escape from the elves by hiding in barrels and shooting the rapids. You don't need to try this yourself to feel nature's power, however. In the summer months, the dam gates open at 10am, noon, 2pm, and 4pm and during the winter at 10am, noon, and 2pm.

Here's something you can try if you've spent all your money on greens fees: Win dinner or your hotel accommodation at the **Lake Taupo Hole in One Challenge** (www.holein1.co.nz; ℂ **07/378-8117**). The idea is to whack your golf ball 115m (378 ft.) over the water, trying to get it into the tiny hole in the middle of a floating pontoon: a hole in one. Apparently they get roughly one winner per week, scoring free entry into attractions, products, adventure packages, and even overseas trips. It costs NZ$1 per ball, NZ$15 for 18 balls, or NZ$20 for 25 balls. It's open daily from 8am till late in summer, closing at 8pm in winter.

KAYAKING Canoe & Kayak (www.canoeandkayak.co.nz; ℂ **0800/529-256** in NZ or 07/378-1003) will guide you more gently down the Waikato. Its 2-hour tour includes a swim in a hot spring (NZ$49 adults and NZ$29 children), operating daily in summer. It also offers a Maori carvings tour on the lake for NZ$95 per person. **Taupo Kayaking Adventures,** Acacia Bay Road (www.tka.co.nz; ℂ **027/480-1231**), do similar trips, costing from NZ$45 to NZ$240.

QUAD BIKING Take the driver's seat and sightsee by quad bike with **Taupo Quad Adventures,** 24km (15 miles) north of Taupo on SH1 (www.taupoquads.co.nz; ℂ **07/377-6404**). They'll take you riding over hill and down dale on a 250cc Suzuki for 1, 2, or 3 hours, from NZ$95 to NZ$205.

WALKING Grab the "10 Great Lake Walks" brochure from the Taupo visitor center for details on the most popular tracks in the area, walks ranging from 15 minutes to about 4 hours. A popular option is the 3km (2-mile) Huka Falls Walk from Spa Park, in Taupo, along the riverbank. If you continue on to Aratiatia Rapids, this will take another 2 hours.

Where to Stay
EXPENSIVE
Hilton Lake Taupo ★★ Perched on a hill above the Onekeneke Thermal Valley, this Hilton started life in 1889 as the Terraces Hotel. It's has an old and newer section, and rooms throughout are big with views of the lake or the geothermal area. By all means appreciate the historic building, but the new suites and fully self-contained apartments are more suited to the task, especially if you are traveling with kids. They have private terraces or balconies, very nice if you're gazing out at the lake. The Hilton is also home to one of Taupo's best restaurants, **Bistro Lago** (see p. 170).

80–100 Napier Rd., Taupo. www.hilton.com/LakeTaupo. ℂ **07/378-7080.** 113 units. Rooms NZ$190–NZ$1,700. **Amenities:** Restaurant; bar; concierge; outdoor geothermally heated pool and children's pool; sauna; geothermally heated Jacuzzi; gym; tennis court; room service; valet parking NZ$35; Wi-Fi (free in public areas; NZ$10/per 30 min. and NZ$120/per week in rooms).

Huka Lodge ★★★   Really, I could rave on for pages about this superlative, standard-setting lodge, which has won every local and international award in creation. But I only need recall my exquisite embarrassment upon arriving here, having my aging Subaru conk out at reception (battery problems), and how effortlessly they made the car disappear without taking my dignity with it. I owe them big for that. Huka Lodge is simply gorgeous, equivalently expensive, and unless there's something wrong with you, you'll love every minute of it, from soup to nuts, as they say. The grounds (7 hectares/17 acres of immaculate riverside privacy), the gorgeous rooms, the wonderful food and—take my word for it—the best service will stay in your memory long after you have moved on. They'll arrange anything you may want to do, but you and the family may find it hard to venture off-lodge. It has numerous places to dine: from the formal Trophy Room, where you'll be watched by lots of dead animal heads, to a nice spot down by the river. A stay in the four-suite **Owner's Cottage** or the two-suite **Alan Pye Cottage** will practically melt your credit card, but you won't regret it. Both have infinity swimming pools and Jacuzzis and many luxurious touches. Enjoy.

271 Huka Falls Rd., Taupo. www.hukalodge.co.nz. ℂ **07/378-5791.** 19 units, 2 cottages. Junior lodge suites NZ$795–NZ$1435 per person; lodge suite NZ$1395–NZ$2662 per person; Owner's Cottage from NZ$1098–NZ$4620 per person; Alan Pye Cottage from NZ$1390–N7$4620 per person. Rates include breakfast, cocktails, five-course dinner, free Taupo airport transfer, and use of lodge facilities. Off-peak rates. **Amenities:** Dining room; bar and 30,000-bottle wine cellar; babysitting; free use of bikes; concierge; Jacuzzis in cottages; library; massage; outdoor heated pool; room service; all-weather tennis court; pétanque; Wi-Fi (free).

Poronui ★★★   This is primarily a luxury hunting and fishing lodge, so best avoid if you're not keen on the idea of killing things (although it pays to remember that most creatures legally killed for sport in this country are introduced pests). It's a bit like Huka Lodge (see above) but on a smaller scale, with an opulent European-style lodge for main meals (which may include game or fish you've caught yourself) and a roaring fire to relax by. There's even a dedicated fly-tying bench for important angling business. It's set on 6,475 hectares (16,000 acres) of wilderness, and hunting and fishing expeditions can be arranged, or you might choose to just go walking in the native bush or take a horse trek. You'll have three accommodations options to choose from: the lodge cabins, luxury riverside camping at Safari Camp, or the elegant Blake House.

Taharua Rd., Taupo. www.poronui.com. ℂ **07/374-2080.** 7 cabins; Blake House; Safari Camp with 2 luxury tents. Lodge rooms NZ$595–NZ$850; Blake House NZ$850–NZ$1030 per double room; Safari Camp NZ$605 per person. Lodge rates include all meals, including pre-dinner drinks and two-course gourmet dinner; same-day laundry service and use of lodge facilities. Off-peak rates. **Amenities:** Dining room; bar and 10,000-bottle wine cellar; massage and spa treatments; library; room service; Wi-Fi (free).

River Birches ★★★   This lovely boutique luxury lodge is tucked away on the banks of the Tongariro River in Turangi, at the southern end of Lake

Taupo. The flyfisher in your party will love being in Trout Fishing Central (there's a webcam that spies on the fish to find the best spots!), but it's a perfect haven even if you have no interest in standing up to your waist in cold water. There are three lovely suites in the main lodge and a separate three-bedroom cottage, plus cedar hot tubs, fine food, and beautiful gardens to wander about in.

19 Koura St., Turangi. www.riverbirches.co.nz. $\circ$ **0800/102-025** in NZ, or 07/386-0445. 3 suites. 1 cottage. Suites from NZ$460–NZ$665. Cottage from NZ$435. Rooms NZ$190–NZ$1,700. Rates include breakfast. Three-course dinner available on request for NZ$90 per person. Long-stay rates and special deals available. **Amenities:** Guest lounge; cedar hot tub; gym; DVD library; Wi-Fi (free).

MODERATE

The enormous **Wairakei Resort Taupo ★★**, 640 Wairakei Dr., SH1 (www. wairakei.co.nz; $\circ$ **0800/737-678**), is 7km (4⅓ miles) out of town and set in lovely grounds with glimpses of steam from the nearby geothermal power station. The biggest four-star resort in the North Island is a great base if you're traveling with children—they offer kids' programs and lots of ways for them to blow off steam, so to speak. It has a restaurant, a cafe, two bars, two geothermally heated pools and six Jacuzzis, saunas, a day spa, a children's playground, a 9-hole golf course … The decor is totally stuck in the '90s, but updating all 187 rooms at once would probably bankrupt them. Rooms range between NZ$125 and NZ$250; the Rangatira Suite is NZ$720.

INEXPENSIVE

It seems that Taupo is where motels go to breed, so many are crammed into the small township. With dozens available, choosing one can be hard if motels are your accommodation of choice. The waterfront **Le Chalet Suisse,** 3 Titiraupenga St. (www.lakefrontmoteltaupo.com; $\circ$ **0800/178-378** in NZ), has clean, functional and roomy one- and two-bedroom apartments and is very handy to the main cafe and restaurant strip. Rates are from NZ$135 per night.

The area has lots of campgrounds if you fancy a cabin or somewhere to park your campervan, although these fill up with Kiwis in summer. **Taupo DeBretts Hot Springs,** Napier/Taupo Road, SH5 (www.taupodebretts.co.nz; $\circ$ **07/378-8559**), is another good bet, with the added advantage of its own thermal park: wonderful! The cabins, motel units, and lodges range from NZ$75 to NZ$285 and have free Wi-Fi.

Moon Walk

The **Craters of the Moon** (www.cratersofthemoon.co.nz), off SH1 north of Taupo, is a geothermal area run by a local trust, which means it's super-cheap (NZ$8 adults and NZ$4 children; open daily 8:30am–6pm). The 45-minute walk will take you along boardwalks through a strange and constantly changing landscape that only appeared in the 1950s following the opening of a geothermal power station.

Gourmet Food & Wine Store

"Luxurious taste sensations" is how they describe their wares at **The Merchant ★**, 114 Spa Rd. (www.themerchant.co.nz; © **07/378-4626**), the Central North Island's largest gourmet food and wine store. If you fancy doing a spot of cooking or having a slap-up picnic by the lake, this is definitely the place to go for a vast range of quality local and imported foods such as salmon, cheeses, pasta, sauces, dressings, and salami and many aisles of specialist kitchenware. For a nice wine to go with your purchases, **Scenic Cellars** is the wine shop in the same premises. They're open Monday to Saturday from 9am to 7pm and Sunday from 10am to 5pm.

Where to Eat

If you've come to Taupo hoping to eat some of the region's famed brown or rainbow trout, you'll be disappointed to learn that it's illegal to sell your catch. You can hook and eat it yourself or give it away, but it won't turn up on restaurant menus. However, there is plenty of other tasty stuff to eat around here—you can even catch and eat your own mega-prawns in the cafe at the **Huka Prawn Park** (see "Kid Magnets," above) if that appeals. There are lots of more conventional eateries here, too. Fortify yourself for the day with a beautiful breakfast at **Replete Café & Store ★**, 45 Heuheu St. (www.replete. co.nz; © **07/377-3011**). Simple food achieves the status of high art: I have never seen a more attractively presented plate of muesli with fresh and preserved fruit than the one I ate here on a bright morning with the sun's rays lighting up the offerings on the plate. It was delicious, too! This much-loved, award-winning local eatery sells an eclectic collection of home- and kitchenwares in the shop part of the enterprise, and its deli cabinets are full of tasty things to take home. It's open for breakfast and lunch (weekdays 8am–5pm and weekends 8am–4pm).

Another fabulous, friendly breakfast and lunch spot is **Piccolo Licensed Café ★**, 41 Ruapehu St. (www.taupocafe.co.nz; © **07/376-5759**), which was voted "Best Hospitality Business" in Taupo and the second-best cafe in the Central North Island by *Café* magazine. High praise indeed, but the signature French toast with berries, banana bacon, and maple syrup more than lives up to its reputation. Opening hours are 7am to 4pm daily.

Head out to **Café L'Arté and Sculpture Garden ★**, 255 Mapara Rd., Acacia Bay, Taupo (www.larte.co.nz; © **07/378-2962**), for a bit of ceramic craziness with your cafe latte (what else?). Judi Brennan has created a colorful and rather eccentric business out of her two passions, and if you're not fussy about straight lines and sober furnishings, you'll love this place, which is open Wednesday to Sunday 8am to 4pm.

The **Vine Eatery & Bar,** 37 Tuwharetoa St. (www.vineeatery.co.nz; © **07/378-5704**), is a popular, well-established place that specializes in serving shared plates with fine wines and craft beers. It's open every day for a bite and a drink from 11am till late. **Dixie Browns** ★, 36 Roberts Rd. (www.dixiebrowns.co.nz; ✆ **07/378-8444**), is a big, busy eatery right on the lakefront that does breakfast, lunch, and dinner (and even children's birthday parties) with an assured flair. The enormous plate of lunchtime calamari (always a good test of a restaurant) was faultless. They're open daily from 6am to 10pm.

The Bistro ★★★ CONTEMPORARY NEW ZEALAND   Not to be confused with the similar-sounding place above, this restaurant is run by a dynamic young chef with the excellent name of Jude Messenger, who runs a tight ship and has six kids so he knows a thing or two about hard work. It's all worth it; the end product is fabulous. He uses a wealth of New Zealand produce like Waikanae crab, Hawke's Bay fish, and Taupo sirloin to create wonderful, reasonably priced food in a relaxed setting.

17 Tamamutu St. www.thebistro.co.nz. ✆ **07/377-3111.** Reservations recommended. Main courses NZ$24–NZ$35. Daily 5pm till late.

Bistro Lago ★★★ CONTEMPORARY NEW ZEALAND   Kiwi kitchen wunderkind Simon Gault creates the menus for this sophisticated restaurant in the Hilton Lake Taupo, and most discerning types would say it's the best in Taupo. The views are wonderful, the interior is gorgeous, and you'll be ordering things like lime-cured Akaroa salmon with apple jelly, fennel, horseradish, and crème fraîche; or venison with carrot, orange, buffalo ricotta ravioli, and five spice butter. Yum!

Hilton Lake Taupo, 80–100 Napier Rd. www.hilton.com/LakeTaupo. ✆ **07/376-2319.** www.bistrolago.co.nz. Reservations required. Main courses NZ$32–NZ$44. Daily 7am–11pm.

The Brantry Restaurant ★★★ CONTEMPORARY NEW ZEALAND   This fine-dining favorite hides its talents behind the rather uninspiring facade of a 1950s two-story house, but fans return here again and again for its excellent, surprisingly good-value food and friendly service. The sticky date pudding is a winner!

45 Rifle Range Rd. www.thebrantry.co.nz. ✆ **07/378-0484.** Reservations recommended. Main courses NZ$30. Tues–Sat 6pm–late.

Plateau Bar + Eatery ★★★ CONTEMPORARY NEW ZEALAND   If you're looking for award-winning local cuisine with an emphasis on hearty carnivorous fare, you've come to the right place. Plateau has won awards for its beef and lamb and came out top in the 2011 Monteith's Wild Food Challenge, where all sorts of strange things are eaten. But if you want more regular grub, this should also suffice. On a Friday night it's full of happy locals kicking back and enjoying good food and drink in a festive atmosphere. Despite the meaty accolades, they do fish very well, as I can attest: The big, juicy scallops on a bed of cauliflower purée, followed by *terakihi* (a sea fish) on couscous with lemon beurre blanc, were delightful.

64 Tuwharetoa St. www.plateautaupo.co.nz. ✆ **07/377-2425.** Reservations recommended. Main courses NZ$28–NZ$45. Daily midday till late.

En Route to the Ruapehu Region

This is one of the most interesting bits of road in the North Island: The 101km (63-mile) drive to **National Park** (yes, it really is called this!) will take you along the eastern shore of Lake Taupo and down to Turangi at the southern end of the lake. A short detour will take you to the rather low-key but always fetching **Tokaanu Thermal Pools** (𝒸 **07/386-8575**), which I visited almost daily on family holidays as a child. Even if you don't swim, it has a great geothermal walk, and the slightly warm river is full of contented trout. Or call in at the **Tongariro National Trout Centre ★★**, south of Turangi (www. troutcentre.com; 𝒸 **07/386-8085**), which has interactive displays and an underwater viewing chamber so you can see these fish in their natural habitat. You can also see endangered *whio* (blue ducks) from the captive breeding program as they prepare to fly off into the real world. These special birds live on the fast-moving whitewater rivers in the area.

You leave SH1 and take SH47, which will take you into the magical, otherworldly volcanic region—a high plain of tussock, scoria plains, stunted forests, and awe-inspiring volcanoes. National Park Village is at the junction of SH4 and SH47 and is the entrance to the Tongariro National Park, which gives the tiny township its rather imprecise name, but it's 15km (9 miles) from the Whakapapa skifield.

THE RUAPEHU REGION ★★★

101km (63 miles) SW of Taupo; 143km (89 miles) NE of Wanganui

Stretching from the volcanoes of Tongariro National Park to the banks of Whanganui River within the Whanganui National Park, the Ruapehu Region is a simply breathtaking part of New Zealand.

Tongariro is the country's oldest national park (the fourth oldest in the world) and a UNESCO dual World Heritage Area, recognized, unusually, for both its outstanding natural and cultural features. The name refers to the three sacred peaks Mount Tongariro, Mount Ngauruhoe, and Mount Ruapehu. In 1887, Te Heuheu Tukino IV, Paramount Chief of the Tuwharetoa tribe, formed a joint partnership with the government in order to protect the mountains forever.

Today, the park covers an area of about 796 sq. km (495 sq. miles). **Mount Ruapehu**, at 2,797m (9,174 ft.), is the highest mountain in the North Island and the main skiing area of the North Island, comprising the Whakapapa, Turoa, and Tukino skifields. This volcano is by no means extinct: The last eruption, in 2008, was a small one that trapped a hiker when a rock thundered through his tramping hut high on the mountain. He survived, although he lost a leg. A sophisticated early-warning system is in place, so it's extremely unlikely you'll run into trouble.

Mount Ngauruhoe is a perfect cone rising 2,290m (7,513 ft.). It's also active, but its last temper tantrum was in 2011, when it sent clouds of ash spewing from its crater.

Mount Tongariro is the lowest and northernmost of the three, at 1,968m (6,455 ft.), although you can see by its shape that it must have been absolutely enormous once. Its peaks form the end of a volcanic chain that extends to the islands of Tonga, 1,610km (1,000 miles) away. Tongariro had a little burst of activity in 2012, the first since 1897.

National Park village is the major settlement closest to the Whakapapa skifield, on the western side of Mount Ruapehu. If you travel south on SH4, you'll come to the small mountain town of Ohakune, at the southern end of the park, which is the home base for the Turoa skifield. (Tukino is a private club skifield.) It's also the gateway to other key activities in the region, including mountain biking and adventures on the Whanganui River.

Essentials

GETTING THERE & GETTING AROUND **By Plane** No airlines fly into this region, although **Fly My Sky** (www.flymysky.co.nz; ☎ **0800/222-123** in NZ, or 09/256-7026) runs a helicopter service from Taumarunui airport, on request. **Mountain Air** (www.mountainair.co.nz; ☎ **0800/922-812** in NZ, or 07/892-2812) specializes in scenic flights (see "Exploring the Mountains," below) but also does charter flights to and from the smaller local airports, including the Chateau airfield (near Whakapapa village) and Turangi and Taupo airports. **Air New Zealand** (www.airnewzealand.co.nz; ☎ **0800/737-000**) flies to the closest airports: Taupo and Whanganui.

By Train **KiwiRail**'s Northern Explorer train (www.kiwirailscenic.co.nz; ☎ **0800/872-467** in NZ) stops at National Park and Ohakune every day of the week except Wednesday: from Auckland on Monday, Thursday, and Saturday and from Wellington on Tuesday, Friday, and Sunday.

By Coach (Bus) **InterCity** (www.intercity.co.nz; ☎ **09/583/5780**) provides services from the major cities to the national park.

By Car A ring of state highways runs around the mountains, and National Park Village lies on the western side, with SH4 running through the middle of it. SH1 runs along the eastern side of the park. Mount Ruapehu is about 4½ hours' drive from Auckland and Wellington.

VISITOR INFORMATION Go to **www.visitruapehu.com**, the website for **Visit Ruapehu,** the region's tourism arm. The **Ohakune i-SITE and DOC Visitor Centre,** 54 Clyde St., Ohakune (☎ **06/385-8427**), is open daily from 8am to 5:30pm and has loads of information on skiing, hiking, cycling, hunting, fishing, and river adventures. The **Tongariro National Park Visitor Centre,** Whakapapa village (www.doc.govt.nz; ☎ **07/892-3729**), is run by DOC and has a fascinating display on the region's volcanoes. It's also a cozy place to thaw out if it's freezing outside! The village is at the base of the Whakapapa skifield and is actually on the mountain. Open daily from 8am to 6pm in summer (till 5pm in winter), it has the latest and best volcanic, weather, and track and Whakapapa skifield information, as well as hut and camping passes, maps and brochures, hunting permits, and some warm-clothing items.

The **Taumarunui i-SITE Visitor Centre,** 116 Hakiaha St., Taumarunui (© **07/895-7494**), is open daily from 8:30am to 5:30pm.

Exploring the Mountains
ON THE SNOW

The Ruapehu region is lucky enough to be one of the few places in New Zealand where summer and winter are equally popular. Far from shutting down when it gets cold, the mountain and its tourism infrastructure are a buzzing hive of activity during the skiing and snowboarding season, usually between June and October.

Mount Ruapehu erupted quite spectacularly in September and October of 1995 and then again in June 1996, shortly after scientists downgraded its danger rating after 8 months of relative inactivity. This led to the closure of the Whakapapa and Turoa skifields for 2 years. Nature has found its balance again: The mountain is quiet and the skiing is good, provided enough snow falls in wintertime. If you want an up-to-date picture of volcanic activity on the mountains, visit **www.geonet.org.nz** for the best scientific information. The two fields have more than 1,050 hectares (2,594 acres) of patrolled, skiable terrain and almost the same amount off-trail, with plenty of facilities and geographical variety to satisfy the most ardent powderhound. Since 2001, Whakapapa and Turoa have been collectively known as Mount Ruapehu, making it New Zealand's largest ski area. Lift passes operate on either field.

The **Whakapapa Ski Area** (www.mtruapehu.com; © **07/892-4000**), which sits above the lovely old Chateau Tongariro hotel, is New Zealand's largest. Unfortunately it also attracts large numbers of skiers compared with the ski fields in South Island. But it has trails and runs to suit visitors of all abilities— from the beginners' slope on Happy Valley to the 24 black and black diamond runs over the back. Whakapapa shares some reciprocal privileges with its sister resort, Copper Mountain, in Colorado in the U.S.

During the season the ski lifts operate daily from 9am to 4pm. An all-mountain all-day pass costs NZ$95 for adults, and NZ$57 for children 5 to 18. Sightseeing passes are NZ$30 and NZ$18, and NZ$69 for a family. Multi-day and season passes are also available. Whakapapa has two gear rental outlets, hiring out skis, snowboards, toboggans, and clothing. Day rental of skis, boots, and poles is NZ$41 adults, NZ$35 children 5 to 18, and free for the wee ones. A snowboard and boots is NZ$49 adults and NZ$41 children. There are lots of other ski and snowboard rental companies dotted all over the region, but these are certainly the handiest.

You can get individual and group skiing and snowboarding lessons on the mountain as well; bookings are only necessary for private lessons. Private lessons range from NZ$130 for 1 hour to NZ$450 for 6 hours and run throughout the day. Ninety-minute group lessons are NZ$60 per person.

Major accommodation providers run their own shuttle service to the skifield. **Plateau Shuttle,** 17 Carroll St., National Park Village (www.plateaulodge.co.nz); © **07/892-2993**), has a shuttle service to and from National Park Village to Whakapapa all year round for NZ$35 adults and NZ$30 children.

Roam (www.roam.net.nz; ℰ **0800/762-612**) does the same thing for NZ$40 return or NZ$20 one-way.

For summertime activities in the Whakapapa area, see "On Foot," below.

Turoa Ski Area (www.mtruapehu.com/winter/Turoa; ℰ **06/385-8456**), which sits above Ohakune, attracts fewer people. It offers the longest vertical descent in Australasia and the highest ski lift in New Zealand and, like Whakapapa, has great terrain for skiers and snowboarders of all abilities, with a beginners' area (the Alpine Meadow) right through to exciting backcountry trails and 25 black and black diamond runs. The ski lifts operate daily from around 9am to 3:45pm, depending on the weather. Turoa has one gear rental outlet. Prices for lift passes, gear rental, and lessons are the same as at Whakapapa, except that a sightseeing pass is NZ$20 adults and NZ$14 children 5 to 18, or NZ$46 for a family.

Dempsey Snow Express (www.dempseybuses.co.nz; ℰ **06/385-4022**) runs a regular daily shuttle service between Ohakune and Turoa skifield. It's NZ$28 return for adults and NZ$20 for children 5 to 16. One-way is NZ$25.

The Turoa skifield is only open during the winter (late June to late Oct).

This is an alpine environment and needs to be treated with the greatest respect. The weather in the park is very changeable, and many park users have been caught out, even in the summer months. Always get the latest trail and weather details before entering the park, or you might find yourself enjoying an unscheduled helicopter ride. To get the latest snow conditions and ski information, call **Ruapehu Alpine Lifts** (ℰ **07/892-4000**) or check www.mtruapehu.com.

ON FOOT

Unless you're an ace mountaineer, you'll probably want to do your hiking in the warmer months. All three mountains have some truly fantastic walks—there aren't too many regions in the world where you can do short or multi-day routes in two national parks. The DOC brochure "Walks in and Around the Tongariro National Park" will give you plenty of ideas—treks range from 20 minutes pottering around the Alpine Garden Nature Walk on Mount Ruapehu to 3 days exploring the mountains. You'll be happy to do quite a few unguided, and some require transport at one or both ends, if you don't have your own vehicle.

For a really brief stroll, the **Tawhai Falls Walk** is just 20 minutes and takes in a waterfall, alpine vegetation, and a beech forest. It's accessed 4km (2⅕ miles) below the Tongariro National Park Visitor Centre on SH48. The **Taranaki Falls Walk** ★ is a delightful 2-hour, 6km (4-mile) loop track that starts above Whakapapa village and takes you through native bush and alpine tussock vegetation to Taranaki Falls, which falls 20m (66 ft.) over the edge of a large lava flow that was spat out of Mount Ruapehu some 15,000 years ago. The 7km (4⅓-mile) **Silica Rapids Walk** takes 2 to 3 hours and also starts above Whakapapa Village. You walk to the rapids' creamy-white terraces and follow the cascading stream down through beech forest and subalpine vegetation to the mountain road a short way from where you started. You'll need more time for the **Tongariro Northern Circuit** ★★ (typically 3–4 days), hiking your way around the mountain and staying in backcountry huts, but if

THE BEST 1-DAY walk IN THE WORLD?

The famed **Tongariro Alpine Crossing** (www.doc.govt.nz), at 19.4km (12 miles) long, arguably wins this title: It's definitely one of the finest day walks in New Zealand. The walk usually takes between 7 and 8 hours, and most people start at the Mangatepopo Valley end. You climb up Tongariro's Devil's Staircase and over a saddle between this mountain and its charmingly named "parasitic cone," Mount Ngauruhoe, through stunning volcanic terrain to the Red Crater and the extraordinary Emerald Lakes and Blue Lake.

You can do a couple of side trips while you're up there: to the summit of Mount Ngauruhoe (about 3 hr. up and down) or Mount Tongariro (about 90 min.). After a very scenic lunch, you descend via a zigzag track down through tussock land and native bush to the Ketetahi car park, where your transport will (hopefully) be waiting. The hike involves an overall climb of 800m (2,600 ft.), with a couple of short, steep sections. Excluding total couch potatoes, most reasonably active folk can manage it. Being underprepared is far more of a hazard—people forget that this alpine environment can also be dangerous in summer. So be sure to bring plenty of warm layers, raingear, and drinking water. The walking season is usually November to May, but it's open

year-round. (If you go between the end of Dec and the first couple of weeks in Jan, it's a circus.)

Whether you are a freedom walker or do a guided trip, you'll need transport at either end. Many operators service this track: **Adrift Guided Outdoor Adventures,** corner of SH4 and SH47, National Park Village (www.adriftnz.co.nz; ✆ **0800/462-374** in NZ, or 07/892-2751), does summer and winter guided trips; it's NZ$225 per person in summer and NZ$175 in winter. **Adventure Outdoors Tongariro NZ,** 60 Carroll St., National Park Village (www.adventure-outdoors.co.nz; ✆ **0800/386-925** in NZ), is another good operator that does summer and winter guided trips; cost is NZ$225 per person in summer and NZ$185 in winter.

If you prefer to go unguided, **Plateau Shuttles,** 17 Carroll St., National Park village (www.plateaulodge.co.nz; ✆ **0800/861-861** in NZ), will pick you up, drop you at the start of the track, and retrieve you at the other end, for NZ$35 adults and NZ$30 children; NZ$30 for adults one-way. They also offer accommodation. **Tongariro Track Transport,** 21 Carroll St., National Park Village (www.thetongarirocrossing.com; ✆ **0800/872-258** in NZ), will also get you from A to B and back again for NZ$35 adults and NZ$25 one-way.

you're a keen walker, this designated Great Walk is a fantastic experience. If you aren't particularly well-equipped but want to do a multi-day expedition, several operators will rent you tramping boots, packs, and so on, including **Edge to Edge** (www.edgetoedge.co.nz; ✆ **07/892-3867**).

The busy people who run the Whakapapa ski field never rest, it seems, and also offer walks on Mount Ruapehu in the summer months (www.mtruapehu. com; ✆ **0508/782-734**). The 6-hour **Guided Crater Lake Hike & Cultural Experience** starts with a scenic chairlift ride over ancient lava flows followed by a 2-hour hike up 2,670m (8,760 ft.) above sea level and then back down through a glacial valley. It runs from mid-December to the beginning of May and costs NZ$99 for adults and NZ$75 for children 5 to 18.

BACK IN THE spotlight

The **Forgotten World Highway (SH43)** ★★★ is a remote and rural 155km (96-mile) stretch of road that runs between Taumarunui in the Ruapehu region and Stratford in Taranaki. Until a few years ago, few people used it, which is a shame because it's a scenic gem, with steep, bush-covered gorges and passes, plunging rivers, and even a hand-hewn, single-lane road tunnel, known by locals as "the Hobbit's Hole." It follows ancient Maori trade routes and pioneers' farm tracks, through tiny settlements and the fiercely independent township of **Whangamomona,** which declared itself a republic in 1989 after local boundaries were changed and the people found they were no longer Taranaki-ites but residents of the Manawatu-Wanganui region. To mark this spirited uprising, "Whanga" holds a Republic Day every January, and a new president is elected. **Forgotten World Adventures,** 9 Hakiaha St., Taumarunui (www.forgottenworldadventures. co.nz; ✆ **0800/724-522-78** in NZ, or 07/895-7181), offers an unusual way to explore this route—on decommissioned railway lines using golf carts that have been adapted to run along the rails. There are six tours, ranging from the 1-day 10 Tunnel Tour (NZ$230 per person) to the the 4-day Epic, which is 2 days on the railway line and 2 days on the Whanganui River (NZ$1,950 per person). Tours depart from Taumarunui, Whangamomona, and Stratford.

For **scenic flights, Mountain Air** (www.mountainair.co.nz; ✆ **0800/922-812** in NZ, or 07/892-2812) conducts year-round scenic flights over the mountains of Tongariro National Park. Its most popular flight is the 35-minute Volcanic Explorer, from NZ$235 per person from the Chateau airport, near Whakapapa village. It also departs from other local airports. Flights are daily, from 8am, although this is weather dependent.

BY BIKE

The Ruapehu region is an exciting place for adventurous cyclists to explore. Two of the 22 rides on the New Zealand Cycle Trail originate or finish here, depending on which way you go. One is the **Timber Trail,** which ends in Ongarue, north of Taumarunui (see chapter 7). If you want to do this one from the Ruapehu end, **Epic Cycle Adventures** (www.epiccycleadventures.com; ✆ **022/023-7958**) provides transport, bikes, and "glamping" (luxury camping for softies!). Shuttles are NZ$40 or NZ$50 per person, depending on which circuit of the trail you do, and bike hire is NZ$60 per day.

The other trail is the awesome **Mountains to Sea Trail** ★★ (www.mountainstosea.co.nz), which is typically tackled from the Ohakune Old Coach Road on Mount Ruapehu—starting with a thrilling 1,000m (about a half mile) descent from the Turoa ski field—through both national parks, along the Whanganui River Road, and finishing up in Whanganui, where the river meets the Tasman Sea. The trail is divided into five sections, usually done over 3 days, but a 1-day ride that also includes a jetboat trip to Pipiriki on the Whanganui River is a popular option. **Whanganui River Adventures** (www.whanganuiriveradventures.co.nz; ✆ **0800/862-743** in NZ) will sort you out with this option, including the jetboat ride, bike hire, and drop-off transport, as well as for other sections of the trail. It's NZ$140 per person. **Mountain Bike Station,** 60 Thames St., The Junction, Ohakune (www.mountainbikestation. co.nz; ⓒ **0800/385-879** in NZ, or 06/385-8797), will rent you a bike and organize transport for this and other bike trails in the region. Bikes are NZ$50 a day for adults and NZ$30 for children. **My Kiwi Adventure** (www.mykiwiadventure.co.nz; ⓒ **0800/784-202** in NZ) specializes in the **Ohakune Old Coach Road** ride, the Grade 2, 15km (9⅓-mile) first section of the Mountains to Sea trail. They'll rent you a bike and do a return transfer from National Park Village from just NZ$45 per day.

The famous **42 Traverse** is one of the most popular 1-day mountain bike rides in the North Island, but the 46km (29-mile) route is not for sissies! The Grade 3 trail follows old logging tracks through scenic native bush and streams from the Tongariro Forest near National Park to Owhango, with an overall descent of 570m (1,870 ft.) and some uphill bits as well. Ask for the "Mountains to Sea and Other Great Local Rides" and "Timber Trail and Other Great Local Rides" brochures from the Ohakune visitor center for the full rundown on biking in the region.

Exploring Farther Afield
THE WHANGANUI RIVER & WHANGANUI NATIONAL PARK
The mighty mountains are this region's biggest stars, but this is also the place to embark on an adventure on or around the Whanganui River. The 64km (40-mile) **Whanganui River Road** runs from the little settlement of Pipiriki to Whanganui. It's narrow and winding but well worth the effort: You'll drive past isolated *marae* and historic river settlements, including Hiruharama (Jerusalem), where a Catholic Maori mission was founded in the 1890s by Sister Mary Joseph. Jerusalem was home to the New Zealand poet James K. Baxter in the 1970s during his hippie dropout phase, and he established a similarly inclined community there, which vanished after he died.

At the Taumarunui end of the river road, shortly before it meets the **Forgotten World Highway** (see below), you may be surprised to suddenly come across **Lauren's Lavender Farm,** 1381 River Rd., Aukopae, Taumarunui (www.laurenslavender.co.nz; ⓒ **07/896-8705**). This particularly purple place (when the lavender's in flower, from the end of Dec until early Mar) is beside the Whanganui River, but it looks like France. You can stroll around the lovely lavender fields (admission is free), have a tasty bite at the onsite cafe, and buy lavender candles and beauty products at the shop. The farm is open from the end of October till the end of May; the cafe is open daily from 9am till late in summer and 10am to 3pm in winter.

Navigating the Whanganui River is, oddly enough, one of New Zealand's Great Walks: It has some 239 listed rapids, but it's a Grade 2 river, so most people could have a crack at it in a kayak and come out smiling. The **Whanganui Journey** can take up to 6 days, staying at DOC huts or camping along the way (see below for operators), or you can just do a little watery joyride.

One of the most popular—and rather poignant—destinations is the **Bridge to Nowhere,** a sturdy concrete creation that was built in 1935 deep in the Park north of Pipiriki at Mangapurua Gorge. Returning servicemen from World War I established a farming community here with their families, but life was tough, and by 1944 the valley was deserted. But the bridge remains, and you can get to it by jetboat (see below). Go to **www.whanganuiriver.co.nz** for details on different ways to explore the river. Here are a few to get you started:

KAYAKING/CANOEING Canoe Safaris (www.canoesafaris.co.nz; ℂ **0800/272-3353** in NZ) has 2- to 5-day guided trips between Taumarunui and Pipiriki (NZ$475–NZ$1,075 adults and NZ$350–NZ$695 children). **Whanganui River Canoes** (www.whanganuirivercanoes.co.nz; ℂ **0800/408-888** in NZ or 06/385-4176) offers 3- to 6-day guided canoe trips from NZ$665 to NZ$885 per person. Freedom hire (unguided rentals) is NZ$160 to NZ$180 per person for 3 to 4 days.

Where to Stay

These days, National Park Village is the poor relation where decent accommodation is concerned, and Ohakune and Whakapapa village have quite a good range of places to stay. As usual, the watchword is to book ahead because of this region's year-round popularity, for the snow in winter and the tramping and mountain biking in the warmer months. Taumarunui and points west are still a bit limited.

IN OHAKUNE

Because it's handy to the Turoa skifield and only about an hour's drive to the Whakapapa field, Ohakune has plenty of lodging options. Built in 1995, the **Powderhorn Chateau,** 194 Mangawhero Terrace (www.powderhorn.co.nz; ℂ **06/385-8888**), used to be the most upmarket place to stay in Ohakune. It may have lost that distinction (see reviews below), but it still holds the title for "closest accommodation to the Turoa field" for its location at the bottom of the mountain road. It's an imposing structure that's wall-to-wall pine inside and out—you'll swear you're in a European ski lodge halfway up the Swiss Alps. The large-format tartan carpet might confuse your compass a little, but this large establishment provides a cozy, comfortable bulwark against bad weather. It has two good restaurants and 30 suites (NZ$215–NZ$240), a luxury apartment that sleeps eight (NZ$750), and a separate, self-contained chalet (NZ$350–NZ$400). **The Peaks Motor Inn,** 128 Mangawhero Terrace (www. thepeaks.co.nz; **0508/8437-3257** in NZ, or 06/385-9144; from NZ$125), is a very pleasant motel with warm, self-contained units and a sauna and Jacuzzi for chillier months. **Cairnbrae House,** 1450 Mangawhero River Rd. (www. cairnbraehouse.co.nz; ℂ **06/385-3002;** NZ$220–NZ$320), is a charming rural B&B that makes the most of the region's bounty. Sample homegrown honey, fruit, veggies, and even venison, although you may feel like skipping this last item after you fall in love with the local herd of enchanting Mesopotamian fallow deer. If you stay in December, you'll probably see fawns!

Ruapehu Country Lodge ★★ Five minutes' drive out of town, this very lovely boutique B&B is one of the most upmarket places around. Relax with a glass of mulled wine in front of the open fire in winter and gaze at the mountains from the perfectly manicured gardens in summer. It also backs onto the Waimarino Golf Course, for those interested in playing a round. This is a beautiful property, inside and out, and you'll get a very warm welcome from your hosts Heather and Peter.

630 Raetihi–Ohakune Rd. www.ruapehucountrylodge.co.nz. ⓒ **06/880-0494.** 4 suites. Suites are from NZ$220–NZ$287. Rates include breakfast. **Amenities:** Guest lounge; gym; Jacuzzi; Wi-Fi (free).

Rocky Mountain Chalets ★ These neat little stand-alone cottages are rather like Doctor Who's Tardis: They're an awful lot bigger than they look on the outside, but the room rate is a lot smaller than you would expect. The cozy, stylish homes-away-from-home have two or three bedrooms; a couple of "executive" versions come with a fireplace and an outside Jacuzzi. Each is welcoming, luxurious, and fully self-contained, including a washing machine and dryer. Ride out a wet day watching the 50+ Sky channels or pop over to the gym and games room, which has two more Jacuzzis attached.

20 Rangataua Rd. www.rockymountainchalets.com. ⓒ **06/385-9545.** 42 chalets. Two bedroom chalets from NZ$155; three bedroom chalets from NZ$195; executive chalets from NZ$340. **Amenities:** Guest lounge/games room; gym; Jacuzzis; sauna; Wi-Fi (free).

Tongariro Suites @ The Rocks ★★★ Sophisticated, eco-friendly luxury comes to the country. This heavenly B&B is in Horopito, 7km (4⅓ miles) from Ohakune, and every beautiful, spacious suite frames Mount Ruapehu. Elspeth and Carl can't part the clouds, but they are available if you need anything. You probably won't: So much thought has gone into this property, which opened in 2014, down to the wineglass, candle, and Elspeth's home-made essential-oil-infused bath salts over the deep soaker tub. Landscaping extends to leaving the wild alpine desert "garden" alone, with its tussock and volcanic boulders, although they've fashioned a pond and added a couple of very realistic decoy ducks to encourage wild ones to stop by. Apparently, a visiting professor asked what breed they were.

27 Hutiwai Rd., Horopito. www.tongarirosuites.co.nz. ⓒ **022/088-7529.** 4 suites. Suites from NZ$185–NZ$275. Rates include breakfast pack in rooms. **Amenities:** Guest lounge; mountain bikes; laundry; Wi-Fi (free).

IN NATIONAL PARK VILLAGE

The pickings are pretty slim here, and what's available tends to be the backpacker variety. If you really want to stay in National Park Village, **Howard's Mountain Lodge,** 43/45 Carroll St. (www.howardslodge.co.nz; ⓒ **07/892-2827**), is probably your best bet. It offers guests free shuttle transport on the Tongariro Alpine Crossing and will rent you any gear you might need. It also offers a number of walking, biking, and skiing/snowboarding packages. In addition to backpacker dorms and rooms with shared facilities, the lodge has a range of rooms with en-suite bathrooms from NZ$75 to NZ$195.

IN WHAKAPAPA VILLAGE

The village on the ski field is a bit of a magnet for party-hearty ski bunnies in the winter, but there are a couple of good choices. The **Skotel Alpine Resort,** 1 Ngauruhoe Place (www.skotel.co.nz; ℓ **0800/756-835** in NZ, or 07/892-3719), is a big chalet-style place for rooms for every budget, from backpacker accommodation to superior rooms and self-contained cabins. It's pretty self-contained, with a restaurant and bar, sauna and Jacuzzis, so you won't have to leave the premises. Rooms range from NZ$35 to NZ$100 for backpacker rooms and NZ$175 to NZ$230 for superior rooms and cabins. The resort offers ski and equipment rentals in winter and transport to walks.

Chateau Tongariro Hotel ★★★ It's an overworked expression, but the neo-Georgian Chateau really does deserve the label "iconic": It's one of New Zealand's most recognizable and grand old ladies. It surely has one of the best locations: Built in 1929, it sits solid and majestic at the base of Mount Ruapehu and feels like a haven in any weather. The hotel has a glorious ballroom with enormous chandeliers, a lovely fine-dining restaurant, and a wonderful sense of history. Plus it has one of the world's most bizarre swimming pools: down in the bowels of the building and uplit with blue and green lights. Taking a dip is like being in an aquarium on drugs! You might prefer to play golf on New Zealand's highest 9-hole golf course (NZ$10 per round). Splash out on a suite for a truly memorable stay, especially if the weather is clear.

SH48. www.chateau.co.nz. ℓ **0800/242-832** in NZ, or 07/892-3809. 109 rooms. Standard rooms from NZ$125; Tongariro and Heritage rooms from NZ$160; family rooms from NZ$165; superior rooms from NZ$255; executive spa suite from NZ$325; McLaren suite from NZ$450; Te Heu Heu suite from NZ$1000. Railway station transfers NZ$30 per person return. **Amenities:** 2 restaurants, 2 cafes, 1 bar; free in-house 60-seat cinema; heated indoor pool; gym; guest lounges; billiards room; pétanque court; sauna; Wi-Fi (free up to 250Mb then NZ$5 for 75Mb).

IN TAUMARUNUI

Forgotten World Motel, 9 Hakiaha St. (www.forgottenworldmotel.co.nz; ℓ **0800/101-941** in NZ, or 07/895-7181), is owned by the people who run **Forgotten World Adventures** (see "Back in the Spotlight," above). Whether you're contemplating this journey or just want good proximity to the mountains or the river, this is a good base. The motel has free Wi-Fi in the rooms, which range from studio units (from NZ$100) to deluxe two-bedroom apartments (from NZ$140).

ALONG THE RIVER

The **Bridge to Nowhere Lodge** ★, Ramanui Landing, Whanganui River (www.bridgetonowhere.co.nz; ℓ **0800/480-308** in NZ), is so remote you arrive by jetboat! It's NZ$145 per adult with breakfast and dinner or NZ$50 self-catering in comfortable rooms with extraordinary views.

Blue Duck Station ★, Oio Road, Whakahoro (www.blueduckstation. co.nz; ℓ **07/895-6276**), is a wonderful, multi-purpose operation situated on a working 2,500-hectare (6,177-acre) sheep and beef farm on the banks of the Whanganui and Retaruke rivers. It's about an hour's drive from National Park

Village along roads that are sometimes steep and windy and unsealed in places—basically in the middle of nowhere, which is a great part of its charm. Whakahoro is the starting point for many kayakers on the Whanganui River, and these good people offer jetboating (see "Exploring Further Afield," above), horse trekking, hunting, and bush safaris. The property is also heavily committed to species conservation, in particular the native blue duck *(whio)*, and works in association with DOC. Volunteer assistance is welcome. The station offers two lovely places to stay. The fully self-contained **Blue Duck Lodge** has three bedrooms and a large kitchen/dining/lounge area. Because of the wet climate, the cottage is covered in lichen, but it's a real treasure, set high above a spectacular gorge. The lodge is NZ$195 for the first two people and NZ$37 for every additional adult or NZ$20 for children 12 and under. The very eco-friendly **Frontier Lodge** is also fully self-contained and has three bedrooms at NZ$195 per room per night.

Where to Eat
IN OHAKUNE

Ohakune has gone from being an egg-and-chips kind of town, where filling up fast was the order of the day, to a place with a number of good eateries. The other settlements don't fare quite as well, but hearty food is never far away, even if it's not exactly fine dining. The **Powderhorn Chateau** (www.powderhorn.co.nz; *©* **06/385-8888**) has two restaurants: The **Powderkeg** has hearty but surprisingly sophisticated food (although it turns into a party zone in winter), and the **Matterhorn** serves equally good tucker in an atmosphere that's a little more refined. The former is open daily from 7am till late; the latter is open Wednesday to Sunday from 5:30pm. In Ohakune township, **The Cyprus Tree,** corner of Clyde and Miro streets (www.cyprustree.co.nz; *©* **06/385-8857**), is a warm, attractive-looking spot where you can enjoy a mulled cider by the log burner or chill out with a craft beer in the summer. It's open for brunch from 10am to 3pm daily except Wednesday and daily for dinner from 5pm. **The Bearing Point Restaurant & Bar,** 55 Clyde St. (*©* **06/385-9006**), is another popular place for an evening meal, impressing locals and visitors alike with its excellent food and friendly staff. It's open daily 7am to 9pm. Two cool and welcoming breakfast and lunch spots also on the main drag are **Utopia Café,** 47 Clyde St. (*©* **06/385-9120**), which is stylish and informal downstairs and has an incredible view of Mount Ruapehu upstairs (daily 7:30am–3pm; yummy muffins!), and **Eat,** 49 Clyde St. (*©* **0274/431-426;** Tues–Sun 9am–4pm), a cool, stripped-back, diner-style place that puts the emphasis on healthy stuff, and all the packaging is recyclable. Try the delicious torpedo sandwiches with names like "Funguy" and "Veganator"; the cauliflower cheese soup with bread is fabulous.

IN NATIONAL PARK VILLAGE
The village stills struggles with its "truckstop and backpacker" image, but you'll get a fun if not quiet dining experience at **Schnapps Bar,** corner of SH4 and Findlay Street (www.schnappsbarruapehu.com; *©* **07/892-2788**). You'll

recognize it by the enormous driftwood kiwi sculpture outside. Predictably for an outdoor-adventure type of region, the lamb shanks served on potato and *kumara* (sweet potato) mash is the top seller. It's open daily from midday till late. The **Station Café,** 18 Findlay St. (www.thestationcafe.co.nz; ℂ **07/892-2881**), in the historic National Park train station, is a bit quieter than Schnapps—unless a locomotive happens to be passing by (it's the halfway point for the Northern Explorer train that runs between Auckland and Wellington). This cozy spot does the usual range of breakfast and lunch food and is famous for its lemonade scones. Trust me, they're delicious. It's open daily from 9am.

IN WHAKAPAPA VILLAGE

You might find yourself sharing the **Terrace Restaurant and Bar** at the **Skotel** (see "Where to Stay," above) with a party of starving trampers or ski-ers, but you won't go away with a rumbling stomach. It does breakfast and dinner for guests and others (no lunch) and is open daily. For lunch, you could try the Chateau Tongariro's **Fergusson's Café,** SH48, Whakapapa village (www.chateau.co.nz; ℂ **07/892-3809**), which is fine for a fill-up, and often excellent. It's open Monday to Friday 7am to 3pm.

Ruapehu Restaurant ★★ PACIFIC RIM For fine dining with even finer views, head for the flashy restaurant at the Chateau Tongariro Hotel. It's an elegant step back in time in sumptuous surroundings, but this is still a family establishment and (well-behaved) children are welcomed. Not surprisingly, the most popular dish is the Chateaubriand for two, which tastes and looks great.

SH48, Whakapapa village. ℂ **0800/242-832** in NZ, or 07/892-3809. www.chateau.co.nz/ruapehu-restaurant. Reservations required for lunch and dinner. Main courses NZ$30–NZ$40. Daily 6:30am till late.

ALONG THE RIVER

The **Bridge to Nowhere Lodge** and **Blue Duck Station** (above) both offer food: The latter has a cafe that's open all day in summer for breakfast and lunch (evening meals available on request). Winter is a time for lovely home-made soups, lasagne, and other hearty items, and in the summer lighter fare is served. There's no cellphone coverage around the station (its remoteness is what makes it special), but if you absolutely must have a look at your Face-book account, satellite Wi-Fi is available at the cafe (NZ$2 for 20Mb to NZ$10 for 100Mb).

En Route to Wellington

The quickest way is to get back onto SH1 (enjoy the atmospheric Desert Rd.!) and follow it all the way down (or all the way up, if you're heading to Auck-land and points north). Visit the very good **National Army Museum** ★★ in Waiouru (www.armymuseum.co.nz; ℂ **06/387-6911**) before you leave the region. Kids can clamber on the old military vehicles, but adults will probably want to ponder the sacrifices made by so many Kiwis in wartime. It's open daily from 9am to 4:30pm and has a cafe, a kids' area, and a gift shop.

EASTLAND & HAWKE'S BAY

astland, also known as the East Coast, is quintessential rural New Zealand: a wild and beautiful region where mass tourism is something best left to other places. Here Maori kids canter their horses bareback through tiny towns, and you can drive for miles along scenic coastal roads to deserted white-sand beaches but still find a restaurant that serves magnificent local wine and seafood.

Travel south and you'll reach the Hawke's Bay region, where you'll find equally appealing lush vineyards and wealthy towns full of boutiques, B&Bs, and upmarket foodie fare. But both the East Coast and Hawke's Bay share a divine climate with long sunshine hours and fertile soil. In Hawke's Bay it's put to good use growing grapes (it's New Zealand's second-largest wine region, after Marlborough), orchard fruit and vegetables, and fat, contented livestock. And it's got a gannet colony where these majestic birds have been living out their lives under the gaze of humans for decades.

GISBORNE & EASTLAND

293km (182 miles) NE of Rotorua; 298km (185 miles) SE of Tauranga; 504km (312 miles) SE of Auckland

Gisborne (population 35,400) was nearly blinded by the glare of publicity it received when the year 2000 rolled around, on account of the fact that it was the first city on earth to greet the sun of a new century. Fittingly, the Maori name for Gisborne is *Te Tai Rawhiti*—the Coast of the Sunrise. The place got a bit of a facelift for the occasion, the sky didn't fall in, and things soon went back to the way they used to be up that way. Stuff happens when it happens. No worries, mate!

Gisborne might be a small town with a leisurely pace of life, but it has a busy river port and an active commercial center and is New Zealand's third-largest grape-growing district, producing about 13% of the country's wine. It's sometimes called the Chardonnay Capital—which accounts for more half of all plantings—but this is underselling it a bit, since the region also produces terrific gewürztraminer, viognier, pinot gris, merlot and malbec. And although you probably don't want to do this after you've been sampling the grape, Gisborne is also a surfing mecca that attracts wavehounds from all over the world, with fabulous, deserted beaches that stretch on forever.

The East Coast is also a place where biculturalism is a living, breathing way of life, not something put on for the tourists. More than 50% of the population in some areas of the region is Maori—the highest proportion of people of Maori descent anywhere in New Zealand—and the Maori language, or *te reo,* is commonly heard in everyday life.

Essentials
GETTING THERE & GETTING AROUND
BY PLANE   Air New Zealand (www.airnewzealand.co.nz; ℂ 0800/737-000 in NZ) has daily flights from major North Island cities. SunAir (www.sunair.co.nz; ℂ 0800/786-247 in NZ) flies to Gisborne's small regional airport (http://gisborneairport.com) from Tauranga, Rotorua, and Napier. There aren't any dedicated airport shuttle operators in Gisborne, but the airport arrivals hall has a number of rental-car companies including **Hertz** (www.hertz.co.nz; ℂ 06/867-5204) and Avis (www.avis.com; ℂ 06/868-9084). The airport is only 5km (3 miles) from the city center.

BY COACH (BUS)   InterCity (www.intercity.co.nz; ℂ 09/623-1503) has a daily bus service to Gisborne from Auckland, Wellington, and Rotorua.

BY TAXI   Call **Gisborne Taxis** (ℂ 0800/505-555 in NZ or 06/867-2222).

BY CAR   If you're coming from Opotiki, east of the Bay of Plenty, you can cut through to Gisborne via the Waioeka Gorge, which has its charms, but you'll miss the East Cape—that quintessential and isolated heartland that gives the region its character. This is **SH35,** one of New Zealand's great coastal road trips, which offers breathtaking scenery and more than an even chance that your journey will be delayed by stray livestock all over the road or possibly people driving them on horseback. This windy 334km (207-mile) route will take about 6 hours at a reasonably brisk pace, but give yourself lots more time and stop overnight if you can. Pick up a copy of the free "Pacific Coast Highway" guide, available from i-SITE visitor centers.

VISITOR INFORMATION
The official tourism website for **Tourism Eastland** is **www.gisbornenz.com**. The **Gisborne i-SITE Visitor Information Centre,** 209 Grey St. (ℂ 06/868-6139), is open Monday to Friday 8:30am to 5pm, Saturday 9am to 5pm, and Sunday 10am to 4pm—and you can play a round of East Coast–themed mini-golf while you're there. The **Wairoa i-SITE Visitor Information Centre,** corner of SH2 and Queen Street (www.visitwairoa.co.nz; ℂ 06/838-7440), is open Monday to Friday 8am to 5pm and weekends 10am to 11am and 3:15pm to 4pm. The **Opotiki i-SITE Visitor Information Centre,** 70 Bridge St. (www.opotikinz.com; ℂ 07/315-3031), is open Monday to Friday from 9am to 4:30pm and on weekends from 9am to 1pm.

ORIENTATION
The city of Gisborne and the key population center of the region lies at the northern end of Poverty Bay. Two rivers, the Waimata and the Taruheru, meet to form the Turanganui River, the country's shortest at just 1,200m (3,900 ft.).

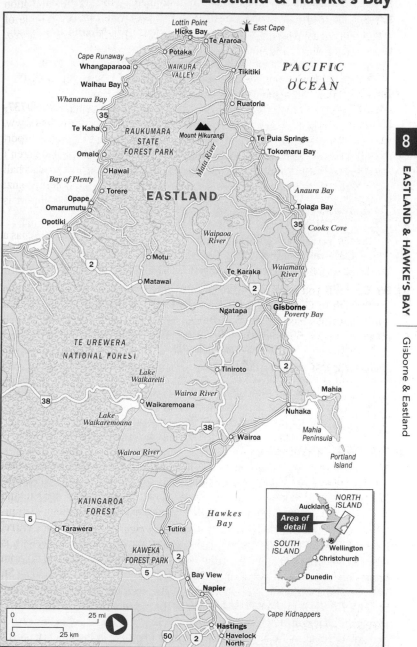

It's a small city with a population of only about 35,000, so the city center is compact. **Awapuni Road** will bring you into the city on SH35; **Gladstone Road** is the main street, and **Centennial Marine Drive** runs from the port area around the bay to the mouth of the Waipaoa River. **Moana Road** is the main thoroughfare south on SH35.

The seaside town of **Opotiki** sits at the eastern end of Bay of Plenty and is the gateway to the **East Cape,** the final stage of the Pacific Coast Highway (SH35), which runs from Auckland all the way down to Napier in Hawke's Bay.

Wairoa is 99km (61 miles) south of Gisborne and is undistinguished but for the fact that it is the gateway to magnificent Lake Waikaremoana inside the Urewera Forest (which was, until recently, a national park). The 3-day hike around the lake is one of the Department of Conservation's Great Walks of New Zealand (see "Outdoor Pursuits," below, and also chapter 9).

SPECIAL EVENTS

The **Sunsplash Summer Festival** is a week-long miscellany of sporting, cultural, and family events that takes place around the third week of January. For details, go to www.gisbornenz.com.

The **Gisborne Wine & Food Festival ★** takes place annually at Labour Weekend, which is at the end of October; for information, contact the **Gisborne Wine Centre** (www.gisbornewineandfoodfestival.co.nz; ✆ **06/867-4085**).

Rhythm and Vines (www.rhythmandvines.co.nz) is a 3-day music festival that runs from December 31 to January 1 (making it the largest gathering of people to see the first sunrise of the New Year in the world!) and boasting six stages with top local and international artists.

Exploring Gisborne

You'll get an amazing view of the city, the surrounding area, and much of Poverty Bay if you hike up to the **Kaiti Hill Lookout.** Walk to the northern end of Gladstone Bridge and follow the signposts, or you can drive to the lookout. At the foot of the hill you'll find **Te Poho-o-Rawiri Marae,** home to one of the largest Maori *whare runanga* (meetinghouses) in New Zealand. It was built in 1925 and one of the first to be constructed from modern materials, but it still features beautiful traditional detailed *tukutuku* (woven wall panels) and *kowhaiwhai* (painted scroll ornamentation) on the rafters. You'll need permission to enter the meetinghouse (✆ **06/866-3659**).

All that walking is likely to make you thirsty (you did walk, didn't you?), so pop along to **The Cidery,** 91 Customhouse St. (✆ **06/868-8300**), if you fancy a cool, crisp glass of cider from New Zealand's leading Bulmer Harvest brand. It's open weekdays 10am to 4pm and weekends by arrangement. If you're visiting Gisborne in the summer months, consider a leisurely cruise on the **MV** *Takitimu* (✆ **06/867-3541**), one of the oldest wooden pilot boats still plying the waters in New Zealand. If you're lucky, you might get to see whales and dolphins out in the bay. Trips depart from Pier One in the inner harbor at 2pm and 5:30pm every Sunday (weather-dependant) or by private arrangement. The cost is NZ$20 adults and NZ$10 children under 12.

The **Tairawhiti Museum** ★★, 10 Stout St. (www.tairawhitimuseum.org. nz; 🕿 06/867-3832), is an excellent provincial museum with great displays on the Maori and European settlement of the region, as well as geological and natural history, decorative arts, and touring exhibitions. A maritime section includes the two-storied wheelhouse and captain's cabin of the *Star of Canada*, a cargo steamer that was blown onto the rocks on the Gisborne foreshore in 1912. The museum is open weekdays and Saturday 10am to 4pm and Sunday 1:30 to 4pm. Admission is NZ$5 for adults; free for children under 12 (Mon it's free admission for all).

If you're interested in old Kiwi rural ways, check out the **East Coast Museum of Technology (ECMoT)**, 67 Main Rd., Makaraka (www.ecmot. org.nz; 🕿 021/161-0455), situated 6km (4 miles) from town. It has a pretty impressive collection of old-time fire appliances, farm and military vehicles, and home technology from yesteryear. It's open Sunday to Friday 10am to 4pm and Saturday 1pm to 4pm; admission is NZ$5 adults, NZ$2 children 13 to 18, NZ$1 younger children, and free for preschoolers.

For more interesting sights around this part of the city, pick up the brochure "An Historic Walk Through Turanga Gisborne" from the visitor center.

Gisborne wouldn't be the obvious place to find New Zealand's national tree collection, but the internationally recognized **Eastwoodhill Arboretum** ★★, 2392 Wharekopae Rd., Ngatapa (www.eastwoodhill.org.nz; 🕿 06/863-9003), is located just out of town, some 35km (22 miles) west of Gisborne. Eastwoodhill was the singular passion of a "tree nut," one Douglas Cook, who took on the mammoth task of planting the bare-earth site in 1910. All these years later, the 135-hectare (333-acre) paradise boasts some 15,000 exotic and native trees, shrubs, and climbers (including rare species). It's the largest collection of Northern Hemisphere trees in the Southern Hemisphere, so try to come in spring or autumn, when the deciduous specimens are at their showiest. Not surprisingly, Eastwoodhill is a New Zealand Garden of National Significance, with more than 25km (15 miles) of marked tracks to wander and explore. It's open daily all year round from 9am to 5pm; admission is NZ$15 adults and NZ$2 children 5 to 16. You can do a guided 1-hour **Curator's Botanical Tour** for an extra NZ$15, and they now also offer accommodations (from NZ$25 per person).

Farther down Wharekopae Road is a rather eye-catching waterfall, **Rere Falls.** You could sit and admire it or do what I did some years ago and slide down the 60m (197-ft.) **Rere Rock Slide** on a boogie board. Everything was going swimmingly until I whacked my elbow on the rock and ended up in the Gisborne Hospital Emergency Department with a shocker of a lump (but nothing broken).

It must have something to do with the climate: Another tree collection, **Hackfalls Arboretum,** 187 Berry Rd., Tiniroto, is an hour's drive southwest of Gisborne (www.hackfalls.org.nz; (🕿 06/863-7083). This working sheep and cattle station has more than 3,000 species, including spectacular oaks, alders, cherries, magnolias, and maples, plus walking tracks, lakes, and gardens to explore at your leisure. It's open daily from 9am to 5pm by appointment; adults are NZ$10, children are free, and you can also stay in a two-bedroom unit for NZ$140 per night, where the rates include a home-cooked meal.

THE GOOD DROP

Gisborne is one of New Zealand's largest grape-growing regions, and if you like chardonnay, you're in luck: Half of Gisborne's 2,000 hectares (4,942 acres) of vineyards are devoted to producing chardonnay grapes. Gewurztraminer, viognier, pinot gris, merlot, and malbec are also produced in the region. Ask for the Gisborne wine guide at the visitor center but be aware that during the winter months most wineries are only open by appointment.

- The **Gisborne Wine Centre,** Shed 3, 50 The Esplanade (www.gisbornewine.co.nz; ℂ **06/867-4085**): Situated in the city's picturesque inner harbor area, this is a good place to get your oenological bearings. The friendly staff know all about the region's best and can make cellar-door bookings for you. They'll guide you through wine tastings and point you to the on-site wine bar and cafe if you want to linger longer. For an organized wine tour, try **Gisborne Tours** (www.gisbornetours.co.nz; ℂ **021/204 1080**), which charges NZ$80 to NZ$95 per person, depending on numbers, for a tour of three wineries with tasting platters. Tours are year-round, starting around 11am.

- **Poverty Bay Wine Estates and Bridge Estate Cellar Door** ★★, 6 Riverpoint Rd., Matawhero (www.povertybaywine.co.nz; ℂ **029/232-2576**): This attractive vineyard under the big skies west of the city offers such varieties as cabernet merlot, claret, chardonnay semillon, and rosé. The cellar door is open daily from 11am to 6pm (Oct–May), or by appointment.

- **Matawhero Wines** ★★, 189 Riverpoint Rd., Matawhero (www.matawhero.co.nz; ℂ **06/867-6140**): Established in 1968, this vineyard won fame as a producer of excellent gewurztraminer that was apparently enjoyed by the Queen. It's a nice place to sample gourmet platters to accompany your wine. It stages quality concerts and events throughout the year and live music on summer Sundays. It's open weekends noon to 4pm October to November; Wednesday to Sunday 11am to 5pm in December; daily 11am to 5pm December 27 to January 31; and Wednesday to Sunday 11am to 5pm February to March. The winery is closed in the winter.

- **Bushmere Estate** ★★, 166 Main Rd., Matawhero (www.bushmere.com; ℂ **06/868-9317**): Enjoy the grape in a somewhat industrial-looking corrugated-iron building that started out as a kiwifruit and citrus packing shed. It's known for its excellent Gewurztraminer and chardonnay, and it has a very nice restaurant, the Vines (see "Where to Eat"). Come on Sundays for tasting platters and live music. It's open daily from 11am to 5pm in summer and Wednesday to Sunday from 11am to 2pm in winter.

- **Millton Vineyard & Winery** ★★, 119 Papatu Rd., Manutuke (www.mill-ton.co.nz; ℃ **06/862-8680**): This vineyard was founded by James and Annie Millton in 1984 on a site where early settlers first planted grapevines in 1871. The large range of award-winning wines is still made using the bio-dynamic principles that gained them the distinction of being New Zealand's first commercial, fully certified organic winery in 1989. In the summer months you can sit outside in the lovely garden with a platter of local cheeses and cured meats while you quaff one of the Milton wines. It's open summer weekdays from 10am to 4pm or by appointment year-round.
- **Spade Oak Vineyard** ★★, 437A Matawai Rd., SH2 (www.spadeoak.co.nz; ℃ **06/867-0198**): You can sit on chairs crafted out of old wine barrels and look out over the chardonnay and viognier vines. It's open Sunday to Tuesday 2pm to 4pm in summer or by appointment. The vineyard is a 10-minute drive from Gisborne on the Opotiki road.

CULTURE AS A WAY OF LIFE

If you've been to Rotorua you may conclude that cultural performances are very much something that's laid on for the tourists, and you'd be right. But here on the East Coast, tribal tradition and the speaking of *te reo Maori* (the Maori language) are part of everyday life. Eastland has more than 150 *marae* (villages), and they are a central part of life for many Maori communities, used for celebrations, meetings, funerals and tribal events. You can visit many by appointment, but to avoid seriously offending the *tangata whenua* (local people) there are a few rules you must adhere to: You are not allowed to take photos inside *marae* anywhere in New Zealand and you can't smoke or take food in with you. As a rule, you must also take off your shoes before entering a building.

There are remnants of ancient *pa* sites (Maori fortresses) around the region, but don't expect to find stone castle ruins as you would in Europe. Maori generally built using wood, and so very little remains. You might see elaborate trenches (Maori pioneered trench warfare) and indentations that indicated *kumara* (sweet potato) pits but very little else. Still, it's interesting to imagine tribal life in the olden days, and the sites generally occupy spectacular out-looks, ideal locations for spotting the enemy before they arrived. The remains of a formidable fortress can be seen at Ngatapa (northwest of Gisborne), which was the scene of a siege between the famous warrior chief Te Kooti and colonial settlers during the New Zealand Wars in the 1860s.

Two excellent Maori-owned and -operated tour companies will give you an insight into the culture of East Coast Maori. **Tipuna Tours** ★★ (℃ **06/862-6118**) offers tailored individual and group tours to local *marae* and places of cultural interest, including a visit to Whangara village north of Gisborne where the movie *Whale Rider* was filmed. Half-day tours are NZ$60 to NZ$120 per person. **Titirangi Maori Experiences** ★★ (℃ **027/624-4796**) have a range of cultural tours and experiences based at Te Poho-o-Rawiri

Marae at the bottom of Kaiti Hill in Gisborne. *Marae* tours are from NZ$20 per person.

Exploring the East Cape

SH35 between Opotiki and Gisborne is an absolutely glorious coastal road (highway is probably a bit of an exaggeration!) full of stunning bays and white-sand beaches lined with *pohutukawa* trees. Quiet little communities, mostly with their own *marae,* boast their own treasures, such as the numerous historic old churches that dot the coast. It feels like going back in time.

At **Te Kaha,** you must ask permission to see the magnificent Tukaki meeting house with its beautifully carved lintel. There's a good swimming beach at **Whangaparaoa,** which was ideal for hauling up the great migration canoe *Tainui* that landed here. Almost halfway along SH35 is **Hicks Bay** and the splendid **Tuwhakairiora meetinghouse ★★,** one of the best examples of carving on the East Cape. The carving was done in 1872 and is dedicated to local members of Ngati Porou who died in overseas wars. There's another great swimming beach here.

Soon, the road descends to sea level and you'll find yourself in **Te Araroa.** New Zealand's largest and oldest pohutukawa tree (around 600 years old) can be found here, and it's a beauty, especially in the summer flowering months. You should take a 20-minute side trip from here to the very lovely and historic 1906 **East Cape Lighthouse ★★,** but bring your A game, fitness-wise. The views and the lighthouse are worth the 700-step slog up the hill, believe me! Better still, bring picnic food and linger in paradise.

Next is **Tikitiki** and the justifiably famous and very ornate **St. Mary's Church ★★★.** As with many of these structures, it was built in remembrance of Ngati Porou soldiers who died during World War I. If you're even slightly interested in Maori culture you need to see the craftsmanship of this ornate Maori church, built in 1924. The interior is a masterpiece of intricate Maori design, the carvings by local Ngati Porou.

Ruatoria is Ngati Porou Central, where the tribe has its headquarters. Although scattered around the country, they are our second-largest Maori tribe. For more information on Ngati Porou tours, see "Sacred Sunrise," below.

Beautiful **Tokomaru Bay ★★** has a lovely beach and some interesting historic buildings. Take care when swimming in the ocean here.

Then you'll reach **Tolaga Bay ★,** which has New Zealand's longest free-standing wharf at 660m (2,165 feet). It's a lovely place to spend an afternoon, where you can also browse the woolly wares at the fabulous **Tolaga Bay Cashmere Company,** 31 Solander St. (www.cashmere.co.nz; ✆ **06/862-6746**). Selling women's and men's clothing, babywear and homeware, it's open weekdays from 9am to 4pm and closed on the weekends.

For a great 1-hour walk, the **Ernest Reeve Walkway ★** at the northern end of Tolaga Bay will take you to a lookout on the cliffs overlooking the bay. The views are totally memorable. Bring your camera.

Just before Gisborne, if you have any interest in diving or snorkeling, you'll want to check out this great local company that caters to families. **Dive Tatapouri** ★★★, SH35, Tatapouri (www.divetatapouri.com; ② **06/868-5153**), offers very reasonably priced guided 2-hour Reef Ecology Experience tours (adults NZ$40 adults, children 5 to 15 NZ$20, under 5 free) as well as other experiences and diving trips.

Outdoor Pursuits

FISHING Eastland offers everything from freshwater trout fishing to game fishing and surf-casting in the Pacific Ocean, which doesn't require a license. If you're coming from the Opotiki end, ask at the visitor center about local fishing clubs or guides along SH35 for both sorts of fishing. The best rivers for trout fishing are the Motu, Waioka, Hangaroa, and Ruakituri, but you will need a license. For fishing charters as well as shark cage diving and marine mammal expeditions, try **Surfit Enterprises,** 48 Awapuni Rd., Gisborne (info@surfit.co.nz; ② **06/867-2970**), which offers a 7-hour fishing trip for around NZ$150 per person.

GOLF **Poverty Bay Golf Club,** Lytton Road, Gisborne (www.gisbornegolf.co.nz; ② **06/867-4402**), is the country's fifth-oldest and one of New Zealand's links-course golfing treasures. Greens fees are NZ$45 for 18 holes, NZ$30 for 9 holes. The club has a pro shop on-site.

SURFING This area is a surfing mecca. Try the world-renowned **Makorori Point** ★★, **Pouawa, Sponge Bay,** and **Kaiaua** beaches. **Midway Beach** is home to the famous Gisborne pipe, known for its deep barrel rides, and **Waikanae** and **Wainui beaches** are also great for surfing and bodyboarding. If you want to learn how to surf or even if you're experienced, Frank is your man. **Surfing with Frank** (www.surfingwithfrank.com; ② **06/867-0823**) offers everything from a half-day tour for NZ$150 per person (plus petrol) to a deluxe 7-night tour with beach-house accommodation for NZ$3,400 for two people.

WALKING Ask for the brochure "Walks of the Eastland Region" at the visitor center for a guide to rambles in the region. The definitive walk in this area is the Lake Waikaremoana 4-day tramp. See the Rotorua entry for **Walking Legends Guided Walk** in chapter 7.

Where to Stay
IN & AROUND GISBORNE

For a splendid architecturally designed property with extraordinary views of Gisborne and the amazing hinterland around it, try **Ridge House Luxury Accommodation** ★★, 103B Wheatstone Rd., Wainui, Gisborne (www.ridgehousenz.com; ② **06/868-5867**). It's just a 5-minute drive from the city but puts you into a different world. The two gorgeous rooms are NZ$250 to NZ$450 per night.

Located in the middle of the city, the **Quality Hotel Emerald,** 13 Gladstone Rd. (www.emeraldhotel.co.nz; ② **0800/363-725** in NZ, or 06/868-8055), has 48 suites (some of the largest in the country), with something for most budgets and all the pampering pleasures of a day spa, restaurant, gym, and outdoor swimming pool. Rooms run from NZ$249 to NZ$700. If you like apartment hotels, the smart and sophisticated **Portside Hotel** ★★ offers stylish guest rooms and suites, 2 Reads Quay Rd., Gisborne (www.portsidegisborne.co.nz; ℂ **06/869-1000**)—but you'll have to go out for dinner since it has no restaurant. Tariffs are from NZ$155 to NZ$550.

Surf City Lodge ★★   Barry and Ros Thomas' lovely 1920s Californian bungalow makes a great base for exploring Gisborne—it's just 3 minutes' walk to the city center. The B&B lodge has three spacious, comfortable rooms in the house and a self-contained cabin in the garden. It's great value for money: Barry's full breakfast will set you up for the day. You'll probably get bacon, scrambled eggs, sausages, lamb chops, and loads of other hearty things, as well as a Continental breakfast. Dinner is worth that little bit extra. Barry is a great chef, and his food is delicious and thoughtfully prepared: I was told to expect mussel fritters for starters, but a very welcome Thai pumpkin soup was served on a cold night instead, followed by roast pork with all the trimmings and a yummy lemon soufflé. Cheers, Barry!

139 Rutene Rd., Inner Kaiti, Gisborne. www.surfcitylodge.co.nz. ℂ **06/868-3900.** 4 units (includes 1 self-contained cabin). NZ$110–NZ$170. Rates include breakfast and refreshments. Dinner on request: NZ$25 per person, including wine and beer. **Amenities:** Gym; mountain bikes; Wi-Fi (free).

Knapdale Eco Lodge ★★★   For a very special rural experience, come and stay with Kees and Kay Weytmans in their beautiful modern home just 10 minutes' drive from Gisborne. It's filled with New Zealand artwork and pieces from their years working and traveling overseas. The outside—all 32 hectares (80 acres) of it—is a private paradise with deer, Highland cattle, ducks and friendly old dogs. These wonderfully hospitable people are very committed to sustainability, using solar power and lots of energy conservation measures. Kees takes guests around the property (on foot or by 4WD): The highlight is the well-preserved Maori pa site on top of a hill, where you can see evidence of kumara pits and garden terraces. Stunning views and some very fine local wine are guaranteed! It should be noted that just about everybody who stays here requests Kay's wonderful dinners rather than going out, and they're not disappointed. Much of the food is grown on the property; if you're lucky you'll get their specialty, venison back steaks from the family herd.

114 Snowsill Rd, Waihirere, Gisborne. www.knapdale.co.nz. ℂ **06/862-5444.** 2 rooms. NZ$420–NZ$495. Rates include breakfast and a guided farm and forest tour. Dinner on request: NZ$90 per person. **Amenities:** Pétanque court; clay pigeon shooting; free laundry; Wi-Fi (free).

AROUND EAST CAPE
Exciting new things are happening around the East Cape in accommodation options, giving you time to enjoy and explore the area. At Te Kaha, 70km (43 miles) from Opotiki, the lovely **Te Kaha Beach Resort** ★★, SH35, Te Kaha (www.tekahabeachresort.com; ℂ **07/325-2830**), offers one- and two-bedoom apartments set in a fabulous panoramic site that overlooks the Eastern Bay of

SACRED sunrise

Mount Hikurangi, at 1,754m (5,754 ft.), is very sacred to the Ngati Porou people. Situated 130km (81 miles) north of Gisborne, it's also the first place on mainland New Zealand to greet the sun each day. A **guided 4WD tour ★★★** with local Maori is very special, although these are daytime tours. **Te Runanganui o Ngati Porou** is the tribal authority and **Tourism Ngati Porou** is the commercial branch that runs such ventures. You can find them at 1 Barry Avenue, Ruatoria (www.ngatiporou.com; (© **06/864-9004**), or at the main Gisborne office, 50 The Esplanade, Kaiti (© **06/867-9960**).

Guides will take you to the nine Maui Whakairo sculptures two-thirds of the way up the mountain, which were created to mark the new millennium. The 4-hour return trip is NZ$165 per person and includes a light lunch. You can also hike unguided to the summit of the mountain, but this is a challenging 7-hour walk and you must get permission from the tribal authority before embarking on an expedition. If you do wish to do this, you can walk up the night before and stay in the hut, getting up early to see the sunrise (NZ$15 for adults and NZ$10 for children; bookings essential). Ask at the visitor center for more information.

Plenty. Try the circular restaurant for the best views and pretty good prices (main courses NZ$25–NZ$35). Rates are from NZ$160.

For a stay in a quaint, historic property, try the fairly modest but perfectly situated **Waihau Bay Lodge,** Orete Point Road, Waihau Bay (http://thewaihaubaylodge.co.nz; © **07/325-3805**), with a hostel, chalets, and in-house rooms. It isn't fancy, but it's quite a treat anyway. Units are NZ$185. For one of the very best locations, try the lovely and very well-regarded **Rangimarie Beachstay ★★**, 930 Anaura Rd., Anaura Bay (www.anaura-stay.co.nz; © **021/633-372**), above one of the most picturesque beaches on the Cape and surrounded by native bush. It has a selection of options: hosted from NZ$120 and self-contained from NZ$165. The bay area has no restaurants, but host Judy Newell will be happy to arrange lunch or dinner with advance notice; the property also has outdoor cooking facilities.

Where to Eat

As in most provincial centers, the food situation in Gisborne is improving by the year, and you'll find cheap eats and more sophisticated establishments in the city and vineyards. On the Cape, go for the best-looking fish and chip shops!

The Marina Restaurant ★★★, Marina Park, Vogel Street (www.marinarestaurantco.nz; © **06/868-5919**), is Gisborne's top fancy place and is located in the lovely old colonial Lysnar Ballroom on the waterfront, opening for lunch and dinner. The menu is international but makes the most of local treats like seafood and celebrates the region's wines. Another sophisticated place for an evening out is **Soho,** 2 Crawford Rd., Inner Kaiti, Gisborne (www.sohobar.co.nz; © **06/868-3888**), which offers a range of tapas and a la carte dishes from old-fashioned classics such as oysters Rockefeller to more edgy modern fare like Moroccan lamb sliders. The cocktail list is inventive and fun and so much cheaper here than in the big cities. It has live music and DJs later in the evening. For something a bit more relaxed, try the **USSCO Bar & Bistro ★★**, 16 Childers Rd., Gisborne (www.ussco.co.nz; © **06/868-3246**), name-checked by *Cuisine*'s *Good Food Guide* in 2014 and a good place to check out in the evening if you're after stylish food in casual surroundings.

Lunch places abound, but if you love books and are looking for lunch in the city, try the lovely **Muirs Bookshop & Café,** 62 Gladstone Rd., Gisborne (www.muirsbookshop.co.nz; © **06/867-9742**). That increasingly rare entity, an independent quality book shop, also serves great food and coffee, and you can sit on the sun-splashed outdoor balcony and watch the world go by. Also a lunch venue but with a rather different vibe, the award-winning and laid-back **Verve Café,** 121 Gladstone Rd., Gisborne (© **06/868-9095**), is loved for its cool menu, great coffee, and ever-changing art exhibitions. You'll see surfing types and business professionals here. Gisborne can do books and art!

For a superior vineyard lunch in a lovely location, try the **Vines at Bush-mere Estate ★**, 166 Main Rd., SH2, Matawhero (www.bushmerevines.co.nz; © **06/868-9317**), which stays open till 5pm daily in the summer months. Sample sharing platters or à la carte dishes and dine indoors or outdoors. They're happy to pair the food with their very best wines.

En Route to Napier

The spectacular 216km (134-mile) drive to Napier grazes the coast and then heads inland past rugged high-country sheep stations and spectacular gorges. A great place to soak your bones between Poverty Bay and Hawke's Bay is lovely **Morere Hot Springs ★** (www.morerehotsprings.co.nz; © **06/837-8856**), which is located in 364 hectares (899 acres) of native rainforest 57km (35 miles) south of Gisborne. You can have a glorious soak and go for a bush walk (anything from 10 min. to 3 hr.). Admission to the public pools and reserve is NZ$12 adults and NZ$6 children and for the private pools, NZ$15 and NZ$10. It's open daily from 10am and, as is the case just about everywhere these days, has a cafe onsite.

HAWKE'S BAY

216km (134 miles) SW of Gisborne; 423km (262 miles) SE of Auckland; 228km (141 miles) SE of Rotorua

Despite its relative geographic isolation, Hawke's Bay is a favorite weekend destination for Wellingtonians and others wanting to enjoy its lush pastoral charms and stunning scenery. **Napier,** population 61,100, is a delightful little city where Art Deco rules supreme, but the reasons behind this architectural style are tragic. In 1931, the city was at the epicenter of a magnitude 7.8 earthquake that razed the city and severely damaged nearby Hastings and other centers. The quake and subsequent fires killed some 256 people, but

Napier rose again, its 140 new buildings constructed in the Art Deco and Spanish Mission styles in vogue at the time. Today, Napier is considered one of the two best-preserved Art Deco centers in the world, along with South Beach, Miami.

Hastings is home to more people (with a population of 67,800) and is a perfectly nice place but lacks Napier's retro cool. It does have some lovely Spanish Mission–style buildings, however, and is handy to many wonderful wineries.

Essentials

GETTING THERE & GETTING AROUND

BY PLANE **Air New Zealand** (www.airnewzealand.co.nz; ℭ **0800/737-000** in NZ) provides a daily service between Napier/Hastings and Auckland, Wellington, and Christchurch. The airport is a 5-minute drive from the city and a 20-minute drive from Hastings. **Super Shuttle** (www.supershuttle.co.nz; ℭ **0800/748-885** in NZ, or 06/835-0055) charges NZ$20 per person to Napier and NZ$43 to Hastings.

BY COACH (BUS) **InterCity** (www.intercity.co.nz; ℭ **09/623-1503**) operates a daily service between Napier/Hastings and Auckland, Gisborne, Rotorua, Taupo, Tauranga, and Wellington. Buses depart from 12 Carlyle St., Napier (next to Clive Sq.).

BY CAR Hawke's Bay is linked to Wellington in the south and to Gisborne in the north by SH2, to Rotorua and Taupo by SH5 and to Auckland via Taupo on SH5 and SH1. It's a 5-hour drive from Auckland, 4 hours from Wellington, 2½ hours from Rotorua, 3 hours from Gisborne, and 1½ hours from Taupo.

BY TAXI **Hawke's Bay Combined Taxis** (www.hawkes-bay.bluebubble-taxi.co.nz; ℭ **06/835-7777**) is the biggest local company.

VISITOR INFORMATION

The official tourism website for **Hawke's Bay Tourism** is **www.hawkes-baynz.com**.

The **Napier i-SITE Visitor Centre,** 100 Marine Parade (www.napiernz.com; ℭ **0800/847-488** in NZ, or 06/834-1911), is open daily 9am to 5pm, with extended summer hours.

The **Hastings i-SITE Visitor Centre,** corner of Russell Street and Heretaunga Street East (www.visithastings.co.nz; ℭ **0800/429-537** in NZ, or 06/873-0080), is open Monday to Friday 9am to 5pm, Saturday 9am to 3pm, and Sunday 10am to 2pm.

ORIENTATION

Lined with Norfolk pines, **Marine Parade** is Napier's waterfront. **Tennyson Street** is the main thoroughfare in and out. Hastings lies 20 minutes south of Napier, and its main roads are **Hastings Street North** and **Queen Street West,** which bisects it.

The height of summer is when Art Deco madness reaches its annual peak: The **Art Deco Weekend ★★★** is held on the third weekend in February, when up to 40,000 people converge on Napier in their fancy '20s and '30s duds to wine, dine, dance and drive around in vintage cars. Contact the **Art Deco Trust** (www.artdeconapier.com; ℂ **06/835-0022**) for more information—and make sure you learn how to do the Charleston before you get here!

If you've got even a passing interest in horses, Hawke's Bay holds the most prestigious equestrian event in New Zealand, the annual **Horse of the Year Show,** in March (www.hoy.co.nz). It's got everything from show jumping and dressage to heavy horse and miniature classes.

In line with the Bay's status as a center of cuisine excellence, the rather cheekily named biannual **FAWC! Food and Wine Classic** takes place in locations all over the Bay. Foodies can get friendly with chefs, food producers, and winemakers during the 10-day summer series (Nov) of more than 75 events. The winter series is 50 events held across four weekends in June. Go to www.fawc.co.nz for more.

Exploring Hawke's Bay
IN NAPIER

The thing you're going to want to do most of all in Napier is just wander around, possibly pretending you're a 1930s femme fatale or a gangster in spats. Pick up the self-guided walking-tour map (NZ$5) from the visitor center: It'll take you about 2 hours to do the downtown area properly. You can also get it from the **Art Deco Shop ★★**, 7 Tennyson St., which has the biggest selection of styley repro (and retro) gifts from the era—everything from elegant jewelry and feather boas to Bakelite telephones and moustache wax. It's run by the good people at the **Art Deco Trust** (www.artdeconapier.com; ℂ **06/835-0022**), who are clearly nuts about the period, and open daily 9am to 5pm.

The Art Deco Trust also conducts very interesting personalized **guided Art Deco tours** in which a friendly local will walk you around the city center explaining the history and significance of different buildings. Morning tours are 1 hour and 20 minutes and cost NZ$17 adults and NZ$5 children 12–18 (under 12s are free). Afternoon tours are 2 hours and 10 minutes (NZ$20 adults and NZ$5 12–18s). Evening tours are 1½ hours (NZ$19 adults and NZ$5 12–18s) To really get into the swing of things, take a **vintage car tour** through Napier and out to Port Ahuriri, where more delightful Deco awaits. The 1-hour, 15-minute tour costs NZ$160 per car. Bus tours are the same duration and cost NZ$40 and NZ$20; doing it by bike takes up to 3 hours and is NZ$50 per person. Inquire at the Art Deco Shop for these, too.

You might like to carry on that gangster fantasy at the **Napier Prison,** 55 Coote Rd., Bluff Hill (www.napierprison.com; ℂ **06/835-9933**), New Zealand's oldest jail, in use from 1862 until 1993. You can do a self-guided tour (NZ$20 adults and NZ$10 children) or a guided tour (from NZ$25 per person). On monthly Dead Hill Scary Night Tours, you walk through dark corridors and try not to scream (from NZ$25 per person; 16 or over only). Don't forget to get a mug shot—it's the perfect souvenir. It's open 9am to 6pm daily.

MTG Hawke's Bay ★★ The former Hawke's Bay Museum has been reborn as MTG Hawke's Bay, which features a starkly contemporary new wing that has some interesting architectural references to Art Deco without copying the style. MTG stands for "Museum, Theatre, Gallery," and not surprisingly you can have all three cultural experiences here and in the two refurbished buildings nearby. The museum bit focuses on the stories, heritage, and art of this region in particular, and features a good *taonga* Maori (Maori treasures) section. Like most regional museums, it has touring exhibitions from around New Zealand, but the major and permanent exhibit that sets this one apart is the **1931 Earthquake Exhibition.** It's good to see this after the 20-minute film that's on view at the Art Deco Shop, since it puts some context around the material. It takes visitors right through that terrible day, from the day's weather forecast: "Tuesday 3 February: slight northwest breeze, 24°C, blue sky" to the quake, the fires, and the appalling aftermath, using photographs, artifacts, and sound. It's quite moving to hear the quiet, insistent beeping of Morse code messages sent between the HMS *Veronica,* which was in port at the time, and other ships nearby. A translation of the messages is beamed onto a screen. The MTG shop has a nice range of New Zealand gifts, cards, jewelry, and souvenirs—many inspired by the exhibitions.

1 Tennyson St. www.mtghawkesbay.com. © **06/835-7781.** NZ$10 adults, free for children under 15. Daily 10am–5pm.

National Aquarium of New Zealand ★★ You might think that a small provincial city is a funny place to house the country's national aquarium, and you'd be right, but this local gem has a lovely waterfront location where sea water less than 100m (328 ft.) away is pumped directly into the huge tanks. Some fish enthusiasts opened this, the first public aquarium in the country, in 1956, and today the vaguely stingray-shaped building has more than 100 species of mainly aquatic animals and the odd other bit of wildlife from New Zealand and around the world. An enormous oceanarium spotlights five species of shark and other reef fish from the local area, as well as exotic reef and deep-sea fish. There are also alligators, turtles, penguins, and some distinctly non-water-dwelling natives: kiwi and tuatara. And because it's not enough just to look at things these days, you can also have "Experiences," like close encounters with little blue penguins, alligators, or piranha (NZ$65), or swimming with sharks (NZ$82).

Marine Parade. www.nationalaquarium.co.nz. © **06/834-1404.** NZ$20 adults, NZ$10 children 3–14. Daily 9am–5pm.

IN HASTINGS & HAVELOCK NORTH

Hastings has its fair share of Art Deco buildings, but it is the Spanish Mission style for which this town is better known. Some architectural gems are the **Methodist Church, Hawke's Bay Opera House,** and **Westerman's**

TASTE YOUR WAY around the bay

Hawke's Bay is the birthplace of New Zealand's wine industry. French Marist missionaries planted the first vines in 1851, and now the region has more than 100 vineyards and 80 wineries, with some 35 winery cellar doors where you can taste and compare to your heart's content. Soil and climate conditions are perfect for late-maturing varieties like cabernet sauvignon, riesling, and chardonnay. Most wineries open every day for sales, and many have their own restaurants. Pick up a free "Hawke's Bay Winery Guide" and map from the visitor center. Hawke's Bay has six distinct wine regions, and following is, appropriately enough, a taste of some of the best, from north to south.

Note: If you're pushed for time, drop into **Advintage,** 4 Donnelly St., Havelock North (www.advintage.co.nz; 🕻 **0800/111-660** in NZ, or 06/877-9754), which sells a huge variety of local and international wine. **The New Zealand Wine Centre ★★**, 1 Shakespeare Rd., Napier South (www.nzwinecentre.co.nz; 🕻 **06/835-5326**), sells local wines only and has aroma rooms where you can put your senses through their paces.

○ **North of Napier: Esk Valley Estate ★**, 745 Main Rd., Bayview, Napier (www.eskvalley.co.nz; 🕻 **06/872-7430**), is a top boutique winery that still hand-plunges its red wines in the traditional manner. It's on a picturesque terraced site overlooking the sea. **Crab Farm Winery,** 511 Main N. Rd., Bayview, Napier (www.crabfarmwinery.co.nz; 🕻 **06/836-6678**) is a family-owned boutique operation with a restaurant in a sunny courtyard.

○ **Taradale & Surrounds: Brookfields Vineyards & Restaurant,** 376 Brookfields Rd., Meeanee,

Taradale, Napier (www.brookfields-vineyards.co.nz; 🕻 **06/834-4615**), is a little handier to Napier. The region's oldest boutique winery, founded in 1937, also has a popular restaurant. Another older winery, **Church Road ★**, 150 Church Rd., Taradale, Napier (www.churchroad.co.nz; 🕻 **06/844-2053**), does daily winery, museum, and behind-the-scenes tours of its operation, which was established in 1897. The winery is a top outdoor venue where summer concerts are staged, and it has a good restaurant. At the region's original vineyard, **Mission Estate Winery,** 198 Church Rd., Taradale, Napier (www.missionestate.co.nz; 🕻 **06/845-9350**), you can dine in the beautifully restored seminary. A big concert is held here every summer. The wines are pretty good, too!

○ **Central Hastings: Vidal Estate Winery ★★★**, 913 St. Aubyn St. E., Hastings (www.vidal.co.nz; 🕻 **06/872-7440**), was founded in 1905 by Spanish settler Anthony Vidal, who bought the property as a racing stable. This award-winning winery was also the first in New Zealand to establish a restaurant and bar and continues to set standards with its chardonnays and cabernet sauvignons.

○ **West of Hastings: Alpha Domus ★★**, 1829 Maraekakaho Rd., Hastings (www.alphadomus.co.nz; 🕻 **06/879-6752**), is a boutique winery in the Bridge Pa sub-region. The winery's flagship wine, "The Aviator," is one of this country's best Bordeaux-style reds. **Sileni Estates Winery ★★★**, 2016

Maraekakaho Rd., Hastings (www. sileni.co.nz; © **06/879-8768**), has the advantage of being a great winery (making world-class Bordeaux and burgundy varieties) with a fabulous gourmet food store, restaurant, and wine discovery center on-site. **Ngatarawa Wines ★**, 305 Ngatarawa Rd., Hastings (www. ngatarawa.co.nz; © **06/879-7603**), is a really lovely boutique property created from an old racing stable. You'll also find **Farmgate Wines** here. **Te Awa Winery ★★**, 2375 SH50, Hastings (www.teawa.com; © **06/879-7602**), is in the Gimblett Gravels wine-producing area, producing Bordeaux-style reds and top-label chardonnay. it has one of the best winery restaurants around. **Trinity Hill Winery ★**, 2396 SH50, Hastings (www.trinityhill.com; © **06/879-7778**), is another top producer in the Gimblett Gravels area Its tasting room is the winery's old barrel hall and features a spectacular 5m-high (16-ft.) ceiling.

○ **Havelock North & Surrounds: Black Barn Vineyards ★★★**, Black Barn Road, Havelock North (www.blackbarn.com; © **06/879-7603**), produces premium Bordeaux-style varieties but also makes award-winning whites (chardonnay, viognier, and sauvignon blanc). It's a beautifully sited boutique operation, with an amphitheater for live concerts and open-air cinema screenings, a farmer's markets on summer Saturdays, an award-winning bistro (see "Where to Eat"), a kitchen shop, and delightful accommodation options for visitors (see "Where to Stay," below). **Te Mata Estate,** 349 Te

Mata Rd., Havelock North (www. temata.co.nz; © **06/877-4399**), dates back to 1896 and is one of New Zealand's most prestigious wineries, comprising five vineyards that produce some 40,000 cases a year. Established in 2003, **Craggy Range Winery ★★★**, 253 Waimarama Rd., Havelock North (www.craggyrange.com; © **06/873-7126**), sits almost under Te Mata Peak and has a top restaurant (see "Where to Eat," below) and vineyard cottages (see "Where to Stay," below).

○ **Te Awanga: Elephant Hill Estate ★★★**, 86 Clifton Hill, Te Awanga, Hastings (www.elephanthill.co.nz; © **06/873-0400**), is New Zealand's newest winery, and its stunningly modern buildings grace a breathtaking location on the Te Awanga coast. Producing premium single-estate wines, It even has a very fine award-winning restaurant (see "Where to Eat," below). **Clearview Estate Winery ★★**, 194 Clifton Rd., Te Awanga, Hastings (www.clearviewestate.co.nz; © **06/875-0150**), is famed for its chardonnay and full-bodied reds. It's in a lovely spot by the sea with a delightful lunch restaurant (see "Where to Eat," below). Idyllic!

○ **Central Hawke's Bay: Junction Wines,** junction of SH2 and SH50, Takapau Plains (www.junction-wines.co.nz; © **06/855-8321**), is owned by former All Black John Ashworth, who played 24 tests in the front row between 1977 and 1986. Visitors are welcome to taste Ashworth's award-winning reds and whites and even park the campervan overnight!

Fur Goodness' Sake

If you've had enough of Art Deco and don't need another reminder about the 1931 earthquake, here's a slightly crazy shopping experience in central Napier that's good for New Zealand. **Opossum World,** 157 Marine Parade (www.opossumworld.co.nz; ℂ **06/835-7697**), sells beautiful garments, cushions, and rugs made from possum fur and possum/merino wool blend. The Australian brushtail possum is very much an unwanted citizen here (New Zealand has no native land mammals apart from several species of bat). In fact, it's estimated that 70 million possums eat 21,000 tons of leaves each night and also consume birds' eggs. So you're doing a fine thing by buying a possum product—the rich, silky fur is lovely, even if the creatures are not. In addition to having the largest range of possu-blend knitwear in the country, Opossum World has a rather insane static display that tells the story of their non-contribution to the country. It's very entertaining. The shop is open Monday to Friday 9am to 5pm and weekends 10am to 4pm (3pm in winter).

Building, the latter conveniently home to the Hastings i-SITE Visitor Centre and the place to pick up the "Heritage of Hastings" brochure.

The **Hastings City Art Gallery,** 201 Eastbourne St. E. (www.hastingscity-artgallery.co.nz; ℂ **06/871-5095**), is a modern art space for contemporary exhibitions and events that really puts a spotlight on what's happening on the New Zealand art scene. It has a "Retail and Reading" space: **Auaha,** a shop that sells work by some of the best local contemporary artists and craftspeople. Entry to the gallery is free: It's open daily from 10am to 4:30pm (6:30pm on summer Thurs). You might want to pick up the "Public Artworks" brochure, which has information about the dozen or so public sculptures installed in Hastings and Havelock North as part of an award-winning revitalization program.

If you have a vehicle, don't miss the opportunity to drive to the top of **Te Mata Peak ★★★**, about 11km (7 miles) southeast of Hastings. The 399m (1,309-ft.) limestone ridge rises dramatically from the Heretaunga Plains. When it's clear you'll have 360-degree views around the region, including across to the Ruahine, Kaweka, and Maungaharuru ranges with Mount Ruapehu visible in the distance. If you want to stretch your legs on the way up or down, there are walking tracks through native forest. The road to the peak is long, steep, and narrow, so drive with care.

There has been an **Australasian gannet colony** at the craggy peninsula of **Cape Kidnappers ★★★** since the 1870s, and its healthy population now numbers about 6,500 pairs. A half-hour drive from Napier and Hastings, it's the largest mainland gannet colony in the world. The best time to visit is from early November to late February; the sanctuary is closed to the public between July and October during the early nesting phase. To get here, drive 21km (13 miles) south of Hastings to Clifton Domain, and then it's a 2-hour walk along 8km (5 miles) of sandy beach. *Note:* The walk *must* be done at low tide—when the tide is high it reaches the base of the steep cliffs. Check tide times with the visitor centers or the local **Department of Conservation** office (© **06/834-3111**). If you don't want to walk, see "Organized Tours," below.

Organized Tours

If you want to meet a good Kiwi bloke who knows about a thing or three about the good drop, try **Grant Petherick Exclusive Wine Tours,** 805 Fitzroy Ave., Hastings (www.flyfishingwinetours.co.nz; © **06/876-7467**), and meet the man himself. He's very down-to-earth and takes only one to four people at a time. His personalized tours are NZ$125 per hour for the group, including pickup from your accommodation. Grant Petherick has another string in his bow as well: He's also a **fly-fishing** fan. He'll take out anglers of any ability and experience for full- and half-day tours in his 4WD in search of rainbow and brown trout. It's NZ$125 per person for one or two people.

Another fine bloke, Vince from **Vince's World of Wine** (© **06/836-6705**), will pick you up from the Napier visitor center or your hotel at 1pm and take you on a half-day winery tour for NZ$65 per person.

Tours of the **gannet colony** use two methods of transport. **Gannet Safaris Overland,** 396 Clifton Rd., Te Awanga (www.gannetsafaris.co.nz; © **06/875-0888**), is the softies' version. For more than 35 years this company has been running 3-hour tours in an air-conditioned 4WD minibus from September to May, and no walking is required. It departs daily at 9:30am and 1:30pm and costs NZ$80 adults and NZ$40 children ages 7 to 16. Established in 1952, **Gannet Beach Adventures** ★★, 475 Clifton Rd., Te Awanga (www.gannets.com; © **0800/426-638** in NZ, or 06/875-0898), takes you out on a trailer being towed by a 1949 Minneapolis-Moline tractor. This fun 4 hour trip is NZ$42 adults and NZ$24 kids 4 to 15 (NZ$101 for a family) and includes 20 to 30 minutes of walking. Tours operate from October to early May. Both require advance booking.

Outdoor Pursuits

CYCLING The **Hawke's Bay Trails** represent 3 of the 23 routes in the New Zealand Cycle Trails network. That's 200km (124 miles) of mainly off-road rides for all ages and abilities and includes the easy **Water Ride** along the Napier seafront, the beautiful **Landscapes Ride** past coastal communities, and the **Wineries Ride,** which begins in Havelock North and meanders through the Gimblett Gravels and Bridge Pa wine regions.

In the Path of the Ancestors

Take a spiritual journey with local Maori through more than 700 years of the life of the Waimarama people. Descendants of the original tribe have formed **Waimarama Maori Tours** ★ (www.waimaramamaori.co.nz; © **021/057-0935**) and will take you to important sites and share their history and culture. Choose from three 2-hour tours: the Te Mata Peak and Pou tour and Walk with the Ancestors (both NZ$80 per person) or the 5-hour A Day in the Life of a Maori Elder tour (NZ$325 per person, including a *marae* visit). Tours run every day at a time of your choosing.

Takaro Trails ★★★, 9 Nelson Quay, Ahuriri, Napier (www.takarotrails. co.nz; ☎ 06/835-9030), specializes in luxury self-guided 1- to 8-day tours with a gourmet theme that include five-star accommodation, support, and transport of luggage. Self-guided day rides are from NZ$40 per person; privately guided day trips are from NZ$250 per person and multi-day trips are from NZ$2500 to NZ$7995 per person.

On Yer Bike Tours ★★★, 2543 SH50, Hastings (www.onyerbikehb.co.nz; ☎ 06/650-4627), will rent you good-quality bikes for the Wineries' self-guided ride, and the support team will pick up your purchases. It's NZ$60 adults and NZ$30 children 6 to 18, including lunch. **Good Fun Bike Rides,** 8 Donnelly St., Havelock North and 217 Ngatarawa Rd., Hastings (www. goodfunbikerides.co.nz; ☎ 06/650-7722), is ideally situated for the Wineries Ride and the Landscape Ride out to the Tuki Tuki Valley: It's NZ$60 for a full day and NZ$40 for half a day. For ambling around Napier, **Fishbike,** 22 Marine Parade, Napier (www.fishbike.co.nz; ☎ 06/833-6979), rents out a range of bikes from cruisers to tandems, from NZ$15 per hour. **Coastal Wine Cycles,** 41 East Rd., Haumoana (www.winecycles.co.nz; ☎ 06/875-0302), will rent you a groovy cruiser bike and send you on one of two easy routes or you can go your own way; bikes are NZ$40 a day. For more information, pick up the "Hawke's Bay Trails" guide from the visitor center.

GOLF   Established in 1896, the **Napier Golf Club,** Waiohiki, 1215 SH50, Napier (www.napiergolf.club.co.nz; ☎ 06/844-7913), is an 18-hole championship course close to the city. Greens fees are NZ$45 for 18 holes and NZ$25 for 9. **Cape Kidnappers Golf Course ★★★,** 446 Clifton Rd., Te Awanga (www. capekidnappers.com; ☎ 06/873-1018), is one of the finest—and most scenic—courses in the world, and green fees are steep: NZ$313 to NZ$475 for 18 holes.

Where to Stay

Hawke's Bay is full to the brim with delightful places to rest your head, from cozy B&Bs and self-contained accommodation to luxury lodges and stylish apartments.

IN NAPIER

Scenic Hotel Te Pania, 45 Marine Parade (www.scenichotels.co.nz; ☎ 0800/696-963 in NZ, or 06/833-7733), curves elegantly around the Parade, has bright, modern rooms, and is close to the action. You'll pay NZ$276 to NZ$567 for a room or suite. If you like boutique, old-style charm, **The County Hotel ★,** 12 Browning St. (www.countyhotel.co.nz; ☎ 0800/843-468 in NZ, or 06/835-7800), can provide it. This gorgeous and iconic old building (built in 1909) is one of only two significant structures to survive the 1931 Napier earthquake—so it's Edwardian, not Art Deco. Rates range from NZ$380 for a luxury king room to NZ$925 for the Regal Suite. In nearby Ahuriri (5-min. drive from the airport and the city center), the **Navigate Seaside Accommodation,** 50 Waghorne St. (www.navigatenapier.co.nz; ☎ 06/831-0077), is a contemporary boutique hotel that offers stylish rooms, suites, and apartments. This place is great for couples but also has family suites and is right opposite a children's playground. Rooms are from NZ$205 to NZ$650.

Tucked away in the tranquil countryside a few minutes from Havelock North is a superlative art, crafts, and collectibles gallery owned by Zimbabwean expats Bruce and Louise Stobart. The award-winning **Birdwoods ★★**, 298 Middle Rd., Havelock North (www.birdwoodsgallery.co.nz; ℭ **06/877-1395**), situated in a transplanted church hall, stocks a fabulous range of local and African pieces. But there's so much more to this little enterprise. Louise started a business back home producing a range of birds and animals made from recycled 40-gallon drums, and her remaining sculptures have been joined by beautiful large-format stone sculptures chiseled by internationally acclaimed Zimbabwean artists and pieces by New Zealand sculptors. These works are on display in the delightful **sculpture garden,** which also has a pond and water feature and is filled with wildflowers (and sometimes brides!) in the summer. Bruce and Louise have thought of everything: There's a terrific little **cafe** that serves a lemon tart that's famous in these parts. And an old-fashioned **sweet shop** in the one-room colonial cottage is the place to get licorice bullets, gumballs, acid drops, multi-hued bonbons, sugared almonds, and every yummy sugary treat you can think of. Birdwoods is open daily from 10am to 5pm (4pm in winter).

Art Deco Masonic Hotel ★★★ This is, quite simply, a beautiful hotel inside and out. It's been completely renovated and has bucketloads of Art Deco charm and atmosphere plus all the modern conveniences. Rooms are stylish, luxurious, and glamorous, the service is excellent, and the Emporium Eatery & Bar is stunning (see "Where to Eat"). The Royal Suite—from the retro drinks trolley to the thoughtfully appointed writing desk—will make you feel just that, partly because the Queen and Prince Philip actually stayed here during her Coronation Tour of 1953! And you'll find real milk, not UHT, in the fridge—always a bonus. This place won Hospitality New Zealand's Best New/Redeveloped Hotel award in 2014—deservedly so.

Corner Tennyson St. and Marine Parade. http://masonic.co.nz. ℭ **06/835-8689.** 42 units. Rooms, suites and apartments NZ$129–NZ$499. Long-stay and off-peak rates. **Amenities:** 2 restaurants, 2 bars; room service; balcony access; Wi-Fi (free).

The Crown Hotel ★ At the heart of this property in the cool seaside village of Ahuriri just out of the CBD is the beautiful old Spanish Mission–style Crown Hotel, built in 1932. Its lovely frontage faces away from the sea; you can stay here in old-fashioned luxury or in the modern wing, which is equally lavish and offers stunning sea views. In addition to a really nice restaurant, **Milk & Honey** next door (see "Where to Eat"), the hotel also has the Globe Theatrette, a 45-seater boutique cinema that screens movies from Tuesday to Sunday. Hotel guests get a 20% discount on movie tickets.

Corner Bridge St. and Hardinge Rd., Ahuriri, Napier. www.thecrownnapier.co.nz. ℭ **06/833-8330.** 42 units. NZ$175 and up studio double; NZ$199–NZ$650 suite; NZ$500–NZ$1,200 2-bedroom loft apartments. **Amenities:** Restaurant, bar; room service; free bike storage; free parking; daily newspaper; laundry service; Wi-Fi (free).

Breckenridge Lodge ★★ Vineyard views, a warm welcome, and food cooked by Michelin-rated chef Malcolm Redmond—who just happens to own this lovely rural property—make this modern, five-star luxury lodge a top place to stay. If you really fall in love with Malcolm's food, you can always enroll in one of his cooking classes, which will give you the perfect excuse to come back.

1 Breckenridge Lane, Taradale, Napier. www.breckenridgelodge.co.nz. ℭ **06/844-9411.** 5 units. NZ$845 double suite with dinner; NZ$595 without dinner. Rates include breakfast, pre-dinner drinks, and five-course dinner. **Amenities:** Dining room; wine cellar; guest lounge; Wi-Fi (free).

IN & AROUND HASTINGS

The Farm at Cape Kidnappers ★★★ As is increasingly the case with high-end properties in New Zealand, many owners are turning their minds to other things they can do with their iconic bits of Kiwi real estate, other than offering visitors a special place to lay their heads. So it is with **The Farm.** Like its sister property, Kauri Cliffs, in Northland, this extraordinary 2,500-hectare (6,000-acre) working sheep and cattle farm is part of a serious wildlife protection effort. The Cape Sanctuary is the largest privately owned and funded wildlife restoration project in New Zealand and is run in association with the Department of Conservation. A number of endangered species live on the reserve, including kiwi, kakariki, saddlebacks, and tuatara, which gives a very heart-warming feeling to this keen greenie. But the Farm is also an immaculate and stunning place to rest or stretch your wings: a five-star lodge with views you wouldn't waste your time dying for—there's too much to look at. Rolling green pastures and the magnificent, internationally acclaimed Tom Doak–designed golf course lead the eye down to the ocean beyond. You can be energetic or luxuriate in your "rustic elegant" suite, have a spa treatment or take a bike ride. The sumptuous Owner's Cottage has four bedrooms with fireplaces in each room and a full kitchen. The food and service throughout, unsurprisingly, are exceptional. This is no vainglorious "look at me" property: I actually couldn't find it at first and had to ask a local to direct me.

446–448 Clifton Rd., Te Awanga, Cape Kidnappers. www.capekidnappers.com. ℭ **06/875-1900.** 23 units (22 suites, 1 cottage). Hilltop suite from NZ$775 per person; lodge or ridge suite from NZ$890 per person; NZ$5,950–NZ$12,750 owner's cottage. Rates include pre-dinner drinks with canapés, gourmet dinner, full breakfast, complimentary minibar (excluding wine and liquor) and full use of lodge facilities, excluding golf course. Ask about off-peak rates. Activities include clay target shooting, farm and gannet colony tours, wildlife spotting, walking, horse treks, and biking. **Amenities:** Restaurant; bar at clubhouse; babysitting; free use of mountain bikes; concierge; 18-hole golf course with pro shop; gym and health spa; outdoor Jacuzzi in pool complex and one at owner's cottage; outdoor heated pool; room service; Wi-Fi (free).

Millar Road ★★ The idyllic location of this boutique property is but one of its many recommendations. It sits proudly on the Tuki Tuki hills with gorgeous views over a 20-hectare (49-acre) vineyard, the coastal settlement of Te Awanga, and even Mount Ruapehu on a good day. There are two modern villas and the larger two-bedroom Haumoana House, which sleeps up to six people: Everything is beautifully designed, with fine examples of New Zealand art and design on show.

83 Millar Rd., Hastings. www.millarroad.co.nz. ⓒ **06/875-1977.** 3 units (2 villas, 1 house). NZ$400–NZ$600 villa; NZ$650–NZ$950 Haumoana House. Rates include breakfast provisions and bottle of Millar Road's estate wine. Long-stay and off-peak rates. **Amenities:** Bar; outdoor pool; Wi-Fi (free).

Greenhill Lodge ★★   Should you prefer your accommodation a little more traditional in style, Greenhill Lodge will blow you away! From its bay windows to its wraparound verandahs to the extraordinary viewing turret on top, you'll feel as if you've stepped back in time in this very large, grand mansion, built in 1898. It sits regally on a hill, as its name would suggest, overlooking the property's beautiful gardens and rolling countryside beyond and is in the heart of Hawke's Bay's food and wine country. You can stay in a suite or room in the main house or the separate contemporary cottage.

103 Greenhill Rd., Raukawa, Hastings. www.greenhill.co.nz. ⓒ **06/879-9944.** 5 units (1 cottage, 4 rooms). NZ$815–NZ$1,225 double. NZ$1,140–NZ$1,360 cottage. Exclusive use of lodge and cottage NZ$4680 for 10 people. Rates include breakfast, pre-dinner drinks and canapés. Rates including a four-course dinner are from NZ$1115–NZ$1525 for the lodge and suites, NZ$1660 for the cottage and NZ$7750 for exclusive use of the lodge and cottage. Long-stay and off-peak rates. **Amenities:** Dining room; croquet; gym; library and billiards room; pétanque; outdoor pool; wine cellar; Wi-Fi (free).

Clearview Homestead ★★   If you love the idea of sleeping in a vineyard, this character-filled circa-1915 house is right in the middle of the Clearview Estate with views and privacy but also a great restaurant, the **Red Shed** (see "Where to Eat," below), just a few steps away. It's also just a 5-minute walk to the beach for the best of both worlds. The five-bedroom house comes with an "entertainers' kitchen," a deck, and gardens and sleeps 10. It's great for groups, but you can also rent the smaller two-bedroom "Shearer's Quarters," in the rear.

194 Clifton Rd., Te Awanga, Hastings. www.clearviewestate.co.nz. ⓒ **06/875-0150.** 1 5-bedroom house. NZ$220–NZ$250 per night for two people. Extra person $50 per night; extra child $25 per night. Long-stay and off-peak rates. **Amenities:** Restaurant; open fire; barbecue.

IN HAVELOCK NORTH

The pretty village of Havelock North is ringed by beautiful vineyards, with Te Mata Peak on its doorstep. Wonderful and generally upmarket accommodation choices abound here, with the emphasis on self-contained houses and B&Bs. **Cottages on St. Andrews,** 14 St. Andrews Rd., Havelock (www.holiday-cottages.co.nz; ⓒ **06/877-1644**), is just 1km (0.6 miles) from Havelock North village and has smart, modern studio units, three- and four-bedroom cottages, and more accommodation in the main house. Sheep, alpacas, a donkey, and various other pattable creatures roam the 2-hectare (5-acre) property, which also has a heated outdoor pool. Rates are from NZ$125 to NZ$480. The six-bedroom **Lodge on St. Georges** is part of the same property and sleeps at least 12 guests; it's NZ$100 per night.

Black Barn Vineyards ★★★ This very professional operation with a beautiful hilltop vantage point incorporates a splendid boutique vineyard, a bistro with wine-tasting (see "What to Eat"), a kitchen store, a farmer's market and some 16 absolutely sublime "retreats." These lovely self-contained houses are in a number of locations on or near the vineyard, by the river and the beach. All have indoor fireplaces; some have outdoor fireplaces. Half have swimming pools. They include the charming old **Rush Cottage** and the **Black Barn** in the vineyard, the six **River Houses** and the **Beach House.** Sensational!

Black Barn Rd. www.blackbarn.com. © **06/877-7985.** 17 units (houses and cottages). From NZ$390 (Rush Cottage) to NZ$5,000 (Paretai). Rates include continental breakfast. Long-stay and off-peak rates available. **Amenities:** Bistro; amphitheater; bikes; all-weather tennis court; farmer's (grower's) market; kitchen store; swimming pools (River Houses, Riverside Lodges 1, 2, 3, 4, and Summerlee only); Wi-Fi (free).

Where to Eat

Many of the best places to eat are in the wineries around Hastings and Havelock North, but good restaurants and cafes can be found everywhere. The abundance of fresh produce certainly seems to be inspiring restaurateurs in this region.

IN NAPIER

The seaside village of Ahuriri, just around the water from Napier's city center, is a groovy little enclave with a number of good eateries. One of the best is the **Milk & Honey Restaurant** ★, 10 Hardinge Rd., Ahuriri (www.themilkandhoney.co.nz; © **06/833-6099**). It's right next door to the **Crown Hotel,** and even on a recent freezing winter night it was buzzing. The food is lovely, the service warm and friendly, and the extensive beverage list includes some really yummy non-alcoholic cocktails, which work surprisingly well with food. I heartily recommend the Pear Shaped Dreams: apple and pear juice, cinnamon syrup, and cream—delectable and you can always skip dessert if you run out of space. It's open daily from 7am to 10pm (to 4pm on Sun).

For authentic Mexican, **Mexi Mama,** 58 W. Quay, Ahuriri (www.meximama.co.nz; © **021/100-5174**), with great—and amazingly cheap—classics, plus a good range of margaritas. It's a fun place that does a funky take on the Day of the Dead, with skull imagery everywhere. It's open Tuesday to Saturday from 6pm till late. **F.G. Smith Eatery,** 9A Ossian St., Ahuriri (www.fgsmitheatery.co.nz; © **06/834-0404**), is a breakfast, brunch, and lunch spot with a cool industrial vibe; it's open weekdays from 7am to 4pm and weekends from 9am to 4pm.

In Napier itself, also check out **Albion Canteen,** corner of Albion and Hastings streets (www.albioncanteen.co.nz; © **06/650-2888**), which specializes in a great range of fresh, delicious salads and juices but has lots of other yummy lunch choices. It's open weekdays from 7:30am to 3:30pm and Saturday from 9am to 1pm. The locals flock to funky and friendly **Adoro Café,** 142 Hastings St., for great coffee and pastries; it's open weekdays from 7am to 4pm, Saturday from 7am to 3pm, and Sunday from 8am to 2pm.

FOOD, glorious HAWKE'S BAY FOOD

Instead of competing, a bunch of local gourmet food producers have banded together to establish the **Hawke's Bay Food Trail ★★★**. Pick up the free map of the trail from the visitor center and munch your way around a delightful array of emporia selling fine chocolates, olives, bakery items, ice cream, honey, and much, much more. It all comes to a glorious culmination of yumminess at the **Hawke's Bay Farmer's Market ★★★**, held at the Hawke's Bay A&P Showgrounds, Kenilworth Road, Hastings (www.hawkesbayfarmersmarket.co.nz; **027/697-3737**), every Sunday from 8:30am to 12:30pm. The location is fabulous—if you come in spring, the mature trees drop their blossoms all over the stallholders!—and the produce and range are among the very best this country has to offer. There's live music and kids running around happily—it really is a joyful place on a fine day. There's also the **Napier Urban Food Market,** Clive Square East, Napier, held on Saturdays from 9am to 1pm. The food is equally good, but the atmosphere is less laid-back.

A picturesque **Growers' Market ★★★** is held at the Sun Dial in the heart of the Black Barn Vineyards, off Te Mata Road, Havelock North (www.blackbarn.com; **06/877-7985**). Buy the new season's fruit and veggies, baked goods, locally roasted coffee, flowers, meat, preserves, olive oil, lavender products, and more. It happens on summer Saturday mornings from early December to the end of February from 9am to noon and, if you haven't eaten too many of your purchases already, you could then go for lunch or brunch at the **Black Barn Bistro** (see below).

Award-winning ice cream maker **Rush Munro's,** 704 Heretaunga St. W., Hastings (www.rushmunro.co.nz; **06/873-9050**), is an institution in these parts. The Hawke's Bay company has been around since 1926 (it's New Zealand's oldest) and is still delighting its fans with 100% natural flavors like passionfruit, manuka honey, strawberries and cream, blackcurrant, maple and walnut, and hokey pokey (a Kiwi favorite made from vanilla ice cream with bits of honeycomb toffee in it). My small son looked totally disbelieving when he was presented with a sundae that was almost bigger than he was on his first visit—but he manfully worked his way through it. The Ice Cream Garden is open daily from noon to 5pm Monday to Friday and on weekends from 11am to 5pm.

Emporium Eatery & Bar ★★★ CONTEMPORARY NEW ZEALAND   The Masonic Hotel's in-house bar and restaurant is every bit as gorgeous as the hotel itself; in fact it was lauded in worldsbestbars.com in 2013—one of the few establishments in New Zealand to garner this accolade. It's modern yet retro with just enough Art Deco styling. Furnished in dark leather and wood with pale walls, the restaurant features a very long marble bar, and clever uplighting means that certain spots are bathed in a golden aura. The food is equally classy (and surprisingly well-priced), including wood-oven pizzas and interesting small plates and nibbles (Moroccan lamb tagine, Penang chicken curry, salt and pepper squid). The menu includes the history of the hotel in words and photos, so you can browse while you order.

Corner of Tennyson St. and Marine Parade. www.emporiumbar.co.nz. **06/835-0013.** Dinner reservations recommended. Main courses NZ$22–NZ$35. Daily 11am till late.

Pacifica ★★★ CONTEMPORARY NEW ZEALAND   This great little spot presents fine dining without the snooty overtones. You'll find Pacifica in a weathered blue driftwood-studded bungalow on the waterfront where good food and hospitality come before pretense. Pacifica won *Cuisine*'s Best Regional Restaurant in 2015; Chef Jeremy Rameka says his cooking is based on "emotion and bravery, rather than convention." It offers two five-course degustation menus—one seafood-based and one a mix of seafood and New Zealand meat and game. Get there quickly if you're feeling emotional and brave—and even if you're not.

209 Marine Parade. www.pacificarestaurant.co.nz. ℃ **06/833-6335.** Dinner reservations recommended. Degustation menus NZ$50 per person. Tues–Sat 6pm till late.

Mister D Dining ★★ CONTEMPORARY NEW ZEALAND   This very groovy eatery on the main road fairly hums with activity and good vibes. These serious food lovers make all their own bread, pasta, and pastries daily, and everything is fresh and original in its approach. The lamb croquettes with date and preserved lemon chutney and yogurt is a standout. Plan to save room for the white chocolate mousse with candied apples and green apple salad, which is cool and delicious, just like this place.

47 Tennyson St. www.misterd.co.nz. ℃ **06/835-5022.** Dinner reservations recommended. Main courses NZ$25–NZ$33. Sun–Wed 7:30am–4pm; Thurs–Sat 7:30am till late.

IN HASTINGS

It's a bit of a no-brainer that you'll want to head for the excellent winery restaurants in this area (See "Taste Your Way Around the Bay"). **Vidal Estate Winery Restaurant** ★★, 913 St. Aubyn St. E. (www.vidal.co.nz; ℃ **06/872-7442**), is a reliable option and New Zealand's oldest winery restaurant, having opened its doors in 1979. It's open daily for lunch and dinner from 11:30am till late (till 3pm on Sun). For stunning views of the cliffs at Cape Kidnappers, head to Clearview Estate's **Red Shed Restaurant,** 194 Clifton Rd., Te Awanga, Hastings (www.clearviewestate.co.nz; ℃ **06/875-0150**). It does delicious brunches and lunches that lean towards the Mediterranean, from light snacks to substantial ribstickers. You'll sitting among the vines as you quaff your glass of house wine; it's open daily from 10am to 5pm (late on Fri) in summer and daily except Tuesday and Wednesday from 11am to 4pm in winter.

Back in Hastings itself, **Opera Kitchen** ★★, 312 Eastbourne St., Hastings (www.eatdrinksharehb.co.nz; ℃ **06/870-6020**), is a fun and funky place that's generally heaving with people. It's open from Monday to Friday 7:30am to 4pm and weekends from 9am to 3pm, and does pre-theater drinks on nights when there's a show on at the nearby Hawke's Bay Opera House. **Little Black Bird Eatery and Catering,** 108 Market St., Hastings (℃ **06/870-7462**), does terrific coffee and tasty, original food: How about a rhubarb Fair Trade white-chocolate and duck-egg custard tart or salted chocolate profiteroles? These folks are quite committed to Fair Trade and organic produce, and of course heaps of it is grown locally as well. Little Black Bird is open Monday to Friday 7:30am to 3:30pm and Saturday 8am to 2:30pm.

Elephant Hill ★★★ CONTEMPORARY NEW ZEALAND Straight lines and extraordinary vistas are what this architecturally stunning property is all about. The coastal vineyard restaurant overlooks Cape Kidnappers with rows of vines offering perfect sightlines to the sea and the infinity water feature doing the same trick. It's a fine place to be in any weather. The food's not bad, either: Elephant Hill won *Cuisine* magazine's Best Winery Restaurant award in 2014, and you can see why as each monument to style comes out. I actually broke my rule about posting photos of food on Facebook and posted the main course of gnocchi tortellini with ricotta, carrots, black garlic, almond praline, and golden raisin puree as well as dessert: pear and frangipane tart with fig-leaf anglaise, walnut crumble, and stilton (yes, stilton!) ice cream. You'll enjoy the wine, too.

86 Clifton Rd, Te Awanga. www.elephanthill.co.nz. ✆ **06/872-6060.** Dinner reservations recommended. Main courses NZ$35–NZ$39. Daily noon tlll late (dinner Thurs–Sun in winter).

IN HAVELOCK NORTH

An impressive player in the vineyard restaurant stakes is **Black Barn Bistro** ★★★, Black Barn Road, Havelock North (www.blackbarn.com; ✆ **06/877-7985**), a stylish and sophisticated spot where you can sit inside or outside in a courtyard strung with fairy lights and gaze at the Tuki Tuki River and the valley below with drink in hand. In fact, everything about this very attractive place is a winner, and you can take home goodies from the kitchen shop onsite when you've eaten and drunk your fill. It's open for lunch Wednesday to Sunday 11am to 3pm (Fri 6:30–9pm) in the summer.

The lovely **Pipi Café,** 16 Joll Rd,, Havelock North (www.pipicafe.co.nz; ✆ **06/877-8993**), is pink! (A pipi is a New Zealand shellfish, which doesn't explain why this eatery is rosy-hued but there you have it.) This place is popular enough to have its own cookbook, and there's also a Pipi Bar across the road and a mobile Pipi Truck that sells fabulous homemade pizzas. It's open Tuesday to Sunday 4pm to 10pm.

Terrôir ★★★ FRENCH COUNTRY Craggy Range's outstanding restaurant was voted among the world's top 20 winery restaurants by website The Daily Meal in 2013, so it's definitely worth a visit, and *Condé Nast Traveler* said it was "a meal as close as you can get to perfection." As its name suggests, Terrôir is all about the inherent characteristics of the region's soil and climate, as reflected in its magnificent French country–style food and wine. Both are very good indeed, with hearty classics such as coq au vin and boeuf bourguignon usually on the menu.

253 Waimarama Rd., Havelock North. www.craggyrange.com. ✆ **06/873-0143.** Main courses NZ$35–NZ$39. Dinner reservations recommended. Mon–Sun noon–3pm and Mon–Sat 6–8:30pm in summer (Wed–Sun noon–3pm and Wed–Sat 6–8:30pm in winter).

En Route to Taupo

If you're heading along the Napier-Taupo Highway (SH5), it'll take you about 2½ hours. The road is winding in places and climbs to 708m (2,322 ft.) over the Titiokura Saddle, and may be closed by snow in the winter.

TARANAKI & WHANGANUI

Halfway between Auckland and Wellington and pointing into the Tasman Sea, Taranaki is truly out there. It boasts a busy and innovative little port city—New Plymouth—in the north but its heart is the beautiful and almost symmetrical Mount Taranaki, which rises up out on the flat countryside like Mt. Fuji without the concession booths. Taranaki's lush plains make it a leading dairying region but it's also an energy center with reserves of natural gas and oil both on- and offshore. If "white gold" is milk and "black gold" is oil, this is a rich region indeed. Welcome to "Taradise"!

South of Taranaki, Whanganui—or Wanganui as it used to be known: Both are correct—is built around its major waterway, literally and figuratively. The mystical Whanganui River may look tame as it wends its way lazily through the town, but the longest navigable river in New Zealand is rich in history and the biggest draw card for visitors to the region. A journey down the river—one of the Great Walks of New Zealand (go figure!)—is something you will always remember.

NEW PLYMOUTH: GATEWAY TO EGMONT NATIONAL PARK

412km (255 miles) W of Napier; 164km (102 miles) NW of Wanganui; 369km (229 miles) SW of Auckland

The Taranaki region is home to almost 115,000 creative, resourceful souls who love their world-class surf breaks, beautiful parks and gardens, and arts events the rest of the country envies. In 2009, the United Nations–endorsed Livable Communities Award named New Plymouth the best small city in the world and its stunning Coastal Walkway the world's best environmental project. It's buzzing with new projects and creative enterprises and is a fun and invigorating place to be.

Taranaki to Wellington

Waitaanga
Okau
Taumarunui
4
43
Aukopae
Waitara
Kirikau
Okoki
New Plymouth
Waitara River
Kohuratahi
Kaitieke
Oakura
3
3A
Egmont Village
Inglewood
Okato
Mt. Taranaki/ Mt. Egmont
43
WHANGANUI NATIONAL PARK
Orautoha
TONGARIRO NATIONAL PARK
Rahotu
EGMONT NATIONAL PARK
Stratford
Te Mapou
4
Oaonui
Eltham
Matemateaoriga
Whanganui River
Ohakune
Kaponga
Lake Rotorangi
Raetihi
Opunake
Pipiriki Jerusalem
Whangaehu River
Manaia
Normanby
Hawera
Waitotara River
Kakatahi
Mangawhero River
Waverley
Paparangi
Tiriaukawa
Patea
4
Mangamahu
Poukiore
Westmere
Fordoll
Hunterville
Whanganui
3
1
Marton
Halcombe
Bulls
Feilding
Palmerston North
Opiki
Foxton Beach
Foxton
Shannon
Levin
Tasman Sea
NORTH ISLAND
Auckland
Area of detail
SOUTH ISLAND
Wellington
Christchurch
Dunedin
0   25 mi
0   25 km
TARARUA FOREST PARK
Stephens Island
Rangitoto Islands
Waikanae Beach
1
Paraparaumu Raumati
Waikanae
Paekakariki
Masterton
MARLBOROUGH SOUNDS MARITIME PARK
Pukerua Bay
Carterton
Plimmerton
Greytown
Mt. Stokes
Porirua
Tawa
2
Upper Hutt
Martinborough
LOWER HUTT
Havelock
Anakiwa
Picton
WELLINGTON
6
1

Essentials

GETTING THERE & GETTING AROUND   **By Plane**   **Air New Zealand** ✆ **0800/737-000** in NZ; www.airnewzealand.co.nz) provides daily flights from Auckland, Wellington, and Christchurch. New Plymouth Airport is 8km (5 miles) from the city. **Scott's Airport Shuttle** (✆ **0800/373-001** in NZ or 06/769-5974; www.npairportshuttleco.nz) will get you there and back cheaper than a taxi.

By Coach (Bus)   **InterCity** (✆ **09/623-1503;** www.intercity.co.nz) provides a daily coach service from all over the North Island. **Citylink** and **Southlink** (✆ **06/765-7127;** www.trc.govt.nz/bus-routes) operate local city buses.

By Car   New Plymouth, on SH3 is a 5-hour drive from Taupo and Auckland and a 2-hour drive from Whanganui. You could also arrive via the **Forgotten World Highway (SH43)** ★★★, which runs from Taumarunui in the Ruapehu region and Stratford in Taranaki (see p. 176).

By Taxi   Try **New Plymouth Taxis** (✆ **06/757-3000**) or **Energy City Cabs** (✆ **0800/181-525** in NZ or 06/757-5580).

ORIENTATION   **Devon Street East** and **Devon Street West** are the main roads. Running parallel and to the north are the one-way streets **Powderham** and **Courtenay,** and to the west, **Vivian** and **Leach** streets. The main thoroughfare into the city from the south is **Eliot Street.** Once you've got the hang of the one-way pattern, you'll find it easy to find your way around.

VISITOR INFORMATION   Go to **www.taranaki.info**, the website for **Taranaki Venture Trust,** the province's official Regional Development Agency. The **New Plymouth i-SITE Visitor Centre,** Puke Ariki, 1 Ariki St. (www.newplymouthnz.com; ✆ **0800/639-759** in NZ, or 06/759-6060), is open Monday to Friday from 9am to 6pm (Wed until 9pm) and weekends from 9am to 5pm. The **South Taranaki i-SITE Visitor Centre,** 55 High St., Hawera (www.southtaranaki.com; ✆ **0800/111-323** in NZ, or 06/278-8599), is open Monday to Friday from 8:30am to 5pm, and weekends 10am to 3pm, December to April.

SPECIAL EVENTS   October's **Powerco Taranaki Garden Spectacular** (www.taft/gardenfestnz/welcome.html; ✆ **0800/746-363** in NZ or 06/759-8412) is a spring festival that allows you to poke around in local "gardens of

---

The Forgotten World Highway

If you have time and want to see the "backblocks" of the North Island, take the wonderful **Forgotten World Highway (SH43)** ★★★, a 3-hour scenic route between Taumarunui in the Ruapehu region and Stratford in Taranaki.

Note that 8km (5 miles) of the 155km (96-mile) road are unsealed and there are no petrol stations. Visitor centers will have the detailed brochure. For other ways to explore this route, see chapter 8.

New Plymouth: Gateway to Egmont National Park

TARANAKI & WHANGANUI

significance." The **TSB Bank Festival of Lights** ★★ (www.festivaloflights. co.nz; © **06/759-6060**) transforms beautiful Pukekura Park into an illuminated wonderland nightly from mid-December to late January. In March, the TSB Bowl of Brooklands in Pukekura Park becomes the home base for **WOMAD** (www.womad.co.nz), the huge 3-day festival of world music and dance, which has New Zealand acts as well as top international ones. The Bowl also has great local and overseas acts throughout the year.

Exploring the Towns
IN NEW PLYMOUTH
If you're staying in the city, you'll definitely want to check out the **Govett-Brewster Art Gallery/Len Lye Centre** ★★★, corner of Queen Street and Devon Street West (www.govettbrewster.com; © **06/759-6060**). The Govett-Brewster has always been a mainstay of support for contemporary New Zealand art with great permanent and temporary exhibitions. And in July 2015, the brand-new and very striking Len Lye Centre opened next door to the old, refurbished building. Designed to look like one of sculptor Len Lye's works, it has a 62-seat state-of-the-art cinema and bespoke gallery spaces. Born in Christchurch, Lye was an internationally recognized kinetic artist and experimental filmmaker who specialized in extraordinarily dynamic moving sculptures: To see his pieces in action can make you a bit scared of physics! His enormous **Wind Wand** installation on the waterfront has become a city landmark. A gift shop sells merchandise lines created especially for the galleries, as well as publications and other good-quality wares. There's also a very nice cafe, **Monica's Eatery** (Mon–Fri 7am to late and weekends 8am to late). The galleries are open 10am to 6pm daily (closed Tues) and till 9pm on Thursday.

Puke Ariki ★★★, 1 Ariki St. (www.pukeariki.com; © **06/759-6060**), is Taranaki's regional museum, a strikingly modern structure in the city center that also houses the public library and visitor center. It tells the story of Taranaki past and present, its Maori and Pakeha worlds and how they have interacted—sometimes violently, as was the case during the Land Wars of the 19th century. There is a terrific display of Maori *taonga* (treasures), and I like the way it focuses on major themes but also zero in on small stories, like that of Tamanui, the last Taranaki *kokako* (a very rare native bird with an exquisite song). He passed on to the big nest in the sky and is now stuffed and on display—but his progeny are thriving on pest-free islands and are soon to make a comeback to the region. You can watch a lovely short film about Tamanui and his legacy. Kids will love the prehistoric megalodon (like a giant great white shark), grinning and suspended from the ceiling, and the massive sperm whale flipper—who knew whales had great big hands with finger bones?

The complex has two cafes (see "Where to Eat," below). The museum is open Monday to Friday from 9am to 6pm (Wed until 9pm) and on weekends from 9am to 5pm. Admission is free.

If you like old houses, there's one sitting rather incongruously right in the middle of the city next to the ultra-modern Puke Ariki: **Richmond Cottage,** on Ariki Street, is a sweet little stone building from 1853 that was moved from the foreshore in the 1960s after it had served its purpose as a family home. It's open on weekends and public holidays from 11am to 3:30pm.

If you're driving south, take SH45—known around here as **Surf Highway 45**—rather than the more direct but less interesting SH3. Pick up the brochure and map from the visitor center and you'll pass some of the best surfing breaks in the country, as well as some nice little towns and access points to Mt. Taranaki. And if you're interested in the arty folk who live and produce stuff in the area, ask for the **Oakura Arts Trail** brochure while you're at it: It lists 14 creative types from in and around this little village working in a number of different mediums. Three of the best are **Ringcraft Moana,** 109 Surrey Hill Rd., Oakura (www.nzpearl.co.nz; ℂ **06/752-7772**), where goldsmith Rob Wright makes exquisite jewelry, including a Len Lye collection inspired by the artist's work that's also on sale at the new Len Lye Centre (he's got a gorgeous cat, too); **Korver Molloy Gallery,** 1729 South Rd., Tataraimaka (www.korvermolloy.com; ℂ **06/752-4131**), where Anna Korver and Steve Molloy create sometimes huge sculptures out of metal and wood (much of it recycled); and **Susan Imhasly,** 294A Surrey Hill Rd., Oakura (www.twinfelt. com; ℂ **027/976-6586**), who has taken felt-making to another level and crafts gorgeous, colorful clothing items, jewelry, and interior design objects like hobby-horses, cushions, and sculptures out of this versatile and very easy-to-source woolen material.

IN HAWERA

If you want to see New Zealand's history presented in a different way, head to Hawera, an hour's drive south of New Plymouth, to the **Tawhiti Museum ★★★**, 401 Ohangai Rd. (www.tawhitimuseum.co.nz; ℂ **06/278-6837**). The museum has won numerous awards and is regarded as the best private museum in the country. The people behind it are Nigel and Teresa Ogle. Nigel is an amazingly driven former art teacher who has created the whole thing with life-size exhibits and scale models that encapsulate the history of Taranaki. He has cast, painted, and dressed thousands of little figures for the museum's dioramas. In the **Traders & Whalers** section, you ride in a boat propelled by water through the dark and dingy early 19th century, where wild pigs and warriors brandishing muskets leap out at you and fast-talking salesmen do deals with the local Maori. The **Tawhiti Bush Railway** takes passengers on a little logging train around the museum environs. The train operates on the first Sunday of each month and most Sundays during school and public holidays. The museum is open daily 10am to 4pm in summer (Dec 26–Jan 31); Sunday only 10am to 4pm winter (June–Aug), and Friday to Monday 10am to 4pm the rest of the year. The museum and Traders & Whalers are both NZ$15 for adults, NZ$5 for children 5 to 15; the railway is NZ$6 for adults and NZ$3 for children. The museum also has a shop and a cafe.

Gardens Galore

With its warm climate, high rainfall, and volcanic soil, plants love Taranaki and you'll love its gardens. The "Taranaki Parks and Gardens" booklet lists 20 of the best ones, including the three owned and operated by the regional council, which have free admission: **Tupare** ★★, 487 Mangorei Rd., New Plymouth (www.tupare.info; ⓒ **0800/736-222** in NZ), is a gorgeous garden built on a hillside around a 1932 Arts & Crafts homestead that sits by the Waiwhakaiho River. It's open daily from 9am to 8pm in the summer and 9am to 5pm in winter. **Pukeiti** ★★, 2290 Carrington Rd. (www.pukeiti.org.nz; ⓒ **0800/736-222** in NZ), has one of the world's biggest collections of rhododendrons, along with camellia, magnolias, and other showy plants, set in native forest with kilometers of walking tracks. This one is a 30-minute drive from New Plymouth and is open daily 9am to 5pm: It's best to visit between July and December. **Hollard Gardens,** 1686 Upper Manaia Rd., Kaponga (www.hollardgardens.info; ⓒ **0800/736-222** in NZ), is a horticultural oasis out in cow country, with a mix of native forest and colorful flowering plants, productive vegetable garden and food forest. It also has a children's playground. It's open daily from 9am to 8pm in summer and 9am to 5pm in winter.

Pukekura Park and Brooklands ★★★, Fillis Street, New Plymouth (ⓒ **06/759-6060**), is one of the best inner-city parks in New Zealand and a winner on several levels. There's the beautiful park itself; the **Brooklands Zoo** (daily 9am–5pm); the **TSB Bowl of Brooklands,** a top open-air entertainment venue; playgrounds, a fernery, lakes, fountains, waterfalls, and specialist gardens—and it's all free to visit. Try to visit between Christmas and February; that's when the **TSB Bank Festival of Lights** ★★ takes place and the park is lit by millions of colored lights. **Te Kainga Marire,** 15 Spencer Place, New Plymouth (www.tekaingamarire.co.nz; ⓒ **06/758-8693**), is Maori for "peaceful encampment," and you'll understand why when you visit this private inner-city Garden of International Significance, where the focus is on native plants. It's open daily September through April from 9am to 5pm (admission NZ$10 per person).

Exploring Egmont National Park

This well-established national park dates back to 1900. Its 33,534 hectares (82,829 acres) are mainly made up of the volcanic peak of Mt. Taranaki (which was known as Mt. Egmont until 1986, although both names are still used). A spectacularly beautiful mountain 2,518m (8,261 ft.) high, it's made up of a number of different habitats: subalpine forest, volcanic scoria, mountain streams and waterfalls, rainforest, and alpine herb fields, with many kilometers of walks and trails to discover, from a 15-minute stroll to the 8-hour round-trip to the summit. Naturally, the latter and other alpine climbs should only be attempted by experienced hikers who know what they are doing and have the right gear: The weather can change extremely quickly on the mountain, and many people have lost their lives here. If you are going without a guide, always check conditions first with the **Taranaki/Egmont National Park Visitor Centre,** which is also a Department of Conservation office (2879 Egmont Rd., Egmont Village; www.doc.govt.nz; ⓒ **06/756-0990**). A 25-minute drive from New Plymouth on the north side of the

awesome DAWSON

The 18m (59-ft.) **Dawson Falls,** on the southeastern slopes of Mt. Taranaki, are an impressive sight and easy to reach, just a 20-minute walk from the car park. You can learn all about them at the **Dawson Falls Visitor Centre,** Manaia Road, Kaponga (✆ **027/443-0248**), open Thursday to Sunday and school and public holidays 9am to 4pm. There are lots of walks and hikes you can do from this side of the mountain, too. If you're driving, it's about an hour's drive south of New Plymouth on SH3 towards Stratford and is well signposted.

If you'd like to stay on the mountain, the rather wonderful **Dawson Falls Mountain Lodge & Café ★**, located right next to the visitor center (www.dawsonfallsmountainlodge.kiwi.nz; ✆ **06/765-5457**), is something of an institution. It was built in 1896 and these days is done up in Swiss chalet–style (one of the owners is from Switzerland). Rooms are from NZ$190 for a double with breakfast. The lodge has a restaurant (closed Tues–Wed) and cafe (open Thurs–Mon) on-site.

mountain, the visitor center has information about the park's history, geology, and flora and fauna. It's open daily from 8am to 4:30pm from the end of October to Easter and daily from 8:30am to 4pm the rest of the year. A cafe is open daily.

Several companies will transport you to the mountain, and a few also offer guiding services. **The Outdoor Gurus** (www.outdoorgurus.co.nz; ✆ **06/758-4152**) offer a shuttle bus service to the visitor center, picking up from hotels around the city at around 7:30am and returning around 5:30pm (NZ$45 per person or NZ$30 per person for two or more). **Taranaki Tours** (www.taranakitours.com; ✆ **06/757-9888**) does the same thing (NZ$55 for one person or NZ$45 per person for two or more). It also offers tours, including a full-day Around Mt Taranaki tour (NZ$250 for one person and NZ$160 each for two). **Withers Tours** (www.witherscoachlines.co.nz; ✆ **06/751-1777**) also does 2-hour and full-day tours of New Plymouth and the Taranaki region (NZ$55 per person and NZ$125 per person, respectively).

Outdoor Pursuits

KAYAKING   Canoe & Kayak Taranaki, 631 Devon Rd., New Plymouth (www.canoeandkayak.co.nz; ✆ **06/769-5506**), will take you out to the Sugar Loaf Marine Reserve (where you might see seals and other marine life), on the Mokau River, or for a ride on the Grade 2 rapids of the Waitara River. Tours are from NZ$70 per person. It also does kayak and stand-up paddleboard freedom hire (rentals) from NZ$45 and NZ$35.

SURFING   At the Beach Street Surf Shop, 39 Beach St., Fitzroy, New Plymouth (✆ **06/758-0400**), you can rent a board and a wetsuit, buy a secondhand board, get the latest surf conditions, and take some lessons—from beginner to advanced—on Fitzroy Beach with Daisy Day. The guys at Hawera-based **Tangaroa Surf Adventures** (✆ **06/278-1285**) will take you to some of the meanest breaks on Surf Highway 45, supplying transport, gear, and local knowledge.

WALKING There's plenty of that around here, even if you don't venture up the mountain. The booklet "A Walker's Guide" gives the lowdown on a range of walks, from gentle toddles to more active endeavors around the region; it's available at t he visitor center. Walking all or some of the multi-award-winning **Coastal Walkway** ★★★ is a must—and it passes right through the city, so you've got no excuses! It's 13km (8 miles) long and runs from Bell Block in the north to Port Taranaki in the south, and in places the ocean crashes against rocks right beside you—or underneath you if you're on the lookout that juts out into the sea, right by Len Lye's **"Wind Wand"** sculpture. The walkway is such a great addition to the city: Even on a bad day, you'll find people walking, jogging, and cycling its length.

Where to Stay

Taranaki has gone from being a bit of a hick outpost to a hip, happening, and thoroughly liveable (to use a rather horrible term) city in a couple of decades. That extends to its accommodation options: Lovely boutique lodges and smart inner-city pads are breaking out all over. For an economical stay 5 minutes from the city, try **One Burgess Hill,** 1 Burgess Hill Rd. (www.oneburgesshill. co.nz; © **06/757-2056**). Its 15 self-contained units overlooking the Waiwhakaiho River and the mountain run from NZ$140 to NZ$300 per night. Right in town is the modern **State Hotel,** 162 Devon St. E. (www.thestatehotel. co.nz; © **06/757-5162**), which bills itself as "the king of economy"; rooms start at NZ$135. Fifteen minutes from town is the **Taranaki Country Lodge** ★★, 169 Hursthouse Rd. (www.taranakicountrylodge.co.nz; © **0800/395-863** in NZ, or 06/755-0274). This modern, award-winning property has two attractive and spacious suites for NZ$200 to NZ$300 per night. Breakfast is included and you can request a big country dinner as well.

Hosking House ★★★ This lovely boutique B&B is close to beautiful Pukekura Park. It's the labor of love of Kiwi Rodney and New Yorker Rachel, who have turned a beautiful old wooden villa into a welcome oasis of tranquility and comfort. And they're really nice, too! Apart from the luxurious touches you'd expect, there's also fresh homemade cakes in tins and a very nice garden in which to savor them. And my suite had a clawfoot tub for a good old wallow at the end of the day.

1 Victoria St. www.hoskinghouse.com. © **06/758-1681.** 3 suites. NZ$165–NZ$220. Long-stay rates and special deals. Rates includes breakfast. **Amenities:** Wi-Fi.

King & Queen Hotel Suites ★★★ This very chic addition to New Plymouth's high-end accommodation sector makes much of the fact that the hotel is on the intersection of two royal roads. The decor, however, ditches Louis IV for a more modern European/Moroccan (nice comfy leather sofas!) look. The suites are very urban sophisticated without being pretentious; some even have enormous balconies so you can keep an eye on the city action below.

Corner of King and Queen sts. www.kingandqueen.co.nz. © **0800/574-683** in NZ, or 06/757-2999. 17 suites. NZ$220–NZ$415. Long-stay rates and special deals. Free parking. **Amenities:** Bikes; free access to City Fitness gym; dining chargeback facilities for local restaurants; Wi-Fi.

Nice Hotel ★★★ And very nice it is, too. This used to be New Plymouth's only small luxury hotel, and new competition has made it even better. Rooms are stylish and modern with all the right luxuries, and it has a lovely and very popular restaurant downstairs (see "Where to Eat"). The main hotel building is actually New Plymouth's oldest wooden structure, built in 1870; the long-stay suites are in another building next door. The hotel offers little extras like a tropical garden deck, an art collection, and a library where you'll be offered a complimentary drink while you read. But don't bring kids under 12. Apparently, that's not Nice for the other guests.

71 Brougham St. www.nicehotel.co.nz. ✆ **06/758-6423.** NZ$250–NZ$350 (double); suites $500. Long-stay rates and special deals. No children under 12. **Amenities:** Restaurant and private dining rooms; bar; bikes; Wi-Fi.

The Waterfront Hotel ★ Big, bright and modern, these beachfront luxury digs are adjacent to Puke Ariki. The rooms are large and comfortable, and each of the one-bedroom apartments has its own Jacuzzi. The hotel is handy to everything, but with a good restaurant on-site you won't have far to go for a feed.

1 Egmont St. www.waterfront.co.nz. ✆ **0508/843-9282** in NZ, or 06/769-5301. 42 units. NZ$180–NZ$550. Long-stay and off-peak rates and special deals. **Amenities:** Restaurant; bar; airport transport; babysitting; free membership to town gym; room service; Wi-Fi.

IN OAKURA

Ahu Ahu Beach Villas ★★★ Fifteen minutes south of New Plymouth, David and Nuala's lovely beach accommodation defies description. Actually, that's not true: David described at great length the hugely enjoyable effort he went to sourcing, recycling, and upcycling all manner of bits and pieces—100-year-old French clay tiles from Stratford Hospital, timbers from ports here and in Nelson, cross-arms from power poles, curtain rails made of rake handles and driftwood—to fashion these four units and three family villas. They look amazing, and so is their location, in a prime position overlooking the always-animated Tasman Sea. It's luxurious and private and simply sensational, plus you'll feel good that the materials are living their lives all over again with these delightful people.

321 Ahu Ahu Rd., Oakura. www.ahu.co.nz. ✆ **06/752-7370.** 4 villas and 3 family villas. NZ$195–NZ$550. Long-stay rates and special deals. Breakfast available on request. **Amenities:** Bikes available for rent; outside firepit; Wi-Fi.

Where to Eat

New Plymouth has a pretty funky restaurant scene these days. For great rib-sticking hearty food that almost puts this place into gastro-pub territory, try **The Black Harp** ★, 31 Gover St. (www.blackharp.com; ✆ **06/758-5373**). It's an Irish bar with lots of dim, cozy corners lined with books, clocks, stuffed creatures and old photographs and you could nurse a Guinness by the fire quite happily for an afternoon. I arrived on a pouring afternoon and it felt very snug and welcoming: The chicken, leek, and potato pie with parmesan crust served with coleslaw went down a treat with a nice cup of tea.

The award-winning **Table at Nice Hotel** ★★ (www.nicehotel.co.nz; ℂ **06/758-6423**), open daily for lunch and dinner, offers international flavors with a Kiwi twist and is considered one of New Plymouth's finest restaurants. Also vying for that distinction is **Arborio** ★★ (www.arborio.co.nz; ℂ **06/759-1241**), a restaurant, cafe, and bar located on the ground floor at Puke Ariki and serving sophisticated Italian-oriented cuisine daily from 9am until late. Puke Ariki's more informal **Taranaki Daily News Café** (www.pukeariki.com; ℂ **06/758-4544**) is a modern espresso bar with a good collection of newspapers and magazines to read—one newspaper in particular, you can be sure! It's open daily from 9:30am to 3:30pm.

If you crave a curry, **PaNKaWaLLa** ★★, 85 Devon St. W. (www.pankawalla.co.nz; ℂ **06/758-4444**), serves really good Indian food in a contemporary setting and is open daily for lunch and dinner. The folks at **Ozone Coffee Roasters** ★, 47A King St. (www.ozonecoffee.com; ℂ **06/757-5404**), really care about coffee, to the point where they offer domestic barista workshops to make you better at it, too, which doesn't seem to kill business. They serve a pretty limited range of food and sell coffee-making paraphernalia; it's open Monday to Friday 7am to 3:30pm and Saturday 8am to 3pm. The very hospitable people at the **Hour Glass** ★★, 49 Liardet St. (ℂ **06/758-2299**), do their best to make your evening a pleasant one. It's a bar that also serves yummy tapas, a limited menu of mains, and dessert. Down by the port end of town on Ocean View Parade, **Gusto** (www.gustotaranaki.co.nz; ℂ **06/759-8133**) is open all day every day in a light, bright modern building that looks like a boatshed and is so close to the water you could launch a craft without even breaking the froth on your coffee. Have a drink and a meal (lots of seafood on offer), and enjoy the view. Also on the parade is **Bach on Breakwater** (www.bachonbreakwater.co.nz; ℂ **06/769-6967**), which is very popular for Sunday brunch and does a fixed-price three-course menu on Sunday night for NZ$46. It's open all day but closed Monday and Tuesday.

In the quiet farming town of Inglewood, 20 minutes southeast of New Plymouth on SH3, **Caffe Windsor,** 1 Kelly St. (www.caffewindsor.co.nz; ℂ **06/756-6665**)—so named because it's situated within the popular 4.5km (2.7-mile) Windsor Walkway loop trail—is an enduring favorite in a lovely old building. This is where you'll find the locals, especially Thursday to Saturday, when it closes late (it's open daily from 8:30am). If you're heading south via Surf Highway 45, you'll pass through Okato, where the funky little country cafe and restaurant **Lahar** ★, 64 Carthew St. (ℂ **06/752-4865**), serves great food and coffee.

The Social Kitchen ★★ CONTEMPORARY Brand-new, and with a modern industrial vibe, this was the hippest place around when I visited. In a high-ceilinged old Salvation Army citadel, big, dangly lamps have been hung from vintage firemen's ladders and mounted stags' heads have been thrown on the walls (what is it with stuffed dead things around here?). There's a weird art installation of meat cuts and salami (fake) hung on butcher's hooks and the repeated motif of a bull smoking a pipe and wearing a suit: Upmarket slaughterhouse meets gentlemen's club? Whatever it is, the food is great and the staff is very friendly. Plus, they seem to be doing their best to make sherry fashionable again. Shared plates are the thing, but you'll have plenty of meaty main courses to choose from (steaks, venison, free-range pork belly), although vegetarians won't run away in tears. My Queensland banana prawns with lemon, chili, garlic, and herbs and haloumi flamed with ouzo, lemon, and thyme were delicious, as was the baked toffee custard.

40 Powderham St. www.social-kitchen.co.nz. ℰ **0508/843-9282** in NZ, or 06/757-2711. Small plates NZ$4–NZ$35; main courses NZ$23–NZ$63. Daily noon to late.

En Route to Whanganui

If you're driving south, it's a 2½-hour drive from New Plymouth to Whanganui through rolling verdant farmland where cows are king—or queen! Take **Surf Highway 45,** the slightly longer route, if you've got time.

9 WHANGANUI

164km (102 miles) SE of New Plymouth; 141km (87 miles) SW of Tongariro National Park; 193km (120 miles) N of Wellington; 252km (156 miles) SW of Napier

The Whanganui River begins its 290km (180-mile) journey as snow melt in the upper reaches of Tongariro National Park, continues on through parts of beautiful Whanganui National Park, and ends in the city of Whanganui (what else would it be called?), where it flows into the Tasman Sea. Maori have lived in this area for more than 800 years, and one of their traditional proverbs includes the line: "Ko au te awa, ko te awa ko au." ("I am the river, the river is me.") Today, the district has a modest population of only about 43,500, but it punches above its weight in creative terms: Whanganui boasts more than 400 resident artists and has a worldwide reputation as the home of New Zealand art glass, with 40+ glass artists and workers in many other mediums living here. It also has a thriving theater and music scene, and there's a good chance that anything you go and look at in the city will take place in a beautiful old historic building—Whanganui has more heritage buildings than most cities of its size in New Zealand. Its main street, Victoria Avenue, has the added bonus of mature trees all the way along it.

Essentials

GETTING THERE & GETTING AROUND By Plane **Whanganui Airport,** 10 minutes from the city, is served daily by **Air New Zealand** (www.airnewzealand.co.nz; ℰ **0800/737-000** in NZ) for flights from Auckland; and by **Sounds Air** (www.soundsair.com; ℰ **0800/505-005** in NZ) for Wellington flights.

By Coach (Bus) **InterCity** (ℰ **09/623-1503**) has services between Whanganui and Auckland, New Plymouth, National Park Village (in Tongariro National Park), and Wellington. For information on urban buses, go to **www. horizons.govt.nz.**

By Car Whanganui is on state highways 3 and 4. It is a 2½-hour drive from New Plymouth or Wellington, 3 hours from Taupo, and 4 hours from Rotorua.

By Taxi Try **Wanganui Taxis** (ⓒ **0800/500-000** in NZ, or 06/343-5555).

VISITOR INFORMATION Go to the **Visit Whanganui** website at **www. whanganuinz.com**. The **i-SITE Whanganui Visitor Information Centre,** 31 Taupo Quay (ⓒ **0800/926-426** in NZ, or 06/349-0508), is open Monday to Friday 8:30am to 5pm and weekends and public holidays 9am to 5pm in summer (till 4pm weekends and public holidays in winter).

SPECIAL EVENTS More than 150 artists display their glass, ceramics, printmaking, jewelry, and painting during the **Artists Open Studios & Glass Festival** (www.openstudios.co.nz), held over two weekends in late March. If you're an opera fan and you're here in January, check out the highly regarded **Wanganui Opera Week** (www.wow.gen.nz) for recitals, masterclasses, and a gala concert at the Royal Wanganui Opera House.

Exploring Wanganui
THE MAIN ATTRACTIONS

Sarjeant on the Quay ★★★, temporarily at Taupo Quay before returning to Queen's Park in 2019 (www.sarjeant.org.nz; ⓒ **06/349-0506**), is a terrific and highly regarded gallery that has a large collection of overseas works, as well as an excellent New Zealand collection with an emphasis on photography. The historic building is being earthquake-strengthened, but the temporary quarters, opposite the I-SITE, gives you a taste of what's to come and is definitely worth a visit. It's open daily 10:30am to 4:30pm, and admission is free.

The **Whanganui Regional Museum** ★★, Watt Street (www.wrm.org.nz; ⓒ **06/349-1110**), is another very grown-up provincial treasure with passionate staff who just love this region and its stories. It has magnificent *waka* (canoes) and other Maori artifacts, as well as a great natural history section, including one of the biggest collections of moa bones and skeletons in the country. (Now extinct, moa were long-necked birds a bit like ostriches that ranged in size from chickens to the biggest bird that ever lived.) Other permanent and temporary exhibitions shine a light on all sorts of aspects of life here, with plenty of attention paid to the importance of the Whanganui River, present and past. It's open daily 10am to 4:30pm; and admission is free.

Paloma Gardens, Pohutukawa Lane, Fordell, Whanganui (www.paloma. co.nz; ⓒ **06/342-7857**), is a private garden with several distinct zones, including the Palm Garden, the Desert House, and the rather unfriendly sounding Garden of Death! The entry fee is NZ$10, and it's open year-round (but a bit coy about naming which days; call before you go). It's a Garden of National Significance, along with **Bason Botanic Gardens** ★★, 552 Rapanui Rd. (www.basonbotanicgardens.org.nz), which is 11km (7 miles) out of town and has loads of rare orchids, native and exotic trees, and places to picnic. Entry is free, and it's open daily from 8am until dusk.

Culture vultures should pick up the "Whanganui Arts Guide" from the visitor center for the lowdown on where to find the region's top artists in many mediums. Lots of studios and galleries are scattered around town. **Chronicle Glass Studio,** 2 Rutland St. (www.chronicleglass.co.nz; ✆ **06/347-1921**), is the open workspace of talented local glass blowers Katie Brown and Lyndsay Patterson, who also display the work of other glass artists.

Virginia Lake, on St. John's Hill (www.wanganui.govt.nz), is a nice place for a stroll. There are ducks, swans, pukekos, an aviary, the Winter Gardens (daily 9am–5pm), an Art Garden, and a fountain that lights up at night. It takes about half an hour to walk around the lake. The local New World supermarket sells bags of day-old bread for NZ$1 if you want to feed the birds.

Here's a well-disguised little treasure: **St. Paul's Memorial Church,** in Putiki across the bridge from town (20 Anaua St.), has had its wooden exterior plastered over and looks like any small Anglican parish church from the outside. But go in and you'll be overwhelmed by a completely different view: The whole interior is covered with Maori carvings and *tukutuku* (wall panels). If you go on a Sunday, you can attend the local service. Otherwise, pick up the key from the i-SITE. It's NZ$2 per person plus a refundable deposit of NZ$2.

EXPLORING THE WHANGANUI RIVER & WHANGANUI NATIONAL PARK

There are a number of ways to explore the Whanganui River and the road that winds alongside it. Both dip in and out of the southern part of beautiful Whanganui National Park, which was established in 1986, protecting one of the largest tracts of lowland forest remaining in the North Island. Confusingly, however, much of the national park and river are within the Ruapehu Region (see chapter 8), and many people access the river from there. Listed below are activities that are based in the Whanganui region.

BY CAR You can drive the 64km (40-mile) Whanganui River Road from Whanganui to the little settlement of Pipiriki, which is just over the Ruapehu border, and the famous Bridge to Nowhere. The isolated and winding but very scenic road has numerous points of historical interest along the way, including the beautifully restored Kawana Mill, Atene (Athens), Koroniti (Corinth),

---

Moving Up in the World

Built in 1919, the **Durie Hill Elevator and Tower,** Victoria Avenue, is New Zealand's only public underground lift and one of only two in the world. A pedestrian tunnel burrows 215m (699 ft.) into the hillside, and then the elevator swoops you 66m (216 ft.) to the summit, where you get some great views of the Tasman Sea and mountains Ruapehu and Taranaki on a good day. If you've got the energy for it (or are highly caffeinated), you might want to then tackle the spiral staircase, 176 steps up the Memorial Tower. It's open daily Monday to Friday 8am to 6pm and weekends and public holidays 10am to 5pm: Entry to the tunnel is free and a trip in the elevator costs NZ$2 one-way for adults and NZ$1 for children.

The River Traders & Whanganui Farmer's Market

Farmer's markets are everywhere these days, but this one combines fresh local produce with choice wares from some of the region's cleverest arty people at great wholesale prices. It's held every Saturday from 9am to 1pm beside the river behind the Whanganui Riverboat Centre (www.therivertraders.co.nz; ℭ 06/343-9795). While you're there, you'll see the **Tram Shed** (www.tramwayswanganui.org.nz; ℭ **06/345-7034**), a wee museum about all things tram-related, as well as Whanganui's lovingly restored Number 12 tram. You can jump in, have a look, and even go for a ride every Sunday between 12:30pm and 3:30pm (NZ$2 per person).

Ranana (London), and Hiruharama (Jerusalem). The redoubtable Sister Mary Joseph founded a Catholic Maori Mission, the Daughters of Our Lady of Compassion, in 1892, and the tiny settlement was home to New Zealand poet James K. Baxter in the 1970s.

BY AERIAL CABLEWAY The Flying Fox ★★ (www.theflyingfox.co.nz; ℭ 06/342-8160) is a slow and gentle way to view the river from above. This delightful slice of hospitality in the middle of nowhere is a 45-minute drive from Whanganui. (Nowhere is quite a popular destination out this way!) You get here by aerial cable car (or "flying fox," although a true Kiwi flying fox is actually a zipline). Never mind: This is very cool, and you can also stay in one of the cute cottages (see below). To get here, take a jetboat tour or drive up Whanganui River Road. A number of tours stop here (see "By Bus," below).

BY BUS Help deliver the post with the popular **Whanganui River Road Mail Tour** ★★ (www.whanganuitours.co.nz; ℭ 06/345-3475) as the posties wend their way to remote locations. They travel on weekdays (NZ$63 per person). Or ride a customized minibus tour with **Whanganui River Road Tours** (www.whanganuiriverroad.com; ℭ 0800/201-234 in NZ). A 5-hour trip is NZ$80 per person.

BY KAYAK The Flying Fox (see above) offers a 3-hour kayak or canoe trip for NZ$85 per person and a half-day jetboat/kayak trip for NZ$160 per person. (For longer trips, most of which leave from Taumarunui in the Ruapehu district, see chapter 8.) These trips can be booked from Whanganui.

BY RIVERBOAT The "Waimarie," New Zealand's only coal-fired paddle steamer, was built in 1890, sank in 1952, and was salvaged in 1993. It was lovingly rebuilt at the **Whanganui Riverboat Centre,** 1A Taupo Quay (www.riverboats.co.nz; ℭ 06/347-1863), a museum chronicling the history of riverboats in the area. Daily 2-hour cruises travel up the Whanganui River (summer at 2pm, with reduced cruises in winter; NZ$39 adults and NZ$15 children 5–15). The center is open Thursday to Saturday from 11am to 2pm; admission is free.

ON FOOT The **Department of Conservation,** Whanganui Area Office, 34 Taupo Quay (www.doc.govt.nz; ℭ 06/349-2100), has information on a range of walks. Among them, the **Skyline Walk** is 6 to 8 hours but reward you with fabulous views of Mt. Ruapehu and Mt. Taranaki. The **Matemateaonga Track** takes 3 to 4 days.

Outdoor Pursuits

BEACHES   **Castlecliff Beach,** 9km (5½ miles) from town, is a wild West Coast beach with black iron sand—good for swimming and surfing and patrolled by lifeguards in summer. Near the airport, **South Beach** is great for surfing and fishing, and **Kai Iwi Beach,** 14km (8½ miles) west of Whanganui, has very photogenic cliffs and is safe for kids.

GOLF   The **Wanganui Golf Club,** Clarkson Avenue (www.wanganuigolf-club.co.nz; ✆ **06/349-0559**), is an 18-hole championship course. Greens fees are NZ$40 for 18 holes and NZ$25 for 9 holes.

Where to Stay

It is fair to say that Whanganui is not teeming with upmarket hotels. There are lots of motels and homestays, and, thankfully, some nice B&Bs are getting established. So this is the ideal opportunity to try something different. Whanganui is good at that!

The **Flying Fox ★★**, 45 minutes out of town (www.theflyingfox.co.nz; ✆ **06/342-8160**), is a case in point, given that you arrive via an aerial cableway (see above). It has three two-bedroom cottages hand-built out of recycled native timbers (NZ$200 for two) and a tiny cabin on wheels, the "Glory Cart" (NZ$100 for two). They'll do breakfast or just hang out with you under the huge walnut trees. Unique enough for you?

The **Dunes,** 137 Karaka St., Castlecliff, Whanganui (✆ **021/635-507**), is a nice, modern beach house right on the seafront with all the modcons (including a full kitchen) and still close to town. It sleeps six people and is from NZ$170 per night. **Gumnut House,** 21 Ikitara Rd. (www.gumnuthouse.co.nz; ✆ **06/343-3276**), is a lovely house on a big property just a 10-minute walk along the riverbank to Whanganui's main street. Rooms are from NZ$120 per night including breakfast. The luxury apartment motel **Aotea Motor Lodge,** 390 Victoria Ave. (www.aoteamotorlodge.co.nz; ✆ **06/345-0303**), is even closer to the action. You won't get stunning views or the quirkiness factor of a B&B, but everything is immaculate and where you'd expect to find it and it's got giant two-person spa baths for companionable soaking. Tariffs are NZ$150 to NZ$210 per night.

Where to Eat

Once you've checked out the visitor center, have a bite at **Mud Ducks Café,** 31 Taupo Quay (✆ **06/348-7626**), next door. Walk a few steps down to the river at low tide, and you'll see why it is so named. It does the coffee-and-cabinet-food thing very well, with cheerful service, and is open daily 8:30am to 4pm. For something a bit fancier, try lunch or dinner at **Element Café and Bistro,** 26 Victoria Ave. (✆ **06/345-7028;** www.elementcafe.co.nz), which is very centrally located in a grand old building on the main street; it does country-sized portions of good standards like chowder and red pork curry. The **Yellow House Café ★★**, 17 Pitt St. (© **06/345-0083**), serves healthy homemade lunches and solid coffee from its suburban location near the river. It's open Monday to Friday 8am to 4pm and weekends 8:30am to 4pm.

The Red Lion Inn ★ CONTEMPORARY   Have a drink in the public bar, a casual meal downstairs, or a flasher one upstairs, or host a function: You can do it all in this lovely old historic house right by the river. In the upstairs restaurant, the portions are huge, but the prices aren't—each of the hearty, satisfying mains (pork, lamb, beef, chicken, done imaginatively) is NZ$30. It's warm and welcoming, with friendly, unpretentious service. The **Café Bar** downstairs does NZ$8 burgers on Monday and Tuesday nights.

45 Anzac Parade. www.redlioninn.co.nz. © **06/348-4080.** Main courses NZ$30. Daily 10am till late.

En Route to Wellington

You can get to Wellington on SH1 down the coast via Levin, Waikanae, and Paraparaumu (the better road), or via Palmerston North and the Wairarapa (see chapter 10). Both trips take about 2½ hours. The **Palmerston North City & Manawatu i-SITE,** The Square, Palmerston North (www.manawatunz. co.nz; © **0800/626-292** in NZ, or 06/358-8414), can help with accommodations and local highlights. It's open Monday to Friday 9am to 5pm and weekends 9am to 3pm.

WELLINGTON & THE WAIRARAPA

Wellington might be our seat of government—you'll see more suited civil servants here than anywhere else—but Wellingtonians sure know how to party when the ties come off! This is New Zealand's coolest and most sophisticated city, a population little more than 200,000 shoehorned between a mercurial harbor and the hills, with the South Island on its doorstep and the rest of the North Island at its back. Wellingtonians live with its bracing breezes and love it just the same: As the saying here goes, "You can't beat Wellington on a good day!" Take the cable car up to Kelburn, find a shady hideaway in the Botanic Gardens, see rare native animals at the Zealandia Wildlife Sanctuary, get in touch with your funky self on Cuba St.—just jump right in.

Over the hill—in a geographic sense only!—lies the appealingly flat region known as the Wairarapa. It's where Wellingtonians come for weekend rebalancing: to sip wine from some of the best boutique vineyards in the land, to chill out in the delightful little towns, and to experience the splendid isolation of its wild, unpeopled coast. But Wairarapa is full of pretty special locals, too, who are coming up with all sorts of interesting ways to celebrate their special place.

WELLINGTON

Essentials

GETTING THERE & ARRIVING

BY PLANE **Wellington International Airport** (www.wellingtonairport.co.nz) is 8km (5 miles) is southeast of the CBD, via the Mount Victoria tunnel or, more scenically, Oriental Parade. It's a 15- to 20-minute drive (but can take longer during rush hours). **Air New Zealand** (www.airnewzealand.co.nz; ✆ **0800/737-000** in NZ); **Qantas** (www.qantas.com; ✆ 0800/808-767 in NZ); **Fiji Airways** (www.fijiairways.com; ✆ 0800/800-178 in NZ); **Jetstar** (www.jetstar.com/nz; ✆ 0800/800-995); and **Virgin Australia** (www.virginaustralia.com; ✆ 0800/670-000 in NZ) are the major international carriers at this point.

The main domestic airlines that fly into Wellington are **Air New Zealand, Jetstar,** and **Sounds Air** (www.soundsair.com; © **0800/505-505** in NZ). For **arrival and departure information** for all of these, call © **04/388-9900.**

The Wellington airport terminal has nine cafes and restaurants in a large food hall, as well as car-rental desks, duty-free stores, gift shops, a Travelex Foreign Exchange service, free Wi-Fi, and ATMs. Coin-operated lockers are on the ground floor.

Super Shuttle (www.supershuttle.co.nz; © **0800/748-885** in NZ, or 04/472-9552) runs between the airport, the city, and the railway station Monday to Friday for NZ$25 per person. Several shuttle operators provide door-to-door service for a bit more.

The **Airport Flyer** (www.airportflyer.co.nz; © **04/569-2933**) goes into the inner city and then on to Queensgate in Lower Hutt. It operates every 20 minutes, 365 days a year, from 6:30am to 9pm. It's NZ$6 to NZ$12 for adults and NZ$4 to NZ$7 for children one-way.

A **taxi** from the CBD to the airport costs around NZ$35. Taxi stands are located directly outside the main terminal. **Eco Taxis** (www.ecotaxis.co.nz; © **027/750-2075**) have a fixed fare of NZ$25 into the city (if you pay cash).

BY TRAIN & COACH (BUS) **Wellington Railway Station** is on Waterloo Quay. For long-distance **rail** information, check out www.tranzscenic.co.nz (© **0800/802-802** in NZ or 04/495-0775). Most major hostels and hotels are within a short taxi ride of the station. For travel by **coach,** call **InterCity** (www.intercity.co.nz; © **09/623-1503**).

BY CAR SH1 and SH2 lead into Wellington: It's 195km (121 miles) from Wanganui (about 2 hr.), 460km (285 miles) from Rotorua (about 5 hr.) and 655km (406 miles) from Auckland (about 8 hr.). The motorway terminates right in the city.

BY FERRY Two operators run passenger and car ferries across the Cook Strait from Picton to Wellington: the **Interislander** (www.interislander.co.nz; © **0800/802-802** in NZ) and **Bluebridge** (www.bluebridge.co.nz; © **0800/844-844** in NZ). Both operate year-round and charge about NZ$55 per adult foot passenger; the trip takes about 3 hours. It's about NZ$230 for a small car and two adults. Cook Strait can be vile in bad weather, so if you're prone to seasickness, take precautions!

VISITOR INFORMATION

The official website for **Positively Wellington Tourism** is **www.wellingtonnz.com**. The **Wellington i-SITE Visitor Centre,** 101 Wakefield St., Civic Square (© **04/802-4860**), is open Monday to Friday from 8:30am to 5:30pm (Tues till 5pm) and weekends from 9:30am to 4:30pm. In addition to providing the usual local information, it's got a cafe.

SPECIAL EVENTS

Run by Wellington City Council, the **Summer City Festival** (www.wellington.govt.nz; © **04/499-4444**) is 4 months of free concerts and fabulous fun that runs from the beginning of December until the end of March, typically

Wellington City

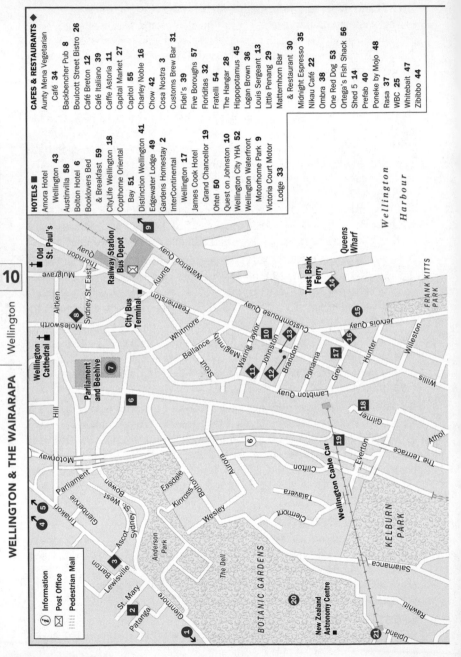

CAFES & RESTAURANTS ◆

Aunty Mena Vegetarian Café **34**
Backbencher Pub **8**
Boulcott Street Bistro **26**
Café Breton **12**
Café Italiano **39**
Caffe Astoria **11**
Capital Market **27**
Capitol **55**
Charley Noble **16**
Chow **42**
Cosa Nostra **3**
Customs Brew Bar **31**
Fidel's **39**
Five Boroughs **57**
Floriditas **32**
Fratelli **54**
The Hangar **28**
Hippopotamus **45**
Logan Brown **36**
Louis Sergeant **13**
Little Penang **29**
Matternhorn Bar & Restaurant **30**
Midnight Espresso **35**
Nikau Café **22**
Ombra **38**
One Red Dog **53**
Ortega's Fish Shack **56**
Shed 5 **14**
Prefab **40**
Poneke by Mojo **48**
Rasa **37**
WBC **25**
Whitebait **47**
Zibibbo **44**

HOTELS ■

Amora Hotel Wellington **43**
Austinvilla **58**
Bolton Hotel **6**
Booklovers Bed & Breakfast **59**
CityLife Wellington **18**
Copthorne Oriental Bay **51**
Distinction Wellington **41**
Edgewater Lodge **49**
Gardens Homestay **2**
InterContinental Wellington **17**
James Cook Hotel Grand Chancellor **19**
Ohtel **50**
Quest on Johnston **10**
Wellington City YHA **52**
Wellington Waterfront Motorhome Park **9**
Victoria Court Motor Lodge **33**

Information ⓘ
Post Office ✉
Pedestrian Mall ┊┊┊

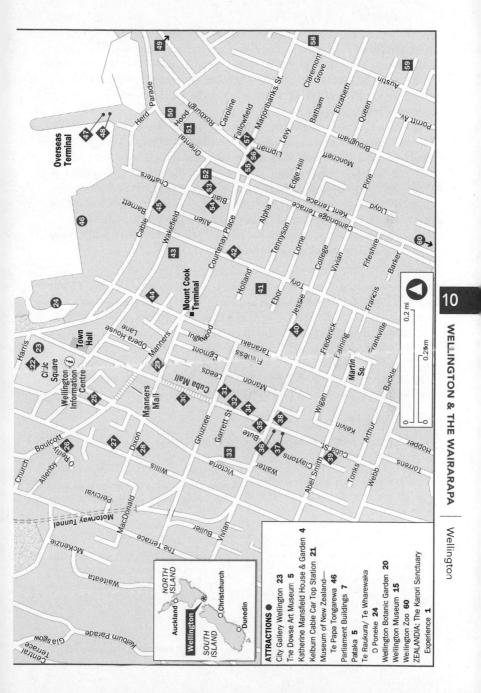

featuring more than 100 events all over town. The country's biggest cultural event takes place in Wellington late in February every 2 years (the even-numbered ones): The **New Zealand Festival** ★★★ (www.festival.co.nz; ✆ **04/473-0149**) is an eagerly anticipated celebration of the very best in local and international creativity—music, dance, theater, comedy—from all corners of the globe. Its oddball offsider, the **Wellington Fringe Festival** ★★ (www.fringe.org.nz; ✆ **04/212-4725**) takes place at the same time but is a separate event and is held annually.

In mid- to late August, foodies gather like sharply dressed vultures for the 2-week **Wellington on a Plate** ★★ (www.wellingtononaplate.com; ✆ **04/473-8044**), the capital's premier celebration of the best in food, wine and hospitality, with culinary events taking place all over the region. The **World of Wearable Art Awards Show** ★★★ (www.worldofwearableart.com; ✆ **03/547-0864**), known as "WOW," bills itself as an event "where fashion and theatre collide." Taking place late in September, it's an annual costume extravaganza that began life in a tent in Nelson in 1987 and now attracts audiences of more than 20,000 during its 3-week run.

ORIENTATION

From the railway station end of town, the major thoroughfare **Lambton Quay** runs roughly parallel to the harbor, and many shops, offices, and government buildings can be found here. **The Terrace,** where some of the larger hotels and apartment complexes are found, is on a hill up above this flat area. **Willis Street, Manners Street,** and **Courtenay Place** (the last having a large concentration of restaurants and bars, along with **Wakefield, Blair,** and **Allen sts.**) are other key roads that follow the line of the harbor, leading towards **Oriental Bay. Cuba Street** runs perpendicular to these.

Neighborhoods in Brief

Thorndon A top suburb full of cute Victorian houses and high-ranking government folk, including politicians who have their capital-city crash pads here. It's super-close to the inner city or the delightful Botanic Garden, with great views and some lovely B&Bs. Parts of it are close to the motorway, however, and parking can be a problem.

Kelburn Full of university students and academics, Kelburn is an up-and-down suburb with gorgeous houses, narrow streets, and million-dollar views. It's easily accessed

via the Cable Car from Lambton Quay; this is another way to access the Botanic Garden.

Mount Victoria See the city from the other side: Mount Vic is at the Courtenay Place end of town—great for eating out and partying the night away. Most of the parking is residents-only during business hours, but it's a free-for-all after 6pm.

Oriental Bay A little farther around, this is blue-ribbon Wellington, a stone's throw from the CBD so you won't need a car. The area has a number of hotels and some very good cafes and restaurants.

GETTING AROUND

Wellington has the country's best public transport system, so you shouldn't need a car. Go to **www.metlink.org.nz** for information about all forms of public transport.

BY BUS GO Wellington (www.gowellingtonbus.co.nz; ✆ **04/387-8700**) has information on all urban services. Buses operate daily from 7am to 11pm on most routes and you can get a city map that shows major bus routes and timetables from the visitor center. The main city bus terminal is **Lambton Interchange.** It's adjacent to the main railway station on Bunny Street.

A **Metlink Explorer Pass** (NZ$21) offers unlimited travel for 1 day after 9am on weekdays and all day on weekends and public holidays on bus and train services around Wellington and the Hutt Valley, and children up to 15 are free. A **BusAbout Pass** (NZ$9.50) is the same but for buses only. A stored-value **Snapper Card** (www.snapper.co.nz; ✆ **0800/555-345**) is NZ$10 for adults and children. You load on as much money as you like and use it for bus and Cable Car fares and even everyday items.

BY TAXI You'll find taxi stands throughout the CBD. To phone for one, call **Gold & Black Taxis** (www.taxisgb.co.nz; ✆ **04/388-8888**) or **Wellington Combined Taxis** (www.taxis.co.nz; ✆ **04/384-4444**).

BY TRAIN **Tranz Metro** operates the train service from Wellington to the outer suburbs. Trains arrive at the city's railway station on Bunny Street; from there you can walk or take a bus to most places of interest. A **Group Rover Pass** (NZ$40) offers unlimited travel for a day for up to four people traveling together, valid on the Johnsonville, Kapiti, and Upper Hutt lines. A **Day Rover Pass** is NZ$14. Call ✆ **0800/801-700** in NZ, or check www.metlink. org.nz or www.tranzmetro.co.nz for timetable and fare information.

BY CAR Don't rent a car in the city if you don't have to. Parking is expensive and traffic can't get pretty snarled up during business hours. If you must, the inner city has plenty of 24-hour parking buildings. Rates range from NZ$3 per hour to NZ$16 per day. There are also lots of pay-and-display parking areas—but if you don't buy (or display) a ticket, the parking wardens will not be kind. Council-owned parks tend to be free on the weekends, but you can only stay for a maximum of 2 hours. Also, don't try to beat the resident parking zone system.

BY CABLE CAR The historic **Cable Car** (www.wellingtoncablecar.co.nz; ✆ **04/472-2199**) runs between Lambton Quay and Kelburn every 10 minutes, with a stop at Victoria University on the way. It runs daily from Monday to Friday 7am to 10pm; weekends and public holidays 9am to 10pm. A round-trip ticket costs NZ$7.50 adults, NZ$3.50 children 5 to 15 and NZ$19 a family, or you can use your Snapper card (see above).

BY FERRY The **Dominion Post Ferry** runs daily between Queen's Wharf, Matiu Somes Island, Eastbourne, and Days Bay wharf. The trip to Days Bay takes 30 minutes one-way, and Eastbourne village is about 15 minutes farther on. The one-way fare costs NZ$11 for adults and NZ$6 for children; a family pass is NZ$61 return. For timetable information, go to www.eastbywest.co.nz (✆ **04/499-1282**).

10

WELLINGTON & THE WAIRARAPA | Wellington

Area Code Wellington's telephone area code (STD) is **04.**

Dentist Contact the **Wellington Hospital dental department** (☏ **04/385-5999**).

Doctor The **Wellington Urgent Medical Centre,** 17 Adelaide Rd., Newtown (www.wamc.co.nz; ☏ **04/384-4944**), is open daily 8am to 11pm. See also **Hospitals,** below.

Emergencies Dial ☏ **111** to call the police, report a fire, or request an ambulance.

Hospitals **Wellington Hospital,** Riddiford Street, Newtown (www.ccdhb.org.nz/patient/visiting_info_Wellington.htm; ☏ **04/385-5999**), has an emergency department.

Newspapers Wellington's morning newspaper, the *Dominion Post,* is published Monday to Saturday. On Sundays, get the nationwide *Sunday Star-Times.* Overseas newspapers are sometimes available at newsstands and in the reading room of the National Library, Molesworth Street (☏ **04/474-3000**).

Pharmacies There are late-night pharmacies at 17 Adelaide Rd., Wellington (☏ **04/385-8810**), and 729 High St., Lower Hutt (☏ **04/939-6669**).

Police See "Emergencies," above.

Post Office The main post office is at 7 Waterloo Quay (www.nzpost.co.nz; ☏ **0800/501-501** in NZ). The *poste restante* office at **NZ Post** is at 43 Manners St. (☏ **04/473-5922**). Most post shops are open Monday to Friday 9am to 5pm, and some, including Manners St., are open on Saturday from 9am to 3pm.

10

Where to Stay

Despite its charms as a tourist destination, Wellington still tends to look toward the corporate market, so accommodation rates can be higher from Monday to Thursday than on weekends. In fact, great deals are often on offer on the weekends, but the best times are over December and January (probably because this is when "the suits" are on holiday). There are now lots of inner-city apartment complexes if you prefer a self-catering option, but remember the city fills up quickly when major events are on, so book in advance.

IN THE INNER CITY
EXPENSIVE

You'll find **CityLife Wellington** ★★, 300 Lambton Quay (www.heritagehotels.co.nz; ☏ **0800/368-888** in NZ, or 04/922-2800), right above the city's best shopping district. It offers 70 modern, self-contained apartments with all the mod-cons from NZ$199 to $399 for a one-bedroom suite, and NZ$260 to NZ$589 for two- and three-bedroom suites respectively. Self-parking is available at NZ$21 per night.

Amora Hotel Wellington ★★ The Amora offers some of the most spacious guest rooms and suites in Wellington. The harbor-facing rooms frame the picturesque waterfront and city and afford panoramic views. Choose from deluxe rooms or relax and enjoy the benefits of the Club Rooms and Club Suites (especially if you get a weekend deal), complete with access to the exclusive Club Lounge.

170 Wakefield St., Wellington. www.wellington.amorahotels.com. © **0800/655-555** in NZ, or 04/473-3900. 192 units. NZ$450 deluxe; NZ$500 club; NZ$550 club suite; extra person NZ$35. Off-peak rates and special deals. Valet parking NZ$25. **Amenities:** Restaurant; bar; babysitting; concierge; well-equipped gym; 24-hr. room service; Wi-Fi (free).

InterContinental Wellington ★★★ You'll feel like a rock star as you sweep into the lobby of this plush palace in the heart of the CBD. Perhaps less so if you've just dropped off a tiny Mazda and not a Bentley, but whatever—they'll still park it for you. Make yourself comfortable and go for a top-floor Club Room if you really want to live the high life. You'll get access to the Club Lounge too, offering perks like free breakfast and Wi-Fi. Even the less rarefied rooms are cool and elegant (the hotel underwent a major refurbishment in 2014). The hotel participates in the international Green Engage System, which tracks its environmental performance in energy use and water use and waste management and looks at ways to improve it.

2 Grey St. www.intercontinental.com/wellington. © **0800/500-619** in NZ, or 04/472-2722. 232 rooms and 7 suites. NZ$250 classic queen; NZ$290 superior; NZ$375 club king; NZ$575 club executive; from NZ$1900 presidential suite. Extra person NZ$35. Children 15 and under stay free in parents' room. Long-stay, off-peak and special deals. Valet parking NZ$30. **Amenities:** 2 restaurants; 2 bars; charged airport transfers; babysitting; concierge; well-equipped gym; Jacuzzi; heated indoor pool; sauna; room service; day spa and beauty treatments; Wi-Fi (free for InterContinental members; NZ$25/ per night otherwise).

Museum Art Hotel ★★★ Sumptuous is probably the best word to describe this large hotel, which was transformed into a sort of contemporary New Zealand art gallery with the addition of many works that err on the eccentric side. Paintings sit alongside sculptures (you can't ignore Michel Tuffery's life-size bull made out of corned-beef cans). If you smoosh them all together with the bright and brilliant decor and some well-chosen and eclectic pieces of furniture, this is what you get: the perfect spot for the traveler who is over understated, neutral tones! Even the bathroom toiletries are little works of art. The hotel is right next to Te Papa and in the thick of the city's restaurant and bar action and offers rooms and two-bedroom apartments in separate wings.

90 Cable St., Wellington. www.museumhotel.co.nz. © **04/802-8900.** 165 units. Rooms NZ$239–NZ$289 double; NZ$299–NZ$959 apartment. Long-stay and special deals. Valet parking NZ$20. **Amenities:** Restaurant; cafe, bar; babysitting; concierge; free Wi-Fi in lobby; well-equipped gym; Jacuzzi; heated indoor lap pool; room service; sauna; Wi-Fi (free in public areas; NZ$12/day in room).

MODERATE

Close to bus, train, and ferry terminals, **Quest on Johnston ★**, 35 Johnston St. (www.questonjohnston.co.nz; © **0800/508-021** in NZ), is a perfectly located 18-level apartment complex where there's always a great deal to be had. Its 67 studios and 1-, 2-, and 3-bedroom apartments are definitely worth a look (NZ$105–NZ$225). **CQ ★**, 213 Cuba St. (www.comfortwellington. com and www.qualitywellington.com; © **04/385-2153**), is two hotels in one, a perfectly good budget option in the old part of the building and a more upmarket option with all the trimmings in the new wing. The other cute things about this place are (A) its name (CQ stands for Comfort and Quality, but it's also right in the heart of the Cuba Quarter—clever, eh?), and (B) the two electric bikes they've recently invested in for guest use. Room rates are NZ$109 to NZ$150 in the old section and NZ$290 for NZ$500 in the new wing.

Bolton Hotel ★★

This multistory, apartment-style hotel has an elegance and style that exceeds some of its bigger capital-city cousins. The hotel was built with energy and water conservation in mind, and its Qualmark Enviro-Gold rating indicates a commitment to all avenues of sustainable tourism. Owners have paid meticulous attention to guest preferences, and rooms abound with luscious textural fabrics and unexpected extra touches—a comprehensive minibar, for instance, that includes an umbrella and disposable raincoat, the importance of which can't be overestimated in Wellington. It's colorful, crisp, modern, and close to the heart of the city, but above all, its rates are enticing. Ask about the classy Bolton suite if you want to indulge; it's very reasonably priced and ideal for families or couples traveling together.

Corner of Bolton and Mowbray sts., Wellington. www.boltonhotel.co.nz.ⓒ **0800/996-622** in NZ, or 04/472-9966. 139 units. NZ$199–NZ$239 studio; NZ$249–NZ$445 1-bedroom suite; NZ$500 2-bedroom suite. Long-stay, off-peak, and special deals. Valet parking NZ$30 per night. **Amenities:** Restaurant; tiny lobby cafe; bar; airport transfer (NZ$70); babysitting; concierge; gym; Jacuzzi; heated indoor lap pool; sauna; Wi-Fi (free).

Distinction Wellington ★

If you're looking for a smart yet functional base during your stay, the self-contained units in this complex have a lot going for them. They're nicely furnished and it's a great location in that you can walk everywhere from here. Happily it's just a few steps from the fabulous Moore Wilson's store, where, if you're like me and love good produce and deli items, you can spend many happy hours browsing.

70 Tory St., Wellington. www.distinctionhotelswellington.com. ⓒ **04/8011-0780.** 89 studios and apartments and 4 penthouses. NZ$149–NZ$450 double. Car parking onsite NZ$20. **Amenities:** Concierge; Wi-Fi (free).

James Cook Hotel Grand Chancellor ★

Highly recommended for its great rates in a prime location. And if you're happy to pay a little extra for a Club Room (on Level 26) you'll get a complimentary breakfast as well as various goodies in the Club Lounge. With its views of the bustling city, direct access to shopping on Lambton Quay, and commerce on The Terrace, this hotel is the perfect base for business or pleasure—and don't forget to ask about the cheaper weekend rates. The hotel runs recycling and power-saving programs and has a Qualmark Enviro-Gold award.

147 The Terrace, Wellington. www.grandchancellorhotels.com. ⓒ **0800/27 53 37** in NZ, or 04/499-9500. 268 rooms. NZ$149–NZ$450 double. Long-stay, off-peak, and special deals. Valet parking NZ$29. **Amenities:** 2 restaurants; 2 bars; babysitting; concierge; limited gym onsite w/use of full-size off-site gym; day spa and beauty treatments; Wi-Fi (free).

Victoria Court Motor Lodge ★   No need for a car when you check in to this tidy, convenient complex—it really is quite close to the heart of Wellington. The 25 units might not be the last word in luxury, but they have much to offer in terms of value and comfort. The two-bedroom units especially are a gift for traveling families, and when you see the smart kitchens (with stovetops and microwaves), you might even feel inspired to cook. Best of all, it's just behind my favorite part of town—Cuba Mall.

201 Victoria St., Wellington. www.victoriacourt.co.nz. © **0800/282-850** in NZ, or 04/472-4297. 25 units. NZ$150–NZ$205 double. Extra person NZ$20. Long-stay, off-peak, and weekend rates. Victoria St. is one-way heading west so enter it off Vivian or Dixon sts. **Amenities:** Babysitting; Wi-Fi (free).

INEXPENSIVE

There's been quite an increase over recent years in the number of campervans on the road, especially during New Zealand's summer months. Those nomadically inclined will appreciate the centrally located **Wellington Waterfront Motorhome Park** (www.wwmp.co.nz) within 3 minutes of the Interislander Ferry terminal and right next to many of Wellington's top attractions. Well signposted on Waterloo Quay, the park offers 30 powered sites, an ablutions block, and a daily onsite manager (available 7am–7pm) at a cost of NZ$50 per vehicle per day.

IN THORNDON/KELBURN

Gardens Homestay ★   Neil Harrap and Sally Guinness like to say that guests are simply friends they haven't yet met. Neil has an extensive knowledge of tourism, which he delights in sharing with those lucky enough to score a bed in this grand 1892 Victorian home filled with antiques. The large two-bedroom, upstairs suite (with one smallish bathroom) is ideal for two couples or family members traveling together. It's quiet and private and has lovely views over one of Wellington's premier residential areas.

11 St. Mary St., Thorndon, Wellington. www.gardenshomestay.co.nz. © **04/499-1212.** One 2-bedroom suite. NZ$295 double. Long-stay and off-peak rates. Rates include breakfast. **Amenities:** Free bikes; heated outdoor pool; Wi-Fi (free).

IN MOUNT VICTORIA/ORIENTAL PARADE

The **Copthorne Oriental Bay** ★, 100 Oriental Parade and 73 Roxburgh St., Mt. Victoria (www.millenniumhotels.co.nz; © **0800/808-228** in NZ, or 04/385-0279), has 118 recently refurbished rooms, some with a private balcony, affording some of the best views in Wellington. Rates range from NZ$175 to NZ$225.

Austinvilla ★★   Zarli Sein and Mark Bodt offer two self-contained apartments in their early-1900s Mt. Victoria home, Austinvilla. Each has private access. The Studio Suite has a queen bed, ensuite, and kitchenette. The Garden Suite adds a living and dining room and French doors opening onto a private patio and garden. Both are elegantly furnished, with attractive views across the city. A continental breakfast is delivered the evening before, so guests can eat at leisure. Zarli and Mark live and work upstairs, so are on hand

10

when needed—Zarli says Austinvilla is ideal for people looking for a homey environment without sharing facilities. The bars and restaurants of Courtenay Place are only 10 minutes away—though as with much of Wellington, there's a slight walk up the hill to get back.

11 Austin St., Mt. Victoria. www.austinvilla.co.nz. ℂ **04/385-8334.** NZ$195–NZ$245 double. Rates include breakfast. Long-stay rates. No smoking. Not suitable for children. **Amenities:** Guest laundry; off-street parking; Wi-Fi (free).

Booklovers Bed and Breakfast ★★
Journalist and author Jane Tolerton offers four large rooms in her two-story Victorian home, and she's a terrific and knowledgeable hostess who knows just when to leave you alone. My pick is the downstairs room, but all are lovely. The whole place heaves with books—if you dabble in the bookshelves you may never want to leave! It's just a short walk from Courtenay Place, or hop on one of the buses that stop right outside the gate.

123 Pirie St., Mount Victoria. www.booklovers.co.nz. ℂ **04/384-2714.** 4 units. NZ$180–NZ$240. Long-stay and off-peak rates. Rates include breakfast. **Amenities:** Babysitting; Wi-Fi (free).

Ohtel ★★★
You may never want to check out of this small, chic boutique hotel with its great location, striking individuality, and total commitment to sustainability. Stylishly furnished throughout, with the owner's collection of midcentury-modern furniture and German ceramics (no two rooms are the same), it is perfectly placed, overlooking Te Papa and Oriental Parade. All rooms are large, but the six front-facing are the best for views. Then there are the wonderfully indulgent bathrooms, where the clever design makes them part of the total space (but a strategically positioned curtain guarantees privacy). Staying here is indeed a full sensory experience.

66 Oriental Parade, Mount Victoria. www.ohtel.com. ℂ **04/803-0600.** 10 units. NZ$200–$360 studio; NZ$250–$550 deluxe; NZ$350–$600 suite. Long-stay and off-peak rates. **Amenities:** Lobby cafe for breakfast and cabinet food; bar; babysitting; concierge; small cardio/weights gym and full-size gym nearby; nearby pool; limited room service; infra-red sauna; Wi-Fi (free).

Roseneath House ★★
The view from the private guest balcony is one of the best in Wellington: through bush across the Oriental Bay beach to the port and city center. It's just as spectacular at night. Internationally exhibited potter Linda Forrest offers one ensuite room and warm hospitality—breakfast is whatever you want it to be. Her pottery is displayed attractively around the house (and she can make pieces to order). Her house, a lovely Victorian villa, is accessed by steps or a new, enclosed cable car—a much more civilized ride than some of the Cresta Run contraptions seen at neighboring properties. It's a challenging walk up the hill, but worth it for the view—and a taxi from Courtenay Place is under $10.

58 Palliser Rd., Roseneath. www.roseneathhouse.co.nz. ℂ **04/384-5501.** $NZ195 double. Rates include breakfast. Two-day minimum stay. **Amenities:** Garage parking; laundry service; Wi-Fi (free).

Brentwood Hotel ★, 16 Kemp St., Kilbirnie (www.brentwoodhotel.co.nz; © **0508/273-689** in NZ, or 04/920-0400), will do the trick if you need to leave town at an unreasonable hour. It offers a free 24-hour shuttle service and has an onsite restaurant. Rooms range from NZ$138 to NZ$350.

Edgewater Lodge ★ Formerly known as the Edge Water Homestay, this is something of a mecca for *Lord of the Rings* fans: It still contains the giant rush-watching screen of one-time owner Barrie Osborne, the LOTR producer, and is within walking distance of Richard Taylor's Weta Cave. Its attractions extend beyond Tolkein, though: Karaka Bay is a very agreeable spot, the rooms are sumptuous, and owner Stella Newman is a former restaurateur who makes the bread, muffins, preserves, and so on for breakfast. Her approach, she says, is simply to make people feel at home. Of the three units, two are double ensuite rooms (one with its own private deck) and one a suite with two bedrooms. All have captivating views across Wellington Harbor. It's about 15 minutes' drive along the winding coastal road to the city center, 10 minutes to the airport, and the bus stops outside the door.

423 Karaka Bay Rd., Miramar Peninsula. www.edgewaterwellington.co.nz. © **04/388-4446** or 021/613-357. 3 units. $270–$520 per night. Rates include breakfast. **Amenities:** Laundry service; off-street parking; tours available; Wi-Fi (free).

Where to Eat

Wellington is crammed with eating places of every stripe from many different cultures. You can generally walk to where you want to go in the inner city, or catch a cab if it's a bit farther out. Grab the "Wine & Food Guide" from the visitor center: It's got the lowdown on what's good. Cuba Street and Courtenay Place are the best places to go for ethnic restaurants and hip eateries; the more traditional places tend to be closer to the waterfront and in suburbs like Thorndon, Mount Victoria, and Oriental Bay. The food is great and the wine is abundant, given that Wellington sits between the top winegrowing regions of Marlborough and the Wairarapa.

IN THE INNER CITY
EXPENSIVE

Boulcott Street Bistro ★ INTERNATIONAL This well-established, well-regarded restaurant has been pleasing lovers of classic cuisine with a twist for many years now. First-time visitors will be especially delighted by the setting in a heritage Victorian cottage right in the heart of the city. If you're in town on a Sunday night, I heartily recommend booking for the Sunday Roast: a hearty two courses (roasted pork loin, roasted Hereford rump, cornfed chicken) and a glass of red for NZ$45.

99 Boulcott St. www.boulcottstbistro.co.nz. © **04/499-4199.** No reservations. Main courses NZ$34–NZ$45. Lunch Sun–Fri 11:30am–3pm; dinner daily 5:30–9:30pm.

Charley Noble Eatery & Bar ★★ INTERNATIONAL If you haven't heard of him, that's because Charley Noble isn't the name of the chef at this

Apart from the other cafes reviewed in this section, you'll find excellent coffee and good atmosphere at **The Hangar,** 119 Dixon St. (ⓒ **04/830-0909**); **Prefab,** 14 Jessie St. (ⓒ **04/385-2263**); **Fidel's** at 234 Cuba St. (ⓒ **04/801-6868**); and **Mojo,** which had at last count over a dozen establishments scattered over town, the latest of which is **Poneke by Mojo** on Clyde Quay Wharf (ⓒ **04/979-9283**), a fairly salubrious address. And for serious caffeine aficionados, you can't beat **Customs Brew Bar ★** at 39 Ghuznee St. (ⓒ **04/473-7697**).

upmarket establishment: There's a long preamble printed on the menus about how the place got its name. It's to do with old seafaring tradition—Charley Noble was the nickname for the galley chimney on board ship—but you don't need to know this to enjoy Paul Hoather's new venture in the historic Huddart Parker Building. It has a great seafood bar (with fresh-shucked oysters), and you can choose from homemade pasta, small plates (chicken liver parfait, bruschetta), large plates (house potpie, market fish), wood-fire-grilled meats, and an array of interesting sides (sesame slaw, fire-roasted portobellos).

1 Post Office Square. www.charleynoble.co.nz. ⓒ **0508/242-753** in NZ. No reservations except for large groups. Main courses NZ$26–NZ$56. Mon–Fri 11:30am–midnight; weekends 5pm–midnight.

Hippopotamus ★★ FRENCH If dinner is not possible, consider breakfast or maybe even a weekend high tea at this most amazing restaurant. From the moment you emerge from the lift you'll notice all manner of wonderful touches, including the herd of hippos marching stoically across the ceiling. Once through the doors you'll want to order whatever tipple you fancy from the curved mirrored bar and then sink into one of the decadently upholstered armchairs to contemplate the menu. Ah yes, the menu … although most dishes are French classics, they tend to feature modern twists, so seared venison filet comes with pickled baby beetroot, port-wine drunken prunes, salted caramel ganache, spiced red-wine jus reduction, and chili and chocolate crumble. Who needs dessert? Actually, I do, and my first choice here are crepes Suzette, flambéed in great style at your table. Ooh-la-la indeed!

Museum Hotel, 90 Cable St. www.hippopotamus.co.nz. ⓒ **04/802-8935.** Main courses from NZ$45. Mon–Fri noon–2pm; daily 6–10pm.

Logan Brown ★★★ INTERNATIONAL Very much a culinary icon on the Wellington map, this is probably the city's best-known restaurant. And although it has retained its reputation for truly excellent food, the ambience is not as formal as it once was—even though the leather-upholstered booths, white-clothed tables, Corinthian pillars, and chandeliers big enough to swing on are still very much in place (quite ironic when you consider its location on the inner city's funkiest street). The food, billed as "honest and simple," focuses on fish and game (the whitebait I had here was outstanding). If you want to sample Logan Brown without emptying your wallet, go for the bistro lunch or choose the pre-theater menu, but remember you have to be out by 7:30pm.

Cuba and Vivian sts. www.loganbrown.co.nz. ⓒ **04/801-5114.** Reservations recommended. Main courses NZ$40–NZ$45. Wed–Thurs noon–1:30pm; Fri–Sat noon–2pm; Tues–Sun 5:30pm–late. High tea Fri & Sat 2:30–3pm.

Zibibbo ★★ MEDITERRANEAN   Located in an attractive old building very close to the heart of town, this is another well-established restaurant that caters to both high- and middle-range budgets. Think tapas and pizza in the bar if you're in the latter range; otherwise head upstairs and contemplate night-roasted free-range pork accompanied by some seriously good wine from the very extensive list, which, by the way, features everything from a pleasant local varietal to Chateau d'Yquem Sauternes (at a mere NZ$700). Don't hesitate to advise them of any special dietary requirements you might have; they are happy to adapt most dishes to suit.

25 Taranaki St. www.zibibbo.co.nz. ⓒ **04/385-6650.** Reservations recommended. Main courses from NZ$35. Fri 11:30am–late; Mon–Thurs & Sat–Sun 4pm–late.

MODERATE

One of the great things about the New York–style eatery **Five Boroughs** is that it looks as if it's been here forever—nothing too flashy or upmarket about it, just a comfortable place to slide into if you're in need of some delicious deli nosh (hot pastrami sandwich, anyone?). You'll find it at 4 Roxburgh St., just off Courtney Pl. (www.fiveboroughs.co.nz; ⓒ **04/384-9300**).

Caffe Astoria ★ MODERN CAFE/LIGHT FARE   This upmarket cafe has a prime setting in the center of Lambton Quay's little green space, and during the week it's well patronized by businesspeople and earnest-looking Wellingtonians, especially those looking for an early dinner before heading home. In the weekend it attracts a much more laid-back clientele, especially for brunch. Despite its rather cavernous interior, it has a great atmosphere, and if you're lucky enough to get a table near the windows, you can enjoy the green aspect of the small but perfectly formed park beyond.

159 Lambton Quay. ⓒ **04/473-8500.** www.astoria.co.nz. Main courses NZ$19–NZ$22. Mon–Fri 7am–7:15pm; Sat–Sun 8am–4pm.

Capitol ★ ITALIAN   Another stalwart on the local scene, Capitol puts an emphasis on casual but quality dining. It's quite an intimate setting: It only seats 44 and has the tiniest kitchen you can imagine, from which comes, among other good things, delicious light and fluffy gnocchi. You'll need to book for lunch, but walk-in diners are welcome in the evening.

10 Kent Tce. www.capitolrestaurant.co.nz ⓒ **04/384-2855.** Main courses from NZ$20–NZ$38. Lunch 7 days; Dinner Sun–Thurs 5.30–9.30pm, Frid & Sat 5.30–10pm.

Chow ★★ SOUTHEAST ASIAN   With its casual, modern interior and the extensive range of noodles, grills, steamed dishes, and salads combined with wine, sake, cocktails, and teas, this place is a winner with busy professionals.

Cool Culinary Quarter: Hannah's Laneway

In the center of town you'll find the **Hannah's Laneway** precinct of seriously cool food purveyors (behind Dixon St.). At the **Wellington Chocolate Factory,** 5 Eva St (www.wcf.co.nz), extraordinarily good chocolate is made with a commitment to ethical trade, with wrappers designed by local artists. At the same address you'll find **Fix and Fogg** (www.fixandfogg.co.nz), two fellows who got sick of being lawyers and now make premier peanut butter in their Nut Buttery. It made locals cry with relief when brothers Jess and Shep opened the

Leeds Street Bakery, 14 Leeds St. (www.leedsstbakery.co.nz), after walking away from Ti Kouka Café; their salted caramel cookies are worth hoofing all over town for. On the same site, the **Red Rabbit Coffee Co.** (www.redrabbit-coffee.co.nz) turns out stunning brews and serves food from the guys next door. For a cold drink with attitude, go to **Six Barrel Soda,** 33 Dixon St. (www.sixbarrelsoda.co.nz), which produces fresh and funky sodas with flavors like feijoa, celery tonic, and hibiscus. Cheers!

Servings are tapas style (I can never get past the salt and pepper squid—which manages to be crunchy and tender at the same time), so it's best to order two or three menu choices.

45 Tory St. and 11 Woodward St. www.chow.co.nz. ✆ **04/382-8585** or 04/473-4474. Main courses NZ$16–NZ$26. Daily noon–midnight.

Floriditas ★ EUROPEAN   A simple one-page menu makes for easy choices in this paisley-embellished corner retreat. European-inspired dishes like vegetable and ricotta lasagna and polenta-dusted calamari make a delicious lunch or light dinner, and the generally friendly staff is knowledgeable about the good wine list. It's also an excellent coffee stop, and daily sweet treats line the countertop. Don't resist the urge to partake. I like the buzzy atmosphere, and it's a favorite with all ages, but it's enormously popular (especially on weekends), so be prepared to wait for a table.

161 Cuba St. www.floriditas.co.nz. ✆ **04/381-2212.** Reservations recommended for dinner. Main courses NZ$18–NZ$25. Mon–Sat 7am–11pm; Sun 8am–5pm.

Fratelli ★ ITALIAN   This is the place to come for reliably fresh, 100% homemade pasta, gnocchi, risotto, and pizza. Chefs here blend traditional Italian cooking styles with new ideas to create great-value meals like risotto with slow-cooked rabbit, button mushrooms, mascarpone, and preserved lemon. Traditional Italian desserts like tiramisu, *panforte,* and gelato round off a very fulfilling evening.

15 Blair St. www.fratelli.net.nz. ✆ **04/801-6615.** Reservations recommended. Main courses NZ$22–NZ$30. Mon–Sat 5:30pm–late.

Nikau Café ★ CAFE   With its focus on seasonal local food, this super-popular daytime cafe has a menu that changes regularly, except for a couple of permanent items such as kedgeree, so good here I could eat it every day for at least a week. Given its central and attractive location (it's named for the metal nikau palms that are a head-turning decorative element of Civic Square), bookings are pretty much essential, although if you do have to wait, the tables turn over fairly quickly.

Wellington City Art Gallery, Civic Square, 101 Wakefield St. http://nikaucafe.co.nz. ℂ **04/801-4168.** Mon–Fri 7am–4pm; Sat 8am–4pm.

Shed 5 ★★ CONTEMPORARY SEAFOOD   As the name implies, this is a huge restaurant, but its popularity and award-winning status are such that, even on a quiet night, there is a decent crowd. If you like good seafood, this is the place to find it—right on the edge of the wharf. The menu also includes lamb, beef, venison, and chicken, and the service is friendly and unobtrusive.

Shed 5, Queen's Wharf. www.shed5.co.nz. ℂ **04/499-9069.** Reservations recommended. Main courses NZ$32–NZ$38. Daily 11am–late.

WBC ★★ MODERN   Although it took a major effort to find this place (it's upstairs and the signage is a bit on the modest side), it was really worth the hunt. Plenty of other people think so too—the place is usually packed. FYI, the initials stand for the Wholesale Boot Company, which once occupied the premises and which the current owners clearly wanted to honor. But let's concentrate on the food, which is mostly about sharing platters, both large and small, raw oysters and clams, and interesting toasts (asparagus and romesco; spicy beef tartare). My standout dishes were the spicy chicken wings with lemon labne and Thai grilled eggplant salad. Yum.

107 Victoria St. www.wbcrestaurant.co.nz. ℂ **04/499-9379.** Reservations essential. Sharing platters from NZ$31. Mon–Fri 11:30am–10pm; Sat–Sun 4:30–10pm.

INEXPENSIVE

All cities have good, cheap ethnic eateries. Ask at the visitor center for in-the-know favorites. For fantastic and ridiculously cheap Malaysian and South Indian food, go to **Rasa,** 200 Cuba St. (ℂ **04/384-7088;** www.rasa.co.nz). You'll stuff yourself for NZ$15 or NZ$20; the masala dosai is fabulous! It's open daily noon to 11pm. Then there's **Little Penang,** 40 Dixon St. (ℂ **04/382-9818**), for authentic and delicious Penang-style street food. If you're non-carnivorous or just crave good, healthy food, try **Aunty Mena Vegetarian,** 167 Cuba St. (ℂ **04/382-8288**). It doesn't look very flash, but this Malaysian food is even cheaper than Rasa's and it's open every day. For

---

Patisserie Perfection

Should you find yourself craving something small, sweet, and perfectly formed, then get yourself to **Louis Sergeant,** 146 Featherston St. (www.louissergeant.co.nz; ℂ **04/499-8475**), a contemporary tea salon where, after sampling the handiwork of chef de patisserie and owner Louis Sergeant, you may think you've died and gone to pastry heaven. Then ask them to pack up as many delicacies as you think you might need to enjoy later.

SEE YOU IN cuba

Cuba Street is bohemian, hipster, scruffy, exuberant—and that's just the shops. The people who frequent this part of Wellington are very different from the suited and booted folk who haunt the business end of town. Go and hang out at **Midnight Espresso ★★**, 178 Cuba St. (**℃ 04/384-7014**), for an hour of so. This old Cuba St. institution has great food (dog roll, anyone? Actually, it's made from chickpeas and is very nice) and serves well into the night. For more sophisticated fare, try **Caffe Italiano,** 229 Cuba St. (**℃ 04/385-2703**), with its excellent deli and a lively weekend brunch scene that often includes the Italian community. Farther down the street, the French-owned bistro **Le Metropolitain,** 146 Cuba St. (**℃ 04/801-8007; www.lemetropolitain.co.nz**), has legions of fans that love the authentic provincial dishes and noisy atmosphere. **Matterhorn Bar & Restaurant ★★**, 106 Cuba St. (**℃ 04/384-3359; www.matterhorn. co.nz**), is a popular, award-winning choice—a dark, moody place where both the food and the service are superb. It turns into a classy nightspot after dinner and is also open for lunch. **Ombra ★★**, 199 Cuba St. (**www.ombra.co.nz;** **℃ 04/385-3229**), is a stylish bar with great food and a wonderfully convivial atmosphere. Until not so long ago it was the home of an adult supplies (aka sex) store. There's no evidence of its former activities, though—in fact, it's had a major makeover to make it resemble a traditional Venetian wine bar. Don't miss out on the Wellington Night Markets on Friday and Saturday nights (see "Specialist Food Markets," below)

wood-fired pizzas and pasta delivered with a smile, go to **One Red Dog,** 56 Customhouse Quay (www.onereddog.co.nz; ℃ **04/918-4723**). If you're not sure what you feel like having, visit the **Capital Market,** 151 Willis St. (www.capitalmarket.co.nz), a recent addition to the city's many and varied food markets. Each of the more than 20 market stalls emit the most delicious aromas; expect to pay around NZ$10 to $12 for the meal of your choice, which you can take away with you or perch at one of the tables and enjoy on the spot. The Breton *galettes* (crêpes) served up at **Café Breton,** 20 Brandon St. (www.cafebreton.co.nz; ℃ **04/473-6576**), are not only easy on the pocket (around NZ$17 each) but hard to beat in terms of a light, savory taste of France. The choice was tough, but I eventually settled on La Bergère, packed with a generous amount of goat cheese, spinach, and walnuts.

IN THORNDON/KELBURN

The **Backbencher Pub & Café,** 34 Molesworth St. (opposite Parliament; ℃ **04/472-3065**), is still a great place to visit for a beer alongside a light meal and a chuckle at the way the place lightheartedly mocks the local parliamentarians. Up the road and on the way to Kelburn, combine the obvious pleasures of the Wellington Botanic Garden with lunch at the **Picnic Café** (http://picniccafe.co.nz; ℃ **04/472-6002;** daily 8:30am–4pm). The cheese scones are truly legendary. On Upland Road in the village of Kelburn, seek out the pocket-size delights of **Kelburn Café,** 87–89 Upland Rd., Kelburn (℃ **04/475-8381**), serving great coffee and fabulous cakes daily from 9am to 5pm.

Right in the heart of Tinakori Village, **Tinakori Bistro** (✆ **04/385-8555**), **Aubergine** (✆ **04/471-2500**), and **Cosa Nostra** (✆ **04/473-3005**) are all recommended and moderately priced options, especially if you are staying locally and don't want to venture too far afield.

IN MOUNT VICTORIA/ORIENTAL PARADE

Is it a gorgeous evening and do you want a complete change? In that case, I suggest you indulge in what Kiwis call a "takeaway" meal (as opposed to "takeout") from **Mt. Vic Chippery,** 5 Marjoribanks St. (www.thechippery. co.nz; ✆ **04/382-8713**), where really good and very fresh fish and chips can be had for a modest sum. With Oriental Bay just around the corner, you will easily find a spot where you can enjoy the view and your fragrant package of goodies.

Ortega Fish Shack & Bar ★★ SEAFOOD   A long-time Wellington favorite, and for good reason: The food is fresh, elegant, and imaginative, without being fussy. Gurnard with black risotto, clams, and chorizo is a standout, as are crepes with orange caramel sauce. Unsurprisingly, fish is the focus, but you can also get a good steak. Decor is eccentric and nautically themed (the original Ortega was a Caribbean fisherman and cook who apparently inspired Hemingway's *The Old Man and the Sea*).

16 Marjoribank St. www.ortega.co.nz. ✆ **04/382-9559.** Main courses NZ$35–NZ$40. Tues–Sat 5.30pm–late.

Whitebait ★★ SEAFOOD   Although a relative newcomer, this smart restaurant has already picked up a major award and is a great place for a special lunch or dinner on one of those days when Wellington puts its best weather forward. When you've had enough of the glorious view over the marina, cast your eyes upward and admire the stunning much-larger-then-life abalone shells (known as *paua* in this part of the world) suspended from the ceiling. Then turn your attention to the menu and prepare yourself for some really good seafood. As for me, I always start with their oysters. Whitebait works hard at reducing its carbon footprint and is an accredited member of Conscious Consumers.

Clyde Quay Wharf. www.whitebait.co.nz. ✆ **04/385-8555.** Reservations recommended. Main courses NZ$35–NZ$40. Tues–Fri 11:30am–2.30pm and Tues–Sat 5:30pm–late.

NEAR THE AIRPORT

Named, perhaps, for the wind that roars in from the sea (but I couldn't swear to this), **Elements,** 144 Onepu Rd., Lyall Bay (✆ **04/939-1292**), does a roaring trade in tasty brunches and lunches (Mon–Fri 7:30am–4pm and Sat–Sun 8:30am–5pm). A word of advice: Get here early during the weekend as the locals tend to congregate in serious numbers. **Maranui Café** (✆ **04/387-2829**), on the Parade, Lyall Bay, is a quirky joint located in the distinctive Maranui Surf Life Saving Club building on the windy waterfront. It's a terrific place for coffee, big cakes, and light lunches, and with gulls soaring just outside the upstairs windows at table level, you'll soon forget all about the rush of the city. It's open daily 7:30am to 5pm. The newest cafe in this area is the **Spruce Goose** (www.sprucegoose.net.nz; ℂ **04/387-2277;** Sun–Thurs 7am–2am and Fri–Sat 7am–midnight), at 30 Cochrane St. and Moa Point Road, Lyall Bay—very near the Wellington International Airport. Its proximity to the airport is not necessarily why so many people flock here, nor is the industrial-looking exterior of the building much of a drawing card. It's all about the great atmosphere and fantastic view of Wellington's occasionally inhospitable coast—plus lots of live music and no neighbors to complain. Oh, and the food is pretty good, too.

Exploring Wellington
THE TOP ATTRACTIONS
Museum of New Zealand–Te Papa Tongarewa ★★★   New Zealand's much-anticipated "national" museum (don't tell Aucklanders that!) opened its doors in 1998 and has become the capital's top attraction. Te Papa, as it's usually known, aims to bring the fun into the museum experience without dumbing it down. Interactive technology and world-class exhibitions eloquently tell the story of New Zealand—its art, culture, history, and environment. Te Papa also happens to looks pretty incredible: a beacon of modernity sitting proudly on the waterfront.

It would take days to properly digest all the permanent and short-term exhibitions on the museum's six levels, but if you've got kids or think like one, the colossal squid (dead) and the dinosaur skeletons (also dead) are pretty memorable, according to my 9-year-old. (Also the 3D movie about life as a squid!) On a more serious note, **Gallipoli: The Scale of Our War** is an absolute must-see. Opening in 2015 and scheduled to run through 2019, it commemorates the first battle involving New Zealand troops in World War I, which resulted in a 93% casualty rate. It really has to be seen to be believed—the eight individuals on which much of the exhibition is based were real-life soldiers, and with the expert involvement of Weta Workshop they have been brought back much larger than life (seriously, they are actually 2.4 times larger than life). The exhibition does an excellent job of providing a very real glimpse of what life in the trenches was really all about.

The permanent exhibitions include **Mountains to Sea**—the story of New Zealand's biodiversity, with loads of interactivity and animation, plus the squid; **Blood Earth Fire/Whangai Ahi Ka,** revealing the changing landscape of this country, including the "earthquake house," another favorite with kids; **Te Marae,** an authentic carved Maori communal meeting place and a great introduction to our precious indigenous culture; **Slice of Heaven 20th Century Aotearoa,** a look at what united and divided Kiwis over the past century; and **Nga Toi/Arts Te Papa,** art from the national collection and other places.

Although general admission is free, Te Papa offers a range of tours that cost extra, from the hour-long **Introducing Te Papa Tour** (NZ$14 adults and NZ$14 children 15 and under) and the **Maori Highlights Tour** (NZ$20 and

SPECIALIST food MARKETS

Wellington is a city of sophisticated eaters who are increasingly demanding and expecting top-quality artisanal food products, which is why the specialist food markets are always crammed with locals. Start with the **Wellington Night Market,** 116 Cuba St. (www.wellingtonnightmarket. co.nz), which sprawls all over Cuba Mall on Friday night from 5pm to 10:30pm. It's a mélange of sights and smells as a huge variety of ethnic food sellers compete for your taste buds and live music keeps you entertained. It now also hosts a Saturday Night Market on Lower Cuba St. (5–10:30pm). On Sunday (7:30am–2pm), you'll find the **Harborside Market** next to Te Papa on the waterfront with around 50 vendors (www.harboursidemarket. co.nz). Buy the freshest fish straight out of Nino's fish boat, which is moored alongside the action. You can also find Hungarian chimney cakes, Stewart Island smoked salmon, organic honey, and much more. Next to this in the historic Chaffers Dock building is the undercover **City Market** (www.citymarket.co.nz; Sun 8:30am–12:30pm), founded by capital foodie legends Martin Bosley and Rachel Taulelei. It has so many delectable treats, including Argentinian cakes filled with dulce de leche; tasty morsels from the House of Dumplings; and fabulous cheeses, jam, organic veggies and meats, beverages, and Martin Bosley's special sauces and dressings. If you're not totally satiated by now, have a look at the truly amazing **Moore Wilson's Fresh,** 93 Tory St. (http://moorewilsons.co.nz), a fourth-generation business that used to sell mainly to caterers and restaurateurs until the public begged to be let in. This is the fresh food and grocery store/deli of your dreams, with a dazzling array of the very best and its own demonstration kitchen. It's open Monday to Friday 7:30am to 7pm, Saturday 7:30am to 6pm, and Sunday 9am to 5pm with branches in Porirua, Lower Hutt, and Masterton.

NZ$10) to private tours (from NZ$14/NZ$7 to NZ$45/NZ$33). You can pick up a self-guided tour booklet, and audio guides are available in several languages. If you're hungry or need an energy boost, head to the **Te Papa Café** or the **Espresso Bar.** The gift shop, **Te Papa Store,** is full of high-quality and desirable arts, crafts, and New Zealand books and toys.

55 Cable St. www.tepapa.govt.nz. (2) **04/381-7000.** Free admission; fees for some activities, tours, and short-term exhibitions. Daily 10am–6pm (Thurs till 9pm).

Wellington Cable Car ★★★ Five minutes of seemingly vertical climbing through native bush and over quaint wooden houses with one of the best views of the city and its magnificent harbor—that's the experience you'll be getting for a handful of bucks. (For more details, see "Getting Around," above.) It's also the easiest way to get to the **Wellington Botanic Garden** (see below). Learn all about the history of this service (which has been running since 1902) at the **Cable Car Museum** (www.museumswellington.org.nz; (2) **04/475-3578;** free admission; daily 9:30am–5pm), located in the original winding house at the top.

Cable car runs between Lambton Quay and Kelburn. Round-trip ticket NZ$7.50 adults, NZ$3.50 children 5 to 15, and NZ$19 a family (you can also use your Snapper card; see "Getting Around," above). Mon–Fri 7am–10pm; weekends and public holidays 9am–10pm.

WELLYWOOD'S weta wonders

New Zealand's movie industry was long a low-key enterprise, but all that changed when director Peter Jackson and **Weta Workshop** founder Richard Taylor created the special effects for the blockbuster *Lord of the Rings* trilogy. Since then, the multiple-award-winning Weta operation has sprinkled high-tech magic on numerous films such as *King Kong, Avatar,* and *Rise of the Planet of the Apes*—and of course the three *Hobbit* movies. You can visit the **Weta Cave** and get up close and personal with characters, props, and displays from the Tolkien films and many others. Take something special home from the **Weta Cave Shop,** which has a huge range of collectibles, miniatures, jewelry, books, posters, clothing, and sculptures. Admission is free or you can book a 45-minute behind-the-scenes tour (NZ$24 adults and NZ$12 children 6–12). Weta Workshop is on the corner of Camperdown Rd. and Weka St., Miramar (www.wetanz.com; ✆ **04/909-4000**). It's open daily from 9am to 5:30pm. Take bus route 2 toward Miramar.

Wellington Botanic Garden ★★★ What sets Wellington's Botanic Garden apart from many others of its type is that it's an inner-city haven. Here you'll find a range of flat and wonderfully hilly areas, secret paths heading off in all directions, and spectacular views of the city. I think I spent more time here than at the nearby university in my younger days! A brochure and map are available from the Wellington visitor center or the Treehouse Visitor Centre inside the garden. A Garden of National Significance, it was established in 1868 and is now 25 hectares (62 acres) in all, with a nice mix of native forest, really quite old exotic trees, and plant collections with seasonal floral displays. The **Lady Norwood Rose Garden,** with 110 beds, is one of the more formal parts of the garden and is at its best from November to May. The lovely old **Begonia House** is full of tropical and temperate plants, including orchids and waterlilies, with a gift shop and the **Picnic Café** next door. There are numerous other little places of interest, like a **Peace Garden,** a **World War I commemorative poppy field,** and some naturally occurring **glowworms.**

Space Place at Carter Observatory ★★★, 40 Salamanca Rd., Kelburn (www.carterobservatory.org; ✆ **04/910-3140**), in the Botanic Garden and a 2-minute walk from the Cable Car terminus, is a world-class digital planetarium and your best chance to see the Southern Hemisphere's night sky. Learn about Maori cosmology, go on a virtual space journey, adopt a star, or peer into a Black Hole. There's also a good sciencey gift shop. Admission is NZ$13 for adults and NZ$8 for children 4 to 16.

Access the gardens from the Cable Car or Centennial entrance on Glenmore St., Thorndon. www.wellington.govt.nz. ✆ **04/499-1400** for Treehouse Visitor Centre. Free admission. Daily dawn–dusk. Treehouse Visitor Centre Mon–Fri 9am–4pm and weekends 9am to 3pm in summer. Begonia House Gift Shop & Cafe Oct–March 9am–5pm, April–Sept 9am–4pm; closed Tues. Take Karori Bus 3 or Mairangi Bus 13 from Lambton Quay.

ZEALANDIA: The Karori Sanctuary Experience ★★ This is something really special: the world's first urban wildlife sanctuary, which opened its gates in 2002. It's no mere park: Zealandia is a 252-hectare (623-acre) forest paradise created from a rather photogenic reservoir catchment just minutes from the inner city, and rare native species such as kiwi, saddlebacks, stitchbirds, kaka, and tuatara now call the pest- and predator-free valley home. You can do a self-guided walk or a 45-minute guided tour (included in the admission price), see wild species being fed, or come back at night to spot kiwi, tuatara, and other nocturnal creatures at work and play. This is a far more rewarding experience than seeing captive animals. It has an excellent visitor center and a cafe and gift shop onsite.

31 Waiapu Rd., Karori. www.visitzealandia.com.℗ **04/920-9200.** NZ$18 for adults, NZ$9 children 5–18, NZ$44 family; night tours are NZ$75 for adults and NZ$36 for children 12–18 or NZ$85 and NZ$41 for daytime admission and the night tour. Daily 9am–5pm. Free hourly shuttle bus from the i-SITE or take a public bus: 3, 13, 18, 21, 22 or 23.

Parliament Buildings ★★

The country's seat of government on Molesworth Street is just moments from Lambton Quay. The 1970s architectural wonder known as the **Beehive** sits by the Edwardian neoclassical **Parliament House.** Join the free daily 1-hour tour of these and the Victorian-Gothic **Parliamentary Library;** they contain some outstanding examples of New Zealand art. The Maori Affairs Select Committee Room, at the front of Parliament House, has specially commissioned carvings and weavings that are worth seeing, too.

The magnificent **Old Government Building,** built in 1876, is across the road. It's the largest wooden office building in the southern hemisphere and now houses Victoria University of Wellington's law faculty. It's only open to the public on Saturday from 1:30pm to 4pm. Close by is the **National Library of New Zealand,** 70 Molesworth St. (www.natlib.govt.nz; ℗ **04/474-3000**), which houses the **Alexander Turnbull Library** (Mon–Sat 8:30am–5pm). This is the research wing of the National Library and holds vast numbers of historic photos, drawings, paintings, maps, books, recordings, manuscripts, and archives from around New Zealand and the Pacific.

Molesworth St. www.parliament.nz. ℗ **04/817-9503.** Free admission. Hourly tours Mon–Fri 10am–4pm; Sat 10am–3pm; Sun 11am–3pm.

Old St. Paul's ★★

While you're in the area, have a look at Old St. Paul's—a stunningly beautiful Anglican church built in 1866 entirely from native wood and one of the best examples of timber Gothic Revival architecture in the world. Inside, the church positively glows with all that polished wood and stained glass—and perhaps a bit of divine spirit.

34 Mulgrave St. www.oldstpauls.co.nz. ℗ **04/473-6722.** Entry by donation. Hourly tours NZ$5 adults and NZ$3 children. Daily 9:30am–5pm.

Katherine Mansfield House & Garden ★

This is the childhood home of a creative New Zealander who was less famous in her time but is probably our best-known author. Mansfield was born in 1888 and left New Zealand for the U.K. permanently in 1908 at the age of 19, where she lived a spirited life in the company of such literary greats as Virginia Woolf, D.H.

Lawrence, and T.S. Eliot. Even if you've never heard of her, a visit to this charmingly restored two-story house is a pleasant diversion. Events such as art exhibitions and garden parties (very appropriate, if you're familiar with her work) are held here from time to time; check the website for details.

25 Tinakori Rd., Thorndon. www.katherinemansfield.com. *℗* **04/473-7268.** NZ$8 adults and free children under 18. Guided tours NZ$10 per person. Tues–Sun 10am–4pm.

City Gallery Wellington ★★ City Gallery Wellington—in the gorgeous old Art Deco Wellington Public Library building—will definitely challenge you with its thought-provoking and sometimes avant-garde collections (painting, sculpture, film, video, industrial and graphic design and architecture). It can be a bit pointy-headed; you'll notice this more if you've come straight from the fairly populist Te Papa nearby, but a visit will get you bang up to speed with what's happening in contemporary art in this country. Don't miss the dedicated Maori and Pacific galleries; it has some outstanding international exhibitions, too. The very good **Nikau Café** is onsite if you need to declutter your brain afterwards.

Civic Sq., 101 Wakefield St. www.citygallery.org.nz. *℗* **04/801-3021.** Admission is by donation; some international exhibitions may have entry fee. Daily 10am–5pm.

Wellington Museum ★★ We're pretty proud that this has been rated one of the 50 best museums in the world by *The Times* in the U.K. Its aim is "to take you back 1,000 years and lead you to a vibrant, present-day Wellington," and it doesn't hurt that the museum is located in the historic 1892 Bond Store. The museum presents the capital's social, cultural, and nautical history in interesting ways, using technology to enhance but not overpower the precious artifacts here. Kids will love the holograms and interactive displays. Permanent exhibits include a film about the 1968 **Wahine** ferry disaster that claimed 51 lives in Cook Strait; the maritime paraphernalia of **Jack's Boathouse;** and a reproduction of the historic Bond Store—complete with virtual vermin.

3 Jervois Quay, Queens Wharf. www.museumswellington.org.nz. *℗* **04/472-8904.** Free admission. Tours from NZ$10. Daily 10am–5pm.

Organized Tours & Cruises

Wellington Hop On Hop Off Scenic Tours (www.hoponhopoff.co.nz; *℗* **0800/246-877** in NZ) takes visitors around the top sights in mini-buses. Highlights of the 2-hour, 17-stop guided tour include the **Mt. Victoria Lookout, Zealandia,** the **Weta Cave, Te Papa,** and the **Wellington Museum.** Pickup is at the i-SITE visitor center on the hour from 10am (last departure 2pm). It's NZ$45 adults and NZ$30 children under 14.

Alternatively, you could try **Hammonds Wellington Tours** (www.wellingtonsightseeingtours.com; *℗* **04/472-0869**). Its 2½-hour **Wellington City Sights & Coastline Tour** has a similar itinerary to the one above except that it has a different style, plus it includes a bit of the rugged south coast as well. It's NZ$55 adults and NZ$28 children 4 to 14. Tours depart daily at 10am and

KID magnets

Wellington Zoo, 200 Daniell St. (www.wellingtonzoo.com; (C) **04/381-6755**), is a great place to visit, but in terms of seeing things here that you won't see anywhere else, it comes in second to **Zealandia** (see above), where you'll encounter only native creatures in the wild. It is, however doing sterling work— and a section of its animal hospital, The Nest, deals with injured native wildlife brought in from outside. It's NZ$21 adults and NZ$11 children 3 to 14 and is open daily 9:30am to 5pm. If you're traveling with really little ones, **StoryPlace** at Te Papa, Cable Street (www.tepapa.govt.nz; (C) **04/381-7000**), will take the kid-entertaining pressure off you for a bit. It's a magical place for the under-5

set with dressing up, storytelling, songs, and art activities. It's open Monday to Friday 10:15am to 4:30pm, and daily sessions are 45 minutes long (NZ$2 per preschooler and adult). If your kids are a bit bigger, send them around the waterfront on **in-line skates** and **bikes** rented from **Fergs Kayaks,** Shed 6, Queen's Wharf (see "Outdoor Pursuits," below). If you're in the city during a weekend or on a public holiday, have fun exploring the waterfront on a two- or four-seater cover bike rented from **The Enormous Crocodile Company,** 1 Herd St., Clyde Quay ((C) **027/276-2269**). Even the name will make you smile: Two-seaters are NZ$15 for 30 minutes and NZ$25 for 1 hour (four-seaters NZ$25 and NZ$40).

2pm. **Capital Personalised Tours** (www.captours.co.nz; (C) **021/280-2406**) will take you around in a sole-use SUV for customized golf, food and wine, sightseeing, or whatever tours you want, from NZ$150 adults and NZ$75 children for half a day.

Flat Earth ★★ (www.flatearth.co.nz; (C) **0800/775-805** in NZ, or 04/472-9635) has a range of excellent specialty half- and full-day tours, including **Maori Treasures, Capital Arts,** and **Middle-earth Film Locations** tours. Half-day tours are from NZ$174 adults and NZ$119 children; full-day tours are from NZ$385 adults and NZ$265 children. For the more Tolkien-obsessed, **Wellington Movie Tours** (www.adventuresafari.co.nz; (C) **027/419-3077**) focuses solely on *Lord of the Rings* locations with tours that include a visit to the Weta Cave (p. 246) onsite movie clips and props. Tours are NZ$70 to NZ$140 adults and NZ$42 to NZ$57 children. Or consider a **There & Back Again** ((C) **04/909-4000**) guided 2½-hour tour for NZ$65, where you'll see props, models, and much more in the Weta Workshop.

Zest Food Tours ★★ (www.zestfoodtours.co.nz; (C) **04/801-9198**) are designed for foodies who really care about what they put in their mouths. **Capital Tastes** and **Walking Gourmet** are their most popular tours. The first (daily from 9:30am) is an excellent 3½-hour meander that leaves from the visitor center and takes in some of the best purveyors of cheese, gelato, coffee, chocolate, and other delights, including markets, if you do it on a Sunday. You'll end the tour very impressed by Wellington's artisan food scene and probably not wanting lunch! It's NZ$169 per person. The second is a 4½-hour culinary journey that ends with a three-course tasting lunch with New Zealand

EXPLORING THE kapiti coast

Situated just 40 minutes' drive from Wellington, the **Kapiti Coast** is a wonderful blend of stunning scenery and the characterful individuality that makes capital dwellers and their coastal cousins so special. It's got beaches that range from endless expanses of sand to rugged, rocky bays; cute villages jammed full of creative endeavours; a great network of mostly flat cycling and walking tracks and—the jewel in its crown—**Kapiti Island.**

You can take the train all the way to Waikanae or drive. The **Paraparaumu i-SITE Visitor Information Centre,** 132 Rimu Rd., Paraparaumu (www.escapeto-kapiti.co.nz; © 04/298-8195), has information on the Kapiti Coast. It's open Monday to Friday from 9am to 5pm and weekends from 10am to 2pm.

If you want to break up the journey in the city of Porirua, 15 minutes north of Wellington (take the Porirua motorway exit), check out the always interesting **Pataka Art + Museum** ★★, corner of Norrie and Parumoana streets (www.pataka.org.nz; © 04/237-1511). This modern gallery truly celebrates Porirua's multicultural mélange and showcases Maori, Pacific Island, and Pakeha (European) arts with fascinating exhibitions. Admission is free and it's open Monday to Friday 10am to 4:30pm and Sunday 11am to 4:30pm.

I can never resist a walk on **Pukerua Bay beach** when visiting the capital. Having grown up in this area, I find myself being drawn back to its wild beauty as the waves crash onto the rocks, with only Kapiti Island to break the intensity of the ocean. It's an ever-changing stretch of water that's always invigorating.

Stop off in the delightful village of **Paekakariki,** a little farther north. This community of creatives and people who don't care much for city life has a gentler stretch of beach and a nifty little collection of offbeat shops. Have an excellent coffee and a florentine at **Beach Road Deli** ★, 5 Beach Rd. (© 04/902-9029), which sells great food and deli items (and has a tips jar with a sign that reads: "AFRAID OF CHANGE? WE'RE NOT"). Then climb the stairs to the **Alan Wehipeihana Studio and Gallery,** 1 Beach Rd. (© 04/905-9250), where this local artist has a very informal studio that was previously a panelbeating shop (Fri–Sun 11am–4pm). He creates thought-provoking paintings, sculpture, and carvings and shares his space with other artists—especially offbeat ones who like to upcycle and create new works with recycled bits and bobs.

Just north of Paekakariki village, **Steam Incorporated** (www.steaminc.org.nz; © 0800-783-264 in NZ) is an organization dedicated to keeping the romance of steam trains and diesel locomotives alive. Steam Inc. runs monthly excursions on the main trunk line to destinations that include the Wairarapa, Hawke's Bay, and Wellington and is open Monday to Saturday, when it's busy restoring and maintaining its rolling stock.

A little bit farther north again is **Queen Elizabeth Park,** Mackays Crossing, Paekakariki (© 04/292-8625), comprised of

wine. It also departs from the visitor center (Mon–Sat 9:30am), and costs NZ$279 per person.

For something a bit different, the **Seal Coast Safari** ★ (www.sealcoast.com; © 0800/732-527 in NZ, or 04/801-6040) will take you out to Red Rocks on the south coast in an SUV to visit the resident seal colony. It's NZ$125 for adults and NZ$63 for children up to 14 years.

650 hectares (1,606 acres) of native bush, walking tracks, and the last area of natural dunes on the Kapiti Coast. This was where 20,000 U.S. Marines were camped during World War II.

A visit to **Kapiti Island** ★★★ (www. doc.govt.nz/parks-and-recreation/places-to-go/wellington-kapiti/places/kapiti-is-land-nature-reserve/) is an absolute must. The 1,965-hectare (4,854-acre) island has been a nature reserve for more than 100 years, and many native species here are very rare or extinct from the mainland, such as little spotted kiwi, kaka, saddle-backs, and takahe. You can do a day trip or stay over, but you must go with an approved operator and book in advance. Two recommended operators are **Kapiti Island Nature Tours** (www.kapitiisland-naturetours.co.nz; ✆ **0800/547-5263** in NZ) and **Kapiti Tours** (www.ngatitoaka-pititours.co.nz; ✆ **0800/527-484** in NZ).

Kapiti Island Nature Tours offers transport, guided walks and tours, and overnight accommodation, from luxury tenting to four-bed cabins to a two-bed-room cottage, and the main lodge has a dining room. It offers half- and full-day guided nature walks and nighttime kiwi-spotting tours, as well as traditional flax weaving and seafood gathering. The ecologically switched-on Maori family who runs this operation has been living on Kapiti since the 1820s. Prices range from NZ$75 for ferry transport only to NZ$405 per person for transport, the kiwi tour, and accommodation in the cottage.

Kapiti Tours is run by Maori from the local Ngati Toa *iwi* (tribe). It offers ferry transport only for NZ$75 (NZ$40 children 17 and under); add a 1-hour guided walk and the cost is NZ$95 for adults and NZ$50 for children 5 to 17. Kapiti Tours also offers several other island tours.

Kapiti is surrounded a marine reserve, and swimming, snorkeling, and scuba diving are also possible. You will need a Department of Conservation (DOC) per-mit to land on Kapiti (the tour operator will organize these). Ferries depart from Kapiti Boating Club, corner of Marine Parade and Kapiti Road at Paraparaumu Beach daily at around 9am (both compa-nies) and 2:30pm (Kapiti Island Nature Tours).

If you choose not to stay on Kapiti Island, the mainland has a couple of lovely lodging options. **Greenmantle Estate Lodge,** 214 SH1, Paraparaumu (www.greenmantle.co.nz; ✆ **04/298-5555**), is the only luxury lodge on the west coast of the lower North Island and boasts six beautiful suites, a heated swimming pool and Jacuzzi, and a fine-dining restaurant. Tiger Woods stayed here, if that's a recommendation! Rates are from NZ$575 to NZ$950 for two people. **103 Cottage at Sudbury,** 101 Te Hapua Rd., Pekapeka (www.sudbury. co.nz; ✆ **06/364-3064**), is situated between Waikanae and Otaki. It's part of a fancy-events venue, but the two-bed-room, five-star accommodation is very private and secluded with lovely country views. It's NZ$550 per night.

And if you like the idea of enjoying the city from a great height, one of the best ways to do it is with **Wellington Helicopters,** centrally located at Shed 1, 19 Jervois Quay (www.helicopers.net.nz; ✆ **04/472-1550**). Choose from a variety of flights ranging from short but perfectly scenic (NZ$120 per person) to a longer experience that may cost up to NZ$399 per person but allows for photo opportunities if the weather permits.

Outdoor Pursuits

CYCLING   That would be Ferg again. Bike rental is from NZ$20 for an hour to NZ$80 for a day.

GOLF   You'll find top courses within an hour of the Wellington CBD. The **Royal Wellington Golf Club,** 28 Golf Rd., Heretaunga, Upper Hutt (www. rwgc.co.nz; ℂ **04/528-4590**), is ranked the best members' club in New Zealand by this country's PGA. Greens fees are NZ$195. It's got a 27-hole course, a swimming pool, and three all-weather tennis courts. **Paraparaumu Beach Golf Club,** 376 Kapiti Rd., Paraparaumu Beach (www.paraparaumubeachgolfclub.co.nz; ℂ **04/902-8200**), is considered to be one of the best links courses in the Southern Hemisphere and has hosted the New Zealand Open 12 times. Greens fees are NZ$150; be sure to book well in advance. Closer to the city is the 18-hole **Karori Golf Club,** South Makara Road, Wellington (www. karorigolf.co.nz; ℂ **04/476-7337**), where a round will cost you NZ$30 during the week and NZ$35 on weekends.

IN-LINE SKATING   Ever the entrepreneur, Ferg (see "Kayaking," above) also rents out in-line skates and bikes. There's nothing like whizzing along the waterfront on wheels. Skate rental is from NZ$15 for an hour to NZ$35 for a day; bikes are from NZ$20 for an hour to NZ$80 for a day.

KAYAKING   **Fergs Kayaks,** Shed 6, Queen's Wharf (http://fergskayaks. co.nz; ℂ **04/499-8898**), is owned by New Zealand's Olympic gold medal–winning paddler Ian Ferguson. Freedom hire is from NZ$20 to NZ$50 for an hour and up to NZ$80 to NZ$180 for a day, or join a guided group. Tours range from NZ$210 to NZ$340. Be prepared, though: The harbor can get pretty rough.

MOUNTAIN BIKING   You'll need pretty good legs for this one—Wellington is not the world's flattest capital city! **Mud Cycles,** 421 Karori Rd., Karori (www.mudcycles.co.nz; ℂ **04/476-4961**), is based near challenging Makara Peak, about 30 minutes' drive from the CBD. Mud Cycles rents out bikes for NZ$35 to NZ$50 for 4 hours, all the way up to NZ$240 to NZ$320 for a week. Check out **Bike Wellington** (www.bikewellington.co.nz; ℂ **021/026-48153**) for information about the best places to go.

WALKING   This is a great city for walking—you can stroll around the **waterfront** from Oriental Bay to Queen's Wharf or wander through the lovely **Botanic Garden,** hike up **Mount Victoria,** or enjoy the inner-city wilds of **Central Park.** The visitor center has brochures on self-guided walks, including "Heritage Trails," "Explore Wellington" (themed walks around the city) and "Five Lunchtime Walks."

Shopping

Pick up the free shopping guides "The Fashion Map" and "The Arts Map" in the visitor center to help you navigate your way around areas of interest. City shops are usually open from Monday to Friday 9am to 5:30pm, Saturday from 9am to 4:30pm, and Sunday from 10am to 2pm.

ART PIECES TO treasure

If you're looking for really high-quality souvenirs, you can't beat the **Te Papa Store ★★★**, Museum of New Zealand –Te Papa Tongarewa, Cable Street (℗ **04/381-7013;** www.tepapastore. co.nz). It has simply beautiful things—books, artwork, homewares, jewelry—and you won't have to pay the local tax (GST) if you're sending gifts overseas. The following shops are also worth seeking out but away from the main shopping streets: **Avid,** 48 Victoria St. (www. avidgallery.co.nz; ℗ **04/472-7703**), is a gallery that showcases locally made contemporary art objects and handmade

jewelry. **Kura,** 19 Allen St. (www.kuragallery.co.nz; ℗ **04/802-4934**), is an art and design gallery that showcases work by New Zealand artists, especially Maori, and has a nice range of Maori carving and *pounamu* (greenstone). Also on Allen Street, **Ora Gallery** (www.oragallery.co.nz; ℗ **04/384-4157**) stocks a fine collection of local art and design. It has a cafe onsite, so you can sip a coffee while you're considering what to buy. **Vessel,** 87 Victoria St. (www.vessel.co.nz; ℗ **04/499-2321**), has a great selection of ceramic domestic ware from some of New Zealand's best artists.

Start on **Lambton Quay**—known as "the Golden Mile"—for department stores and designer shops. This is lunchtime shopping country for civil servants, so it's crammed with shoe shops, boutiques, great bookstores, and those increasingly rare shops that sell music CDs. Wellington's most famous and classy department store, **Kirkcaldie & Stains,** has of 2016 been taken over by the Australian department store giant David Jones. The historic Bank of New Zealand building is now the **Old Bank** (www.oldbank.co.nz; ℗ **04/922-0600**), a posh retail arcade featuring top local and international stores with cafes, restaurants, and designer clothing shops.

Moving on to **Willis Street,** you'll find more fashion, books, and music. **Quoil ★★**, 149 Willis St. (℗ **04/384-1499;** www.quoil.co.nz), is a gallery space that shows work by New Zealand's top contemporary jewelers. If you turn down Manners Street, you can make a right into **Cuba Steet,** with its wonderful mix of the strange, the quaint, and the shops that have been there for decades! **Cuba Mall** has the beloved '70s-era Bucket Fountain, the landmark tipping-bucket installation that has been fascinating kids of all ages for many a year. The funkiest cafes are here, as are a good number of the city's bohemian set—many of them wearing cool vintage gear from shops like **Hunters & Collectors,** 134 Cuba St. (℗ **04/384-8948**); **Ziggurat,** 144 Cuba St. (℗ **04/385-1077**); and **Emporium Vintage Boutique,** 103B Cuba St. (℗ **04/381-4544**). (This neighborhood is also the very best place to get a tattoo, a piercing, or your fix of adult entertainment.)

All the upmarket suburbs have lovely shops to browse, but **Tinakori Rd. Village** is particularly good. **Millwood Gallery ★★**, 291B Tinakori Rd. (www.millwoodgallery.co.nz; ℗ **04/473-5178**), is a haven of fine art, books, and fancy stationery. You could buy a piece of original New Zealand art—perhaps a representation of this eminently paintable city. **Tinakori Antiques ★★**,

291 Tinakori Rd. (© **04/472-7043**), will be fatal for lovers of fine, old things. **Secondo,** 289 Tinakori Rd. (© **04/472-1400**), a recycled clothing boutique rather different from those found in Cuba St., has some very expensive items worn once or twice at swanky dos and passed on.

At the other end of town, if you hanker after a big, fluffy sheepskin, the **Sheepskin Warehouse,** 56 Kingsford Smith St., Rongotai (© **04/386-3376**), has the biggest range of skins and woolen products around and will post overseas. GST is deductible.

Wellington After Dark

Wellington is such a fun, creative city by day it should come as no surprise that it parties hard at night. Whether you want cool bars, hot dance clubs, or something a bit more refined, there'll be something on that appeals. Pick up *Capital Times* and *What's On* (both free) at the visitor center for listings.

THE PERFORMING ARTS

Wellington stages the biggest performing-arts festival in the country (see "Special Events"). It's also home to the **New Zealand Symphony Orchestra,** the **Royal New Zealand Ballet,** two thriving **professional theater companies,** the **New Zealand School of Dance,** and the **New Zealand Drama School.**

The lovely Edwardian **St James Theatre,** 77–87 Courtenay Place (www.pwv.co.nz/our-venues/st-james-theatre/; © **04/801-4231**), boasts both a preserved heritage theater and state-of-the-art technology. You can see top-quality musical shows and professional opera here, and it's also the permanent home of the Royal New Zealand Ballet Company. The rather stylish 1920s **Embassy Theatre,** 10 Kent Terrace (www.eventcinemas.co.nz/cinema/the-embassy; © **04/384-7657**), now functions as a cinema and was done up for the big, star-studded world premieres of *The Lord of the Rings: The Return of the King* and *The Hobbit: There and Back Again.* It's got a huge screen and flash digital sound system, plus a cafe and bar.

Circa Theatre, 1 Taranaki St. (www.circa.co.nz; © **04/801-7992**), has a great waterfront location next to Te Papa and presents high-quality, interesting productions, some homegrown. Dine on a preshow meal at its Encore Restaurant. Tickets range from NZ$20 to NZ$51. **Bats Theatre,** 1 Kent Terrace (www.bats.co.nz; © **04/801-4175**), is New Zealand's top developmental theater, putting on new and experimental plays and dance at great prices (NZ$14–NZ$20).

CLUBS & BARS

Wellington has an abundance of these, the most raucous being around the **Courtenay Place** area. If you wish to avoid heavily imbibing young people, go somewhere else if it's a Thursday, Friday, or Saturday night.

The bar scene, of course, is in constant motion, and what's hot today might be a cool-zone ghost town in 6 months' time. Ask around for the happening (or, alternatively, the quiet but atmospheric) places. Closing times vary and

Wellington is crazy for **craft beers,** lovingly made creations that are as individual and nuanced as good wine. Pick up a copy of the **Craft Beer Capital self-guided trail map** from the visitor center: It highlights 16 bars, eight breweries, and four bottle stores that stock the top local brews. Don't miss these ones: **Goldings Free Dive,** 15 Leeds St. (ℂ 04/381-3616), is a cool, colorful, and rather expensive little brewbar where you can buy your beers by the jug—a good, old-fashioned Kiwi tradition. Tuatara's microbrewery **The Third Eye,** 30 Arthur St., is set up in an old printing works and serves Tuatara beers as well as other trendy brews. From Wednesday to Saturday, the Goose Shack truck parks up in the beer garden and serves great grub. The rest of the time it's toasted sandwiches and bar snacks! **Grill Meats Beer,** 227 Cuba St. (ℂ 04/801-8787), is an offshoot of the fabulous **Logan Brown** restaurant that's dedicated to perfectly matching food and beer. **Hashigo Zake,** 25 Taranaki St. (ℂ 04/384-7300), describes itself as a cult beer bar. You can expect to find some serious ale geeks here. A little way up the Aro Valley, you'll find **Garage Project,** 68 Aro St. (www.garageproject.co.nz), a brewery that was so small when it started out it was more nano than micro. Their ethos hasn't changed, but this bunch of beardie guys is now pumping out some seriously good beer.

depend on whether it's summer or winter and what kind of liquor license the establishment holds. Most Wellington bars stay open until midnight to 2am during the summer months.

Established in 1963, **Matterhorn ★★★**, 106 Cuba St. (www.matterhorn. co.nz; ℂ **04/384-3359**), serves fabulous cocktails and food and transforms into a very groovy nightspot later in the evening (which always makes me laugh—I used to work here as a poor student when it was a rather pretentious coffee bar run by a grumpy Swiss-German couple). **Motel Bar ★★**, Forrester's Lane (www.motelbar.co.nz; ℂ **04/384-9084**), does a Pacific Island retro thing, serving tropical cocktails in tiki-shaped mugs, parrot heads, skulls, and fresh pineapples. You could hula on down here after a bite at the popular **Chow** restaurant next door. **The Apartment ★★**, 25 Allen St. (www. theapartment.co.nz; ℂ **04/385-9771**), is done up to look like a chic New York loft space with bookshelves, lounge and dining room, leather sofas, a terrace, and even a bedroom. Great food and drink, too. Carrying on the theme of bar-as-theater, **Duke Carvell's Emporium,** 3 Swan Lane (www.dukecarvell. co.nz; ℂ **04/385-2240**), is decked out like a stately old home and is supposedly run by an impoverished noble of indistinct European origins. Or not, as the case may be. . . .

The **Library ★**, 53 Courtenay Place (www.thelibrary.co.nz; ℂ **04/382-8593**), is a lounge bar and reading room (yes, there are plenty of books) with live music, food (fabulous desserts!), and a cool, slightly distressed vibe. Two converted historic cottages down an alley, **Havana,** Wigan Street (www.havanabar.co.nz; ℂ **04/382-8593**), is lots of fun with a lovely staff and terrific

Cuban-themed everything. **CGR Merchant & Co.,** 46 Courtenay Place
(⦿ **04/384-6737**), is famous right now for its salted caramel rum (the CGR
stands for coffee, gin, and rum and tends to appear in everything), but who
knows what it will be tomorrow? **The Bresolin,** 278 Willis St. (www.thebre-
solin.co.nz; ⦿ **04/801-5152**), invites you to celebrate in its classy Edwardian
villa, where it serves sophisticated pub food and drink.

THE GAY SCENE

It should be noted that Wellington is a very liberal city, so a gay "scene" isn't
strictly necessary, but a number of bar and clubs do label themselves as such.
Ask at the visitor center for information on gay-friendly accommodations and
bars/clubs other than the ones listed here, or phone the Wellington **Gay and
Lesbian Helpline** (www.gaywellington.org.nz; ⦿ **04/473-7878**), open only
on Sunday from 7:30pm to 9:30pm.

Some good places to check out include **S&M's (Scotty & Mal's),** 176
Cuba St. (www.scottyandmals.co.nz; ⦿ **04/802-5335**), a classy cocktail and
lounge bar with a B&D (basement and dance) space downstairs that's open on
Friday and Saturday nights and has a resident DJ; and the fun **Ivy Bar and
Cabaret,** 49 Cuba St. (www.ivybar.co.nz; ⦿ **027/325-8306**), which hosts such
events as karaoke, jelly wrestling, and Mr. Gay Wellington. Both are closed
on Monday. **Checkmate,** open daily from noon, bills itself as "The Number
One True Blue Kiwi Gay Sauna"; it's at 15 Tory St. (www.checkmatesauna.
co.nz; ⦿ **04/385-6556**).

En Route to the Wairarapa

The Wairarapa is separated from Wellington by the Rimutakas, a range of hills
that can experience all of the capital's breeziest conditions plus a scattering of
snow in the winter. Always take care on this road, which is a mix of two and three
lanes. It's 62km (39 miles) from Wellington to Featherston, about an hour's drive
in normal conditions. Before you reach "the hill," you'll pass through the **Hutt
Valley,** which is made up of two cities, Upper Hutt and Lower Hutt. It's long
been a bit of a poor cousin to Wellington, but if you're happy to make a bit of a
detour, the seaside suburbs of **Eastbourne** and **Days Bay** are very pretty for a
stroll, a coffee, and something nice to nibble on. Try **Chocolate Dayz café,**
Marine Drive, Days Bay (www.chocolatedayzcafe.co.nz; ⦿ **04/562-6132**). The
Dowse Art Museum, 45 Laings Rd., Lower Hutt (www.dowse.org.nz; ⦿ **04/570-
6500**), is a really innovative gallery that holds one of New Zealand's largest and
most significant public art collections *and* the best collection of craft art. Entry is
free, and it's open daily from 10am to 5pm.

THE WAIRARAPA

There's so much innovation in this rural region it's barely recognizable from
the collection of quiet towns where just a couple of decades ago little was
happening except the Golden Shears sheep-shearing competitions. Now it's
busting out all over with innovative new ways to show itself off—but always

in a nice way. Filmmaker James Cameron liked it so much he bought a big chunk of farmland and is contributing to the local economy with his newest venture (p. 263).

Most of the region's infrastructure is based in **Masterton** (population 23,350), the largest town. **Martinborough** has an abundance of great vineyards and restaurants and is a very attractive heritage village. Crammed with Victorian buildings and boutique shops, historic **Greytown** is one of the prettiest little towns in New Zealand. Nearby **Carterton** is hot on its heels, and **Featherston** keeps coming up with new ways to reinvent itself. Oh, and there's space, space, and a bit more space to roam.

Essentials

GETTING THERE If you're driving from the south, take SH2 from Wellington, over the Rimutakas (see above). If you're coming from the north, it's about a 3-hour drive from Napier to Masterton and 1 hour from Palmerston North, or you can take the regular commuter train from Wellington all the way to Masterton. Go to **www.metlink.org.nz** for more information. If you've got deep pockets, you could fly in by helicopter: A flight from Wellington to Martinborough takes about 15 minutes. Try **Amalgamated Helicopters** (www.amalgamatedheli.co.nz; ✆ **06/379-8600**).

VISITOR INFORMATION The website for the region's official tourism arm, **Destination Wairarapa,** is **www.wairarapanz.com.**

The **Masterton i-SITE Visitor Centre,** corner of Dixon and Bruce streets (✆ **06/370-0900**), is open daily Monday to Friday 9am to 5pm and weekends 10am to 4pm, with extended hours in summer. The **Martinborough i-SITE Visitor Centre,** at 18 Kitchener St. (✆ **06/306-5010**), is open Tuesday to Saturday 9am to 5pm and Sunday and Monday 10am to 4pm.

SPECIAL EVENTS **Martinborough Fair** ★★ (www.martinboroughfair. org.nz; ✆ **06/304-9933**) is a great chance to buy quality New Zealand–made goods in a delightful setting. The fair takes place annually on the first Saturday in February and the first Saturday in March and is widely thought to be one of the best crafts events in the country. If you want something really authentic, get yourself to Masterton's **Golden Shears** (www.goldenshears. co.nz; ✆ **06/378-8008**), the world's biggest shearing and wool-handling competition. It's 3 days of bleating, baahing hard yakka, held late in February or early in March each year. A bit more refined is **Toast Martinborough** ★★★ (www.toastmartinborough.co.nz; ✆ **06/306-9183**), a top wine, food, and music festival that takes place in November. A special festival train runs from Wellington and shuttle buses run continuously around the 9 or 10 vineyards taking part, so you can taste without having to drive.

Exploring the Area

Featherston is the first settlement you reach if you're coming from Wellington. This little town almost tucked into the base of the Rimutakas has spread its wings in recent years, although one thing that seems to have been here forever is the **Fell Locomotive Museum,** SH2 (www.fellmuseum.org.nz; ✆ **06/308-9379**). It's home to H1999, the last remaining locomotive of its type in the world and one of six engines designed for use on the Rimutaka Incline. (You can climb up and look at its hard, pointy bits—the levers, knobs, valves, and switches.) These grunty little characters are an important part of the area's history—they had to climb gradients as steep as 1 in 13 to grind their way up to the summit of the ranges. The museum is open daily (10am–4pm); admission is NZ$5 adults, NZ$2 children over 5, and NZ$12 a family. If you have a car, this is the departure point for the rugged south coast and **Cape Palliser.** This very scenic drive takes you past the spectacular **Putangirua Pinnacles,** fluted columns of rock formed by the rather quaintly termed "badlands erosion" of an ancient gravel deposit—it's a 30-minute walk to get to them. Back in your car, carry on past the rough-and-ready fishing village of **Ngawi** to the lovely **Cape Palliser Lighthouse** (built in 1897) and the very accessible but rather pungent **fur seal colony.** This is breathtaking country: Life is hard out here, even for the wildlife!

From here, you'll probably want to visit **Martinborough,** known best as a top winemaking region, with more than 20 vineyards in one small area (see "The Wineries," below). You can rent a bike from one of several operators in the village and cycle from vineyard to vineyard—carefully!

Back on SH2, continue north to **Greytown,** which has the best collection of Victorian buildings of any town in New Zealand—as well as fabulous cafes and boutique shops. But if history is your thing, check out **Cobblestones Museum,** 169 Main St., an interesting collection of pioneer buildings and memorabilia (www.cobblestonesmuseum.org.nz; ℭ **06/304-9687**) on the original site of the stables operated by Cobb & Co, which shifted mail and passengers to Wellington from 1866. It's open daily 10am to 4pm, and entry is free.

On the outskirts of Greytown you'll find Neil and Greg and their collection of farm pets at the lovely **Kahikatea Gardens ★,** 60 Wilkie St. (www.kahikateagardens.co.nz; ℭ **06/304-9461**). I was met at the gate by Neil and two enormous ex-pet lambs on leads, and we proceeded around the garden together, past native trees, exotic flowering shrubs, and fruit and nut trees. In pride of place is a giant 900-year-old kahikatea tree. The excess produce from the fruit and nut trees is turned into Neil and Greg's Rexworthy Cottage chutneys, jams, walnuts, and hazelnuts. Admission to the gardens and farm is NZ$15 adults and NZ$10 children, and a deluxe tour with morning or afternoon tea and a visit to the homestead is NZ$25; bookings essential.

Masterton is the "big smoke" around here. It's not that fascinating as a regional center, but it has a great museum (see "L.A. Meets Masterton," below), and it's where you take the hour-long drive out to **Castlepoint.** This is a fabulously wild environment with one of our most famous lighthouses and a couple of no-nonsense cafes. Plus, if you visit on a late-summer Saturday, you'll come across the iconic **Castlepoint Beach Races,** which have been, er, running since 1872. You might want to learn more about the farming backbone of this region at **The Wool Shed—National Museum of Sheep and Shearing,** 12 Dixon St., Masterton (www.thewoolshednz.com; ℭ **06/378-8008**). It's built around two historic woolsheds, one dating back to the 1880s, and if you can possibly think of any sheep-related question this place doesn't answer, you can ask one of the friendly volunteers. Admission is NZ$8 adults, NZ$2 children, and NZ$15 per family. It's open daily from 10am to 4pm.

Some 27km (17 miles) north of Masterton on SH2 is the must-see **Pukaha Mount Bruce National Wildlife Centre ★★★** (www.pukaha.org.nz; ℭ **06/375-8004**). Its star attractions are the rather odd white kiwis that have been born here, numbering five since 2010. But this is no freak show: Pukaha is a serious player in the conservation of endangered native birds, fish, and reptiles, and the entry fee covers six daily talks and feeds, as well as entry to the nocturnal house, where you can see Manukura, the only white kiwi on public display in the world. She really is something to behold and, without wanting to be too anthropomorphic, seems to have a fair bit of rock-star attitude for one so perilously rare! Pukaha is open daily from 9am to 4:30pm. Admission is NZ$20 adults, NZ$6 children 5 to 15, and NZ$50 per family.

L.A. Meets Masterton

Aratoi: Wairarapa Museum of Art and History, corner of Bruce and Dixon streets, Masterton (www.aratoi.org.nz; ℂ 06/370-0001), is a lovely and innovative museum and art gallery that has a globetrotting Kiwi at its helm. Director Alice Hutchison left New Zealand more than 20 years ago to work in top U.S. art spaces, including L.A.'s Ace Gallery, where she was the curator and associate director for 5 years. Now back on home soil, she's enjoying bringing the stories of Wairarapa to a varied audience. Aratoi has a significant collection of Maori and European *taonga* (treasures) and contemporary New Zealand and international artworks, as well as interesting temporary exhibitions about the region and the wider world. It's open daily 10am to 4:30am: Admission is by gold coin donation.

THE WINERIES

Lots of sunshine and low autumn rainfall give the Martinborough region a distinct advantage and are contributing factors in the rather impressive success of the 30-plus small boutique wineries in this area. Add to this another handful in Gladstone and Masterton, and you'll realize you're in one of the world's top pinot noir and sauvignon blanc regions. Pretty cool, eh? This is the heart of the **Classic New Zealand Wine Trail,** which comprises Hawke's Bay, Wairarapa, and Marlborough. Most of the wineries love to have visitors and are open for tastings when they have enough wine in stock, and some are open year-round—but many of the very best sell out by mail order within a few weeks of release, so there's not much point in mentioning them. Visit from late October to early March, when new wine stocks have been released. Pick up a wine map from one of the i-SITE visitor centers; your only problem will be deciding which wineries to visit. "Favorite" is a pretty subjective term, but the following all have excellent reputations and are open daily. All are in the Martinborough region except for **Gladstone Vineyard.**

And if you can't make up your mind where to go or are short on time, drop in to at **Martinborough Wine Centre,** 6 Kitchener St. (www.martinborough-winecentre.co.nz; ℂ 06/306-9040), which has a very clever staff, a comprehensive range of wines in stock, and lots of yummy things to buy that go particularly well with wine. You can taste their wares and even rent a bike to wobble around the vineyards (NZ$40/full day; NZ$30/half-day).

○ **Ata Rangi** ★★ (Puruatanga Rd.; www.atarangi.co.nz; ℂ 06/306-9570): One of the region's original vineyards, Ata Rangi sells its outstanding pinot noir in more than 25 overseas markets. You can buy (and taste) it here, along with chardonnay, riesling, rosé, and a cabernet/merlot/syrah blend.

○ **Poppies Martinborough** ★★ (Puruatanga Rd.; www.poppiesmartinborough.co.nz; ℂ 06/306-8473): Poppy makes the wine and Shayne does the outdoor stuff. This young couple is passionate about their chosen life, and this is the only place you can buy what they make over the counter (pinot gris, sauvignon blanc, riesling, gewürztraminer, chardonnay, rosé, pinot noir). Enjoy it with an absolutely delicious platter of local seasonal foods such as dolmades, tapenade, artichokes, stuffed peppers, Indian relish, and local meats.

o **Martinborough Vineyard** ★ (Princess St.; www.martinborough-vineyard. co.nz; ℂ **06/306-9955**): Another founding vineyard and one that claims to have the oldest pinot noir vines in the region. What started as a family business is now a major player that exports around the world. It produces exceptional pinot noir, chardonnay, riesling, sauvignon blanc, syrah viognier, and pinot gris.

o **Palliser Estate** ★★ (Kitchener St.; www.palliser.co.nz; ℂ **06/306-9019**): This "boutique Martinborough vineyard with an international outlook" is where chief winemaker Allan Johnson makes award-winning chardonnay, pinot noir, sauvignon blanc, and pinot gris and a nice bubbly. He produces wines under the Palliser Estate and Pencarrow labels.

o **Te Kairanga Wines** (Martins Rd.; http://tkwine.co.nz; ℂ **06/306-9122**): Another oldie, Te Kairanga comprises four fully sustainable vineyards in the region, each with distinct characteristics. The Martinborough Terrace vineyard specializes in high-quality pinot noir, but the winery also makes chardonnay, riesling, pinot gris, and sauvignon blanc and holds a farmer's market on summer Sundays.

o **Gladstone Vineyard** ★★ (Gladstone Rd., Carterton; www.gladstonevineyard.co.nz; ℂ **06/379-8563**): This Vineyard is delightful to look at, the award-winning sauvignon blanc, pinot gris, rosé, pinot noir, and viognier vintages (including the Jealous Sisters range!) are lovely to drink, there's a cafe onsite (open weekends only), and if you really can't face leaving, it also has boutique apartment-style accommodations. If you're here in April, you can do a behind-the-scenes tour.

Organized Tours

While we're on the subject of wine—and this does start a lot of conversations in the region—you might want to enjoy the grape without even driving over the hill. If so, hop aboard the **Tranzit Gourmet Wine Tour** ★★ (www.tranzittours.co.nz; ℂ **0800/471-227** in NZ). You can catch a train in Wellington for a scenic journey to the Wairarapa, pick up a coach tour (or skip the train part), visit four vineyards for tastings, have lunch, and take a trip to the Martinborough Wine Centre (NZ$197 round-trip per person from Wellington, NZ$173 from elsewhere in the Wairarapa, and NZ$152 from Martinborough). Tours run daily. **Zest Food Tours** ★★★ (www.zestfoodtours.co.nz; ℂ **04/801-9198**) runs a private **Martinborough Food and Wine Producers Tour** for two to four people that will take you around the region to meet artisan food producers and taste their wares (NZ$429 per person; daily by arrangement).

You'll be exercising different muscles, but the **Rimutaka Cycle Trail** ★★★ (www.nzcycletrail.com/rimutaka-cycle-trail) is hugely popular among two-wheel fans and has opened up areas that we previously whizzed past in a car. You can do all or part of the 115km (71-mile) Wellington to Wairarapa trail, classed as one of New Zealand's "Great Rides," making it one of the top 23 cycle trails in the country. The trail starts on the Petone Foreshore in Lower Hutt, passes alongside the Hutt River, through tunnels under the Rimutaka Ranges, peaceful farmland, and native forest, and out to the rugged Wairarapa south coast. Ride with the **Green Jersey Cycle Tour Company** (www.greenjersey.co.nz; *℡* **021/0746-640**) for from NZ$999 per person, including the bike and selected accommodations. Green Jersey also offers guided daylong Wairarapa wine trail tours and multi-day explorer tours.

The delightfully named **To the Coast with the Post** (http://tothecoastwiththepost.co.nz; *℡* **027/430-8866**) is a very laid-back tour with a very laid-back guy—Gordon the local postie (mailman). Join him as he does his rounds in a van through scenic South Wairarapa all the way to the Cape Palliser lighthouse. It's NZ$85 per person, including snacks and a homemade picnic lunch, and runs Monday to Friday 8:30am to 4pm.

Where to Stay

Weary Wellingtonians need somewhere to park their pooped public-service personages on the weekend, and Wairarapa has an abundance of delightful, relaxing accommodation options, including many lovely historic cottages and some properly upmarket ones. Here's a taste:

The Martinborough Hotel ★★, The Square (www.martinboroughhotel.co.nz; *℡* **06/306-9350**), is a fine old building with wide, covered verandas, from which you can watch the comings and goings in and around the village's central square. The 1882 hotel has been beautifully restored—they must have bought every clawfoot bathtub in the Wairarapa—and the 20 rooms are sophisticated and elegant. Some are in the old hotel, and others are new rooms in the garden courtyard. Have a meal in the very nice restaurant or chuck down a beer in the public bar. The very reasonably priced range from NZ$150 to NZ$240.

Peppers Parehua ★, New York Street West, Martinborough (www.peppers.co.nz/parehua/; *℡* **0800/448-891** in NZ, or 06/306-8405), is not historic at all, but its large, modern cottages and villas are perfect for a luxurious country stay. Opposite the Palliser vineyards, you can hole up here and eat at the restaurant, swim, play tennis, pétanque, or croquet, or venture out on a bike and cycle around the vineyards. Rates range from NZ$149 to NZ$548 and include breakfast. At the northern end of Greytown you'll find **Briarwood ★**, 21 Main St. (www.briarwoodgreytown.co.nz; *℡* **06/304-8336**), a five-star boutique lodging with three suites that treads the line between urban chic and Victorian elegance. It's luxurious and peaceful, despite being within strolling distance of a wealth of cafes and interesting shops. Rooms are NZ$250 to NZ$350.

If you want to stay in Masterton, the **Copthorne Hotel & Resort Solway Park,** High Street (www.solway.co.nz; *℡* **0800/808-228** in NZ, or 06/370-0507), can't fully escape its 1970s roots, but it's a great place to bring the kids. It's set on 10 hectares (24 acres) and has a gym, heated indoor pool, Jacuzzi, indoor squash court, tennis and volleyball courts, a playground, a 10-bay golf driving range, a high-ropes course—and a malt whisky bar with around 60 kinds of Scotch for mum and dad! Rooms range from NZ$126 to NZ$280.

GOURMET grazing

The Wairarapa is known for its fabulous artisanal food products—you'll be tripping over them everywhere you go these days. Here are a few foodie highlights, starting with the best deli products and the best name:

o **C'est Cheese** For a great selection of cheeses (mainly New Zealand but some imported), olive oils, cured meats, chutneys, and other delights, C'est Cheese is open daily. It also stocks a range of local-ish preserves with another great name: Snooty Fruit! (19 Fitzherbert St., Featherston; *© 06/308-6000*).

o **Food Forest Organics** The owner is Hollywood director James Cameron, whose nearby farms supply much of the organic vegan produce sold in the store. Try beetroot noodles, coconut chocolate butter, and quinoa pasto, as well as more prosaic fare. It's open Wednesday to Sunday 9:30am to 4:30pm (101 Main St., Greytown; www.foodforestorganics.co.nz; *© 06/304-9790*).

o **Kingsmeade Cheese** Producing award-winning sheep-milk cheese

and selling lots more—chutneys, chocolates, sauces, specialty pastas—besides (8 First St., Masterton; www.kingsmeadecheese.co.nz; *© 06/378-7178*).

o **Olivo** Among the ever-increasing number of olive-oil producers in the Wairarapa, the oldest and still one of the best is Olivo, which produces award-winning extra-virgin and infused olive oils. The tasting room on the beautiful property is open on weekends from 10:30am to 5pm and by appointment (Hinakura Rd., Martinborough; www.olivo.co.nz; *© 06/306-9074*).

o **Schoc Chocolates** Schoc produces more than 85 different flavors of deliciousness, under the watchful eye of chocologist Murray Langham. A few to ponder: lavender salted caramel, lemon thyme, smoked tea, and carrot and coriander. Oh, and things like strawberry as well! It's open Monday to Friday 10am to 5pm and weekends 10:30am to 4:30pm (177 Main St., Greytown; www.schoc.co.nz; *© 06/304/8960*).

Summit Lodge ★★ A special place with special people, Summit Lodge is perfect if you want a serene stay where you get to chat with the owners, Tracey and Jim, in their shared kitchen/dining room space. The large, modern house in rural Gladstone has two separate wings, so you can get peaceful privacy when you want it or join other guests in the large lounge. This is a five-star, Qualmark Enviro-Gold property, which means they're doing things in an environmentally friendly way. Tracey will cook a lovely dinner if you require it and take you for a walk around the place to meet the friendly alpacas, along with several cats and Dexter the Labrador if you're lucky.

4 Admiral Rd., Gladstone. www.summitlodge.co.nz. *© 06/372-7757.* 3 units. NZ$285 suite. Rates include breakfast and pre-dinner drinks and canapés. No children under 18. Dinner on request: NZ$60 for three courses or NZ$85 with wine. Off-peak rates and special deals. **Amenities:** Jacuzzi; guest lounge with open fire; Wi-Fi (free).

Wharekauhau Country Estate ★★★ Would William and Kate, the Duke and Duchess of Cambridge, have stayed here if it wasn't pretty damned exceptional? No doubt the royals were blown away at their first sight of this beautiful accommodations on a 2,000-hectare (5,000-acre) working sheep station. The views out over rugged Palliser Bay hit you like a keening southerly, but in the nicest possible way. The estate has won two prestigious Andrew Harper awards (www.andrewharpertravel.com), among many others, and your luxury and comfort are assured. For a memory to treasure, go horseback riding and take a gallop along the cliffs. Even my husband, who has ridden more camels than horses, loved this added extra.

Western Lake Rd., Palliser Bay, RD3, Featherston. www.wharekauhau.co.nz. ℭ **06/307-7581.** 13 cottages. NZ$1978 cottage suite. Rates include breakfast, pre-dinner drinks and canapés, and four-course gourmet dinner. Off-peak rates and special deals. **Amenities:** Bar; babysitting; bikes; concierge; farm tours; gym; horseback riding; heated indoor pool; day spa; all-weather tennis court; Wi-Fi (free).

Where to Eat

You'll probably find that you spend as much time eating in winery restaurants and grazing in specialty food shops as going to dedicated eateries, but this abundant region has plenty of good places to get a feed. In Tauherenikau, just out of Featherston, is a country pub that's been here forever: The **Tin Hut ★**, SH2, Tauherenikau (ℭ **06/308-9697**), has had a serious makeover and now borders on flash with a nice garden, but you can still dine on its famous homemade pies, roast pork, and other tasty stuff. *Note:* Management of the restaurant was in flux at press time, so call ahead. It's open for lunch Friday to Sunday from 11am and dinner on Tuesday to Sunday from 5pm.

MARTINBOROUGH

In Martinborough, the little **Village Café** in the Wine Centre, 6 Kitchener St. (ℭ **06/306-8814**), is a great place to dine and stock up on essential deli items and fine wine (daily 8am–4pm and until 9pm on Fri). Nearby is one of Wairarapa's best cafes: **Café Medici,** 9 Kitchener St. (www.cafemedici.co.nz; ℭ **06/306-9965**), serving terrific local, seasonal food, and great Mojo coffee daily from 8:30am to 4pm. If you're looking for a dinner venue, the well-regarded **Pinocchio Martinborough,** 3 Kitchener St. (www.pinocchiomartinborough.co.nz; ℭ **06/306-6094**), transforms from a lunch cafe by to a dinner bistro at night, serving a la carte dishes like a line-caught snapper in an herb emulsion to the signature confit duck leg; it also has a seven-course tasting menu. Pinocchio is closed on Monday and Tuesday.

GREYTOWN

Greytown has a wealth of lovingly created restaurants. The long-established **Main Street Deli Café,** 88 Main St. (ℭ **06/304-9022**), sells great food and deli items, including its own Cocodeli products made from organic coconut sugar—very hot right now! It's open daily from 8am to 5pm. **Jack & Jill Café,** 65 Main St. (www.jackandjillgreytown.com; ℭ **06/304-9645**), is getting a reputation for its savory coffee and classics like eggs benedict and French toast; it's open daily from 7am. **Bar Saluté,** 83 Main St. (www.salute.net.nz; ℭ **06/304-9825**), is a Euro-style bar that does terrific tapas to go with its extensive wine and beer list. It's open till late and closed on Monday and Tuesday. For more substantial meals, two venerable favorites serve hearty country food: **Turkey Red,** 53 Main St. (www.turkeyredhotel.co.nz; ℭ **0274/994-394**), and the **Greytown Hotel,** 83 Main St. (www.greytownhotel.co.nz; ℭ **06/304-9138**). Both are open daily.

CARTERTON

Carterton boasts what locals reckon is the best French cafe in the lower North Island, lovingly run by a delightful Parisian gentleman named Olivier and his Kiwi wife, Megan, who is the Cordon Bleu–trained chef. **Café Mirabelle ★,** 31 High St. N. (https://cafemirabelle.wordpress.com; ℭ **06/379-7247**), does out-of-this-world French pastries and standards like French onion soup and— *zut alors!*—snails. It's open Wednesday to Friday 9 to 3:30pm, Saturday 10am to 2:30pm, and Friday and Saturday from 7pm.

A little farther up the road, Mike and Rose Kloeg create delectable treats in an old Brethren church. The **Clareville Bakery ★,** 3340 SH2, Carterton (http://theclarevillebakery.co.nz; ℭ **06/379-5333**), is home to New Zealand's best pie for 2016: a rather startling lamb cutlet and kumara mash treat that I guarantee is unlike anything you have ever tasted. They also run a European-style cafe here, open Monday to Saturday 7:30am to 4pm and Wednesday 6pm to 10:30pm. Mike's citron tart is easily the best I've ever tasted, and he's also very passionate about his award-winning breads. An out-of-town institution that has had a facelift since its days as a rural boozer is the **Gladstone Inn,** 571 Gladstone Rd. (ℭ **06/372-7866**), which opened its doors as a ferry house in 1871. In addition to serving some quite fancy stuff for lunch and dinner, it also has a dedicated pizza chef for dine in and take out. It's open daily 11am till late (till 3pm on Mon).

MASTERTON

In Masterton, **Entice Café ★★,** corner of Bruce and Dixon streets (www.entice.co.nz; ℭ **06/377-3166**), serves great food, and you'll be dragged in here for yummy treats by the kids after they've visited Aratoi museum, which is in the same building. It's open daily from 8am to 4pm. **The Farriers Bar & Eatery,** 4 Queen St. (www.thefarriers.co.nz; ℭ **06/377-1102**), is an upmarket, all-occasion pub with friendly service and good-value meals that's open daily.

MARLBOROUGH & NELSON

So here you are on the South Island—the Mainland, so named for its large land mass—population 1,058,500. Because some 3½ million people live on the smaller North Island, there will be times when you think you have the huge spaces of the South Island completely to yourself. Relax. Even those who of us have lived our entire lives here know the feeling. We call it "loving the wide open spaces."

The long distances between settlements in the South Island means that flying is a popular travel option, but when it comes to leaving the North Island and traveling south, we recommend arriving by sea. Cook Strait is a narrow but stormy piece of water, and although bridges and tunnels have been considered, the difficulty of construction means crossings are by ferryboat. This is a benefit: Sailing through the calm, green, bush-lined waterways of the Marlborough Sounds is pure magic.

There are three main sounds: **Kenepuru, Pelorous,** and **Queen Charlotte.** The port town of **Picton** in Queen Charlotte Sound is the gateway to **Blenheim** and the province of **Marlborough,** and to the wider regions of **Nelson, Tasman,** and **Golden Bay.**

PICTON ★★

146km (91 miles) E of Nelson and 27km (17 miles) N of Blenheim

Picton is a quiet, easygoing town in the Marlborough province. Picton, in Queen Charlotte Sound, has a population of just 3,000, but with over 1,500km (930 miles) of accessible shoreline in and around the Sounds, is an obvious kickoff place for water sports— sailing, kayaking, fishing—and bush walking. It's got plenty of beautiful places but plenty of action as well.

Essentials

GETTING THERE & GETTING AROUND

BY PLANE   Air service between Picton and Wellington is provided by **Sounds Air** (www.soundsair.com; ✆ **0800/505-005** in NZ). **Picton Airport** (also known as **Koromiko Airport**) is about a 10-minute drive from the port. Contact **A1 Picton Shuttles** (www.a1pictonshuttles.co.nz; ✆ **800/A1PICTON**) for airport and ferry transfers.

Air New Zealand (www.airnewzealand.co.nz; ℂ **0800/737-000**) flies into nearby Blenheim (27km/17 miles from Picton). **Marlborough Shuttle Services** (www.marlboroughsoundsshuttles.co.nz; ℂ **03/572-9910**) provides airport and ferry transfers in Blenheim.

BY TRAIN The Coastal Pacific provides daily rail service between Picton and Christchurch. The trip takes about 5½ hours. Contact **KiwiRail Scenic Journeys** (www.kiwirailscenic.co.nz; ℂ **0800/872-467** in NZ) for departure and arrival times.

BY COACH (BUS) **InterCity** coaches (www.intercity.co.nz; ℂ **09/583-5780**) connect Picton with Blenheim and Christchurch, Nelson, the West Coast, and Otago. **Naked Bus** (https://nakedbus.com) operates similar routes.

BY CAR Picton is 20 minutes' drive time from/to Blenheim. For Nelson allow 2½ hours. If heading south to Christchurch via Kaikoura, allow 2 hours to Kaikoura and another 2½ hours to Christchurch.

BY FERRY Both **Interislander** (www.interislander.co.nz; ℂ **0800/802-802** in NZ) and **Bluebridge** (www.bluebridge.co.nz; ℂ **0800/844-844** in NZ) offer regular daily ferry service across Cook Strait between Wellington (North Island) and Picton (South Island). It's a 3-hour, 92km (57-mile) beautifully scenic ride.

BY WATER TAXI **Cougar Line** (www.cougarlinecruises.co.nz; ℂ **0800/504-090** in NZ), **Endeavour Express** (www.boatrides.co.nz; ℂ **03/573-5456**), and **West Bay Water Transport** (ℂ **03/573-5597**) provide regular services throughout Queen Charlotte Sound.

VISITOR INFORMATION

For travel guidance and comprehensive information, check out the region's official tourism websites: **www.marlborough.co.nz** and **www.picton.co.nz**.

The **Picton i-SITE Visitor Centre,** London Quay (www.lovemarlborough. co.nz; ℂ **03/520-3113**), is open daily 8am to 6pm.

ORIENTATION

The town faces Queen Charlotte Sound. London Quay runs along the foreshore, with the ferry terminal at one end and the town wharf at the other. The small shopping area is centered on High Street.

[FastFACTS]

Emergency For ambulance, fire, police, call (toll-free) ℂ **111. Picton Police Station** (ℂ **03/250-3120**). Directory assistance: 018.

Hospital **Wairau Hospital,** Blenheim (ℂ **03/520-9991**).

Exploring Picton

2014 was the 50th anniversary of the cessation of commercial whaling in New Zealand waters, and the same year saw the opening of the **National Whale Centre** ★ (www.aworldwithwhales.com; Wed–Sun noon–5pm; longer hours

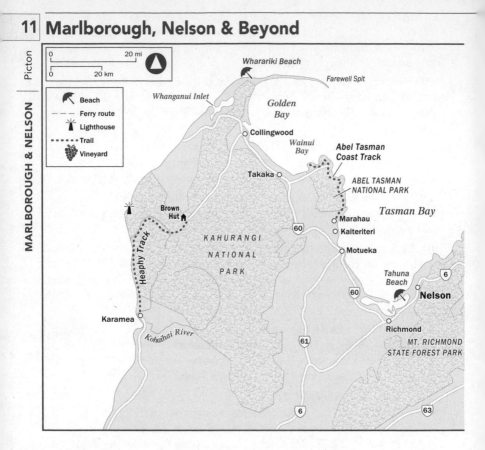

0	20 mi
0	20 km

- ☂ Beach
- – – – Ferry route
- ⚡ Lighthouse
- •••• Trail
- 🍇 Vineyard

Wharariki Beach

Farewell Spit

Whanganui Inlet

Golden Bay

Collingwood

Wainui Bay

Abel Tasman Coast Track

Takaka

ABEL TASMAN NATIONAL PARK

Tasman Bay

Brown Hut

Marahau

Kaiteriteri

60

Motueka

KAHURANGI NATIONAL PARK

Heaphy Track

Tahuna Beach

6

Nelson

60

Karamea

Kohaihai River

Richmond

61

MT. RICHMOND STATE FOREST PARK

6

63

in summer), which addresses New Zealand's 170-plus years of whaling and subsequent shift to sustainable marine industries and ecotourism. It's located to the rear of the i-SITE Information Centre and Department of Conservation Building, London Quay.

The waterfront at Picton has a surprise for art collectors. Barbara Speedy, director of the **Diversion Gallery** ★, 10 London Quay (www.thediversion. co.nz; ✆ **03/573-9069**), is not only an agent for some of the country's best artists, but she has a number of pieces for sale, including works by Grahame Sydney, Nigel Brown, Michael Smither, and Bing Dawe. Exhibitions of new artists are held regularly, and the gallery is well worth a lingering visit.

Don't expect giant tanks of stingrays or squid in the slightly seen-better-days facility at **EcoWorld Picton Aquarium** ★, Picton Foreshore, 1 Dunbar Wharf (www.ecoworldnz.co.nz; ✆ **03/573-6030**). The emphasis here is on rehabilitating injured creatures of the sea, including penguins. Children *love* the feeding times (11am and 2pm) and the accompanying chit-chat from the guide/feeder. A turtle and a spiky old tuatara (a rare native lizardlike reptile)

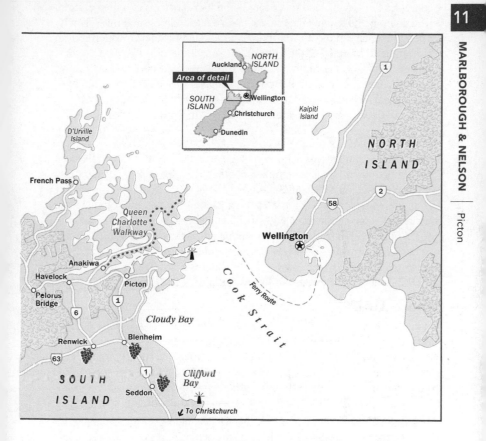

can be studied in close quarters. Admission is NZ$22 adults, NZ$11 children 3-14, NZ$59 family pass; it's open daily from 9:30am.

Tours

- The **Cougar Line,** London Quay (www.cougarlinecruises.co.nz or www. queencharlottetrack.co.nz; ✆ **0800/504-090** in NZ), has a range of cruise options for Queen Charlotte Sound. If your time is limited, we recommend the 3-hour **Sounds Delivery Cruise ★**, departing daily from Picton at 10am, returning at 1:30pm (NZ$75 adults, NZ$38 children 5–15).

- Although passengers on any vessels may see dolphins, **Dolphin Watch Ecotours ★**, London Quay (www.naturetours.co.nz; ✆ **0800/945-3543** in NZ), makes these incredible marine creatures the focus of its tours. Watch the fun and flips on a Dolphin Viewing Ecotour (NZ$100 adults, NZ$60 children 5–15) or get wet along with the dolphins on a Dolphin Swimming Ecotour (NZ$160 adults, NZ$100 children 8–15).

- The **Marlborough Travel Greenshell Mussel Cruise ★★** (www.green-shellmusselcruise.co.nz; ✆ **0800/990-800** in NZ, or 03/577-9997) combines food, wine, and water touring on half-day trips to a mussel farm, where you get to sample the biggest and sweetest Greenshell mussels with a complimentary glass of a Marlborough sauvignon blanc. Cruises run from November to March (NZ$125 adults, NZ$45 children 5–15).

o A wine tour with the **Sounds Connection ★★**, 10 London Quay (www.soundsconnection.co.nz; © **0800/742-866** in NZ, or 03/573-8843), has half- and full-day excursions to Marlborough vineyards/wineries from NZ$65 to NZ$150. Groups are small and the choice of vineyards is varied.

Where to Stay

Should holiday fatigue attack, slip yourself into the silent beauty of Queen Charlotte Sound and book a night at **Lochmara Lodge ★★**, Lochmara Bay (www.lochmara.co.nz; © **0800/562-462** in NZ or 03/573-4554). This wilderness experience comes with the satisfying comfort of family-motel-style units, chalets, and studio units with spellbinding views of the bay and bush-covered hills. The lodge has a restaurant/bar on-site, a bathhouse to unkink travel aches, bush walks to stretch the legs, and free use of kayaks when you want to get onto the water. *Bonus:* It also houses a wildlife recovery center and exhibits art. Nightly rates are from NZ$95 to NZ$295.

Where to Eat

Picton eateries come and go, but one enduring favorite is **Le Café ★★**, London Quay (© **03/573-5588**). As a restaurant in a prime tourist spot, it could serve as an example to others in a similar situation. The food is consistently good, the staff are unfailingly pleasant, and it is open all day, every day. Coffee is excellent, and the mussels (many options) with fries are a perfect example of good, fresh local food. The vibe is casual and prices are moderate.

Havelock: The Mussel Pot ★ SEAFOOD   The giant mussel shells on the restaurant roof tip you off to what's on the menu. This is *the* place for fresh mussels. Fresh steamers are served in the shell, fresh flats are grilled in the half shell, and the mussel chowder is never less than excellent. Reservations required for dinner. Havelock is 33km (20 miles) from Picton.

73 Main Rd., Havelock. www.themusselpot.co.nz. © **03/574-2824.** Main courses NZ$19–NZ$31. Daily 10:30am–2:45pm and 5:30pm–late.

BLENHEIM ★★

117km (73 miles) SE of Nelson and 27km (17 miles) S of Picton

Another quiet, easygoing town in the Marlborough province, Blenheim has a population of over 30,000. It lies at the heart of New Zealand's largest wine region. Stand on any high point around Blenheim and as far as the eye can see, the land is peppered with grapevines. Two decades ago thousands of sheep were farmed here, grown for meat and wool, but older farmers in the region will tell you that only about 10% of arable land now supports sheep. In just over 25 years, Marlborough has established itself as one of the world's premier wine-producing regions, responsible for over 63% of New Zealand's total wine production. There are about 170 wineries in the area, and around 45 of these are open for cellar door sales and have tasting rooms and restaurants or cafes.

Essentials

GETTING THERE & GETTING AROUND

BY PLANE **Air New Zealand** has direct flights from Auckland, Wellington and Christchurch (www.airnewzealand.co.nz; © **0800/737-000** in NZ). The **Marlborough Airport** (www.marlboroughairport.co.nz) is 10km (6 miles) from its town center and has car-rental agencies and taxi stands; it's a 15- to 20-minute drive from the airport to central Blenheim. **Marlborough Shuttle Services** can provide airport and ferry transfers (www.marlborough-soundsshuttles.co.nz; © **03/572-9910**).

BY TRAIN The Coastal Pacific provides daily rail service between Picton and Christchurch via Blenheim. Contact **KiwiRail Scenic Journeys** (www.kiwirailscenic.co.nz; © **0800/872-467** in NZ) for updated seasonal fares and timetables.

BY COACH/BUS **InterCity** buses (www.intercity.co.nz; © **09/583-5780**) links Blenheim with Picton, Nelson, Kaikoura, Christchurch, and other centers in the South Island. **Naked Bus** (https://nakedbus.com) provides a similar route/service.

BY CAR Take SH1 from Picton (a 20-min. drive); SH6 from/to Nelson; SH1 from/to Kaikoura and Christchurch.

VISITOR INFORMATION

The **Blenheim i-SITE,** 11 Sinclair St, SH1 (© **0800/777-181** in NZ, or 03/577-8080), is open from 8:30am to 5pm weekdays (9am–3pm weekends).

[FastFACTS]

Emergency For ambulance, fire, police, call (toll-free) © **111. Blenheim Police Station** (© **03/578-5279**).

Medical **Wairau Hospital,** in Blenheim (© **03/520-9991**).

Exploring Blenheim

Omaka Aviation Heritage Centre ★★★ This remarkable collection of aircraft and aviation history would be a big drawcard in any country, in any city, and to find it in a small-town aerodrome is amazing. A display of combat aircraft eventually became an air show to rival Warbirds over Wanaka, but its size and scope increased exponentially when "Lord of The Rings" movie director, Sir Peter Jackson, an avid collector of World War 1 aircraft, added the Knights of the Sky exhibition with the assistance of Weta Workshop and Wingnut Films. It is a dramatic extended arrangement consisting of original and full-scale replica aircraft and a number of compelling tableaux showing wartime scenes such as ditched aircraft, surrenders, and the crash that killed the Red Baron. A guided tour costs extra, but the volunteer guides are experienced in aviation ways, know their aircraft, and generally bring the show to life. Every second year the Centre hosts the **Classic Fighters Air Show** (the next show is in 2017).

79 Aerodrome Rd. www.omaka.org.nz. *(C)* **03/579-1305.** Daily 10am–4pm. Admission NZ$25 adults, NZ$10 children 5–15, NZ$55 family.

WINERY TOURS

New Zealand wine buffs still marvel at the juggernaut that is the country's wine industry. In the late 1960s, a smattering of two or three quite ordinary wines were produced from vines only a year or two old. Today wine is now among New Zealand's top exports, and vineyards and wineries throughout the country rate "of special interest" to visitors. Marlborough was an early starter, thanks to wineries such as Brancott Estate, and Drylands. It was when Marlborough sauvignon blanc came to the attention of international winemakers, however, that the region became widely known as a producer of wines with intense flavors and aromas.

For roads and routes, a copy of **"The Marlborough Wine Trails"** from Blenheim's i-SITE or online at www.marlborough.co.nz is invaluable.

Self-Drive Winery Visits ★★

o **Auntsfield Estate** (270 Paynters Rd.; www.auntsfield.co.nz): The first wines were planted in the early 1900s, but the wine was not produced commercially. Today's owners have replanted and expanded and produce small batches of handcrafted wines.

o **Brancott Estate** (180 Brancott Rd.; www.brancottestate.com): Huge plantings of grapes throughout the countryside belie the personal touch and helpful friendliness of this behemoth. An eco-friendly cellar door, restaurant, and visitor center tucked into a fold of the hills looks over the original vineyard.

o **Cloudy Bay** (Jacksons Rd., a very visible signpost; www.cloudybay.co.nz): Sauvignon blanc is on wine lists from Tuscany to Timaru, so a visit to this cellar door/winery might surprise. From the outside it looks like a big shed, but step inside and be wowed.

o **Forrest** (19 Blicks Rd.; www.forrest.co.nz): The doctor owners have planted vineyards in different regions of the South Island in their quest to find the perfect site for riesling grapes. They have succeeded.

o **Hans Herzog Estate** (81 Jeffries Rd.; www.herzog.co.nz): The owners came to New Zealand from Switzerland, searching for the world's best terroir for the vines they wanted to plant and the wines they wanted to make.

o **Huia** (22 Boyces Rd.; www.huia.net.nz): This is not the biggest vineyard, but there are times when small is good. The fragrant gewürztraminer should be sampled.

o **Seresin** (the cellar door is at 85 Bedford Rd.; www.seresin.co.nz): These organic biodynamic vineyards in the Wairau and Omaka valleys are owned by cinematographer Michael Seresin, who lives sometimes in the

Marlborough Sounds, sometimes in London, sometimes in Italy. A delicious olive oil is also produced.

o **Wither Hills** (211 New Renwick Rd., RD2; www.witherhills.co.nz): A string of successes from the early vintages on. Sample in the large and welcoming cellar door/tasting room/restaurant.

o **Yealands Family Wines** (corner of Seaview and Reserve roads, Seddon; www.yealands.co.nz): An international winner in sustainable wine tourism, the owner has built an impressive winery and an equally impressive cellar door/tasting room.

Organized Wine Tours
Highlight Wine Tours takes small groups (van transport) to five or six wineries in the Blenheim/Renwick area, with a lunch at one of the wineries and a sweet little side visit to Makana Boutique Chocolate Factory (www.highlightwinetours.co.nz; ✆ **03/577-9046;** half-day tours 11:30am–5pm: NZ$75 per person).

For those who like to bike as well as tour wineries, **Bike Hire Marlborough ★** provides bikes, helmets, and maps (www.bikehiremarlborough.co.nz; ✆ **0800/397-027** in NZ; NZ$25 for 3 hr., includes transport to/from Blenheim and Renwick; lunch extra).

Where to Stay
Hotel d'Urville ★★ This hospitable hotel offers a mix of slightly faded grandeur and style. The decor in the 11 rooms is eclectic, maybe even eccentric, but charming (love the Raja room). The hotel has been created in what was a typical small-town grand old office building in central Blenheim, circa 1920s, and its generous spaces have allowed large, comfortable bed/bathrooms, a small restaurant, and two sitting rooms. Upstairs the sofas huddle around a side table sporting a decanter of port; guests help themselves to a complimentary snifter. The latest addition is an inside-outside cocktail bar. Service is good.

52 Queen St. www.durville.com. ✆ **03/577-9945.** 11 units. B&B from NZD$225. Rates come with full breakfast. **Amenities:** Restaurant; bar; Wi-Fi (free).

Marlborough Vintners Hotel (Heritage Boutique Collections) ★ Situated in a vineyard, this five-star hotel has large, comfortable apartment-style units with small kitchens, ideal for self-catering travelers. The garden views from the Vintners Room, the hotel restaurant, includes the dining room's colorful kitchen garden of herbs and vegetables. This section of Raupara Road is home to a number of Marlborough winery restaurants with easily accessed cellar doors, wine, and food tastings.

190 Raupara Rd. www.mvh.co.nz. ✆ **0800/684-190** in NZ 03/572-5094. NZ$250 suite. **Amenities:** Vintners Room restaurant; gym; outdoor spa; Wi-Fi (free).

Where to Eat
If you're looking for hearty snacks or picnic food, swing by the **Burleigh ★** (72 New Renwick Rd.; ✆ **03/579-2531**), a pickup-and-go stop with such goodies as pork belly or steak and cheese hand pies. The goodness includes excellent coffee.

Arbour ★★★ SEASONAL NEW ZEALAND/INTERNATIONAL   Ignore the unassuming appearance, the casual outdoor dining option, the minimal decor. Study the wine list and note its famous wine names from France, Australia, and just up the road. At the newly christened Arbour (formerly Gibbs on Godfrey), the menu is tight, but trust owner/chef Bradley Hornby and order the "Many," his seven-course degustation menu produced with amazing tastes from regional ingredients, or his smaller but equally thoughtful four-course "Just Feed Me" option. It's hard to choose a star, but the ravioli stuffed with smoked eggplant, any Cloudy Bay clam dish, or indeed any dish matched with Greywacke wild yeast sauvignon blanc, ensures a sublime food/wine experience. High praise for the restaurant, chef, and his partner Lizz Buttimore (front of house). Note to wine buffs: Greywacke Wines are made by winemaker Kevin Judd, who has moved on from Cloudy Bay to his own winery.

36 Godfrey Rd. www.arbour.co.nz. ℂ **03/572-7989.** Main courses NZ$31–NZ$38. Tues–Sat from 6pm.

Herzog Winery & Restaurant ★★★ INTERNATIONAL   Enjoy world-class wine and food in a lovely, old-fashioned garden. The vineyard provides the background to glorious food and impeccable service. Hans and Therese Herzog came to Marlborough from Zurich, leaving an established winery and a Michelin-starred estate restaurant, and from bare land and a rambling homestead they have created a remarkable enterprise. That award-winning wines, a cellar boasting 500 wines, and a team of talented European and New Zealand chefs are available in this rural setting is a continuing surprise. For a superb food and wine-matching experience, we suggest A Tasting Menu, three or five courses if time and budget allows (NZ$136–NZ$197).

81 Jeffries Rd. www.herzog.co.nz. ℂ **03/572-8770.** Bistro daily noon–5pm and 6–10pm (Oct–May) and Wed–Sun noon–3pm and 6 to 8pm (May–Oct). Restaurant Wed–Sun 7pm to late (closed May–Oct). Bistro main courses NZ$24–NZ$34. Restaurant main courses NZ$31–NZ$43.

Wither Hills Winery ★ REGIONAL   The restaurant enjoys a splendid setting in a gardenscape of white and green. The Wither Hills restaurant is a pleasant place for lunch at any time of year, but in warmer weather it is pure magic, especially if there is an interest in matching the winery's new vintage light and floral whites with one of the menu's Asian-inspired dishes. We recommend

The Scenic Winding Road

As an alternative route to the more direct SH6 from Picton to Nelson, the **Queen Charlotte Drive** offers good views of the Marlborough Sounds, but it's a narrow, winding road that needs to be driven with care. There are several good lookout stops along the way. The road meets up with SH6 at Havelock to continue to Nelson. The whole trip should take about 2½ hours.

the salt and pepper squid or the simple filet of fish with the pinot gris. Stop off in the large cellar door and tasting room if you'd like to take some wines home.

211 New Renwick Rd. www.witherhills.co.nz. ℰ **03/520-8284.** Daily from 11am. Main courses NZ$25–NZ$30.

NELSON ★★★

144km (89 miles) W of Picton; 226km (140 miles) NE of Westport; 424km (263 miles) N of Christchurch

Nelson is our sunshine place. It's 2,500 hours of annual sunshine, golden-sand beaches, vineyards, and impressive—and different—museums (fashion as art—and motorcycles?). Got to be different!

Essentials

GETTING THERE & GETTING AROUND

BY PLANE Nelson City Airport (www.nelsonairport.co.nz) is the fourth-busiest airport in New Zealand, with regular direct flights to and from Auckland, Wellington, Christchurch, and major provincial centers. It's serviced by **Air New Zealand** (www.airnewzealand.co.nz; ℰ **0800/737-000** in NZ) and several regional airlines including **Sounds Air** (www.soundsair.com; ℰ **0800/505-005** in NZ).

The airport is located about 8km (5 miles) from the Nelson city center. Several international rental-car companies have branches located just outside the terminal entrance. Taxis are also located at the terminal front, or call **Nelson City Taxis** (ℰ **03/548 8225**). Super Shuttle (www.supershuttle.co.nz; ℰ **0800/748-885** in NZ) operates regularly between the airport and the city center for NZ$19.

BY COACH (BUS) InterCity (www.intercity.co.nz; ℰ **03/548-1538**) and **Naked Bus** (https://nakedbus.com) connects Nelson with numerous towns and cities.

BY CAR The scenic drive from Picton to Nelson, via Queen Charlotte Sound (narrow and winding), takes about 2½ hours. SH6 (more direct) takes approximately 2 hours without stops. If you're coming from the West Coast, the drive from Westport takes approximately 3½ hours; from Christchurch via Lewis Pass, about 5 hours, or Christchurch via Kaikoura-Blenheim, 6 hours.

VISITOR INFORMATION

The Nelson i-SITE Visitor Centre, **Millers Acre Centre,** 77 Trafalgar St. (www.nelsonnz.com; ℰ **0800/635-827** in NZ or 03/548-2304), is open Monday to Friday from 8:30am to 5pm, and 9am to 4pm on weekends.

ORIENTATION

The city is not large, but in case you lose your bearings Nelson's Christ Church Cathedral on Church Hill rears above Trafalgar Street. Architecturally speaking, the cathedral is less than inspirational—but it's a useful landmark.

KID magnets

o **Nelson Fun Park** Give the kids a chance to burn off some excess energy at Nelson Fun Park, adjacent to Tahuna Beach and just a 5-minute drive from central Nelson. They can unwind on the hydroslide, play miniature golf, or have fun on bumper boats (*C* **03/548-6267**).

o **Natureland Zoo** Also at Tahuna Beach, this zoo lets kids get up close with wallabies, meerkats, otters, monkeys, and exotic birds (www.naturelandzoo.co.nz; *C* **03/548-6166**).

o **Happy Valley Adventures** ★★ Hit the heights on the Skywire, a sort of flying fox meets ski chairlift. Fly on the Skywire for over 3km (1¾ miles) for NZ$85 adults and NZ$55 children 16 and under (194 Cable Bay Rd., Nelson; www.happyvalleyadventures. co.nz; *C* **0800/157-300** in NZ, or 03/545-0304).

o **Penguino Gelato Café** ★★ This gelateria has "bambinos" for children and a big four-flavor cone for the ambitious (85 Montgomery Sq., Nelson; www.penguino.co.nz; *C* **03/545-6450**).

o **Nelson Provincial Museum** ★★ The "especially for children" section concentrates on interactive activities, including a Taniwha Cave (a taniwha is a mythical creature that lives in water) and a touchscreen showing the region's geological features (corner of Trafalgar and Hardy sts.; www.nelsonmuseum.co.nz; *C* **03/548-9588**).

[FastFACTS]

Emergency For ambulance, fire, police, call (toll-free) *C* **111. Nelson Police Station:** *C* **03/546-3840.**

Medical Nelson Hospital: *C* **03/546-1800.**

Exploring Nelson
MUSEUMS

Nelson Provincial Museum ★★ This well-curated museum is not overly large, but you could easily spend many hours among both permanent collections and changing exhibitions. The first section of the gallery features the geological features of the region, and with some clever utilization of space lays them out in map style. View this section before you visit Farewell Spit and the Boulder Bank to further your appreciation. The "listening posts" will fascinate anyone who likes family stories of past days and ways, and the centennial commemoration of World War I is recommended.

Corner Trafalgar and Hardy sts. www.nelsonmuseum.co.nz. *C* **03/548-9588.** Weekdays 10am–5pm; weekends 10am–4:30pm. NZ$5 adults, schoolchildren NZ$3, free for preschoolers and all New Zealand residents.

The World of Wearable Art (WOW) & Classic Cars Museum ★★★
This two-museums-in-one combo is a must-see. WOW is an outstanding

collection of some 600 winning entries exhibited in the World of Wearable Art Awards, an annual event that has captivated artists and fashion designers the world over. For many years it was staged in Nelson, and when it packed up to Wellington, having a museum to show off the winning designs was a sop for locals. But it has morphed into a special showcase. Dresses cut from suitcases follow hot on the heels of robots, warriors, and devils of the dance all leading the way to an explosive mashup of art and fashion. WOW owes its beginning (and continuing fame) to Nelson artist Suzie Moncrieff (now Dame Suzie Moncrieff), who in 1987 reasoned that by taking art off the wall and turning it into a stage show, she could raise funds for a rural art gallery. The first show was staged by volunteers, and the first audience numbered about 200. WOW is now presented in Wellington, where in 2014 the audience numbered 50,000.

If art, clothing, and classic cars seem an odd combination, who could argue? But the collector behind the **Classic Car Museum** had the space that WOW needed in order to show its collection at its best, and, now the adjoining collections complement each other. The cars are some of the most sought-after models in the classic motoring world, and from first sight of the huge pink and white Cadillac to the distinctly curious Messerschmitt two-seater, the viewer's attention is captured. It is a world-class exhibit.

Cadillac Way, off Quarantine Rd. www.wowcars.co.nz. ℰ **03/547-4573.** Daily 10am–5pm. NZ$24 adults, NZ$10 children 5–14; family discounts available.

NZ Classic Motor Cycles ★ Motorcycle naysayers should keep an open mind, as these two floors of motorcycles include those that were first wheeled out between 1902 and 1920. Collected by American and now Nelson resident Tom Sturgess, the exhibits hit all the buttons. Close to 300 machines (sidecars and so forth) restored and polished to perfection hang from the walls, fill the aisles, and look ready to ride again. As a side hobby the owner/collector also exhibits the original art behind the early advertisement/posters. Download the museum app to your smart phone to get the insider info.

75 Haven Rd. nzclassicmotorcycles.co.nz. ℰ **03/546-7699.** Mon–Fri 9am–4pm, Sat & Sun 10am–3pm. $20 adults, $10 children 5–15, free children 4 and under.

ARTS & CRAFTS
The essence of Nelson province is in its abundance of top-quality arts and crafts. The city boasts some 300 practicing artists and 40 galleries and studios.

Jens Hansen Gold & Silversmith ★★★, 320 Trafalgar Sq. (www.jenshansen.com; ℰ **03/548-0640**), is a name associated with quality New Zealand–made gold and silver jewelry—*and* the handmade rings and jewelry used in the "Lord of the Rings" trilogy.

Royce McGlashen Pottery ★★★, 128 Ellis St., Brightwater (www.roycemcglashen.co.nz; ℰ **03/542-3585**), is another high point. A renowned ceramic artist, he uses color with artistic abandon, but anyone seeking a hand-thrown matte-black dinner set will find it in this studio.

Flame Daisy, 324 Trafalgar Sq. (www.flamedaisy.com; ℰ **03/548-4475**), is a glass-art gallery with a wide variety of well-priced items.

Boulder Bank is a natural 13km (8-mile) spit of boulders reaching into Tasman Bay. An 8km (5-mile) **walkway** ★ along the bank is not your usual stroll by the sea—"exhilarating" is more like it. Check tides and times with the Department of Conservation or Nelson i-SITE. Take sturdy shoes and all-weather clothing. If driving to the start of the walk is not an option, the **Ferry** (on-demand cruises), Nelson, can oblige ((ℂ **03/539-1116;** from NZ$22).

Outdoor Pursuits

BEACHES Nelson has dozens of fabulous beaches. Close to the city, the best bet is **Tahuna Beach** (also known as Tahunanui), which offers excellent swimming. Farther afield, there is the hugely popular **Kaiteriteri Beach ★★.** From here you can take a water taxi to **Abel Tasman National Park,** where there are more beaches and bays than you can poke a driftwood stick at.

KAYAKING **Cable Bay Kayaks ★,** Cable Bay Road, Nelson (www.cablebaykayaks.co.nz; ℂ **0508/222-532** in NZ, or 03/545-0332), specializes in half- and 1-day tours that take in bird colonies, caves, and coves for NZ$65 to NZ$145 per person.

UP IN THE AIR **Happy Valley Adventures ★★,** 194 Cable Bay Rd., Nelson (www.happyvalleyadventures.co.nz; ℂ **0800/157-300** in NZ, or 03/545-0304), has come up with its version of a flying fox experience, the Skywire. A cross between the zippity line of a flying fox and the seated comfort of a ski chairlift, this 3km (1¼ miles) ride climbs high—so not only thrills galore but great views too. A ride on the Skywire costs NZ$85 adults, NZ$55 children 16 and under.

Where to Stay

Rutherford Hotel Nelson ★, T27 Nile St. W. (www.heritagehotels.co.nz; ℂ **0800/368-888** in NZ, or 03/548-2299), is a good, centrally located spot that always appeals. It has an outdoor pool, two restaurants, a bar, and a cafe.

Tahuna Beach Holiday Park ★★, 70 Beach Rd., Tahunanui (www.tahunabeach.co.nz; ℂ **0800/500-501** in NZ, or 03/548-5159), is the largest motor camp in New Zealand. Accommodation ranges from motel units to cabins to tentsites. It offers free barbecues, three playgrounds, and mini golf.

Wakefield Quay House B&B ★★★ When host/owners Woodi and Johnny Moore say "our B&B has quite possibly the best sea views in Nelson," believe them. From the deck of this historic villa (1905) high above the quay you are in *the* place to watch ships and tugboats, swimming races, yacht races, and Tasman Bay's amazing sunsets. You'll have those same views from your luxurious en suite room, with a comfy queen bed, fresh flowers, and all the modcons you desire. Some of Nelson's best restaurants are but a stroll away, and as longtime locals the Moores can direct their guests to artists, vineyards, and activities not widely known.

385 Wakefield Quay. www.wakefieldquay.co.nz. © **03/546-7275.** 2 units. NZ$295–NZ$335. Rates include full breakfast and complimentary pre-dinner drinks (including local wines) and canapés. **Amenities:** Wi-Fi (free).

Grand Mercure Monaco Nelson Hotel & Resort ★★★ When you are completely over another night in a cabin or backpacker dorm, treat yourself to a stopover in a cute brick cottage that might have strayed from your favorite storybook. The rows of cottages are more apartments than motel units, with ivy clambering around the casement windows. Reside in comfort in a paneled sitting room with soft leather chairs, with French doors opening to a village green and ensuite bedrooms with big, soft beds. Impressed? Add on-site restaurant, the **Monaco Kitchen,** and you might not want to leave.

6 Point Rd., Monaco. www.monacoresort.co.nz. © **03/547-8233.** 84 units. NZ$195–NZ$385. **Amenities:** Restaurant; gym; jewelry shop; solar-heated outdoor pool; health & beauty spa; Wi-Fi (free).

Where to Eat

Nelson is recognized as seafood central, so yes, expect restaurants to excel in fresh fish preparations and shellfish dishes.

Boat Shed Cafe ★ SEAFOOD The over-the-water setting puts this busy Nelson landmark in top place from the start. Famous for its upbeat take on fish dishes, the Boat Shed has a good wine list, and the waitstaff are quick to recommend locally brewed beers. It can be noisy and crowded, but those are the signs of a popular place the world over. Shared Plates and Trust The Chef choices are available, but on a busy night these dishes can arrive randomly. A better bet is to order the dishes you want to eat. "Over the water" means what it says—so snag a seat on the (enclosed) veranda, and kick back to the swish-swash of water lapping. It's colorful and fun, with good food. Reservations essential for dinner.

350 Wakefield Quay. www.boatshedcafe.co.nz. © **03/546-9783.** NZ$32–NZ$44. Weekdays 10am–late; weekends 9:30am–late.

Jellyfish Café & Bar Shed ★★ MEDITERRANEAN Chef Mark Mehalski was declared Nelson's best in 2012, and his style of simple and fresh continues to impress. This is a lovely, casual place on the Mapua wharf, with

---

Bambinos from Penguino

For the best and biggest range of ice cream in town, head for **Penguino Gelato Café** ★★, where you'll find 18 flavors made from traditional Italian recipes. Try the gelato, sorbet, sundaes, "bambinos" for children, and the big four-flavor cone for the ambitious. It's open daily in summer from noon to 5pm (85 Montgomery Sq., Nelson; www.penguino.co.nz; © **03/545-6450**).

With a strong hop-growing history, it's not surprising that Nelson delivers on the beer front. Two breweries to visit are **Founders Organic Brewery ★**, Founders Historic Park, 87 Atawhai Dr., Nelson (www.biobrew.co.nz; ✆ **03/548-4638**), the country's first certified organic brewery complete with a cafe that serves great lunches; and the **Vic Brew Bar ★**, 281 Trafalgar St., Nelson (www.macs.co.nz; ✆ **03/548-7631**), which serves a range of premium award-winning beers; it's open daily from 11am until late.

good beer and wine lists and an eclectic menu frequently featuring Moroccan flavors: eggplant with lamb, sumac on the salad, and an unusual lemon za'atar. The summer season starts in September, and once again Jellyfish will be doing dinners. *Tip:* Should the Seifried Sweet Agnes riesling be on the dessert wine list, do sample a glass.

1 Mapua Wharf, Mapua. www.jellyfishmapua.co.nz. ✆ **03/540-2028.** NZ$24–NZ$34. Daily 9:30am–3pm and Tues–Sat 5pm–late.

River Kitchen ★★ SEASONAL NEW ZEALAND   Open for breakfast and lunch, this is a lovely place to sit and sip (a nice assortment of beer and wine) and dig into good mussels and great calamari (spiced with an unusual pepper), not to mention seafood risotto, a creamy seafood chowder, and burgers that range from standard beef to deep-fried fish or chickpea patty. Expect excellent coffee and good service—and it's nice to see walkers with dogs welcomed.

81 Trafalgar St., Nelson (the address of the large building in which it's located; the restaurant opens to the pathway beside the Matai River). www.riverkitchennelson. co.nz. ✆ **03/548-1180.** Lunch main courses NZ$18–NZ$28. Mon–Fri 7:30am–5pm, Sat 8am–5pm, and Sun 8:30am–5pm.

ABEL TASMAN NATIONAL PARK & GOLDEN BAY ★★★

Marahau, the southern gateway to the park: 67km (42 miles) NW of Nelson; Takaka, the gateway to Golden Bay: 109km (68 miles) NW of Nelson

Abel Tasman is New Zealand's smallest national park. It protects 23,000 hectares (57,000 acres) of easily accessible coastline, offering limestone and sandstone cliffs and coves, golden-sand beaches and forested headlands. **Marahau** and **Kaiteriteri** are the main gateways to the park, 1½- and 2½-hour drive, respectively, from Nelson.

Farther north, Golden Bay sits peacefully beyond the twists and turns of Takaka Hill, opening out in a spread of forested parks, golden beaches, and so much beauty that the term "breathtaking scenery" is no cliché. The population is an interesting mix of dairy farmers, employees in the hospitality industry, amateur and professional artists, and those wanting a back-to-nature lifestyle.

Essentials

GETTING THERE & GETTING AROUND

BY PLANE   Golden Bay Air has scheduled flights between Wellington and Takaka (www.goldenbayair.co.nz; ℭ **0800/588-885** in NZ).

BY COACH (BUS)   Abel Tasman Coachlines (www.abeltasmantravel. co.nz; ℭ **03/548-0285**) operates year-round daily service from Nelson to Kaiteriteri, Marahau, Totaranui, and Abel Tasman National Park. It also provides connecting service to Kahurangi National Park and the north entrance to the Heaphy Track. **Golden Bay Coachline** (http://goldenbaycoachlines.co.nz; ℭ **03/525-8352**) operates a daily service to Takaka, Collingwood, and the north entrance to the Heaphy Track.

BY CAR   The trip from Nelson to Takaka in Golden Bay via State Highway 60 takes about 2 hours and includes the long, steep, winding Takaka Hill. To reach Marahau, in Abel Tasman National Park, turn right at the bottom of Takaka Hill, just past Motueka (don't go over Takaka Hill), and drive through Kaiteriteri. The trip takes about 1½ hours.

VISITOR INFORMATION

The **Golden Bay i-SITE Visitor Centre,** Willow Street, Takaka (www.nelsonnz.com; ℭ **03/525-9136**), is open daily from 9am.

Exploring Abel Tasman National Park ★★★

Abel Tasman is the jewel among popular national parks. It's a sea kayaker's paradise and has good swimming beaches. The **Abel Tasman Coastal Track** is one of the Department of Conservation's eight identified Great Walks and the only track of its kind in the country. It can be done in 3 to 5 days, and can be combined with water taxis or sea kayaks.

Abel Tasman Kayaks ★, Main Road, Marahau (www.abeltasmankayaks. co.nz; ℭ **0800/732-529** in NZ, or 03/527-8022), pioneered sea kayaking in this region. Full-and multi-day guided excursions may include walks and/or swimming with seals, or both. Prices range from NZ$110 for a 1-day guided tour to approximately NZ$5600 for a private 3-day kayak-camping (fully catered) guided tour (not available for children under 14). Prices include pickup and transport from Motueka. Return transport to Nelson costs NZ$30.

Wilsons Abel Tasman ★, 265 High St., Motueka (www.abeltasman.co.nz; ℭ **0800/223-582** in NZ, or 03/528-2027), operates buses, launches, beachfront lodges, guided walks, and guided sea-kayaking experiences, up to 5-day guided walks and sea-kayaking trips (from NZ$85).

Abel Tasman Aqua Taxi ★, Main Road, Marahau (www.aquataxi.co.nz; ℭ **0800/278-282** in NZ, or 03/527-8083), has a half-day cruise that visits points of interest along the park beaches and the fur-seal colony on Tonga Island (NZ$77 adults, NZ $39 children 5–14). If you're short on time, do the cruise if nothing else, or you'll miss seeing this spectacular unspoiled coast.

WHERE TO STAY

Abel Tasman Ocean View Chalets ★   These private, salf-contained, and well-appointed timber chalets were built on a bush-lined elevated site. You'll have stunning sea views, and it's just a short stroll to a beach of golden sand and blue-green water. Each unit has TV, phone, and broadband—and did we mention views? Marahau restaurants are within walking distance, and convenient water taxi pickup is available. Activities available include sailing, kayaking, paddle-boarding, and horseriding. Buffet breakfasts are available, and in-room amenities include fresh-ground coffee, tea, and cookies.

305 Sandy Bay Rd., Marahau. www.accommodationabeltasman.co.nz. © **03/527-8232.** 8 units. NZ$145–NZ$290. **Amenities:** Wi-Fi (free).

Peppers Awaroa Lodge ★★   This ecolodge is a feature destination of the Abel Tasman Coastal Track. It is quite possibly the perfect leave-it-all-behind place. The buildings are set among untouched bush, but the wilderness stops at the door. Inside all is warm and spacious, with a fireside lounge and a library, a bar, and a restaurant. There is no road access; you arrive/depart by foot, kayak, water taxi, catamaran, helicopter, or small, fixed-wing aircraft. Kayaking trips, helicopter flights, bush walks, are all here for the doing, and glowworms, fur seals, penguins, and dolphins are all here for viewing.

Abel Tasman National Park. www.awaroalodge.co.nz. © **0800/448-891** in NZ, or 03/528-8758. 26 units. NZ$275–NZ$589. No cell phone or Internet access due to isolated site. Open Oct–April.

WHERE TO EAT

Fat Tui ★★ BURGERS   A burger truck with the biggest, untidiest, most amazing burgers in these parts. The mussel burger, for instance, is a whopper pattie of the lovely shellfish, wrapped in a matching whopper bun piled high with fresh salady things and all utterly delicious. Then there are the burgers with funny names as in Ewe Beaut (a lamb burger named for a lady sheep). Park yourself on a picnic bench nearby and rejoice in New Zealand's take on good, simple, food. In fact, the burgers were awarded best-in-the-land status in 2014 by online newspaper www.stuff.co.nz. Believe the raves.

Franklin St., Marahau. www.facebook.com/The-FAT-TUI-486460701371881. © **03/527-8420.** Main courses NZ$13–NZ$17. Wed–Sun noon–8pm.

Shoreline Café ★ CAFE   On the beach in Kaiteriteri, this cafe enjoys a perfect setting for a casual meal. The emphasis here is on fresh and local (fish, vegetables, shellfish, craft beers, lamb, and beef), and the inexpensive dishes are fuss-free. Very relaxing.

Corner of Inlet and Sandy Bay roads, Kaiteriteri. www.shorelinekaiteriteri.co.nz. © **03/527-8507.** Main courses NZ$26–NZ$30; burgers NZ$18–NZ$22. Daily 8:30am–4pm.

Exploring Golden Bay ★★★

The main town is Takaka, which has a tiny resident population of 1,100 and many long-term visitors who love the alternative lifestyle. Collingwood,

28km (17 miles) north, is more a settlement than a town but features lovely old colonial buildings.

Golden Bay is rich in natural attractions, notably **Te Waikoropupu Springs** ★★ (Pupu Springs, if you want to sound like a local). The rushing, bubbling water is said to be the clearest freshwater in the world. It's signposted just north of Takaka township.

Cave formations are also common; one of the most famous, **Harwood's Hole,** plummets 180m (600 ft.) straight down. Take the signposted road off the Takaka Hill Road and then the slow 12km (7-mile) drive over a metal road, followed by a lengthy hike through a rather magical beech forest. Prepare to be underwhelmed when you arrive at Harwood's Hole, however, as you don't get to peer down the "hole." If you prefer your cave explorations guided, head back on the hill road, where **Ngarua Caves** offers guided tours, revealing stalactites, and moa bones. Tours are offered on the hour from 10am to 4pm (NZ$18).

Wharariki Beach ★★, 20 minutes from Collingwood to the carpark, then a 40-minute walk, features immense carved limestone cliffs and caves. It faces west, where the Tasman Sea can be a roar of hammering surf or (occasionally) as flat as a millpond—but be warned: This is a beach for walkers, *not* swimmers. Visit at low tide to take in the whole beach. **Farewell Spit** ★★, 26km (16 miles) north of Collingwood, is a unique curve of sand dunes and shoreline reaching out in a gentle 35km (22-mile) curve into Golden Bay. Its sand dunes are huge but fragile, and freedom walkers are restricted to 4km (2.4 miles) from just below the Spit's cafe. It is only about half a mile wide, although low tide reveals countless sandbanks blanketed with migratory birds making their first or last landing in New Zealand. The channels of sandbanks have been known to trap whales in the shallow water, beaching them. To capture Farewell Spit in its entirety, take a guided tour. **Farewell Spit Eco Tours,** 6 Tasman St., Collingwood (www.farewellspit.com; ✆ **0800/808-257** in NZ, or 03/524-8257), offers a range of tours from 2 to 6½ hours (NZ$125–NZ$160).

WHERE TO STAY

The comfortable, affordable studio, one-, and two-bedroom units at **Anatoki Lodge Motel,** 87 Commercial St. (the main drag), Takaka (http://anatokimotels.co.nz; ✆ **0800/262-333** in NZ, or 03/525-8047), lie just over the road from a good restaurant. All rooms have kitchen facilities, and the motel has an indoor pool.

The **Collingwood Park Motel,** Tasman Street, Collingwood (www.collingwoodpark.co.nz; ✆ **0800/270-520** in NZ, or 03/524-8499), offers double, studio, and family units with kitchen facilities. The hospitable hosts have good knowledge of sightseeing attractions in the wider region. The motel is a short drive to Farewell Spit and Wharariki Beach.

Ratuni Lodge ★★ For a touch of luxury near the beach, the Ratuni features elegant accommodation and a dining room and bar resplendent with with period furnishings and white table linens. Three-course fixed-price dinners with polished service and delicious food are available with reservations made before noon that day. A weekly menu is available online. The wine list features a number of Nelson wines, and the predinner cocktails are very good. Flight/tour packages are available. Not suitable for children under 12.

818 Abel Tasman Dr., Pohara. www.ratunilodge.com. © **03/525-7998.** NZ$174–307. Rates include continental breakfast. 9 units. **Amenities:** Restaurant; saltwater pool; spa; Wi-Fi (free).

WHERE TO EAT

Popular with the indie music crowd, the moderately priced **Brigand ★**, 90 Commercial St., Takaka (© **03/525-9636**), offers big servings, a good chowder, and an excellent steak served on a mountain of mashed potatoes. It's open Monday to Saturday from 11am to late.

  The Mussel Inn, 1259 SH60, Onekaka (www.musselinn.co.nz; © **03/525-9241**), is woodsy and friendly, and in truth could do with a refreshing, though regulars who love it for the atmosphere might object. It offers good beer (try a pint of the Captain Cooker manuka beer, brewed, so they say, to prevent scurvy), hearty, inexpensive food (mussels!), and live music. It's off the road, halfway between Takaka and Collingwood, with an almost hidden entrance, so look for the sign. It's open daily from 11am to late.

  Enjoy casual, inexpensive food (pizza, burgers) at the **Penguin Café & Bar,** 822 Abel Tasman Dr., Pohara (http://penguincafe.co.nz; © **03/525-6126**), with a glass or wine and a pint of beer in a bar overlooking the beach. It's open from 9am daily.

WEST COAST & THE GLACIERS

There's no disputing that the "Coast," as it's colloquially known, is a different region from the rest of New Zealand. It's more length than breadth, with its natural resources and beauty locked between the Tasman Sea on one side and the long chain of Southern Alps on the other. Its very narrowness provides ever-changing scenery. One minute you're looking at a long sweep of empty beach, then around the corner an icy glacier fills a mountain valley.

WESTPORT ★

Westport: 101km (63 miles) N of Greymouth; 226km (140 miles) SW of Nelson

Westport is a small town with big surprises, including a guided train journey into a historic (nonworking) coal mine and rafting through underground limestone caves.

Essentials

GETTING THERE & GETTING AROUND

BY PLANE **Sounds Air** (www.soundsair.com; © **0800/505-005** in NZ) offers daily scheduled flights from Wellington.

BY COACH (BUS) A number of daily bus service operate to/ from Westport/Nelson/Christchurch/Greymouth/Hokitika/Glaciers, among them **InterCity** (www.intercity.co.nz; © **64/9/583-5780**) and **Naked Bus** (https://nakedbus.com).

BY CAR From Nelson to Westport via Buller Gorge takes approximately 3½ hours. The spectacular drive to/from Greymouth via SH6 (also signposted as the Great Coast Rd.) is about 2 hours. From Christchurch via Lewis Pass (forest, plains, mountains, rivers, bush) and the Buller Gorge is 331km (205 miles) and takes around 4 hours. The area has a number of single-lane bridges, so watch for signs instructing you to proceed or stop.

VISITOR INFORMATION

The **Westport i-SITE Information Centre,** Coal Town Museum, 123 Palmerston St., Westport (www.westport.org.nz; © **03/789-6658**), is open Monday to Sunday 9am to 5pm (Sat–Sun 10am–4pm in May–Aug) and 10am to 4pm on public holidays.

[FastFACTS]

Emergency Emergency toll-free calls (ambulance, fire, police): ✆ **111. Westport Police Station:** ✆ **03/789-7339.**

Medical Buller Hospital: ✆ **03/788-9030.**

Exploring Westport

The South Island town of Westport is 1 of 28 known "Westports" in the world, with most being a historical reference to Ireland's Westport. The town had its origins in the goldrush days of the 1860s, but the major source of wealth for most of its history has been "black gold": coal. Now, in the 21st century, tourism is the earner.

The town is built around the mouth of the Buller River, a stretch of water that offers the calm of deep trout pools as well as the rush of whitewater that draws river rafters and jetboaters.

Coal Town Museum The Coal Town Museum offers insights into what was once the region's main source of wealth: coal and the mining of it. This small, well-presented museum is best visited *after* the Denniston Experience (p. 288) for the full picture of coal mining.

123 Palmerston St. www.buller.co.nz/southisland-newzealand-activities/coaltown-museum. ✆ **03/789-6658.** Mon–Fri 9am-4:30pm, Sat and Sun 10am–4pm (daily 9am–5pm in summer). NZ$10 adults, NZ$2 children.

Outdoor Pursuits

HORSE TREKKING Get up close with the scenery around the Buller River on a trail trek on horseback with **Buller Adventure Tours** (www.adventuretours.co.nz; ✆ **0508/486-877** in NZ). Make it a family outing and ride with the kids; it's suitable for beginners (horses can be led) to experienced riders. Can include horse swimming. Treks last 1½ hours and cost NZ$89 adults, NZ$69 children.

WALKING Tauranga Bay ★★★ has a beautiful coastline and a number of short walking tracks. A seal colony has been in residence for years and is worth a walk to see (but note that seals are smelly and territorial, so keep to the track). Pick up the Department of Conservation's brochure with maps from the visitor center.

WHITEWATER RAFTING Whitewater rafting is a prime sport in this area, so if you've always wanted to try it, this is your chance to tackle the Buller River Earthquake Rapids (plenty of adrenaline rush action) with **Wild Rivers Rafting** (www.wildriversrafting.co.nz; ✆ **0508/467-238** in NZ). Guides give full rafting safety instructions, and your time on the river is 2½ hours. Allow 4 hours total for the trip.

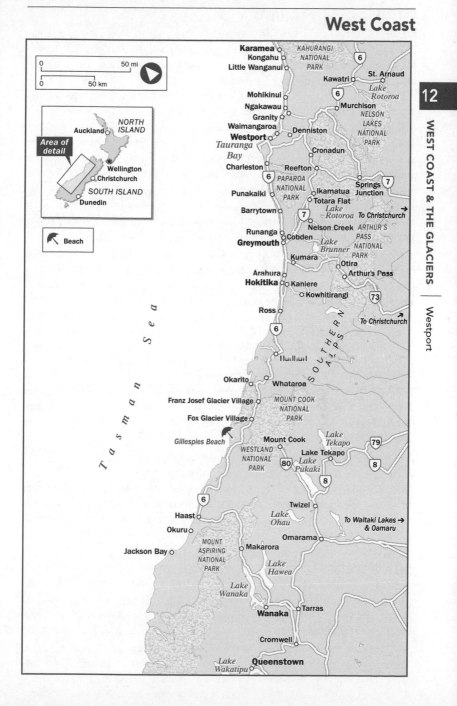

0   50 mi
0   50 km

Beach

NORTH
ISLAND

Auckland

Area of
detail

Wellington
Christchurch

SOUTH ISLAND

Dunedin

Karamea
Kongahu
Little Wanganui

KAHURANGI
NATIONAL
PARK

6

Kawatri

St. Arnaud
Lake
Rotoroa

Mohikinui
Ngakawau
Granity
Waimangaroa
Westport
*Tauranga
Bay*

6

Murchison

NELSON
LAKES
NATIONAL
PARK

Denniston

Cronadun

Charleston

6

Reefton

PAPAROA
NATIONAL
PARK

Ikamatua
Totara Flat

Springs
Junction

7

Punakaiki

Barrytown

7

Lake
Rotoroa

To Christchurch

Nelson Creek

ARTHUR'S
PASS
NATIONAL
PARK

Runanga
Greymouth

Cobden

Lake
Brunner

Kumara

Otira
Arthur's Pass

Arahura
Hokitika   Kaniere

Kowhitirangi

73

Ross

6

To Christchurch

S O U T H E R N   A L P S

T a s m a n   S e a

Okarito   Whataroa

Franz Josef Glacier Village

Fox Glacier Village

Gillespies Beach

MOUNT COOK
NATIONAL
PARK

Mount Cook

WESTLAND
NATIONAL
PARK

Lake Tekapo

Lake
Tekapo

79

80

Lake
Pukaki

8

8

6

Haast
Okuru

Jackson Bay

MOUNT
ASPIRING
NATIONAL
PARK

Makarora

Twizel

Lake
Ohau

Omarama

To Waitaki Lakes →
& Oamaru

Lake
Hawea

Lake
Wanaka

Wanaka   Tarras

Cromwell

Lake
Wakatipu   Queenstown

Outlying Attractions

DENNISTON Coal was discovered on this coal-rich subalpine plateau, 25km (15 miles) northeast of Westport, in 1863, and by the early 1900s was being delivered to a rail terminus at the base of the plateau by a unique rail line, the Denniston Incline. The rail track fell 510m (1,640 ft.) in 1.7km (1 mile). The full coal trucks going down pulled the empty wagons up the line. Apart from a steep rough hillside track, the wagons were the only way the residents of the small town could reach or leave the settlement.

The last delivery of coal down the Incline was in 1968. Visitors today will find a tiny settlement—a scattering of historic dwellings—with well-marked walking trails up to and around what was once the thriving township.

GLOWWORM CAVES & UNDERGROUND RAFTING ★ Discover many intriguing caves and underground pools in the area on a cave tour with **UnderWorld Adventures,** Charleston, SH6, 30km (19 miles) south of Westport (www.caverafting.com; ✆ **0800/116-686** in NZ, or 03/788-8168). On the 3½-hour **Glowworm Cave Tour** (NZ$110 adults, NZ$85 children 5–15, NZ$340 family), you'll take a "rainforest train" to Nile River caves that feature glowworms, stalactites, and stalagmites. Wear sturdy shoes and a jacket; you'll need to be able to walk unassisted on uneven surfaces.

Where to Stay

Carters by the Sea ★ A motel with stylish studio units, Carters opened in early 2015. It has large bathrooms, small but well-designed kitchens, and huge windows facing the town green and the open sea. Nearby amenities include a cafe, bar and bakery next door, and an 18-hole golf course.

7 Marine Parade, Carters Beach, Westport. www.cartersbythesea.co.nz. ✆ **03/789-8169.** 10 units. NZ$160–NZ$184. Rates include free airport transfers. **Amenities:** Wi-Fi (500MB free).

Art Hotel ★ Owned by an artists' cooperative, this is a welcoming, good-value lodging. The decorative entrance opens onto a vintage hotel that had its heyday in the 19th century. It has no bar or cafe (these are available close by), but rooms are warm and quiet and beds are comfortable. Kitchen facilities are available—and yes, the walls are hung with an array of interesting artworks, in rotating exhibits.

10 Brougham St., Westport. www.arthotel.co.nz. ✆ **03/789-8203.** 10 units. NZ$30 single; NZ$50 double; NZ$60 triple; long-stay rates available. **Amenities:** Art gallery; bike rentals and storage; kitchen & herb garden; studio and workshop space; Wi-Fi (free).

Birds Ferry Lodge ★★★ Some 150 years ago a Mr. Bird operated a ferry at Charleston. His name lives on in the lodge, comprised of two ensuite B&B rooms and Ferry Man's Cottage, both owned and operated by Alison and Andre Gygax. Originally from Scotland (Alison) and South Africa (Andre), the couple have years of international hospitality experience between them but are now so embedded in the New Zealand landscape that they own 33 acres of it. It's a stylish haven, and guests benefit from Alison's excellent culinary talents with a breakfast that may include free-range eggs, homemade muesli, and fresh-baked bread. The turnoff to the property is well-signposted, and the gravel drive in includes some "out-there" landscaping: How about an eight-oar rowing scull going nowhere but looking magnificently eccentric in a small pond? The cottage, set on 12 landscaped acres of the property's 33 acres alongside a serene lake, sleeps up to five people and has a fully equipped kitchen and two outdoor garden baths.

Birds Ferry Rd., off SH 6, 20 min. south of Westport. www.birdsferrylodge.co.nz. ℰ **0800/212-207** in NZ, or 03/429-1604. 3 units. NZ$399 lodge double. NZ$300–NZ$450 cottage; $60 each extra person per night. Rates include full breakfast; dinner extra. Children under 12 welcome in the cottage only. **Amenities:** Hot tub; Wi-Fi (free).

Where to Eat

The Bay House ★★ REGIONAL   This restaurant is almost on the beach, with rocky inshore islands and breaking surf filling the landscape. Once a private holiday house, it has been a restaurant off and on for some 12 years. The brunch/lunch menu is not large but delivers good options ranging from calamari salad to a hearty seafood chowder. The menu for evening diners is similarly compact, with good variety. The focus is on produce grown (or raised) in the neighborhood: berry fruits, venison, lamb, beef, and, perhaps most important, seafood. Here the fish dish of the day might feature turbot or hoki (from the southern seas) or John Dory, gurnard, rig, or snapper landed by smaller local boats. Shellfish might include Marlborough mussels or Nelson scallops. Threads of seasonality ripple through the dessert menu as well; should crème brûlée with rhubarb compote show up on the menu, we recommend ordering it.

Tauranga Bay, RD2, Westport. www.bayhouse.co.nz. ℰ **03/789-4151.** Main courses NZ$25–NZ$34. Wed–Sat 10am–3:30pm and 5:30–8:30pm; Sun 10am–3:30pm. Closed Mon–Tues.

Denniston Dog ★ KIWI   The name is a historic remnant from the days when Denniston (p. 288) was a flourishing mining town and had a pub known as the Red Dog Saloon. This Westport restaurant/cafe/bar makes an effort to serve local produce, and the fish is always a good choice. Order turbot if it's on the menu. A notable feature is the size of the portions; "generous" is an understatement. It is a popular place, but the kitchen is small and diners may face a wait for their meals.

18 Wakefield St., Westport. www.dennistondog.co.nz. ℰ **03/789-5030.** Main courses NZ$25–NZ$36. Daily 9am–late.

KARAMEA ★

96km (60 miles) NE of Westport

The road from Westport ends at the charming settlement of Karamea, close to the beginning (or end) of the **Heaphy Track,** one of New Zealand's top nine hiking trails. There is plenty of natural beauty here, with nikau palms studded among the native tree ferns. Geographically, it is part of the huge limestone/sandstone area of this corner of the South Island. A must-see is the **Oparara (river) Basin** with its limestone arches and river tunnels.

Essentials

GETTING THERE & GETTING AROUND

BY PLANE   Fixed Wing Charter (☎ 03/548-2800) from Nelson for up to six passengers.

BY COACH (BUS)   Karamea Express (☎ 03/782-6757 for fares and schedules) travels daily from Westport.

BY CAR   Karamea is 96km (60 miles) north of Westport, but you should allow 1½ to 2 hours for the drive—at least 25km (15 miles) of roadway is steep and winding, especially over the Karamea Bluff.

VISITOR INFORMATION

The **Karamea Information & Resource Centre** (www.karameainfo.co.nz or www.westcoast.co.nz; ☎ 03/782-6652), in the village of **Market Cross,** is open daily from 9am. The township has cafes, stores, and motels.

Exploring Karamea

Top of your list should be a visit to **Oparara Arch ★★** (www oparara.co.nz), the biggest limestone arch of its type in the Southern Hemisphere. It is not an easy drive and a guided tour is advised. Tours from 2½ to 5 hours are available; admission is NZ$95 to NZ$224 adult (child rates available). For tour companies, contact the **Karamea Information & Resource Centre,** Market Cross, Karamea (☎ 03/782-6652).

Outdoor Pursuits

CANOEING   Rent a canoe from the **Last Resort** (www.lastresort.co.nz; ☎ 03/782-6617) to paddle about in the lagoon—but be aware of the tides as the lagoon empties completely at low tide.

FISHING   The 40km (25 miles) of coastline are suitable for surfcasting, and the Karamea River offers good trout fishing. Daily, weekly, or full-season licenses are available in Karamea. Visitors to Karamea (and the entire West Coast) between September 1 and November 4 have the opportunity to try the uniquely New Zealand foraging/food gathering hobby: netting whitebait. On a tidal river. Get rules and regulations from the Department of Conservation office and the **Karamea Information & Resource Centre** (☎ 03/782-6652).

MOUNTAIN BIKING   This is a popular sport with designated tracks. Bikes can be rented; inquire at the Karamea Information and Resource Centre.

WALKING   Karamea has two major hiking trails (for treks up to 5 days) but many 1-day tracks, so consult the experts (the Karamea Information and Resource Centre, above) to find the right trail for you. They guide newbies to a track befitting age and fitness levels.

The Denniston Mine Experience

Travel north on SH67 and turn right at Waimangaroa. From here the Denniston Hill road twists and turns for 8km (5 miles), taking about 20 minutes to arrive at the **Denniston Mine Experience** ★★ (www.denniston.co.nz; ✆ **0800/881-880** in NZ, or 64/21/936-094). This is a unique immersion in the life and times of underground coal miners and mining, a lifestyle unlikely to ever return to this region. Travel into one of the country's best-known (now nonworking) coal mines. Narrow-gauge rail carriages carry visitors and guides along a 170m (185-yard) track into a mine first mined in 1879. It is stable, undamaged, and non-gaseous, strengthened with modern support systems and equipped with natural ventilation shafts and extensive safety equipment. Visitors must be able to walk at least 500m (half a mile) over damp, uneven ground. Clearly, this is not suitable for anyone with claustrophobia. The 2-hour tour is NZ$99 adult, NZ$40 children 5 to 14 (minimum age 5).

Where to Stay

With nine studio and one- and two-bedroom units, **Karamea River Motels** ★, 31 Bridge St. (www.karameamotels.co.nz; ✆ **0800/527-263** in NZ, or 03/782-6955), is good for families or travelers aiming to spend a few days in the area (NZ$129–NZ$169 double).

Last Resort ★★ Opened as budget accommodation in 1991, by 2015 the Last Resort had added a restaurant, cafe, and bar to a comprehensive range of accommodations to suit all budgets. All buildings are sited to best advantage on the generous grounds, which also accommodate a number of picnic tables and barbecue areas. The cottages are ideal for families and groups—each sleeps five and is self-contained and private. The comfortable studio ensuite units sleep up to three and are popular with couples and small families. The ensuite lodge units have a private shower and toilet and sleep up to four people. The twin room lodges have two single beds and sleep two; linens are provided, and bathroom and kitchen facilities are shared. The lodge double (Room 16) sleeps two in a double bed; linens are provided, and kitchen and bathroom are shared. The backpacker dorm Room is school-dormitory style, sleeping five; all linens are provided, and bathroom and kitchen facilies are shared.

71 Waverley St., Karamea. www.lastresortkaramea.co.nz. ✆ **0800/505-042** in NZ, or 03/782-6617. 26 units. NZ$50–NZ$155. Free parking. **Amenities:** Restaurant; cafe; bar; Wi-Fi (free).

Where to Eat

For such a small settlement, the options are pleasing, thanks in no small measure to the spate of hikers coming off the trails wanting good food and a cold beer (or chilled wine). The **Last Resort** ★, 71 Waverley St. (www.lastresort-karamea.co.nz; ✆ **0800/505-042** in NZ, or 03/782-6617), boasts a bar, cafe, and a 96-seat restaurant. The cafe has made-to-order burgers and very good fish and chips along with cabinet food—baked goods such as cakes, pie slices, cookies, sandwiches, and filled rolls, all set out in glass-fronted cabinets. The restaurant is open for breakfast and dinner, and common to both menus is the substantial size of the dishes. Dinner guests will find good lamb dishes (lamb shanks and rack of lamb are always popular), steaks are noteworthy for their size and spot-on cooking (order "rare" and it will be), and, of course, the ubiquitous "best whitebait pattie."

The **Karamea Village Hotel restaurant** ★, Waverley Street (www.karameahotel.co.nz; ℂ **03/782-6800**), a restored historic building, comes as a happy surprise given that it looks more like an archetypal New Zealand country pub. Service is friendly but professional, and the menu is an eclectic list of New Zealand classics and ethnic foods. A good curry competes with the "roast" (meat) of the day, which comes with an impressive gravy. (For the uninitiated, a roast gravy is somewhere between a roux-based sauce and a meaty jus, and a good restaurant never stints on the amount added to the dish.) Dishes are prettily presented, with vegetables carved into delicate petals.

EN ROUTE TO GREYMOUTH: PUNAKAIKI

The drive between Westport and Greymouth has some of the best coastal views in the country: Native trees brush the highway on the inland side, while rocky offshore islands not much bigger than a tree are photogenic gems. Dozens of walkways lead to natural attractions including the world-famous **Punakaiki Pancake Rocks and Blowholes** ★★★. The coastal rocks, 45km (28 miles) north of Greymouth, are pancakelike limestone layers formed by sea and seismic action aeons ago. The best viewing is at high tide when there is a westerly swell running; the sea surges into deep caverns before spouting high in the air. The walkway to the Rocks is wide, well maintained, and easily negotiable. Put on your walking shoes, get out your camera and get ready for awesome. Expect crowds February through March. For more details, contact the **Punakaiki-Paparoa National Park Visitor Centre (i-SITE),** SH6, Punakaiki (www.punakaiki.co.nz; ℂ **03/731-1895**), and the **Department of Conservation** (www.doc.govt.nz; ℂ **03/731-1895**).

Outdoor Pursuits

HORSEBACK RIDING   Ride on the beach, cross rivers, and soak up spectacular scenery on a morning or afternoon horseback trek with **Punakaiki Horse Treks** ★★ (www.pancake-rocks.co.nz; ℂ **03/731-1839**). With horses and rides to suit all abilities, Punakaiki offers nature tours into the magnificent Punakaiki Valley. Treks are around 2½ to 3 hours. Punakaiki is located 600m (656 yards) south of the Pancake Rocks.

WALKING/TRAMPING   Both the **Truman Track** ★★ and the **Punakaiki Cavern** walk ★★ are under an hour and suitable for the entire family. The Truman Track takes walkers through coastal forest to a beach with caves and a waterfall. The **Pororari River Track** starts at the bridge over the Pororari

Shopping for Local Crafts

You are in the heartland of crafts here. Across the road from the track entrance, you'll find a gathering of cafes and stores, including **Punakaiki Crafts** ★★ (www.punakaiki.co.nz/crafts/; ℂ **03/731-1813**), a cooperative with an innovative stock that includes hand-blown glass, pottery, and carvings of native wood and limestone often embellished with the attractive blue-green lining of the paua shell, a type of shellfish found throughout New Zealand; it's open daily from 8:30am to 6pm.

River, 1km (just over half a mile) north of the visitor center. It passes through dense bush, with a popular swimming hole about 15 minutes down the track. Allow 2½ hours return.

Where to Stay

A welcoming place with 10 cabins, a communal kitchen, hot showers, and a lovely site, **Punakaiki Beach Camp** ★, Owen Street, off SH6 (www.punakaikibeachcamp.co.nz; ℂ **03/731-1894**), is an easy walk from the Pancake Rocks. Cabins run from NZ$68 for two people. **Punakaiki Resort** ★, SH6 (www.punakaiki-resort.co.nz; ℂ **0800/706-707** in NZ, or 03/731-1168), opened in 2001 just a stone's throw from the sea. It offers 58 rooms with ocean or bush/garden views, a restaurant, and a bar. There have been some complaints about service in high season, but we find that tends to be a recurring issue in a number of out-of-the-way hotels. Rates are from NZ$259 (hotel room) to NZ$315 for an eco-suite.

Where to Eat

As the name suggests, **Pancake Rocks Café Punakaiki** ★ (ℂ **03/731-1122**) honors the Pancake Rocks that dominate the coastline here. Carrying the theme further, the cafe's speciality is pancakes, with the all-day menu featuring sweet (with cream and berries) and savory (served with bacon) options for NZ$19. The cafe's roadside site ensures that it is busy, busy with independent travelers as well as coach passengers. In addition to cabinet food offerings, the cafe sells made-to-order steak sandwiches and an open fish and salad sandwich featuring filet of terakihi. It's open daily 8am to 5pm, with evening meals available from 5pm in the summer season (Dec–Apr).

GREYMOUTH

101km (63 miles) SW of Westport; 45km (28 miles) N of Hokitika; 290km (180 miles) SW of Nelson

The landing place for Maori canoes traveling to the southern region seeking greenstone (jade), or *pounamu,* Greymouth is embraced by the Grey River. Greenstone was prized for its decorative beauty and its suitability as weaponry (it can be ground to a sharp edge).

Today, tourism, along with beer and brewing, is the name of the game in Greymouth. Monteith's Brewery is a big company, and it sponsors and supports many West Coast organizations and public endeavours. Make time for a brewery tour and a meal in its good cafe.

Essentials

GETTING THERE & GETTING AROUND

BY PLANE   Daily flights between Christchurch and Hokitika are operated by **Air New Zealand** (www.airnewzealand.co.nz; *℗* **0800/737-000** in NZ). A shuttle service carries visitors the extra 30 minutes by road from/to Greymouth.

BY TRAIN   The **TranzAlpine** (www.kiwirailscenic.co.nz; *℗* **0800/872-467** in NZ) runs daily between Christchurch and Greymouth.

BY COACH (BUS)   **InterCity** buses (www.intercity.co.nz; *℗* **64/9/623-1503,** or 03/768-7080) connect Greymouth with all main South Island centers including Queenstown, Fox Glacier, Franz Josef, Nelson, and Westport.

BY CAR   Greymouth is reached via SH6 from Hokitika and Westport. From Christchurch via Lewis Pass and Reefton take SH7 or SH73 via Arthurs Pass. Allow approximately 4 hours.

VISITOR INFORMATION

The **Greymouth i-SITE Visitors Information,** 164 Mackay St., Greymouth (www.westcoasttravel.co.nz; *℗* **0800/473-966** in NZ, or 03/768-7080), is open Monday through Friday 9am to 5pm and Saturday, Sunday, and public holidays 9:30am to 4pm. It also serves as the Department of Conservation agency for the region.

[FastFACTS]

Emergency   Ambulance, fire, police: toll-free *℗* **111. Greymouth Police Station:** *℗* **03/768-1600.**

Medical   **Grey Base** hospital: *℗* **03/769-7100.**

Exploring Greymouth

History buffs and kids of all ages will find **Shantytown Heritage Park ★★**, 316 Rutherglen Rd., 10km (6 miles) south of Greymouth (www.shantytown.co.nz; *℗* **03/762-6634**), a pleasure. The replica West Coast gold-mining town includes some 30 historic buildings, a steam train that tootles along a track through bush, and a gold-panning experience that usually delivers some "color," in gold-mining terms. It might sound like early Disneyland, but Shantytown is an engaging experience, especially for kids. It's open daily 8:30am to 5pm (NZ$32 adults, $16 children, NZ$74 family passes).

On a different tack, take in one of the changing exhibitions in the **Left Bank Art Gallery ★**, 1 Tainui St., on the left bank of the Grey River (www.

leftbankarts.org.nz; ℂ **03/768-0038**). The artworks are usually interesting and sometimes outstanding. If you're looking for quality souvenirs, the gallery gift shop has good art and crafts by West Coast artists. It's open Monday through Friday from noon to 4pm and Saturdays 11am to 2pm.

Beer enthusiasts should make a beeline for a tour at **Monteith's Brewery ★★**, Herbert Street (ℂ **03/768-4149**). The company brews small batches, and its range is intriguing, to say the least: Ginger beer? Chocolate ale? It's all here for the sampling. Tours are at 10:30am, 3pm, 4:30pm, and 6pm.

Outdoor Pursuits

OFF-ROAD BIKING It's "muddy great fun" as you zoom through privately owned rainforest along off-road tracks with **On Yer Bike ★★** (www. onyerbike.co.nz; ℂ **0800/669-372** in NZ, or 03/762-7438). Choose from quad biking, go-karting, or an 8WD Argo that's like a rollercoaster without the tracks. It spins, slides and floats! It carries up to five passengers and is ideal for families including smaller children. On Yer Bike is located 5 minutes north of Greymouth and is well signposted. Rides are from NZ$115.

RAFTING New Zealand Discovery Adventures ★ (www.fun-nz.com; ℂ **0800/946-543** in NZ or 03/768-6649) offers serious adventure seekers a 5-hour cave rafting trip deep into an underground world of water and glowworms. For those who prefer tamer pursuits, the company offers guided walks, birdwatching tours, photographic tours, and greenstone (jade) and gold hunts.

WALKING The **Point Elizabeth Walkway ★★** starts at Rapahoe and follows the coast south around the headland to the Cobden Beach road end. The track takes under 2 hours one-way. If the tide is low, return along the beach. Go in early evening to enjoy one of Greymouth's fabulous sunsets.

Where to Stay

GREYMOUTH

Greymouth Seaside Top 10 Holiday Park ★★ Greymouth has tent and caravan sites, cabins, studio units, motel units, and two- and three-bedroom apartments. Configurations are many, with some units (such as small cabins) sharing bathroom and kitchen facilities; other larger cabins and motel and studio units have private facilities. In 2014 two- and three-bedroom apartments were added to the accommodation options; these are popular with larger families and groups who plan a few days' holiday by the sea. The park enjoys an enviable site practically on the beach, with the sounds of the sea lulling tired travelers to sleep. An ideal departure point for the West Coast Wilderness (bike) Trail.

2 Chesterfield St. www.top10greymouth.co.nz. ℂ **0800/867-104** in NZ, or 03/768-6618. 58 units. $NZ374 apartment; NZ$65 cabins; NZ$45 powered sites. **Amenities:** Barbecues; children's playground; coin-operated Internet.

A SUPERB DAY OUT VIA scenic train & plane ★★★

This opportunity to experience two of the major South Island experiences is not necessarily only for the time-poor. Quite simply, it is a superb day out, traveling Christchurch to Greymouth by train, taking a scenic flight over national parks, the mountains, and glaciers of the Southern Alps, then returning passengers to Christchurch.

The **KiwiRail Scenic Journeys TranzAlpine train** (www.kiwirailscenic.co.nz; ☏ **0800/872-467** in NZ) departs Christchurch at 8:15am and travels to Greymouth via Springfield, Arthur's Pass, Jacksons, and Moana. The rail track crosses the Canterbury Plains and traverses the Southern Alps via tunnels and viaducts and long bridges over wide, straggling rivers. The landscape changes dramatically near the mountain divide at Arthur's Pass before the long final tunnel

into the West Coast's green landscape of native bush, forests, and shimmering lakes. Arrival time at Greymouth is 12:45pm. At that point **Air West Coast** (www.airwestcoast.co.nz; ☏ **03/738-0524**) offers one of the region's great-value scenic flights. Departing from Greymouth Airport in a six-seater Cessna, the flightpath includes Franz Josef (with an optional heli-flight to the snow), the lonely majesty of Aoraki/Mount Cook, the Tasman Glacier, the Alps, and northern Mackenzie Country before landing at Christchurch airport at around 3:30 or 4pm. The TranzAlpine Christchurch to Greymouth flight: from NZ$99 adult, NZ$69 child. The Air West Coast alpine scenic flight from Greymouth to Christchurch: from NZ$515 (Franz Josef landing and heli-flight additional NZ$210).

Coleraine ★   Coleraine caters to leisure travelers and the corporate market with spacious suites and apartments: one- or two-bedroom suites, executive rooms, and spa studio rooms. All units are large and nicely decorated with quality furnishings and linen. Service is excellent, with a very helpful reception staff. A central location allows for an easy walk to Greymouth's main attractions. Breakfast is available in-house, and guests will find Buccleugh's On High restaurant across High Street a fine option for dinner.

61 High St., Greymouth. http://colerainegreymouth.nz. ☏ **0800/270-077** in NZ. 22 units. NZ$165–NZ$255 double. **Amenities:** Free pickup from TranzAlpine; Wi-Fi (free).

KUMARA

The Theatre Royal Hotel ★★★   Comfort rules at this 1876 relic of gold-mining days in Kumara (20 min. south of Greymouth/north of Hokitika). The owners rescued a derelict building that was a saloon (pub) and dance theater during gold-rush days, and spent many months and even more money to create a haven of hospitality. Completed in 2012, the revamped hotel offers rooms, suites, and cottages with beds that are plump puffs of softness, providing deep sleep comfort. Bedrooms in the main building are decorated in a style familiar to travelers in Victorian times—lace curtains, flowery wallpaper, brass bedheads, and freestanding wardrobes—though are now outfitted with TVs and tea/coffeemaking units rather than crinolines and top hats.

Ensuite bathrooms are large, heated, and luxurious, the Victorian and Edwardian-era furniture has been restored, and the rooms and narrow staircases now boast plush carpeting rather than druggets. In addition to the main building, an old bank building opposite has been completely restored and now comprises two lavish suites where once were teller's counters and an old gold office. Renovated miner's cottages nearby are also lodging options. The hotel bar and restaurant (see "Where to Eat," below) in the original hotel opens off the long veranda.

81 Seddon St., Kumara. Turn at Kumara Junction and take SH73 to Kumara. www.theatreroyalhotel.co.nz. ℭ **03/736-9277.** 13 units. NZ$115–NZ$250 double. **Amenities:** Restaurant; cafe; bar; Wi-Fi (free in some rooms).

Where to Eat
GREYMOUTH

At the family restaurant **Buccleugh's on High** in the Recreation Hotel at 68 High St., Greymouth (www.rechotel.co.nz; ℭ **03/768-5154**), the menu features blue cod, one of the South Island's most popular fish varieties, here poached in ginger and shallot cream. Braised lamb shanks and Buccleugh's surf 'n' turf (a ribeye steak topped with scallops and prawns) are menu standards that also enjoy enduring popularity. Open for breakfast and dinner every day, lunch Friday Saturday, Sunday. It's open for breakfast and dinner everyday and and lunch on Friday, Saturday, and Sunday.

The popular **Priya INDIAN** ★, 84 Tainui St., Greymouth (ℭ **03/768-7377**), is open for lunch and dinner. Layers of spices—not necessarily hot—and the expected ginger and fenugreek flavor dishes might have been purposely designed to accompany a cold beer.

For good coffee in Greymouth, head to **DP1 café** ★, 108 Mawhera Quay (ℭ **03/768-4005**). **Ali's Café** ★, 9 Tainui St. (ℭ **03/768-5858**), does a roaring trade despite a bland exterior. Inside the little cafe are interesting displays of local artwork, a warm welcome, and good food, especially the baked goods (great cakes!) and handpies. It's open daily from 9 to 8:30pm.

KUMARA

The Theatre Royal Hotel ★★ REGIONAL   Continental breakfasts are available for hotel guests who rise early, but we suggest you sleep in and wait for the cooked breakfasts—which could also be lunch, since the menu is available from 10am to 3pm. Enjoy a feast featuring venison sausages with hash browns, whitebait sandwiches, or beer-battered turbot with fries. The dinner menu includes the Coaster Platter, which offers tastes of the West Coast: blackball salami, smoked salmon, wild pork sliders, and apple chutney. If the salad of smoked venison is on the menu, consider it a must: The tender, smoky meat is tossed with beetroot, walnuts, bleu cheese, salad leaves, and a lovely raspberry vinegar dressing.

81 Seddon St., Kumara. www.theatreroyalhotel.co.nz. ℭ **03/736-9277.** Main courses NZ$21–NZ$35. Cafe daily 10am–9pm. Dinner a la carte menu Thurs–Sat 6–8pm.

HOKITIKA: GREENSTONE, GLOWWORMS & GOLD

45km (28 miles) S of Greymouth; 147km (91 miles) N of Franz Josef Glacier

Hokitika is a buzzy, hip destination, albeit not as buzzy as it was in the gold-rush years when some 102 pubs were scattered about the town. Today the focus is on greenstone (jade), the beach, the surrounding lakes, and the many excellent stone carvers, glass artists, wood turners, and potters who ply their craft here.

Essentials

GETTING THERE & GETTING AROUND

BY PLANE Air New Zealand Link (www.airnewzealand.co.nz; ℭ 0800/737-000 in NZ) has air service between Hokitika and Christchurch.

BY TRAIN The only train access is to/from Christchurch/Greymouth on KiwiRail's daily **TranzAlpine train** (www.kiwirailscenic.co.nz; ℭ 0800/872-467 in NZ).

BY COACH (BUS) InterCity (www.intercity.co.nz; ℭ 64/9/623-1503) and **Naked Bus** (https://nakedbus.com) have daily departures from Hokitika to Nelson, Westport, Greymouth, and Fox Glacier.

BY CAR Hokitika is reached from the north and south via SH6.

VISITOR INFORMATION

The **Hokitika i-SITE Visitor Centre,** 36 Weld St., Hokitika (www.hokitika. org; ℭ 03/755-6166) is open Monday to Friday 8:30am to 6pm and Saturday to Sunday 9am to 6pm (Nov–Feb); Monday to Friday 8:30am to 5pm and Saturday to Sunday 10am to 3:15pm (Mar–Nov).

[FastFACTS]

Emergency Ambulance, fire, police: toll-free ℭ **111. Hokitika Police Station:** ℭ **03/756-8310.**

Medical **Westland Medical Centre:** ℭ **03/755-8180.**

Exploring Hokitika

West Coast history—not to mention geography—is enriched by *pounamu:* the green jade prized by Maori for its beauty, strength, and cutting edge. It is found exclusively in the South Island and mainly on the West Coast. To appreciate its importance to the local Ngati Waewae people and to the Ngai Tahu tribe in general, visit **Te Waipounamu Maori Heritage Centre ★★**, 39 Weld St. (ℭ **03/755-8304**). Those wanting to purchase a piece are assured of its provenance, since no imported jade or unlicensed removal of local greenstone is permitted. Public fossicking (prospecting) is still permitted on the beaches but restricted to that which an individual can carry out within a 24-hour time limit (to stem the illegal lifting of greenstone boulders). Admission is free.

A big spread of sand and sea, **Hokitika beach** ★★★ is just a few steps from the main street. It's a lively promenade of runners, dogs, and strollers. The annual Beach Sculpture event here is a don't miss, where clever hands create figures and shapes (including dinosaurs, stick people, and crinoline-gowned belles) from found objects on the beach (mostly driftwood). On the main beach-walk entrance there's a series of unique seats from the Take A Seat public art project, with flat sculptures of seated women and a plaque commemorating Westland women as the "the heart of our community."

The Hokitika Museum ★   This small but carefully curated museum is in a restored Carnegie Public Library building, circa 1908. The collections include artifacts from the 1860s gold-mining era and an excellent exhibition of the people and places of the early district by photographer Charles Robert Kirk (1876–1954). The photographs of Maori leaders are compelling, as is the audiovisual section on greenstone (jade) and gold. For visitors curious about the strange appeal of whitebait, the museum has answers to frequently asked questions. A recent addition (and definite oddity): a Meccano model of a river dredge.

17 Hamilton St. www.westlanddc.govt.nz/hokitika-museum. Ⓒ **03/755-6898.** Daily 10am–5pm (10am–2pm May–Oct). Admission $6 adults, $3 schoolchildren.

National Kiwi Centre ★   Housed in a nocturnal setting, kiwi can be viewed at close quarters through glass, scratching around in their habitat. Giant eels are the other main attraction, and these are so tame they are handfed by visitors at 10am, noon, and 3pm.

64 Tancred St. www.thenationalkiwicentre.co.nz. Ⓒ **03/755-5251.** NZ$22 adults, NZ$55 family pass. Daily 9am–5pm.

SCENIC WATERWAYS

Take a 1½-hr **paddle boat cruise** ★, down the Mahinapua Creek and Lake. The lake was originally a coastal lagoon, but the sand dunes gradually built up, cutting off access to the sea. Now it is part of an interesting scenic water reserve and campground. The entrance is via a turnoff from SHW6, 10km (6¼ miles) south of Hokitika opposite the Maninapua pub. It's NZ$35 adults, NZ$20 children 5 to 12 (Main Rd. S.; Ⓒ **03/755-7239** or 03/755-6166). The **Hokitika Gorge Scenic Reserve** presents a startling combination of brilliant blue water and dark green bush. Well-defined walking paths and bridges provide picturesque views.

Shine On, Glowworm Dell

The town hosts the largest outdoor gathering of glowworms in New Zealand. Once the sun has set, bring along a torch (flashlight) and follow the signposted area just north of the town on SH6 to the glowworm dell, where glowworms are clustered on and over damp banks of bush. Walk quietly, don't speak, and turn off the torch, and the glowworms will shine on you. It's a magic moment, and absolutely free.

SHOPPING

There must be something in the water that entices so many arts-and-crafts talents to move to this town. The **Hokitika Craft Gallery ★★**, 25 Tancred St. (ⓒ **03/755-8802**), is a cooperative of 15 artists and craftspeople. Standards are high and if a unique souvenir is sought, this address is where to start looking. A number of greenstone carvers work in Hokitika, and many retail outlets sell their work. We recommend **Westland Greenstone Ltd.**, 34 Tancred St., Hokitika (ⓒ **03/755-8713**).

Where to Stay

Stumpers ★★   As centrally located as you can get, Stumpers has 23 units with a range of options from full-facility premium and family ensuite rooms to studio units and backpacker accommodation with shared bathrooms/kitchens. For the convenience of its central location, on-site restaurant and bar, and affordability, Stumpers is a traveler's joy. The bar/restaurant/cafe is bright and busy. There is a retro twist to the dinner menu, with options like deep-fried Camembert, chicken schnitzel, and tournedos Rossini, as delicious here as they must have been back in the day. The breakfast menu features an option rarely seen in a cafe, oatmeal porridge. Served with brown sugar and a sprinkle of cinnamon, it is as good as grandma's ever was.

2 Weld St. www.stumpers.co.nz. ⓒ **03/755-8007.** 23 units. NZ$35 per person to NZ$130 double. **Amenities:** Bar; cafe; Wi-Fi (free).

Teichelmann's Bed & Breakfast ★★   Owners Brian Ward and Frances Flanagan go the extra distance to make visitors welcome, and Teichelmann's has built a big reputation for its hospitable ways. Situated opposite the museum, the elegant heritage home was built for a Dr. Teichelmann in 1910 and has been lovingly restored. Guest rooms exude comfort with large beds, down blankets, and central heating. The hospitality extends to very good breakfasts, which come with homemade preserves and jam. The B&B is opposite the Hokitika Museum and well-served by a number of good restaurants, cafes, and bars. It's a very popular B&B, so booking ahead is advised.

20 Hamilton St. www.teichelmanns.co.nz. ⓒ **03/755-8232.** 6 units. NZ$165–NZ$240. **Amenities:** Wi-Fi (free).

Stations Inn ★★   Blue Spur was a gold-mining site in 1867, and the original Station Hotel lay at the end of a tram track. In 2004 Hugh and Glenda Little built Stations Inn on this historic site, creating a bar, restaurant, and accommodations (stylish units with lavish ensuite bathrooms). The restaurant has won awards for its New Zealand beef and lamb. Of its fish selection, turbot—caught in the southern seas off the West Coast—is frequently on the menu, carefully dressed with chef Drew Boyling's secret lemon and butter sauce. The restaurant building is apart from the accommodation and looks over a large water wheel, with tame farm animals grazing in the green pastures.

Blue Spur Rd. www.stations.co.nz. ⓒ **03/755-5499.** 10 units. NZ$170–NZ$300. **Amenities:** Restaurant; bar; Wi-Fi (free).

BIRDING cruise TO WHITE HERON SANCTUARY

If you're driving from Hokitika to Franz Josef (2 hr.), be sure to stop at **Whataroa,** 35km (22 miles) north of Franz Josef, the starting point for a remarkable bird-watching expedition. November to February is the nesting season for the *kotuku* (white heron), and the **White Heron Sanctuary Tour** ★★★ (www. whiteherontours.co.nz; ℂ **0800/523-456** in NZ, or 03/753-4120) takes you downriver in a 20-minute scenic jetboat ride to the Waitangiroto Nature Reserve and the country's only white heron nesting colony.

Entry is restricted, and the tour operator is the only one hereabouts to hold the necessary permits. From the landing stage it is a 500m (half a mile) walk over a forest boardwalk to a hide, a disguised cabin that looks straight across the river to lofty trees populated with large white birds, spoonbills as well as white herons, parent birds and chicks. In late February, the chicks are making floppy aerial attempts. Tour times are at 9am, 11am, 1pm, and 3pm and cost NZ$120 adults, NZ$55 children 12 and under.

Where to Eat

Fat Pipi Pizzas ★★★, 89 Revell St. (ℂ **03/755-6373**), makes the best pizza this side of New York. If you have gotten this far without trying whitebait, do try the world's first whitebait pizza, which comes with whitebait, mozzarella, capers, and lemon on a garlic buttered crust. Seriously yum. Zucchini, spinach, mushrooms, feta, olives, red onion, and a roasted red pepper pesto make the Greenpiece pizza a winner for vegos. The Chicken Lickin pizza comes with smoked chicken, mushrooms, cream cheese, and a sweet and spicy sauce of apricot and red capsicum. Pasta dishes, soup, salad—oh, and more pizzas—are also available. Pizzas run from NZ$20 to NZ$30. Yes, there can be queues.

Clocktower Café ★★, Weld Street (ℂ **03/755-7737**), opposite the very visible Clock Tower, serves up award-winning hand pies (NZ$5). The venison pie is a winner, but oyster and beef has to be a close second.

Self-catering types will appreciate **Stella Cafe** ★, 84 Revell St. (ℂ **03/755-5432**), but this warm coffee shop (very good coffee, we might add) is also a whizz at baking, with treasures including batches of famous-in-Hokitika cheese scones. In fact, the cafe has its own cheese shop.

FRANZ JOSEF & FOX GLACIERS ★★★

Franz Josef: 188km (117 miles) SW of Greymouth; 24km (15 miles) N of Fox Glacier; 134km (85 miles) SW of Hokitika

It seems improbable that you could find a glacier on a South Pacific island and ice in a temperate rainforest, but that's New Zealand for you—full of surprises. Nowhere else in the world (outside Arctic regions) will you find glaciers 300m (1,000 ft.) above sea level and just 12km (7½ miles) from the sea.

The Franz Josef and Fox glaciers are a small part of the 115,000-hectare (284,000-acre) **Westland National Park,** an impressive area of high mountains, glaciers, rushing rivers—not to mention Fox Glacier and Franz Josef villages. The park is popular for tramping, mountain climbing, fishing, canoeing, hunting, and horse trekking.

Essentials

GETTING THERE
BY COACH (BUS) **InterCity** (www.intercity.co.nz; © **64/9/623-1503**) and **Naked Bus** (https://nakedbus.com) have daily scheduled services.

BY CAR The **World Heritage Highway** (SH6) follows the coast from Whataroa to Franz Josef Glacier and Fox Glacier to Haast and over the Haast Pass. Roads in this area should always be treaded carefully, especially in stormy, wet, or icy conditions.

GETTING AROUND
Fox Glacier and Franz Josef villages are small; either can be walked end to end in under 15 minutes. Bike rentals are also available. You can travel between the two villages by **InterCity coach** (www.intercity.co.nz).

VISITOR INFORMATION
The **Westland National Park Visitor Centre and i-SITE,** SH6 (www.doc.govt.nz and www.glaciercountry.co.nz; © **03/752-0796**), has literature, maps, displays, and activities. It's open daily in summer 8:30am to 6pm (till 5pm in winter).

Exploring the Glaciers
Conditions are always changing in the glacier valleys, and viewpoints may be meters from the face of the glacier, but barriers must *never* be crossed. To get the latest information, visit the **Westland Tai Poutini National Park Visitor Centre and i-SITE** in Franz Josef, or the **South Westland Weheka Area Office** in Fox Glacier, or check the website of the **Department of Conservation** (www.doc.govt.nz/visittheglacierssafely).

Aerial sightseeing of the glaciers is a moving experience. Helicopters have been the workhorses of these mountainous regions for over 25 years and provide one of the best ways to capture a glacier experience. Be aware, however, that conditions on the glaciers may close flights. If your time is short, take the first flight available lest you miss out, because to travel this distance and not experience the amazing closeup views may cause a lifetime of regret. *Note:* Fitness levels for heli-hiking should be discussed when booking.

A number of options are available including private charters, but the most popular heli-tours are scenic flights with landing and a 2-hour guided walk/hike (from NZ$425) and 30-minute flights covering both glaciers (from NZ$300). Flights from the Westland glaciers to Aoraki/Mount Cook take in the west face of the mountain (from NZ$440).

Helicopter operators and their offices pepper the settlements of Fox and Franz Josef, giving visitors a number of pricing and viewing options. Among them:

- Fox and Franz Josef Heliservices (www.scenic-flights.co.nz; ℂ 0800/800-793 in NZ, or 03/751-0866 in Fox Glacier; or 03/752-0793 in Franz Josef).
- Fox Glacier Guiding ★★★ 44 Main Rd., Fox Glacier (www.foxguides.co.nz; ℂ 0800/111-600 in NZ, or 03/751-0825).
- Franz Josef Glacier Guides, 6 Main Rd., Franz Josef (www.franzjosefglacier.com; ℂ 0800/484-337 in NZ, or 03/752-0763).
- Glacier Helicopters (www.glacierhelicopters.co.nz; ℂ 0800/800-732 in NZ, or 03/752-0755 in Franz Josef; or 03/751-0803 in Fox Glacier).
- The Helicopter Line ★★★ (www.helicopter.co.nz; ℂ 0800/807-767 in NZ, or 03/752-0767 in Franz Josef; or 03/751-0767 in Fox Glacier).
- Mount Cook Ski Planes ★★, New Zealand's only fixed-wing glacier landing experience (www.mtcookskiplanes.com; ℂ 0800/368-000 in NZ, or 03/752-0714 on the West Coast; or 03/430-8034 at Mount Cook).

Beyond the Glaciers: What to See & Do

The **seal colony at Gillespies Beach** ★ is a resting colony for seals during winter months and a great tramping spot, with five walking tracks. Take Cook Flat Road from Fox Glacier township and turn onto Gillespies Beach Road. Half of the 13-mile journey is on a narrow unsealed road, so take care to stay on the left and keep your speed down. The "beach" is all but covered with schitz and quartz (rocks), mountains of driftwood, and the rusted remains of old gold-working machinery—and lies just past Gillespies Point. Of the five walking tracks, the shortest, the **Miners Cemetery Walk,** is a poignant history lesson. The area was once extensively worked for gold and had a considerable population, as the headstones reveal. The longest walk, the **Galway Beach Tramping Track,** is a 3½-hour roundtrip from the Gillespies Beach carpark. Follow the signposts for the track through rimu native trees to the remote beach. Stay clear of the seals, however, never putting yourself between them and the sea (their escape route).

Safety tip: The weather can change rapidly in Westland, and it is important to take warm/waterproof clothing in case of sudden storms. Check track conditions and weather forecasts at the **Westland Tai Poutini National Park Visitor Centre,** 13 SH6 Franz Josef (ℂ 03/752-0796). Insect repellent is a must—the sandflies here are huge.

The **Glacier Hot Pools** ★★★, Cron Street, Franz Josef (www.glacierhotpools.co.nz; ℂ 0800/044-044 in NZ, or 03/752-0099), look as if they have been in the native bush for eons, but these are not natural springs but a trio of cleverly created pools nestled into the rainforest. It's pretty wonderful, nonetheless. The glacier water is heated to between 36°C and 40°C and is chlorinated. Large sail-like canopies keep the weather at bay. The facility has three public pools, three private pools, and a massage section. It's open from noon to 10pm (NZ$26 adults, NZ$22 children).

West Coast Wildlife Centre ★★★ It's worth the basic All-Day Pass alone to see the wildlife center's interactive glacier exhibits, but we recommend purchasing a **VIP Backstage Pass,** which includes admission to the center's glacier attractions and historic displays plus a guided tour of the indoor hatching home of the Rowo kiwi. This is New Zealand's rarest kiwi, and until recently it on the verge of extinction. The opportunity to see baby Rowo kiwi scuttling round their nocturnal enclosure is a special moment. Enjoy **Café Wild** (free Wi-Fi with your coffee), and shop for classy souvenirs in the **Wild West Shop.**

Cron St., Franz Josef. www.wildkiwi.co.nz.ℂ **03/752-0600.** All-Day Pass: NZ$35 adults, NZ$20 children 5–15, and NZ$85 family of five. VIP Backstage Pass: NZ$55 adults, NZ$35 children 5–15, and NZ$145 family of five. Daily 8:30am–5:30pm. Rowo kiwi tours daily 11am, 12:30pm, 2:30pm, and 4pm.

Where to Stay
IN FRANZ JOSEF

As ever with the Top 10 brand, the emphasis at the **Franz Josef Top 10 Holiday Park** ★, Main Road (www.top10.co.nz/parks/franz-josef; ℂ **0800/467-897** in NZ, or 03/752-0735), is on convenience, service, and value for money. It offers powered camping sites, cabins (from NZ$75 per night double), a lodge, tourist cabins, and motel units.

A short walk to shops and cafes, **Glenfern Villas** ★, SH6 (www.glenfern. co.nz; ℂ **0800/453-633** in NZ, or 03/752-0054), has 18 comfortable one- or two-bedroom villas (apartments) with fully equipped kitchens for from NZ$230 to NZ$289, plus bike rentals and a playground.

Across the road from the Glacier Hot Pools, the 20 units in the **Punga Grove Motel & Suites** ★, 400 Cron St. (www.pungagrove.co.nz;ℂ **0800/437-269** in NZ, or 03/752-0001), are surrounded by huge tree ferns and rainforest (NZ$165–NZ$275). Each unit comes with fully equipped kitchenettes. Executive studios have gas fires and ensuite spa baths.

IN FOX GLACIER

With a central location just 6km (4 miles) to the glacier and 400m (440 yards) to village cafes, **Lake Matheson Motel** ★, Cook Flat Road (wwwlakemathe-son.co.nz; ℂ 0800/452-243 in NZ), offers comfortable, spacious, quiet accommodations from NZ$105 double. It has an outdoor garden and barbecue area and covered parking.

The 21 rooms are stylish and spacious at **Distinction Te Weheka** ★, 15 Main Rd., SH6 (www.distinctionfoxglacier.co.nz; ℂ **0800/313-414** in NZ, or 03/751-0730), with king or twin beds, big bathrooms, and balconies. It also has an onsite restaurant, a guest lounge, and a library (from NZ$395 double).

Where to Eat
IN FRANZ JOSEF

Don't expect anything posh, but if you like good coffee and hearty, filling nosh, **Full of Beans Café** ★, 24 SH6 (the highway is the settlement's main street; ℂ **03/752-0139**), is the place. Full of Beans is popular for breakfast, and the all-day menu offers burgers, blue-cod fish and chips, and good hand pies (main courses NZ$15–NZ$25). It's open daily from 7am.

You can't miss the **Blue Ice Restaurant & Bar** ★, 12 SH6 (📞 **03/752-0707**): The owner's Hummer sits right outside, ready for the evening pickup service for township visitors who don't want to walk or drive from their accommodation. The fully licensed restaurant has a good wine list and a menu that showcases New Zealand produce and features a number of Asian-influenced dishes. It's more than a fish and chips joint (although it's on the menu), but it does offer takeout pizza (main courses NZ$28–NZ$36).

A good-value option is the **Landing** ★, Main Road (📞 **03/752-0229**), a popular sports bar serving pizza, snacks, and platters.

IN FOX GLACIER
In the same building as Fox Glacier Guiding (and booking office!), **Hobnail Café** ★, 44 SH6, Fox Glacier (www.foxguides.co.nz; 📞 **03/751-0005**), has a busy buzz, everyone working at top speed. It offers to-order breakfast and lunch items such as colcannon patties (bubble and squeak cakes), sausage rolls, and toasted sandwiches as well as filling cabinet food. It's open daily 7:30am to 3pm for breakfast, lunch, drinks, and all-day snacks (NZ$8–NZ$18).

HAAST ★
121km (75 miles) S of Fox Glacier

A series of small settlements, Haast is the big outdoors personified, with hunting, hiking, and fishing the most popular pursuits. The main settlements are **Haast township** and **Haast Junction** on SH6, and **Haast Beach** on Jackson Bay Road. In 1934 Haast Beach was the unlikely landing place for the first commercial flight in New Zealand.

Essentials
GETTING THERE & GETTING AROUND
BY COACH (BUS) InterCity (www.intercity.co.nz; 📞 **09/623-1503**) and **Naked Bus** (https://nakedbus.com) provide daily scheduled services to/from Haast and on to Wanaka and Queenstown.

BY CAR The **World Heritage Highway** (SH6) follows the coast from Whataroa to Franz Josef Glacier and Fox Glacier to Haast and over the Haast Pass on the Haast Highway.

VISITOR INFORMATION
There are **I-SITE offices** and **Department of Conservation** offices in Franz Josef (www.doc.govt.nz and www.glaciercountry.co.nz; 📞 **03/752-0796**) and Queenstown.

SPECIAL EVENTS
Whitebait season opens September 1 through to November 14.

Where to Stay
Offering good value and comfort, **Asure Haast Aspiring Court Motel** ★, Marks Road, Haast township (www.aspiringcourtmotel.com; 📞 **0800/500-703**

in NZ or 03/750-0703), is also close to shops and cafes. It has 13 one- or two-bedroom units (from NZ$98).

Wilderness Lodge Lake Moeraki ★★★ With 28 splendid rooms, the Wilderness Lodge at Lake Moeraki has forged a solid international reputation in ecotourism, offering guests opportunities to explore the surrounding rainforest, lake and river, and coastline in the South West World Heritage Area of Te Wahipounamu. It is an isolated area, but the lodge offers sophisticated and stylish accommodation, superb food, and every possible comfort. It has all been built with concern for the unique surroundings, and nothing jars. The Riverview Premier rooms have private sundecks overlooking river rapids, large bedrooms, and bathrooms with spa baths (Jacuzzis). Rainforest rooms look onto the native rainforest. Garden rooms overlook the Lodge's private gardens. The rates include bed, breakfast, dinner, and two complimentary guided activities on the river and in the rainforest. Other excursions are available to the nearby coast to spot dolphins, penguins, and seals; fishing rods (and guides) can be hired; and there are guided half- and full-day tramps to the upper valleys.

Hwy. 6. 30km (19 miles) north of Haast (driving time more of an indication of distance as roads can be tricky). www.wildernesslodge.co.nz. *C* **03/750-0881.** 28 units. NZ$350–NZ$589 per person per night. Rates includes gourmet dinner, full breakfast, two guided nature trips, and 15% tax. **Amenities:** Restaurant; kayaks; walking trails; wine cellar; Wi-Fi (free).

Where to Eat

If a camo-covered **Land Rover ★★** towing a coffee cart is parked up in Haast township, stop for a coffee and a whitebait sandwich—both the best for miles around. Note that the owner occasionally takes the day off.

In the 1970s Haast was an isolated settlement where daring young men and their helicopters captured live wild deer to establish deer farms and begin the production of farmed venison. The past lives on in the decor of the **Hard Antler Bar & Restaurant ★**, Marks Road, in Haast township (*C* **03/750-0034**), with many sets of antlers fastened to the roof beams. The restaurant has the air of a country pub, but the food is better than that in most such establishments. Lunchers should try the whitebait patties or the fish and chips, and diners keen on a good steak will find it here. It's open for lunch and dinner from 11am to 9pm (main courses NZ$20–NZ$30).

En Route to Wanaka & Queenstown

The highway between Haast and Wanaka is magnificent, moss-covered, and often misty. It follows the course of the Haast River for much of the way. High peaks rise up on either side of the road. The route took 40 years to build and is 563m (1,847 ft.) above sea level. Frequent stops are advised for self-drivers but only if conditions allow. The Department of Conservation has created many walks along the way, including to the wonderful Blue Pools. Traveling nonstop, the trip to Wanaka will take at least 3 hours. If traveling on to Queenstown, allow another 1 to 2 hours.

CHRISTCHURCH & ENVIRONS

F or 150 years pretty Christchurch was known as the Garden City. All that changed in February 2011 following the second destructive earthquake in 5 months. Today, in its post-earthquake garb, Christchurch is less about prettiness and more about rebuilding and reinvention. A sense of excitement and positivity has replaced the angst that swept through 5 years ago. In every way, it is a city on the rise—literally, as architects, designers, and developers combine skills to reshape the past. New cafes, bars, and hotels are opening, and the business district and central city are at work again.

A bit of geography: The region of Canterbury extends from the Southern Alps to the Pacific Ocean, and its physical attractions are many. Within and just beyond Christchurch are rivers, harbors, hills, bays, and mountains. From this new-look city to French-settled Akaroa on Banks Peninsula, and the sea-girt town of Kaikoura, the region is buzzing with new purpose.

CHRISTCHURCH

366km (227 miles) north of Dunedin, 350km (217 miles) south of Picton

ESSENTIALS
GETTING THERE
BY PLANE **Air New Zealand** (www.airnewzealand.co.nz) operates domestic and international flights from/to the city. The economy airline **JetStar** (www.jetstar.com) connects the city with Wellington, Auckland, Queenstown, Melbourne, Sydney, and Brisbane. A growing number of Asian airlines operate direct flights to the city. **Christchurch International Airport** (www.christchurchairport.co.nz) is 10km (6 miles) from Cathedral Square and welcomes over 7 million passengers a year. Terminal 1 has restaurants, shopping, ATMs, currency exchange, help desks, Internet access (with 30-min.-free Wi-Fi), an i-SITE Information Centre, car-rental counters, baggage storage facilities, and postal services.

Transfers from/to the airport include **Super Shuttle** (www.supershuttle.co.nz; © **0800/748-885** in NZ) with a 24-hour daily service (around NZ$24 from the airport to the central city). All taxi

Christchurch

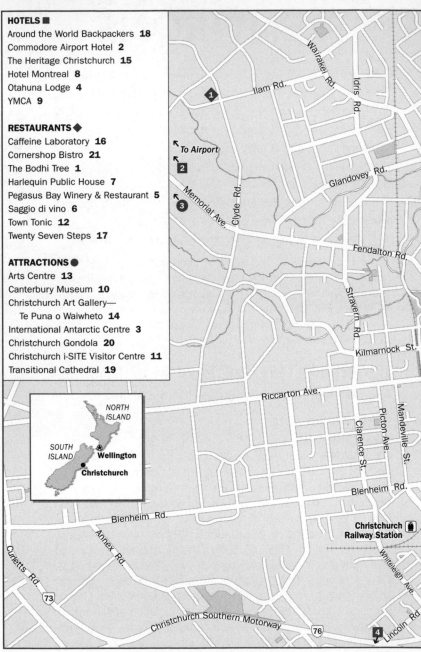

13

Christchurch

CHRISTCHURCH & ENVIRONS

companies work the airport; taxi fares run around $50 to the central city. The airport is also on the bus route: Purple Line (www.metroinfo.co.nz).

BY TRAIN **KiwiScenic Rail** (www.tranzscenic.co.nz; $\mathcal{C}$ **0800/872-467** in NZ, or 03/341-2588) has a daily service to/from Greymouth (**TranzAlpine;** see p. 7317), West Coast, and Glaciers, and a daily **Coastal Pacific** service to/from Picton/Christchurch. A summer-season (Sept–Apr) train journey between Christchurch and Kaikoura includes a special Escape Day Trip (p. 323). There are no passenger trains operating south of Christchurch. The **Christchurch Railway Station** is on Clarence Street, Addington.

BY COACH (BUS) **InterCity** (www.intercity.co.nz; $\mathcal{C}$ **0800/468-372** in NZ, or 64/03/365-1113) and **Naked Bus** (https://nakedbus.com) have scheduled services to/from Christchurch, linking the city to all main centers and tourist attractions in the South Island.

BY CAR From the north, SH1 enters the city through the northwest suburb of Papanui. Drive time is 5 hours from Picton and 2½ hours from Kaikoura. From the south (Dunedin, Oamaru, Timaru, Ashburton), SH1 enters the city at Hornby. Drive time from Dunedin is 5 hours and Oamaru 3 hours.

GETTING AROUND
BY PUBLIC BUS **Metro** (www.metroinfo.co.nz; $\mathcal{C}$ **03/366-8855**) operates bus services in the Christchurch area. Check the website for comprehensive information on fares, timetables, and routes. The **Bus Interchange** near the corner of Lichfield and Colombo streets has a staffed MetroInfo kiosk, undercover waiting rooms, amenities, and a real-time bus tracking system that tells you how many minutes until your bus arrives. The Interchange sells **Metrocards** and **Metrocard All Day Passes.** If visitors plan to be in the city for more than a day and use the bus system to move around the city, purchasing an All-Day Pass makes sense.

Many Metro routes are identified by color, repeated in timetables, bus colors, and stops. For example, if traveling to the airport from the Interchange, you hop on the Purple Line traveling on a purple bus.

BY TRAM The **Christchurch Tram** (www.welcomeaboard.co.nz; $\mathcal{C}$ **03/366-7830**) runs on a short tramway that is not part of the city transport system. It is designed to show off some of the CBD's highlights via vintage tramcars. The 17-stop journey is enhanced by the frank driver commentary. Tickets are NZ$20, valid for 1 full day. The tram runs from 9am to 6pm in summer, 10am to 5pm in winter. Tickets are available in the Tramways office at Cathedral Junction or from the tram driver.

BY TAXI Taxi stands are scattered around the inner city and at all transport terminals. Taxis are unlikely (but not unknown) to respond to being hailed within a quarter-mile of a stand.

BY CAR Limited parking and roadwork will continue for some time as the city rebuilds. It's probably easier to take a bus (see above) or a guided tour.

TWO earthquakes IN 5 MONTHS: A PERSONAL STORY

In September 2010, an early spring brought blossoms and birdcall to Christchurch. At 4:34am on Saturday, September 4, most of the city was asleep. Then: A tremendous noise ripped the dark apart and the world rocked and shook.

I could hear furniture falling, plates crashing. Had a truck hit the house? Had a plane crashed? My husband located a battery radio. The news crackled: We had had a 7.2 earthquake. At daylight the neighborhood gathered, a surreal scene of dozens of people on the street in their nightclothes asking, "Are you alright?" The sun came up and we got on with the day, cleaned up the mess, took the dogs for walks, shared experiences. There was damage in pockets, and when we went to work on Monday some buildings were roped off. Road cones appeared. A few demolition notices were posted. We put it behind us.

Five months later, at 12:51pm, February 22, 2011, a 6.3 earthquake. Lunchtime. A shallow and violent quake. We fell as we tried to run. Buildings fell. People were trapped; some died. The central city, the port town of Lyttelton, Sumner village, New Brighton—all suffered massive destruction. Brick dust, sirens, aftershocks, buildings collapsing, sand and water bursting through bricks and asphalt. We clustered and crouched in the streets as the aftershocks rattled on and on. Cellphone towers were down, water and sewer pipes all ripped up. If we'd taken a car to work it was going to be months before we saw it again. Gadually we patched information together. Safety was the first priority.

Commercial businesses moved to the outskirts of the city, and for months the retail heart of the city was Zoned Red and inaccessible to all apart from those working on the rebuild. Some 1,200 buildings, many of them listed as heritage, had been destroyed. With repairs and the rebuild underway, businesses gradually moved back, a skyline of cranes the new norm.

Now? Well, we have learned to accept a different city. It will never replace the old one, with its Gothic towers and twisted lanes, its boisterous reinvented buildings that saw department stores turned into pizza joints, coat factories into nightclubs. But often we can't even remember what was here, or there. We have moved on from 2011 and mostly come to terms with the gaps in our lives, and our streets. Now it's all about the future and new opportunities.

—Kate Fraser

VISITOR INFORMATION

Go to **www.christchurchnz.com**, the official website for Christchurch & Canterbury Tourism. The **Christchurch & Canterbury i-SITE Visitor Centre** (✆ **0800/423-783** in NZ, or 03/379-9629) is on Rolleston Avenue by the Canterbury Museum/Botanic Gardens. It provides comprehensive information and bookings for tours, transport, and accommodation in Christchurch, Canterbury, and the South Island. The center is open from 8:30am to 5pm.

ORIENTATION

Cathedral Square (aka **The Square**) is the centerpoint of the city, with the main streets laid out in a grid system, surrounded by four main avenues—**Bealey, Moorhouse, Deans,** and **Fitzgerald.** *Note:* At press time, the 19th-century cathedral had yet to be rebuilt or repaired. The transitional cathedral (p. 315) is located on the Madras Street/Hereford Street corner. The **Avon River** curves through Hagley Park and the central business district. The **Port Hills,** south of the city, are a useful landmark when you need to get your bearings.

Key Neighborhoods in Brief

A strange anomaly in Christchurch is the upside-down-ness of what makes a neighborhood desirable. While the leafy suburb **Fendalton,** with its expensive homes, sits close to the airport, the beachside suburb of **New Brighton** struggles (possibly because of the chilly easterly winds that whip off the sea).

Sumner, a sheltered bayside village and a popular destination for recreational cyclists, has busy cafes and a beach that's favored by walkers. Visitors to New Zealand will note that our beaches are open to all, never roped off, and in the case of Sumner, seldom cleared of driftwood and kelp. **Woolston,** once an industrial area, has been reinvented as a shopping destination, with its hub the elegant Edwardiana-influenced shopping and hospitality complex the Tannery. Toward the hills, the old suburb of **Sydenham** is newly popular, especially around the Colombo, a food, entertainment, and shopping complex.

Papanui Road in the northwest of the city and **Riccarton Road** in the northeastern segment are lined with accommodation options—motels mostly, but also B&Bs and apartments.

Lyttelton has been a port town since the first settlers arrived in the 1880s. It was damaged in the 2011 quake, but its quirky streets and heritage houses have a timelessness that embraces the new and retains the old. It is a hot spot for coffee aficionados and those who like to dine well.

SPECIAL EVENTS

Christchurch is the festival capital of New Zealand—no matter when you visit, it's bound to coincide with a festival of some sort. The **World Buskers Festival** ★★★ (www.worldbuskersfestival.com) held mid- to late January, is the largest street performance festival in the Southern Hemisphere. You'll be treated to jazz and comedy shows, as well as acts of juggling, contortionism, and more. The **Christchurch Arts Festival** ★★★ (www.artsfestival.co.nz) is

---

Hagley Park: A Happening Urban Oasis

In 1855 the Canterbury Provincial government set aside 165 hectares within the planned city for a public park.

Hagley Park ★★★ extends from the inner city (Rolleston and Park aves.) to Riccarton, Merivale, and Addington; it is not gated and can be entered at any accessible place. Within its boundaries are a golf course, polo grounds, winter and summer sports fields, tennis courts, a cricket oval, botanic gardens, walking and running tracks, and boatsheds renting out canoes and kayaks. It also has a restaurant (the **Curator's House**), a cafe (**Ilex**), and a children's playground. The **Canterbury Museum,** the **Arts Centre,** and the **Christchurch Art Gallery** are nearby, as are a number of cafes and restaurant/bars.

staged every 2 years (July–Aug) as a showcase for local and international talent. The next one will be held in 2017.

The **New Zealand Cup & Show Week** ★★★ (www.nzcupandshow. co.nz), the second week of November, is a mixed bag of celebratory events, from Canterbury's anniversary day to racing events, fashion shows, and a rollout of the best of the country's agriculture and pastoral farming industry, the **Canterbury Agricultural and Pastoral (A&P) Show** (www.theshow. co.nz), where the farming community brings its best to town. This ranges from dressage and show jumping to wood chopping and sheep shearing to a grand parade of prize-winning animals, and tent after tent of award-winning wines, oils, cakes, jam, along with the fun of fair stalls and sideshows. At the same time, the horse-racing fraternity arrives in Christchurch for the New Zealand Cup national trotting cup and race day with a gold cup for thoroughbreds (gallops). Tickets for race meetings, the A&P Show, and other promoted events are available from the website.

[FastFACTS]

Banks/ATMS You'll have no trouble finding banks or ATMs in Christchurch, including several branches of the **Bank of New Zealand** (www.bnz.co.nz) and **WestPac** (www.westpac.co.nz); check websites for locations. Note that New Zealand is a heavy user of EFTPOS (Electronic Funds Transfer at point of sale), and even small businesses offer the service.

Currency Exchange The best place for currency exchange currently is at Christchurch Airport, where six Travelex stores provide service.

Emergency For ambulance, fire, police, call toll-free ℂ **111.** Christchurch Police (nonemergency calls): ℂ **03/363-7400.**

Hospital The public hospital **Christchurch Hospital** is at Oxford Terrace and Riccarton Avenue (ℂ **03/364-0640**). **24 Hour Surgery** (private) is always available for medical care (corner of Colombo St. and Bealey Ave.; www.24hoursurgery.co.nz; ℂ **03/365-7777**).

Exploring Christchurch

Arts Centre ★★ An important cluster of Victorian Gothic-style buildings, holding, you guessed it, arts organizations, the Arts Centre is being restored to its former glory after considerable earthquake damage. Contributions towards the millions of dollars required for the work have flowed in from admirers all over the world. Its street market might take a year or two to return, but other areas have re-opened (check the website).

Bounded by Worcester Blvd., Rolleston Ave., Hereford St., and Montreal St. www. artscentre.org.nz. ℂ **03/363-2836.**

Canterbury Museum ★★ The Canterbury Museum has something for everyone, but particularly kids, with a Discovery Centre (and Discovery Club for ages 3–13) where predator spiders and other creepy-crawlies can be viewed in glass-topped drawers. Its Antarctic display offers a compelling history of Antarctic exploration and so makes an excellent corollary to a visit to the International Antarctic Centre (near the airport). Among its crowd-pleasers are a re-creation of a Victorian street, scenes depicting Maori life before European settlement and the Special Exhibitions Hall, where changing and often controversial exhibitions (like one on T-shirts and a Whole House Re-Use event) are housed. It has a museum shop and cafe (daily 9am–4:30pm).

Rolleston Ave. www.canterburymuseum.com. ℂ **03/366-5000.** Admission free but donations requested (fees may be charged for special events). Free guided tours Tues–Thurs 3:30–4:30pm (meet in museum foyer). Daily 9am–5pm (till 5:30pm Oct–March).

Christchurch Art Gallery Te Puna o Waiwhetu ★★
Curving glass facades, spectacular outdoor sculpture, and one of the largest permanent collections in New Zealand establish the gallery's importance on the larger cultural scene. The collection of more than 5,500 paintings, sculptures, prints, drawings, and crafts emphasizes work from the Canterbury region, but the gallery also hosts regular touring international and national shows.

Worcester Blvd. and Montreal St. www.christchurchartgallery.org.nz. ℂ **03/941-7300.** Free admission (fees may be charged for special exhibitions). Daily 9:30am–5pm.

Christchurch Botanic Gardens ★★
The turquoise-and-yellow Peacock Fountain by the main entrance on Rolleston Avenue makes a colorful splash, heralding the beauty of the 23 hectares (57 acres) of gardens, with one of the finest collections of exotic and local plants in the country, including heritage roses, a tropical conservatory, and an herb garden. Guided tours in an all-weather electric vehicle are offered by Caterpillar Gardens Tour (pickup by entrance gate or Visitor Centre; NZ$20 adult and NZ$9 children). A map of the gardens with suggested walking tracks is available from the Visitor Centre.

6 Rolleston Ave. www.ccc.govt.nz. ℂ **03/941-8999.** Free admission. Botanic Gardens open daily 7am–6:30pm. Ilex cafe open daily 8:30am: 5:30pm.

Christchurch Gondola ★
The gondola (or cable car) climbs 862 horizontal meters (2,828 ft.) from the Heathcote Valley to the terminal at the top of Mount Cavendish Walk. You're outside and walking on the edge of an extinct crater rim with views across the Canterbury Plains to the Southern Alps. The terminal has a "Time Tunnel Heritage" show and the Red Rock Café.

10 Bridle Path Rd. www.gondola.co.nz. ℂ **03/384-0310.** Admission NZ$26 adults; NZ$12 children 5–15; NZ$60 families. A return shuttle operates on the hour from i-Site Rolleston Ave (NZ$10 adults, $5 children). Daily 10am–5pm.

International Antarctic Centre ★★
If you've ever wanted to romp with penguins, stroke a leopard seal, climb aboard a snowmobile, explore a snow cave, and feel the icy wind chills of Antarctica, this is probably as close as you'll ever get. It takes more of a geographic/natural history approach than the Canterbury Museum's Antarctic exhibition, and seeing the one in junction will give you a healthy appreciation for life on the ice. The **Antarctic**

Hagglund Ride is 15-minute experience that promises an insight into the planning of Antarctic journeys, but it's a bigger hit with kids than adults.

Orchard Rd., adjacent to the Christchurch International Airport. www.iceberg.co.nz. ℂ **0508/736-4846** in NZ, or 03/353-7798. All-day pass with unlimited Hagglund Rides and entry to 4D Extreme Theatre NZ$59 adults, NZ$29 children 5–15, NZ$149 families. The complimentary Penguin Express Shuttle leaves i-Site on the hour 9am–4pm (from 10am Apr–Sept), and returns on the half-hour 9:30am–4:30pm. Daily 9am–5:30pm year-round.

Orana Wildlife Park ★   Set on 80 attractively laid-out hectares (198 acres), this park is New Zealand's largest wildlife reserve, with the emphasis on a natural environment (so few fences and cages). The park hosts cheetahs, lions, rhino, giraffe, monkeys, and meerkats. The most popular activity for visitors? Helping to feed the giraffes!

743 McLeans Island Rd. www.oranawildlifepark.co.nz. ℂ **03/359-7109.** Admission NZ$35 adults age 15 and up, NZ$9.50 children 5–14, f20-min. drive from central city and well signposted from the airport. Free parking. Daily 10am–5pm.

Transitional Cathedral ★★★   Christchurch's iconic Anglican Cathedral was severely damaged in the 2011 earthquake, and a question mark hangs over its future. A Transitional Cathedral was opened in 2013 on Hereford Street/Latimer Square after Japanese architect Shigeru Ban gifted his time and design. Ban's so-called "Cardboard Cathedral" makes use of varied construction materials, from cardboard tubes to timber beams, structural steel, and concrete. It also incorporates a unique "rose window" that features images from the original cathedral's rose window.

T234 Hereford St. www.cardboardcathedral.org.nz. ℂ **03/366-0046.** Daily 8:30am–5pm.

Willowbank Wildlife Reserve ★   The wide area of waterways, islands and trees here are home to wallabies, otters, an alpine aviary with kea, deer, and a number of heritage farm animals including a Clydesdale and kunekune pigs. Kiwis can be seen in the always-nighttime nocturnal house. On a different note, the reserve offers the Ko Tane Maori cultural experience: a performance by a local kapa haka group and a *hangi* meal. The best deal is the combination entry, including the guided Kiwi Experience tour and Ko Tane experience with meal.

60 Hussey Rd. www.willowbank.co.nz or www.kotane.co.nz. ℂ **03/359-6226.** Wildlife Reserve only: NZ$28 adult, NZ$11 children 5–14, free children 4 and under; Ko Tane, *hangi* meal, reserve entry & guided Kiwi tour: NZ$165 adult, NZ$80 children, free children 4 and under. Daily 9:30am–7pm summer (last entry 6pm); 9:30am–5pm winter. Guided tour 4.30pm; Ko Tane Cultural Performance check-in time 5:15pm.

THE WINERIES

Home to more than 80 wineries, the Canterbury region is now the fourth-largest winemaking area in the country. The combination of long hours of sunshine; stony, free-draining soils; low rainfall; extended autumns; and cool winters produces grapes with complex and developed flavors. The region is well suited to the production of red wines such as cabernet, merlot, and pinot noir. The main growing areas are Waipara, Christchurch, Burnham, and Banks Peninsula.

For details on the **Waipara Wine & Food Festival,** held in late March annually, visit www.waiparawineandfood.co.nz or call ℂ **0800/166-071** in New Zealand.

Wine Tours & Trails

○ **Discovery Travel Ltd.** Discovery offers customized tours of the Waipara region for 2 to 250 wine enthusiasts with tastings at four wineries and a vineyard lunch. Depending on availability, the wineries may include Pegasus Bay, Waipara Hills, Greystone, Waipara Springs, Black Estate, and Terrace Edge (www.discoverytravel.co.nz; ℂ **0800/372-879** in NZ and 03/357-8262; prices vary depending on numbers, transport used, and participating wineries).

○ **Canterbury Leisure Tours** Canterbury offers tours to the Waipara wine region with four wineries and a platter lunch at one vineyard restaurant. Comfortable transport, knowledgeable guides, and groups of no more than 10 are hallmarks of this experience (www.leisuretours.co.nz; ℂ **0800/484-485** in NZ, and 03/384-0996; NZ$130 per person).

○ **Canterbury Food & Wine Trails** The network of wineries and vineyards in the wider Canterbury region, including those on Christchurch's doorstep of Mid Canterbury, Banks Peninsula, and Selwyn can be viewed/downloaded on www.canterburyfoodandwinetrails.co.nz. They include **Lone Goat** (608 Burnham Rd.) and **Rossendale Wines** (122 Old Tai Tapu Rd.).

Outdoor Pursuits

BIKING Christchurch has a reputation as a cyclist's paradise thanks to its overall flat terrain. Bike lanes have been marked off in several parts of the city, and parking lots provide bike racks. For rentals, contact **City Cycle Hire** (www.cyclehire-tours.co.nz; ℂ **0800/343-848** in NZ, or 03/339-4020), which will deliver bikes directly to your accommodations. It has road and mountain bikes plus tandems, and all are supplied with locks and helmets. Half-day, 1-day, and long-term rentals are available.

BOATING **Punting** is a fun activity, especially since someone else is doing all the work. You'll spot the young men from **Punting on the Avon** in straw hats pushing their way up the Avon River round the Oxford Terrace and Worcester Boulevard. You can reserve a ride at the visitor center (www.welcomeaboard.co.nz; ℂ **03/366-0337;** NZ$25 adults, NZ$12 children; daily from 9am). If canoeing is your thing, rent from **Antigua Boatsheds** (2 Cambridge Terrace; http://boatsheds.co.nz; ℂ **03/366-6768**) for NZ$12 per hour. It opens at 9am; the last boats go out at 5pm.

MOUNTAIN BIKING The Port Hills are a favorite place for mountain biking. The **Mountain Bike Adventure Co.** (ℂ **0800/424-534** in NZ) makes it possible to take the Christchurch Gondola to the top and then bike down one of the hill tracks. Mountain-biking reservations can be made at the visitor center; day packages or off-road bike rental from NZ$70.

Tours

If you are traveling without a car, **Canterbury Leisure Tours** ★★ (www. leisuretours.co.nz; ℭ **0800/484-485** in NZ) can get you to the area's top sights, including Willowbank Wildlife Reserve, the International Antarctic Centre, Christchurch Tram, the Gondola, and Lyttelton. Prices vary by what you include in the itinerary. **The Big Five Tour** (NZ$210 per person) offers a set tour of Willowbank and the Antarctic Centre, rides the Christchurch Tram, takes a Lyttelton Harbor excursion with Christchurch Wildlife Cruises, and rides on the Christchurch Gondola.

For a look at the quake and its aftermath, ride the **Red Bus** (www.redbus. co.nz) on its 1.5-hour **Rebuild Tour** ★★, with the before, during, and post-earthquake narrative fully covered by driver or guide commentary. Tours are offered daily from 11:30am. Bookings, tickets, and departure from i-SITE, by the Canterbury Museum on Rolleston Avenue (NZ$29 adults and NZ$15 children).

Hassle-free Tours ★★ (www.hasslefreetours.co.nz; ℭ **0800/427-753** in NZ) delivers on the promise of its name with a 3.5-hour Discover Christchurch Tour in and around the city (NZ$69 adults, NZ$35 children); or a 1-hour tour (NZ$35 adults, NZ$19 children) covering the basics in the central city. Tickets, bookings, and departure from i-SITE by Canterbury Museum Rolleston Avenue, daily from 10am.

The **TranzAlpine** ★★★ is rated as one of the five most spectacular train journeys in the world. The train travels from the east coast, over the Canterbury Plains and through the heart of the Southern Alps to the West Coast. It's a super-easy way to see a lot in a day although there is only a 1-hour stop in Greymouth before the return trip departs (or see p. 296 for a scenic return flight option). The train leaves from Christchurch's main railway station at 1 Clarence St., Addington. Food is available in the buffet car. For reservations contact **KiwiRail Scenic Journeys** (www.kiwirailscenic.co.nz; ℭ **0800/872-467** in NZ).

Where to Stay

EXPENSIVE

Hotel Montreal ★★★ The theme of this stylish boutique hotel (25 suites and a penthouse suite) is polo, reflecting the owning family's involvement in the sport. But don't come expecting saddle chairs and paintings of horses: The decor is more for the "horsey set," with lots of leather, velvets and tony neutral colors (the contemporary art and comfy furniture throughout is so outstanding that guests often inquire about purchasing). The hotel has a swank bar and restaurant (cocktails and tapas anyone?), courtyard with pizza oven, and a croquet green. All is possible for this crack staff, and inquiries are welcomed by the front desk.

363 Montreal St. http://hotelmontreal.co.nz. ℭ **03/943-8547.** 26 units. NZ$450–NZ$1,600 suite. **Amenities:** Restaurant; bar; croquet green; in-room iPads; fitness center; Wi-Fi (free).

Otahuna Lodge ★★★ A mansion, no less, nestled into gentle green hills, with a kitchen garden and orchard, a kitchen with chef Jimmy McIntyre at the helm, and all the fittings and furbelows that might befit the lifestyle of Canterbury's landed gentry. Owned and hosted by Hall Cannon and Miles Refo, this Relais & Chateaux property successfully combines the style of the Edwardian era with the amenities of today. It's wrapped in comfort and luxuries. Yes, it's pricy, but rates include bed-and-breakfast and a five-course seasonal degustation dinner. The hotel is happy to arrange fly-fishing, golfing, horseback riding, and heli-touring excursions.

Rhodes Rd., Tai Tapu, Christchurch. www.otahuna.co.nz. ℂ **03/329-6333.** 7 units. NZ$2,300–NZ$12,760 suite. Rates include breakfast and five-course degustation dinner. **Amenities:** Restaurant; bar; bikes; concierge; gym; outdoor pool; hard-surface tennis court; walking & biking trails; wine cellar; Wi-Fi (free).

MODERATE

Commodore Airport Hotel ★★ A sizable property with 156 rooms, the Commodore has been owned and run by the Patterson family since 1971. The great service, staff, and ambience are as far removed from the standard airport hotel experience as it gets. For starters, the property is not "at" the airport, but sited on Memorial Avenue, a route from the CBD to the airport via the leafy suburb of Fendalton, which also explains the lush sprawl of the hotel's 7-acre grounds. A five-star property, it's a winning combo of charm, outstanding staff (no request is too difficult for this competent team), and full-service facilities.

449 Memorial Ave., Burnside, Christchurch. www.commodorehotel.co.nz. ℂ**0508/266-663** in NZ, or 03/358-8129. 156 units. NZ$230–NZ$500 double. Free parking on-site. **Amenities:** Restaurant; bar; babysitting; bike rental; business center; dry cleaning; fitness center; heated indoor pool; complimentary shuttle transfer to/from airport; Wi-Fi (free).

The Heritage Christchurch ★★ Offering charm and character in what was originally the Old Government Building (ca. 1913), the Heritage has huge spaces, scads of elegant details (tessellated entry tiles, brass railings, French doors, Scarlett O'Hara staircase), and a central-city site. The accommodation comprises good-size, fully self-contained one-, two-, and three-bedroom suites, each with kitchen (including dishwasher) and living area.

28–30 Cathedral Sq., Christchurch. www.heritagehotels.co.nz. ℂ **0800/936-936** in NZ. 35 units. From NZ$240. **Amenities:** Breakfast available in ground-floor restaurant; babysitting; dry cleaning; gym; indoor pool; tour desk; Wi-Fi (free; $10/day for extra 1GB).

INEXPENSIVE

Around The World Backpackers ★★ ATW, as it's known to thousands of travelers, is not fancy, but the shared facilities are pristine, and the atmosphere is welcoming. Accommodation includes four-bed dorms, twin rooms, and double rooms.

314 Barbadoes St. www.aroundtheworld.co.nz. ℂ **03/365-4363.** 36 units. NZ$38–NZ$77. Free off-street parking. **Amenities:** BBQ grill; Wi-Fi (free).

YMCA ★★ Situated in an enviable site opposite the Botanic Gardens, close to the Canterbury Museum and Arts Centre, this is much sought-after accommodation, with facilities running the gamut from shared dorm rooms to en-suite rooms to a self-contained apartment. All are spotless. A restaurant/bar and coffeehouse share the building, and there is a communal kitchen.

12 Hereford St., Christchurch. www.ymcachch.org.nz. © **0508/962-224** in NZ, or 03/366-0689. 104 units. NZ$33–NZD$220. Free off-street parking. **Amenities:** Restaurant; cafe; self-catering kitchen; 24-hr. reception; Wi-Fi.

Where to Eat

EXPENSIVE

Pegasus Bay Winery ★★★ EUROPEAN   This lunch-only restaurant, set in an internationally recognized winery, offers a foodie experience as opulent and fulfilling as any found after the sun sets. Dishes are created around the wine list (each dish is presented with a wine suggestion) and are quite creative, ranging from cured fish topped with wasabi sorbet, to goat cheese "cigars" to Muscovy duck for two. The menu is seriously seasonal—with herbs and veggies from the on-site garden—and so changes regularly.

Stockgrove Rd., Waipara (35 min. north of Christchurch). www.pegasusbay.com. © **64/03/314-6869.** Main courses NZ$36–NZD$44. Thurs–Mon noon–4pm.

Saggio di Vino ★★★ EUROPEAN   With its extensive wine list and menu created from the best ingredients owner Lisa Scholz can source—everything from wild rabbit to venison to the finest cheeses of the region   Saggio has been an enduring success. Located in the Carlton Butchery Building, it's a good special occasion choice, with a well-curated tasting menu.

179 Victoria St., Christchurch. www.saggiodivino.co.nz. © **03/379-4006.** Main courses NZ$40–NZD$62. Daily 5pm till late.

MODERATE/INEXPENSIVE

The Bodhi Tree ★★ BURMESE   Owned by its Burmese chef and his New Zealand wife, this small establishment has been a favorite since it opened in 2001. The small-plates menu is designed to sample and share. The most popular items on the menu (deservedly so) are the refreshing and complex salads, particularly the tea salad and the shredded papaya salad. Bodhi Tree has many vegetarian options and a small wine list, but is also licensed as BYO.

399 Ilam Rd. www.thebodhitree.co.nz. © **03/377-6808.** Main courses NZ$20–NZ$30. Tues–Sat 6–10pm.

Caffeine Laboratory ★★★ INTERNATIONAL   Sure it's small, but this little eatery packs a punch, thanks to fantastic coffee and food that's big on flavor and innovation (such as fish tacos slathered in saffron-infused mayo with cucumber cress and radish salad, house-smoked salmon, and doughnuts filled with raspberry jam and cardamom mascarpone!). Burgers come meatful and meat-less but you don't give up on taste with the latter, particularly the

Bondie burger, a big patty of quinoa and almond, topped with a grilled mushroom, haloumi, mung bean, and beetroot with sriracha mayo on a brioche bun. 1 New Regent St., www.caffeinelab.co.nz. © **03/350-3600.** Burgers $14; dinner main courses NZ$24–NZ$26. Mon–Fri 7:30am–9pm.

Cornershop Bistro ★ REGIONAL   This neighborhood restaurant in the seaside suburb of Sumner draws a citywide clientele. In 2015 chef/owner Rod Cross and his wife, Kathryn, marked 11 years in business and, as published reviews constantly note, they still come up with fresh ideas. Cross is a chef who embraces seasonality, and his menu celebrates special arrivals—asparagus! whitebait! autumn lamb! spring lamb!—as well as a rollout of locally grown and reared produce. Friday to Sunday sees the brunch crowd enjoying such dishes as coddled egg with creamed potatoes and smoked fish. 32 Nayland St., Sumner. www.cornershopbistro.co.nz. © **03/326-6720.** Main courses NZ$28–NZD$36. Wed–Sun 5:30pm–late; Fri–Sun brunch 10am–3pm.

Harlequin Public House ★★★ BISTRO   The name may suggest ye olde pub days, and it's located in a wooden heritage building that might have been a public house before living memory, but HPH is a slicker operation than any public house we ever imagined. The restaurant offers a serious and wholly seasonal approach to stylish food, with inventive dishes such as ox-tongue Caesar, steak and oyster tartare, and duck crackling. 32 Salisbury St. www.hphchch.com. © **03/377-866.** Dinner main courses NZ$28–NZD$36; lunch main courses NZ$22–NZD$26. Daily noon–10pm.

Town Tonic ★ CONTEMPORARY   This unassuming cafe/bar/restaurant has a simple menu, but the food shines—it's fresh, and seasonal. Service slips occasionally, but the kitchen has talent. It's open for breakfast, lunch, and dinner. Look for eggs, French toast, and avocado many ways at breakfast (smashed, with bacon, in Mexican salad); intriguing lunch mains like a crunchy chicken parfait (crispy chicken skin, toast, almonds, seeds, and red-wine-poached prunes); and such dinner dishes as venison tartare and salmon and cream-cheese fingers. Town Tonic also has an interesting wine list. 335 Lincoln Rd., Addington, Christchurch. www.towntonic.co.nz. © **03/338-1150.** Lunch main courses NZ$18–NZD$23; dinner main courses NZ$28–NZD$44. Mon–Fri 7:30am–late; Sat 8:30am–late; Sun 8:30am–3:30pm.

Twenty Seven Steps ★★ RUSTIC EUROPEAN   Twenty Seven Steps makes much of its site on New Regent Street, known for its quirky, charming Spanish-Mission architecture. Here, four adjoining first-floor spaces have been opened up, renovated, and enhanced to spectacular result. The glorious arched windows are not about the views but the space within: elegant in a non-fussy simplicity. The Seven Steps menu is in the same vein. Look for generous dishes such as a chargrilled Canterbury steak crusted with beef bone marrow or free-range poussin with faro, vegetables, and lemon cream. Twenty Seven Steps also has an intriguing cocktail menu, good wines, and craft beers. 16 New Regent St., Inner Christchurch. www.twentysevensteps.co.nz. © **03/366-2727.** Main courses $29–$40. Tues–Sat 5pm–midnight.

Nightlife & Entertainment

An arts-and-entertainment precinct featuring the new **Christchurch Music Centre** and the restored **Isaac Theatre Royal** (glowing like a CBD jewel) will soon be joined by the **Christchurch Town Hall,** the city's vaunted performing-arts center, which began its post-quake restoration journey in 2015 bringing joy to concert singers and orchestras that value its world-recognized acoustics.

BARS

Dux Live, 363 Lincoln Rd. (www.duxlive.co.nz; © **03/366-6919**), has had a reputation for hospo since its first appearance in Christchurch. The good times continue with exceptional beer and an outstanding gig list. **The Last Word,** 31 New Regent St. (www.lastword.co.nz; © **03/928-2831**), is a whisky-cum-cocktail lounge in a small space—but it works. It's charismatic, cozy and cute, and has an outstanding list of whiskies and a sprinkling of top-drawer wines.

Opened to great acclaim immediately post-quakes as a bar-in-a-bus with some tented shelter, **Smash Palace,** 172 High St. (http://thesmashpalace. co.nz; © **03/366-5369**), now has a permanent site, but the bus, et al., remain, along with house beer on tap, books to browse, burgers made from scratch, and motorbike night (Thurs). Mad and marvelous.

Part of the Cassels & Sons brewing business on the site of The Tannery complex, **The Brewery,** 3 Garlands Rd., Woolston (http://casselsbrewery. co.nz; © **03/389-5359**), has long been a pioneer in the brewing of big, bold beers. The brewpub has a huge following of craft-beer enthusiasts.

Pomeroys Old Brewery Inn, 292 Kilmore St. (http://pomspub.co.nz; © **03/365-1523**), is a family-owned and -operated pub in the Wards Brewery, with good food, its own craft beer, and a great atmosphere.

SIDE TRIPS FROM CHRISTCHURCH

Akaroa ★★★

After French whaler Jean Francois Langlois took word of New Zealand's rich land and forests back to France, a handful of Gallic settlers set sail in 1840 to colonize Akaroa Harbour. They were too late, however—the British had beaten them to it with the signing of the Treaty of Waitangi. The colonization plan was abandoned, but the settlers stayed on. Today they are remembered in small settlements around Akaroa: Le Bons Bay, Duvauchelle, and French Farm. Other than its street names, Akaroa is not particularly French in style, but it is a pretty town and makes a fun day trip from Christchurch.

ESSENTIALS

GETTING THERE By Car From Christchurch, take the SH75. Allow 1½ hours' drive time.

By Coach Daily coach/shuttle transport is available. Book online or purchase tickets at i-Site Rolleston Avenue (also the pickup place). **Akaroa**

French Connection (www.akaroabus.co.nz; 🕐 **0800/800-575** in NZ, or 03/366-4556) has daily departures at 9am from i-Site Christchurch, with a 4pm return from Akaroa (NZ$45 round-trip). The **Akaroa Shuttle** (www. akaroashuttle.co.nz; 🕐 **0800/500-929**) has daily departures from Christchurch at 8:45am, with a return departure time of 3:45pm (NZ$50 adults, NZ$40 children). Both companies also offer scenic tours; reservations essential.

VISITOR INFORMATION The **Akaroa i-Site Visitor Centre** (www. akaroa.com; 🕐 **03/304-8600**), 120 Rue Jolie, opens daily at 9am.

EXPLORING AKAROA

The Town

Pick up the brochure for the self-guided **Akaroa & Bays Art Trail** ★, which leads to the homes and studios of 18 local artists and craftspeople. One of the most striking and unusual artist environments is the **Giant's House—Linton** ★★★, 68 Rue Balguerie (www.linton.co.nz; 🕐 **03/304-7501**), where sculptor Josie Martin has surrounded her historic home (B&B loding available) with landscaped gardens and amazing mosaic sculptures. Children love it, and it's bound to be one of your lasting Akaroa memories as well. The garden is open daily noon to 4pm December to March, and 2 to 4pm April through November. Admission is NZ$20 adults, NZ$12 children, and a cafe is on-site.

The Harbor

Pohatu Sea Kayaking ★ (www.pohatu.co.nz; 🕐 **03/304-8552**) offers **guided kayak tours** in the Flea Bay Marine Reserve (from NZ$90 per person). Tour guides are also volunteers working on penguin conservation. Evening tours and 4WD tours/packages are available as well.

Take a 2-hour **scenic harbor cruise** with **Akaroa Harbour Nature Cruises** ★ (www.blackcat.co.nz; 🕐 **0800/436-574** in NZ, or 03/304-7641). *The Cat* takes 90 people and offers great views along the long harbor including ancient volcanic sites (Scenery Nook) and a salmon farm. You'd have to be quite unlucky *not* to see the charming Hector's dolphins. Departs daily from Main Wharf 11am and 1:30pm (from NZ$74 per person).

WHERE TO EAT

Bully Hayes Restaurant & Bar ★, 57 Beach Rd. (www.bullyhayes.co.nz; 🕐 **03/304-7533**), is a lovely waterfront spot with a hearty seafood-centric menu and craft beers. Reservations recommended. It's open daily from 8:30am to late. **L'Escargot Rouge Deli** ★, 67 Beach Rd. (www.lescargotrouge.co.nz; 🕐 **03/304-8774**), opens its doors daily at 8am, offering pastries and breads, juice, and coffee with French bread sandwiches and very Parisian breakfasts.

Kaikoura ★★★

The coastline along the seaside settlement of Kaikoura, 2½ hours from Christchurch, is rugged—the Seaward Kaikoura Mountains crouch almost to the sea in places, and the cliffs are so close that the roadway has to go through short tunnels at a couple of points. Rocky outcrops rear out of the waves, to the

wildlife EXPERIENCES IN KAIKOURA

Whales and other marine mammals are the big drawing card in Kaikoura. Here are some of the best ways to encounter the area's marine animals, including seabirds.

o **Whale Watch Kaikoura ★★★** is an awe-inspiring outing that gives passengers a good chance of having a close encounter with a giant sperm whale and spotting dolphins and seals along the way. An award-winning, locally owned tourism company, Whale Watch is the only operator permitted in this protected marine area. It has excellent guides. Sperm whales cruise and snack about 7 miles offshore, so the likelihood of seeing one has a success rate of 98%! (A partial refund covers the disappointment of a no-show.) There are four 2½-hour tours daily (www.whale-watch.co.nz; 𝄐 **0800/655-121** in NZ, or 03/319-6767; NZ$145 adults and NZ$60 children 3–15;

not suitable for kids 2 and under).

o **Wings Over Whales ★** offers an airborne perspective on whale-watching via a 30-minute flight (NZ$165 adults/$75 children). Success rate is around 90%, and although it lacks the drama of sharing a space of sea with a giant whale, it is a good alternative. If you're short on time, this is probably the best choice (www.whales.co.nz; 𝄐 **0800/226-629** in NZ, or 03/319-6580).

o **Albatross Encounter ★★** is a guided birdwatching cruise with the focus on seabirds, including albatross, mollymawks, gannets, and petrels. They put on quite a circus wheeling and skimming the waves. Great pix! (www.albatrossencounter.co.nz; 𝄐 **0800/733-365** in NZ, or 03/319-6777; NZ$120 adults and NZ$60 children 8–14)

pleasure of the seal colonies that thrive in these fish-rich waters. The marine life is remarkable, with several breeds of whales, dolphins, and seals feeding in the area. Kaikoura is a town that makes the most of its natural attributes and welcomes all-comers during its long tourist season. It was also the first local body authority in the world to achieve Green Globe 21 certification, proving the town's commitment to reducing environmental impacts.

ESSENTIALS

GETTING THERE **By Car** Travel from Christchurch via main North Road Papanui/Belfast SH1 to Kaikoura.

By Coach **InterCity** (www.intercity.co.nz; 𝄐 **03/365-1113**) has two daily return services between Christchurch and Kaikoura. Fares vary, but expect to pay around NZ$15 to NZ$20. **Naked Bus** (https://nakedbus.com) has Christchurch-Kaikoura service; book online or at i-Site.

By Train In summer (Oct–Apr), **KiwiRail** (www.kiwirailscenic.co.nz) offers a special Web-only "Escape" fare between Christchurch and Kaikoura for a day trip that allows 5 hours in Kaikoura. The fares are one-way, and to/

Maurice and Heather Manawatu of **Maori Tours Kaikoura ★★** (www. maoritours.co.nz; ℃ **0800/866-267** in NZ, or 03/319-5567) offer what is quite possibly the finest learning experience of a New Zealand holiday, awarded New Zealand's "Best Cultural Experience" four times. Their half-day tour covers ancient Maori sites, explores native bush, and reveals the traditional Maori uses of plants. Wear walking shoes. The 3- to 4-hour tour (max 10 people) begins at 9am and/or 1:30pm and costs NZ$134 adults, NZ$74 children ages 5 to 15. A real winner.

from trips need to be booked separately online (from NZ$59 adults; NZ$41 children). The train departs Christchurch at 7am and returns at 7pm.

VISITOR INFORMATION   The **Kaikoura i-SITE Visitor Centre** (www. kaikoura.co.nz or www.naturallykaikoura.co.nz; ℃ **03/319-5641**) is located at the south end of the town's main carpark, West End.

WHERE TO EAT

Hislops Wholefoods Café ★, 33 Beach Rd. (℃ **03/319-6971**), has an organic focus, but think fresh salads with organic meat rather than mountains of chickpeas; it's open daily from 9am in summer. **Kaikoura Seafood BBQ Kiosk ★★**, Fyffes Quay (℃ **03/319-6971**), is a busy spot, but service is swift and smiling and the fish is fresh-caught. The mussels are fantastic. The vintage style of the **Pier Hotel,** 1 Avoca St. (www.thepierhotel.co.nz; ℃ **03/433-9691**), draws you in—you might almost expect Mis' Bella-Mae to be in charge. But no, it's staffed by international young'uns working hard to deliver good food, including succulent crayfish. It's open for lunch and dinner.

QUEENSTOWN, WANAKA & FIORDLAND

The South Island's southwestern section has outstanding areas of natural beauty in its lakes and fiords (sounds). For all their lonely majesty, they sit easily with New Zealand's most popular resort city, Queenstown. The town and its upbeat neighbors offer extreme-adventure activities, along with top restaurants, winning wineries, cocktail bars, and casinos.

14

QUEENSTOWN ★★★

404km (250 miles) SW of Franz Josef; 263km (163 miles) SW of Mount Cook; 117km (73 miles) S of Wanaka; 172km (107 miles) NE of Te Anau

What's not to love about a major metropolitan area that's also a summer lake resort, a winter ski resort, and an all-year-round wine and food, eat and drink destination? Queenstown is busy, often crowded, noisy, and colorful, and then—only a mile or so from the bustle of the waterfront—you can be in the hush of a forest or the silence of the tussock lands. One thing is certain: Boredom doesn't get a look in.

Essentials

GETTING THERE & GETTING AROUND

BY PLANE **Queenstown Airport** (www.queenstownairport. co.nz) is well serviced by **Air New Zealand** (www.airnewzealand. co.nz; ℭ **0800/737-000** in NZ) with domestic services to/from Christchurch, Wellington, and Auckland, and to/from Brisbane, Melbourne, and Sydney. **Jetstar** (www.jetstar.com; ℭ **0800/800-995** in NZ) operates flights from Wellington and Auckland, Melbourne, Sydney, the Gold Coast, and Brisbane. **Virgin Australia Airlines** (www.virginaustralia.com; ℭ **0800/670-000** in NZ and **Qantas** (www.qantas.com.au; ℭ **0800/808-767** in NZ) operate frequent scheduled flights to/from Queenstown/Melbourne, Sydney, and Brisbane.

Super Shuttle (www.supershuttle.co.nz; ℭ **0800/748-885** in NZ) offers transport to/from airport/downtown Queenstown; it's a

20-minute ride (NZ$10 per person). **Connectabus** (www.connectabus.com; 🕿 **03/441-4471**) operates scheduled services between the airport, Queenstown, Arrowtown, major attractions, hotels, and shopping centers. The trip to/from the airport and downtown Queenstown is about 25 minutes and costs NZ$12 adults, NZ$5.50 children. **Taxis** are available at the airport; it's a 15-minute taxi drive from the airport to downtown Queenstown (around NZ$30). Several major **rental-car agencies** are located in the airport, including **Avis** (🕿 **03/442-3808**) and **Hertz** 🕿 **0800/654-321** in NZ).

BY COACH (BUS) InterCity (www.intercity.co.nz; 🕿 **64/9/583-5780**) has daily services connecting Queenstown to Christchurch, Dunedin, Fox Glacier, Franz Josef, Invercargill, Milford Sound, Aoraki/Mount Cook, Te Anau, and Wanaka. **Naked Bus** (https://nakedbus.com) operates similar routes.

BY CAR Allow 5 to 6 hours from Christchurch, 3½ hours from Dunedin, 5½ hours from Franz Josef, 2½ hours from Te Anau, 5 hours from Milford Sound, and 2½ hours from Invercargill. Roads affected by weather always have warnings or closures signposted well in advance. Major **rental-car and motor-home agencies** have offices in Queenstown.

BY TAXI Queenstown Blue Bubble Taxis (http://queenstown.bluebubbletaxi.co.nz; 🕿 **0800/788-294** in NZ) has a 24-hour manned call center. Fares from the town center to most accommodations are between NZ$15 and NZ$30.

VISITOR INFORMATION

The website for the official regional tourism organization **Destination Queensland** is www.queenstownnz.co.nz. The **Queenstown i-SITE Visitor Centre,** corner of Shotover and Camp streets (🕿 **03/442-4100**), is open daily from 7am. The **Department of Conservation Information Centre** is at 50 Stanley St. (www.doc.govt.nz; 🕿 **03/442-7935**).

ORIENTATION

Queenstown is a compact lakefront town, with shops, restaurants, and amenities within easy walking distance. It has no public bus system, but the Connectabus (see above) provides excellent all-day service. The central shopping area is bordered by Marine Parade on the lakefront, Camp Street to the north of that, and Shotover Street, which runs into Lake Esplanade. The shopping area at Remarkables Park, close to Queenstown Airport, is open daily and has 700+ parking spaces. Street parking in Queenstown is limited and expensive. Wilson Parking has carparks in Church Street and Stanley Street.

The township of **Arrowtown** is 20km (12 miles) northeast of Queenstown. Quieter and less frenetic than the lakeside resort, Arrowtown offers museums, heritage sites and walkways, cafes, restaurants, and some interesting shopping.

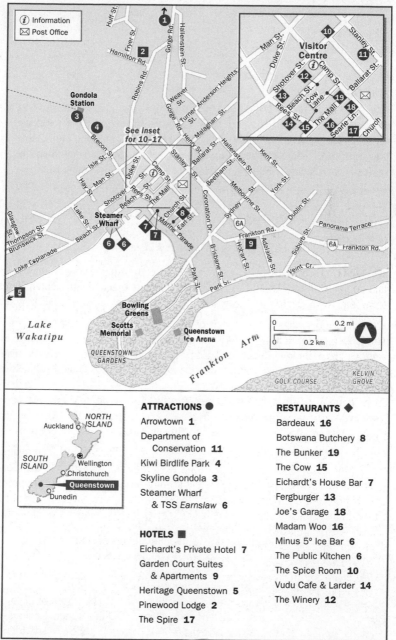

Central Queenstown

(i) Information
⊠ Post Office

Gondola Station

See inset for 10-17

Visitor Centre

Steamer Wharf

Lake Wakatipu

Bowling Greens

Scotts Memorial

Queenstown Ice Arena

QUEENSTOWN GARDENS

Frankton Arm

GOLF COURSE

KELVIN GROVE

0   0.2 mi
0   0.2 km

NORTH ISLAND
Auckland

SOUTH ISLAND
Wellington
Christchurch
Queenstown
Dunedin

ATTRACTIONS ●
Arrowtown **1**
Department of Conservation **11**
Kiwi Birdlife Park **4**
Skyline Gondola **3**
Steamer Wharf & TSS *Earnslaw* **6**

HOTELS ■
Eichardt's Private Hotel **7**
Garden Court Suites & Apartments **9**
Heritage Queenstown **5**
Pinewood Lodge **2**
The Spire **17**

RESTAURANTS ◆
Bardeaux **16**
Botswana Butchery **8**
The Bunker **19**
The Cow **15**
Eichardt's House Bar **7**
Fergburger **13**
Joe's Garage **18**
Madam Woo **16**
Minus 5° Ice Bar **6**
The Public Kitchen **6**
The Spice Room **10**
Vudu Cafe & Larder **14**
The Winery **12**

14

QUEENSTOWN, WANAKA & FIORDLAND | Queenstown

327

[FastFACTS]

Emergencies Ambulance, fire, police: toll-free ℂ **111. Queenstown Police Station:** ℂ **03/441-1600.**

Medical Lakes District Hospital, Frankton: ℂ **03/441-0015.**

Exploring the Area
IN QUEENSTOWN

It's easy to meander the compact center of Queenstown. Have a picnic on the little beach along Lake Wakatipu. Walk the paths in and around the extensive grounds of the **Queenstown Gardens.** If it's Saturday, visit the **Queenstown Arts & Crafts Market** (http://marketplace.net.nz) at Earnslaw Park near Steamer Wharf (9am–4:30pm). Watch the **TSS** *Earnslaw* (www.tssearnslaw. co.nz), one of the last remaining coal-fired passenger-carrying vessels operating in the Southern Hemisphere, ply the lake. The sight of steam and smoke, not to mention the ship's toot-toot, is a lovely connection with old ways.

There is no better place to get the measure of Queenstown than from the heights. The **Skyline Queenstown** gondola ★★, Brecon Street (www.skyline. co.nz; ℂ **03/441-0101**), offers not only an impressive ride up and down what is a very steep site, but the view from the top is all-encompassing. The complex includes a cafe for coffee and a snack, a restaurant for lunch and dinner, a luge (about 1km/half a mile) good for kids and adults, **Stargazing,** an after-dark opportunity, and a small theater complex for Maori cultural performances. A range of ticket options is available that offer one or all options—for example, the Gondola Lunch and Luge Rides includes return ride on the gondola, five luge rides, and lunch at the restaurant for NZ$92 adults, NZ$61 children 5 to 14, and free 4 and under.

The **Kiwi Birdlife Park** ★, Upper Brecon Street (http://kiwibird.co.nz; ℂ **03/442-8059**), is set in parklike grounds near the base of the gondola. In around 40 minutes, visitors get to see birdlife and tuatara close up. It opens at 9am, with daily conservation shows at 11am and 3pm and kiwi feeding sessions at 10am, noon, 1:30pm, and 4:30pm daily. Admission is NZ$43 adults, $22 children, and NZ$98 family pass for 5.

An opportunity to cycle around some of New Zealand's most photographed scenery comes with the added advantage of an easy ride when **ChargeAbout Queenstown** (www.chargeabout.co.nz; ℂ **0800/324-536** in NZ) gets involved. We're talking electric mountain bikes! ChargeAbout bikes are mountain bikes with a small electric motor that kicks when you need some extra oomph (perhaps going uphill). Take a water taxi from Queenstown across to ChargeAbout at the Hilton on the Kelvin Heights Peninsula, then ride your eBike to the Gibbstown Valley wineries, or take the other road to Jacks Point. From Queenstown, pick up a rental eBike from Alta at 8 Duke Street. Recharge locations are established throughout the 110km of cycle trails. Most riders will get 40 to 60km (25–31 miles) before a recharge is needed (half-day rental NZ$79; full day NZ$119).

KID magnets

Many Queenstown adventures have high minimum-age requirements, but these fun, family-friendly activities don't.

o **Family Adventures ★★★** Scenic four-wheel-drive excursion into Skipper's Canyon allow visitors to see old mining relics and jetboats in action, before embarking on a 1½-hour gentle rafting tour down the safest section of the Shotover River. Good for people looking for a scenic river experience, for newbies to rafting, and for children under 13 (4 Brecon St.; www.familyadventures.co.nz; ℃ **03/442-8836;** from NZ$179 adults and NZ$125 children 3–16; not available for kids 2 and under).

o **Caddyshack City Mini Golf ★** This indoor miniature-golf experience is popular with families (25 Brecon St.; ℃ **03/442-6642;** daily 10am–8pm; NZ$20 adults, NZ$13 children 5–14; not suitable for children under 4).

o **Kiwi Birdlife Park ★** This is a good introduction to conservation and New Zealand birdlife. The **Skyline Luge ★★★** is great fun for all ages, as is Real Journey's **Walter Peak Farm**

Excursion ★★ (see "Lake Cruises," below), which includes a steamship cruise and a farmyard tour, where children can help feed the animals. The **Underwater Observatory** will also amuse the kids. Fish are fed each day (a coin-operated fishfeed machine for participating visitors; Main Pier; http://kiwibird.co.nz; ℃ **03/442-8538;** NZ$8 adults, NZ$3 children, and NZ$13 for a family pass).

o **The Queenstown Ice Arena ★★** Located in the Queenstown Gardens, the rink is open year round; skate rental included in the entry price. A plus: The cafe has good food and very good coffee (www.queenstownicearena.co.nz; ℃ **03/441-8000;** daily 10am–5pm; Fri Night Lights Session 5:30–9:30pm; NZ$19 adults, NZ$15 children, NZ$7.50 4 and under).

o **ChargeAbout** Electric mountain bikes (eBikes) can be rented for children 10 and over. Children's half bikes and toddler trailers are available to attach to adults' eBike (ChargeAbout Queenstown; www.chargeabout.co.nz; ℃ **0800/324-536** in NZ).

IN NEARBY ARROWTOWN

For an enjoyable outing and a less hectic pace, visit Arrowtown, 20km (12 miles) to the northeast of Queenstown, on the banks of the Arrow River. Gold was discovered here in 1862, and the township retains a number of heritage sites and buildings. The **Lakes District Museum,** 49 Buckingham St. (www.museumqueenstown.com; ℃ **03/442-1824**), an interesting but not particularly well-curated selection of exhibits, includes a blacksmith forge (the smithy), a schoolroom, Victorian-era medical items, and detailed descriptions of gold-mining methods. It's open daily from 8:30am (NZ$8 per person).

The restored **Chinese Camp ★**, on Bush Creek at the northern end of town, demonstrates the hard and lonely lives of the Chinese migrants who arrived on the Arrow goldfield to try their luck. The tiny rooms of Ah Lum's General

Store (and informal bank if the barred windows are any indication) and the very humble dwellings tucked under rocky outcrops are quite moving when you consider that it was not that long ago that Arrowtown's Chinese community lived and worked here. The first "dwelling" on the path into the settlement is an open-fronted long-drop (toilet), which may be interesting to some but of doubtful authenticity to others.

An eclectic bunch of shops on **Buckingham Street** offers the expected outdoor clothing as well as cute shops down tiny alleyways. **Blue Moon Rummage** (http://bluemoonrummage.co.nz) stocks clothing, handmade gifts (knitted toys, for example), pottery, witty cards, furnishings, and even vintage skis. A few steps along, **Ogle** (www.myogle.co.nz) has clever books and cards, satchels, hip flasks, games, and more.

Where to Stay in Arrowtown

Arrowtown Lodge ★, 7 Anglesea St., Arrowtown (www.arrowtownlodge. co.nz; © **0800/258-802** in NZ, or 03/442-1101; NZ$195–NZ$395), has individual semi-detached cottages that replicate something of Arrowtown's goldrush heritage. Owners Richard and Sally Hoskin revamped the lodge for the 2016 summer season, adding outdoor barbecues and outdoor firepits. It's a 2-minute walk to cafes and shops.

Millbrook Resort ★★★ This award-winning resort is so generously sized it's almost a village. Three minutes from Arrowtown and 20 minutes from Queenstown, the hotel offers a range of lodging options, from studio, one-, and two-bedroom suites to good-value two, three-, and four-bedroom self-contained cottages (ideal for families or friends traveling together) to luxurious fairway homes. Numerous on-site dining options—the **Clubhouse ★★** (breakfast), the casual **Hole in One Café ★★** (breakfast, lunch, and dinner), the **Millhouse Restaurant ★★★** (dinner serving international cuisine incorporating local produce), and **Kobe Cuisine ★★** (dinner serving Japanese cuisine)—means you never have to leave the property to eat out. You'll find good walks around and alongside the extensive grounds, not to mention one of the best championship golf courses in the country. Even non-golfers are wowed by the handsome imaginative landscaping.

Malaghans Rd., Arrowtown. www.millbrook.co.nz. © **0800/800-604** in NZ, or 03/441-7000. 160 units. NZ$210–NZ$493 suite. NZ$505–NZ$680 cottage. From NZ$1,230 fairway home. Seasonal rates apply; packages available. **Amenities:** 4 restaurants; bar; babysitting; bike rentals; children's programs; 27-hole golf course and driving and putting greens; gym/fitness center; outdoor hot pools; lap pool; room service; spa; tennis courts; Wi-Fi (free).

Where to Eat in Arrowtown

Amisfield Winery & Bistro ★★★ CONTEMPORARY NEW ZEALAND With its scenic site by Lake Hayes, Amisfield can claim to be both an Arrowtown and a Queenstown restaurant. The menu changes daily according to what is in season and/or available. Some recommendations: any asparagus dish, seared salmon, beef tartare, and southern hapuka with clams and karengo, or just go with the sharing-style "Trust The Chef" menu. The wine list is magnificent, and the sommelier's advice is trustworthy. You may remember hearing about Amisfield, because it was visited by the Prince and Princess of Wales in 2014. Kate quashed pregnancy rumors by chugging some of the wines here (okay, she didn't chug, but she drank enough to make people stop speculating about her fertility).

10 Lake Hayes Rd. www.amisfield.co.nz. (C) **03/442-0556.** A la carte main courses NZ$18–NZ$40. "Trust the Chef" menu NZ$70–NZ$120 per person. Reservations recommended. Daily 11:30am–8pm.

Chop Shop Food Merchants ★★ ECLECTIC Initially, chef Chris Whiting and his maitre'd wife, Fiona, were looking for premises suitable for food prep for their catering business. The upstairs area of what had been the Laneway Café proved to have enough space and facilities for a daytime cafe as well. A hit from opening day, the Chop Shop has an eclectic menu that's a mix of breakfast, brunch, and lunch options. A blackboard menu lists items only available for a day, or seasonally (e.g., whitebait, and wild rabbit) with the printed menu offering a number of wide-ranging options. Dishes such as Turkish poached eggs; salads of crispy duck breast with pink grapefruit segments and tangles of pickled daikon; and beetroot-cured salmon are already proven winners. The decor features kitchen counters faced with large panels of pressed tin that were probably ceilings in an old Edwardian-era homestead, but they look quite at home in the industrial-chic space. Indoor and outdoor tables offer winter and summer dining.

8 Arrow Lane, off 44 Buckingham St., Arrowtown, (C) **03/442-1116.** Main courses NZ$19–NZ$25. Daily 8am–4pm.

Postmasters House ★★ NEW ZEALAND/INTERNATIONAL This charming cafe/restaurant occupies Arrowtown's venerable postmasters' home. Indoors the tables extend to include what was a many-windowed sunporch, and outdoors the gardens have been paved to create a large courtyard opening off the street. It's open for breakfast, lunch, and dinner, with a kids' menu for all-day and breakfast; coffee and cakes are available all day. The seasonal dinner menu is a showcase of New Zealand ingredients: Stewart Island salmon, green-lipped mussels, Fiordland venison, blue cod, and Cardrona lamb. Venison enthusiasts should try the entrée (first course) option of seared Fiordland venison carpaccio with Parmesan and white truffle oil.

54 Buckingham St. www.postmasters.co.nz. (C) **03/442-0991.** Main courses NZ$25–NZ$39. Daily from 9am.

Saffron ★★ NEW ZEALAND/ASIAN The lunch menu at this perennial hot spot has a number of Asian-influenced dishes: Thai beef curry with pineapple, a salad of crispy pork and squid with yellow soybean dressing, green-lipped mussels with white wine and lemongrass. Dinner features more traditional European options incorporating the best of locally grown, reared, or caught produce including puff pastry wrapped around a filling of wild boar, smoked bacon, and house-made black pudding. For those who dislike the taste of grass-grazed beef, Saffron's Wakanui eye filet steak comes from animals that have had 3 months of grain feed. Blue cod is given an Asian tweak with grilled filets served with Vietnamese rolls on a sweetcorn and lemongrass purée.

18 Buckingham St. www.saffronrestaurant.co.nz. © **03/442-0131.** Main courses NZ$39–NZ$49. Daily noon–3pm and 6pm–late.

Organized Tours

○ Guided astronomy tours atop the Skyline Queenstown gondola with **Skyline Stargazing** ★★ (www.skyline.co.nz/stargazing; © **03/441-0101**) allow visitors to explore the night sky with professional astronomy guides and top-of-the-line Celestron telescopes. Everything is provided, including down jackets (but wear shoes suitable for walking). The 1-hour tours depart nightly after sunset, weather dependent; booking ahead is essential.

○ Take a **scenic cruise of Lake Wakatipu** ★★★ aboard a catamaran or a vintage steamship. The catamaran cruise aboard the *Spirit of Queenstown* with Southern Discoveries (www.southerndiscoveries.co.nz; © **0800/264-536** in NZ) is not only a blissful experience (sun, water, large viewing windows, indoor seating, wide decks), but the running commentary from the skipper, closeup views of Bob's Cove, and farm tours of Mount Nicholas High Country Farm (a working merino-sheep farm) are a real immersion in the local culture. Scenic cruises run from NZ$55. Then there is the lady of the lake herself, the 1912 vintage steamship **TSS** *Earnslaw.* Originally built to connect with the railway at Kingston and carry the goods to Queenstown, the steamer also serviced remote farms, sometimes carrying 1,500 sheep and 30 cattle on her decks. Today, scheduled excursions aboard the TSS *Earnslaw* are offered by **Real Journeys** (www.realjourneys.co.nz; © **0800/656-503** in NZ, or 03/442-7500). The 1½-hour **Walter Peak Cruises** to Walter Peak Farm run up to six times a day year-round (with a reduced winter schedule), costing NZ$55 adults and NZ$22 children 5 to 14. Real Journeys' Walter Peak 3½-hour farm excursion includes a country-style morning or afternoon tea, sheep shearing and mustering demos, and the perennially popular spinning exhibitions (NZ$72 adults, NZ$22 children 5–14).

Wine, Wine, Wine
ORGANIZED WINE TOURS
Central Otago's rugged hillsides and sunny valleys are clad in vineyards that produce some of the country's most distinctive wines. Pinot noir (85% of the total plantings), chardonnay, sauvignon blanc, pinot gris, and riesling wine flows from over 85 (and growing) vineyards. Wine buffs who prefer to visit wineries on their own will find the "Central Otago Wine Map," produced by the **Central Otago Winegrowers Association** (www.cowa.org.nz), invaluable. It is informative, comprehensive and widely available. At all i-SITE information offices in Central Otago has copies.

Skippers Canyon, 22km (13 miles) from Queenstown, at the head of the Shotover River, is another area that opened up with the discovery of gold (in 1862). Within 4 months of that first find, more than 10,000 miners were in the canyon, living in "hellish hard conditions." The hills and gullies are treeless, and even campfire cooking is near-impossible without fuel. Yet the miners still came, and eventually the rough camps became settlements with grog shops, schools, and stores. The harsh climate and time itself has seen the settlements disappear but for a few isolated dwellings. The road to Skippers is frequently described as narrow and winding, but in truth it is more akin to driving along a shelf. Built of rock. We recommend taking a tour with someone else at the wheel. Tour companies offering 4WD tours include **Queenstown Heritage Tours ★★★** (www.qht.co.nz; ℂ 03/409-0949; from NZ$160). Limited to four to six people, the half-day tour includes a picnic. **Nomad Safaris** (www.nomadsafaris. co.nz; ℂ 0800/688-222 in NZ) offers a 4-hour 4WD safari into the canyon for NZ$175 adults and NZ$80 children ages 4 to 14.

14

Join the 5-hour personalized Original Wine Tour with tastings at four wineries with **Queenstown Wine Trails ★★** (www.queenstownwinetrail.co.nz; ℂ **0800/827-8464** in NZ, or 03/441-3990). The tour includes time for an optional winery lunch (own expense); cost is NZ$155 per person. The 4.5-hour Private Twilight Wine Tour includes wine tastings at three vineyards and dinner at Amisfield bistro (NZ$399 per person).

Appellation Central Wine Tours ★★ (www.appellationwinetours.nz; ℂ **03/442-0246**) offers small-group (max. 11 people) tours. A half-day Boutique Wine Tour includes wine tastings at four vineyards in Gibbston and Bannockburn with a platter lunch at Carrick Winery. The Gourmet Wine Tour is a full day covering five vineyards in Gibbstown, Bannockburn, and Cromwell, with a wine cave tour, cheese tasting, and a platter lunch included. Tours cost NZ$185 to NZ$230 per person. Appellation Central also does helicopter wine tours and golf and wine tours.

SELF-DRIVE WINERY VISITS

o **Amisfield Winery ★★★**, 10 Lake Hayes Rd. (www.amisfield.co.nz; ℂ **03/442-0556**): Producing award-winning pinot noir, aromatic whites, and sparkling wines, this winery has one of the best restaurants in the region. It's 10 minutes from Queenstown.

o **Carrick ★★**, 247 Cairnmuir Rd., Bannockburn (www.carrick.co.nz): This certified organic vineyard offers lovely pinot noir, chardonnay, and a rich pinot gris. As well as a cellar door, the winery has a good restaurant with a wonderful view of the "burn" (creek) and hills that were riddled by sluice-mining guns in gold rush days.

o **Chard Farm Vineyard ★★**, SH 6, 20 minutes from Queenstown (www. chardfarm.co.nz; ℂ **03/442-6110**): Just past the Kawarau bungy bridge is one of the most spectacularly situated vineyards in the country. Straddling a narrow ledge between rugged mountains and the river gorge, it's reached via the narrow Chard Road above the Kawarau River. Sample its pinot noir, riesling, pinot gris, and gewürztraminer.

o **Gibbston Valley Wines ★★**, SH 6, Gibbstown Valley (www.gibbstonvalley.com; (C) **03/442-6910**): Producing award-winning single vineyard reserve wines, pinot noir, pinot blanc, pinot gris, and rosé, Gibbston also has a wine cave, a cellar door, cheeseries, and a gift shop.

o **Mt. Difficulty Wines ★★**, 319 Felton Rd., Bannockburn (www.mtdifficulty.co.nz; (C) **03/445-3445**): This winery is a leading producer of pinot noir, as well as riesling, chardonnay, pinot gris, and merlot. It also has a pleasant lunch cafe.

o **Peregrine ★★**, SH6, Gibbstown Valley (www.peregrinewines.co.nz; (C) **03/442-4000**): Named after the falcon now found only in the Central Otago region, Peregrine produces excellent pinot noir, pinot gris, riesling, and rosé.

o **Wild Earth Wines ★★**, SH6 (www.wildearthwines.co.nz; (C) **03/445-4841**): Wild Earth hangs its sign from the popular Goldfields (mining) Centre in the Kawarau gorge. Good wines, good food, and a unique barbecue experience using wine barrel cookers.

Outdoor Pursuits

BUNGY JUMPING Queenstown has three bungy-jumping sites, and **A. J. Hackett Bungy ★★★** (www.bungy.co.nz; (C) **0800/286-4958** in NZ) now operates them all. **Kawarau Bridge,** at 43m (140 ft.) high, was the world's first commercial bungy operation. It's just 23km (14 miles) from Queenstown, and the full package, including jump, T-shirt, video, photos, and transport, costs NZ$175 adults, NZ$145 children ages 10 to 15. The **Nevis-Highwire Bungy ★★★** is the highest bungy site in New Zealand. The full package costs NZ$355. The **Nevis Swing** requires a walk across a 70m (230-ft.) suspension bridge to the launching pad, and then a free fall some 160m (525 ft.) down (NZ$275).

CANYONING Participants in this extreme sport make their way through river canyons: rappelling, walking, climbing, jumping, and swimming. Options from **Canyoning NZ** (www.canyoning.co.nz; (C) **03/441-3003**) range from NZ$195 and can include a half-day Queenstown trip or the more expensive full-day Routeburn canyoning trip for NZ$260. *Note:* Know that for half the trip time you will be wet.

JETBOATING Shotover Jet **★★★** (www.shotoverjet.com; (C) **0800/746-868** in NZ, or 03/442-5591) is a **do-not-miss experience.** It's a real adrenaline rush as you blast along the rocky river canyon, its boulders and walls mere inches from the boat. Cost is from NZ$145 adults and NZ$80 kids ages 5 to 15; seasonal rates apply, and family packages and combo tickets available.

LUGE The Skyline Luge **★★★** (www.skyline.co.nz; (C) **03/441-0101**) is nearly 1km (½ mile) of downhill fun. Various packages are on offer, including

SIDE TRIPS TO milford sound ★★★

It's 179 miles by road from Queenstown (a 5-hr. drive each way) to Milford Sound, but most find the time flies by. The scenery along the way varies from lakeside highway to sheep and dairy farms, river flats, and forests. A tunnel is followed by some narrow mountain roads, then finally the sheer glaciated walls of the Sound (fiord) appear, with cascades of water tumbling to the deep waters far below. Near the sea mouth, the mighty slab of Mitre Peak appears to rise in a perfect peak from the fiord floor, but sightseeing from a boat reveals that the majestic peak is actually one of many in a range split by hanging valleys and distant glaciers. If you'd prefer not to tackle the long drive from Queenstown to Milford Sound yourself, numerous tour operators offer day tours, including: **Great Sights** (www.greatsights.co.nz; ✆ **0800/744-487**); **Real Journeys** (www.realjourneys.

co.nz; ✆ **0800/656-503**); and **Southern Discoveries** (www.southerndiscoveries. co.nz; ✆ **0800/264-536** in NZ, or 03/441-1137).

Flightseeing is a smart option for those short on time (the coach journey takes 12 hr., with 10 of those in transit). Options for scenic flights from Queenstown to Milford include flights to/from Queenstown with a landing and transfers to a launch for a cruise on the Sound; **overflights**—over glaciers, lakes, and Milford Sound; and **fly-cruise-fly options** that take in other areas such as Glenorchy. All options can be booked at local i-SITE centers; prices range from NZ$185 to NZ$990. Note that trips that incorporate fly/cruise/coach are cheaper and also provide on-the-ground viewing of the remarkable landscape between Queenstown and Fiordland.

several rides and gondola transport. Luge ride is only NZ$35 adults, $25 children. Multi-ride deals are also available. Purchase tickets at the Skyline Gondola terminals. It's open daily from 10am.

SKIING   From late June to September, international skiers and boarders flock to Queenstown to enjoy the accessible slopes of **Coronet Peak** and the **Remarkables;** the wide open cruisy slopes at **Cardrona;** and the challenging downhills at **Treble Cone. Heli-skiing** is hot in these mountain regions with plenty of thrills (and fresh powder), so your little black trip book should include **Harris Mountains Heliski** (www.heliski.co.nz; ✆ 03/442-6722); **HeliGuides** (www.flynz.co.nz; ✆ 03/442-7733); and **Glacier Southern Lakes Heliski** (www.glaciersouthernlakes.co.nz; ✆ 03/442-3016).

The ski fields are constantly upgrading and installing new facilities. In 2015, **Cardrona** (www.cardrona.com) extended its season to October 11; the **Remarkables** (www.nzski.com/queenstown/the-mountains/the-remarkables) opened a new base lodge with seating capacity for 644, and three outdoor sundecks; **Treble Cone** (www.treblecone.com) built an alfresco cafe on the top of Home Basin with a barista and a chef in charge of coffee and grill respectively; **Glacier Southern Lakes Heli-Ski** (see above) developed Sessions, its ski and lunch package, for Wanaka and Queenstown heli-ski areas (one heli-ski run and a barbecue lunch NZ$385; every additional run NZ$85).

WALKING   There are at least 10 walks of 1 to 8 hours in and around town. A reasonably testing walk is the 2- to 3-hour uphill **Queenstown Hill Track,** which starts and finishes on Belfast Trace. There are also several excellent walks around **Lake Wakatipu,** including the easy **Bob's Cove Track and Nature Trail ★★**, which starts 14km (9 miles) from Queenstown on the road to Glenorchy. **Guided Walks of New Zealand ★★★** (www.nzwalks.com; ℭ **0800/455-712** in NZ) specializes in hikes with an emphasis on nature interpretation. Half- and full-day options for a maximum of seven people cost from NZ$125 to NZ$455 per person.

Where to Stay

Queenstown has more than 20,000 guest beds, ranging from backpacker hostels to new apartments, international-class hotels to family lodges, and they keep coming. Even with multiple new additions, it still pays to book well in advance when planning your Queenstown stopover.

EXPENSIVE

Eichardt's Private Hotel ★★★   The property claims to have New Zealand's most prominent lakeside address. No argument there: Lake Wakatipu's little waves wash gently on the narrow beach just across the street. The original hotel was a Victorian hostelry, but clever design (including a classy glass-walled addition) has transformed the 19th-century structure into a small, luxurious boutique hotel with five suites, four two-bedroom apartments, and one three-bedroom lakeside residence—all with fireplaces (the residence comes with a fully equipped European kitchen). A bar/restaurant at the hotel's entrance offers a la carte breakfasts and tapas-style evening menus. A splendid old-school upstairs room titled The Parlour offers hotel guests a whisky nightcap.

Marine Parade. www.eichardts.com. ℭ **03/441-0450.** 10 units. NZ$1,300–NZ$2,100 Rates include full breakfast, complimentary evening drink, and a nightcap from the whisky lounge. **Amenities:** Restaurant; bar; babysitting; library; Wi-Fi (free).

The Spire Hotel ★★   A true boutique hotel with updated Mid-Century Modern furnishings (love the Eames-style lounge chairs), lots of burnished woods and leather, the Spire has10 suites, each comprising a large bedroom, a bathroom, and a generous balcony with comfortable outdoor furniture. Church Lane links the lakefront to the town's main throughfares and business center, and a number of good cafes and restaurants are close by, including Botswana Butchery. Excellent onsite food is provided by **No5 Church Lane** restaurant & bar (www.no5churchlane.com; daily 7–11:30am, noon–4pm, and 5pm–late), its kitchen overseen by Eichardt's chef Will Eaglesfield. We had to knock off one star, however, for the noise in rooms that face the nightclub across the street (ask for a quiet room when you book).

3–5 Church Lane. www.thespirehotel.com. ℭ **03/441-0004.** 10 units. NZ$550–NZ$1,300 suite. Rates include complimentary a la carte breakfast, evening aperitif, and valet parking. Seasonal rates apply. **Amenities:** Restaurant; bar; concierge; pillow menu; 24-hr. room service; Wi-Fi (free).

MODERATE

Garden Court Suites & Apartments ★★   This mix of motel units and contemporary apartments offers good value in a top location. We especially like the two-bedroom apartments with their cozy living areas, kitchens, and downstairs bathrooms (the two bedrooms upstairs). Some 18 spacious one-bedroom, one-bathroom apartments are also available. Room amenities include small laundry facilities, a boon for travelers who have been on the road for a few days. The site is ideally situated out of the hurly-burly of downtown Queenstown's traffic, but only 10 to 15 minutes' walk to the center. Frankton Road sits above the Frankton Arm of Lake Wakatipu and offers swell views of The Remarkables, the picturesque mountain range towering above the lake.

41 Frankton Rd. www.gardencourt.co.nz. ℂ **0800/427-336** in NZ. 54 units. NZ$200–NZ$375 (2-bedroom apartment) on Connectabus route. Seasonal rates available. **Amenities:** Breakfast restaurant; bikes for hire; Wi-Fi (free).

Heritage Queenstown ★★   The Heritage isn't in Queenstown proper, but nestled into an alpine setting of pine trees, mountain peaks, and a lake of deep blue. Its views of that lake that make it special, so be sure to ask for a room that fronts the water when booking. As for the accommodations: The digs range from studio suites to two-bedroom suites, family rooms, and three-bedroom villas with full kitchen and laundry facilities. All are contemporary in their styling and well-maintained, though some find the beds a bit soft. The lake-view hotel restaurant is a bonus for guests who prefer not to go back into town to dine.

91 Fernhill Rd. (20-min. walk to town). www.heritagehotels.co.nz. ℂ **0800/424-988** in NZ, or 03/450-1500. 175 units. NZ$195–NZ$295 deluxe double, NZ$220–NZ$299 lakeview deluxe double. Seasonal rates may apply. **Amenities:** Restaurant; bar; indoor/outdoor heated pool; room service; shuttle service; Wi-Fi (500MB free daily per room).

Pinewood Lodge ★★   Rob and Rose Greig have created one of the best budget options in the area. A number of houses—from small to quite large (sleeping from 1 to 24)—are scattered over a tree-covered hillside, some with dorm rooms, others with nicely outfitted apartments. Each house has its own lounge and fully equipped kitchen. With facilities such as hang-up bike storage and bike wash, the lodge is an unofficial headquarters for mountain bikers. A sociable atmosphere and location close to town add to the appeal.

48 Hamilton Rd. www.pinewood.co.nz. ℂ **0800/746-3966** in NZ, or 03/442-8273. 33 units. From NZ$28 dorm bed to NZ$200 apartment. **Amenities:** Bike rental; Jacuzzi rental; Wi-Fi (free).

Where to Eat

Queenstown has so many good cafes and bars, cocktail joints, and fine-dining restaurants that the various establishments jostle for space and visitor attention. During high-season months (Nov–Mar), dinner reservations are recommended.

EXPENSIVE/MODERATE

Botswana Butchery ★★★ UPMARKET GRILL Established in a historic cottage close to the garden-peninsula areas of the lakefront, Botswana Butchery specializes in aged beef and lamb cuts, game, and fish (brill, farmed salmon, Pacific tuna). The food is outstanding, and for unique South Island produce it is hard to pass on the Fiordland crayfish salad, sautéed *paua* (abalone), or the venison tartare (wild Fiordland red deer). The restaurant has a lively atmosphere, with dining spaces divided into a main downstairs restaurant and Garden Room, with private dining rooms and a lounge bar upstairs. On evenings when the mountain air is nippy, log fires warm the cottage. Fixed-price menus are available in addition to the extensive main menu. During the day an Express Lunch service delivers quick dishes.

17 Marine Parade (garden end). www.botswanabutchery.co.nz. ℭ **03/442-6994.** Main courses NZ$32–NZ$44. Reservations recommended. Daily noon–late.

The Bunker ★★★ INTERNATIONAL Don't judge a book by its cover—or The Bunker by its outward appearance. The wooden, basic, slightly battered entrance door is a carefully designed secret, with no signs, no posted menus. But inside it's all soft lights, sparkling glassware, delicious food fragrances, and, if it's a chilly night, a log fire. Luxury! The menu is resplendent with flavorful tastes: Abalone agnolotti, a risotto with veal sweetbreads, and a confit pork belly with a sensational tamarillo purée are wonderful successes. A "taste of the south" degustation menu offers a comprehensive rollout of speciality (and often local) ingredients: scallops, paua, wild hare, merino lamb, salmon, Manuka honey, saffron, and cheeses. The bar upstairs offers smooth single malts and a dizzying cocktail list.

Cow Lane. www.thebunker.co.nz. ℭ **03/441-8030.** Reservations essential. Main courses NZ$36–NZ$45. Daily 5pm–4am.

Eichardt's Bar ★★★ TAPAS This small, popular streetside bar fronts Eichardt's Private Hotel on the waterfront. Both lunch and evening menus offer an innovative range of small dishes for sharing (recommended: the Cromwell parsnip and potato rosti with wild-thyme-flavored mushrooms and house-made black pudding). Chef Will Eaglesfield is knowledgeable about local produce, and his tapas include Bluff oysters (in season), rillettes of wild hare and duck, fig and goat cheese mousse, seared monkfish chunks on eggplant purees, marinated merino lamb with hummus—and the best potato chips (fries) in the south. Hand-cut, served with olive salt and a mellow garlic aioli, they're sensational.

Marine Parade. www.eichardtsbar.com. ℭ **03/441-0450.** Tapas N$Z7.50–NZ$26. Reservations recommended. Daily 7:30-11am and noon–late.

Madam Woo ★★★ CHINESE/MALAY For some 125 years, 5 Ballarat Street has housed food businesses, including a long-time grocery store, a vegetable and lolly shop, and, since 1972, a number of restaurants now relegated to history. When Madam Woo opened in 2014, it (she?) introduced a new style of eating to Queenstown: Asian street food in a comfortable restaurant. The decor captures the faded grandeur of colonial Malaysia and Singapore—charming if ever so slightly kitsch—and makes the best of what was a rambling country store with family quarters above. A large bar takes center stage, the longest wall has bench and cushion seating for small tables, the old shopfront window spaces are ideal for banqueting tables, and The Parlour Bar upstairs was likely the parlor of the family who lived above the shop. The menu is based on the street food of Malaysia. Hawker's rolls as offered by Madam Woo show an Indian influence, with sturdy *roti* (flat breads) acting as edible plates. Held cup-shaped in one hand, they are filled with steamed or fried mains (fish, shellfish, pork, chicken), crisp greens, chilies, herbs, and sauces. Chef Jane Leong's menu also offers substantial dishes such as fish curry with tamarind, chili and lemongrass, pork spare ribs, wonton soup, and shredded duck with cabbage salad.

5 The Mall, waterfront end of Lower Ballarat St. www.madamwoo.co.nz. *©* **03/442-9200.** Main courses NZ$16–NZ$32. Daily noon–late.

Public Kitchen & Bar ★★ KIWI Public's mission statement has it that "Clever kiwis farm it, catch it, brew it, and grow it. We cook it, pour it. You eat it." Which explains the main menu divisions of venison, bird, lamb, beef, pork, and seafood with the provenance of each item included. The venison and lamb, for example, come from the rich grasslands of Athol, a farming settlement some 60 miles down the road that leads to Te Anau and beyond. There is a hint of old school to the menu (Joe's housemade corned beef and mustard with cream sauce) as well as classics such as rack of lamb with mint pesto. Among the surprises are whole baked flounder and grilled skirt steak. Food aside, the restaurant site on Steamer Wharf has an outdoor area that makes the most of its lakeside position with huge views and the scent of fresh water all around.

Ground floor, Steamer Wharf, Beach St. www.publickitchen.co.nz. *©* **03/442-5969.** Main courses NZ$22–NZ$45. Daily 9am–11pm.

INEXPENSIVE

A little pizzeria den of great-value tastes, the **Cow ★**, Cow Lane, off Beach Street (www.thecowrestaurant.co.nz; *©* **03/442-8588**), is woody, moody, and very popular. If your budget has taken a beating on your trip, console yourself with the pepperoni pizza, pasta bolognese with fresh green salad, or one of the homemade soups. This good family restaurant is open daily noon to midnight.

Fergburger ★★★ BURGERS This extraordinary burger joint (with a slightly mad website) serves extremely large burgers of the best lamb, beef, venison, bacon, salad, vegetables (beetroot is a traditional burger inclusion in New Zealand), relishes, and sauces. It's a shiny wood and big counter place, but too small for every customer to eat in-situ, so the routine is to order and pay at the counter, receive a numbered receipt, wait where you can see the big signboard, then eat in or out. Fillings have politically incorrect titles such as Sweet Bambi (venison), Little Lamby (ground lamb), and Southern Swine (bacon and beef). The Big Al burger is a high stack of double beef burgers, bacon, cheese, two eggs, slices of beetroot, tomato and red onion, relish, and sauce. Fries are extra (NZ$4.50 per serving). Its fame has spread, and queues can form.

Note that next door is **Fergbaker,** selling sweet and savory pies, cakes, croissants, Boston cream doughnuts, and other treats to go. It's a Ferg empire.

42 Shotover St. www.fergburger.com. (*C*) **03/441-1232.** Burgers NZ$12–NZ$18; sandwiches & main courses NZ$10–NZ$15. Daily 8:30am–5am (next day).

The Spice Room ★★ INDIAN   The complex flavors of the Indian subcontinent are used here in some typically New Zealand dishes, including barbecued venison, South Island goat curries, and Nelson scallops. An early bird Indian feast (5–7pm) of curry, rice, naan, and papadum is a bargain at NZ$20 per person. A children's menu is available, as are gluten-free and vegan dishes.

15 Shotover St., 1st floor. http://spiceroom.co.nz. (*C*) **03/442-5335.** Main courses NZ$20–NZ$26. Daily 10am–noon lunch; from 5pm dinner.

Vudu Café & Larder ★★ CAFE   First established on Beach Street, Vudu Café now has a cafe and larder on Rees Street that's bigger and brighter. Breakfast is a hearty workout here; for example, poached eggs come on whacking great slices of granary bread with perfectly grilled halloumi cheese and radish salad. Lunch may be a free-range lamb shoulder shepherd's pie or a vegetable and pinenut kofta. The ordering system is slightly fiddly—you have to quickly read the menu, quickly make a decision, then quickly find a table holding on to your number. But it works. It's open for breakfast, lunch, and tea.

16 Rees St. www.vudu.co.nz. Main courses NZ$12–NZ$20. Daily from 8am.

Queenstown Nightlife

BARS & CELLAR DOORS

A cluster of nightspots draws after-dark crowds.

- **The Bunker** ★★★, Cow Lane (www.thebunker.co.nz; (*C*) **03/441-8030**), plays on no advertising, no signs, and the fact that it's hard to find. It's a first-rate restaurant (p. 338) and a *very* popular cocktail bar.

- **Bardeaux** ★★, Eureka Arcade, 11 The Mall ((*C*) **03/442-8284**), is a classy wine bar with a huge range of Central Otago wines.

- **Minus 5° Ice Bar,** Steamer Wharf (www.minus5icebar.com; (*C*) **03/442-6050**), lets you spend the night on ice—literally—in its 80-ton ice bar. It's all about hand-sculpted ice furnishings and famed vodka cocktails. Big coats and woolly gloves are provided.

- The **Dux de Lux** ★, 14 Church St. (www.thedux.co.nz), draws big crowds with its specialty beers and fun atmosphere. Next door is the ever-popular **Monty's Bar** ★★, 12 Church St. (www.montysbar.co.nz). Both are cool places to meet and greet and have a glass or three, especially when the music cranks up.

- **The Winery** ★, 14 Beach St. (www.thewinery.co.nz; (*C*) **03/409-2226**), is the resort's in-town cellar door, where you can sample wines from a selection of over 80 varietals. It also has whisky (mostly the Scottish variety) and honey tastings.

CASINOS

Queenstown has two casinos: **SKYCITY Queenstown Casino,** 16–24 Beach St. (www.skycityqueenstown.co.nz; ℭ **03/441-0400**), has more than 80 gaming machines and the usual table games such as roulette, blackjack, and baccarat, not to mention Wild Thyme Bar & Restaurant; the casino is open daily noon to 4am. **Lasseters Wharf Casino,** Steamer Wharf (www.lasseterswharfcasino.co.nz; ℭ **03/441-1495**), is a boutique operation with much the same on offer in the way of games (and The Waterfront bar and bistro). It's open daily from 11am to 3am. In both casinos, you must be 20 and over and smartly dressed to enter.

LAKE WANAKA ★★★

145km (90 miles) S of Haast; 117km (73 miles) N of Queenstown

The town of Wanaka has Lake Wanaka as its focus point, with the mountain backdrop always in view. The gateway to Mount Aspiring National Park, it is under the jurisdiction of the Department of Conservation (DOC), which translates to maintained walking tracks, excellent maps, and weather guidance for those going into wilderness areas.

Wanaka is the perfect place to spend a couple of days recharging. The lakeside town has seen huge growth in the past 10 years, with high-(ish) rise apartments overlooking the lake, stylish home and holiday houses perched hillside and lakeside, and a buzzing cosmopolitan center with good shops, restaurants, cafes, and bars.

Essentials

GETTING THERE & GETTING AROUND

BY AIR The **Wanaka Airport** (ℭ **03/443-1112**), 9km (5 miles) from Lake Wanaka township, has no scheduled commercial flights operating, but small fixed-wing planes and helicopters provide sight/flightseeing opportunities.

BY COACH (BUS) **InterCity** (www.intercity.co.nz; ℭ **64/9/583-5780**) provides coach services linking Wanaka to the West Coast, Christchurch, Dunedin, Mount Cook, Queenstown, Te Anau, and Milford Sound. **Wanaka Connexions** (www.alpinecoachlines.co.nz; ℭ **0800/244-844** in NZ) runs between Wanaka and Queenstown several times a day, and also has a daily service to Invercargill, Dunedin, and Christchurch. Contact **Yello** (www.yello.co.nz; ℭ **0800/443-5555** in NZ) for charter transport and getting around places other transport doesn't go (you can't miss this transport operator—it's all yellow!).

BY CAR Wanaka is a 4- to 5-hour drive from Christchurch, 3½ hours from both Dunedin and Te Anau, and 1¼ hours from Queenstown. A shorter 1-hour route to/from Queenstown crosses the Crown Range (SH89) but is sometimes closed in winter due to snow/ice/flood.

VISITOR INFORMATION

The official website for **Lake Wanaka Tourism** is **www.lakewanaka.co.nz**. The **Lake Wanaka i-SITE Visitor Centre,** 100 Ardmore Rd. (© **03/443-1233**), is open daily from 8am. The **Department of Conservation (DOC),** Ardmore Street and Ballantyne Road (© **03/443-7660**), provides information on Mount Aspiring National Park and all DOC tracks in the area.

[Fast FACTS]

Emergencies   Ambulance, fire, police: toll-free © **111. Wanaka Police Station:** © **03/443-7272.**

Medical   **Wanaka Medical Centre:** © **03/443-7811.**

SPECIAL EVENTS

The **Warbirds Over Wanaka International Air Show** ★★★ (www.warbirdsoverwanaka.com) combines classic vintage and veteran aircraft, machinery, fire engines, and tractors with dynamic Air Force displays and aerobatic teams in the natural amphitheater of the Upper Clutha Basin. It's one of the top four Warbirds air shows in the world and is held every second Easter in even-numbered years.

Exploring Wanaka

Since 1973, Stuart Landsborough (aka Professor Puzzle) has drawn thousands of visitors to the confusing passageways of his elaborate Great Maze at **Stuart Landsborough's Puzzling World** ★★, SH89, 2km (1¼ miles) from Wanaka (www.puzzlingworld.co.nz; © **03/443-7489**). The crazy Tilted House, Leaning Clock Tower, and a Hologram Hall will further test your perceptions. It's always interesting and a great place for kids, especially on a rainy day. Admission is from NZ$15 adults and NZ$10 children 5 to 15; it's open daily from 8:30am, with last admission at 5:30pm in summer (5pm winter). Allow a good 2 hours for your visit.

New Zealanders are collectors of machines that move (or once moved), from vintage tractors to vintage fighter planes. In 2011 the outstanding New Zealand Fighter Pilots' Museum merged with the **Warbirds & Wheels Museum** ★★★ (http://warbirdsandwheels.com; © **0800/927-247**). Located at the Wanaka Airport, the museum contains a collection of fighter aircraft (warbirds), classic cars (including a Duesenberg), and a pictorial history of New Zealand aviation legend Sir Tim Wallis. It's open daily 9am to 5pm, and admission is NZ$20 adults and NZ$5 children 5 to 15.

A stone's throw away, the **National Transport & Toy Museum** ★ (www.nttmuseumwanaka.co.nz; © **03/443-8765**) has a huge collection of every toy you've ever heard of—from teddy bears to Barbie dolls, Lego to Meccano sets. A massive collection of cars and trucks and tractors and tanks sprawls through hangers and Quonset huts. The collections and exhibitions are well done. *Note:* A Russian MIG jet set on a plinth by the museum suggests that

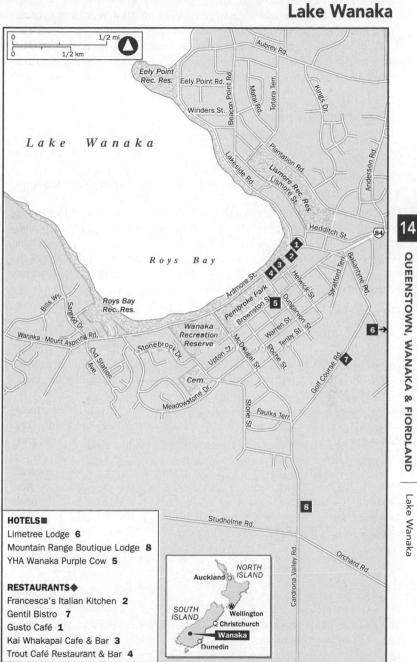

Lake Wanaka

0   1/2 mi
0   1/2 km

Aubrey Rd.

Eely Point
Rec. Res.

Eely Point Rd.

Winders St.

Beacon Point Rd.

Matai Rd.

Totara Terr.

Kings Dr.

Lake   Wanaka

Plantation Rd.

Lakeside Rd.

Lismore Rec. Res.

Lismore St.

Anderson Rd.

Hedditch St.

84

Roys   Bay

Ardmore St.

Helwick St.

Stratford Terr.

Ballantyne Rd.

Roys Bay
Rec. Res.

Pembroke Park

Brownston St.

Dungarvon St.

Bills Wy.

Sargood Dr.

Wanaka - Mount Aspiring Rd.

Wanaka
Recreation
Reserve

Stonebrook Dr.

Warren St.

Tenby St.

Roche St.

Golf Course Rd.

Old Station Ave.

Upton St.

McDougal St.

Cem.

Meadowstone Dr.

Stone St.

Faulks Terr.

Studholme Rd.

Cardrona Valley Rd.

Orchard Rd.

HOTELS■
Limetree Lodge **6**
Mountain Range Boutique Lodge **8**
YHA Wanaka Purple Cow **5**

RESTAURANTS◆
Francesca's Italian Kitchen **2**
Gentil Bistro **7**
Gusto Café **1**
Kai Whakapai Cafe & Bar **3**
Trout Café Restaurant & Bar **4**

NORTH
ISLAND
Auckland

SOUTH
ISLAND

Wellington
Christchurch
Wanaka
Dunedin

this is the fighter aircraft museum, but oops, that's the Warbirds & Wheels next door. It's open daily 8:30am to 5pm, and admission is NZ$17 adults and NZ$5 children 5 to 15.

If all that museumgoing becomes thirsty work, take a break at **Wanaka Beerworks** ★ (www.wanakabeerworks.co.nz; ℂ **0800/273-9754** in NZ), situated between the two museums at the airport. This boutique craft beer brewery is open daily.

Organized Tours

○ **Lake & Island Cruise/Tour:** Chris Riley of **Lakeland Adventures** (www. lakelandadventures.co.nz) offers a unique tour involving a boat cruise on Lake Wanaka, landing on the island of Mou Waho, and an hour's guided walk to the summit of the hill to a lake upon a mountain upon a lake. Magic!

○ **Motorcycle Wine Tour: Wanaka Trike Tours** (www.wanakatriketours. co.nz; ℂ **0800/874-537** in NZ) has taken the motorcycle to greater lengths—a rider upfront and two passengers behind—and ridden off not into the sunset but to the vineyards. Decked out with safety helmet and jacket, riders head for **Rippon, Maori Point,** and **Swallows Crossing** wineries. (The signs announcing the vicinity of Swallows Crossing cellar door has led more than one visitor to ask, "Exactly why do swallows want to cross the road anyway?" Confusion, likely thanks to many rural signposts announcing cows or trucks crossing.) Trike Tour operator Ian Piercy in particular enthuses over Swallows Crossing's GSpot wine, a white wine blend of gerwurztraminer, pinot gris, and riesling. Tours run from 2 to 3 hours or longer if required. Two trikes carry up to four passengers (from NZ$199 per person).

○ **Photo Safari:** Photographer Gilbert van Reenen of **Clean Green Phototours,** 641 Ballantyne Rd., Wanaka (www.cleangreen.co.nz; ℂ **03/443-7951**), will tailor a photographic expedition to suit individual interests. He includes photographic tips and advice, and because he knows the area forwards and backwards, grand landscapes are a given. Prices vary depending on numbers and distances, but expect to pay from NZ$350 per person.

Beanbags & Cocktails: A Night at the Movies

See a flick and soak up some local flavor at **Cinema Paradiso** ★★★, 72 Brownston St. (www.paradiso.net.nz; ℂ **03/443-1505**). This unique twin-screen movie theater has been celebrated since it opened in the 1990s for its quirky take on a night at the movies. Vintage sofas, big soft chairs, cushions and beanbags say sit down, sprawl out, and have a good time. Homemade cookies and secret-recipe ice cream is served, and light meals can be ordered. **Ruby's Cinema & Bar** ★, 50 Cardrona Valley Rd., on the outskirts of town (www.rubyscinema.co.nz), is a classy little theater that draws big crowds, with the look of a cocktail bar and the feel of a funky Greenwich Village arthouse cinema. Come to think of it, Ruby's actually *is* a cocktail bar, serving drinks and snacks to movie patrons.

WINE TOURS

Wine buffs are in for a treat in Wanaka with a couple of innovative wine tours.

o **Funny French Cars Wine Tours** (http://funnyfrenchcars.co.nz; © **027/866-932** in NZ): Julie Nicholson and her husband, Deane, have taken their interest in wine and the famous French Citroen 2CV to put together Funny French Cars Wine Tours. Julie picks up visitors, and everyone rattles merrily off into a hinterland of vineyards. Her beat includes **Aitken's Folly** (www.aitkensfolly.co.nz), where Fiona and Ian have planted a vineyard of chardonnay and pinot noir on Riverbank Road. Fiona, from Scotland, is the viticulturist in the family, and by the couple's second vintage it would seem "folly" may be a misnomer. The rosé is rather special, but most of the interest is likely to be in Aitken's Folly pinot noir wines.

o **Maori Point Vineyard,** 413 Maori Point Rd., Tarrus (www.maoripoint. co.nz; © **03/428-8842**): Take a tour of Maori Point with winemaker Matt Evans. Matt arrived at Maori Point Vineyard via Princeton, UC Berkeley, and careers in banking and solar technology, during which he was quietly developing his interest in wine. Six years ago he began winemaking commercially and now works double vintages, jetting between Anderson Valley, California, and Central Otago, New Zealand. The team at Maori Point is comprised of Matt, his wife, Maggie, and vineyard owners Dr. John Harris and Dr. Marilyn Duxson. The wine list includes impressive successive pinot noir vintages, pinot gris, riesling, and the unique Gold Digger, a "sparkly" presented in crown-capped small beer bottles. It always sells out. Tours run from 3 hours. Expect to pay around $100 per person.

Outdoor Pursuits

ECORAFTING This is an easy adventure for those who aren't ready to risk whitewater rafting, as well as for less active people and children. It's all about learning as you paddle, as guides enlighten you about flora and fauna along the way. **Pioneer Rafting ★★** (www.ecoraft.co.nz; © **03/443-1246**) conducts half- and full-day excursions down the Upper Clutha Mata-Au River, the country's largest river. The trip is suitable for all ages. A half-day trip costs NZ$135 adults and NZ$75 children ages 5 to 15 (no kids 4 and under).

FLIGHTSEEING Southern Alps Air, 48 Helwick St. (www.southernalpsair.co.nz; © **0800/345-666** in NZ), has an excellent range of options, from short flights (NZ$99) to a Milford Sound flight-and-cruise for NZ$490 adults and NZ$280 children 5 to 15. All passengers get a window seat for superb views over glaciers, snowcapped mountains, rivers, forests, and the two national parks. CEO and pilot Paul Cooper, who has been flying the route for 25 years, says the aircraft is his office. "My office window has the best view in the world and I am always impressed by the effect on passengers. Most say they had no idea of the magnificence of the mountains—it's not unknown for people to get tears in their eyes."

MOUNTAIN BIKING The Department of Conservation's leaflet on bike trails in the Wanaka area is available from its office at Ardmore Street and

Ballantyne Road. Mountain bikes can be rented from **Racer's Edge/Mountain Bikes Unlimited,** 99 Ardmore St. (www.racersedge.co.nz; ℂ **03/443-7882**). Good bikes are also available from **Lakeland Adventures** (ℂ **03/443-7495**). There are excellent biking tracks around the lakeshore that are ideal for young (and older) cyclists.

ROCK CLIMBING   The Wanaka area offers lots of excellent, stable climbing. **Wanaka Rock Climbing,** 7 Apollo St. (www.wanakarock.co.nz; ℂ **03/443-6411**), can introduce you to all the best places. You'll pay from NZ$120 for a range of options.

Where to Stay

The Mountain Range Boutique Lodge ★★, Heritage Park Cardrona (www. mountainrange.co.nz; ℂ **03/443-7400**), is a great choice for groups. This charming eight-bedroom house (big rooms, big bath tubs) sleeps 16 and has a fully equipped kitchen, two living/dining areas, office with printer, and a games room, bikes, and hot tubs. It's close to Florence's Food Store and Lone Star restaurant and runs around NZ$1,200 per night for 16 people. Heritage Park is just off Cardona Valley Road, 2km (1¼ miles) from Wanaka.

The 11-unit **YHA Wanaka Purple Cow ★★**, 94 Brownston St. (www.yha. co.nz; ℂ **0800/772-277** in NZ, or 03/443-1880), is frequented by budget-minded travelers from throughout the world. It's just a step or two from town and has dorm beds from NZ$28 to NZ$35 per person and ensuite doubles from NZ$86 to NZ$130.

Limetree Lodge ★★★   True luxury boils down to a few elements: genuinely warm hospitality, beauty (in the natural surroundings and in the guest rooms), and good food. Limetree Lodge scores on all those points. Visitors stay either in one of four large ensuite guestrooms, each with French doors leading to a veranda; or in one of two suites (the most fabulous is the Black Peak Suite, with two bedrooms, a private lounge with fireplace, and a kitchenette). All are outfitted with special comforts—heated floors, fresh flowers, high quality mattresses, special teas and chocolate. The lodge has a saltwater pool for hot days and a lounge with log fires for wet days. Breakfasts are true feasts and run the gamut from house preserves and granola to hot meals incorporating eggs from the resident hens. For those wanting to dine in, hosts Pauline and John will arrange for a guest chef or food delivered from a restaurant—or prepare an in-house gourmet evening meal themselves. A truly special place.

Ballantyne Rd., RD2. www.limetreelodge.co.nz. ℂ **03/443-7305.** 6 units. NZ$350–NZ$550 (dinner extra). Rates include complimentary shuttle service to/from Wanaka restaurants, full breakfast, all-day coffee, tea, and muffins, and complimentary evening aperitifs. **Amenities:** Croquet lawn; on-site helipad; Jacuzzi; petanque courts; pitch-and-putt golf; saltwater pool; spa pool; Wi-Fi (free).

Where to Eat
EXPENSIVE
Gentil Bistro ★★★ FRENCH   French owner Luc Bohyn and English-trained executive chef James Stapley provide a powerhouse combination of

KID magnets

- **Stuart Landsborough's Puzzling World ★★** An elaborate Great Maze, a crazy Tilted House, a Leaning Clock Tower, and a Hologram Hall (SH89, 2km [1¼ miles] from Wanaka; www.puzzlingworld.co.nz; ✆ **03/443-7489;** daily from 8:30am; last admission 5:30pm in summer [5pm winter]; NZ$15 adults and NZ$10 children 5–15).

- **National Transport and Toy Museum ★** A huge collection of every toy we've ever heard of, from teddy bears to Barbie dolls, Lego to Meccano sets, not to mention a massive collection of cars, trucks, tractors and tanks. Watch for the signposting near Wanaka Airport (www.nttmuseum-wanaka.co.nz; ✆ **03/443-8765;** 8:30am–5pm; NZ$17 adults and NZ$5 children 5–15).

- **Pioneer Rafting ★★** Take the family on a leisurely raft cruise on a half-day trip along the Clutha River (no kids 4 and under; www.ecoraft.co.nz; ✆ **03/443-1246**).

largesse and talent. The bistro itself has a number of unique advantages including an extensive kitchen garden and orchard and Luc Bohyn's own brand of Provencal olive oils and Swiss-made balsamic vinegars. The lunch menu features a fixed price three-course meal and delicate treats from the afternoon tea menu with petite gateaux and complex chocolate creations. The dinner menu is a triumphant rollout of South Island grown produce such as *sous vide* salmon with an oyster beignet, Canterbury duck, and Cardrona lamb. The international wine list has at least 24 wines available by the glass, thanks to the bistro's enomatic wine system, which keeps opened wine fresh. 76A Golf Course Rd. www.bistrogentil.co.nz. ✆ **03/443-2299.** Main courses NZ$34–NZ$42; 7-course degustation menu NZ$120 per person. Daily 11am–late (closed Mon–Tues in Nov).

MODERATE

Trout Café Restaurant & Bar ★★ NEW ZEALAND First, know that there is no trout on this menu, or any other menu. In New Zealand trout is only for those who catch it. The Trout Bar has plenty of other tasty regional options, however, including a lovely lamb rack with a beetroot puree, and a crispy salmon (the skin is cooked to a smoky, delicious char). This is a restaurant that gives presentation its full attention, and the chef's modernist take on a prawn cocktail might surprise. An extra bonus is the view: From where you sit (across the road from the lakeshore), the wide waters of Lake Wanaka and the high peaks of Mount Aspiring National Park are in full view. The bar serves a large range of craft beers and Central Otago wines by the glass. 151 Ardmore St. www.troutbar.co.nz. ✆ **03/443-2600.** Main courses NZ$24–NZ$34. Daily 8:30am–late.

Francesca's Italian Kitchen ★★★ ITALIAN Just reading the menu is enough to spark the taste buds. The food, as expected, is traditional Italian, but the dishes here seem cleaner and more flavorful than those in any other Italian lakeside resorts. "Best pizza ever" is the common unsolicited comment passed on by locals. It's hard to pick an absolute star—every dish tried was excellent—but the cauliflower risotto is a fantastic, surprising dish. Coffee is simply great.

93 Ardmore St. http://fransitalian.co.nz. © **03/443-5599.** Main courses NZ$20–NZ$26. Daily noon–3pm and 5pm–late.

INEXPENSIVE

The popular, casual **Kai Whakapai Café & Bar** ★, Lakefront at the corner of Ardmore and Helwick streets (© **03/443-7795**), is good for pizzas and well-stuffed sandwiches and coffee. It's also a favorite bar for those who seek local brews on tap (good wine list, too.) Busy bar in the evening and a great people-watching place all day (daily 7am–11pm).

TE ANAU ★★

172km (107 miles) SW of Queenstown; 116km (72 miles) S of Milford Sound; 157km (97 miles) NW of Invercargill

Te Anau is the hub of Fiordland National Park, a 1.2-million-hectare (3-million-acre) World Heritage Site. The resort township is built around the foreshore of Lake Te Anau, the largest of the South Island lakes. It has a permanent population of about 4,000, which swells to over 10,000 in summer.

Lake Te Anau's eastern shoreline, where the township is located, is virtually treeless, with about 76cm (30 in.) of annual rainfall, while its western banks are covered in dense forest nurtured by more than 254cm (100 in.) of rain each year. The lake includes three long "arms" that are more fiord than lake in appearance as they reach far into virgin forests. The area has excellent hiking trails and walking tracks, good cafes, and places to stay. If you're coming to explore Fiordland's waterfalls, virgin forests, mountains, rivers, and lonely fiords, this is the place to base yourself.

What attracts visitors to New Zealand's second-largest lake are the opportunity for watersports and the proximity to Milford Sound, 116km (72 miles) away. The sound, which is actually a fiord, reaches 23km (14 miles) in from the Tasman Sea, flanked by sheer granite peaks and traced by playful waterfalls. Its waters and surrounding land have been kept in as nearly a primeval state as humans could possibly manage without leaving them totally untouched. Yes, facilities have been built to enable good visitor experiences, which has had the slightly unfortunate outcome of drawing more and more visitors to the region. But Milford Sound continues to exude a powerful sense of nature's harmony and beauty.

Shoo-fly

Many visitors ask why the magnificent trees along the town's lake foreshore are Australian native eucalyptus. The answer, according to every local resident asked, is that "the scent of eucalyptus keeps sandflies away." True or not, the town has a noticeable absence of the pesky biters.

Te Anau & Fiordland

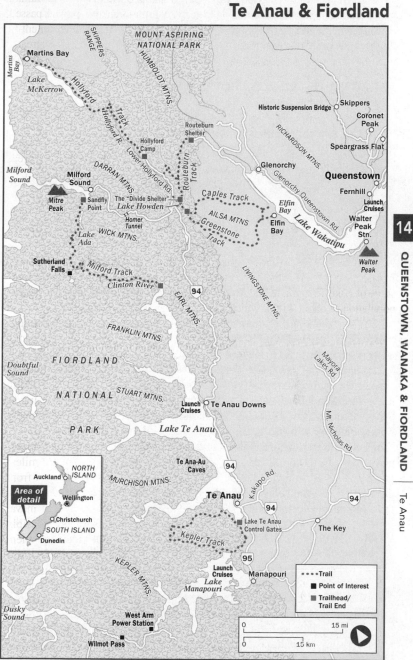

Milford Sound may be the most famous and accessible of the fiords, but Doubtful Sound is the deepest and, according to some, the most beautiful. Even farther south, Dusky Sound may well qualify as the most remote and mysterious of the famous trio.

Essentials

GETTING THERE & GETTING AROUND

BY PLANE   Air services to Te Anau and Fiordland are available as charter flights or scenic overflights, with landings in Milford Sound, with **Air Fiordland Ltd.** (www.airfiordland.com; ℂ **0800/107-505** in NZ).

BY COACH (BUS)   **InterCity** (www.intercity.co.nz; ℂ **64/9/583-5780**) operates daily coach services between Te Anau and Invercargill, and Te Anau and Queenstown, where they connect with scheduled routes to Christchurch or Dunedin.

BY CAR   From Queenstown, take SH6, via Frankton, Kingston, and Athol, then SH94 from Mossburn. The journey takes approximately 2½ hours.

ORIENTATION

Te Anau's main street is SH94 (known as Milford Rd. within the township). This is where to find restaurants, grocery stores, a supermarket, and most shops. The majority of hotels and motels are on Lakefront Drive. The small township is very easy to negotiate on foot or by car.

VISITOR INFORMATION

The **Fiordland i-SITE Visitor Centre,** Lakefront Drive, Te Anau (www.newzealand.com; ℂ **03/249-8900**), shares the same office as **Real Journeys** (www.realjourneys.co.nz; ℂ **0800/656-501** in NZ), open daily from 8:30am. The **Fiordland National Park Visitor Centre,** Lakefront Drive, Te Anau (www.doc.govt.nz; ℂ **03/249-7924**), is a must for anyone contemplating doing either short walks or the well-known multi-day tramps (hikes)—Hollyford, Routeburn, Milford, Kepler, and Caples. It's open daily from 8:30am.

Exploring Te Anau

Dedicated trampers can hook up with **Tracknet ★★** (www.tracknet.net; ℂ **0800/483-262** in NZ), a track-and-transport passenger bus that links the starting and finishing points of Great Walks tracks and many smaller tracks with Te Anau, Milford, Invercargill, and Queenstown.

Cruise Te Anau (www.cruiseteanau.co.nz; ℂ **03/249-8005**) offers a 3-hour cruise in the serenity of the South Fiord (Arm) of Lake Te Anau. A track from the jetty leads to the Hidden Lakes, a secret place still unseen and unknown to many. This is a boutique tour in the nicest sense of the word—with only 12 passengers on a comfortable lake cruiser per tour.

Offering a daily screening of "Ata Whenua"—not just a movie but Fiordland on film—**Fiordland Cinema ★★**, 7 The Lane, Te Anau (www.fiordlandcinema.co.nz; ℂ **03/249-8844**), is a cool movie house (seating 52) with a wine bar so you can sip while you watch the show.

Where to Stay

Numerous motel complexes line the waterfront, and backpackers are well served. The 25-unit **Te Anau Lakefront Backpackers** ★, 48–50 Lakefront Dr. (www.teanaubackpackers.co.nz; ℂ **0800/200-074** in NZ; or 03/249-7713), has dorm beds from NZ$25 to NZ$30 and ensuite doubles for NZ$75 to NZ$95. It has barbecue grills as well as car and gear storage.

    Amber Court Motel ★, 68 Quintin Dr. (www.ambercourtteanau.co.nz; ℂ **0800/188-779** in NZ; or 03/249-7230), has 12 studio and one- to three-bedroom apartments, all with kitchen facilities. It's pleasant and private, but only a short walk from town, the supermarket, and cafes. A good family-stay option. Rates run NZ$150 to NZ$300.

Te Anau Lodge ★★   The old-world charm of Te Anau Lodge can be traced back to the building's 1936 origins as a convent in the Southland township of Nightcaps (and relocated here), although it's more likely a result of the attention it has received from its owners/restorers. Large rooms and bathrooms glory in such titles as Mother Superior's Room, the Music Room, and the Belfry. Breakfasts are served amid stained-glass windows in the old chapel or outdoors in the courtyard—and you can choose from full or continental.

52 Howden St. www.teanaulodge.com. ℂ **03/249-7477.** 9 units. NZ$240–NZ$350 double. Rates include full or continental breakfast, and refreshments in library. **Amenities:** BBQ grills; bikes; laundry; library; guest communal lounge; Wi-Fi (free).

Where to Eat

The town's original Italian restaurant, **La Toscana** ★, 108 Town Centre (www.latoscana.co.nz; ℂ **03/249-7756**), serves inexpensive pasta and pizza along with craft beers and wines from an Italian and South Island wine list. It's open daily from 5:30pm. The terms laid-back, casual, and friendly were invented for **The Fat Duck Café & Restaurant** ★, 124 Town Centre (ℂ **03/249-8480**), which must have hungry hikers in mind when they prepare their very hearty food, always freshly made with good local produce and generous servings. Breakfasters will find the expected egg dishes, but we also recommend the fish (particularly the blue cod), and for dinner you can sample bone-on cuts of Fiordland venison shanks and ribs. This popular family restaurant offers snacks and treats (and a kids' menu) throughout the day; it's open daily from 8:30am to 11pm for breakfast, lunch, and dinner.

    The Redcliff Café ★★, 12 Mokonui St. (www.theredcliff.co.nz; ℂ **03/249-7431**), in a converted vintage cottage, offers good food, a garden bar, and live music daily. The dinner menu includes New Zealand venison and wild hare and Fiordland fish. **Sandfly Café** ★★, 9 The Lane (ℂ **03/249-9529**), is a favorite Te Anau cafe—friendly, with excellent, quirky fare (banana and chocolate chip muffins, bacon and Parmesan scones, sushi, venison pie) and open daily from 7am. It's good for a quiet wine or beer after a busy day.

EXPLORING THE SOUNDS OF FIORDLAND

Milford Sound ★★

119km (74 miles) NE of Te Anau; 286km (177 miles) NW of Queenstown

No matter what the weather is like, Milford Sound is memorable. Its 14 nautical miles length is scene after scene of misty peaks, and sheer rocky mountains, reaching heights of 1,800m (5,900 ft.). Forster's fur seals laze on rocky shelves, and dolphins play in water that reaches depths of 600m (2,000 ft.).

It rains a lot and the weather is extremely changeable, even in summer, so come prepared. You may not glimpse the mountaintops through the rain, but you'll see and hear hundreds of waterfalls.

In summer, coaches pour in at a rate of 100 per day for the launch cruises—that's up to 5,000 people joining you for a look at this special place. If you can overlook these numbers you'll be rewarded with unforgettable landscapes.

THE MILFORD ROAD

The road to Milford Sound from Te Anau, SH94, can be driven in 2 to 3 hours, but allow for stops to photograph the many natural attractions, including the lake's islands and bush-covered shores on your left. The drive is often a slow one, especially in wet conditions, as you make your way through steep gorges and between walls of solid rock and moss-covered inclines. We would discourage anyone from taking a motor home on this road as it is narrow, steep, and winding with a lot of bus traffic—and if that doesn't put you off, the dark, narrow tunnel might. The road is usually very busy in summer and there can be delays, especially at Homer Tunnel. *Note:* There are no fuel stops between Te Anau and Milford, so make sure your tank is full.

The road winds via the **Eglinton** and **Hollyford valleys,** then up to the narrow **Homer Tunnel,** which pierces the Main Divide (wild mountain terrain looms along the road). The tunnel emerges into the light at the head of the **Cleddau Valley,** leading to Milford Sound.

EXPLORING THE SOUND
Cruising

To be fully appreciated, Milford Sound must be seen from the deck of one of the cruise vessels. Prices differ depending on whether you join the cruise vessel in Queenstown, Te Anau, or at Milford Sound, and whether you choose coach, fixed-wing, or helicopter connections. Fares and inclusions vary from operator to operator, and seasonal rates may apply, but expect to pay around NZ$175 adult, NZ$88 child for coach/cruise/coach tour from Te Anau, and NZ$190 adult, NZ$95 child from Queenstown. Fly/cruise/fly tours from Queenstown will cost around NZ$470 adult, $306 child.

One of the best Milford experiences is waking up in the watery light of a new day on the sound itself after an overnight stay. **Real Journeys** (www.realjourneys.co.nz; ✆ **0800/656-501** in NZ or 03/249-7416) offers overnight cruises aboard the "Milford Mariner" (with private two- and four-bunk cabins and ensuites) and the "Milford Wanderer" (twin-share cabins and shared bathrooms; from NZ$340 adult, NZ$170 child). Meals are included, but transport to Milford is extra.

Southern Discoveries (www.southerndiscoveries.co.nz; © **0800/264-536** in NZ, or 03/441-1137) offers Milford Sound cruises including the good-value "Discover More Cruise" comprising a cruise on the Sound, a picnic lunch, and **Milford Deep Underwater Observatory** ★★, where visitors descend 10m (33 ft.) beneath the fiord surface to observe underwater life (NZ$99 adult, NZ$35 child).

Kayaking

Kayaking has rapidly become another popular activity here. It is quite something to be gliding over the dark green water in your own kayak. **Rosco's Milford Kayaks** (www.roscosmilfordkayaks.com © **03/249-8500**) offers several Milford Sound kayaking adventures, including a "Milford Paddle 'n Walk," with a scenic paddle around the sound's Deepwater Basin and a walk along the final section of the Milford Track (NZ$115).

Southern Discoveries (www.southerndiscoveries.co.nz; © **0800/264-536** in NZ, or 03/441-1137) offers a "Cruise & Kayak Milford Sound" itinerary, with a stop (and underwater viewing) at its Milford Discovery Centre and a guided paddle around Harrison Cove (NZ$166).

WHERE TO STAY

Milford Sound Lodge, SH94, Milford Sound (www.milfordlodge.com; © **03/249-8071**), offers a number of options, including chalets, cabins, and dorm beds as well as campsites (chalets from NZ$345; cabins NZ$99; dorm beds NZ$33). The lodge has the Pio Pio cafe and bar on site.

Doubtful Sound ★★★

Doubtful Sound is remote, silent, and 10 times the size of Milford Sound. **Real Journeys** (www.realjourneys.co.nz; © **0800/656-501** in NZ or 03/249-7416) offers wilderness tours of Doubtful Sound, taking passengers from Manapouri, on a launch to West Arm, and a 20km (12-mile) coach trip to Deep Cove in Doubtful Sound. The coach travels over Wilmot Pass, 662m (2,171 ft.) above sea level, stops to visit **Manapouri Power Station,** 225m (750 ft.) downward, to view the seven immense underground turbines. A second launch cruises the sound with its resident pod of dolphins, fur seals, and rare crested penguins (NZ$198–NZ$265 adults, NZ$65 children 5–14; from Te Anau, add about NZ$25, and about NZ$75 from Queenstown).

AORAKI/ MOUNT COOK, MACKENZIE COUNTRY & WAITAKI DISTRICT

This may be the region that captures the essence of New Zealand's South Island: small in size, huge in diversity. The expansive landscape stretches from the massive peaks of World Heritage–listed Aoraki Mount Cook National Park, across the savannah-like Mackenzie basin with its high country lakes and rivers, to a seaside town rich in original Victorian architecture. A determined traveler could skim it in a day, but its geological, geographical, and historical points are so different, so outstanding, it would be like sitting down to a banquet and eating only bread and water. This is a must-do.

THE MACKENZIE COUNTRY

Christchurch to Aoraki/Mount Cook 331km (206 miles)

There is a point on SH79 winding inland from the small town of Geraldine where the landscape changes abruptly, shedding its Canterbury "Englishness" (tree-lined roads and neat green fields) to slip into the dry emptiness of the Mackenzie Country. From the road above Fairlie the scene is of a vast bowl-shaped acreage embraced by high hills in the foreground, lined with jagged mountains in the distance. Ahead but unseen lie Lakes Tekapo and Pukaki, Aoraki/Mount Cook National Park, Lake Ohau, and the long run of the Waitaki River valley to Oamaru on the coast.

Then, just as you sight Lake Tekapo, the mountains loom overhead and then—suddenly—the recognizable tent-like peak of Aoraki/Mount Cook dwarfs everything. The entire landscape is painted in shades of blue. Sky, water, ice: sensory overload!

rustler OR SHEPHERD?

The Mackenzie Country owes its name to a sheep rustler named James Mackenzie. He seems to have spent not much more than 2 years in New Zealand after his arrival from Scotland, but he left behind a legend that lives on.

In March 1855 Mackenzie was arrested after being found "in possession of 1000 sheep" near Tekapo. At his trial he claimed that he was a drover was moving sheep to pasturelands for another person. He was convicted but eventually pardoned, and it is assumed he left the country. It is said that Mackenzie was a good drover and had a "guid way wi dogs." He spoke in the Gaelic and had little English. For years it was believed he had discovered the hidden pass that led to a huge tussocky basin in the shadow of the Southern Alps, but that honor goes to one Michael John Burke of Raincliff who discovered "Burkes" Pass following public interest in Mackenzie's arrest and trial. That Maori from near Christchurch had used the route for hundreds of years before settlers arrived was forgotten.

For over 100 years the Mackenzie was sheep country. In the early 2000s, following the construction of canals and lakes for hydroelectricity, irrigation transformed the dry tussock lands into grasslands, and dairy farming became a sustainable option.

LAKE TEKAPO ★★

225km (140 miles) or 3 hr. from Christchurch

Lake Tekapo is one of three large lakes in the Mackenzie Country, and its village is a popular stopover for those making the long journey to Queenstown, the Southern Lakes, and Fiordland. Attractions include hot pools for soaking and cool pools for swimming, an ice rink, a ski field (seasonal), fixed-wing and helicopter flightseeing options, and an important observatory. On the shores of the lake, the Church of the Good Shepherd, one of the country's most photographed country churches, is a gnarly little beauty built of local stone, but most of the houses around are fashioned of wood and iron and have very large windows. Most are holiday homes, or *baches,* as they are known here. In the winter months snow and frost are constants, but in summer Lake Tekapo and its village bake dry under a hot sun.

Essentials

GETTING THERE & GETTING AROUND The region is well served by public transport, including **InterCity Coaches** (www.intercity.co.nz; © **64/9/583-5780,** or 09/623-1503 Auckland call center), with daily connections to Christchurch and beyond, Queenstown, and Fiordland. Private operator **Cook Connection** (www.cookconnect.co.nz; © **0800/266-526** in NZ) runs a daily return service from September to May linking Lake Tekapo and Twizel to Mount Cook.

VISITOR INFORMATION The official tourism website for the Lake Tekapo region is **www.tekapotourism.co.nz.** The **i-SITE Information Centre** is located by the Godley Hotel in the cluster of shops, accommodation, cafes, and bars in the Lake Tekapo village center (in a layby alongside SH8; ℰ **03/680-6579**).

Exploring Tekapo

STARGAZING **Mount John Observatory** is perched on what is more high mound than mountain. Thanks to its unusually high number of clear nights and skies largely free of light pollution, it has been recognized as a Gold Status Starlight Reserve. (It helps that the good folk of Tekapo village keep their lights dimmed to preserve the clarity of the starry darkness.) The Mt. John University Observatory is one the world's southern-most astronomical research facilities. It's easily accessed, and day tours are available. Interesting though these are, the popular vote goes to evening tours, when good eyesight, laser-gun beams, and powerful telescopes reveal the Milky Way galaxy, seasonal planets, and constellations such as the Southern Cross and nearby Jewel Box. Tours are subject to weather conditions, so it is advisable to check in with tour operator **Earth and Sky** (www.earthandskynz.com; ℰ **03/680-6960**) on the day for availability. The company also operates night skygazing at Aoraki/Mount Cook village.

SWIM & SKATE **Tekapo Springs,** 6 Lakeside Dr., Tekapo (www.tekapo-springs.co.nz; ℰ **0800/235-3823** in NZ), is an innovative enterprise that uses the heat reversal technique to heat water *and* make ice, thus creating hot pools side by side with an ice rink. The complex includes three hot pools, three new cool pools, an outdoor skating rink (open Apr–Sept only), a day spa with sauna, a tubing slide (kids love it), an aqua play area, and a cafe with an all-day menu, blackboard specials, and good coffee. It's open daily from 10am, and all-day passes cost from NZ$22.

Where to Stay

Many of the holiday homes (baches) in Tekapo are available to rent. Go to **www.bookabach.co.nz** who will work online with you to find the right place. **Lake Tekapo Motels and Holiday Park ★★,** Lakeside Drive: Talk about rooms with views! This holiday park (known locally as "the camping ground") enjoys a prime spot on the lake front. Options include backpacker style cabins, chalets and family motels with kitchens. A small supermarket in the village has everything a self-caterer needs. **Amenities:** Kitchens, barbecues, Wi-Fi (pay) kiosks. From NZ$30 to NZD$150 per night (www.laketekapo-accommodation.co.nz; ℰ **0800/853-853** in NZ, or 03/680-6825).

    Peppers Bluewater Resort ★ is in the same neighbourhood as Tekapo Springs and the Holiday Park. It presents as a long curve of units (132) sprawled across the high ground above SH8 with great views of lake and mountains. Small rooms but well styled with touches of luxury. From NZD$143-$500, with seasonal rates available. **Amenities:** Restaurant/bar, babysitting service, concierge, Internet access (www.peppers.co.nz; ℰ **0800/275-373** in NZ).

Where to Eat

If you're looking for a hearty breakfast or lunch to set you up for a big day of touring, **Run 76 Café ★**, Main Street, Tekapo village, SH8 (www.run76laketekapo.co.nz; ✆ **03/680-6910**), serves up pancakes, omelets, manuka-smoked bacon, and fresh-baked country bread. Serving food daily from 7:30am to 2:30pm, the cafe has a deli selling local condiments, cheeses, and more (open till 4pm) and a window for hot coffee to go (open till 6pm).

For a moderately priced taste of Japan—lunch or dinner—seek out **Kohan ★★**, Tekapo village, SH8 (www.kohannz.com; ✆ **03/680-6688**), in the village cluster. Countless visitors have commented on the surprise of finding a restaurant of such excellence in this distant place. Look for fresh sushi and sashimi (the salmon comes directly from a nearby salmon farm), tempura, and noodle soups. Do try the restaurant's signature green tea ice cream.

LAKE PUKAKI

45km (28 miles) from Lake Tekapo

Less than an hour after heading southwest of Lake Tekapo, your car window will once again be filled with lake views and cloud-piercing peaks as you skirt the shoreline of Lake Pukaki and its colors of deep blue (lake), gold (tussock), green (pine trees), and snowy Alps. If you're looking for the perfect photo op, pull off the highway at the turnoff to the architecturally interesting former Information Centre, where the famous shot of Aoraki/Mount Cook is yours for the taking. *Note:* The i-SITE Information Centre has moved to the center of Twizel and the former center here is now a shop front for Mount Cook Salmon Farm, but it offers plenty of parking.

Aoraki/Mount Cook Village ★★

Aoraki/Mount Cook Village is known throughout the world for its alpine beauty and remoteness. It sits within the 70,000 hectares (173,000 acres) of **Aoraki/Mount Cook National Park,** some 753m (2,470 ft.) above sea level and surrounded by 140 peaks over 2,100m (6,888 ft.) high, 22 of which are over 3,000m (9,840 ft.). Most famous of all is **Aoraki/Mount Cook,** which rises 3,695m (12,120 ft.) into the sky. "Aoraki" means "cloud piercer" in Maori. A third of the park is permanent snow and ice, and the **Tasman Glacier** (although retreating) is approximately 29km (18 miles) long and 3km (2 miles) wide.

ESSENTIALS

GETTING THERE & GETTING AROUND

BY COACH/BUS Daily **InterCity** buses (www.intercity.co.nz; ✆ **64/9/583-5780**) link Aoraki/Mount Cook and Christchurch, Queenstown, and Timaru. The **Cook Connection,** Twizel (www.cookconnect.co.nz; ✆ 0800/266-526 in NZ), offers daily return trips from Lake Tekapo and Twizel to Aoraki/Mount Cook village from October through May (departs 8am Tekapo, NZD$65; 10am Twizel NZD$46; bikes NZD$15 each).

15

AORAKI/MOUNT COOK | Lake Pukaki

Note to drivers: There is only Fuel Card gas (petrol) service in Mount Cook Village, so fill up before leaving Tekapo or Twizel. If driving in this region during winter, make sure you have antifreeze fluid in your car radiator.

BY CAR The settlement almost at the foot of Aoraki/Mount Cook is Aoraki/Mount Cook Village. It is reached via SH80 (the turnoff from SH8 is well signposted 200m before the turnoff). Note that care should be taken on all area roads during fall/winter when surfaces can become icy and slippery.

VISITOR INFORMATION

The **Aoraki/Mount Cook National Park Visitor Centre ★★**, 1 Larch Grove, Mount Cook Village (www.doc.govt.nz; ✆ **03/435-1186**), is open daily in summer from 8:30am. Operated by the Department of Conservation (DOC) which offers constantly updated information on weather, track, and road conditions. A stop is highly recommended: The center has excellent displays detailing the natural and human history of the national park (including the heart-tugging audiovisual "The Race to be First") as well as interesting art by Julius von Haast and famed guide and mountaineer Duncan Darroch.

Also go to **www.mtcooknz.com**.

ORIENTATION

A T-intersection at the end of the highway marks the entrance to Aoraki/Mount Cook Village. Turn left and you'll pass Glencoe Lodge, a modern motor hotel, the youth hostel, and the Aoraki/Mount Cook National Park Visitor Centre. Turn right at the intersection for the Hermitage Hotel. There are no ATM machines or petrol/service stations other than a Fuel Card stop in the village.

Exploring the Area

The **Sir Edmund Hillary Alpine Centre ★★**, the Hermitage Hotel (www. hermitage.co.nz/en/the-sir-edmund-hillary-alpine-centre; ✆ **0800/686-800** in NZ, or 03/435-1809), is a must-do, particularly for its small cinema with two big attractions: "Hillary on Everest," a 75-minute documentary on Sir Ed and how he conquered Mount Everest; and the 20-minute "Mount Cook Magic," a 3D movie that replicates the thrill of aerial sightseeing. It also has a planetarium and a museum/gallery documenting pioneering days and Sir Ed's long association with the region. Admission is NZD$20 adults, NZ$10 children.

AERIAL FLIGHTSEEING **Mount Cook Ski Planes,** Mount Cook Airport, SH80 (www.mtcookskiplanes.com; ✆ **0800/800-702** in NZ, or 03/430-8034), is licensed to land scenic flights on Tasman Glacier and in Aoraki/Mount Cook National Park (up to NZ$560; seasonal rates apply). The **Helicopter Line,** Glentanner Park, Aoraki/Mount Cook (www.helicopter.co.nz; ✆ **0800/650-651** in NZ, or 03/435-1801), has several tours, including the popular 60-minute flight over Aoraki/Mount Cook, the Main Divide, and Tasman Glacier (NZ$620 per person; seasonal rates apply).

TASMAN GLACIER BY BOAT Glacier Explorers ★★★ (www.glacier-explorers.com; ℂ **0800/686-800** in NZ) offers an incredible 3-hour boat ride on Tasman Glacier terminal lake. As the glacier retreats (melts), the lake grows, and more icebergs "calve" (break away from the main river of ice). Glacier Explorer employs five Zephyr boats for seven tours a day (8am, 9:30am, 11am, 12:30am, 2pm, 3:30pm, and 5pm), with excellent guides providing interesting commentary, and the opportunity for a short walk through the alpine park (NZ$155 adults, NZ$78 children 4–14; Sept–May only).

SHORT WALKS

○ **Governors Bush Nature Trail (45 min.):** A pleasant walk even in the rain, the trail begins at the public shelter in Mount Cook Village. You'll see plenty of birdlife, one of the last stands of silver beech in the country, alpine plants, rainforest canopy, and ground-cover ferns. Good views up the Hooker Valley to Aoraki/Mount Cook.

○ **Bowen Bush (1 hr.):** An extension of Governors Bush Walk, it begins near the petrol (gas) station opposite Alpine Guides, in Mount Cook Village. In summer the mountain ribbonwood (*houhere*) is in flower and the thin bark *totara* and *taramoa* (bush lawyer) should be showing fruit. On the forest floor, look for mosses, spleenwort ferns, and, if you are lucky, Mount Cook buttercup (incorrectly named Mount Cook lily). Birds common to beech forest include gray warblers, tomtits (*miromiro*), fantails (*piwakawaka*), and the tiny rifleman (*tiitipounamu*).

○ **Kea Point Track (2 hr. return):** Start at the DOC Visitor Centre and cross the road to Hooker Valley. A gentle winding track through tussock and scrub leads to the Mueller Glacier moraine wall. The track follows an old stream bed and ends at a viewpoint with grandstand views of Mount Sefton, the Footstool, Mueller Glacier lake, and Aoraki/Mount Cook.

Where to Stay

The **Mount Cook YHA Hostel** ★, Bowen Drive and Kitchener Avenue (www.yha.co.nz; ℂ **0800/278-299** in NZ, or 03/435-1820), has 72 beds in 17 rooms, including six twins and two doubles, plus a shop, a sauna, a video library and TV lounge, luggage lockers, and a ski drying room. Reservations are essential from November to April (NZ$38–NZ$137).

Aoraki/Mount Cook Alpine Lodge ★, Bowen Drive, Aoraki/Mount Cook (www.aorakialpinelodge.co.nz; ℂ **0800/680-680** in NZ, or 03/435-1860), offers 16 rooms with lovely views, a fun and friendly communal dining and lounge area, and a fully equipped kitchen for self-caterers (NZ$169–NZ$240).

The Hermitage Hotel ★★ The Hermitage was smartly refurbished in 2010, and although today's tall, rectangular hotel is a far cry from the post-colonial swagger of the original the original humble building built of cob and handmade bricks in 1884. The views are now, as then, beyond splendid: The mighty Aoraki/Mount Cook (the cloud piercer) stands proud in a majestic huddle of massive peaks. The hotel has a Qualmark Enviro-Gold rating and takes part in local native planting programs and a conservation program for native flora in the area. Attention to guest comfort is noticeable throughout the property, from Premium-Plus rooms on the top floor of the hotel, with their huge picture windows facing Mount Cook, through Premium and Standard rooms (with Mount Cook views). Alpine open-plan self-contained chalets 200m (218 yards) from the main building include kitchenettes, and a free shuttle service is available on request to/from the main building. The hotel has three good dining options (see "Where to Eat," below).

Terrace Rd., Aoraki/Mount Cook Village. www.hermitage.co.nz. ℗ **0800/686-700** in NZ, or 03/435-1809. 216 units. NZ$255–NZ$610. Seasonal rates available. **Amenities:** 3 restaurants; lounge; Wi-Fi (free).

CAMPING & CARAVANNING

Camping and caravaning are permitted in Aoraki/Mount Cook National Park at designated sites with water and toilets available. Check sites at the **Aoraki/ Mount Cook National Park Visitor Centre ★★**, 1 Larch Grove, Aoraki/ Mount Cook Village (www.doc.govt.nz; ℗ **03/435-1186**).

Where to Eat

The **Panorama Restaurant ★★**, the Hermitage Hotel's fine-dining signature restaurant in Aoraki/Mount Cook Village (www.hermitage.co.nz; ℗ **03/435-1809**), has stunning wraparound views (hence its name) and a standout menu. Highlights include grilled Aoraki farmed salmon with a maple syrup and soy glaze, Canterbury rack of lamb with lavender jus, and wild tahr with juniper jus. As expected, such fine food is matched with an extensive wine list offering New Zealand's best wines. The Hermitage's other eateries, **Alpine Restaurant** (serving buffet brunches, lunch, and dinner) and the **Sir Edmund Hillary Café & Bar** (a self-service cafe open daily 8am–5pm), are more casual in style, but the food is as ever taken seriously. Like the hotel's main restaurant, the Alpine offers New Zealand specialities, such as kumara and orange salads, mussel dishes, and venison pies. The Sir Edmund Hillary Cafe has a selection of hand pies, stuffed breads, pizzas, sandwiches, and beverages. In summer, the bar stays open until the sun sets.

Old Mountaineers' Café, Bar & Restaurant ★ next to the DOC Visitor Centre (http://mtcook.com/restaurant; ℗ **03/345-1890**), serves big homestyle breakfasts and good coffee until 11:30am, then an all-day menu kicks in, offering salads, pizzas, pies, and burgers. The dinner menu from 6pm is slightly more formal with main dishes of grilled steaks, salmon filets, and a hearty sausage dish served with potatoes and gravy. The difference with the food here is the emphasis on organic and free-range produce—an admirable aspiration but no easy task in a small mountain village. Chapel-style windows frame the views, the ambience is casual, and the mountaineering memorabilia around the walls will capture will interest. Service, however, can be brusque. It's open from 10am until late.

THE long ride: ALPS TO OCEAN CYCLE TRAIL

The longest continuous cycle ride in New Zealand, the **Alps 2 Ocean (A2O) Cycle Trail** begins at Aoraki/Mount Cook and ends in Oamaru 6 days and 301km (187 miles) later. It takes in some remarkable scenery as it showcases the unusual geological and geographical aspects of a route that reaches from the Southern Alps to the Pacific Ocean. Riders pass through national parks and heritage centers, skirt glacial lakes, limestone cliffs, and vineyards, take in Maori rock art, and stop over in colorful villages. Yet with all these superlatives, it is suitable for beginner to medium-grade cyclists.

The bike trail starts 2km (1.2 miles) north of Aoraki/Mount Cook Village. The first section includes a short helicopter flight to Tasman Point, although options are available to access the track at points that don't require a helicopter hop.

Over the course of the trail the tracks vary from gravel to country roads to concrete roads crossing hydroelectric dams to SH83 and many miles of specially constructed bike-riding paths. The trail has been designed to allow overnight accommodation in places with good amenities and interesting attractions. Highlights include the otherworldly **Lake Ohau; Omarama,** with its clear skies, glider planes, and strangely fluted **Clay Cliffs;** the **Otematata-to-Aviemore section,** which can include a crossing of the Waitaki river via two huge hydroelectric dams; the **Kurow-Duntroon-Oamaru leg** that includes caves sheltering Maori rock art, fossil sites, and weird rock formations (Elephant Rocks); and finally the **neoclassical limestone buildings** in the coastal town of Oamaru.

Accommodation ranges from farm cottage to B&B homesteads to historic buildings to clever conversions (the Railway Station, Duntroon, has the style of a New York loft apartment), and the homesteads of Tokarahi and Burnside offer insights into the grand homes of old North Otago. Some offer accommodation only; others offer eateries only, and still others have both. Get the details of affiliated tour operators, accommodations, and eateries at **Tourism Waitaki** (www.tourismwaitaki.co.nz) and the **Mackenzie Country** (wwwmackenzie.govt.org.nz) websites. You can also see it all on video. The Alps 2 Ocean (www.alps2ocean.com) website details the trail with maps, comprehensive information on stopovers, and a video of the experiences.

ORGANIZERS/TOUR PROVIDERS

o **Alps 2 Ocean Cycle Trail** (www.alps2ocean.com; (©) **03/434-1655**) provides a comprehensive website with maps, weather information, trail status and accommodation options for each of the eight sections.

o **Helibike,** Twizel (http://helibike.com; (©) **0800/435-424** in NZ, or 64/21/435-424), is a heli-bike alternative.

o **Kiwistyle Lake Tekapo** ((©) **64/21-288-0100**) has fully supported tours, bike hire, and luggage transfers.

o **A2O Cycle Journeys,** Twizel ((©) **03/435-0578** in NZ), provides bike hire, daily luggage movement, shuttles, accommodation bookings.

o **Adventure South NZ** (www.advsouth.co.nz; (©) **0800/001-166** in NZ, or 03/942-1222) operates scheduled tours from October to April, cycling 30 to 50km a day. Private trips can be organized.

o **Tuatara Tours,** Christchurch (www.tuataratours.co.nz; (©) **0800/377-378** in NZ, or 03/962-3280), organizes and books packages, everything from bike porterage to accommodations and all meals dining out.

AORAKI/MOUNT COOK | Lake Pukaki

En Route to Waitaki District: Twizel

Twizel was once a company town. The town was built in 1968 by the Ministry of Works to house all those who worked on the hydroelectric canals, dams, and lake schemes. It is now a vacation spot with enviable weather, rivers, lakes, and scenery. It has good lodging and food options if the weather in Aoraki/Mount Cook National Park is iffy and visitors decide to wait it out. The staff at **Twizel i-SITE,** Twizel Events Centre, Market Square (② **03/435-3124**), can help in any aspect of travel planning and will organize and book tours, activities, and transport. The visitor center has restrooms, showers, a gym, Internet facilities, and souvenir shopping.

Twizel has two supermarkets, a number of cafes, bars, takeout joints, and an ATM in the shopping center. It also boasts a jolly-good what-ho chaps! flightseeing option in a **Red Cat biplane ★★★** with **Red Cat Scenic Flights,** SH8 (near Twizel; www.redcat.co.nz; ② **0800/733-228** in NZ). This is an over-the-top experience, with passengers dressed for the event in (provided) leather flying jackets, goggles, and helmets. It offers six flight options, including the unique "Wild Wilderness" into the Ahuriri Conservation Area over Mount Barth Glacier, and the "Dambusters," which features a landing for coffee at the Omarama airstrip where the country's most expensive gliders wait for the wind beneath their wings. Check for availability and seasonal rates.

WHERE TO STAY

Parklands Alpine Tourist Park ★★, 122 Mackenzie Dr. (wwwparklandtwizel.co.nz; ② **03/435-0507**), is a tidy conversion of what was once the township's maternity hospital. It is now a holiday park in a pretty setting (plenty of roaming space for kids) with cabins, tent/campsites, and cottages (NZ$36–NZ$150). Wi-Fi and bike rental are available.

Matuka Lodge B&B ★★★ This is a homestead of grace and charm. Hosts Jo and Peter have traveled extensively and understand the difference that warm and welcoming hospitality can make to travelers who are far from home. The spacious accommodation offers privacy and elegance throughout, with a guest lounge, den and TV room, and four guest bedrooms (two deluxe rooms with ensuite spa bathrooms and two ensuite king rooms). The views across the trout pond and golden tussocks to the ring of mountains (the property is only 45 min. from Aoraki/Mount Cook) are simply beautiful. Breakfast includes house-made preserves and conserves (jams) along with local bacon, eggs, salmon, sausages, fruit and vegetables, breads, and very good coffee.

395 Glen Lyon Rd., Twizel. www.matukaluxurylodge.com. ② **03/435-0144.** NZ$285–NZ$300. Rates include full cooked breakfast and pre-dinner aperitif and canapés. **Amenities:** Wi-Fi (free).

WHERE TO EAT

Make your breakfast stop at the **Musterers Hut ★**, 20 Ruataniwha Rd. (www.musterershut.com; ② **03/425-0241**), for local (framed) smoked salmon with

KID magnets

o **Tekapo Springs** This water playground has three hot pools, three new cool pools, an outdoor skating rink (Apr–Sept only), a tubing slide, an aqua play area, and a cafe with an all-day menu. It's open daily from 10am, and all-day passes cost from NZ$22 (6 Lakeside Dr., Tekapo; www.tekaposprings.co.nz; ℂ **0800/235-3823** in NZ).

o **Mount John Observatory** Evening tours with guides, laser beams, and powerful telescopes reveal the wonders of the stars in the night sky. See the Milky Way galaxies, planets (Saturn!) and constellations such as the Southern Cross and nearby Jewel Box. Tours are subject to weather conditions, so check in with tour operator **Earth and Sky** (www.earthandskynz.com; ℂ **03/6806-960**) on the day for times, tours, and availability.

o **The Sir Edmund Hillary Alpine Centre** Featuring "Hillary on Everest," a 75-minute documentary on how Sir Ed conquered Mount Everest, and the 20-minute "Mount Cook Magic," a 3D movie that replicates the thrill of aerial sightseeing, this center also has a planetarium (Hermitage Hotel, Aoraki/Mount Cook Village; www.hermitage.co.nz/en/the-sir-edmund-hillary-alpine-centre; ℂ **0800/686-800** in NZ, or 03/435-1809; NZD$20 adults, NZ$10 children).

o **The Vanished World Centre** Displaying mammal fossils uncovered from the district's limestone formations, the center also lets kids extract their own fossils from blocks of local rocks. The village has a restored heritage blacksmith's forge, an old gaol, and the "brewer's hole," a deep, spring-fed body of water with a viewing platform (7 Campbell St., Duntroon, Waitaki Valley, SH 83; www.vanishedworld.co.nz; ℂ **03/431-2024;** admission NZ$10 adults, free children 12 and under).

o **Children's Playground** Overlooking Friendly Bay on Harbour Street in Oamaru (the inner harbor; good for swimming and rowing), this playground has penny farthing bikes for climbing up, over, on, and even swinging from and on tunnels and futuristic slides, "trees" that look like the War of the Worlds passed this way, and a big playground elephant.

scrambled eggs. If you're here for lunch, add a Kurow Valley wine to the order. Breakfast is served from 9am to 11:30am, and lunch is served from 11:30am to 2pm.

Shawty's Café ★★ CAFE/PIZZA Shawty's is known for its pizzas, but it does a good breakfast, lunch, and dinner as well. The breakfast menu has a different take on kasundi eggs, with its stack of savory fritters (patties), bacon, and eggs topped with a kasundi-style relish. The lunch menu offers the aforementioned pizzas, but don't overlook meat-in-a-bun options like lamb burger and rib-eye steak sandwich. If pizza, steak, or lamb rack for dinner don't appeal, the menu has an interesting pork-belly cut on leek tart with broad beans (fava beans) and mustard sauce. It's a kid-friendly place, but the kid's menu is basically pasta or pizza and ice cream.

4a Market Place, Twizel. www.shawtys.co.nz. © **03/435-3155.** Main courses NZ$26–NZ$36; pizzas NZ$16–NZ$20. Daily 8am–late.

Ministry of Works Bar & Eatery ★ REGIONAL/INTERNATIONAL
In late 2015 Troy and Rachel Sheridan, the owners of Shawty's Café, bought the empty premises of Hunters restaurant next door and opened a bar and eatery to fill a gap in Twizel's social life: an evening-only bar and eatery with live music. The name comes from the town's one-time main employer the Ministry of Works, which built not only the town but the lakes, canals, and dams behind the giant hydroelectric scheme that reshaped the Mackenzie Country and the neighboring Waitaki Valley from the 1930s to the 1980s. Craft beers are on tap, and good Canterbury and Otago wines are listed. Rather than being divided into entree, mains, and tapas, the menu is described as Bedford, Lorry, and Dinkies—which to workers on the projects indicated the size/horsepower of various vehicles they drove. So, a blue cod taco (NZ$14) is a Bedford, a T-bone with mash and coleslaw (NZ$35) is the Lorry, and chicken wings (NZ$8.50) are Dinkies. In a nod to history, the owners have given over a wall to original street maps of Otematata and Twizel townships, inviting all those who ever worked and lived there to add their family names on the addresses.

2 Market Place, Twizel. © **03/435-3155.** Main courses NZ$14–NZ$35. Daily 4pm–midnight.

Lake Ohau

As SH8 leaves Twizel heading for Omarama, large signposts indicate that the turnoff ahead will bring you to a lake, a ski field, and a lodge. Take the turn; you won't regret your discovery of this piece of wilderness. For a few kilometers the landscape looks more like moonscape: barren, empty, almost treeless. Then up a rise and voila! Lake Ohau in all its blue glory and Aoraki/Mount Cook in the distance. Travel past a smaller lake (Lake Middleton) on the other side of the road from the "big" lake and soon you will be at **Lake Ohau Lodge,** 2295 Lake Ohau Rd. (www.ohau.co.nz; © **03/438-9885**). Even if you only stop for lunch on the deck you will treasure the silence, the peace, and the scents of beech forest, willow herb, and fresh water. Stay if you can; ask about the bed, breakfast, and dinner rate.

WAITAKI DISTRICT

203km (126 miles) from Aoraki/Mount Cook; Omarama 30km (18 miles) from Twizel

In the 1880s, Omarama was a staging post for the coach from Oamaru to Wanaka. Today the attractions of this small town include **gliding** (www.glideomarama.com; © **03/438-9555**), **sheep-shearing** demonstrations (www.thewrinklyrams.co.nz; © **03/438-9751**), and **hot tubbing** in pure mountain water (http://hottubsomarama. co.nz; © **03/438-9705**). The road ahead, SH8, leads to the Lindis Pass and into Central Otago, but if you take the turn into SH83 you'll discover one of the South Island's best kept-secrets: the Waitaki Lakes and Waitaki Valley.

The Waitaki Lakes & Waitaki Valley

The Waitaki Lakes—Benmore, Aviemore, and Waitaki—are manmade, created between 1928 and 1968 when three hydroelectric power stations were built on the Waitaki River and lakes spread out behind the dams. From Omarama, SH83 skirts Lake Benmore briefly, but the size of the lake is better appreciated from the top of Benmore Dam. The formation of Lake Aviemore in the 1960s created a lake in what had been a deep river bed. This huge body of water is bordered with willows and grassy banks. The last lake, Waitaki, was built by hand for a Depression-era make-work project—no bulldozers, no excavators, only shovels and picks. A cluster of houses built in the 1940s as homes for permanent workers remains. In the past, plagues of rabbits periodically denuded the farmlands and hills, but now with the Waitaki tapped for its water and the drylands irrigated, the region is prosperous.

Kurow is only the second point where the Waitaki is bridged, linking Otago to Canterbury. It's a typical rural town, with a few shops and cafes lining the highway through the township. The old village post office has been converted to a cellar door for the local wineries, and some Victorian-era buildings still stand, including the pretty vicarage and chapel of St. Albans, although others have suffered unfortunate conversions or stand empty. The **Kurow Museum,** 57 Bledisloe St. (www.kurow.org.nz; © **03/436-0950**), in the main thoroughfare, is an excellent example of a country museum with local history put into wider perspective from the days when big, high-country sheep runs were divided and sold as smaller properties. It includes a homage to local rugby heroes All Black player Philip Gard (1971) and All Black captain (2004–2015) Richie McCaw.

A feature of Duntroon is its limestone cliffs and escarpments. Fossilized mammals discovered in the limestone star at the **Vanished World Heritage Centre,** 7 Campbell St., Duntroon, SH 83 (www.vanishedworld.co.nz; © **03/431-2024;** admission NZ$10 adults, free children 12 and under; Maori rock art and the strange formations of "Elephant Rocks" are part of the same limestone feature). The village, which also has a restored blacksmith's forge and an old gaol, is a pleasant place to explore especially for those who are participating in the Alps 2 Ocean Cycle Trail (see "The Long Ride: Alps to Ocean Cycle Trail," p. 361) and stopping over. Stately accommodation options at the homesteads of Tokarahi and Burnside offer visitors (and cyclists on the trail) an insight into the grand homes of old North Otago.

OAMARU ★★★

112km (70 miles) north of Dunedin (about a 1½-hr. drive) on SH1; 203km (126 miles) from Aoraki/Mount Cook, on SH80; 43km (27 miles) from Duntroon, on SH83

This quiet, coastal town is home to the largest collection of **Victorian heritage buildings** in the country. Built in locally hewn, creamy-white limestone, many of the hefty, ornate buildings, complete with enormous Corinthian columns, are decidedly European in concept and construction, and stand out

A VICTORIAN heritage

Some 150 years ago Oamaru was known as the best-built town in the country, especially its commercial center, which extended from the small harbor and creek. Today, many of the grand neoclassical Victorian-era buildings—public houses and hotels, warehouses, offices, banks, bakeries, and shops selling everything from patent medicines to fancy feathered hats—have been returned to useful life. Thanks, in large part, to limestone.

When the town was first established, it was discovered that local limestone hills could be quarried. Oamaru limestone is soft to cut, easy to carve, reasonably easy to build with, and improves with age. As it weathers, it hardens. The 19th-century streetscapes in Oamaru were fine examples of space and grace. Then the port began to falter, and the business center moved to Thames Street. Harbour Street and neighboring Tyne and Itchen streets became a backwater. It was not until 1985, when a film crew sought permission to use the streets as a backdrop for a Victorian setting, that Oamaru fully realized what was in its midst. In 1987 the formation of the Oamaru Whitestone Civic Trust enabled the purchase and restoration of many of the old buildings, and that, combined with support from the New Zealand Historic Places Trust, has seen Oamaru regain its status as an architectural prize.

among colonial-era homes. Then there is the town's growing fame as the Steampunk capital of Australasia, maybe the world. It's a strange mix, but in Oamaru the grandeur of one and the inventiveness of the other come together brilliantly.

Essentials

GETTING THERE & GETTING AROUND

BY PLANE   Oamaru has an airport, but no commercial flights currently operate there.

BY COACH (BUS)   InterCity Coaches (www.intercity.co.nz; ✆ **09/583-5780**) has daily scheduled services operating from main centres north and south of Oamaru (✆ **09/623-1503**). **Naked Bus** (https://nakedbus.com) has daily services to/from Christchurch and Dunedin.

BY CAR   Take SH1 from Dunedin. SH1 from Christchurch, and SH83 from Omarama via Waitaki Lakes, Kurow, and Duntroon.

VISITOR INFORMATION

The Oamaru **i-SITE Visitor Centre,** 1 Thames St. (www.visitoamaru.co.nz; ✆ **03/434-1656**), is close to the **Victorian Oamaru Historic Precinct** (www.victorianoamaru.co.nz). Like every i-SITE center, it provides expert travel recommendations and bookings services for transport and accommodation.

ORIENTATION

Oamaru is on the coast, but the port no longer operates as a commercial venture. SH1 from Dunedin becomes Severn Street at the top of the South Hill. SH83 joins SH1 at Pukeuri, which leads to the north end of the town. **Thames Street** is the main thoroughfare through the shopping/business district.

[FastFACTS]

Emergencies Ambulance, fire, police: toll-free $\textcircled{C}$ **111. Oamaru Police Station:**
$\textcircled{C}$ **03/433-1400.**

Medical   Oamaru Hospital: $\textcircled{C}$ **03/443-0290.**

Exploring Oamaru

The **Victorian Oamaru Historic Precinct** ★★★, on Harbour and Tyne
streets (www.victorianoamaru.co.nz), is a restoration marvel. Elegant buildings rescued from obscurity now house artists, crafts, cafes, and pubs.
Michael O'Brien Bookbinder ★★★, 7 Tyne St. ($\textcircled{C}$ **03/434-9277**), is a
renowned craftsman making books by traditional hand-bound methods. Like
many others who run businesses in the precinct, he lives a Victorian lifestyle
and dresses in period costume. **Oasis** ★ (http://oasisnz.com) is a large shop/
storehouse of bibelots, paintings, books, collectibles, and antiques with an
interesting and knowledgeable owner sitting quietly with his dog in the midst
of the treasures. A bakehouse, fudge shop, gift shops, good art galleries, cafes,
a whisky distillery, and a brewery keep the buzz alive in the area.

A leaflet available from the Oamaru i-SITE Information Centre lists those
buildings of heritage significance that are accessible to visitors. Among them
are the **Harbour Board Office** (built in 1876), Harbour Street; the **Criterion
Hotel** (1877), Tyne Street; The **ANZ bank** (1871), Thames Street; the **Opera
House,** Thames Street, and the **Forrester Gallery,** Thames Street.

For some 10 years Oamaru has had a reputation among steampunk enthusiasts for its support for the movement. Steampunk, for those who don't know,
is where sci-fi meets the Victorian age of steam, a retro-futuristic mashup of
Victorian and industrial. **Steampunk HQ** ★★★, 1 Itchen St. (http://steam-
punkoamaru.co.nz), in a restored building built in 1883 when Oamaru claimed
to be larger than Los Angeles, is a mad mix of whimsical sci-fi art, sound and
light shows, film, and "War of the Worlds." There's a lot to see, and most
exhibits warrant a second look. It's open daily 10am to 5pm (NZ$10 adults,
NZ$2 children, NZ$20 family pass).

Take in the machinations, then mosey along the street toward the beachfront
and see what steampunk style has wrought in the **Children's Playground** ★★
overlooking Friendly Bay (the inner harbor; good for swimming and rowing).
Surely a one-off, this child-pleaser features penny-farthing bikes for climbing
up, over, on and even swinging from and on, tunnels and futuristic slides,
"trees" that look like the War of the Worlds passed this way, and, yes, even a
big fake playground elephant.

Wildlife enthusiasts won't want to miss a tour of the **Oamaru Blue Penguin Colony** ★, Waterfront Road (www.penguins.co.nz; $\textcircled{C}$ **03/433-1195**).
Many of the penguins spend the day at sea (guided day tours of breeding area:
NZ$16 adults, NZ$8 children 5–17) and return to their colony under the harborside cliffs at night. Book your spot for the evening viewing (NZ$28 adults,

NZ$14 children 5–17; rates higher for premium seating)—and don't be late or you might miss the rush as the little penguins scurry in from the sea. Wear your warmest clothes; it can get cold.

Where to Stay

Highfield Mews ★, corner of Thames and Exe streets (GPS #26 Exe St.; www.highfieldmews.co.nz; ✆ **0800/843-639,** or 03/434-3437), offers comfortable, compact, well-designed motel units, good for self-catering, with free parking, and the free use of bikes and barbecue grills. Rates from NZ$165.

Another venerable Victorian building (ca. 1881) holds the **Brydone Hotel,** 115 Thames St. (www.brydonehotel.co.nz; ✆ **03/433-048;** from NZ$115). The building has been altered, but a number of historic details remain, including the staircase. The hotel has a restaurant and bar and same-day laundry service.

Pen-y-bryn Lodge ★★★ Pen-y-bryn is Welsh for top of the hill, an apt address for this impressive Victorian heritage homestead. Hosts James Glucksman and James Boussy came to Oamaru in 2010 in search of their ideal house and found it in this inspirational building. The large timbered home has a Category One listing with the New Zealand Historic Places Trust, and the generously sized billiards room, library, and drawing room reflect the lodge's journey from Victorian times to the 21st century. In 2015 the lodge was revamped, resulting in the seamless expansion of the Garden, Nest, and Park rooms to incorporate sitting areas, super-king beds, and bathrooms with shower and bath. Antique furniture, artworks, magnificent paneling, and oak parquet flooring are background constants in the public rooms, but huge log fires, flowers, and soft, elegant furnishings remind that this is a home where guests are welcome. If the dinner option is included in the stay, chef James (Glucksman) is happy to organize his kitchen and menu to allow an evening viewing at the Blue Penguin Colony.

41 Towey St. www.penybryn.co.nz. ✆ **03/434-7939.** 5 units. NZ$625–NZ$750 double. Rates include breakfast, pre-dinner drinks, and canapés. NZ$875 with 4-course dinner. **Amenities:** Concierge; laundry service; Wi-Fi (free).

Where to Eat

A little coffeebar/cafe with the big vibe, **Tees Street Café ★★**, 1 Tees St., Oamaru (www.teesst.com; ✆ **03/434-7004**), lies just around the corner from Cucina 1871 (see below), facing the church of St Luke. It does an excellent breakfast with a menu that may feature black pudding or shakshuka eggs. The cabinet food is on the decadent side (lots of caramel), but the herb scones are very good. Excellent coffee and local Craftwork brew beer are also available. It's open 6:30am to 4pm weekdays; 7:30am–4pm weekends.

Fat Sally's ★, 84 Thames St. (✆ **03/434-8368**), serves good, inexpensive pub food in a relaxed atmosphere that is also buzzing with bar patrons.

Scotts Brewing Company ★, Wansbeck Street (http://scottsbrewing.co.nz; ✆ **03/432-2244**), is a purpose-built craft brewery and cafe and so close to the historic precinct it qualifies as the neighborhood brew bar. The deck is a fine place to sample one of its nine craft beers. If Tar Pot Mary or Wainak Witbier is available, do try. The kitchen also turns out some classy pizzas with tongue-in-cheek titles (smoked penguin, anyone?) from NZ$18.

Cucina 1871 ★★ ITALIAN   An interesting venue with food prepared by a chef who clearly understands Italian cuisine, Cucina 1871 is located in one of the city's elegant heritage Victorian buildings. The menu ripples with classics: arancini, duck ragu, seafood linguine, risotto, affogato, panna cotta—and all are as they should be. The good wine list includes local Waitaki wines but is dominated by Italian varietals; trust the sommelier.

1 Tees St., corner Itchen St. www.cucina1871.co.nz. Ⓒ **03/434-5696.** Main courses NZ$29–NZ$33. Daily 4pm–late.

Riverstone Kitchen ★★★ INTERNATIONAL   A short drive north (12km/8 miles) of Oamaru, and out on its own in a rural setting, this is a classic destination restaurant, with many awards and many fans. Bevan and Monique Smith (chef and maitre 'd, respectively) own and operate a cafe by day and an evening restaurant on farmland alongside busy SH1. The availability of space could have seen a sprawling coachstop eatery, but the husband-and-wife team came to Oamaru from the famed bistro d'ecco in Brisbane, Australia, to create one of New Zealand's best establishments. The name comes from the local river stones (greywacke) washed to a smooth pale grey by glacial ice and the Waitaki River. The restaurant space is large, light, and calm, cool on hot days and warmed by a huge fireplace on chilly days and nights. Outside a well-equipped playspace delights the kids, and a large kitchen garden and orchard supplies seasonal fruit and vegetables. Locally produced foods include early potatoes (jersey bennes), stonefruit, berries (blackcurrants and raspberries), pork, lamb, and venison. The food positively sings from breakfast to dinner. Maybe pork and fennel sausages with harissa for brekkies? Otago's blueskin bay clams, then saltimbocca chicken with burnt butter sauce and new potatoes for dinner? Do dessert too, especially if blackcurrant ice cream or a soufflé is on the menu.

1431 SH1. www.riverstonekitchen.co.nz. Ⓒ **03/431-3505.** Main courses NZ$22–NZ$32. Thurs–Mon 9am–5pm and Thurs–Sun 5–9pm.

DUNEDIN, SOUTHLAND & STEWART ISLAND

V isitors tend to overlook the areas covered in this chapter, which is seriously unfortunate because Dunedin, Southland, and Stewart Island offer some of the country's more diverse and fascinating flora and fauna; intriguing rural towns; and probably one of the least harried travel experiences in all of New Zealand.

Some geography before we get down to the advice. Otago encompasses a number of districts and towns. The district of Dunedin includes the Otago Peninsula, the town of Mosgiel, and the Taieri Plains. The Waitaki district extends from Mackenzie Country (p. 354) to the towns of Oamaru and Palmerston. The Catlins, Gore, and Invercargill are in Southland, the country's coolest region, but the rainfall and temperatures produce the grasslands that support intensive dairy-sheep and dairy farming. Stewart Island, the third-largest island of New Zealand, is an unspoiled area rich in native birds and vegetation.

DUNEDIN ★★★

283km (175 miles) S of Queenstown; 366km (227 miles) S of Christchurch; 220km (136 miles) N of Invercargill

Dunedin is a city of grand Victorian architecture befitting its 19th-century status as the top dog in New Zealand's wealthiest region. That status disappeared with the demise of gold mining, and today the city is best known as a university town. The **University of Otago,** New Zealand's oldest university, was established in 1869, and the original buildings (following the design of Glasgow University) have retained their handsome bluestone and slate detailing. A conglomerate of less ornate but more functional 20th- and 21st-century university buildings now spread throughout North Dunedin.

Although Dunedin is Otago's main business center, the city has a quaint Scottish soul and a penchant for quirkiness. You can have a dress kilt made up in your clan tartan, love or hate the music of dozens of indie music bands, and applaud the work of international up-and-coming fashion designers on a railway station platform disguised as a catwalk. That's in addition to touring a Chinese garden, an elegant 19th-century family home, a chocolate factory, and an albatross colony. All in all, Dunedin is an über-cool packet of pleasures, large and small.

ESSENTIALS

GETTING THERE

BY PLANE   **Air New Zealand** flies to/from Dunedin, Sydney, Melbourne, and Brisbane, as well as major NZ centers (www.airnewzealand.co.nz; ✆ **0800/737-000** in NZ). **Virgin Australia** (www.virginaustralia.com) has flights from/to Dunedin and Brisbane, Australia. **Jetstar** (www.jetstar.com) operates scheduled domestic and to/from Australia flights to main centers in New Zealand.

The **Dunedin Airport** (www.flydunedin.com) is 40 minutes south of the city, and taxis charge approximately NZ$90 for the trip into town. Door-to-door shuttle services with **Airport Shuttles Dunedin** (www.airportshuttles-dunedin.co.nz; ✆ **0800/477-800** in NZ) cost considerably less, with discounted fares for two or more passengers. The cost per passenger if more than 5 passengers are riding is NZ$12.

BY COACH (BUS)   **InterCity** (www.intercity.co.nz; ✆ **03/471-71433**) and **Naked Bus** (https://nakedbus.com) provide daily coach connections throughout the South Island, linking main centers and visitor hotspots.

BY CAR   SH1 is the main route in and out of the city. Dunedin is 366km (227 miles) and approximately a 5-hour drive south of Christchurch; 220km (136 miles) and 2 to 3 hours northeast of Invercargill; and 4 hours from Queenstown, if driving inland through Central Otago.

GETTING AROUND

BY BUS   The **GoBus** service (www.orc.govt.nz; ✆ **0800/474-082** in NZ) is run by the Otago Regional Council. Most city buses leave from the vicinity of the Octagon. Bus timetables are available from the Dunedin i-SITE at 50 The Octagon. Distances are divided into zones with fares ranging from Zone One NZ$2.20 to Zone Seven NZ$6.70. If you're planning extensive bus travel in Dunedin and/or Queenstown it might pay to purchase a GoCard which provides a 10 per cent discount on every trip. These concession cards cost NZ$5 to issue and a minimum of NZ$10 must be loaded. The cards are also valid on Queenstown's Connectabus services.

BY CAR   Once you familiarize yourself with the one-way systems and the interrupted street pattern around the Octagon, Dunedin is easy to negotiate, but a GPS system is a good investment. Most central streets have "pay and display" **metered parking** for 2 to 3 hours at a time, and there are public car park buildings in Lower Moray Place between Lower Stuart Street and Burlington Street and in Great King Street between St. Andrew and Hanover streets. Permitted times and payment methods are clearly posted.

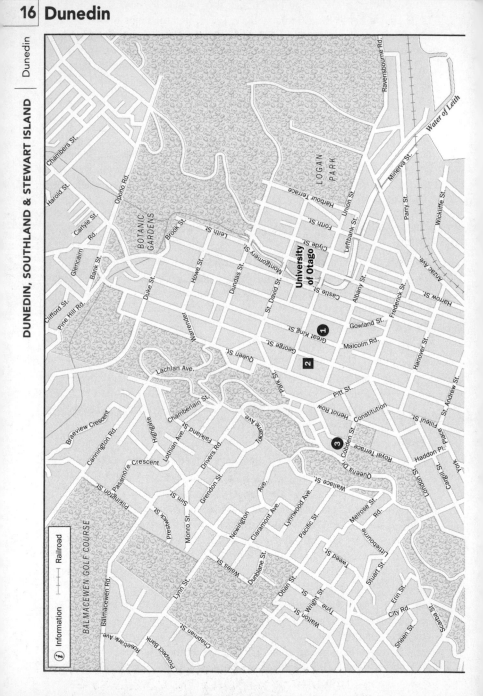

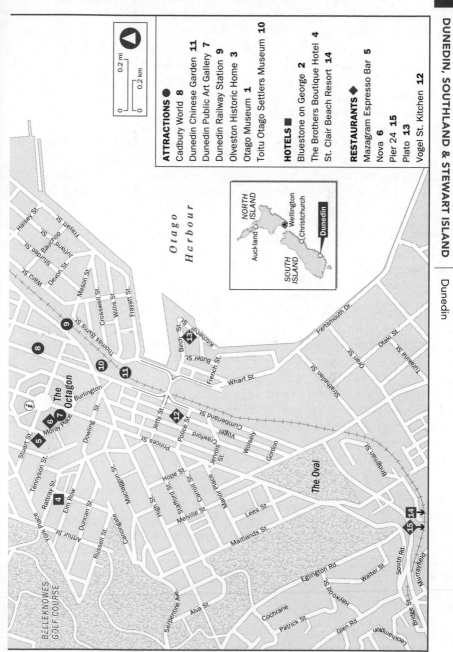

ATTRACTIONS ●
Cadbury World **8**
Dunedin Chinese Garden **11**
Dunedin Public Art Gallery **7**
Dunedin Railway Station **9**
Olveston Historic Home **3**
Otago Museum **1**
Toitu Otago Settlers Museum **10**

HOTELS ■
Bluestone on George **2**
The Brothers Boutique Hotel **4**
St. Clair Beach Resort **14**

RESTAURANTS ◆
Mazagram Espresso Bar **5**
Nova **6**
Pier 24 **15**
Plato **13**
Vogel St. Kitchen **12**

Otago Harbour

NORTH ISLAND
Auckland
Wellington
Christchurch
SOUTH ISLAND
Dunedin

VISITOR INFORMATION

The **Dunedin i-SITE Visitor Centre,** 50 The Octagon (www.dunedin.govt. nz/isite; ⏰ **03/474-3300**), is open Monday to Friday 8:30am to 6pm and Saturday and Sunday 8:45am to 6pm (till 5pm Apr–Oct).

ORIENTATION

Rather than having the usual square at its heart, Dunedin has the tree-lined **Octagon,** which acts as a central meeting place. This is where you'll find municipal chambers, a cathedral, many cafes, wine bars and pubs, Dunedin Art Gallery, design outlets, good shops, and a massive statue of the Scottish bard Robbie Burns, who sits in majesty "with his back to the kirk and his face to the pub." The Octagon divides the city's main street into **George Street** to the north and **Princes Street** to the south. A popular shopping area is to be found in the George Street section. The city center is at the head of Otago Harbour, and is encircled by a 200-hectare (500-acre) strip of land, the **Green Belt.**

[FastFACTS]

Emergencies   Ambulance, fire, police: toll-free ⏰ **111. Dunedin Central Police:** ⏰ **03/471-4800.**

Medical   Dunedin Public Hospital: ⏰ 03/474-0999.

Exploring Dunedin

Dunedin's **Railway Station** at 20 Anzac Avenue could have fallen from the pages of a fairy story with its slightly mad turrets, colonnades, and imposing stained-glass windows depicting lit-up steam engines (in the ticket hall). Its style was described as Flemish Renaissance by designer George A. Troup, and it has changed little since its opening in 1906, other than no longer being a stopping place for daily passenger trains. If you're nearby, do visit.

The Dunedin Chinese Garden ★★   Dunedin has a considerable Chinese community, many of whom have roots back to the Chinese gold miners of the 1860s Otago gold rush. The Scholar's Garden sprang from the sentiment that the Chinese had played an important part in local history and their efforts should be acknowledged. So this gated oasis of water and graceful trees (between the harbor and the business district) was designed and built in Shanghai, dismantled, shipped to Dunedin, reconstructed, and opened in 2008. Despite the unusual provenance, the gardens don't have an artificial atmosphere; instead they offer an aura of scholarly calm. The garden also has a good, albeit small, gift shop.

Corner of Rattray and Cumberland sts. www.dunedinchinesegarden.com. ⏰ **03/477-4000.** Admission NZ$9 adults, NZ$6 students, free for children under 13. Daily 10am–5pm.

Dunedin Public Art Gallery ★★   Who would have thought a department store could convert to such a splendid art gallery? Congratulations to the staff of the Dunedin Public Art Gallery who pulled this feat off. The gallery opened in 1996 in the rambling premises of the Dominion Importing Company (DIC), which stocked everything from shoes to silverware. It has significant holdings of European art, Japanese prints, French Impressionist works (including the only Monet on the continent), and a collection of contemporary and early New Zealand art. A groovy foyer shop sells arty things.

30 The Octagon. www.dunedin.art.museum. ℂ **03/474-3240.** Free admission. Daily 10am–5:30pm.

Olveston Historic Home ★★★ Olveston is one of the country's best examples of an old-fashioned stately home. Designed by London architect Sir Ernest George, the 35-room, Jacobean-style mansion was built between 1904 and 1906 for the wealthy Theomin family. It is said that traveling and shopping was a hobby of the family patriarch—and didn't he do well? Inside this delightful residence you'll find a trove of Eastern decorative arts—in bronze, cloisonné, ivory, ceramics, jade—and over 250 paintings. My favorite part? The formal dining room with its grand banquet table set for dinner. If the room seems dark on a sunny day, it's the protective UV-ray film on the windows. Touring this house is time-travel at its best— it's been meticulously preserved, so it really feels like the family popped out for a minute, leaving you to look around. Viewing by guided tour only.

42 Royal Terrace. www.olveston.co.nz. ℂ **03/477-3320.** NZ$20 adults, NZ$19 seniors and students, NZ$11 school-age children. Six 1-hour tours daily between 9:30am and 4pm.

Otago Museum ★★★ Established in 1868, this is New Zealand's fourth-largest museum, with over 1.7 million items; most people are surprised by the depth of its large ethnographic, natural-history, and decorative-arts collections. These include **Southern Land Southern People ★★** a superbly curated exhibition of southern Maori art and artifacts, their stories and treasures; and **Discovery World Tropical Forest** (on the same level) which draws visitors into a re-created, and quite humid, rainforest, home to **First Flight ★★★**, a three-level butterfly experience. Constantly changing exhibitions are mounted; should **Ice Lab ★★★** be on during your visit—it features fascinating examples of Antarctic architecture—make it a must-see. The **Museum Café** features the region's famed cheese rolls among its selections; these are an Otago/Southland specialty (but you might wonder why).

419 Great King St. www.otagomuseum.govt.nz or www.discoveryworld.co.nz. ℂ **03/474-7474.** Donation admission to museum; World Tropical Forest NZ$10 adults, NZ$5 children 2–18 (free under 2), NZ$25 family pass (2 adults, 2 children), NZ$9 students and seniors. Daily 10am–5pm; tours daily at 2pm.

Toitu Otago Settlers Museum ★★★ Originally conceived as the Early Settlers Museum, the institution had a major revamp in 2012 and now draws raves for its brilliantly curated exhibits. These range from a re-creation of a family cabin in a sailing vessel, simulating the voyage that brought settlers from Scotland to this distant place in the Pacific (an evocative display of comforts and hardships) to a vintage Buick and the country's first coal-fired ovens. Especially moving: a poignant tribute to Otago's men and women who fought in World War I (1914–1918) far across the seas in Europe. This special exhibit that will remain in place until 2018, 100 years after "the war to end all wars" ended. Every corner of this vast building holds much of interest.

31 Queens Garden. www.toituosm.com. ✆**03/477-5052.** Free admission. Daily 10am–5pm.

Just Outside the City: The Otago Peninsula

The 33km (20-mile) Otago Peninsula is a busy ecotourism corridor, particularly at the headland area known as Taiaroa Head. It is home to a number of bird and sea mammal colonies that shelter royal albatross, Little Blue Penguins, yellow-eyed penguins, fur seals, and Hooker sea lions. Of these, the most important is the royal albatross protected rookery at the Royal Albatross Centre (see below).

To see the adorable Little Blue Penguins, we highly recommend booking a tour with a naturalist from the Royal Albatross Centre. The best option for those planning on seeing a variety of sites on the peninsula is the **Pukekura Blue Penguin Tour** ★★ (www.albatross.org.nz; ✆ 03/478-0499; NZ$25 adults, NZ$10 children, NZ$60 family pass two adults, up to three children), which takes place at dusk nightly, when the small penguins come ashore at Pilots Beach below the cliffs of the headland. For those without a car, the **Tiki Tour Little Blue Penguin Tour** ★★ (www.albatross.org.nz; ✆ 03/478-0499; NZ$65 adults, NZ$50 children over 5, NZ$40 children under 5) includes transport from the Octagon in Dunedin to Pilots Beach.

Larnach Castle ★★   Larnach Castle may be small by European standards, but it's clear William Larnach had more than a simple bungalow in mind when he set about constructing this marvelous edifice in 1871. No doubt keen to impress his French heiress wife, he hired 200 workmen for 3 years just to build the shell; a host of European master craftsmen took another 12 years to complete the interior. The carved foyer ceiling alone took three craftsmen 6½ years to finish. The Georgian hanging staircase is the only one in the Southern Hemisphere. Larnach came to New Zealand from Australia in the late 1860s to set up the first Bank of Otago. He later became a member of Parliament, but with three marriages behind him and a family history dotted with scandal and misfortune, he committed suicide in the Parliament Buildings in Wellington. (His first two wives both died at the age of 38, and his third dealt him a fatal emotional blow by dallying with a

Chocolate Heaven

Nirvana for fans of sweets, **Cadbury World,** 280 Cumberland St. (www.cadburyworld.co.nz; ✆ **03/467-7967**), is chokka with chocolate and open for visitors. Daily guided tours of the factory depart from the foyer every half-hour from 9am until 3:15pm. Both the 75- and 45-minute tours include a few surprises, such as a chocolate waterfall (very Willy Wonka, we must say). Generous samples of the product are handed out, which is possibly why tours get thumbs up from the kids.

Relax in heated salt-water pools as you listen to the crash of waves on the rocks outside at the **St. Clair Hot Salt Water Pool,** a pool complex tucked between the rocky shore and the open sea. Pool temps are always maintained at a pleasing 82°F (28°C). The complex is open from late October through March, Monday through Friday 6am until 7pm (weekends 7am–7pm). Admission is NZ$6 adults, NZ$3 children 5 to 15, and NZ$13 family. St. Clair beach is also a popular surfing beach for those learning the sport and hot shots in competition (the 2016 Billabong National Surfing Championship was held here). Early morning and evening sees youngsters getting the hang of it all, with help from parents or pro surf instructors.

son from his first marriage.) After his death, the crown used the castle as a mental hospital.

145 Camp Rd., off Highcliff Rd. www.larnachcastle.co.nz. © **0800/527-6224** in NZ or 03/476-1616. NZ$30 adults, NZ$10 children, NZ$70 family. Daily 9am–5pm.

Monarch Wildlife Cruises ★★★   Established in 1983 by owners with degrees in biology and a wealth of experience on research vessels, these cruises offer an excellent way to see a variety of wildlife along the peninsula. Crews are experienced in conservation and know everything about the albatrosses, New Zealand fur seals, yellow-eyed penguins, and other species you're likely to see.

www.wildlife.co.nz. © **0800/666-272** in NZ, or 03/477-4276. Tours from 1 hr. (NZ$49) to half- and full-day (NZ$275, NZ$160 for children). Pickup from accommodation included.

Royal Albatross Centre ★★★   The only mainland colony of albatross in the world, this protected rookery offers a unique opportunity to see these endangered birds at unusually close range (sometimes visitors can get as close as 12 ft. away from the birds). Albatross have such huge wingspans they can fly nonstop for weeks, and during nesting/feeding season (Jan–Mar, the best times to visit), when the chicks are hatching, you can see the magnificence up close when a parent bird leaves or returns to the nest; in late afternoon, you'll see courtship displays. Be sure to bring binoculars and a camera. All tours are guided, many by volunteers, and their knowledge and patience is impressive. It's a 2-minute walk up a path to the observatory; mobile carts are available for visitors with disabilities. A souvenir shop, cafeteria, and wildlife displays are on the grounds.

1260 Harrington Point Rd., Taiaroa Head. www.albatross.org.nz. © **03/478-0499.** Free admission to Albatross Centre. Daily tours from NZ$45 adults and NZ$15 children. Reservations essential. Daily 11:15am–9:15pm.

Where to Stay in Dunedin

Bluestone on George ★★   The Bluestone accomplishes the neat trick of answering each and every traveler's need (even some they may not have realized they had). I'm talking free Wi-Fi that's lightning-fast, a washer/dryer

A day trip **TO MORAKI**

The highway (SH1) between Oamaru (p. 365) and Dunedin hugs the coast for many miles, providing sea views on one side of the road, rolling farmland and gentle bush-clad hills on the other. Two recommended places to visit are Moeraki Boulders and Fleur's Place, 3km (1¾ miles) away in Moeraki township.

Moeraki Boulders ★ is a collection of large, weirdly round boulders, popping up like giant eggs along the shoreline—a surprising sight. The boulders, classified as septarian concretions, were formed in ancient sea secretions—not unlike the formation of pearls in oysters. You'll find them, well signposted, some 36km (23 miles) south of Oamaru and 75km (47 miles) north of Dunedin. More information can be found at www.moerakiboulders.co.nz.

But the real reason to head this way is for a meal at the extraordinary **Fleur's Place ★★★** (169 Haven St., Moeraki; www.fleursplace.com; ✆ 03/439-4480). Owner Fleur Sullivan is one of the most hospitable women in the restaurant business, and her face is known internationally thanks to all of the selfies visitors feel compelled to take with her. Simple cooking techniques allow Sullivan's dishes to "sing of the sea" as a world-famous visiting chef once told the world—particularly true of the house-smoked fish, a specialty. Fleur's is open Wednesday through Sunday from 10:30am, with the last orders for dinner taken at 7:30pm. Advance reservations are essential.

and fully stocked kitchen in each unit, bathrooms with heated floors, and comfy beds with a choice of fiber or feather pillows. Heck, they will even deliver your free continental breakfast to your room if you request it. Located on a quiet street that's an easy walk from the Octagon and all its action, this motel even has hotel-like decor, all done up in soothing, silvery grays and blues. A top pick.

571 George St. www.bluestonedunedin.co.nz. ✆ **03/477-9201.** 55 units. NZ$190–NZ$260 basic double, more for bigger apartments. Rates include breakfast and free parking. **Amenities:** Business center; gym; Wi-Fi (free).

The Brothers Boutique Hotel ★★ Formerly a residence for men in the Christian Brothers' Order, the accommodation in this stately 1920s brick building has been converted from prosaic hostel-style lodging to elegant, albeit small guestrooms with leather furnishings, generous comfortable beds, fine linens, tiled bathrooms, and, in one suite, exquisite stained-glass windows. Rattray Street is a hillside address, and the excellent views from rooms and the four balconies look to the cathedral opposite, the city and harbor below.

295 Rattray St. www.brothershotel.co.nz. ✆ **0800/477-004** in NZ, or 03/477-0043. 15 units. NZ$240–NZ$395. Rates include breakfast, pre-dinner drinks, and free parking. **Amenities:** Wi-Fi (free).

Larnach Castle Lodge ★★ First things first: Lodgings here are not actually *in* the historic mansion (see our review of that in "Exploring Dunedin" above). But they are in structures purpose-built in the middle of the estate's spectacular gardens, meaning that guests get the same eye-candy views the castle's founder had (guests also get free tours of the mansion). As for the rooms, they're handsome and contemporary but with touches that recall the castle next door, like four-poster beds, walls painted in richly saturated Victorian-era colors, and overstuffed armchairs (note that the more economical "stable" rooms are less elegant than the lodge rooms). You can also stay in the very glam Camp Estate, a five-bedroom country house on the castle grounds. Many guests add an elegant dinner served in the castle to their stay.

145 Camp Rd., Otago Peninsula. www.larnachcastle.co.nz. ℂ **03/476-1616.** 19 units. NZ$155 stable room; NZ$290 lodge room; from NZ$460 camp estate. Meals and activity packages available. **Amenities:** Guest laundry; Wi-Fi (free).

Where to Eat

As a university town, Dunedin has many cafes and bars that cater to the student population, but that doesn't mean only fast-food outlets (though there are plenty of these). In this intellectual hangout, good wine, good food, and good coffee are more important than chicken nuggets and a burger, so you'll find plenty of posh as well as budget options.

Mazagram Espresso Bar ★ ESPRESSO BAR   A treat for the coffee connoisseur, this roastery supplies java for most of Dunedin's leading cafes (a telling recommendation). There's a small selection of pastries to go with your coffee (NZ$4.50 a cup). Credit cards not accepted.

Upper Moray Pl. ℂ **03/477-9959.** Open Mon–Fri 8am–6pm, Sat 10am–2pm.

Plato ★★★ SEAFOOD   Chef Nigel Broad opened this popular restaurant in 2002, and it has been a star on the Dunedin culinary scene from day one. Situated in what was once a "seafarer's rest" (a cheap, 19th-c.-era accommodation for merchant seamen) on the wharves and decorated with a quirky collection of teapots, kitchen utensils, and other bric-a-brac, it is pleasantly eccentric-looking place. But you come here for the seafood, which is super-fresh and often served in creative preparations (you might get a curry, a side of melon salsa, or something else interesting). Craft-beer fans come for the pilsner that's brewed on-site. For value, the two-course set menu (NZ$54) is hard to beat. Take a cab; it's easy to get lost in the wharf area.

2 Birch St., Inner Harbour Warehouse Area. www.platocafe.co.nz. ℂ **03/477-4235.** Main courses NZ$28–$38. Mon–Sat noon–2pm and 6pm–10pm; Sun 11am–2pm and 6–9pm.

Scotia Restaurant & Whiskey Bar ★★★ SCOTTISH   Haggis, hot pot, smoked steak, and clootie dumpling are the stars of the menu here, fitting for this Scots-obsessed city. It's all quite expertly cooked and served in an exceedingly pleasant heritage house, with framed prints of Scottish heroes on the cream-colored walls and a roaring fire (many nights) in the fireplace. Oh, and a staggeringly large choice of whiskeys makes this a popular watering hole.

199 Upper Stuart St. www.scotiadunedin.co.nz. ℂ **03/477-7704.** Main dishes NZ$34–NZ$38. Tues–Sat 5pm–2am.

The **Taieri Gorge Railway ★★★** (www.dunedinrailways.co.nz; *©* **03/477-4449**) is surely the most beautiful 47-mile train ride I've ever experienced. First there's the golden landscape: towers of schist rock, tussock grasses and wildflowers, tumbling waterfalls scattering precious water on the arid land. Then there's the engineering prowess that allowed the original steam trains to climb from sea level to the high plains of the Maniototot. It's a 4-hour roundtrip ride from Dunedin to Pukerangi (NZ$89), and 6 hours between Dunedin and Middlemarch (NZ$110). Best months for the trip are October to early April.

The Central Otago Rail Trail ★★★ is another beaut, following the (long-gone) railway line between Middlemarch and Clyde. Opened to the public for biking and walking in 2000, it is now one of the country's most popular trails. It can be done in either direction, finishing or starting at either Middlemarch or Clyde. It takes about 4 days to bike it with 4 to 6 hours of cycling each day (no very steep climbs, but a good level of fitness and some cycling experience makes the journey more pleasurable). The track goes through rail tunnels and over viaducts as it presents up-close heartland Otago, with its tawny landscape of tussock grass, wild herbs, and rocky uplands. For bike rental and accommodation information, go to www.otagocentralrailtrail.co.nz. Fully supported tours are offered by **Off the Rails** (www.offtherails.co.nz) and **Shebikeshebikes** (http://shebikeshebikes.co.nz; *©* **03/447-3271**).

Vogel Street Kitchen ★★ COMFORT FOOD   Opened late 2014 by Cantabrian Riah McLean, this is the first cafe bar to open in what was a street of warehouses. Echoing concrete floors and hissing espresso machines cannot quite smother the sounds of young corporates out for lunch or chasing after-work drinks. The menu includes standout wood-fired pizzas, some with odd names, like the Trotters Gorge (it's covered with pancetta but named for a nearby river gorge). The well-curated wine list features South Island wines; Emerson beer is on tap and the coffee is excellent.

76 Vogel St. www.vogelskitchen.co.nz. *©* **03/477-3623.** Main courses NZ$8.50–NZ$20. Mon–Thurs 7:30am–4pm; Fri 7:30am–late; Sat 8:30am–late; Sun 8:30am–4pm.

Shopping

Dunedin offers some unique shops. Most open Monday through Friday from 9am and Saturday and Sunday from 10am to 4pm. The **Scottish Shop ★★**, 17 George St. (www.scottishshop.co.nz; *©* **03/477-9965**), stocks tartan and heraldic goods, including ties, shields, brooches. **Lure ★★**, 130 Lower Stuart St. (*©* **03/477-5559**), exhibits and sells the works of leading New Zealand jewelers, much of it exquisite statement jewelry. **Dada Boutique ★★**, 28 Moray Pl. (*©* **03/477-0250**), has a small but excellent selection of New Zealand fashion labels, including knitwear. It opens at noon during the week.

En Route to Invercargill & Stewart Island

Two main roadways link Dunedin with Invercargill. **SH1** is the more direct route via Balclutha, Gore (see p. 382 for the John Money Collection at the

East Otago Gallery Gore), and Edendale (see p. 386 for a detour to Wyndham and the Maple Glen Gardens). Or leave SH1 in central Balclutha and take the well-signposted **Southern Scenic Route** to Invercargill via Owaka and The Catlins.

THE CATLINS ★★

Owaka 113km (70 miles) SW of Dunedin

Situated along the Southern Scenic Route, **The Catlins** contains the most significant area of native forest on the east coast of New Zealand. Rain falls in this area 214 days a year, but don't hesitate to step into the weather. Good walking tracks wind through forests of rimu and totara, and big sweeps of empty beach are never far away, making the soggy tramp worth it.

Scenes of natural beauty are not in short supply in New Zealand, but The Catlins have so many they can overwhelm. That's when it's time to stop for a breather and a walk in the wilderness. **Nugget Point** to **Waikawa** and **Purakaunui Falls** is a 20-minute round-trip walk through beech and podocarp forest. The 80-minute round-trip walk to/from the **Cathedral Caves** (18km/11 miles from Papatowai; www.cathedralcaves.co.nz, NZ$5 per-person entrance fee) starts in the sign-posted car park 2km (1¼ miles) off the Southern Scenic Highway. The track is through coastal bush to Waipati Beach and the 200m/200 yards-long sea-formed caves. Access to the caves is restricted to 2 hours on either side of low tide during October through to May. Tide timetables are published in regional daily newspapers and on the website, but this is a remote area, so check the notice boards at the carpark entrance for updated information. Weather or tide conditions can prevent access. A torch (flashlight) is necessary, sand-fly repellent is advised, and expect to get your feet wet. Do not disturb penguins and fur seals sheltering in the caves!

At **Curio Bay** you will see imprints of ancient trees and ferns; then, at low tide, look for fossilized tree remnants. Yellow-eyed penguins are often seen in the bay area in late afternoon.

There is more to the Catlins than raw beauty, however. **The Owaka Museum,** 10 Campbell St., Okawa (www.owakamuseum.org.nz; ℂ **03-415-8371**), is a trove of information about the area and its marine history (it's also the site of the Caitlins Info Centre). This rugged coastline is still described as a "shipwreck coast," and the museum houses relics from the wreck of the liner *Manuka,* which sank on a reef in 1929. Admission is NZ$5 adults, free children.

The Catlins: Visitor Info

In Owaka, head to the **Catlins Info Centre** at 10 Campbell St. (ℂ **03/415-8371**) for maps and travel advice (it's also the site of the Owaka Museum; see below). For more information on The Catlins, go to **www.catlins.org.nz**. The largest township, **Owaka,** has a small supermarket with an ATM. Service stations for petrol (gas) are situated in Owaka, Papatowai, Tokanui, and Fortrose.

In Papatowai look for the big green housetruck signposted **The Lost Gypsy Gallery,** where creator, designer, and craftsman extraordinaire Blair Somerville produces curiosities for collectors. "Whimsical toys" is one description offered, but the pieces are so clever in their in-out, up-down movements and so beautifully constructed from bits and pieces of what is basically junk (old tins, broken shells, screws, twists of wire), whimsy doesn't begin to describe them.

Where to Stay

Nugget View Kaka Point Motels ★   The best thing you can say about these simple motel units, set just a (steepish) 300m (328 yards) walk from the beach, are their views. That's not a knock: The digs here are dated, but clean, well maintained, and an excellent value. A cafe is nearby.

11 Rata St., Kaka Point. ℂ **0800/525-278.** NZ$100 economy units, NZ$165 units with spa baths. **Amenities:** Wi-Fi (free).

Pounawea Motor Camp ★   This motor camp has an enviable site on a sheltered waterfront. Right by the estuary, with well-fitted and -kitted (if small) cabins, and powered sites for campers and campervans, this property should fit the bill for many travelers—especially those with kids, thanks to the abundant birdlife and good bush walks from the camp. Another plus: Visitors have use of a well-stocked communal kitchen and a large table to share.

Park Lane Pounawea, Owaka. www.catlins-nz.com/pounawea-motor-camp/. ℂ **03/415-8483.** NZ$45–NZ$80 cabins; NZ$36 RV sites. **Amenities:** Nature trails; playground; pool; Wi-Fi (free).

GORE

190km (118 miles) S of Queenstown; 217km (135 miles) SW of Dunedin; 67km (42 miles) northeast of Invercargill

This pretty, pleasant rural Central Southland town has two important stops for visitors. Three, if you happen to be a country music fan and are in the neighborhood late May to early June, when the annual **Gold Guitar Week** kicks off. Yee-ha!

The big must-see is the **John Money Art Collection ★★★** on permanent display at the **Eastern Southland Gallery** at 14 Hokonui Dr. (www.esgallery. co.nz; ℂ **64/5/208-9907**). Money was New Zealand–born, but his academic career led him to Harvard University and then John Hopkins in Baltimore, where he was professor of medical psychology and pediatrics. The collection isn't medical, though: Money was a collector of indigenous art for most of his life, and, concerned that his collection would be broken up after his death, he bequeathed it all to the gallery in Gore. It is astounding that 300 high-quality pieces of art would land in a small country town, in a building that was once the town's public library. Native African, Australian, Maori, and Pacific art, and a collection of New Zealand artists Ralph Hotere and Rita Angus are on exhibit. Admission is free.

Lake Te Anau
↑ To Milford Sound
Te Anau
94
↑ To Queenstown
6
8

O T A G O

Lake Manapouri
Five Rivers
Mossburn
FIORDLAND

Lumsden
NATIONAL
6
94
Dipton
Riversdale
Lake Mahinerangi
90
8
To Dunedin →
1

PARK

Nightcaps
Gore
1
Waipahi
Milton

Winton
96
Mataura
1
Balclutha

Te Waewae Bay
Macarewa
1
Windham
Nugget Point

Riverton
Invercargill
See detail inset
1
Fortrose
Waimahaka
Owaka
Papatowai
PACIFIC OCEAN

Bluff
Lands End Boutique Hotel
Tokanui
Otara
Waikawa
Curio Bay
Chaslands Mistake

Foveaux Strait

Codfish Island
Ruapuke Island

Mason Bay
Oban
Halfmoon Bay

Mt. Allen

FRASER PEAKS

STEWART ISLAND

0 — 20 mi
0 — 20 km

Invercargill

Victoria Ave.
(i) QUEENS PARK
Southland Museum and Art Gallery
Gala St.
6
Leet St.
Water Tower
Victoria Railway Hotel
Yarrow St.
Spey St.
Don St.
Railway Station
Esk St.
Otepuni Creek
The Crescent
Tay St.
1
To Transport → World
Wood St.
Forth St.
Otepuni Gardens
Tyne St.
St. Mary's Basilica
Eye St.
To ← Airport
Tweed St.
Teviot St.
Ettrick St.
Bowmont St.
Crinan St.
1
Earn St.
(i) Information
✉ Post Office
Balmoral Dr.
Dalrymple St.
0 — 0.5 mi
0 — 0.5 km
Grace St.

Bond St., Mersey St., Leven St., Dee St., Kelvin St., Deveron St., Jed St., Doon St., Queens Dr., MacMaster St., Annan St., Liddel St., Clyde St., Nith St., Conon St., Ythan St., Ness St., Elles Rd., Princes St.

NORTH ISLAND
Auckland
SOUTH ISLAND
Wellington
Christchurch
Dunedin
Area of detail

Next stop: **The Croydon Aircraft** ★ on the outskirts of Gore at the old Mandeville Airfield, 1558 Waimea Hwy. (www.croydonaircraft.com; ⓒ **03/208-9755**), to see restored vintage aircraft. You may even get to take a flight in an open-cockpit Tiger Moth.

Gore's best restaurant is **Howl at the Moon** ★, 2 Main St. (ⓒ **03/208-3851**). Ignore the daft if memorable name and enjoy the unadventurous but well-prepared menu. My favorite dish? The lamb rack on roasted kumara with a red currant port sauce.

INVERCARGILL

190km (118 miles) S of Queenstown; 217km (135 miles) SW of Dunedin

Originally settled by Scottish immigrants in 1853, this southernmost city was surveyed in 1856 by New Zealand's first surveyor general, J. Thomson, who decided the main streets (named for Scottish rivers) would be 40m (130 ft.) wide, giving the city its extremely spacious, windy streets. Unfortunately, outside of business hours these same wide streets can present a "no-one lives here" appearance. Don't judge this book by its cover, however; Invercargill's population of roughly 53,000 is extremely social: They like to shop, eat out, and enjoy good beers and wine just as much as folks in larger cities do. And then there's the hug factor. You may get some, unexpectedly. Cargill residents are keen to share their part of New Zealand with you, the visitor, and they let you know they're happy to see you.

Like much of Southland, Invercargill's prosperity owes much to the region's lush grasslands. Farming is the backbone of the economy, and just beyond the city boundaries dairy, venison, and lamb producers earn millions. Wilderness areas offer adventures as disparate as shark-cage diving, kayaking, and hiking. With Invercargill as a base, the adventure tourism industry is roaring ahead. With its more than 1,000 motel and hotel beds, the city is the ideal jumping-off place for the wilderness areas of Fiordland, The Catlins, and Stewart Island.

Essentials

GETTING THERE & GETTING AROUND **By Plane** **Air New Zealand** (www.airnewzealand.co.nz; ⓒ **800/737-000** in NZ) has services between Invercargill and Auckland, Wellington, and Christchurch. **Stewart Island Flights** (www.stewartislandflights.com; ⓒ **03/218-9129**) has daily scheduled flights to/from Invercargill/Stewart Island.

By Coach (Bus) **InterCity** (www.intercity.co.nz; ⓒ **03/471-71433**) and **Naked Bus** (https://nakedbus.com) have daily coach services linking Invercargill with all South Island main centers and visitor hotspots.

By Car Take SH6 from Queenstown or SH1 from Dunedin.

VISITOR INFORMATION The **Invercargill i-SITE Visitor Centre** is open daily from 8am in the Southland Museum and Art Gallery, 108 Gala St. (www.southlandnz.com; ⓒ **03/211-0895**).

The main thoroughfares are Tay Street and Dee Street. Many of the principal shops and office buildings are found at their intersection.

[FastFACTS]

Emergencies Ambulance, fire, police: toll-free ⓒ 111. Invercargill Police Station: ⓒ 03/211-0400.

Medical **Southland Hospital: ⓒ 03/218-1949.**

Exploring Invercargill

It's hard to miss the big white pyramid of the **Southland Museum and Art Gallery** ★★ at 108 Gala St. (www.southlandmuseum.com; ⓒ **03/219-9069**), near the main entrance to Queens Park. A wide range of exhibits brings the region to life. The biggest attraction of all, the **Tuatarium,** should not be missed. Here you'll find the fascinating tuatara—strange prickly reptiles that are descendants of the dinosaurs and now exceptionally rare. The museum breeding program is the only one in the world. The star of the exhibit is the very ancient Henry (somewhere over 100 years old), who lives with the still-breeding reptiles Albert, Mildred, and Lucy. The conservation and breeding facilities at the museum are also hand-rearing kakapo chicks to help save it from extinction. A permanent exhibition that speed fiends will appreciate recounts the story of **Burt Munro** (a name familiar to those who saw the movie *The World's Fastest Indian*), the local man who bought and modified motorcycles for some 62 years. He achieved a (still-standing) speed record when he was 68 years old with his 47-year-old bike on the Bonneville Salt Flats (USA). The museum is open Monday through Friday 9am to 5pm and Saturday, Sunday, and holidays 10am to 5pm. Admission is free, but a fee may apply to some exhibits.

More **Burt Munro** memorabilia can be seen at **E Hayes** ★★ at 168 Dee St., a hardware/gift store that had a long association with Munro. The **E Hayes Motorwork Collection** includes Munro's workbenches, his bikes, and his tools, as well as vintage vehicles, bikes, trikes, and machinery.

Speaking of days past, **Invercargill Heritage Trail** is an excellent self-guided tour produced by the New Zealand Historic Places Trust (the brochure is available at the visitor center). It highlights 18 of the city's finest architectural specimens, including St. Mary's Basilica, on Tyne Street, and the town's famous 43m (139-ft.) red-brick Romanesque water tower.

Transport World ★★★ Reportedly the largest collection of Ford vehicles on the planet, Transport World showcases a 1940 Dodge Airflow fuel tanker (built for the Texaco Oil Company in 1939), seemingly every Ford truck made, and seven rare examples of the eight production models made before the Model T Ford, which was released in 1908 (the missing car is the Model B). The museum is a work in progress and likely ever thus—its owners are avid collectors. Open year-round to the public, it has a cafe and a Lego World on-site to keep the little kids busy, while the big kids go car crazy over anything with wheels, like a replica of the 1896 Ford Quadricycle—a star turn.

491 Tay St., Hawthorndale; www.transportworld.co.nz; ✆ **03/217-1600**). NZ$25 adults, NZ$15 children ages 5–14; guided tour NZ$45 per person. Daily 10am–5pm.

PARKS & GARDENS

The main entrance to **Queens Park** is near Southland Museum and Art Gallery. This cool, green 80-hectare (200-acre) oasis is a perfect place to wander. You'll find formal rose gardens, a rhododendron walk, an iris garden, a Japanese garden, a wildlife sanctuary, a walk-through bird aviary, duck ponds, tennis courts, and an 18-hole golf course. The aviary has a good parrot collection and is best visited in early morning or late afternoon when the birds are most active.

Maple Glen Gardens and Nursery, in nearby rural Wyndham (www. mapleglen.co.nz; ✆ **03/206-4983**), is a remarkable private garden and exotic bird haven that every gardener should see. It's open daily from 9am to 5pm. A guided walk costs NZ$8 per person, but otherwise admission is free.

Where to Stay

Ascot Park Hotel ★★ It may not the prettiest building on the block with its clunky 1980s architecture, but for quiet, comfortable accommodation at a very good price and with darn good amenities (indoor pool, sauna, and restaurant), Ascot Park nails it. And really, the extensive and pleasant gardens and lawns do much to improve the ambience. The hotel has large, attractive king and queen rooms and self-contained one-bedroom apartments. The less expensive but still quite nice motel units are self-contained studios with parking.

Corner of Tay St. and Racecourse Rd. www.ascotparkhotel.co.nz. ✆ **0800/272-687** in NZ NZ$150–NZ$250 double. Rates include free parking and free shuttle service from/ to airport and Central Business District. **Amenities:** Restaurant; bar; fitness area; indoor pool; Wi-Fi (free).

Safari Lodge ★★ This stately brick Tudor home, built in 1902 and meticulously restored to its Edwardian grandeur, would make a lovely honeymoon option. African pieces add a touch of whimsy to the romantic period decor (four-poster beds, flocked wallpaper, and the like)—owners Ray and Trish lived for a time in Mozambique. The day starts off with a feast of a breakfast, included in the price and cooked to order.

51 Herbert St. www.safarilodge.co.nz. ✆ **03/214-6329.** 4 units. NZ$200–NZ$320 double. Rates include full breakfast. **Amenities:** Billiards room; indoor spa pool; Wi-Fi (free).

Victoria Railway Hotel ★★ Set in one of the city's architectural landmarks, the Railway Hotel is a rambling structure. Some 22 of the suites have been refurbished, standard twins and studios, all with en-suite bathrooms. The decor is a mashup of colonial, Edwardian, Victorian, and current-day fussy, but unless a guest is a decorating purist, it comes across as charming. Rooms are large, bathrooms warm, and the stairs are a good workout (sorry, there's no elevator). Good service and attention to details from hosts Aaron and Georgie make the place feel even more special, as does the elaborate etched-glass door leading to the bar (rumored to be from a London gentleman's club!).

Corner Leven & Esk sts., Invercargill. www.vrhotel.co.nz. © **0800/777-557** in NZ. 22 units. NZ$120–NZ$195. Rates include free parking. **Amenities:** House bar and dining room; Wi-Fi (free).

Where to Eat

The Batch ★★ CAFE   The Batch is a favorite of locals not just for remarkably pleasant atmosphere (light, bright, and warm), but for the seriously good food and coffee—and it has a row of awards to attest to its winning ways. The menu includes fresh salads, substantial breakfast and lunch dishes (favorites include chowder and scones, and any of the blue cod options), plenty of sugary treats, and maybe the best brownie in the Southern Hemisphere.

173 Spey St. © **03/214-6357.** Main courses NZ$16–NZ$20. Mon–Fri 7am–4:30pm; Sat–Sun 8am–4pm.

Kiln ★★ INTERNATIONAL   This restaurant is also a brewery, but the menu of hearty favorites is more sophisticated than just pub food. Cheers for the lamb selections, especially the smoked back straps. For those who know and appreciate nose-to-tail cuisine, look for the sweetbreads. Beer, especially Monteith's, is the focus of the beverage list, but a comprehensive wine list offers plenty of options.

7 Don St. www.thekiln.co.nz. © **03/218-2258.** Main courses NZ$29–NZ$35. Mon–Wed & Sun 11am–midnight; Thurs 11am–1pm; Fri–Sat 11am–3am.

Louie's Café and Tapas Bar ★★★ INTERNATIONAL   If you ask locals where to go for a special meal, they'll likely point you to Louie's, which may have the most innovative menu in town. It borrows from a number of different cultures, so you might find yourself sampling salt-and-pepper squid, Mexican soft tacos, or one of the best chicken salads you've ever tasted (the lamb liver pate is also delish). The mixology is also solid, so order up a cocktail.

142 Dee St. © **03/214-2013.** Main courses NZ$28–NZ$35. Tues–Sat 5:30pm–late.

BLUFF

27km (17 miles) from Invercargill.

Bluff is known throughout the country for its namesake shellfish, Bluff oysters. One of the few wild oyster beds still producing a yearly harvest lies under Foveaux Strait (the stretch of sea separating the mainland from Stewart Island and the Southern Ocean). The flavor of Bluff oysters is briny, and markedly different from that of farmed oysters. The season's duration is determined by the Bluff Oyster Management Company, but it usually opens in March and closes in July. The annual **Bluff Oyster & Southland Seafood Festival** ★★★ is held between late April and May (www.bluffoysterfest.co.nz).

Where to Stay & Eat

Bluff Fish and Chips Shop ★ SEAFOOD   Takeout fare moves up a notch when you get a steamy parcel of battered oysters as close to the catch as this. The batter is not doughy, the oysters are fat and whole, the chips long but not too thin, and plenty of salt is scattered around. Oh, and vinegar is the sauce du jour, so don't go asking for a lemon and garlic vinaigrette.

42 Gore St. ℂ **03/212/7391.** Oyster prices depend on the seasonal set price but expect to pay at least NZ$2.50 an oyster; fish NZ$4–NZ$6 a piece, chips (fries) NZ$3. Sun–Thurs 11:30am–8pm; Fri–Sat 11:30am–9pm.

Lands End Boutique Hotel ★★   This is as far as the road goes; SH1 ends (or starts) here. So this small hotel, big on style and comfort, is also wonderfully serene. Spacious en-suite bedrooms (super-comfortable beds) and sea views also recommend it. The Oyster Cove Café next door (see below) is open daily, but evening dining in this predominately lunch cafe/bar is limited (dinner is served Wed–Sun until 8pm). Good thing, then, that the hotel may be opening its own bistro in the near future. Otherwise, host Lynda Jackson is happy to recommend Bluff pubs and eateries if guests want to explore.

SH1, 10 Ward Parade, Stirling Point. www.landsendhotel.co.nz. ℂ **03/212-7575.** 5 units. NZ$180–NZ$220. Rates include continental breakfast and off-street parking. **Amenities:** Wi-Fi (free).

Oyster Cove Café/Bar ★ SEAFOOD   A personable approach to hospitality by the owners makes this a crowd-pleaser. Ditto the freshness of the seafood. We recommend anything/everything that features blue cod, bluff oysters, or mussels. Be aware that "mutton bird" is not a type of flying sheep but the young of a variety of gull. It is a local delicacy. And an acquired taste.

SH1, 8 Ward Parade, Stirling Point ℂ **03/212-8855.** Main courses NZ$18–NZ$33. Mon–Tues 10am–4pm. Wed–Sun 11am–8pm.

STEWART ISLAND ★★

30km (19 miles) SW of Bluff, across the Foveaux Strait

Stewart Island, the third-largest island in New Zealand, is an area rich in native birds and vegetation. It's larger than Singapore but has a population of only 400. Almost without exception, first-time visitors are surprised by its temperate climate and sense of tranquility. Only 1% of the island is inhabited—the rest is given over to natural native bush, beaches, bird sanctuaries, and all-round ruggedness. The village of **Oban** in Halfmoon Bay is where most islanders live and work (fishing and tourism) and the main point of entry.

Originally called "Te Punga o Te Waka a Maui" by the Maori, which translates as "The Anchorstone of Maui's Canoe," the island is also known by the Maori name Rakiura, which means "Land of Glowing Skies," in reference to the vivid colors of dawn and twilight skies. A giant anchor-chain sculpture on the beach at Stewart Island provides a literal translation of the Maori anchorstone legend.

ROUGH sailing

If you're taking the ferry, know that Foveaux Strait is one of the most unpredictable passages in the world, and seas can be extremely rough. If you're prone to seasickness, come prepared and ask staff for rough-weather tips. It may be a short trip (1 hr.), and the large catamaran boats are known for their stability in rough seas, but the swells can be huge. Because bookings are heavy for flights, It is not always possible to swap the ferry return trip for a flight, but the "ferry one-way, fly one-way" option can be booked ahead. This gives you two perspectives and eliminates a difficult water crossing if the oceans are up.

Essentials

GETTING THERE

BY PLANE   Air transport to Stewart Island is provided by **Stewart Island Flights** (www.stewartislandflights.com; ℂ **0800/737-000** in NZ) from Invercargill airport/Stewart Island Airport. The round-trip fare NZ$195 adults, NZ$115 children. **Rakiura Helicopters,** on Stewart Island (www.rakiurahelicopters.co.nz; ℂ **03/219-1155**), offers scenic flights, transfers to/from Bluff (NZ$250 per person), and charter flights for hikers and hunters.

BY BOAT   The passenger-only ferry, operated by **Stewart Island Experience** (www.stewartislandexperience.co.nz; ℂ **0800/000-511** in NZ, or 03/212-7660), will have you on Stewart Island in an hour. It departs the Bluff ferry terminal September through April daily with at least three runs between 8:30am and 4pm (departure times change in May–Aug). The ferry deposits you on the wharf at Oban within a few hundred meters of the center of the small village. One-way fares are NZ$69 adults, NZ$35 children. Secure car and campervan parking (extra cost) is available near the Bluff ferry terminal.

GETTING AROUND

Most things on the island are within walking distance, though reaching some spots will mean an up and downhill walk. You can rent cars, mountain bikes, and motor scooters from the **Stewart Island Visitor Terminal,** on the wharf (www.stewartislandexperience.co.nz), and the **Stewart Island Flights Depot,** Elgin Terrace (www.stewartislandflights.com; ℂ **03/219-1090**). Charter boats and water taxis can be arranged for sightseers, hunters, divers, trampers, and fishermen; make reservations at the **Stewart Island Visitor Terminal** (www. stewartislandexperience.co.nz; ℂ **03/219-0034**).

VISITOR INFORMATION

The **Stewart Island i-SITE Visitor Information Centre** at 12 Elgin Terrace (www.stewartisland.co.nz; ℂ **03/219-1400**) is open daily 9am to 7pm. The Department of Conservation (DOC) has a big presence here. All trampers (hikers) must report to the **Rakiura National Park Visitor Centre,** 15 Main Rd. (www.doc.govt.nz; ℂ **03/219-0009**), in the DOC building, for walking-track and hut passes. Staff are extremely well informed on all aspects of exploring Stewart. It's open weekdays 8am to 5pm and weekends 9am to 4pm.

Emergencies Ambulance, fire, police: toll-free ℰ **111. Stewart Island Police:** ℰ **03/219 0020.**

Medical Stewart Island Health Centre (24-hr. call service: ℰ **03/219-1098**).

Exploring the Island

At press time, a brand-new NZ$2.8-million heritage center was under development on the island to house the voluminous collection of the **Rakiura Museum,** currently at Ayr Street, Halfmoon Bay (www.rakiuramuseum. co.nz; ℰ **03/219-1221**), which has some 5,000 artifacts and items showcasing the island's history, from early Maori settlements (archeologists have discovered a cooking site dating from the 13th c.) through the many business endeavors that had their moment, particularly whaling, tin mining, timber milling, and commercial fishing. The exhibits include an extensive and intriguing collection of Stewart Island shells, a drawing card for the many shell collectors the island attracts. The museum is open from 10am but is run by volunteers so hours are limited. The new heritage center will also house the city's Information Centre.

FISHING/SHELLFISH DIVING Full-day fishing charters are a highly popular way to pass the time on Stewart. Would-be fishers should pick up the Department of Conservation leaflet called "New Regulations for Fishing in Paterson Inlet, Stewart Island," then check the availability of charter boats at i-SITE. The seawater around Stewart Island is very clear, making it ideal for diving for crayfish (lobster) and shellfish.

HIKING Stewart Island hikes range from 15 minutes to 7 hours and spread out in a number of directions from Oban. They include comfortable walks to Observation Rock, Golden Bay, Lonneckers Bay, Lee Bay, and Ringaringa Beach (a great spot for shellseekers), and a longer walk to Garden Mound (5-hr. round-trip).

Note that the bush and the podocarp forest crowd the roadways and look benign, but five steps in and you can lose sight of the road. So stick to the tracks. They are well marked and well cared for, and include long sections of boardwalk to protect the native plants. It can be muddy, so wear sturdy walking shoes or boots. Expect the weather to change and carry a waterproof. Consult the experts at DOC if you are unsure about any track.

> ### Money Business
>
> There are no banks on the island itself; the nearest bank is located at Invercargill. Traveler's checks and foreign cash can be difficult to change, so bring New Zealand dollars. Most businesses on Stewart Island have EFTPOS and credit-card facilities.

SHARK DIVING The waters in this region also host a large number of Great White sharks, so if the idea of eyeing one of these large

SPOTTING the kiwi

The claim that Stewart Island is the only place in the country where you can be absolutely sure to spot a kiwi seems to be accurate. The Stewart Island kiwi, *Apteryx australis lawryi*, a larger bird than most with longer legs and a bigger beak, can often be seen at daylight on beaches foraging for sandhoppers among the kelp, but they are more easily spotted in the evening light. Phillip and Diane Smith operate **Bravo Adventure Cruises** (www.kiwispotting.co.nz;

✆ **03/219-1144;** NZ$140 per person), taking 15 passengers on the 52-foot MV *Wildfire* on a twilight sail from Halfmoon Bay to the beach at Glory Bay. With the help of flashlights or headlamps, they spot the ungainly birds which, patter and plod, stop and start as they seek out their evening meal. The expedition lasts about 4 hours, requires a reasonable level of fitness, and is not suitable for children under 15—but it's both fascinating and unique.

mammals through the bars of an underwater cage appeals, here's your chance. **Shark Experience** (www.sharkcagediving.co.nz; ✆ **03/212-7112**) operates from December through June out of Bluff and dives near Edward Island, Foveaux Strait. A reasonable level of fitness is necessary, and a scuba certification is preferable though not essential, since a scuba introduction is provided before the dive. Day trips run from 7:45am to 5pm and include time needed to get to the dive area (NZ$430; scuba introduction $99). Wetsuits can be provided, and a camera with waterproof casing is recommended.

Shark Dive New Zealand (wwwsharkdivenz.com; bookings only by email: dive@sharkdivenz.com) operates from Stewart Island. Divers do not need to be experienced or certified—the surface cage has air delivered to your regulator via hose from the deck—although snorkeling experience is beneficial. It operates from January to June (NZ$620 per diver; includes lunch).

ORGANIZED LAND TOURS

Village & Bays Tours ★ (www.stewartislandexperience.co.nz; ✆ **0800/000-511** in NZ, or 03/212-7660) gives a 1½-hour tour of Oban village and the surrounding bays, providing a real insight into island life, thanks to the chatty commentary from the driver of the small bus. The beaches revealed on this short trip are beautiful (pity about the temperature of the water), as are the views from the hilly areas. Bottom line: This is a history and geography lesson in one and well worth the price (NZ$45 adults, NZ$22 children 5–14).

Beautiful **Ulva Island** ★★★ is frequently described as the "jewel in Stewart Island's crown." The guided **Ulva Stewart Island Experience** (www.stewartislandexperience.co.nz; ✆ **0800/000-511** in NZ, or 03/212-7660; NZ$90 per person) takes in both Paterson Inlet and Ulva Island. Leaving from the Ferry Wharf at Halfmoon Bay, it includes a gentle ferry cruise that hugs the shore for sightings of old whaling stations, early settlers' huts, and boatbuilding endeavors. On Ulva, a guide takes the group along well-formed tracks through native forest and bush with birdlife fluttering ahead, behind, and over. Tour guides are impressively knowledgeable, and time passes too quickly.

Where to Stay

Observation Rock Lodge ★★★   Just how special is Observation Rock Lodge? A wild parrot stops by each evening to meet the new guests and peck at their palms for cashew nuts. We actually feel sorry for the parrot—he's missing the exquisite feasts that host Annett serves up for guests both morning and evening (she's a trained chef, and it shows). And poor bird: He doesn't get to bed down in rooms where the mattresses are first-rate, the decor both cheery and elegant, and the windows open to views of the magnificent grounds that surround the lodge. Lastly, Annett's husband, Phil, has a kayaking business and can set you up with either guided tours or wondrous kayaking excursions in Ulva Inlet. This may well be the best place you stay in all of New Zealand.

7 Leonard St., Halfmoon Bay. www.observationrocklodge.co.nz. *©* **03/219-1444.** 3 units. NZ$195–NZ$395, depending on room and add-on extras (meals, tours). Rates include free transfers to/from ferry and airport. No credit cards. **Amenities:** Hot tub; Wi-Fi (free).

South Sea Hotel ★   A Stewart Island icon thanks to its longevity and good looks—for many years the waterfront hotel was featured on countless postcards. It retains a measure of fame for its friendly bar service, fish dishes on the (cafe) menu (daily 7am–9pm), and a Sunday-night pub quiz that is louder, funnier, and ruder than most visitors expect (HRH Prince Harry was a keen participant in 2015). Accommodations options range from backpacker rooms with shared facilities to self-contained motel units.

Halfmoon Bay; 3-minute walk from ferry wharf. www.stewart-island.co.nz. *©* **03/219-1059.** 42 units. NZ$115–NZ$170 double. **Amenities:** Cafe; bar; Wi-Fi (NZ$2 per hour).

Stewart Island Lodge ★★★   Spot this from the jetty and you will hope that is your accommodation. It oozes comfort with wide verandas, large terraces through gardens and native bush, and huge windows facing the sea. Promise becomes reality as you and bags are transported up the (steep) hill. Bedrooms are oversized and pleasant king or twin rooms. All bedrooms open to a balcony/veranda, and a light-filled guest lounge offers great views.

14 Nicol Rd., Oban. www.stewartislandlodge.co.nz. *©* **0800/656-6501** or (in NZ) 03/219-0085. Rates NZ$195–NZ$220 double. Rates includes continental (cold) breakfast and free airport/ferry transfers. **Amenities:** Wi-Fi (free).

Where to Eat

Church Hill Café & Restaurant ★★, at 36 Kamahi Rd., on the hill overlooking Oban (www.churchhillrestaurant.com; *©* **03/219-1323**), specializes in locally caught or grown produce (fish, herbs, vegetables, fruits) and is widely respected for its seafood dishes (NZ$37–NZ$49). It's open daily 6pm until last orders at 8pm. **KaiKart Takeaways** (www.kaikartstewartisland.com; *©* **03/219-1225**) is a mobile caravan on Ayr Street, Oban, beside the museum and school. Its fish and chips are fast becoming visitors' favorite takeout, closely followed by venison burgers. KaiKart is open Thursday to Sunday 11am to 2pm and 5pm till late in summer (from NZ$6).

PLANNING YOUR TRIP TO NEW ZEALAND

A small country overflowing with intriguing sights and thrilling activities, New Zealand has the welcome mat out at all times. This chapter has been designed to smooth your journey to New Zealand, providing the low-down on those practicalities that can occasionally trip up the unprepared, such as road rules, currency issues, power voltage, even how to catch a cab. As ever, it is simply a matter of knowing what to expect.

ENTRY REQUIREMENTS

Passports & Visas

A **passport** is required for all entering visitors, and it must be valid for at least 3 months beyond your departure date from New Zealand.

Canada, France, Germany, Ireland, the Netherlands, and the U.S. are a few of the 56 countries that have **visa-waiver arrangements** with NZ allowing a stay for up to 3 months, providing there is a return or onward ticket paid for, credit card, or NZ$1,000 per month showing sufficient monetary support while in the country. Australian citizens do not need visas. U.K. passport holders who can produce evidence of the right to reside permanently in the U.K. can be granted a visitor visa for up to 6months upon arrival in New Zealand.

For further information of visa-waiver countries or general queries on work or study visas, contact a NZ embassy or consulate or the **New Zealand Immigration Service,** Wellington, NZ (www.immigration.govt.nz).

Customs

For information on what you're allowed to take into New Zealand, contact **New Zealand Citizens: New Zealand Customs,** The Customhouse, 17–21 Whitmore St., Box 2218, Wellington, 6140 (www.customs.govt.nz; © **04/473-6099** or 0800/428-786).

For details on what you're allowed to bring home, contact the following:

U.S. Citizens: U.S. Customs & Border Protection (CBP), 1300 Pennsylvania Ave. NW, Washington, DC 20229 (www.cbp.gov; ✆ 877/287-8667).

Canadian Citizens: Canada Border Services Agency, Ottawa, Ontario, K1A 0L8 (www.cbsa-asfc.gc.ca; ✆ 800/461-9999 in Canada, or 204/983-3500).

U.K. Citizens: HM Customs & Excise, Crownhill Court, Tailyour Road, Plymouth, PL6 5BZ (www.hmce.gov.uk; ✆ 0845/010-9000; from outside the U.K., 020/8929-0152).

Australian Citizens: Australian Customs Service, Customs House, 5 Constitution Ave., Canberra City, ACT 2601 (www.customs.gov.au; ✆ 1300/363-263; from outside Australia, 61/2-6275-6666).

GETTING THERE

The cost of getting to New Zealand is likely to be your single biggest cash outlay, so it makes sense to shop around. Remember to check out recommended agents and hot travel offers listed for your country of origin on the Tourism New Zealand website, **www.newzealand.com**. Also go to Air New Zealand's website at **www.airnewzealand.com** for special deals.

By Plane

Air New Zealand (www.airnewzealand.co.nz; ✆ 0800/737-000 in NZ) is the dominant airline on the U.S.–N.Z. Pacific route with nonstop flights operating from Los Angeles, San Francisco, and Houston. From Asia a number of airlines, including Air New Zealand, **Singapore Airlines** (www.singaporeair.com), and **Qantas** (www.qantas.com), fly direct to New Zealand. From Australia many airlines have connecting services from Europe, India, Asia, South and North America. From the wider Pacific, **Air Tahiti Nui** (www.airtahitinui.com), **Fiji Airways** (www.fijiairways.com), and Air New Zealand have direct flights to New Zealand.

Auckland Airport (www.aucklandairport.co.nz; ✆ 0800/247-767 in NZ or 09/275-0789) is the major hub for most airlines coming in to New Zealand, followed by **Christchurch International Airport** (www.christchurchairport.co.nz). If you plan to spend most of your time in the South Island, it makes sense to fly into Christchurch, but depending on your airline, you may have to fly into Auckland and then transfer to domestic flights to other centers.

Airline prices vary according to seasonal demand, as well as capacity. New Zealand's **peak tourist season** is December through February; **shoulder season** is usually regarded as from late March can include September and October. **Low season** runs from April through to August, but this excludes those areas that have ski/snow seasons.

By Boat

New Zealand is a popular **cruise-ship destination** with over one-third of passengers coming from the United States.

Most cruises coming to New Zealand also visit Australia and are typically 12 to 16 days in duration. New Zealand cruise ports include **Bay of Islands, Auckland, Tauranga, Napier, Wellington, Lyttelton (Christchurch), Akaroa, Dunedin,** and **Milford Sound.** You can fly to Australia or New Zealand to join a cruise, or you can take a segment on a world cruise that includes New Zealand.

Cruise lines with New Zealand on its itineraries: **Cunard** (www.cunard.com; ✆ 800/717-286273); **Silversea** (www.silversea.com; ✆ 877/276-6816); **Holland America Line** (www.hollandamerica.com; ✆ 877/932-4259); **Regent Seven Sea Cruises** (www.rssc.com; ✆ 877/505-5370), **Princess Cruises** (www.princess.com; ✆ 800/774-6237); **P&O Cruises** (www.pocruises.com; ✆ 0845/678-0014); **Fred.Olsen Cruise Lines** (www.fredolsencruises.com; ✆ 44/01473-746175); and **Oceania Cruises** (www.oceaniacruises.com; ✆ 800/531-5619).

GETTING AROUND

By Plane

Air New Zealand (www.airnewzealand.co.nz, ✆ **0800/737-000** in NZ, or 64/9/357-3000), along with its **Air New Zealand Link,** is the dominant domestic carrier, linking many of the smaller centers (such as Invercargill and Napier) to main centers. **Jetstar** (www.jetstar.com; ✆ **0800/800-995**) has daily scheduled flights between Auckland, Wellington, and Christchurch, and Auckland, Wellington, and Queenstown. Other smaller airlines are operating on internal routes; see the "Getting There" section in the individual destination chapters for details.

Air New Zealand is a good source of special deals. The airline regularly offers packages and deals of the month, but these must be purchased outside of New Zealand. Once you're here, Air New Zealand's **Grabaseat** (https://grabaseat.co.nz) daily deals are a great option for finding the cheapest seat available. Grabaseat is also available as an app, with customized alerts to price drops or real-time sales.

By Car, Motorcycle, or RV

To travel into the heartland, to roam the big spaces, it is necessary to hit the road, either via coach (bus) or by driving a rental car, motorcycle, or motorhome. If the holiday is planned around only three or four destinations, combining air travel with a self-drive rental could be the best choice.

New Zealand's roading network encompasses State Highway One (SH1) running the length of both islands and a number of regional highways. Two-lane single carriageways are the norm, with dual motorway sections near Auckland, Hamilton, Wellington, Christchurch, and Dunedin. Motorway sections are likely to be sealed with smooth asphalt, but other highways/roads have a rough surface of chipped stones sealed with a film of bitumen. Its virtues are low cost, suitability for varied temperatures, and longer life, but most

RULES FOR safer driving

Road safety is a major concern to the authorities, particularly driving at excessive speeds, illegal overtaking, and failure to keep left.

o **Drive on the left.** Keep left.

o Wearing a **seatbelt** is compulsory.

o **Speed limits** are in kilometers per hour, not miles per hour. On the open road the maximum speed is 100kmph. In built-up areas it is 50, although lower speed limits may apply. These will be signposted.

o No **overtaking on yellow lines** or at any time the driver cannot see a clear road for 100m.

o A **red traffic light** means stop. No turning allowed.

international drivers find it rougher and noisier than expected. Many roads have unsealed shoulders, so drivers must take care not to drift off the sealed surface. Expect unsealed gravel roads in rural/farmland areas.

New Zealand motorists have an unfortunate reputation for aggressive driving, but strict policing is having its effect, and road manners have improved markedly in recent years.

If planning to rent a car and self-drive on your holiday, consider joining the **New Zealand Automobile Association** (AA; www.aa.co.nz; ✆ **0800/500-444** in NZ). Nationwide offices provide maps, drive-times, breakdown services, and advice. For those belonging to a similar organization elsewhere, membership is free, so carry a membership card.

Tip: If driving on the left is a concern, AA has an excellent multiple-choice online driving program that can allay worries. Go to **www.aa.co.nz/travel/visitors-to-new-zealand/visiting-driver-training-programme** and get comfortable with the NZ ways. Some rental-car companies, including Thrifty and Europcar, will even provide a discount to those drivers who successfully complete the program certificate.

Petrol (gas) prices in New Zealand fluctuate greatly. At press time, gas cost NZ$2.21 per liter for 91 octane, NZ$2.12 for 95 octane, and NZ$2.02 to NZ$1.90 per liter for diesel. Service (gas) stations have clear displays of prices.

Most towns and all main centers have **metered street parking** accepting payment by coins or credit card or via mobile phone. Instructions are marked clearly on each meter. If metered times are exceeded, the fines are heavy.

RENTING A CAR

Having a car is a great way to see the country. Every major New Zealand city has rental-car companies, including local companies (see below) and international brands such as **Avis** (www.avis.com), **Budget** (www.budget.com), **Hertz** (www.hertz.com), and **Thrifty** (www.thrifty.com). Most accept overseas booking.

Visitors planning to self-drive a rental car or motor home (RV) should be over 21 years of age, although some firms require a minimum of 23 years and a maximum of 75 years. A current license/international license is required. There is a car at the right price for every driver. In the low, low budget range, cars will be older but roadworthy. Inclusions are not a given, but at an average of NZ$25 per day for a high-mileage used compact car, what you see is pretty much what you get. The newer, late-model rental cars from international firms (Hertz, Budget, Avis) average around NZ$100 a day, but discounts are often available depending on seasonal availability and length of rental. Daily rates can range from NZ$55 (for example, Toyota Yaris) to NZ$107 (Toyota Corolla) a day. During the high-season months of January through March, don't expect too many discounts, but always check for inclusives such as free airport/depot transfers, free AA roadside assistance, reduced credit card fees, and unlimited kilometers.

Recommended local firms include **Jucy** (www.jucy.co.nz; ℂ **0800/500/079** in NZ), which has a range of vehicles, from "el cheapo" compacts from NZ$38 a day to upmarket 4WDs from NZ$95 a day. Jucy has locations in Auckland (city and airport) and at the Wellington, Christchurch, Dunedin, and Queenstown airports. For good service and an excellent range of used well-maintained vehicles, the South Island company **Affordable Rental Cars** (www.affordablecars.co.nz; ℂ **0800/233/678** in NZ) has rentals ranging from NZ$44 a day (a compact two-person) to NZ$78 (a family SUV Prado). Affordable has depots in Christchurch and Queenstown.

To search for low-priced car-rental deals and compare rates in New Zealand, go to the regional online travel agency **WebJet** (http://cars.webjet.co.nz).

RENTING A MOTORCYCLE

You can rent motorcycles or purchase tour packages with or without guides. You'll need to have your full motorcycle license. Motorcycles for rental are newer models. Most companies have offices/depots in Auckland and Christchurch and offer motorcycle tours as well as rentals.

For motorcycle rentals, **Auckland Motorbike Hire** (www.aucklandmotorbikehire.com; ℂ **09/536/6884**) has a wide range of vehicles. The daily rate for a 7-day hire of a Suzuki bike is NZ$125; the daily rate for a 7-day hire of a BMW is NZ$200. Rental extras include GoPro cameras, tents, and bike-to-bike communications. **New Zealand Motorcycle Rentals & Tours** (www.nzbike.com; ℂ **09/486/2472**), which has offices in Auckland, Christchurch, and Wellington, offers fully guided tours as well as rentals; the daily rate for a 7-day hire of a Yamaha Classic is NZ$120; the daily rate for a BMW K50 is NZ$270. **Paradise Motorcycle Tours NZ** (www.paradisemotorcycletours.co.nz; ℂ **09/473/9404**), with offices in Auckland and Christchurch, offers both guided and self-guided motorbike tours and rentals; the daily rate for a 7-day rental of a 2015 Indian Scout NZ is $199.

Adventure New Zealand Motorcycle Tours & Rentals, Nelson, South Island (www.gotournz.com; ℂ **64/3/548-5787**), offers deluxe tours with top-class bikes and upmarket accommodation for the 35 to 65 set.

Freedom Rules

If "freedom camping"—camping out in your vehicle by rivers or lakes, in the bush, or simply off the road—is your preferred camping mode rather than staying in designated camping sites or holiday parks, be aware that in 2012, rules were drawn up to guarantee safe freedom camping. Many regions now only permit freedom camping when the vehicle (campervan/motor-home etc) is a certified self-contained vehicle. The vehicle must display a warrant on the front window and a sticker on the rear window or bumper to verify its status under the NZ Standard for Self Containment of Motor Caravans and Caravans, NZS 5465:2001: "Responsible freedom camping can be achieved in a certified self-contained vehicle, as these vehicles have the necessary facilities on-board to contain all the occupants' waste for a minimum of three days."

RENTING A MOTORHOME (RV)

For holidays free of accommodation and transport reservations, consider renting a motorhome, aka campervan or RV (recreational vehicle). These rolling, self-contained vehicles are outfitted as living quarters with toilet, kitchen facilities, and generally the option of two or more sleeping berths.

Note: Although New Zealanders often say "campervan" whether describing a van, camper, or motorhome, strictly speaking a campervan is a van that has sleeping quarters but is not self contained. Think of a camper as backpacker accommodation on wheels: The driver's cabin fronts the bed/bunk area, and there are no bathroom or cooking facilities. Campervans without bathroom facilities are not permitted to freedom camp (see "Freedom Rules," below).

Motorhomes, on the other hand, have kitchens, showers, toilets, and berths to accommodate two to six people, all tucked neatly behind the driver's cabin. Camping is permitted in wilderness and freedom-camping areas and at the many designated motorhome camps.

For motorhome rentals, **Jucy** (www.jucy.co.nz; ℂ **0800/500/079** in NZ) has depots in Auckland, Wellington, Christchurch, Dunedin, and Queenstown. The daily rate for a 7-day hire for a four-berth self-contained motorhome is from NZ$235.

Britz (www.britz.co.nz; ℂ **800/200/80801**) has depots in the Auckland, Christchurch, and Queenstown airports. The daily rates for a 7-day rental for a four-berth self-contained motorhome is from NZ$107.

Wilderness (www.wilderness.co.nz ℂ **09/282/3606**) has depots in Auckland and Christchurch. The four-berth Alpine self-contained motorhome offers a touch of luxury (daily rates from NZ$475), but cheaper options are available.

By Taxi

Taxi stands featuring a number of different licensed taxi companies are located at all transport terminals and in major shopping and accommodation areas of cities and towns. Driver identification and rates should be clearly displayed. Taxis are unlikely (but not unknown) to respond to being hailed within a quarter-mile of a stand. Drivers don't expect a tip, but if they handle a lot of luggage or perform other special services, a tip will be accepted.

The global on-demand taxi service **Uber** (www.uber.com) has been available in Auckland and Wellington since 2014. The service is expected to be up and running in Christchurch by 2016. Uber cars are provided by private car drivers.

By Interisland Ferry

Crossing Cook Strait by ferry is not just a travel option; it's a wonderful tourism experience. Leaving or arriving at Wellington presents a vista of the hills hugging the harbor. The journey to and from Picton is magical; the ferry travels at slow speed through the waterways of the Marlborough Sounds, with likely sightings of seals and dolphins. It's a 3-hour, 92km (57-mile) beautifully scenic ride.

Two ferry companies operate between Wellington and Picton. The **Interislander** ferry system (www.interislander.co.nz; ✆ **0800/802-802** in NZ) has six daily crossings and three fare options. **Bluebridge Cook Strait Ferry** (www.bluebridge.co.nz; ✆ **0800/844-844** in NZ) sails four times daily. Fare bookings are transferable until 24 hours before travel, subject to availability, but are nonrefundable. Ferry facilities include licensed bar/cafe TV lounges and children's play areas.

Note: All ferry passengers should be aware that high swells and severe winds can affect scheduled departures of Cook Strait crossings.

By Coach (Bus)

Coach travel is a cost-effective, worry-free way of getting around New Zealand. Most provide some kind of commentary and stop frequently for refreshments. Smoking is not permitted. **InterCity** (www.intercity.co.nz; ✆ **09/583-5780** in Auckland, and ✆ **03/377-0951** in Christchurch) operates three-star coaches on New Zealand's most comprehensive coach network, visiting some 600 towns and cities, with daily schedulaed services. **Naked Bus** (https://nakedbus.com) operates on many of the same routes but is more budget-class that tourist-class, offering cut-rate fares. *Reminder:* Book coach journeys in advance during peak travel periods (summer and holidays).

InterCity offers discounts to students, seniors (65 and over), YHA members, and VIP Backpackers cardholders. **An InterCity Flexi-Pass** allows travelers to buy blocks of travel time up to 40% cheaper than standard fares on all InterCity routes. **Naked Bus Passports** offer a similar option.

Tip: Map out an itinerary, taking into account travel time, destinations, and timetables, and lock in the discounts.

Shuttles (minivans) offer a transport alternative to/from main centers and to/from tourist hotspots. Fares and schedules vary according to seasonal demand. Check shuttle services at local i-SITE offices.

By Train

KiwiRail Scenic journeys (www.kiwirailscenic.co.nz; © **0800/872-467** in NZ) operate three long-distance train routes: **Northern Explorer** from/to Auckland and Wellington; the **Coastal Pacific,** to/from Picton and Christchurch; and the **TranzAlpine,** to/from Christchurch Greymouth. The trains are modern and comfortable, heated and air-conditioned. Scenic Rail Passes offer fixed passes for 7, 14, and 21 days; Freedom Passes are pre-purchased travel days (minimum 3) for any day during summer season. The Fixed Pass makes sense only if a leisurely trip through the country is planned since train journeys are limited to only three routes.

TIPS ON ACCOMMODATIONS

As a free-market country, New Zealand does not impose regulatory rates on accommodations businesses. The government agency **Tourism New Zealand** has responsibility for the marketing of New Zealand to the world as a visitor destination and works with accommodations and hospitality business owners to deliver promises made in international campaigns. One of its more prominent exercises has been the development of **Qualmark** (www.qualmark. co.nz), its official mark of quality. It means that every type of accommodation has been independently assessed as professional and trustworthy and graded one star (acceptable), two stars (good), three stars (very good), four stars (excellent), or five stars (exceptional or among the best in New Zealand). There are even Qualmark Endorsements for visitor activities (bungy jumps, say, or hiking trails) and Qualmark Enviro Awards for sustainable tourism practices.

It should be noted, however, that within the Qualmark system, a three-star hotel is not the same as a three-star B&B or a three-star lodge, and that a five-star B&B is not the same as a five-star hotel. Each category of accommodations is assessed on different criteria. It is also worth noting that many accommodations operators have little faith in this rating system because it's voluntary, and only those properties that request assessments are included.

Nonetheless, before leaving on your holiday, go to www.qualmark.co.nz or pick up the free **Qualmark Accommodation Guide** from visitor centers when you arrive. The guide has the complete list of all participating accommodations options and tourism businesses.

Please note that because accommodation rates are not standardized what you get for NZ$150 can be much better than something for two or three times the price. Best advice: Ask around, and don't assume that all places in the same price range offer the same standard of accommodations. (They probably do in the Expensive range, but certainly not in the Moderate and Inexpensive categories.)

Note that New Zealand now has an across-the-board legal ban on smoking in public buildings. That includes hotels and restaurants. Therefore, you should assume that accommodations listed throughout this guide have a non-smoking policy. It is also a legal requirement that all public buildings have reasonable access for travelers with disabilities. You should therefore assume that properties reviewed in this guide offer rooms with reasonable and adequate access for travelers with disabilities, although in the case of B&Bs and backpacker lodgings, it pays to double-check before booking.

New Zealand has a multitude of available lodging options. Here's a rundown on what you'll find. Price ranges are based on the following scale: **Inexpensive** (NZ$30–NZ$150); **Moderate** (NZ$151–NZ$300); and **Expensive** (NZ$301–NZ$1,600 and up). An excellent website for information on the many and varied type of options (including family-focused, budget, LGBT, single women, luxury, and camping), go to **www.tourism.net.nz/accommodation**.

HOTELS & MOTELS A **hotel** is a hotel the world over. Facilities are often extensive (spa, gym, pool, tennis courts) but invariably include a bar and restaurant. The advertised rate (aka rack rate) for hotel rooms is often fluid, depending on the day and the season. **Luxury resort hotels** offer nothing but the best and may include a restaurant with a famous chef, its own label wine, and even tours. A **lodge** has come to mean an upmarket B&B with luxury accommodation for at least four guests, often including private dining room, pool, and even helipads. A **pub** is a country hotel that offers accommodations of a more modest nature. Some rooms have shared bathrooms, and meals are often served in the bar. Pubs can provide a colorful experience. New Zealand has plenty of franchised **motels** offering comfortable units with kitchen facilities and parking.

BED & BREAKFASTS (B&B) These range from a guest room with shared facilities and home-cooked breakfasts to upmarket luxury lodges with pools, helipads, and more. For options go to **www.bnb.co.nz** and **www.bed-and-breakfast.co.nz**.

APARTMENTS, CONDOS & HOLIDAY HOMES An apartment of condo unit is generally self-catering, with full kitchen facilities, living areas, multiple bedrooms and bathrooms, and sometimes an outdoor terrace or patio. Washer-dryers are often on-site.

Private Home Hosting in New Zealand

It started with couch-surfing in a host home, and now private home hosting is all the rage practically everywhere. It's a great way to live like a local, and it's often more cost-efficient than staying in a hotel. **Homestay** (www.homestay.com), **VRBO** (www.vrbo.com), and **airbnb** (www.airbnb.com) have all infiltrated New Zealand. VRBO has nearly 10,000 listings alone. These homestays range from renting a room with a local family to booking fully outfitted homes or apartments, some with pools, tennis courts, and more.

Holiday homes are privately owned holiday houses usually in popular visitor spots, including lake, beach or mountain resorts and famous bike trails. For options check out **www.bookabach.co.nz**.

Rated by "Condé Nast Traveler" as 1 of only 49 villa rental agents world-wide best qualified to match its readers with suitable holiday properties, **Touch of Spice,** Queenstown (www.touchofspice.co.nz; ℂ **03/442-8672**), is a meticulous concierge and luxury lifestyle specialist offering a range of luxury properties from inner-city apartments to country hideaways and private island retreats—five-star quality and with staff if required.

HOSTELS & BACKPACKER RESORTS Hostels and backpacker resorts vary from a bunk bed in a dorm room to family rooms with en-suite facilities, but in general amenities are few, the fundamentals are spare, and low costs appeal to budget travelers. Go to **VIP Backpacker Resorts of New Zealand** (www.vip.co.nz; ℂ **09/827-6016**) for listings. Facilities in **hostels,** with single or double rooms and dorms available, range from en-suite bathrooms to shared bathrooms. Kitchens and dining areas are usually communal, although some hostels have cafes and bars. Go to **YHA New Zealand National Reservations Centre** (www.yha.co.nz; ℂ **03/379-9808**).

FARMSTAYS Farmstays present an ideal opportunity to get a feel for New Zealand's rural life. For options go to **Accommodation New Zealand** (www.accommodation-new-zealand.co.nz; ℂ **09/444-4895** or 03/487-8420) or **Hospitality Plus,** the New Zealand Home & Farmstay Company (www.hospitalityplus.co.nz; ℂ **03/693-7463**).

HOLIDAY PARKS & CAMPSITES For powered sites for motor homes and campsites for tents, cabins, and motel-style units, check out: **Top 10 Holiday Parks** (www.top10.co.nz; ℂ **0800/867-836** in NZ, or 03/377-9950) and **Holiday Accommodation Parks New Zealand** (www.holidayparks.co.nz; ℂ **04/298-3283**).

RESPONSIBLE TOURISM

Responsible tourism is conscientious travel. It means taking care in the environments you explore and respecting the communities you visit.

Ecotourism

The **International Ecotourism Society** (TIES; www.ecotourism.org) defines ecotourism as responsible travel to natural areas that conserves the environment and improves the well-being of local people. You can find some eco-friendly travel tips and statistics, as well as touring companies and associations—listed by destination under "Travel Choice"—at the **TIES** website.

Volunteer Travel

Volunteer travel has become increasingly popular among those who want to venture beyond the standard group-tour experience to learn languages, interact with locals, and make a positive difference while on vacation. Volunteer

If you'd like to work in New Zealand during your trip, you'll need to acquire a working holiday permit. There are usually plenty of short-term working opportunities, especially in the summer when orchards, market gardens, and vineyards need part-time workers. Go to **www.** **seek.co.nz**, **www.nzrecruitme.co.nz**, or **www.seasonaljobs.co.nz**. The New Zealand hospitality industry also employs large numbers of working tourists. Details of visa and work permit requirements are available from **New Zealand Immigration** (www.immigration.govt.nz).

travel usually doesn't require special skills—just a willingness to work hard—and programs vary in length from days to weeks. Committing a day or two of volunteer work while you're on vacation is another popular option.

Volunteering New Zealand (www.volunteernow.org.nz) focuses on putting the age, wisdom, and acquired experience of those from age 55 to 65 to good use. The website lists volunteer positions in different regions of the country. The **Global Volunteer Network** (www.globalvolunteernetwork.org) operates in many countries, including New Zealand. Programs here include assistance to conservation groups and conservation projects. Volunteers are involved in habitat restoration, predator control projects, tree planting, invasive weed removal, monitoring re-vegetation growth rates, and more. This program is based in Wellington, and you need to be moderately fit, proficient in English, and 18 or over to participate.

[FastFACTS] NEW ZEALAND

ATMs ATMs are common throughout New Zealand and can be found inside and outside banks, in major shopping centers, in supermarkets and gas stations. Some smaller towns and remote locations don't have ATMs but an EFTPOS or debit card that can be used at a local retail outlet will also give change.

Business Hours Banks are open Monday through Friday 9:30am to 4:30pm and on weekends in some shopping malls. **Shopping hours** are generally 9am to 5:30pm, with malls and large retail outlets open until 6pm and from 10am

weekends. Many service (gas) stations operate 24 hours.

Cellphones Using your own phone on "roam" can be prohibitively expensive. The simplest way to keep in touch is to either have a GSM unlocked phone that will allow a local SIM card and a prepaid plan. Or purchase a cheap cellphone (not necessarily a smartphone) on arrival, a SIM card, and a pay-as-you-go plan. These are widely available; shop at any branch of **The Warehouse** (www.thewarehouse.co.nz; ✆ 0800/422-276 in NZ) or any **Dick Smith store** (www.

dicksmith.co.nz; ✆ 0800 373 347 in NZ).

Disabled Travelers New Zealand is a relatively good destination for visitors with disabilities. Since 1975, every public building and major renovated structure in the country has been required by law to provide reasonable and adequate access for those with disabilities. In addition, accommodations with five or more units must provide at least one room for guests with disabilities. For general information, see the CCS Disability Action (www.cccdisabilityaction.org.nz or www.weka.net.nz).

Drinking Laws The minimum drinking age is 18 in pubs, and proof of age may be required. Beer and wine can be purchased from most supermarkets and spirits, beer and wine from liquor stores. Wine can also be purchased from specialty wine shops and wineries. New Zealand police stage random drug and alcohol testing on roads in major cities to check for drinking and driving; you must stop on request and are required to take a breath test.

Electricity The voltage is 230 volts in New Zealand, and plugs are of the flat, three-pronged variety (with the top two prongs angled). If you bring a hair dryer, it should be dual-voltage, and you'll need an adapter plug. Most motels and some B&Bs have built-in wall transformers for 110-volt, two-prong razors. Other electrical equipment will require its own transformer.

Health Vaccinations are not required to enter New Zealand. Make sure your health insurance covers you when you're out of the country; if it doesn't, consider buying travel insurance before leaving home. Health insurance is strongly advised because New Zealand's public and private medical/hospital facilities are not free to visitors, except in the event of accidents. New Zealand healthcare includes a no-fault accident scheme that extends to visitors to the country. The Crown entity Accident Compensation

Corporation (ACC) provides cover in the form of medical expenses and some hospital expenses to visitors who may be injured in an accident.

Visitors arriving in New Zealand with prescription drugs should have a doctor's letter or certificate confirming their prescription drug requirements to avoid problems with Customs at point of entry. It is not necessary to pack anti-diarrheal and/or anti-emetic products as these are available over-the-counter in New Zealand pharmacies—as are most generic prescription drugs for common problems like headaches, coughs, fevers, and influenza. Even small towns have a pharmacy or chemist shop for OTC remedies, and medical centers are available nationwide.

Bugs, Bites & Wildlife Concerns New Zealand has no man-eating animals, snakes, or poisonous toads. There are areas that are plagued by wasps in summer, and sandlies all year round. But new controls for wasps are in place, sandflies and bush flies (sometimes known as blue-bottles) are best dealt with via personal repellent, and mosquitoes repelled with citronella coils or sprays. Katipo spiders can inflict painful bites, but these spiders are rare. Anyone allergic to insect stings/bites should carry antihistamine products.

Extreme Weather Extreme weather conditions can spring up out of nowhere. A change in the

wind direction can mean gale-force hot winds, or cold driving southerly storms of hail, even snow in midsummer. Storms in the mountain ranges that divide the North and South Island into West Coast and East Coast regions cause rivers to rise suddenly—so trampers/hikers planning to be 2 or 3 days in mountain regions must check in with DOC or track authorities and leave notice of departure/return dates and planned routes. NZ has an excellent Search and Rescue service, but the exercises are expensive and not taken lightly. Go to www.adventuresmart.org.nz for the complete picture.

Sunburn New Zealand's clear air and fierce sun are a dangerous combination, and the country has an extremely high incidence of melanoma (cancer). Vacationers in the mountains or near water (lakes, rivers, beaches) should apply a good suncream, wear hats, and keep necks, arms, and backs covered especially between the hours of 11am and 4pm.

Internet & Wi-Fi More and more hotels, resorts, airports, cafes, and retailers offer free Wi-Fi access. Most upscale accommodations and many B&Bs in New Zealand offer free Wi-Fi service. Most **youth hostels** have at least one computer you can use for Internet access. Most **public libraries** in New Zealand offer Internet access free, or for a small charge, as do many **i-SITE visitor centers.**

New Zealand's dominant telecommunication company, **Spark** (previously Telecom NZ), has wireless hot spots throughout the country (see call boxes in main centers). For notebook users, Vodaphone and Spark sell prepaid USB dongles and local SIM cards. Both have prominent service outlets in shopping malls, or go to www.spark.co.nz or www.vodaphone.co.nz.

A computer **connection kit** of the right power and phone adapters is an important accessory.

LGBT Travelers   Gay and lesbian travelers should feel at ease in New Zealand, especially in Auckland and Wellington. For information, go to **New Zealand Gay and Lesbian Travel Association** (www.iglta.org; (T) **04/917-9184**); **Pink Pages New Zealand** (www.pinkpagesnewzealand.com); **Queer Resources Aotearoa** (www.qrd.org.nz); and **Gay Queenstown** (www.gayqueenstown.com). The **International Gay and Lesbian Travel Association** (**IGLTA;** www.iglta.org) has an online directory of

gay- and lesbian-friendly travel businesses and tour operators.

Mail   It costs NZ$2.50 to NZ$5.40 (depending on size) to send an airmail letter to the United States, Canada, United Kingdom, or Europe. Overseas postcards cost NZ$2. New Zealand post offices will receive mail and hold it for you for up to 2 months. *Poste restante* (held mail) service operates in main towns and centers. Due to the closing of some postal outlets, check current postshops/centers to decide where and when you can be to receive mail, then arrange mail delivery. Have the parcel addressed to you c/o Poste Restante at the postshop of the town you'll be visiting. Go to www.nzpost.co.nz/personal/receiving-mail/*poste-restante*. Parcels and documents can also be sent by tracked post for extra security. You can follow the progress of all tracked items on the New Zealand Post website, www.nzpost.co.nz.

Money & Costs   From-mer's lists exact prices in the local currency. For daily

currency conversions, check at any bank or currency exchange office. *Tip:* Have a mix of cash, credit cards, and traveler's checks to cover every option on your holiday. Carry enough cash to cover airport incidentals, tipping, and transportation to your hotel, or withdraw money upon **arrival at an airport ATM.**

It is important to ensure that your **ATM card** is compatible with New Zealand systems. The machines generally accept four-digit PINs, but it always pays to check with your bank branch or office before leaving home.

Most New Zealand businesses take **MasterCard** and **Visa.** American Express and Diners Club are likely to be accepted in resort areas and major cities but not in smaller towns.

Safety   New Zealand is one of the world's safest holiday destinations; nevertheless individuals must expect to assume responsibility for personal health and possessions. Street crime—mugging and pickpocketing—is rare, but use common sense and be wary of ill-lit streets or drunken

WHAT THINGS COST IN NEW ZEALAND	NZ$
Taxi from the airport to downtown Auckland	NZ$50–NZ$90
Double room, moderate	NZ$350–NZ$600
Double room, inexpensive	NZ$150–NZ$250
Three-course dinner for one without wine	NZ$60–NZ$90
Bottle of beer	NZ$3.50–NZ$8
Cup of coffee	NZ$3.50–NZ$4.50
Admission to most art galleries and museums	Free or by donation

groups. Police do not carry guns as a general rule but are armed with tasers, sprays, and batons. Policing is by car and in cities by foot patrols. CCTV coverage is widespread. There is concern about the growth of a drug culture in New Zealand, so there is heavy surveillance at the points of entry. Buying or selling illegal drugs incurs stiff penalties.

Senior Travel Discounts for those 65 and over are increasingly available in New Zealand, so inquire when making reservations for accommodations and attractions. Carry photo identification. Good websites are **Grey Power** (www. greypower.co.nz) and **Age Concern** (www.ageconcern. co.nz).

Smoking New Zealand has an across-the-board legal ban on smoking in public buildings. It is already widely discouraged in public places (parks, pavements, bus shelters) and banned in hospitals, restaurants, trains, planes, buses and most accommodation options. It is not unusual for a smoker to be told to "pick up your butts" if seen smoking in public. Packets of cigarettes currently cost NZ$20, a figure that should only go up. The general plan is that New Zealand will be smoke-free by 2026.

Student Travel The **International Student Identity Card (ISC;** www.

isic.org) qualifies students for substantial savings on rail passes, plane tickets, entrance fees, and more. The ISIC card is accepted by many New Zealand tourism operators, including hotels, bars, transport providers, theaters, major attractions, and tour companies. It also provides students with basic health and life insurance and a 24-hour help line. The card is valid for a maximum of 18 months.

Taxes A national 15% **Goods and Services Tax (GST)** is a government tax levied on all goods and all services no matter how large or small, including restaurant bills. A new tax applicable to air travel was announced in June 2015. Termed a "border clearance levy," it is expected that arriving passengers will pay NZ$22 and departing passengers NZ$16, but at press time the exact amount had not yet been announced.

Time New Zealand is located just west of the International Date Line, and its standard time is 12 hours ahead of Greenwich Mean Time. Thus, when it's noon in New Zealand, it's 7:30am in Singapore, 9am in Tokyo, 10am in Sydney; and—all the previous day—4pm in San Francisco, and midnight in London. In New Zealand, daylight saving time begins late October and goes to mid-March.

Tipping Generally speaking, tipping is not customary in New Zealand, with a few caveats: Taxi drivers appreciate a fare being rounded up, as in "keep the change, driver." Tipping in restaurants is optional, but hospitalilty staff always appreciate a tip if a meal/drink has been delivered swiftly with care and precision (no more than 5%–10%).

Visitor Information The official **Tourism New Zealand** website is **www. newzealand.com**, where you can get comprehensive details for every aspect of your trip. **I-SITE** is New Zealand's official visitor information network (a Tourism New Zealand initiative), with more than 80 **i-SITE Visitor Centres** (www.i-site.org.nz) scattered around the country. These i-SITES are New Zealand's secret vacation weapon—they provide **free** services and maps, and the staff is friendly and ready to advise and book, free of fees, accommodations, activities, travel, tours, and events. They even sell stamps and phone cards. **Department of Conservation (DOC) offices** (www. doc.govt.nz) are staffed by friendly, knowledgeable, helpful men and women whose main task is to preserve our conservation areas and national parks. They too are happy to pass on local knowledge and essential visitor information.

Index

Map List

Photo Credits

p. i: © Woody Ang / Shutterstock; p. ii: © Naruedom Yaempongsa; p. iv: © Jiri Foltyn; p. v, top: © Rob Suisted; p. v, bottom: © russellstreet; p. vi, top left: © Yevgen Belich / Shutterstock.com; p. vi, top right: © Eli Duke; p. vi, bottom left: © HeliHead; p. vi, bottom right: © gracethang2; p. vii, top: © ChameleonsEye / Shutterstock.com; p. vii, bottom: © Jo Moore; p. viii, top: © Tom Hall; p. viii, bottom left: © Madeleine Deaton; p. viii, bottom right: © D Coetzee; p. ix, top left: © Evgeny Gorodetsky; p. ix, top right: © anoldent; p. ix, bottom: © Amesbury School; p. x, top: © Gary Bembridge; p. x, bottom: © Tez Goodyer; p. xi, top left: © Nicram Sabod; p. xi, top right: © Nicram Sabod; p. xi, bottom left: © Andrea Schaffer; p. xi, bottom right: © Kwang Chun Gan / Shutterstock.com; p. xii, top: © Steve Gardner; p. xii, bottom: © Alan Lam; p. xiii, top left: © Steve Watson; p. xiii, top right: Courtesy of Minus 5[dg] Ice Bar; p. xiii, bottom: © Tim Cuff / Alamy Stock Photo ; p. xiv, top: © Roderick Eime; p. xiv, bottom: © Ruklay Pousajja; p. xv, top: © alarico / Shutterstock.com; p. xv, middle: © Konrad Mostert; p. xv, bottom: © Greg Balfour Evans / Alamy Stock Photo ; p. xvi, top left: © Jane Nearing; p. xvi, top right: © nobleIMAGES / Alamy Stock Photo; p. xvi, bottom: © Stanislav Fosenbauer

IN MEMORIAM

This book is dedicated to the memory of Diana Balham, who passed away in late 2015 while she was writing the North Island section of this guide. Her zest for life, particularly for travel and adventure, and her quirky sense of humor will be sadly missed by all who knew her.

Frommer's New Zealand, 8th Edition

Published by
FROMMER MEDIA LLC

Copyright © 2017 by Frommer Media LLC. All rights reserved. No part of this publication may be repro-
duced, stored in a retrieval system, or transmitted in any form or by any means, electronic, mechanical,
photocopying, recording, scanning or otherwise, except as permitted under Sections 107 or 108 of the
1976 United States Copyright Act, without the prior written permission of the Publisher. Requests to the
Publisher for permission should be addressed to the support@frommermedia.com.

Frommer's is a registered trademark of Arthur Frommer. Frommer Media LLC is not associated with any
product or vendor mentioned in this book.

ISBN 978-1-62887-252-1 (paper), 978-1-62887-253-8 (e-book)

Editorial Director: Pauline Frommer
Editor: Alexis Lipsitz Flippin
Production Editor: Heather Wilcox
Cartographer: Roberta Stockwell
Cover Design: Dave Reidy

For information on our other products or services, see www.frommers.com.

FrommerMedia LLC also publishes its books in a variety of electronic formats. Some content that appears
in print may not be available in electronic formats.

Manufactured in the United States of America

5 4 3 2 1

DISCARD

ABOUT THE AUTHORS

Auckland-based **Diana Balham** was many things before her untimely death in September 2015, including musician and keen conservationist, but travel writing was her forte and her passion. Her articles have appeared in a number of publications, but most regularly in the *New Zealand Herald* and the *New Zealand Listener*. Diana also wrote *Undiscovered Auckland: 70 Great Spots Waiting to be Explored* (New Holland Publishers, 2008).

From her home in the South Island of NZ, **Kate Fraser** has pursued a career in words, initially as a copy director in advertising agencies, then as a lifestyle journalist, followed in turn by her work as a section editor for *The Press* and restaurant reviewer for *Cuisine* magazine. Kate's writing awards include two Qantas Awards and Culinary Quills from the Guild of Food Writers. Her work has been published in newspapers and magazines, and she is an occasional contributor to Radio New Zealand. She has traveled extensively and visited (and eaten well) in both well-known and yet-to-be-discovered places.

Renée Lang has been involved in the world of books for most of her working life and has edited and published numerous titles. More recently she has written a few too, including *101 Must-Do Weekends*, *Auckland Harbour Bridge: 50 Years of a City Icon*, *Explore New Zealand*, and *Urban Chicks*.

ABOUT THE FROMMER TRAVEL GUIDES

For most of the past 50 years, Frommer's has been the leading series of travel guides in North America, accounting for as many as 24% of all guidebooks sold. I think I know why.

Though we hope our books are entertaining, we nevertheless deal with travel in a serious fashion. Our guidebooks have never looked on such journeys as a mere recreation, but as a far more important human function, a time of learning and introspection, an essential part of a civilized life. We stress the culture, lifestyle, history, and beliefs of the destinations we cover, and urge our readers to seek out people and new ideas as the chief rewards of travel.

We have never shied from controversy. We have, from the beginning, encouraged our authors to be intensely judgmental, critical—both pro and con—in their comments, and wholly independent. Our only clients are our readers, and we have triggered the ire of countless prominent sorts, from a tourist newspaper we called "practically worthless" (it unsuccessfully sued us) to the many rip-offs we've condemned.

And because we believe that travel should be available to everyone regardless of their incomes, we have always been cost-conscious at every level of expenditure. Though we have broadened our recommendations beyond the budget category, we insist that every lodging we include be sensibly priced. We use every form of media to assist our readers, and are particularly proud of our feisty daily website, the award-winning Frommers.com.

I have high hopes for the future of Frommer's. May these guidebooks, in all the years ahead, continue to reflect the joy of travel and the freedom that travel represents. May they always pursue a cost-conscious path, so that people of all incomes can enjoy the rewards of travel. And may they create, for both the traveler and the persons among whom we travel, a community of friends, where all human beings live in harmony and peace.

Arthur Frommer